17th International Conference on Parsing Technologies (IWPT 2021)

Including the IWPT 2021 Shared Task

Online
6 August 2021

ISBN: 978 1 7138-3377-2

Printed from e-media with permission by:

Curran Associates, Inc.
57 Morehouse Lane
Red Hook, NY 12571

Some format issues inherent in the e-media version may also appear in this print version.

Association for Computational Linguistics
209 N. Eighth Street
Stroudsburg, Pennsylvania 18360

Phone: 1-570-476-8006
Fax: 1-570-476-0860

acl@aclweb.org

Additional copies of this publication are available from:

Curran Associates, Inc.
57 Morehouse Lane
Red Hook, NY 12571 USA
Phone: 845-758-0400
Fax: 845-758-2633
Email: curran@proceedings.com
Web: www.proceedings.com

IWPT 2021

The 17th International Conference on Parsing Technologies

Proceedings of the Conference (Including the IWPT 2021 Shared Task)

August 6, 2021
Bangkok, Thailand (online)

Preface

Welcome to the 17th International Conference on Parsing Technologies (IWPT 2021), which this year (for only the second time since 2007) is co-located with the Annual Meeting of the Association for Computational Linguistics and of the Asian Federation of Natural Language Processing (ACL-IJCNLP). The IWPT meeting series, hosted by the ACL Special Interest Group in Natural Language Parsing (SIGPARSE), has been held biennualy since its inaugual meeting in 1989 in Pittsburgh, PA (USA).

For 2021, the SIGPARSE steering group decided to continue an experiment started last year, co-location with the main ACL meeting in the form of a reduced one-day IWPT programme. The main motivation for this move was to reduce fragmentation (and travel) and to increase IWPT visibility in the broader ACL community. We believe that both these goals have been attained in 2020 and hope to see this development continue this year. At the same time, IWPT has launched its own series of parsing shared tasks since 2020, which strengthens the experimental and applied perspective on parsing technologies in the conference programme.

The IWPT 2021 shared task focuses on the parsing of Enhanced Universal Dependencies (EUD) over 17 languages, continuing on from a successful EUD parsing shared task in 2020. This is the second time that graph-based representations of syntactic structures are evaluated on such a large scale, and we believe it will pave the way for research on richer models and representations. The shared task attracted system submissions from nine teams from around the world and, thus, establishes a highly relevant point of comparison for this line of syntactic analysis. We are very grateful to everyone who contributed to this shared task, starting with the data providers who worked hard to meet our deadline. Thanks to the participant teams who worked tirelessly in a short time period to provide such a set of great and interesting systems!

Owing to the ongoing pandemic, the meeting will regrettably once again be held entirely virtual, where for IWPT we have adopted a mostly-asynchronous format: Accepted papers (of four different types, long, short, shared task, and findings) will be presented through pre-recorded talks, which become available on-line for individual viewing before the actual conference day. On the day of the conference, August 6, there will be a four-hour live session, scheduled so that the timing should be convenient (all things considered) for participants around the world: 13:00–17:00 UTC+0, which translates, for example, into a starting time at 6:00 in the morning at the US West Coast and wrapping up at 1:00 in the morning in Melbourne, Australia. The live sessions will be devoted exclusively to questions and answers, organized into six thematic sessions. Authors of papers associated with each session will be available to answer questions and discuss their work (possibly also among themselves).

There has been (and to some degree still is) much uncertainty about the format of ACL-IJCNLP and IWPT this year, and in a sense we were positively surprised to receive a number of submissions comparable to recent IWPT instances. Out of 24 regular paper submissions, the programme committee accepted 13 for presentation at the conference. The IWPT 2021 programme is complemented by one invited talk, by Emily Pitler of Google Research (to whom we are immensely grateful for honoring her commitment despite the mostly-asynchronous, virtual format), by four papers adopted from the Findings of ACL-IJCNLP 2021, and by an overview paper and nine system descriptions from the IWPT 2021 shared task. We further gratefully acknowledge the work, flexibility, and collegiality of authors and reviewers, as well as of the ACL-IJCNLP workshop and publication chairs, who had to shepherd our community through a difficult logistics process.

Davis, Groningen, Oslo, Paris, Prague, and Tel Aviv

Gosse Bouma, Stephan Oepen, Kenji Sagae,
Djamé Seddah, Reut Tsarfaty, and Dan Zeman

Organizers:

Stephan Oepen, University of Oslo (General Co-Chair)
Kenji Sagae, University of California at Davis (General Co-Chair)
Reut Tsarfaty, Open University of Israel (General Co-Chair)
Gosse Bouma, University of Groningen (Shared Task Co-Chair)
Djamé Seddah, University Paris-Sorbonne (Shared Task Co-Chair)
Dan Zeman, Charles University in Prague (Shared Task Co-Chair)

Program Committee:

Omri Abend
Željko Agić
Mark Anderson
Miguel Ballesteros
James Barry
Gosse Bouma
Marie Candito
Xavier Carreras
John Carroll
Maximin Coavoux
Éric de la Clergerie
Miryam de Lhoneux
Agnieszka Falenska
Jennifer Foster
Annemarie Friedrich
Stefan Grünewald
Carlos Gómez-Rodríguez
Zixia Jia
Yong Jiang
Lifeng Jin
Nikita Kitaev
Mateusz Klimaszewski
Marco Kuhlmann
Jonathan K. Kummerfeld
Sandra Kübler
Joseph Le Roux
Yusuke Miyao
Mark-Jan Nederhof
Joakim Nivre
Stephan Oepen
Barbara Plank
Roi Reichart
Corentin Ribeyre
Kenji Sagae
Giorgio Satta
Natalie Schluter
Djamé Seddah
Tianze Shi
Reut Tsarfaty

Gertjan van Noord
David Vilares
Daniel Zeman
Yi Zhang
Yue Zhang
Lilja Øvrelid

Invited Speaker:

Emily Pitler, Google Research

Table of Contents

Conference Program

Friday, August 6, 2021 (All Times in UTC+0)

13:00–13:30 Session 1: Regular Papers Q&A

Generic Oracles for Structured Prediction
Christoph Teichmann and Antoine Venant

Proof Net Structure for Neural Lambek Categorial Parsing
Aditya Bhargava and Gerald Penn

Findings: Neural Combinatory Constituency Parsing
Zhousi Chen, Longtu Zhang, Aizhan Imankulova, Mamoru Komachi

Findings: Rule Augmented Unsupervised Constituency Parsing
Atul Sahay, Anshul Nasery, Ayush Maheshwari, Ganesh Ramakrishnan, Rishabh Iyer

13:30–14:05 Session 2: Regular Papers Q&A

The Reading Machine: A Versatile Framework for Studying Incremental Parsing Strategies
Franck Dary and Alexis Nasr

Semi-Automatic Construction of Text-to-SQL Data for Domain Transfer
Tianyi Li, Sujian Li and Mark Steedman

Levi Graph AMR Parser using Heterogeneous Attention
Han He and Jinho D. Choi

Translate, then Parse! A Strong Baseline for Cross-Lingual AMR Parsing
Sarah Uhrig, Yoalli Garcia, Juri Opitz and Anette Frank

Great Service! Fine-grained Parsing of Implicit Arguments
Ruixiang Cui and Daniel Hershcovich

Friday, August 6, 2021 (All Times in UTC+0) (continued)

14:05–14:35 Session 3: Regular Papers Q&A

A Falta de Pan, Buenas Son Tortas: The Efficacy of Predicted UPOS Tags for Low Resource UD Parsing
Mark Anderson, Mathieu Dehouck and Carlos Gómez-Rodríguez

Multilingual Dependency Parsing for Low-Resource African Languages: Case Studies on Bambara, Wolof, and Yoruba
Cheikh M. Bamba Dione

Findinigs: Climbing the Tower of Treebanks: Improving Low-Resource Dependency Parsing via Hierarchical Source Selection
Goran Glavaš, Ivan Vulić

Findings: Annotations Matter: Leveraging Multi-task Learning to Parse UD and SUD
Zeeshan Ali Sayyed, Daniel Dakota

14:35–15:05 Session 5: Regular Papers Q&A

Bidirectional Domain Adaptation Using Weighted Multi-Task Learning
Daniel Dakota, Zeeshan Ali Sayyed and Sandra Kübler

Strength in Numbers: Averaging and Clustering Effects in Mixture of Experts for Graph-Based Dependency Parsing
xudong zhang, Joseph Le Roux and Thierry Charnois

A Modest Pareto Optimisation Analysis of Dependency Parsers in 2021
Mark Anderson and Carlos Gómez-Rodríguez

Applying Occam's Razor to Transformer-Based Dependency Parsing: What Works, What Doesn't, and What is Really Necessary
Stefan Grünewald, Annemarie Friedrich and Jonas Kuhn

Friday, August 6, 2021 (All Times in UTC+0) (continued)

15:05–15:15 Break

15:15–16:00 Session 4: Invited Talk

Incorporating Compositionality and Morphology into End-to-End Models
Emily Pitler

16:00–16:45 Session 6: Shared Task Q&A

From Raw Text to Enhanced Universal Dependencies: The Parsing Shared Task at IWPT 2021
Gosse Bouma, Djamé Seddah and Daniel Zeman

COMBO: A New Module for EUD Parsing
Mateusz Klimaszewski and Alina Wróblewska

Splitting EUD Graphs into Trees: A Quick and Clatty Approach
Mark Anderson and Carlos Gómez-Rodríguez

Graph Rewriting for Enhanced Universal Dependencies
Bruno Guillaume and Guy Perrier

Biaffine Dependency and Semantic Graph Parsing for EnhancedUniversal Dependencies
Giuseppe Attardi, Daniele Sartiano and Maria Simi

Enhanced Universal Dependency Parsing with Automated Concatenation of Embeddings
Xinyu Wang, Zixia Jia, Yong Jiang and Kewei Tu

RobertNLP at the IWPT 2021 Shared Task: Simple Enhanced UD Parsing for 17 Languages
Stefan Grünewald, Frederik Tobias Oertel and Annemarie Friedrich

The DCU-EPFL Enhanced Dependency Parser at the IWPT 2021 Shared Task
James Barry, Alireza Mohammadshahi, Joachim Wagner, Jennifer Foster and James Henderson

Friday, August 6, 2021 (All Times in UTC+0) (continued)

TGIF: Tree-Graph Integrated-Format Parser for Enhanced UD with Two-Stage Generic- to Individual-Language Finetuning
Tianze Shi and Lillian Lee

16:45–17:00 Session 7: SIGPARSE Business Meeting

End-to-end mBERT based Seq2seq Enhanced Dependency Parser with Linguistic Typology knowledge
Chinmay Choudhary and Colm O'riordan

Generic Oracles for Structured Prediction

Christoph Teichmann
Bloomberg
cteichmann1@bloomberg.net

Antoine Venant
Université Montreal
antoine.venant@umontreal.ca

Abstract

When learned without exploration, local models for structured prediction tasks are subject to exposure bias and cannot be trained without detailed guidance. *Active Imitation Learning* (AIL), also known in NLP as Dynamic Oracle Learning, is a general technique for working around these issues by allowing the exploration of different outputs at training time.

AIL requires *oracle feedback*: an oracle is any algorithm which can, given a partial candidate solution and gold annotation, find the correct (minimum loss) next output to produce.

This paper describes a general finite state technique for deriving oracles. The technique described is also efficient and will greatly expand the tasks for which AIL can be used.

1 Introduction

Structured Prediction tasks, e.g., POS tagging, machine translation or syntactic parsing, are central to NLP and are commonly solved with machine learning based models. There are two main ways of approaching these problems: in one, a model scores fragments of possible outputs and an efficient decoding algorithm finds the highest scoring solution, e.g., using conditional random fields and the forward-backward algorithm. In the second approach a model produces an output through a sequence of decisions, each extending a partial output produced by the previous steps, e.g., picking one word after the other in a sequence to sequence translation system or repeatedly splitting a sentence into constituents. Modern neural models use complex hidden states to express the interdependence between outputs, making efficient decoding difficult and the latter approach ever more important.

When training models to make sequential decisions it is necessary to provide guidance on which actions to take to achieve minimum loss against a gold output. Sometimes there is a clear sequence of correct actions, e.g., when learning to translate or tag, there is the option of simply training the model to follow the gold annotation, which corresponds 1-1 to possible model outputs.

1.1 The Problems Dynamic Oracles Solve

Not all tasks have straightforward gold sequences. Consider the problem of simplifying a sentence by tagging words either to be deleted or replaced with more common, semantically similar words. There may be multiple ways to simplify that generate the same end result. If only a gold simplification is annotated, and no gold sequence of **actions** (*i.e.* deletion or replacement), then it is not clear which sequence of actions to train for. For another example, consider multiple annotations coming from multiple annotators, where it is necessary to interpolate between them.

Furthermore, when only following gold sequences, the model will never learn to recover from incorrect choices, as they are not encountered during training - the so called exposure bias. Consider the following example: assume that we want to map a sentence to a parse tree as in Fig. 1. For a simple sequence to sequence model, a parse tree is produced by outputting opening and closing brackets as well as words and mapping the result to a tree. If the model incorrectly added an NP(bracket right before "hit", then a gold sequence based training would never expose the model to a similar situation. The model would have no knowledge of how to recover from the error with minimal loss, and how to best represent a sequence with a questionable bracket.

Both exposure bias and the absence of clear gold training sequences can be tackled with *active imitation learning* (AIL). AIL uses a source of ground truth to determine the optimal action to take at each step. These sources of ground truth are called *dy-*

Proceedings of the 17th International Conference on Parsing Technologies (IWPT 2021), pages 1–12
Bangkok, Thailand (online), August 6, 2021.

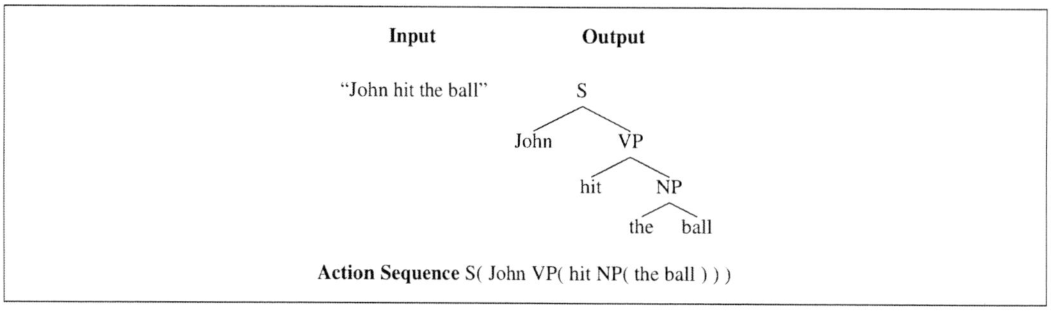

Figure 1: Example structured prediction task for active imitation learning.

namic oracles in the NLP literature, or *experts* in AIL focused works. Dynamic oracles determine what to do for any partially complete solution to minimize the loss relative to a gold annotation and they contrast with static oracles, which only provide a gold output sequence.[1] This paper is concerned with a generic way to build dynamic oracles for NLP problems. In our example of an incorrectly placed NP(, AIL would enable us to create training examples that contain similar errors and show how to recover from them.

1.2 Contribution

Dynamic oracles have been developed for different parsing tasks (Goldberg and Nivre, 2012; Goldberg et al., 2014; Coavoux and Crabbé, 2016; Fernández-González and Gómez-Rodríguez, 2018b; Coavoux and Cohen, 2019; Gómez-Rodríguez and Fernández-González, 2015) and have been shown to improve parsing performance (Ballesteros et al., 2016; Goldberg and Nivre, 2012; Coavoux and Crabbé, 2016; Fernández-González and Gómez-Rodríguez, 2018b). These oracles work for specific output types and losses. It is sometimes possible to use an oracle derived for one problem in a different context, but this transfer is limited. Here we instead give a completely generic technique for deriving dynamic oracles.

We focus on problems that involve mapping an input sequence to an output sequence in left to right order, which also generalizes the task of tagging the sequence. Our approach is general enough to subsume others, e.g., parsers based on transition systems can be encoded through tagging (Gómez-Rodríguez et al., 2020). Our technique is based on encoding possible outputs in a finite state automaton. By incorporating the loss via a transducer, we are able to formulate oracles as a minimum weight problem on regular languages. We also investigate the complexity of repeatedly solving these minimum weight problems.

2 Formal background

Before we describe our approach, we will recap some of the theory of AIL and finite state machines. Through a detailed discussion of both topics in a shared vocabulary, the connection will become clearer. We use the task of mapping sentences to parse trees as our running example.

General Notation We start with generic notations that will be used throughout the paper: we denote by $[k, n]$ the set of natural numbers between k (included) and n (included). For any set Σ we let $\wp(\Sigma)$ denote the powerset (set of all subsets) of Σ, and Σ^* denote the set of sequences of elements of Σ. For such a sequence $\alpha \in \Sigma^*$, $|\alpha|$ denotes the length of the sequence, for an index $i \in [1, |\alpha|]$, α_i denotes the i^{st} element in the sequence α. We also refer to sequences by extensionally listing their elements within angle brackets, as in $\alpha = \langle x_1, \dots, x_n \rangle$.[2] ϵ denotes an empty sequence, as does $\langle \alpha_k, \dots, \alpha_n \rangle$ whenever $n < k$. For two sequences α, β, $\alpha \leq \beta$ holds iff α is a prefix of β. Accordingly $\alpha < \beta$ holds iff $\alpha \leq \beta$ and $\alpha \neq \beta$. $\alpha \bullet \beta$ denotes the concatenation of the two sequences α and β ($\langle \alpha_1, \dots, \alpha_n \rangle \bullet \langle \beta_1, \dots, \beta_m \rangle = \langle \alpha_1, \dots, \alpha_n, \beta_1, \dots \beta_m \rangle$). Finally we adopt the convention that $\min_{x \in \emptyset} f(x) = +\infty$ for any real-valued function f of one variable, and $\arg\min_{x \in E} f(x)$ denotes the set $\{x \in E \mid f(x) = \min_{x' \in E} f(x')\}$.

[1] We occasionally drop the "dynamic" part, as dynamic oracles are a strict generalization of static ones.

[2] In this case, $|\alpha| = n$.

2.1 Active Imitation Learning

Imitation learning is concerned with using supervised feedback in order to learn models which can make sequential decisions. Example NLP problems for which imitation learning can be used are Named-Entity Recognition tagging (Brantley et al., 2020) and shift-reduce dependency parsing (Goldberg and Nivre, 2012). We focus on problems in which the model chooses from a fixed set of actions O at every step (also referred to as the *output lexicon*) and define an imitation learning input as follows:

Definition 1 (Imitation Learning Input). An imitation learning input[3] x consists of a sequence $w = \langle w_1, \dots, w_n \rangle$, a successor function $s : O^* \rightarrow \wp(O)$, and a stopping criterion $t : O^* \rightarrow \{\text{true}, \text{false}\}$.

Intuitively, the successor function s restricts the actions that the model can choose to the set $s(\alpha) \subseteq O$, depending on the sequence of previously taken actions α. Such a restriction is generally needed to ensure that only meaningful output (*e.g.* well-formed trees) are produced for a given input.

For our example of generating a sequence corresponding to a parse tree, the input sequence consists of word tokens. Our output lexicon consists of all possible word tokens that occur in the input, as well as opening brackets labeled with all possible nonterminals in the set N, e.g., NP(or S(, and the closing bracket). The stopping criterion is true once all tokens in the input have been generated in the output and there are no unmatched open brackets. For ease of presentation we will only consider context free parses without unary productions, i.e. we do not allow trees of the form $X(t)$ where t is any complete parse tree. This means the successor function allows generation of) whenever there is at least one more unmatched open bracket, the previous output is either a word token or another) and closing the bracket would not create a unary bracketing. s will allow opening brackets as long as there are more word tokens left to be produced than there are words left to produce and the last output was not a word token. Finally the s function allows w_i after an opening bracket or another word, if w_{i-1} has been produced.

We obtain a solution $\alpha_1, \dots, \alpha_k$ for a given input with a *model* m by repeatedly choosing the next action α_k among the admissible actions in $s(\alpha_1, \dots, \alpha_{k-1})$, according to the scores assigned by m. Whenever $t(\alpha_1, \dots, \alpha_k)$ becomes true, the model will have to score the option of stopping against all possible outputs. This is relevant to problems such as machine translation, where it is possible to continue even after a potential stopping point. Our definition of an input restricts admissible candidate solutions to the set $\tau_x = \{\alpha \in O^* \mid \forall k \in [1, |\alpha|]\, \alpha_k \in s(\alpha_1, \dots, \alpha_{k-1}) \wedge t(\alpha) = \text{true}\}$.

We assume that every imitation learning problem comes with a set Y of possible results, and that every (admissible) action sequence α for an input x can be interpreted as an element $[\![\alpha]\!] \in Y$. In our parsing example, the interpretation function simply takes a valid bracketing and maps it to the corresponding tree with Y being the set of parse trees for the sentence. Another example would be outputting the tokens of an SQL command and mapping them to their evaluation result relative to a database.

Note that $[\![\cdot]\!]$ is not necessarily an injective mapping. For the SQL example, different commands evaluate to the same results. In some settings the interpretation of an action sequences can depend on the words of the input sequence w, e.g., if our outputs were actions in classical shift-reduce parsing. For this reason, we assume a collection of interpretation functions indexed by the input rather than a unique, input-independent one. Finally, in order to unify the treatment of the training and test setting, we generally assume that there is a gold output $g \in Y$. This leads to this definition of an imitation learning problem:

Definition 2 (Imitation Learning Problem). An imitation learning problem P is a set of *instances*, each being a triple $\langle x, g, [\![\cdot]\!] \rangle$ where x is an input, $g \in Y$ is a gold annotation. and $[\![\cdot]\!] : \tau_x \mapsto Y$ is a function interpreting any admissible output action sequence as an outcome in Y.

A model's performance is measured by a *loss function*. A loss function is a function $\mathcal{L} : Y \times Y \mapsto \mathbb{R}^+$. The arguments fed to the loss function typically are the interpretation of an action sequence and the gold annotation. For constituency parsing the loss function for training and testing is 1 minus the F1 score - for a loss function, smaller values should indicate better results. To give another example, for machine translation, a loss would be 1 minus the BLEU score computed between gold translations and the output translation. Because we measure the loss of an (admissible) output ac-

[3] We simplify to just input whenever the meaning is clear.

tion sequence α on a problem instance $\langle x, g, [\![\cdot]\!] \rangle$ through the quantity $\mathcal{L}([\![\alpha]\!], g)$, it is not necessary that the output action sequence and the gold annotation are of the same "type". The comparison is mediated by the interpretation function and training will aim to learn to produce action sequences that interpret to low loss targets.

2.2 Learning Set-Up

How does one learn in this setting? One option is to use reinforcement learning to obtain a model through trial and error feedback coming from the loss function (Sutton and Barto, 2018). This is generally not the most efficient way to use the information available. If it is possible to derive a sequence of outputs $\langle \alpha_1, \ldots, \alpha_m \rangle$ with minimum loss, then this can be used as the basis of standard imitation learning, without any exploration (Hussein et al., 2017). This is known as *static oracle learning* in NLP. In the parsing example this means obtaining the action sequence that is given in Fig. 1, as it corresponds to the "correct" parse tree, and training a classifier to produce $S($ as a first step given the input, then produce $NP($ given the input and $S($ and so on. We can further exploit the knowledge implicit in the loss function through active imitation learning(Hussein et al., 2017; Ross et al., 2011), also known as dynamic oracle learning in NLP (Goldberg and Nivre, 2012). In this setting the learning is active because it obtains feedback for which action is optimal for a given instance and partial action output $\alpha = \langle \alpha_1, \ldots, \alpha_k \rangle$, where we will call α a *prefix*. This makes it possible to learn to adjust for errors that a model is likely to make, and to explore different sequences of actions, in order to find one that is easy to learn.

When teaching a robot how to move, or learning to automatically drive, human intervention might be required in order to give the optimal action for every situation. We are focused on deriving optimal actions directly from gold outputs so that no further annotator intervention is necessary. We define a dynamic oracle as follows:

Definition 3 (Dynamic Oracle). A *dynamic oracle* π for an imitation learning instance $\langle x, g, [\![\cdot]\!] \rangle$ and loss $\mathcal{L}$ is a function such that:

$$\forall \alpha \in O^* : \pi(\alpha) \in \arg\min_{o \in s(\alpha)} \min_{\beta \in \tau_x, \alpha \bullet o \leq \beta} \mathcal{L}([\![\beta]\!], g)$$

To put the definition of π in words: an oracle gives, for every prefix, an action that is the next step in a sequence that has the minimum loss possible for this prefix. Dynamic oracles enable the implementation of special learning algorithms with strong guarantees on test time performance and no exposure bias. One such algorithm is Dagger (Ross et al., 2011), which comes with attractive guarantees on model convergence. For clarity we provide the pseudo-code for Dagger, adjusted for our framing of the problem, in Figure 2, where we denote the *prediction of a model* ϕ for a given instance $in = \langle x, g, [\![\cdot]\!] \rangle$ and action sequence α as $\phi(\alpha, in)$.

- **Inputs**
  - interpolation schedule $\iota_0 \in (0, 1), \ldots$
  - instances $\langle x_1, g_1, [\![\cdot]\!] \rangle, \ldots, \langle x_n, g_n, [\![\cdot]\!] \rangle$
  - dynamic oracle π_j for each $\langle x_1, g_1, [\![\cdot]\!] \rangle$
  - starting model ϕ_0
- $Data = \emptyset$
- **Steps** for $i = 0$ to max steps:
  1. for $j = 1$ to n:
     (a) go to example $in = \langle x_j, g_j, [\![\cdot]\!] \rangle$ and set $\alpha \leftarrow \epsilon$
     (b) iterate:
        i. with probability ι_i set $pred = \phi_i(in, \alpha)$ otherwise set $pred = \pi_j(\alpha)$
        ii. add $\langle in, \alpha, \pi_j(\alpha) \rangle$ to $Data$
        iii. if $pred$ is to stop, end iterate
        iv. set $\alpha \leftarrow \alpha \bullet pred$
  2. train ϕ_{i+1} from $Data$

Figure 2: Pseudocode for Dagger.

The Dagger algorithm alternates between pursuing an optimal action and pursuing one chosen by the current model with probability ι_i. ι_0 is usually set to 0, to train a first model on optimal action sequences. By adding pairs of prefixes that a model visited and the dynamic oracle actions for these prefixes to the training data, models are able to learn what to do for prefixes they are likely to encounter. The last model trained is usually the one used at test time.

We presented dynamic oracles as the solution to an optimization problem over sequences. With this in mind, we will build on concepts from finite state automata in order to make these problems clearer and to solve them efficiently.

2.3 Finite State Machines

Given any finite set Q, called *states*, and finite set Σ, called *alphabet*, we call δ a transition function if δ assigns a weight $w \in \mathbb{R} \cup \{+\infty\}$[4] to any triple $\langle q, o, q' \rangle \in Q \times \Sigma \times Q$. Given such a transition function, we write δ^* for the (weighted) transitive closure of δ. δ^* extends δ to words in Σ^* and is defined inductively:

$$\delta^*(q, \epsilon, q) = 0$$
$$\delta^*(q, \alpha \cdot o, q') = \min_{q''} \delta^*(q, \alpha, q'') + \delta(q'', o, q').$$

Where q, q', q'' range over Q, o over Σ and α over Σ^*, and all free variables are implicitly universally quantified.

In order to later discuss transducers, we will also use the classic extension of transition functions to a pair of a left-hand side alphabet and a right-hand-side alphabet $\langle \Sigma, \Lambda \rangle$. Such an (extended) transition function δ assigns a weight to any quadruple $\langle q, o_1, o_2, q' \rangle \in Q \times (\Sigma \cup \{\epsilon\}) \times (\Lambda \cup \{\epsilon\}) \times Q$.[5] In this extended case, the definition of the (weighted) transitive closure of δ is amended to:

$$\delta^*(q, \epsilon, \epsilon, q) = 0$$
$$\delta^*(q, \alpha, \beta, q') = \min_{\gamma, \lambda, o_1, o_2 \in H(\alpha, \beta)} \min_{q''} \delta^*(q, \gamma, \lambda, q'') + \delta(q'', o_1, o_2, q').$$

Where the first minimum is taken over the set $H(\alpha, \beta) = \{\langle \gamma, \lambda, o_1, o_2 \rangle \in \Sigma^* \times \Lambda^* \times (\Sigma \cup \{\epsilon\}) \times (\Lambda \cup \{\epsilon\}) \mid \langle o_1, o_2 \rangle \neq \langle \epsilon, \epsilon \rangle \text{ and } \langle \gamma \bullet o_1, \lambda \bullet o_2 \rangle = \langle \alpha, \beta \rangle\}$

This paper uses automata exclusively for minimum weight problems. This means that we only focus on tropical weighted finite state automata and transducers (Mohri, 2009), which use the addition and minimum operations. We drop both "tropical" and "weighted" where appropriate.

Definition 4 (Weighted Finite State Automaton). A tropical weighted finite state automaton (automaton) A is a tuple $\langle q_0, Q, \Sigma, \delta, \rho \rangle$ where $q_0 \in Q$ is the start state, Q and Σ are the states and the alphabet, δ is a transition function and $\rho : Q \to \mathbb{R}$ is the final weight function. A defines a function $A(\alpha) = \min_{q \in Q} \delta^*(q_0, \alpha, q) + \rho(q)$. The weighted language $L(A)$ of A is the set $\{\langle \alpha, w \rangle \mid A(\alpha) = w\}$.

We say that a (non weighted) language $L \subseteq \Sigma^*$ is *regular*, iff there exists an automaton A_L such that, for any $\alpha \in \Sigma^*$, $A_L(\alpha) = 0$ if $\alpha \in L$ and $A_L(\alpha) = +\infty$ otherwise. Such an automaton is said to *recognize* L.

Definition 5. A tropical transducer T is a tuple $\langle q_0, Q, \Sigma, \Lambda, \delta, \rho \rangle$, where Σ and Λ are two alphabets, and δ is an extended transition function over theses two alphabets. All other members of T are exactly as in definition 4. T defines a weight function (of two arguments) $T(\alpha, \beta) = \min_{q \in Q} \delta^*(q_0, \alpha, \beta, q) + \rho(q)$. The weighted relation $L(T)$ of T is the set $\{\langle \langle \sigma, \sigma' \rangle, w \rangle \mid T(\sigma, \sigma') = w\}$

The size $|A|$ (resp. $|T|$) of an automaton A (resp. a transducer T) is defined as $|Q| + |\delta|$, where $|\delta|$ is the number of finite-weight transitions. If A and A' are both weighted automata, we write $L(A) \cap L(A')$ to denote the weighted language $\{\langle \alpha, w \rangle \mid w = A(\alpha) + A'(\alpha)\}$. This is the *intersection* of A and A'. If T is a transducer and A is an automaton, we write $L(T) \circ L(A)$ for the weighted relation $\{\langle \langle \alpha, \beta \rangle, w \rangle \mid w = T(\alpha, \beta) + A(\beta)\}$. Symetrically, we write $L(A) \circ L(T)$ for the weighted relation $\{\langle \langle \alpha, \beta \rangle, w \rangle \mid w = A(\alpha) + T(\alpha, \beta)\}$. Both are called *applications* of T to A. Note that the intersection of two automata can be expressed as an finite automaton as well and the application of a transducer can be expressed as another transducer:

Lemma 1. *1. If A and A' are automata, one can construct an automata $A \cap A'$ such that $L(A \cap A') = L(A) \cap L(A')$. Moreover, $A \cap A'$ can be computed in time $O(|A||A'|)$ (Rabin and Scott, 1959).*

2. If A is an automaton and T is a transducer, there exists a transducer $T \circ A$ such that $L(T \circ A) = L(T) \circ L(A)$. Moreover, $T \circ A$ can be effectively computed in time $O(|T||A|)$ (Mohri, 2004). The same holds, up to symmetry, for $L(A) \circ L(T)$, and we write $A \circ T$ for the corresponding transducer.

For all of the above statements the intuition is to construct a new automaton/transducer that has pairs of the two automata's states as its states and has a transition with weight $w + w'$ if the two automata have matching transitions with weight w and w' respectively. As a consequence, if A has m states, u transitions and A' (resp. T) has m' states, u' transitions, then $A \cap A'$ (resp. $A \circ T$ or $T \circ A$) has $O(|k||l|)$ states and $O(|u||u'|)$ transitions.

Definition 6. For any transducer T, we let V_T denote the function which maps every state to the

[4] As we will be reasoning about minimum weight paths, ∞ corresponds to an absent transition.

[5] Note the addition of the empty sequence ϵ to the left-hand-side and right-hand-side alphabets.

minimal score which can be assigned to some sequence read from that state. Formally: $V_T(q) = min_{\alpha,\beta,q'}\delta^*(q,\alpha,\beta,q') + \rho(q')$.

In other words, V_T gives the weight of the minimum weight or *shortest* path to any final state plus the weight of that state (Mohri, 2009).

Lemma 2. *For any transducer T and state q, the set*

$$\{\langle q, V_T(q)\rangle \mid q \in Q\}$$

can be computed in $O(|Q||\delta|)$ (Mohri, 2009).

This is a shortest path problem, solvable by the Bellman-Ford (Mohri, 2009) algorithm. If all weights are positive, this is amenable to $O(|Q|log(|Q|) + |\delta|)$ through Dijkstra's algorithm (Dijkstra, 1959).

3 Finite State Automata Oracles

We now provide generic dynamic oracles, prove the soundness of our constructions and provide complexity upper-bounds. We will encode all the possible action sequences for a given imitation learning problem as an automaton and then retrieve the next transition in a minimum loss complete solution for a given prefix.

The key question is how to derive an automaton of losses from a problem instance without having to explicitly go through all possible action sequences. In order to do this, we need three requirements guaranteeing applicability of finite-state techniques. First, we must be able to build a *decomposition automaton* inverting the interpretation function, and its language must not be empty. Second, we must be able to approximate the loss function with a transducer working over action sequences. Third, there must be an automaton recognizing the set of admissible candidate output action sequences for the considered input. These requirements are formally captured by the following definitions.

Definition 7. $\langle x, g, [\![\cdot]\!]\rangle$ has a *decomposable gold annotation* if the set $[\![g]\!]^{-1} = \{\alpha \in O^* \mid [\![\alpha]\!] = g\}$ is both regular and non-empty. An automaton recognising this set is called a *decomposition automaton*.

In our constituency parsing example, the decomposition automaton for a tree is simply the automaton that accepts the bracketing for the tree, e.g., the one recognizing "S(John VP(hit NP(the ball)))" for the tree in Fig. 1. The automaton recognizing this sequence would have positions in the gold output as states and would have transitions such as $1, John, 2$ or $2, VP(, 3$ with weight 0. For machine translation the decomposition automaton may recognize any of a number of possible gold translations. Note that our notion of "decomposable" is unrelated to the notion of "arc-decomposable" used in previous research on oracles for dependency parsing. Our notions of decomposability is concerned with decomposing every possible way of arriving at the gold output into a sequence of actions, while arc-decomposability tells us about the interaction between added edges during dependency parsing.

Definition 8. We say that $\mathcal{L}$ is *decomposable* if there exists a transducer T such that for any instance $\langle x, g, [\![\cdot]\!]\rangle \in P$ and sequences $\alpha, \alpha', \beta \in O^*$, if $\mathcal{L}([\![\alpha']\!], [\![\beta]\!]) < \mathcal{L}([\![\alpha]\!], [\![\beta]\!])$, then there exists $\beta' \in O^*$ such that $[\![\beta']\!] = [\![\beta]\!]$ and $T(\alpha', \beta') < T(\alpha, \beta)$.

Definition 8 relates the transducer and loss function with an inequality, not an equality. This provides more flexibility: we do **not** require that the loss function be directly computed by a transducer. If we did, then that would rule out very common losses such as F-Score. Rather, we allow transducers which conserve the right minima (see Lemma 3 below). Variations of the Levenshtein edit-distance between the output and gold-sequence are expressible as a (single state) transducer, and provides a generic loss function in practical cases. Consider our example of constituency parsing: the F-Score is the harmonic mean of two measures that require division by the total count of constituents present in a prediction and is hard to express as a transducer. However, as shown by Cross and Huang (2016), for purposes of an oracle, the number of incorrectly inserted and missing brackets (which corresponds to the edit distance between input and output for our setting) fits definition 8 and can thus replace a loss based on the F-Score. An incorrectly inserted bracket will always reduce precision without changing recall and vice versa for dropping a bracket. For our example problem the transducer would have have transitions $0, x, x, 0$ with weight 0, which map every symbol to itself, transitions $0, X(, \epsilon, 0$, $0, \epsilon, X(, 0$ and $0, Y(, X(, 0$ which allow us to delete, insert, or relable any opening brackets $X($, $Y($ with weight 1, as well as transitions $0, X), \epsilon, 0$ and $0, \epsilon, X), 0$ with weight 0.[6]

[6]Because closing brackets need to be matched, each incorrectly inserted one will incur a loss through an incorrect opening bracket

The next lemma states that for any set of action sequences, the input action sequence assigned minimum weight by some decomposition transducer is indeed a minimum loss action sequence out of that set.

Lemma 3. *Let* $\mathcal{L}$ *be decomposable,* $\langle x, g, [\![\cdot]\!]\rangle \in P$*, and* T *be as described in definition 8. For any subset* $D \subseteq O^*$*,*

$$\text{if } \tilde{\alpha} \in \arg\min_{\alpha \in D} \min_{\beta, [\![\beta]\!] = g} T(\alpha, \beta),$$

$$\text{then } \tilde{\alpha} \in \arg\min_{\alpha \in D} \mathcal{L}([\![\alpha]\!], g)$$

Proof. Let $\tilde{\alpha} \in \arg\min_{\alpha \in D} \min_{\beta, [\![\beta]\!] = g} T(\alpha, \beta)$ and $\tilde{\beta} \in \arg\min_{[\![\beta]\!] = g} T(\tilde{\alpha}, \beta)$. If there existed $\alpha' \in D$ such that $\mathcal{L}([\![\alpha']\!], g) < \mathcal{L}([\![\tilde{\alpha}]\!], g)$, it would follow from definition 8 that $\exists \beta', [\![\beta']\!] = [\![\tilde{\beta}]\!] = g$ and $T(\alpha', \beta') < T(\tilde{\alpha}, \tilde{\beta})$, which contradicts the definition of $\tilde{\alpha}$. Hence $\tilde{\alpha} \in \arg\min_{\alpha \in D} \mathcal{L}(\alpha, \beta)$. □

Finally, we need to add the regularity of the possible action sequences:

Definition 9. We say that x has *regular constraints* iff τ_x is regular.

For our context free parsing example, all the possible parses for a sentence can be expressed in a finite state automaton by virtue of the fact that any finite language is regular. We obtain an automaton of size $O(n^2)$ for an input of length n, when we construct states that encode how many brackets are open and which word was last produced. We would have a state $(3, c, t)$, which would be reached after producing, e.g., $((a(bc$ for the input sentence $abcd$. t and f would be use to indicate whether we can still produce closing brackets before outputting the next word, to prevent outputs like $((a(b()$. We would allow, e.g., a transition of the form $(3, c, t),), (2, c, t)$. Note that we only need to maintain numbers up to the length of the inputs sentence, since no more can be used in a permissible parse for the input. Our construction for the action sequence automaton allows for unary bracketings, but since they do not occur in the gold output and would always incur additional loss, this will not constitute a difficulty.

From here on, we assume $\langle x, g, [\![\cdot]\!]\rangle$ to be an instance with both decomposable gold annotation and regular constraints, and $\mathcal{L}$ to be a decomposable loss function. We now proceed to a first oracle construction which follows naturally from these assumptions and some of the properties of finite state machines listed in section 2. Let $\alpha \in O^*$ represent a sequence of k actions that the model has already taken. We can find an optimal action for the next step: consider an arbitrary candidate action $o \in O$ and recall that the oracle must determine which, among the possible choices for o, is part of the minimum loss completion of α into an admissible action sequence. Letting (for any action sequence γ) $\mathsf{cont}_\gamma = \{\gamma' \in \tau_x \mid \gamma' \geq \gamma\}$ denote the set of admissible continuations of γ, we can formally rephrase our objective as choosing an action o minimizing the quantity $\min_{\alpha' \in \mathsf{cont}_{\alpha \bullet o}} \mathcal{L}([\![\alpha']\!], g)$.

To ease notational clutter, let us define $l(\alpha') = \min_{\beta' \in [\![g]\!]^{-1}} T(\alpha', \beta')$. Observe that lemma 3 ensures that we solve the oracle task if we find $\tilde{o} \in \arg\min_{o \in O} \min_{\alpha' \in \mathsf{cont}_{\alpha \cdot o}} l(\alpha')$. For if we find such $\tilde{o}$, letting $\tilde{\alpha} \in \arg\min_{\alpha' \in cont_{\alpha \bullet o}} l(\alpha')$, we have $\tilde{\alpha} \in \arg\min_{\alpha' \in \mathsf{cont}_\alpha} l(\alpha')$ (easily checked from the definition of $\tilde{o}$). Then, from lemma 3 follows that $\tilde{\alpha} \in \arg\min_{\alpha' \in \mathsf{cont}_\alpha} \mathcal{L}([\![\alpha']\!], g)$, which (since $\tilde{\alpha} \in \mathsf{cont}_{\alpha \bullet \tilde{o}}$) finally shows that $\tilde{o}$ is one of the optimal choices for continuing α, *i.e.* $\tilde{o} \in \arg\min_{o \in O} \min_{\alpha' \in \mathsf{cont}_{\alpha \bullet o}} \mathcal{L}([\![\alpha']\!], g)$.

How can we compute this quantity? We first build an automaton $A_{\alpha \bullet o}$ which recognizes the set $\alpha \bullet o \bullet O^*$. This is easily done as depicted below, with the following graphical conventions: states are circled, the start state (0) is marked with a left-dangling incoming arrow, arrows between states represented transitions, annotated with their label(s) and weight (a set of labels like O is a factored representation of one transition for each $o \in O$, all with the same indicated weight), and final weights are given by the downwards outgoing arrows.

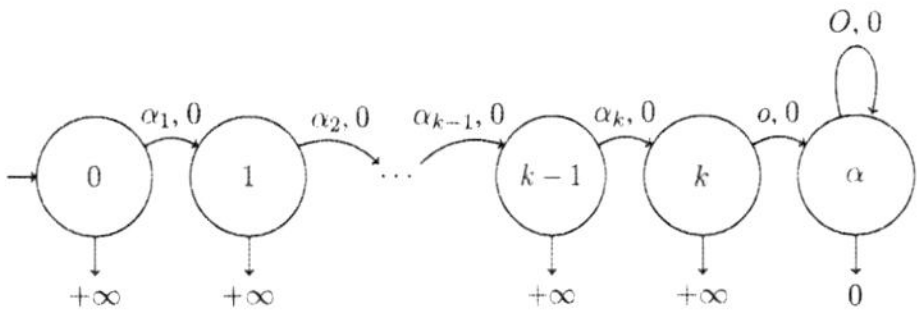

In our example setting, this would be an automaton that accepts the brackets and word tokens produced so far, followed by all possible words and brackets and which assigns weight 0 to each of those transitions.

Let C_x be an automaton recognizing the set τ_x of admissible actions for x (C_x exists since x has regular constraints). In our example this would be an automaton that accepts all the valid bracketings of the input. Note that this can be represented as a finite state automaton, due to the limit on open brackets we stipulated. Observe that $C_x \cap A_{\alpha\bullet o}$ (as provided by lemma 1) recognizes $\mathsf{cont}_{\alpha\bullet o}$.

Let now T be the transducer provided by definition 8, and $\mathcal{D}_g$ be a decomposition automaton for g. Consider the transducer $T_{\alpha\bullet o} = (C_x \cap A_{\alpha\bullet o}) \circ (T \circ \mathcal{D}_g)$ (provided by two successive applications of lemma 1), and let q_0 be its initial state. With a little work (we skip the details here, due to space limitations), one can show that if $\beta' \notin [\![g]\!]^{-1}$ or $\alpha' \notin \mathsf{cont}_{\alpha\bullet o}$ then $T_{\alpha\bullet o}(\alpha', \beta') = +\infty$, and that otherwise $T_{\alpha\bullet o}(\alpha', \beta') = T(\alpha', \beta')$. This guarantees:

$$\begin{aligned} &\min_{\alpha'} \min_{\beta'} T_{\alpha\bullet o}(\alpha', \beta') \\ &= \min_{\alpha' \in \mathsf{cont}_{\alpha\bullet o}} \min_{\beta' \in [\![g]\!]^{-1}} T(\alpha', \beta'). \end{aligned} \tag{1}$$

Recall that $V_{T_{\alpha\bullet o}}(q_0) = \min_{\alpha'} \min_{\beta'} T_{\alpha\bullet o}(\alpha', \beta')$. Equation (1) and preceding observations establish the soundness of the following oracle computation:

Oracle computation for prefix α. For each $o \in O$, construct $T_{\alpha\bullet o}$, then computes $V_{T_{\alpha\bullet o}}(q_0)$. Find and output the action o minimizing $V_{T_{\alpha\bullet o}}(q_0)$.

In terms of our example, this would mean taking the automaton that expresses all possible continuations of a partial parse and intersecting it with the automaton of all possible bracketings of the input. Then we apply a transducer that encodes the edit distance to the gold bracketing and extract the shortest path from the resulting automaton

We now briefly discuss the complexity of a single call to this oracle, and of a sequence of prediction, at each timestep of an input's processing. Recall that $k = |\alpha|$ and observe that $A_{\alpha\bullet o}$ has $O(k)$ states and $O(k)$ transitions. Let m_T, m_g and m_x denote the number of states of T, D_g and C_x resepectively, and e_T, e_g, e_x their respective number of finite-weight transitions. We consider the size of the alphabet O constant and exclude it from the underlying variables of all the asymptotic bounds reported. By lemma 1, computing $T_{\alpha\bullet o}$ is done in time $O(k|D_g||T||C_x|) = O(k(m_g + e_g)(m_x + e_x)(m_T + e_T))$, it has $O(km_g m_T m_x)$ states and $O(ke_g e_T e_x)$ transitions. By lemma 2 computing $V_{T\alpha\bullet o}(q_0)$ is done in $O((km_g m_T m_x)(ke_g e_T e_x))$, and is asymptotically the dominant term. Iterating (a constant number of times) over $o \in O$ leaves the asymptotic bound $O(k^2(m_g m_T m_x e_g e_T e_x))$.

If a machine learning system builds and outputs a (complete) sequence of n actions in processing (entirely) a given input x, and needs to call the oracle at each timestep $k \in [1, n]$ (*i.e.*, there is a call on each prefix of length k of the complete action sequence), the overall cost of oracle calls in the processing of x will then be $O(n^3(m_g m_T m_x e_g e_T e_x))$. If no negative weights are involved, this can be lowered to $O(n^2(m_g m_T m_x log(n m_g m_T m_x) + e_g e_T e_x))$.

This is extremely suboptimal, because the algorithm discussed above is only *superficially* dynamic: at every timestep, an independent computation arises with redundant work all the way up to the prefix α of previous actions disregarding the result of previous timesteps' computations. In fact, shortest path computations can be performed in advance. To this aim, we can work with $T_\epsilon = C_x \circ (T \circ D_g)$, a transducer that combines the automaton of all possible input sequences with the decompositions of the gold output. This transducer is only dependent on the problem and the loss function, hence only needs to be computed once, at the time the corpus is created. We can use the following observation: when we start producing the output sequence, the best action is the first action of the best path from T_ϵ's start state q_0. After outputting an action a, we can obtain a set c of states in T_ϵ that are reachable by reading a from q_0. The best next action must then be the first action of some path from some state $q' \in c$, which is determined according to the cost of reaching q' through a plus the weight of the best path from q'. This updating can be carried forward during the whole decoding process. This frees us from having to repeat a lot of computation, as we will see that we only need to compute the best paths in T_ϵ once. To formalize this: let $T_\epsilon = \langle q_0, Q, O, O, \delta, \rho \rangle$, then

$$\begin{aligned} &\min_{\alpha' \in \mathsf{cont}_\alpha} \min_{\beta' \in O^*} T_\epsilon(\alpha', \beta') \\ &= \min_{q'}(\min_{\beta} \delta^*(q_0, \alpha, \beta, q') + V_{T_\epsilon}(q')). \end{aligned} \tag{2}$$

Let $\mathsf{Pre}_\alpha(q') = \min_{\beta \in O^*} \delta^*(q_0, \alpha, \beta, q')$, the minimum weight of a path reaching q' from the start state with α. Using Eq. (2), we have

$$\begin{aligned} &\arg\min_{o \in O} \min_{\alpha' \in \mathsf{cont}_{\alpha\bullet o}} \min_{\beta'} T_\epsilon(\alpha', \beta') \\ &= \arg\min_{o} \min_{q'} \mathsf{Pre}_{\alpha\bullet o}(q') + V_{T_\epsilon}(q'). \end{aligned}$$

Finally, since by construction $T_\epsilon(\alpha', \beta') \neq +\infty$ entails $[\![\beta']\!] = g$, it is sufficient to find

$$\tilde{o} \in \arg\min_{o} \min_{q'}(\mathsf{Pre}_{\alpha\bullet o}(q') + V_{T_\epsilon}(q')) \tag{3}$$

to solve the oracle problem for prefix α. Our second construction thus proceeds as follows:

Second oracle computation for α. When constructing the problem, compute V_{T_ϵ} for each instance. During iteration, to obtain the optimal next action $o \in O$ for prefix α, choose the minimum of $\mathsf{Pre}_{\alpha \bullet o}(q') + V_{T_\epsilon}(q')$.

What we gain from this obviously depends on the cost of computing $\mathsf{Pre}_\alpha(q')$ for every state q'. The key insight is that $\mathsf{Pre}_{\alpha\bullet o}$ can be computed inductively from Pre_α:

$$
\begin{aligned}
&\mathsf{Pre}_{\alpha\bullet o}(q') \\
&= \min_{\beta \in O^*} \delta^*(q_0, \alpha \bullet o, \beta, q') \\
&= \min_{\beta', \beta'', p} \min_{q''} \delta^*(q_0, \alpha, \beta', q'') \\
&\qquad + \min_{q'''} \delta(q'', o, p, q''') \\
&\qquad\qquad + \delta^*(q''', \epsilon, \beta'', q') \\
&= \min_{q''} \mathsf{Pre}_\alpha(q'') \\
&\qquad + \min_{q'''} \min_{p} \delta(q'', o, p, q''') \\
&\qquad\qquad + \delta^*(q''', \epsilon, \beta'', q')
\end{aligned}
$$

Obverse that in the second equality above, the quantity $\min_{q'''} \min_p \delta(q'', o, p, q''') + \delta^*(q''', \epsilon, \beta'', q')$ depends only on T_ϵ, the states q'' and q', and **not** on the prefix α. We thus refer to this quantity as $\mathcal{C}(q'', q')$. Since it does not depend on α, it can be precomputed once for every pair $\langle q'', q' \rangle$, and reused through every iteration. The cost of this precomputation is asymptotically bounded by $O(|Q|^3)$: the lion's share is computing a table for the (lhs) epsilon closure $\delta^*(q''', \epsilon, \beta'', q')$, for all pairs $\langle q''', q' \rangle$. This is an instance of an all-pair shortest-path problem and solved with the Floyd-Warshall algorithm (Mohri, 2009). This is also akin to considering T_ϵ has an automaton rather than a transducer, using only the 'input' side (lhs) of transitions, and eliminating ϵ transitions. Note in passing, that computing Pre_ϵ is a similar problem and therefore done with the same asymptotic bound.

Because $\mathsf{Pre}_{\alpha\bullet o}$ can be computed inductively, it is possible to update it as the Dagger algorithm is going through a problem instance computing first Pre_ϵ, and then updating by taking a minimum over all possible transitions for the next action produced. The induction step then computes $\mathsf{Pre}_{\alpha\bullet o}(q')$ from the different $\mathsf{Pre}_\alpha(q'')$ and $\mathcal{C}(q'', q')$ in $O(|Q|^2)$ (since for each entry q' we need to range over all q''). This could be reduced to constant time by looking just at the inputs of T_ϵ and making the induced automaton deterministic (Hopcroft et al., 2006), however, that would come at the cost of a worst-case exponentially larger precomputation.

We now turn to the complexity analysis of the refined oracle construction. Computing V_{T_ϵ} is the only precomputation that we have not yet addressed, and can be achieved in time $O(|Q||\delta|)$ before any Dagger iterations. We can bound this with $O(|Q|^3)$ as well. Oracle calls will receive a (possibly empty) prefix of the form α. To compute the oracle we have to compute $\mathsf{Pre}_{\alpha \cdot o}$ from Pre_α, which will cost $O(|Q|^2)$ for a nondeterministic automaton, and then compute the minimum in equation (3). Hence, over a sequence of n actions with oracle calls in one entire pass over input x in Dagger, the total cost of oracle calls will be bounded by $O(|Q|^3 + n|Q|^2)$, or with the same notations as before $O((m_x m_g m_T)^3 + n(m_x m_g m_T)^2)$. Holding other parameters fixed, our second construction is much more efficient with respect to n, the length of the input. We can therefore conclude that our second construction is much more efficient during the actual Dagger training steps, with most of the computation moved into preprocessing, which is only needed once during the lifetime of a corpus.

Applied to our context free parsing example, our analysis bounds an oracle call (and update of Pre) with $O(n^6)$. The precomputation is bounded by $O(n^9)$, and the total of oracle calls in building a complete output is bounded with $O(n^7)$. However, we used here a generic bound that will hold for all instances of our method. No assumption were made on the nature of the automata involved[7], and specific instances will allow more efficient implementation of automata-theoretic operations, with no change to the general framework. We leave discussion of the automata theoretic properties that enable more efficient oracles for future work.

4 Related Work

Our dynamic oracle construction is general and only takes limited bookkeeping as seen in the previous section. However, this computation can still be costly and one topic in existing imitation learning is avoiding oracles computations where possible. A recent approach uses statistical techniques for the so called task of *apple tasting* to learn when it is necessary to call to an expensive oracle and when it is possible to instead use a cheap heuristic (Brantley et al., 2020). We could implement trans-

[7]Also, we relied for simplicity on a worst-case estimation $O(Q^2)$ for the number of transitions of T_ϵ.

ducer application and other computations on the finite state automata in a lazy manner and avoid oracle computations in order to save on computations for the automata and for tracking shortest paths. Other work uses reinforcement learning in order to derive approximate oracles (Yu et al., 2018; Fried and Klein, 2018). By using reinforcement learning to replace many of the oracle evaluation, it would also be possible to save on automaton construction.

The finite state approach we have sketched can give us an optimal action to take next. While this is sufficient to implement active imitation learning with a technique like Dagger, in some settings it can be beneficial to use not just information on what the best next action is, but rather to obtain the minimum loss for every available action in a given state (Ross and Bagnell, 2014) and to then train a loss aware classifier. As we are already computing these quantities, our algorithms would also suitable for this setting.

Related Dynamic Oracles There are a number of previously published oracles that are related to our setting, even if they proceed slightly differently. They are particularly used for dependency or constituency parsing. Note that our approach for constructing an automaton expressing the loss for all possible continuations could be applied to setting where the output is produced in a fashion other than left to right. Assume, e.g., that we use an algorithm which produces parse trees by "splitting" a sentence into sub-sequences repeatedly as in Stern et al. (2017). Let the output generated to far be S(NP(The old baker)VP(uses a sharp knife)). We would then simply construct an automaton equivalent to the regular expression $\mathrm{S(NP(.*The.*old.*}\mathit{baker}.*)\mathrm{VP(.*uses.*a.*sharp.*knife.*))}$, where $.*$ stands for an arbitrary sequence of brackets. Through application of the loss transducer approximating the loss for all possible action sequences, we could retrieve the minimum loss continuation. We leave work on whether this construction allows for more efficient look-up to future work.

A predecessor of the work by Stern et al. (2017) is the paper by (Cross and Huang, 2016) which discusses a shift-reduce system for constituency parsing and gives a constant time dynamic oracle for this system. It would be possible to express their setting, as well as those of Coavoux and Crabbé (2016), Fernández-González and Gómez-Rodríguez (2018b) and the discourse parsing focused on of Hung et al. (2020) in our framework.

Dynamic oracles have also been developed for different formalizations of the dependency parsing problem (Goldberg and Nivre, 2012; Goldberg et al., 2014) for shift reduce parsing. For the projective setting, one could generalize these oracles by translating dependency tree to constituency trees Mareček and Žabokrtský (2011) or tag sequences (Gómez-Rodríguez et al., 2020). Oracles for non-projective dependency and constituency parsing (Coavoux and Cohen, 2019; Nederhof, 2021; Gómez-Rodríguez and Fernández-González, 2015; Fernández-González and Gómez-Rodríguez, 2018a; de Lhoneux et al., 2017; Gómez-Rodríguez et al., 2014) can in certain cases be computed in polynomial time, but would be harder to express in this framework without necessitating extremely large automata as it would be difficult to encode the different admissible sets of actions.

Our idea of using interpretations of action sequences is inspired by Interpreted Regular Tree Grammars (IRTGs) (Koller and Kuhlmann, 2011). Our approach works in terms of automata over string sequences and IRTGs are based on automata over trees. In future work we will use IRTGs to extend our approach to additional domains.

5 Conclusion

This paper gives a generic approach for deriving dynamic oracles for NLP. The oracles make it possible to implement error aware learning and learning in ambiguous environments for a wide range of NLP problems, including most problems that can be approached with sequence to sequence models. There is no need to derive new oracles for every new loss or set of output actions, instead automata can be derived once and reused if only part of a problem changes. We also showed how to substantially improve the efficiency of oracle lookup, by moving most computational cost into a one time pre-computation.

References

Miguel Ballesteros, Yoav Goldberg, Chris Dyer, and Noah A. Smith. 2016. Training with exploration improves a greedy stack LSTM parser. In *Proceedings of the 2016 Conference on Empirical Methods in Natural Language Processing*, pages 2005–2010, Austin, Texas. Association for Computational Linguistics.

Kianté Brantley, Hal Daumé III, and Amr Sharaf. 2020. Active imitation learning with noisy guidance. In

Proceedings of the 58th Annual Meeting of the Association for Computational Linguistics, pages 2093–2105, Online. Association for Computational Linguistics.

Maximin Coavoux and Shay B. Cohen. 2019. Discontinuous constituency parsing with a stack-free transition system and a dynamic oracle. In *Proceedings of the 2019 Conference of the North American Chapter of the Association for Computational Linguistics: Human Language Technologies, Volume 1 (Long and Short Papers)*, pages 204–217, Minneapolis, Minnesota. Association for Computational Linguistics.

Maximin Coavoux and Benoît Crabbé. 2016. Neural greedy constituent parsing with dynamic oracles. In *Proceedings of the 54th Annual Meeting of the Association for Computational Linguistics (Volume 1: Long Papers)*, pages 172–182, Berlin, Germany. Association for Computational Linguistics.

James Cross and Liang Huang. 2016. Span-based constituency parsing with a structure-label system and provably optimal dynamic oracles. In *Proceedings of the 2016 Conference on Empirical Methods in Natural Language Processing*, pages 1–11, Austin, Texas. Association for Computational Linguistics.

E. W. Dijkstra. 1959. A note on two problems in connexion with graphs. *Numer. Math.*, 1(1):269–271.

Daniel Fernández-González and Carlos Gómez-Rodríguez. 2018a. A dynamic oracle for linear-time 2-planar dependency parsing. In *Proceedings of the 2018 Conference of the North American Chapter of the Association for Computational Linguistics: Human Language Technologies, Volume 2 (Short Papers)*, pages 386–392, New Orleans, Louisiana. Association for Computational Linguistics.

Daniel Fernández-González and Carlos Gómez-Rodríguez. 2018b. Dynamic oracles for top-down and in-order shift-reduce constituent parsing. In *Proceedings of the 2018 Conference on Empirical Methods in Natural Language Processing*, pages 1303–1313, Brussels, Belgium. Association for Computational Linguistics.

Daniel Fried and Dan Klein. 2018. Policy gradient as a proxy for dynamic oracles in constituency parsing. In *Proceedings of the 56th Annual Meeting of the Association for Computational Linguistics (Volume 2: Short Papers)*, pages 469–476, Melbourne, Australia. Association for Computational Linguistics.

Yoav Goldberg and Joakim Nivre. 2012. A dynamic oracle for arc-eager dependency parsing. In *Proceedings of COLING 2012*, pages 959–976, Mumbai, India. The COLING 2012 Organizing Committee.

Yoav Goldberg, Francesco Sartorio, and Giorgio Satta. 2014. A tabular method for dynamic oracles in transition-based parsing. *Transactions of the Association for Computational Linguistics*, 2:119–130.

Carlos Gómez-Rodríguez and Daniel Fernández-González. 2015. An efficient dynamic oracle for unrestricted non-projective parsing. In *Proceedings of the 53rd Annual Meeting of the Association for Computational Linguistics and the 7th International Joint Conference on Natural Language Processing (Volume 2: Short Papers)*, pages 256–261, Beijing, China. Association for Computational Linguistics.

Carlos Gómez-Rodríguez, Francesco Sartorio, and Giorgio Satta. 2014. A polynomial-time dynamic oracle for non-projective dependency parsing. In *Proceedings of the 2014 Conference on Empirical Methods in Natural Language Processing (EMNLP)*, pages 917–927, Doha, Qatar. Association for Computational Linguistics.

Carlos Gómez-Rodríguez, Michalina Strzyz, and David Vilares. 2020. A unifying theory of transition-based and sequence labeling parsing. In *Proceedings of the 28th International Conference on Computational Linguistics*, pages 3776–3793, Barcelona, Spain (Online). International Committee on Computational Linguistics.

John E. Hopcroft, Rajeev Motwani, and Jeffrey D. Ullman. 2006. *Introduction to Automata Theory, Languages, and Computation (3rd Edition)*. Addison-Wesley Longman Publishing Co., Inc., USA.

Shyh-Shiun Hung, Hen-Hsen Huang, and Hsin-Hsi Chen. 2020. A complete shift-reduce Chinese discourse parser with robust dynamic oracle. In *Proceedings of the 58th Annual Meeting of the Association for Computational Linguistics*, pages 133–138, Online. Association for Computational Linguistics.

Ahmed Hussein, Mohamed Medhat Gaber, Eyad Elyan, and Chrisina Jayne. 2017. Imitation learning: A survey of learning methods. *ACM Comput. Surv.*, 50(2).

Alexander Koller and Marco Kuhlmann. 2011. A generalized view on parsing and translation. In *Proceedings of the 12th International Conference on Parsing Technologies*, pages 2–13, Dublin, Ireland. Association for Computational Linguistics.

Miryam de Lhoneux, Sara Stymne, and Joakim Nivre. 2017. Arc-hybrid non-projective dependency parsing with a static-dynamic oracle. In *Proceedings of the 15th International Conference on Parsing Technologies*, pages 99–104, Pisa, Italy. Association for Computational Linguistics.

David Mareček and Zdeněk Žabokrtský. 2011. Gibbs sampling with treeness constraint in unsupervised dependency parsing. In *Proceedings of Workshop on Robust Unsupervised and Semisupervised Methods in Natural Language Processing*, pages 1–8.

Mehryar Mohri. 2004. *Weighted Finite-State Transducer Algorithms. An Overview*, pages 551–563. Springer Berlin Heidelberg, Berlin, Heidelberg.

Mehryar Mohri. 2009. Weighted automata algorithms. In Manfred Droste, Werner Kuich, and Heiko Vogler, editors, *Handbook of Weighted Automata*, pages 213–254. Springer Berlin Heidelberg, Berlin, Heidelberg.

Mark-Jan Nederhof. 2021. Calculating the optimal step of arc-eager parsing for non-projective trees. In *Proceedings of the 16th Conference of the European Chapter of the Association for Computational Linguistics: Main Volume*, pages 2273–2283, Online. Association for Computational Linguistics.

M. O. Rabin and D. Scott. 1959. Finite automata and their decision problems. *IBM Journal of Research and Development*, 3(2):114–125.

Stéphane Ross and J. Andrew Bagnell. 2014. Reinforcement and imitation learning via interactive no-regret learning. *CoRR*, abs/1406.5979.

Stephane Ross, Geoffrey Gordon, and Drew Bagnell. 2011. A reduction of imitation learning and structured prediction to no-regret online learning. In *Proceedings of the Fourteenth International Conference on Artificial Intelligence and Statistics*, volume 15 of *Proceedings of Machine Learning Research*, pages 627–635, Fort Lauderdale, FL, USA.

Mitchell Stern, Jacob Andreas, and Dan Klein. 2017. A minimal span-based neural constituency parser. In *Proceedings of the 55th Annual Meeting of the Association for Computational Linguistics (Volume 1: Long Papers)*, pages 818–827, Vancouver, Canada. Association for Computational Linguistics.

Richard S. Sutton and Andrew G. Barto. 2018. *Reinforcement Learning: An Introduction*. A Bradford Book, Cambridge, MA, USA.

Xiang Yu, Ngoc Thang Vu, and Jonas Kuhn. 2018. Approximate dynamic oracle for dependency parsing with reinforcement learning. In *Proceedings of the Second Workshop on Universal Dependencies (UDW 2018)*, pages 183–191, Brussels, Belgium. Association for Computational Linguistics.

Proof net structure for neural Lambek categorial parsing

Aditya Bhargava and **Gerald Penn**
Department of Computer Science
University of Toronto
Toronto, ON, Canada M5S 3G4
{aditya, gpenn}@cs.toronto.edu

Abstract

In this paper, we present the first statistical parser for Lambek categorial grammar (LCG), a grammatical formalism for which the graphical proof method known as *proof nets* is applicable. Our parser incorporates proof net structure and constraints into a system based on self-attention networks via novel model elements. Our experiments on an English LCG corpus show that incorporating term graph structure is helpful to the model, improving both parsing accuracy and coverage. Moreover, we derive novel loss functions by expressing proof net constraints as differentiable functions of our model output, enabling us to train our parser without ground-truth derivations.

1 Introduction

In the family of categorial grammars, combinatory categorial grammar (CCG) has received by far the most attention in the computational linguistics literature. There exist algorithms for both mildly context-sensitive (*e.g.*, Kuhlmann and Satta, 2014) and context-free (typically CKY; Cocke and Schwartz, 1970; Kasami, 1966; Younger, 1967) CCG parsing, and there has been much research on statistical CCG parsers (*e.g.*, Clark and Curran, 2007; Lewis et al., 2016; Stanojević and Steedman, 2020). Another member of the categorial family, Lambek categorial grammar (LCG), has been less well-explored: LCG work has been primarily theoretical or focused on non-statistical parsing.

The recent lack of attention is likely due to two notable results: (1) LCG is weakly context-free equivalent (Pentus, 1997); and (2) LCG parsing is NP-complete (Pentus, 2006; Savateev, 2012). However, neither of these issues is necessarily *practically* relevant. Moreover, LCG presents a number of advantages and interesting properties. For example, LCG provides even greater syntax-semantics transparency than is the case for most CCG parsers because it does not invoke non-categorial rules, maintaining a consistent parsing framework. LCG's rules together define a calculus over syntactic categories that is a subset of linear logic (Girard, 1987).

LCG, like CCG or LTAG, is a highly lexicalized formalism: lexical categories encode substantial syntactic information, and as a result are themselves complex and structured. Despite this, the inner structure of the categories has not been strongly considered in parsers beyond evaluating the category for compatibility with a grammatical rule.

In this paper, we present the first statistical LCG parser. Unlike past parsers for CCG or LTAG, our parser explicitly incorporates structural aspects of the grammar. We base our system on *proof nets*, a graphical method for representing linear logic proofs that abstracts over irrelevant aspects, such as the order of application of logical rules (Girard, 1987; Roorda, 1992). This corresponds to the problem of spurious ambiguity, making proof nets an attractive choice for representing derivations.

Our work has two primary contributions. First, we introduce a self-attention–based LCG parsing model that incorporates proof net structure in multiple ways. We find that minding proof net structure enables us to define a model that is differentiable through this categorial structure down to the atomic categories of the grammar, improving parsing accuracy and coverage on an English LCG corpus.

Second, proof net constraints allow us to define novel grammatico-structural loss functions that can be used as training objectives. This enables us to train a parser *without ground-truth derivations* that has high coverage and even frequently includes the correct parse among the parses that it finds. Our analysis shows that all of our components contribute to the parser's performance, but that planarity information is especially important.

Proceedings of the 17th International Conference on Parsing Technologies (IWPT 2021), pages 13–25
Bangkok, Thailand (online), August 6, 2021. ©2021 Association for Computational Linguistics

$$\frac{\Delta \vdash X/Y \quad \Gamma \vdash Y}{\Delta, \Gamma \vdash X} /_e \qquad \frac{\Gamma \vdash Y \quad \Delta \vdash X\backslash Y}{\Gamma, \Delta \vdash X} \backslash_e$$

$$\frac{\Gamma, Y \vdash X}{\Gamma \vdash X/Y} /_i \qquad \frac{Y, \Gamma \vdash X}{\Gamma \vdash X\backslash Y} \backslash_i$$

$$\frac{}{X \vdash X} \text{axiom}$$

Figure 1: The rules of the associative Lambek calculus without product and allowing empty premises.

2 Background

2.1 Lambek categorial grammar

Lexical categories in LCG, like those of CCG, comprise an infinite set of categories that is formed by the closure of two binary connectives, the forward (/) and backward slash (\), on a small set of **atomic** (*i.e.*, primitive) categories, such as S and NP for sentences and noun phrases. The connectives both create functional categories, and they differ in which of a word or phrase a specified argument must appear. For example, (S\NP)/NP/NP represents a category that combines with two NPs to its right and one NP to its left to yield a valid S.[1] In English, this category might represent a ditransitive verb.

Figure 1 shows the rules of inference for **L***, the associative Lambek calculus without product and allowing empty premises. In L*, statements, called **sequents**, have (ordered) lists of categories as **antecedents** on the left of the turnstile and single categories as **consequents** on the right. The interpretation of a sequent is that its consequent can be derived from its antecedents. The rules have their **premises** above a bar, **conclusions** below, and a label for the rule to the right. Rules $/_e$ and $\backslash_e$ *eliminate* a slashed category, in that it is missing from their conclusions; rules $/_i$ and $\backslash_i$ *introduce* a new slashed functor in the consequent of their conclusions.

Each rule states that its concluding sequent is true (derivable) if and only if all of its premises are. X and Y are variables over categories (atomic or complex) while Δ and Γ are variables over possibly-empty[2] *lists* of categories. A typical application of LCG is to look up a category for each word in a sentence and then inquire whether the consequent S is derivable from the antecedent that lists these categories in the same order as their words.

While some of CCG's rules are not derivable in the Lambek calculus (*inter alia*, crossing composition and substitution), first-degree harmonic composition and type-raising are. At the same time, LCG's introduction rules cannot be derived by any CCG with finite rules (Zielonka, 1981).

Although LCG parsing is known to be an NP-complete problem (Pentus, 2006; Savateev, 2012), Fowler (2010) presented an algorithm that is exponential only in category *order*, a quantity that is bounded to small values in practice (Fowler, 2016).

2.2 Term graphs: enhanced proof nets

Our work in this paper is based on a variety of proof net known as term graphs. A **term graph** is a digraph that represents a sequent proof in the Lambek calculus. The atoms of the sequent correspond to vertices in the graph, and the internal structure of the lexical categories is represented by **regular** edges and **Lambek** edges between the vertices. Together, the vertices, regular edges, and Lambek edges are referred to as a **proof frame**, which is invariant across possible proofs for the sequent. A proof is represented by a proof frame plus by an additional set of regular edges between the vertices called a **linkage**. Different linkages correspond to different proofs, which in turn correspond to different syntactic parses. For a term graph to be valid, the frame-plus-linkage is subject to certain conditions, detailed below.[3]

To construct a proof frame for a sequent $A_1, A_2, \ldots, A_n \vdash B$, the categories in the sequent are first assigned positive or negative polarities. Each lexical category A_i of the antecedent is marked negative (A_i^-), while the consequent B is marked positive (B^+). Each polarized category is decomposed into its polarized atoms according to a set of recursively-applied rules. These rules also specify the regular and Lambek edges between the atoms, represented as solid and dashed edges, respectively. The lexical decomposition rules are:

$$(X/Y)^- \Rightarrow X^- \rightarrow Y^+ \quad (X\backslash Y)^- \Rightarrow Y^+ \leftarrow X^-$$
$$(X\backslash Y)^+ \Rightarrow X^+ \dashrightarrow Y^- \quad (X/Y)^+ \Rightarrow Y^- \dashleftarrow X^+$$

The total order of the frame (indicated left-to-right) is determined by the ordering of the lexical categories in the sequent together with the ordering specified in the decomposition rules above.

A linkage for a proof frame consists of directed edges called **links** from positive vertices to negative vertices of the same atomic category. Valid linkages form perfect matchings: each vertex in the frame

[1] Although LCG's usual notation employs these connectives slightly differently, we use CCG notation here.

[2] There are calculus variants that disallow such empty lists.

[3] See (Fowler, 2009, 2016) for full details.

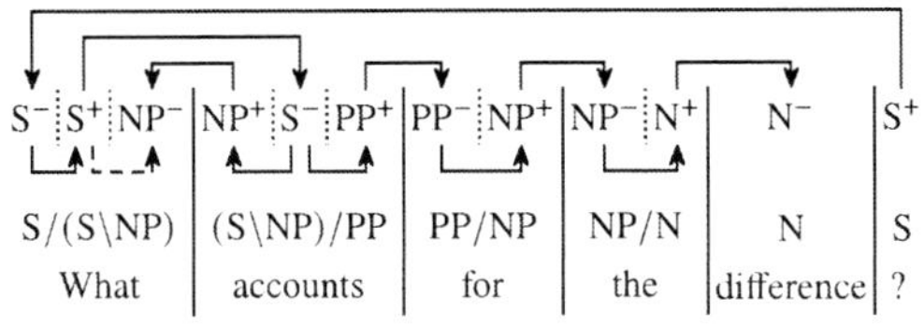

Figure 2: An example term graph. Dotted vertical lines delimit polarized atoms within a word; solid vertical lines mark lexical boundaries. The linkage is shown above the atoms; the proof frame edges are shown below them, with solid regular edges and dashed Lambek edges. The consequent category is aligned with sentence-final punctuation for convenience. This single term graph represents multiple spuriously ambiguous derivations.

has exactly one link, and that link is outgoing for positive vertices and incoming for negative vertices.

A term graph represents a proof in L* (Fowler, 2009), and therefore also an LCG parse, so long as it meets the following conditions:

T1. The linkage is half-planar; *i.e.*, the links can be drawn above the linearly-ordered vertices without crossing.

T2. Treating links as regular edges, the graph is regular-acyclic; *i.e.*, there are no cycles containing only regular edges.

T3. For each Lambek edge $\langle i, j\rangle$, there exists a regular path from i to j.

A term graph that satisfies these conditions is called **L*-integral**. Figure 2 shows an example term graph.

3 Neural network LCG parsing

For categorial and other highly-lexicalized grammatical formalisms, the standard approach to statistical syntactic parsing separates the problem into two steps: (1) a supertagger assigns lexical categories to the words in the input sentence; then (2) a parser uses the supertagger's predictions to produce a predicted parse for the sentence. With proof nets, the lexical categories uniquely determine the proof frame, so supertagging can be seen as predicting a proof frame for the sentence. The second step then corresponds to predicting the linkage for the proof frame. Of course, the linkage must, together with the proof frame, yield an L*-integral term graph.

Our work in this paper focuses on the latter component. Our parser is constructed such that we can separate its aspects that incorporate term graph structure and constraints from a "baseline" model which uses almost no such information. To provide a broad overview, our baseline model runs a Transformer encoder stack (Vaswani et al., 2017) over the proof frame vertices. The top encoder block is truncated, omitting everything after and including the softmax, which directly yields scores for every pair; we mask these scores so that only valid links (*i.e.*, those from positive vertices to negative vertices of the same atomic category) are considered.

We next detail our baseline model in Section 3.1 and then our various methods for incorporating term graph structure in Sections 3.2–3.4. Note that we use named tensor notation (Chiang et al., 2021) in the mathematical descriptions.

3.1 Baseline: parsing by predicting links

3.1.1 Parser inputs

Our baseline model takes as input a sentence, an associated proof frame, and an alignment between the words in the sentence and the polarized atoms that are the proof frame's vertices. We represent each word as a vector of size $|\mathsf{vec}|$ so that a sentence of length $|\mathsf{words}|$ is represented as a matrix $\boldsymbol{H} \in \mathbb{R}^{\mathsf{words} \times \mathsf{vec}}$. For a grammar with atomic categories $\mathcal{T} = \{t_1, t_2, \ldots, t_{|\mathcal{T}|}\}$, the set of possible polarized atoms is $\mathcal{P}_{\mathcal{T}} = \{t_1^+, t_1^-, t_2^+, t_2^-, \cdots, t_{|\mathcal{T}|}^+, t_{|\mathcal{T}|}^-\}$; the proof frame vertices are thus each represented as one-hot vectors of width $|\mathsf{pt}| = |\mathcal{P}_{\mathcal{T}}| = 2|\mathcal{T}|$. A proof frame with $|\mathsf{vtx}|$ vertices is represented by stacking its vertex's vectors, forming a matrix $\boldsymbol{N} \in \{0,1\}^{\mathsf{vtx} \times \mathsf{pt}}$ with $\sum_{\mathsf{pt}} \boldsymbol{N} = 1$. The vtx axis is ordered according to the vertices' total order. Finally, the word-vertex alignment is represented as a matrix $\boldsymbol{M} \in \{0,1\}^{\mathsf{vtx} \times \mathsf{words}}$ where $\boldsymbol{M}_{\mathsf{vtx}(i),\mathsf{words}(j)} = 1$ if and only if vertex i corresponds to word j.

3.1.2 Transformer encoder stack

The Transformer encoder stack as defined by Vaswani et al. (2017) adds positional encoding vectors to the model inputs. In our case, we have two input sequences (polarized atoms and word vectors) of differing lengths, along with an alignment between them. We include the positional encoding vectors over the *word* positions as inputs to the encoder, and apply *relative* positional attention (Dai et al., 2019) during the self-attention step over the *polarized atom* positions. We found this combination most effective during development.

More precisely, we add the usual sinusoidal positional encoding vectors (Vaswani et al., 2017) $\boldsymbol{P}_{\mathrm{w}} \in \mathbb{R}^{\mathsf{words} \times \mathsf{vec}}$ to the word vectors and map the result to the vertex indices. We embed the polarized atoms $\boldsymbol{N}$ via trainable matrix $\boldsymbol{A} \in \mathbb{R}^{\mathsf{pt} \times \mathsf{vec}}$ and add them to their corresponding word vectors to yield inputs $\boldsymbol{X}_0 \in \mathbb{R}^{\mathsf{vtx}\times\mathsf{vec}}$ for the encoder stack:

$$[\mathrm{PE}(p)]_{\mathsf{vec}(i)} = \begin{cases} \sin\left(\frac{p-1}{10^{4(i-1)/|\mathsf{vec}|}}\right) & i \text{ odd} \\ \cos\left(\frac{p-1}{10^{4(i-2)/|\mathsf{vec}|}}\right) & i \text{ even} \end{cases}$$

$$[\boldsymbol{P}_\mathrm{w}]_{\mathsf{words}(p)} = \mathrm{PE}(p)$$

$$\boldsymbol{X}_0 = (\boldsymbol{H} + \boldsymbol{P}_\mathrm{w}) \underset{\mathsf{words}}{\odot} \boldsymbol{M} + \boldsymbol{N} \underset{\mathsf{pt}}{\odot} \boldsymbol{A}$$

The Transformer encoder stack consists of L encoder layers. Denoting the input to layer l as $\boldsymbol{X}_{l-1}$, with $\boldsymbol{X}_0$ as above, each layer computes $\boldsymbol{X}_l$ as:

$$\boldsymbol{T}_l = \mathrm{SelfAttn}_l(\boldsymbol{X}_{l-1}) + \boldsymbol{X}_{l-1}$$
$$\boldsymbol{X}_l = \mathrm{FFN}_l(\boldsymbol{T}_l) + \boldsymbol{T}_l$$

with FFN defined as in (Vaswani et al., 2017).[4]

From a given input sequence, standard self-attention computes query, key, and value tensors. Although all three tensors derive from the same input sequence, the key and value tensors function as "memory" tensors, so their sequence axis is a "lookup" axis distinct from that of the query tensors. In our case, the input sequence axis is vtx, so we preserve this distinction by renaming the vtx axis to vtx′ for the key and value tensors.

We employ relative positional encoding following Dai et al. (2019), allowing our model to directly learn to attend to polarized atoms at positions relative to a given atom. The *relative* positional vectors are represented as a tensor $\boldsymbol{P}_\mathrm{v} \in \mathbb{R}^{\mathsf{vtx}\times\mathsf{vtx'}\times\mathsf{vec}}$ so that $[\boldsymbol{P}_\mathrm{v}]_{\mathsf{vtx}(i),\mathsf{vtx'}(j)} = \mathrm{PE}(i-j)$ is the encoding of position j (on the key/value axis) *relative to* position i (on the query axis).

For multi-headed self-attention, each encoder layer l computes $|\mathsf{heads}|$ attention heads, each of width $|\mathsf{hdim}|$. We thus have trainable parameters $\boldsymbol{W}_{\mathrm{q},l}, \boldsymbol{W}_{\mathrm{k},l}, \boldsymbol{W}_{\mathrm{v},l}, \boldsymbol{W}_{\mathrm{r},l}\boldsymbol{W}_{\mathrm{o},l} \in \mathbb{R}^{\mathsf{heads}\times\mathsf{hdim}\times\mathsf{vec}}$ and $\boldsymbol{b}_{\mathrm{k},l}, \boldsymbol{b}_{\mathrm{r},l} \in \mathbb{R}^{\mathsf{heads}\times\mathsf{hdim}}$ with which we compute the query, key, value, relative position encoding, and attention score tensors $\boldsymbol{Q}_l, \boldsymbol{K}_l, \boldsymbol{V}_l, \boldsymbol{R}_l$, and $\boldsymbol{S}_l$ as:

$$\boldsymbol{Q}_l = \boldsymbol{W}_{\mathrm{q},l} \underset{\mathsf{vec}}{\odot} \boldsymbol{X}_{l-1} \tag{1}$$

$$\boldsymbol{K}_l = \boldsymbol{W}_{\mathrm{k},l} \underset{\mathsf{vec}}{\odot} [\boldsymbol{X}_{l-1}]_{\mathsf{vtx}\to\mathsf{vtx'}} \tag{2}$$

$$\boldsymbol{V}_l = \boldsymbol{W}_{\mathrm{v},l} \underset{\mathsf{vec}}{\odot} [\boldsymbol{X}_{l-1}]_{\mathsf{vtx}\to\mathsf{vtx'}}$$

$$\boldsymbol{R}_l = \boldsymbol{W}_{\mathrm{r},l} \underset{\mathsf{vec}}{\odot} \boldsymbol{P}_\mathrm{v}$$

[4]We apply layer normalization (Ba et al., 2016) as well, but omit it here for concision. We use the "pre-norm" application order (Wang et al., 2019; Nguyen and Salazar, 2019).

$$\boldsymbol{S}_l = \frac{(\boldsymbol{Q}_l + \boldsymbol{b}_{\mathrm{k},l}) \underset{\mathsf{hdim}}{\odot} \boldsymbol{K}_l + (\boldsymbol{Q}_l + \boldsymbol{b}_{\mathrm{r},l}) \underset{\mathsf{hdim}}{\odot} \boldsymbol{R}_l}{\sqrt{|\mathsf{hdim}|}} \tag{3}$$

where vtx → vtx′ denotes renaming axis vtx to vtx′. Next, with final trainable parameter $\boldsymbol{W}_{\mathrm{o},l} \in \mathbb{R}^{\mathsf{heads}\times\mathsf{hdim}\times\mathsf{vec}}$, we compute the $\mathrm{SelfAttn}_l$ output:

$$\mathrm{SelfAttn}_l(\boldsymbol{X}_{l-1}) = \boldsymbol{W}_{\mathrm{o},l} \underset{\substack{\mathsf{hdim}\\\mathsf{heads}}}{\odot} \left(\underset{\mathsf{vtx'}}{\mathrm{softmax}}(\boldsymbol{S}_l) \underset{\mathsf{vtx'}}{\odot} \boldsymbol{V}_l \right) \tag{4}$$

Each encoder layer includes all of these steps except for the final layer $l = L$, where we omit Equation 4.

Finally, we apply a mask $\boldsymbol{F} \in \{0, \infty\}^{\mathsf{vtx}\times\mathsf{vtx'}}$ to ensure that only edges from positive atoms to negative atoms of the same category are considered:

$$\boldsymbol{F}_{\mathsf{vtx}(i),\mathsf{vtx'}(j)} = \begin{cases} 0 & \text{if } \mathrm{atom}(i) = \mathrm{atom}(j) \\ & \text{and } \mathrm{pol}(i) > \mathrm{pol}(j), \\ \infty & \text{otherwise} \end{cases}$$

$$\boldsymbol{S} = \underset{\mathsf{heads}}{\mathrm{mean}}(\boldsymbol{S}_L) - \boldsymbol{F} \tag{5}$$

where $\mathrm{atom}(i)$ returns the category of vertex i and:

$$\mathrm{pol}(i) = \begin{cases} 1 & \text{if vertex } i \text{ is positive,} \\ -1 & \text{if vertex } i \text{ is negative.} \end{cases}$$

3.1.3 Linkage loss function

Given the predicted score matrix $\boldsymbol{S}$, it still remains to specify how to predict candidate linkages. We first note the problem with which we are presented at this stage is exactly that of finding the max-weight (or min-cost) perfect bipartite matching. Ideally, $\boldsymbol{S}$ will provide scores that, when optimized over, yield the desired matching, *i.e.*, the ground-truth linkage.

As we aim to train our parser on a corpus with ground-truth linkages using gradient descent, our perfect matching algorithm must be differentiable for training so that gradients can be back-propagated through it from the loss function; we use Sinkhorn's algorithm (Sinkhorn and Knopp, 1967) with temperature, also known as SoftAssign (Kosowsky and Yuille, 1994; Gold and Rangarajan, 1996b). The procedure, which alternates normalizing the rows and columns of $\exp(\boldsymbol{S}/\tau)$, $\tau > 0$, converges to a doubly-stochastic matrix. In the limit of $\tau \to 0$, this converges to the optimal matching (Mena et al., 2018), thereby providing a means of computing the optimal linkage. Moreover, with the addition of standard Gumbel noise, $\boldsymbol{S}$ can be seen to parameterize a distribution over permutation matrices, with the Sinkhorn operator then functioning as a means of sampling from this distribution.

Importantly for training with gradient descent, the operations of Sinkhorn's algorithm are fully differentiable. For a given doubly-stochastic output matrix from Sinkhorn's algorithm, the negative log likelihood $\mathfrak{J}_{\mathrm{NLL}}$ of the ground-truth linkage $\mathcal{L} = \{\langle i_1, j_1\rangle, \langle i_2, j_2\rangle, \ldots, \langle i_{|\mathsf{vtx}|/2}, j_{|\mathsf{vtx}|/2}\rangle\}$ is a natural choice of loss function for training:

$$Z = \underset{\mathsf{vtx},\mathsf{vtx}'}{\mathrm{Sinkhorn}}(\exp(S/\tau)) \tag{6}$$

$$\mathfrak{J}_{\mathrm{NLL}}(\mathcal{L}, Z) = -\underset{\langle i,j\rangle\in\mathcal{L}}{\mathrm{mean}}\left(\ln[Z]_{\mathsf{vtx}(i),\mathsf{vtx}'(j)}\right) \tag{7}$$

Our base model uses this loss function and is trained with the ground-truth linkages as targets.

3.2 Modelling term graph structure

The model just described is a straightforward application of attention scores and Sinkhorn's algorithm to the problem of finding linkages for a proof frame. However, the only place where the structured nature of the proof net is exploited is in the polarity and category restrictions on the matching; other relevant characteristics are not directly taken into account, such as the proof frame or the validity conditions. Given that the validity conditions cannot even be evaluated without the proof frame edges, we hypothesize that including knowledge of the proof frame structure will help the model to select valid linkages, or even the correct one. Similarly, encoding information about the validity conditions themselves may also be beneficial. We therefore incorporate term graph structure into our model in a number of ways, which we now describe.

3.2.1 Regular and Lambek edges

As is, the parser does not have knowledge of the internal structure of the lexical categories; while it receives as input the atomic category and polarity of each vertex in the proof frame, it has no knowledge of the regular and Lambek edges. We hypothesize that incorporating this structure will boost parser performance, as the edges provide crucial information about which links combinations fail to satisfy the validity conditions for term graphs.

To encode these edges in the parser, we alter the inputs to the encoder's attention blocks. We represent the regular edges as an adjacency matrix $E_{\mathrm{R}} \in \{0,1\}^{\mathsf{vtx}\times\mathsf{vtx}'}$ where $[E_{\mathrm{R}}]_{\mathsf{vtx}(i),\mathsf{vtx}'(j)} = 1$ if and only if the proof frame has a regular edge from (negative) vertex i to (positive) vertex j. Lambek edges are represented similarly as an adjacency matrix E_{L}. For each encoder layer l, we introduce four new transformation matrices $W_{\mathrm{q,R},l}, W_{\mathrm{q,L},l}, W_{\mathrm{k,R},l}, W_{\mathrm{k,L},l} \in \mathbb{R}^{\mathsf{heads}\times\mathsf{hdim}\times\mathsf{vec}}$ and alter Equations 1 and 2:

$$\begin{aligned}
Q_l = {} & W_{\mathrm{k},l} \underset{\mathsf{vec}}{\odot} X_{l-1} \\
& + \left[\left(W_{\mathrm{q,R},l} \underset{\mathsf{vec}}{\odot} X_{l-1}\right) \underset{\mathsf{vtx}}{\odot} E_{\mathrm{R}}\right]_{\mathsf{vtx}'\to\mathsf{vtx}} \\
& + \left(W_{\mathrm{q,L},l} \underset{\mathsf{vec}}{\odot} [X_{l-1}]_{\mathsf{vtx}\to\mathsf{vtx}'}\right) \underset{\mathsf{vtx}'}{\odot} E_{\mathrm{L}} \\
K_l = {} & W_{\mathrm{q},l} \underset{\mathsf{vec}}{\odot} [X_{l-1}]_{\mathsf{vtx}\to\mathsf{vtx}'} \\
& + \left[\left(W_{\mathrm{k,R},l} \underset{\mathsf{vec}}{\odot} [X_{l-1}]_{\mathsf{vtx}\to\mathsf{vtx}'}\right) \underset{\mathsf{vtx}'}{\odot} E_{\mathrm{R}}\right]_{\mathsf{vtx}\to\mathsf{vtx}'} \\
& + \left(W_{\mathrm{k,L},l} \underset{\mathsf{vec}}{\odot} X_{l-1}\right) \underset{\mathsf{vtx}}{\odot} E_{\mathrm{L}}
\end{aligned}$$

Per adjacency matrix, this alteration first computes a transformation of the input for both the query and key aspects of the self-attention transformation. Multiplying by the adjacency matrix then, for each vertex i, sets the value to be equal to the sum of the values of either i's out-neighbours or i's in-neighbours, depending on the particular term. This serves as a form of message passing along the graph edges, similar to some methods in graph-based neural networks (Gilmer et al., 2017).

3.2.2 Planarity-aware attention

Condition T1 requires that term graph linkages be half-planar. We include planar crossing information in the attention scores S_l in Equation 3 for each vertex pair by subtracting the mean attention score of conflicting vertex pairs. More formally, let $\mathcal{X}_{ij}$ denote the set of vertex pairs between which a link would cross with a link between vertex pair (i, j) in the half-plane above the linearly ordered vertices of the term graph. Then we adjust S_l as follows:

$$\begin{aligned}
\mathcal{X}'_{ij} &= \left\{(k,m) \,\middle|\, \begin{array}{l} k < i < m < j \\ \text{or } i < k < j < m \end{array}\right\} \\
\mathcal{X}_{ij} &= \mathcal{X}'_{ij} \cup \{(m,k) \mid (k,m) \in \mathcal{X}'_{ij}\} \qquad (8) \\
[\mu_{\mathrm{cross}}(A)]_{\mathsf{vtx}(i),\mathsf{vtx}'(j)} &= \underset{(k,m)\in\mathcal{X}_{ij}}{\mathrm{mean}}[A]_{\mathsf{vtx}(k),\mathsf{vtx}'(m)} \\
S'_l &= \frac{(Q_l + b_{\mathrm{k},l}) \underset{\mathsf{hdim}}{\odot} K_l + (Q_l + b_{\mathrm{r},l}) \underset{\mathsf{hdim}}{\odot} R_l}{\sqrt{|\mathsf{hdim}|}} \\
S_l &= S'_l - \mu_{\mathrm{cross}}(S'_l)
\end{aligned}$$

3.2.3 Edge filtering

In Equation 5, a mask is applied to the candidate link scores produced by the model to enforce the category and polarity constraints. We augment this mask in two ways. First, we disallow *necessarily* non-planar links, *i.e.*, links that cannot be in any planar linkage. Penn (2004) defined a context-free grammar for *building* planar linkages; we use this CFG with the inside-outside algorithm (Baker, 1979) to identify whether candidate links each exist in any spanning planar linkage.

Second, we disallow intra-word links, *i.e.*, links between any two vertices that map to the same word. Some of these links are permissible according to the rules of L*, but do not occur in our corpus; moreover, their linguistic utility is unclear. Overall, we expect that these restrictions on allowable links will help reduce the size of the search space, thereby improving system performance.

Inspecting Figure 2 exemplifies how these extra filters can be useful. Disallowing necessarily non-planar links eliminates a candidate link from the NP^+ of "for" to the NP^- of "What" as it would prevent the NP^+ and S^- of "accounts" as well as the NP^- of "the" each from having any planar links. This then implies that there must be a link from the NP^+ of "for" to the NP^- of "the", since that is the only remaining option. Similarly, disallowing the S^+ of "What" from linking to its own S^- immediately implies that it must then link to the S^- of "accounts" while also preemptively preventing a violation of condition T2.

3.3 k-best linkages

While Sinkhorn (with Gumbel noise) provides differentiable sampling of matchings, it has two noteworthy drawbacks. First, it sometimes does not converge to an exact permutation and gets stuck with some values very close to 0.5 (Guigues, 2020), requiring some means of or discretizing such cases (*e.g.*, Gold and Rangarajan, 1996a). This does not pose a potential issue for our parser during training, since $\mathfrak{J}_{\mathrm{NLL}}$ does not require a permutation matrix. During inference, however, the parser needs to be able to produce a discrete result as its output parse.

Second, Sinkhorn makes it difficult at best to retrieve multiple matchings from the distribution. Without Gumbel noise (and with sufficiently small τ), it will converge to the *best* permutation, but one cannot specifically retrieve the second-best (etc.) matchings from this. Sampling (via the addition of Gumbel noise) may yield *multiple* matchings, but there is no guarantee of their overall rank; furthermore, if the input matrix represents a very concentrated distribution, retrieving further matchings may require inordinate sampling rounds.

Since there can be multiple valid parses for a sentence, a parser should ideally be able to return multiple parses if they exist. Moreover, there is no guarantee that the predicted linkage $\boldsymbol{Z}$ in Equation 6 will yield an L*-integral term graph, so it is worthwhile to be able to evaluate alternatives. We therefore use Murty's algorithm (Murty, 1968), a k-best optimal matching algorithm, to produce k candidate linkages from $\boldsymbol{S}$. We stably sort the linkages according to the number of term graph conditions that they violate when combined with the input proof frame, allowing fractional violations of condition T3. Enabling the production of multiple candidate parses also makes it possible for the parser to return the correct parse when it otherwise might not have done so.

3.4 L* structural loss

In contrast to other statistical parsers, the system presented thus far does not have any explicit encoding of the rules of the grammar. Since the negative log-likelihood loss function (Equation 7) is based only on the ground-truth linkage, it is not clear how well the model will be able to generalize and return multiple valid linkages when applicable, rather than linkages most similar to the correct one. We therefore introduce loss function terms that directly encode the term graph validity conditions, and posit that they will help the parser produce linkages that, with the input proof frame, yield an L*-integral term graph. These novel loss functions also enable training our model without ground-truth derivations.

For condition T1, we define the planarity loss function $\mathfrak{J}_{\mathrm{T1}}$ as a function of the post-Sinkhorn matrix $\boldsymbol{Z}$ from Equation 6 so that each link in each pair of crossing links is penalized in proportion to the scores given to the pair:

$$\mathfrak{J}_{\mathrm{T1}}(\boldsymbol{Z}) = \sum_{i,j} \left(\boldsymbol{Z}_{\mathsf{vtx}(i),\mathsf{vtx}'(j)} \sum_{(k,m)\in X_{ij}} \boldsymbol{Z}_{\mathsf{vtx}(k),\mathsf{vtx}'(m)} \right)$$

where X_{ij} is defined as in Equation 8. Minimizing $\mathfrak{J}_{\mathrm{T1}}$ then corresponds to minimizing the scores assigned to crossing links.

The remaining loss terms require further computation. Note that conditions T2 and T3 both express constraints on the (non-)existence of certain *regular* paths; the latter is already stated as such while the former can be equivalently restated as barring regular paths from any vertex to itself. Checking for the existence or absence of paths between two vertices of a graph requires traversing graph edges. As graph traversal corresponds to multiplication by the graph's adjacency matrix, this presents a differentiable means of computing the extent to which a candidate term graph meets conditions T2 and T3.

For an arbitrary weighted graph G with vertices $\mathcal{V}$, denote by $\mathcal{W}_{i,j,n}$ the set of all walks of length n from vertex i to vertex j. By definition, each walk $w \in \mathcal{W}_{i,j,n}$ is a sequence of n edges, *i.e.*, $w = (\langle k_1, l_1\rangle, \langle k_2, l_2\rangle, \ldots, \langle k_n, l_n\rangle), k_1 = i, l_n = j$. Let $\boldsymbol{A}$ denote the adjacency matrix of G; then the matrix power $\boldsymbol{A}^n$ represents the sum (over walks) of walk edge products, *i.e.*, $(\boldsymbol{A}^n)_{i,j} = \sum_{w \in \mathcal{W}_{i,j,n}} \prod_{\langle k,l\rangle \in w} (\boldsymbol{A})_{k,l}$. If edges in G have only positive weights, then $(\boldsymbol{A}^n)_{i,j} = 0$ if and only if there are no walks of length n from vertex i to vertex j. It then follows that $(\sum_{n=1}^{N} \boldsymbol{A}^n)_{i,j} = 0$ if and only if there are no walks of length $\leq N$ from vertex i to vertex j. Since a cycle in G can have length at most $|\mathcal{V}|$, G is therefore acyclic if and only if $(\sum_{n=1}^{N} \boldsymbol{A}^n)_{i,i} = 0 \, \forall i \in \mathcal{V}, N \geq |\mathcal{V}|$.

Returning to term graphs, for condition T2 this means that we can detect regular cycles in a candidate graph with $|\mathcal{V}|$ vertices by constructing an adjacency matrix $\boldsymbol{A} \in \mathbb{R}^{|\mathcal{V}| \times |\mathcal{V}|}$ from the regular edges of the proof frame together with the candidate linkage, computing $\sum_{n=1}^{|\mathcal{V}|} \boldsymbol{A}^n$, and then verifying that the diagonal entries are all zero. For condition T3, we can similarly inspect the entries corresponding to the parent and child nodes of all Lambek edges and verify that they are all one, indicating that a regular path exists. We can now see how to specify these conditions as loss functions:

$$\boldsymbol{G} = \sum_{n=1}^{|\mathrm{vtx}|} \boldsymbol{A}^n = \sum_{n=1}^{|\mathrm{vtx}|} (\boldsymbol{E}_{\mathrm{R}} + \boldsymbol{Z})^n$$

$$\mathfrak{I}_{\mathrm{T2}}(\boldsymbol{G}) = \sum_{i=1}^{|\mathrm{vtx}|} (\boldsymbol{G}_{i,i})^2$$

$$\mathfrak{I}_{\mathrm{T3}}(\boldsymbol{G}) = \sum_{i=1}^{|\mathrm{vtx}|} \sum_{j=1}^{|\mathrm{vtx}|} (\boldsymbol{E}_{\mathrm{L}})_{i,j} (\boldsymbol{G}_{i,j} - 1)^2$$

Minimizing $\mathfrak{I}_{\mathrm{T2}}$ and $\mathfrak{I}_{\mathrm{T3}}$ correspond to minimizing violations of conditions T2 and T3, respectively.

We refer to the sum of these three loss functions $\mathfrak{I}_{\mathrm{L*}} = \mathfrak{I}_{\mathrm{T1}} + \mathfrak{I}_{\mathrm{T2}} + \mathfrak{I}_{\mathrm{T3}}$ as the **(L*) structural loss.**

4 Related work

A key aspect of our parser is that it makes use of a structured decomposition of lexical categories in categorial grammars. In this sense, our work follows up on the intuition of recent "constructive" supertaggers, which have been explored for a type-logical grammar (Kogkalidis et al., 2019) and for CCG (Bhargava and Penn, 2020; Prange et al., 2021). Such supertaggers construct categories out of the atomic categories of the grammar; this challenges the classical approach to supertagging, where lexical categories are treated as opaque, rendering the task of supertagging equivalent to large-tagset POS tagging. With this view, it becomes possible for novel categories to be produced; furthermore, the supertaggers are better able to incorporate prediction history and thereby produce grammatical outputs (Bhargava and Penn, 2020).

Recently, Kogkalidis et al. (2020) proposed a system for parsing a "type-logical" grammar that is essentially a modal, non-directional extension of LCG. The Dutch grammar they used is substantially different from our grammar: their connectives are both modal and non-directional; in addition, they have far more atomic categories. While their model is similar to our baseline (Section 3.1), our work here differs substantially in that we incorporate proof-net structural elements and validity conditions, and our system is able to return multiple linkages (Sections 3.2–3.4). Our approach also enables ground-truth–free training.[5]

Lastly, our trained parser operates in polynomial time. Since LCG parsing is NP-complete, our work adds to the body of recent work applying neural networks to NP-hard combinatorial optimization problems to yield polynomial-time approximate solvers (*e.g.*, Li et al., 2018; Gannouni et al., 2020; Sultana et al., 2020; Cappart et al., 2021).

5 Experiments

5.1 Data

We train our models on LCGbank, a semi-automatic conversion of CCGbank to LCG (Fowler, 2016). This conversion necessitated adjusting for instances of CCG's crossing rules that are not permitted in LCG, as well as providing fully categorial parses for the cases in CCGbank where non-categorial rules are used (*e.g.*, unary type-changing).[6] LCGbank also omits features on its categories and includes

[5]Although Kogkalidis et al. (2020) describe their model's training as "end-to-end", their approach is perhaps better described as *joint* training. A truly end-to-end system would allow *differentiation* through the supertagger/proof frame construction, which remains a topic for further investigation.

[6]Refer to (Fowler, 2016) for further conversion details.

Category	Count	Category	Count
NP	1,356,438	,	32
S	563,390	RRB	26
N	419,766	:	16
PP	48,642	.	2
conj	844	LRB	2

Table 1: Counts of atomic categories in LCGbank.

the 274 sentences that were originally excluded from CCGbank. These adjustments substantially increase the number of lexical categories in LCGbank compared to CCGbank. Without the features, CCGbank has 476 unique lexical categories, while LCGbank has 987. Decomposed, the categories yield 10 atomic categories, shown in Table 1.

We follow the CCGbank/PTB tradition of using section 0 for development/validation and section 23 for testing, yielding 1,921 and 2,414 sentences, respectively. For training, however, we use all of the remaining data (sections 1–22 and 24), in contrast to the usual training set for CCGbank (sections 2–21). This is simply to make full use of all available data and yields 44,833 sentences for training.

5.2 Model & training details

We implement our model with PyTorch (Paszke et al., 2019) and PyTorch Lightning (Falcon et al., 2019). Including the truncated top layer, we use three encoder layers (*i.e.*, $L = 3$) with $|\mathsf{vec}| = 384$ and $|\mathsf{heads}| = 4$. We use ReLU activations (Nair and Hinton, 2010) throughout. Parameters are initialized according to PyTorch's defaults. Our transformer uses normalization before each layer rather than after (Wang et al., 2019; Nguyen and Salazar, 2019). To represent the lexical inputs, we use a distilled (Sanh et al., 2019) version of Roberta (Liu et al., 2019) as provided by the Hugging Face Transformers library (Wolf et al., 2020).

For our inside-outside algorithm implementation, we adopt Rush's (2020) overall method for adapting it to GPU matrix operations. We implement the intensive parts of the algorithm as custom CUDA kernels that operate on packed Booleans. We use the fastmurty library (Motro and Ghosh, 2019) for the k-best matchings algorithm.

Training examples are sorted by output sequence length to yield efficient batches; the ordering of the batches is shuffled every epoch. We clip gradients, scaling accordingly, if the sum of gradient norms exceeds 1. We train our models with the AdamW optimizer (Loshchilov and Hutter, 2019; Kingma and Ba, 2014) for 40 epochs, halving the learning rate when performance reaches a plateau with patience of three epochs. We keep the model weights from the epoch with the best development set performance. We report results averaged over three training runs with different random seeds.

We tune hyperparameters with Optuna (Akiba et al., 2019), using the tree-structured Parzen estimator (Bergstra et al., 2011) for sampling and asynchronous successive halving (Karnin et al., 2013; Jamieson and Talwalkar, 2016; Li et al., 2020) for pruning. The initial learning rate and weight decay coefficients are sampled from log-uniform distributions on $[10^{-5}, 10^{-2})$ and $[10^{-7}, 10^{-2})$, respectively. The dropout rate is sampled from a uniform distribution on $[0, 0.6)$. We also use dropout on the input lexical tokens, sampled uniformly on $[0, 0.1)$.

5.3 Experimental conditions and evaluation

We evaluate four conditions: (1) the baseline model (Section 3.1) trained only with $\mathfrak{J}_{\mathrm{NLL}}$; (2) the improved model (Section 3.2) trained only with $\mathfrak{J}_{\mathrm{NLL}}$; (3) the improved model trained with both $\mathfrak{J}_{\mathrm{NLL}}$ and $\mathfrak{J}_{\mathrm{L}^*}$; and (4) the improved model trained only with $\mathfrak{J}_{\mathrm{L}^*}$. The latter condition is trained without ground truth while the others are trained with it. Since comparing the two cases would be unfair (especially on a measure such as sentence accuracy), we evaluate them separately. To evaluate the effect of allowing k-best linkages (Section 3.3), we evaluate all conditions with both $k = 1$ and $k = 512$. Note that with $k = 1$, our baseline model is similar in design to that of Kogkalidis et al. (2020), with minor differences such as model sizes and vector embedding details; this represents the closest point of comparison while controlling for our other model aspects as well as our grammar and corpus.

We evaluate our parser using four measures: (1) **link accuracy**, the percentage of positive vertices that were assigned their correct negative vertex; (2) **sentence accuracy**, the percentage of sentences with 100% link accuracy; (3) **coverage**, the percentage of sentences for which an L*-integral linkage was found; and (4) the average number of unique parses (*i.e.*, L*-integral) found per sentence.

When used for computing $\mathfrak{J}_{\mathrm{NLL}}$, we use Sinkhorn temperature $\tau = 0.01$. We use a separate temperature parameter τ_{L^*} when computing $\mathfrak{J}_{\mathrm{L}^*}$. The intuition behind this is that because $\mathfrak{J}_{\mathrm{NLL}}$

	Condition	LAcc	SAcc	Cov	Parses
$k = 1$	Baseline	97.7	86.2	97.3	—
	+TG	97.9	87.4	98.4	—
	+TG+$\mathfrak{I}_{\mathrm{L}^*}$	97.9	87.2	98.7	—
$k = 512$	Baseline	97.9	87.7	99.8	5.9
	+TG	98.0	88.2	99.96	5.7
	+TG+$\mathfrak{I}_{\mathrm{L}^*}$	98.0	87.8	99.96	5.8

Table 2: Link accuracies (LAcc), sentence accuracies (SAcc), coverage (Cov), and average number of parses per sentence for the $\mathfrak{I}_{\mathrm{NLL}}$-trained systems on the LCGbank test set. +TG refers to the model changes of Section 3.2. +TG+$\mathfrak{I}_{\mathrm{L}^*}$ includes the model changes and is trained with both $\mathfrak{I}_{\mathrm{NLL}}$ and $\mathfrak{I}_{\mathrm{L}^*}$. All values are averages over three random seeds.

permits one specific parse while $\mathfrak{I}_{\mathrm{L}^*}$ permits multiple parses, they may require different levels of uncertainty in their corresponding doubly-stochastic matrices. We treat τ_{L^*} as a hyperparameter with initial values sampled log-uniformly on $[0.01, 10)$.

For the condition that includes both $\mathfrak{I}_{\mathrm{NLL}}$ and $\mathfrak{I}_{\mathrm{L}^*}$, we linearly combine the two to obtain the final objective function $\mathfrak{I} = \alpha\,\mathfrak{I}_{\mathrm{NLL}} + (1-\alpha)\,\mathfrak{I}_{\mathrm{L}^*}$. We tune α as a hyperparameter as well, with initial uniform sampling on $[0.05, 0.95)$.

5.4 Results

5.4.1 Training with ground truth

Table 2 shows the performance of the systems trained against gold-standard linkages. Evaluating multiple linkages from the single score matrix $\boldsymbol{S}$ is clearly beneficial on all accounts. In particular, doing so yields almost complete coverage for all cases, but especially for our two improved versions. The accuracies improve as well; since our sorting of multiple candidates linkages is stable, the improvements to sentence accuracy come from cases where the correct parse was scored higher than other valid parses, but lower than some invalid parses. Here, filtering the list using the term graph validity conditions is clearly useful.

Incorporating term graph structure in the model as described in Section 3.2 improves performance as well, though not by as much as evaluating multiple linkages. While we expected the number of parses per sentence found by the parser to increase due to the presence of grammatico-structural information, in fact it returned fewer parses. With $\mathfrak{I}_{\mathrm{NLL}}$ as the sole training objective, the model uses this extra information solely to increase its performance as measured by that objective. Interestingly, adding $\mathfrak{I}_{\mathrm{L}^*}$ to the model improvements seems to *decrease* accuracy, nearly to the baseline's level for the $k = 512$ case. Coverage remains high, however. In this case, we believe that the two training objectives are somewhat conflicting, with $\mathfrak{I}_{\mathrm{NLL}}$ pushing the model towards the correct linkage but $\mathfrak{I}_{\mathrm{L}^*}$ equally preferring other valid linkages.

5.4.2 Training without ground truth

Training a model without ground-truth linkages impairs system performance substantially, as expected: the model has no signal guiding it to the correct linkage, nor differentiating the correct linkage from other valid ones. With $k = 1$, the system achieves 91.2% coverage on the LCGbank test set.

With $k = 512$, this increases substantially to 96.2%. Here the parser finds an average of 5.9 parses/sentence. Since it did not find a single valid parse for 3.8% of sentences, the number of parses found for *covered* sentences is 6.2. This is further in line with the idea that $\mathfrak{I}_{\mathrm{L}^*}$ "pulls" the model away from the correct parse in the direction of other (valid) parses.

Since the loss function cannot distinguish correct linkages from other valid ones, this configuration cannot be expected to select the correct linkage. Nonetheless, the correct parse appears in the system's set of output parses for 79.0% of sentences, appearing at the top (*i.e.*, the correct sentence is given the highest score) for 53.4% of sentences with $k = 1$ and 54.9% of sentences with $k = 512$.

5.5 Analysis

Finally, we conduct a post-hoc ablation study for the ground-truth–free condition. For each ablated as, we adjust the model or loss function accordingly, and then retrain the model from scratch using the same hyperparameters as the original model. Table 3 shows the results, comparing coverage of the ablated versions with that of the original.

We see that removing all planarity information (*i.e.*, the link filtering, the planarity-aware attention, and the planarity loss term $\mathfrak{I}_{\mathrm{T1}}$) is disastrous; this condition has by far the largest drop in coverage. This is especially notable as LCG proof nets must be half-planar due to the non-commutativity of L*; this useful constraint is not present in type-logical grammars that do not have this property, such as that employed by Kogkalidis et al. (2020).

Other decreases range from moderate to small:

Condition	$k = 1$	$k = 512$
+TG+$\mathfrak{I}_{L^*}$−$\mathfrak{I}_{NLL}$	91.2	96.2
−$\mathfrak{I}_{T1}$	84.5	95.1
−$\mathfrak{I}_{T2}$	72.9	92.9
−$\mathfrak{I}_{T3}$	70.6	93.8
−RL	89.0	95.9
−IW	81.1	91.0
−IW−NP	73.9	85.6
−RL−IW−NP−PA	74.9	90.7
−IW−NP−PA−$\mathfrak{I}_{T1}$	19.2	44.7

Table 3: LCGbank test set coverage under various ground-truth–free training conditions. −$\mathfrak{I}_x$ removes loss term x; −RL removes regular and Lambek edges; −IW removes the filter on intra-word links; −NP removes the filter on non-planar links; −PA removes planarity-aware attention. In contrast to Table 2, here the ablated versions (all but the first line) are results from one single training run each.

- All three loss terms are important, with coverage decreasing notably upon ablation; the decrease is lowest for $\mathfrak{I}_{T1}$, suggesting that its removal is partially ameliorated by the other sources of planarity information in the model.
- Removing the regular and Lambek edge information decreases coverage by a small amount.
- Filtering out intra-word links is surprisingly important; we had suspected that, since the model has information about which words are the same for given atomic category pairs, it would learn to avoid them. If the filter on non-planar links is also removed, coverage drops further. Removing planarity-aware attention and the proof frame edge information (*i.e.*, stripping down to the baseline system of Section 3.1, but here training with the structural loss only) strangely slightly *restores* coverage.

6 Conclusion and future work

We have presented an LCG parser with multiple novel techniques, including neural term graph structure and structural constraint encodings, novel loss functions derived from LCG term graph validity conditions, and a self-attention–based system for returning and efficiently evaluating k-best matchings. Evaluating on a corpus of English LCG proof nets, we found our improvements to be effective, especially the k-best matchings. Our loss functions, furthermore, enable training an LCG parsing model without ground-truth derivations or linkages. Analysis shows that planarity conditions are especially important, but that all of our alterations contribute to the parser's improved performance.

As we saw in Table 2, combining $\mathfrak{I}_{NLL}$ and $\mathfrak{I}_{L^*}$ seems to be detrimental to parser accuracy. The two loss terms have seemingly conflicting objectives, with the former concentrating probability mass around a single solution and the latter spreading probability mass over multiple solutions. We believe it would be worthwhile to explore combining these two in a more congruent manner.

Since our model allows differentiating through the structure of lexical categories, the obvious next step is to incorporate a supertagger and pass gradients down to it. As it stands, supertaggers have rudimentary knowledge of their context, with no notion of how the atomic subcategories of one category might combine with those of another. A tight coupling of the techniques we proposed here with an appropriately designed supertagger would yield a true end-to-end differentiable LCG parser.

Lastly, we believe further investigation of structural constraints and objectives to be promising. Although we still relied on supertags from the corpus, our results with the grammatico-structural loss functions demonstrate the training of a high-coverage parser with a decreased annotation burden. Techniques such as those presented here suggest a potential path to parsing with lower data requirements, or perhaps even to structured, formalism-driven unsupervised parsing.

Acknowledgements

We thank Elizabeth Patitsas as well as our anonymous reviewers for their feedback. This research was enabled in part by support provided by NSERC, SHARCNET, and Compute Canada.

References

Takuya Akiba, Shotaro Sano, Toshihiko Yanase, Takeru Ohta, and Masanori Koyama. 2019. Optuna: A next-generation hyperparameter optimization framework. In *Proceedings of the 25th ACM SIGKDD International Conference on Knowledge Discovery & Data Mining*, KDD '19, pages 2623–2631, New York, NY, USA. Association for Computing Machinery.

Jimmy Lei Ba, Jamie Ryan Kiros, and Geoffrey E. Hinton. 2016. Layer Normalization. In *arXiv:1607.06450 [Cs, Stat]*.

J. K. Baker. 1979. Trainable grammars for speech recognition. *The Journal of the Acoustical Society of America*, 65(S1):S132.

James S. Bergstra, Rémi Bardenet, Yoshua Bengio, and Balázs Kégl. 2011. Algorithms for Hyper-Parameter Optimization. In *Advances in Neural Information Processing Systems*, volume 24, pages 2546–2554. Curran Associates, Inc.

Aditya Bhargava and Gerald Penn. 2020. Supertagging with CCG primitives. In *Proceedings of the 5th Workshop on Representation Learning for NLP*, pages 194–204, Online. Association for Computational Linguistics.

Quentin Cappart, Didier Chételat, Elias Khalil, Andrea Lodi, Christopher Morris, and Petar Veličković. 2021. Combinatorial optimization and reasoning with graph neural networks. *arXiv:2102.09544 [cs, math, stat]*.

David Chiang, Alexander M. Rush, and Boaz Barak. 2021. Named Tensor Notation. *arXiv:2102.13196 [cs]*.

Stephen Clark and James R. Curran. 2007. Wide-Coverage Efficient Statistical Parsing with CCG and Log-Linear Models. *Computational Linguistics*, 33(4):493–552.

John Cocke and J. T. Schwartz. 1970. Programming Languages and Their Compilers: Preliminary Notes, Second Revised Version. Technical report, Courant Institute of Mathematical Sciences, New York University.

Zihang Dai, Zhilin Yang, Yiming Yang, Jaime Carbonell, Quoc Le, and Ruslan Salakhutdinov. 2019. Transformer-XL: Attentive Language Models beyond a Fixed-Length Context. In *Proceedings of the 57th Annual Meeting of the Association for Computational Linguistics*, pages 2978–2988, Florence, Italy. Association for Computational Linguistics.

William A. Falcon, Jirka Borovec, Adrian Wälchli, Nic Eggert, Justus Schock, Jeremy Jordan, Nicki Skafte, Ir1dXD, Vadim Bereznyuk, Ethan Harris, Tullie Murrell, Peter Yu, Sebastian Præsius, Travis Addair, Jacob Zhong, Dmitry Lipin, So Uchida, Shreyas Bapat, Hendrik Schröter, Boris Dayma, Alexey Karnachev, Akshay Kulkarni, Shunta Komatsu, Martin.B, Jean-Baptiste Schiratti, Hadrien Mary, Donal Byrne, Cristobal Eyzaguirre, cinjon, and Anton Bakhtin. 2019. PyTorch Lightning.

Timothy A. D. Fowler. 2009. Term Graphs and the NP-Completeness of the Product-Free Lambek Calculus. In *Formal Grammar*, pages 150–166, Berlin, Heidelberg. Springer Berlin Heidelberg.

Timothy A. D. Fowler. 2010. A Polynomial Time Algorithm for Parsing with the Bounded Order Lambek Calculus. In *The Mathematics of Language*, Lecture Notes in Computer Science, pages 36–43, Berlin, Germany. Springer.

Timothy A. D. Fowler. 2016. *Lambek Categorial Grammars for Practical Parsing*. Ph.D. thesis, University of Toronto.

Aymen Gannouni, Vladimir Samsonov, Mohamed Behery, Tobias Meisen, and Gerhard Lakemeyer. 2020. Neural combinatorial optimization for production scheduling with sequence-dependent setup waste. In *2020 IEEE International Conference on Systems, Man, and Cybernetics (SMC)*, pages 2640–2647, Toronto, Canada. IEEE.

Justin Gilmer, Samuel S. Schoenholz, Patrick F. Riley, Oriol Vinyals, and George E. Dahl. 2017. Neural message passing for quantum chemistry. In *Proceedings of the 34th International Conference on Machine Learning*, volume 70 of *ICML'17*, pages 1263–1272, Sydney, NSW, Australia. JMLR.org.

Jean-Yves Girard. 1987. Linear logic. *Theoretical Computer Science*, 50(1):1–101.

Steven Gold and Anand Rangarajan. 1996a. A graduated assignment algorithm for graph matching. *IEEE Transactions on Pattern Analysis and Machine Intelligence*, 18(4):377–388.

Steven Gold and Anand Rangarajan. 1996b. Softassign versus softmax: Benchmarks in combinatorial optimization. In *Advances in Neural Information Processing Systems*, volume 8. MIT Press.

Laurent Guigues. 2020. Concerning Iterative Graph Normalization and Maximum Weight Independent Sets. *arXiv:2012.07764 [cs, math]*.

Kevin Jamieson and Ameet Talwalkar. 2016. Non-stochastic Best Arm Identification and Hyperparameter Optimization. In *Proceedings of the 19th International Conference on Artificial Intelligence and Statistics*, volume 51 of *Proceedings of Machine Learning Research*, pages 240–248, Cadiz, Spain. PMLR.

Zohar Karnin, Tomer Koren, and Oren Somekh. 2013. Almost Optimal Exploration in Multi-Armed Bandits. In *Proceedings of the 30th International Conference on Machine Learning*, volume 28 of *Proceedings of Machine Learning Research*, pages 1238–1246, Atlanta, USA. PMLR.

T. Kasami. 1966. An Efficient Recognition and Syntax-Analysis Algorithm for Context-Free Languages. Technical Report R-257, University of Illinois Coordinated Science Laboratory.

Diederik P. Kingma and Jimmy Ba. 2014. Adam: A Method for Stochastic Optimization. In *Proceedings of the 3rd International Conference for Learning Representations*, San Diego, USA.

Konstantinos Kogkalidis, Michael Moortgat, and Tejaswini Deoskar. 2019. Constructive Type-Logical Supertagging With Self-Attention Networks. In *Proceedings of the 4th Workshop on Representation Learning for NLP (RepL4NLP-2019)*, pages 113–123, Florence, Italy. Association for Computational Linguistics.

Konstantinos Kogkalidis, Michael Moortgat, and Richard Moot. 2020. Neural Proof Nets. In *Proceedings of the 24th Conference on Computational Natural Language Learning*, pages 26–40, Online. Association for Computational Linguistics.

J.J. Kosowsky and A.L. Yuille. 1994. The invisible hand algorithm: Solving the assignment problem with statistical physics. *Neural Networks*, 7(3):477–490.

Marco Kuhlmann and Giorgio Satta. 2014. A New Parsing Algorithm for Combinatory Categorial Grammar. *Transactions of the Association for Computational Linguistics*, 2:405–418.

Mike Lewis, Kenton Lee, and Luke Zettlemoyer. 2016. LSTM CCG Parsing. In *Proceedings of the 2016 Conference of the North American Chapter of the Association for Computational Linguistics: Human Language Technologies*, pages 221–231, San Diego, California. Association for Computational Linguistics.

Liam Li, Kevin Jamieson, Afshin Rostamizadeh, Ekaterina Gonina, Jonathan Ben-tzur, Moritz Hardt, Benjamin Recht, and Ameet Talwalkar. 2020. A System for Massively Parallel Hyperparameter Tuning. In *Proceedings of Machine Learning and Systems*, volume 2, pages 230–246, Austin, USA.

Zhuwen Li, Qifeng Chen, and Vladlen Koltun. 2018. Combinatorial optimization with graph convolutional networks and guided tree search. In *Advances in Neural Information Processing Systems*, volume 31. Curran Associates, Inc.

Yinhan Liu, Myle Ott, Naman Goyal, Jingfei Du, Mandar Joshi, Danqi Chen, Omer Levy, Mike Lewis, Luke Zettlemoyer, and Veselin Stoyanov. 2019. RoBERTa: A Robustly Optimized BERT Pretraining Approach.

Ilya Loshchilov and Frank Hutter. 2019. Decoupled Weight Decay Regularization. In *Proceedings of the 7th International Conference on Learning Representations*.

Gonzalo Mena, David Belanger, Scott Linderman, and Jasper Snoek. 2018. Learning Latent Permutations with Gumbel-Sinkhorn Networks. In *Proceedings of the 6th International Conference on Learning Representations*, Vancouver, Canada.

Michael Motro and J. Ghosh. 2019. Scaling data association for hypothesis-oriented MHT. In *22nd International Conference on Information Fusion (FUSION)*, pages 1–8, Ottawa, Canada. IEEE.

Katta G. Murty. 1968. An Algorithm for Ranking all the Assignments in Order of Increasing Cost. *Operations Research*, 16(3):682–687.

Vinod Nair and Geoffrey E. Hinton. 2010. Rectified Linear Units Improve Restricted Boltzmann Machines. In *Proceedings of the 27th International Conference on Machine Learning (ICML-10)*, pages 807–814, Haifa, Israel. Omnipress.

Toan Q. Nguyen and Julian Salazar. 2019. Transformers without Tears: Improving the Normalization of Self-Attention. In *Proceedings of the 16th International Workshop on Spoken Language Translation 2019*, Hong Kong. Zenodo.

Adam Paszke, Sam Gross, Francisco Massa, Adam Lerer, James Bradbury, Gregory Chanan, Trevor Killeen, Zeming Lin, Natalia Gimelshein, Luca Antiga, Alban Desmaison, Andreas Kopf, Edward Yang, Zachary DeVito, Martin Raison, Alykhan Tejani, Sasank Chilamkurthy, Benoit Steiner, Lu Fang, Junjie Bai, and Soumith Chintala. 2019. PyTorch: An imperative style, high-performance deep learning library. In *Advances in Neural Information Processing Systems 32*, volume 32, pages 8026–8037. Curran Associates, Inc.

Gerald Penn. 2004. A Graph-Theoretic Approach to Sequent Derivability in the Lambek Calculus. *Electronic Notes in Theoretical Computer Science*, 53:274–295.

Mati Pentus. 1997. Product-Free Lambek Calculus and Context-Free Grammars. *The Journal of Symbolic Logic*, 62(2):648–660.

Mati Pentus. 2006. Lambek calculus is NP-complete. *Theoretical Computer Science*, 357(1-3):186–201.

Jakob Prange, Nathan Schneider, and Vivek Srikumar. 2021. Supertagging the Long Tail with Tree-Structured Decoding of Complex Categories. *Transactions of the Association for Computational Linguistics*, 9:243–260.

Dirk Roorda. 1992. Proof Nets for Lambek Calculus. *Journal of Logic and Computation*, 2(2):211–231.

Alexander Rush. 2020. Torch-Struct: Deep Structured Prediction Library. In *Proceedings of the 58th Annual Meeting of the Association for Computational Linguistics: System Demonstrations*, pages 335–342, Online. Association for Computational Linguistics.

Victor Sanh, Lysandre Debut, Julien Chaumond, and Thomas Wolf. 2019. DistilBERT, a distilled version of BERT: Smaller, faster, cheaper and lighter. In *arXiv:1910.01108 [Cs]*, Vancouver, Canada.

Yury Savateev. 2012. Product-free Lambek calculus is NP-complete. *Annals of Pure and Applied Logic*, 163(7):775–788.

Richard Sinkhorn and Paul Knopp. 1967. Concerning nonnegative matrices and doubly stochastic matrices. *Pacific Journal of Mathematics*, 21(2):343–348.

Miloš Stanojević and Mark Steedman. 2020. Max-Margin Incremental CCG Parsing. In *Proceedings of the 58th Annual Meeting of the Association for Computational Linguistics*, pages 4111–4122, Online. Association for Computational Linguistics.

Nasrin Sultana, Jeffrey Chan, A. K. Qin, and Tabinda Sarwar. 2020. Learning to Optimise General TSP Instances. *arXiv:2010.12214 [cs, math]*.

Ashish Vaswani, Noam Shazeer, Niki Parmar, Jakob Uszkoreit, Llion Jones, Aidan N. Gomez, Łukasz Kaiser, and Illia Polosukhin. 2017. Attention is All you Need. In *Advances in Neural Information Processing Systems*, volume 30, pages 5998–6008. Curran Associates, Inc.

Qiang Wang, Bei Li, Tong Xiao, Jingbo Zhu, Changliang Li, Derek F. Wong, and Lidia S. Chao. 2019. Learning Deep Transformer Models for Machine Translation. In *Proceedings of the 57th Annual Meeting of the Association for Computational Linguistics*, pages 1810–1822, Florence, Italy. Association for Computational Linguistics.

Thomas Wolf, Lysandre Debut, Victor Sanh, Julien Chaumond, Clement Delangue, Anthony Moi, Pierric Cistac, Tim Rault, Remi Louf, Morgan Funtowicz, Joe Davison, Sam Shleifer, Patrick von Platen, Clara Ma, Yacine Jernite, Julien Plu, Canwen Xu, Teven Le Scao, Sylvain Gugger, Mariama Drame, Quentin Lhoest, and Alexander Rush. 2020. Transformers: State-of-the-Art Natural Language Processing. In *Proceedings of the 2020 Conference on Empirical Methods in Natural Language Processing: System Demonstrations*, pages 38–45, Online. Association for Computational Linguistics.

Daniel H. Younger. 1967. Recognition and parsing of context-free languages in time n^3. *Information and Control*, 10(2):189–208.

Wojciech Zielonka. 1981. Axiomatizability of Ajdukiewicz-Lambek Calculus by Means of Cancellation Schemes. *Mathematical Logic Quarterly*, 27(13-14):215–224.

The Reading Machine: a Versatile Framework for Studying Incremental Parsing Strategies

Franck Dary, Alexis Nasr
Aix Marseille Univ, Université de Toulon, CNRS, LIS, Marseille, France
{franck.dary,alexis.nasr}@lis-lab.fr

Abstract

The Reading Machine, is a parsing framework that takes as input raw text and performs six standard NLP tasks: tokenization, POS tagging, morphological analysis, lemmatization, dependency parsing and sentence segmentation. It is built upon Transition Based Parsing, and allows implementing a large number of parsing configurations, among which a fully incremental one. Three case studies are presented to highlight the versatility of the framework. The first one explores whether an incremental parser is able to take into account top-down dependencies (i.e. the influence of high level decisions on low level ones), the second compares the performances of an incremental and a pipe-line architecture and the third quantifies the impact of the right context on the predictions made by an incremental parser.

1 Introduction

Syntactic parsers usually take as input text that has been processed at several levels. It has generally been segmented in sentences, tokenized, POS tagged, and possibly lemmatized and morphologically analyzed. All such steps are realized by other NLP modules that are usually organized in a sequential pattern, called a pipe-line. The pipe-line imposes a rational order on the modules: word boundaries, for example, have to be determined before a word can be associated to a POS tag and syntactic parsing usually comes after POS tagging, for POS tags group words that have close syntactic properties.

The pipe-line architecture offers many advantages, among which, the independence of the modules that compose it. The only constraint for their inter-operability is the compatibility of their inputs and outputs. Once this constraint is verified, each module can be built on any kind of model considered more suitable for the task to perform. Besides, in a pipe-line architecture, every module narrows down the search space of the following modules: a parser, for example, does not have to consider different tokenization hypotheses nor different POS tags for a word. Considering all such decisions can lead to a combinatorial explosion problem and yields huge search spaces.

The pipe-line architecture nevertheless has its limits. It is well known that some low level decisions (made by early modules of the pipe-line) can benefit from high level ones (made by late modules). Some tokenization decisions, for example, can depend on the syntactic structure of the sentence to parse, such as complex prepositions in French, as noted by Nasr et al. (2015). Likewise, sentence segmentation can depend on syntactic structures, especially when punctuation is absent or unreliable, such as in speech transcriptions. Such *top down dependencies* cannot be taken into account in a strict pipe-line architecture. But they are arguably less numerous than *bottom up dependencies* and this is the reason why the pipe-line architecture usually yields good results. One aim of this paper is to propose a framework, called the Reading Machine (RM), that is flexible enough to define several patterns for combining different NLP modules and explore different ways to link decisions made by these modules. We use in this paper the RM framework to define and compare several non sequential machines that model top down dependencies.

There is another, less immediate, reason for studying non sequential architectures, in link with human cognition. Psycholinguistic studies have shown that human language processing is incremental, i.e., people do not wait to see the entire sentence before they start trying to understand it (see Keller (2010) for more details). Such findings have developed interest in using NLP tools to implement cognitively-plausible models of hu-

Proceedings of the 17th International Conference on Parsing Technologies (IWPT 2021), pages 26–37
Bangkok, Thailand (online), August 6, 2021.

man sentence processing (see Hale (2017) for a review). Various "linking hypotheses" have been proposed to relate the models' intermediate states when parsing a given sentence to the behavior of human subjects trying to understand that same sentence. The RM offers a framework to investigate such linking hypotheses by defining machines that implement them and observe their behaviour on human data. In this perspective, the RM has already been used for predicting eye-movements during reading: different RM architectures have been compared on their ability to accurately predict fixation time (Dary et al., 2021a,b). In order to illustrate the kind of experiments that can be conducted in such a perspective, we will define and compare machines that model different perceptual fields and measure their influence on an incremental parsing process.

Technically, RM is an extension of the transition-based parsing algorithm (TBP) (Yamada and Matsumoto, 2003; Nivre, 2003). The reason for this choice is mainly that TBP implements an incremental parsing strategy (Nivre, 2008). We propose to extend this model to define a complete incremental NLP parser that integrates six tasks: tokenization, POS tagging, morphological analysis, lemmatization, syntactic parsing and sentence segmentation. RM borrows from TBP the two key notions of *Configurations* and *Actions* (also called *Transitions*), as well as a greedy algorithm that performs syntactic parsing. We extend these notions by defining an enriched version of a configuration and a richer set of actions. All linguistic decisions, such as word and sentence boundaries detection, POS tagging, lemmatization and, of course, syntactic parsing are realized by actions that are predicted based on configurations. The RM takes as input raw text and greedily predicts a sequence of actions that perform the six tasks mentioned above.

2 Related Work

Solving the circular dependencies that exist between parsing and other pre-processing steps, is an active area of research in the parsing literature. The solution that has been mainly investigated consists in jointly performing syntactic parsing and other pre-parsing steps. If we restrict ourselves to recent approaches to dependency parsing, solutions have been proposed both for graph based parsing (Yan et al., 2020; Lee et al., 2011; Nguyen and Verspoor, 2018; Nasr et al., 2015; Li et al., 2011; Zhang et al., 2015) and transition-based parsing (Yoshikawa et al., 2016; Bohnet and Nivre, 2012; Alberti et al., 2015; Hatori et al., 2012; Honnibal and Johnson, 2014; Constant and Nivre, 2016; Kurita et al., 2017; Wan et al., 2018).

Solutions to this problem differ vastly for these two approaches, mainly because of the different parsing strategies they adopt. This is why we have decided to restrict ourselves to TBP based papers in the remainder of this section.

There have been many propositions to realize simultaneously several linguistic tasks in TBP. Both Bohnet and Nivre (2012) and Alberti et al. (2015), for example, show how a transition system can be extended and trained to jointly predict POS tags and the dependency tree, improving both the accuracy of tagging and parsing. These systems are not strictly incremental across the tasks they realize for they process text that has already been segmented in words and sentences. Besides, the text has been pre-tagged in order to limit the size of the search space.

The closest approach to ours is Kurita et al. (2017), which is based on the work of Hatori et al. (2012). The authors propose an extension of the arc-standard transition system that is able to perform a fully joint prediction of word segmentation, POS tagging and dependency parsing. Their system takes a queue of symbols as input, and process it in an incremental fashion, consuming one symbol at a time. They conducted their experiments on Chinese, and were the first to use a neural network architecture using both word and character based embeddings to achieve fully joint prediction of these three tasks. They showed that their joint architecture was competitive with a pipeline architecture for word segmentation and POS tagging, but fell short on parsing.

For their participation in the 2018 CoNLL Shared Task (Zeman et al., 2018), Wan et al. (2018) also defined an extension of TBP that is close to ours. It is based on the arc-standard system enriched with a swap transition (Nivre, 2009), and is able to jointly perform word segmentation, POS tagging, morphological tagging and dependency parsing. They showed that such a system could get better scores than the shared task's baseline, while still being quite far from the top scoring systems. Their paper focuses on low or even zero resources languages (what the shared task was mainly about), and did not test whether or not the joint prediction of multiple tasks was improving the performances.

Our model has the following characteristics that distinguishes it form the approaches cited above.

The RM performs simultaneously six NLP tasks with the notable inclusion of sentence segmentation which is almost always pre-processed in parsing systems.

The RM allows us to build a machine that is strictly incremental across the six tasks it realizes. There are two reasons for this choice. The first is theoretical, we are interested to know how much information is present in top-down dependencies and whether they can be captured in an incremental setup. The second is related to psycholinguistics: we believe that the definition of a fully incremental RM offers a useful model for simulating human behaviour during reading.

The RM is flexible enough to design machines that implement different strategies in order to compare them. We propose, in section 5, a high-level description format that allows us to define machines that differ on a specific dimension and study the effect of this dimension on the performances of the machines.

3 The Reading Machine

As mentioned in the introduction, the reading machine is an extension of the TBP[1] framework. The details of this algorithm are well known and do not need to be repeated here. We will only introduce the terms that are important for the rest of the paper.

TBP is an algorithm that predicts the dependency syntactic structure of sentences. This task can be viewed as selecting for each word w of a sentence its syntactic governor (another word w' of the sentence) as well as its syntactic function f. A directed arc, referred to as a *dependency*, is built from w' to w, labeled with function f. The graph built at the end of the parsing process is a tree. The TBP algorithm builds the dependency tree by scanning the sentence word by word, in reading order. At each step, an *action*, is predicted and applied to the current *configuration* of the parser and yields a new configuration. The prediction is realized by a classifier that takes as input a configuration and computes a score for every possible action. The parser makes use of a stack containing words that need to be linked to words yet undiscovered.

Four types of actions are defined: SHIFT, pushes the current word on the stack, REDUCE, pops the stack, LEFT_l, creates a left dependency, labeled l, whose governor is the current word and dependent is top element of the stack and RIGHT_l, which creates a right dependency, labeled l, whose dependent is the current word and governor is the top element of the stack.

[1]Several sets of actions have been proposed in the literature, the one used here is known as *Arc Eager*.

SEG	NO	NO	NO	NO	NO	YES
SYN	DET	SUB	ROOT	DET	OBJ	PCT
GOV	+1	+1	0	+1	-2	-3
LEM	@	@	s@	@	@	@
MRF	DEF	SG	P3S	DEF	SG	-
POS	DET	N	V	DET	N	PCT
TOK	the	boy	hits	the	ball	.
INPUT	t h e	b o y	h i t s	t h e	b a l l	.

Table 1: Input and output tapes of a RM after processing the text *The boy hits the ball.*

Before giving a precise definition of the RM, in section 3.1, we describe the directions in which the TBP has been extended.

Tapes: The RM has one input tape, which is a read tape and an arbitrary number of output tapes which are read/write tapes.

The input tape contains the text to parse. It is character based: each cell of the tape contains a character. The text has not been linguistically pre-processed: it has not been segmented into sentences nor into words. The current position of the reading head of the input tape is called the *character index*.

Output tapes are word based: each cell of a tape refers to a word of the input text. Output tapes are used to write the predictions made by the machine, typically one tape per type of prediction. These tapes are synchronized: at all times, the head is at the same position for all tapes. This position is called the *word index*.

Table 1 represents the tapes of a machine after processing the text *The boy hits the ball.* The machine has 7 output tapes and one input tape, represented at the bottom.

Sliding Window: The reading head of the input tape takes the form of a sliding window. It is centered on the cell of the tape pointed by the *character index* and has access to an arbitrary number of cells to the left and to the right of this cell.

States and Transitions: TBP can be seen as a single state machine, in contrast RM are multi-state machines. Every state, or set of states, is devoted to a specific linguistic task and is linked to a classifier. The linking between states and classifiers can range from a single classifier for all states to one classifier per state. States are deterministically linked to each other through transitions that are labelled with action labels. At each step, the classifier of the current state predicts the next action to perform. The action is applied on the configuration and the transition labeled with this action is traversed to reach another state.

Actions: RM actions encompass standard *Arc Eager* actions for parsing and new actions have been defined for performing the other tasks.

Word tagging tasks (POS tagging and morphological tagging) are realized through a single action: TAG_L(t), which simply writes symbol t on tape L at the word index position. For example, action TAG_{POS}(DET) tags the current word as a determiner.

It is not straightforward to cast lemmatization as a classification task, due to the large number of classes (potentially all the lemmas of a language). Besides, lemmatization is, to a large extent, regular. In order to capture this regularity, the classifier that realizes the lemmatization task predicts editing rules of the form `s1@s2` where `s1` is a suffix of the word to lemmatize and `s2` the suffix of the lemma.[2] When applied to a word w, such a rule strips off suffix `s1` from w and appends `s2`, as in the following example *apply(*`s@`*, hits) = hit*.

The actions predicted by the tokenizer are of four types: ADD_n adds the n next characters of the input tape to the current word and moves the character index n positions to the right, IGNORE ignores the current character (typically spaces) and moves the character index to the right, WORD marks the current word as complete and SPLIT^w_W action moves the character index $|w|$ positions to the right and adds the word sequence W in the buffer. This last action is used to expand contractions such as *don't* → *do not*.

Programming an oracle function for actions IGNORE, WORD and SPLIT is straightforward because there is no ambiguity on which is correct at any time. However, the choice of ADD_n is ambiguous: if we consider that the 8 next characters on the input tape are "*academic*", we want to add them to the current word. This could be done using several action sequences, such as "ADD_8", "ADD_4,ADD_4" or "ADD_2,ADD_3,ADD_3,". In our experiments, we chose to limit the size of ADD_n to n=6 and to program the oracle so that it adds the largest number

[2]Of course, such a simple form of rules can only deal with suffixal flexional morphology. More complex morphological phenomena, in templatic morphology for example, ask for more elaborate types of rules.

State	Action	Description
TOK	ADD_n	Adds the n next symbols to b.0.
TOK	IGNORE	Ignores the next symbol.
TOK	WORD	Marks b.0 as complete.
TOK	SPLIT^w_W	Consume symbol sequence w. Add word sequence W in buffer.
POS, MRF	TAG_L(t)	Writes tag t to b.0 on tape L.
LEM	`s@s'`	b.0 lemma := form $- s + s'$.
LEM	CASE_{ul}	b.0 lemma to upper/lower case.
SYN	REDUCE	Pop the the stack.
SYN	SHIFT	Push b.0 on the stack.
SYN	RIGHT_l	Adds arc (s.0,b.0,l). Push b.0 on the stack.
SYN	LEFT_l	Adds arc (b.0,s.0,l). Pop the stack.
SEG	EOS(Y/N)	Mark b.0 as an end of sentence, set sentence root, attach orphans to root then empty stack.

Table 2: Actions used in our RM architecture. b.0 stands for the current word and s.0 for the word on top of the stack.

of characters at once. During training, the correct action sequence would then be: "ADD_6,ADD_2"

Sentence segmentation is realized by a binary action EOS(YES/NO) which tags the current word as the end of the current sentence, or not. Once the end of a sentence has been detected, the deepest element in the stack is marked as the root of the sentence and the potential remaining elements of the stack are attached to the root, before emptying the stack. The complete set of actions is reported in Table 2.

3.1 Formal Definition

A RM, as any formal automata, has an input alphabet Σ_T, which is a set of characters, a set of states $\mathcal{S}$, a transition function δ, an initial state s_0 and a set F of final states. It also has N output alphabets $\Sigma_1, \ldots \Sigma_N$ associated to its N output tapes. Transitions between states are labelled with actions. Moreover, each state is associated, via function γ, to a classifier, which maps configurations to actions, along with a score.

Formally, we define a RM as a tuple $\mathcal{T} = (\Sigma_T, N, \Sigma, \mathcal{S}, s_0, \mathcal{A}, \mathcal{K}, \gamma, \delta, F)$. We develop below the elements of the machine that deserve more explanation.

- $\mathcal{A}$ is a set of actions. Each action can write a symbol on an output tape, move the character head or the word head either to the left or to the right and push or pop the stack (see Table 2).
- $\mathcal{K}$ is a set of classifiers, described in section 3.3
- $\delta : \mathcal{S} \times \mathcal{A} \rightarrow \mathcal{S}$ is a deterministic transition function, also called a *Strategy*. Given the current state and its associated classifier, the action selected by the classifier is performed and control jumps to the destination state of the transition. The strategy defines the order in which the predictions are made. For instance a strategy could force the lemmatization task to happen after the dependency parsing task. Two different strategies are described in section 5.
- $\gamma : \mathcal{S} \rightarrow \mathcal{K}$ is a function that maps each state of the RM to a classifier. This mapping allows several states to share a single classifier which allows in turn jointly training several processes.

3.2 Configuration

Configurations for a RM M and a text T are defined as $(S, T, c, \beta_{1,N}, w, \sigma, H)$, where:
- S is the current state of M.
- T is the input tape
- c is the character index
- $\beta_{1,N}$ is a collection of output tapes.
- w is the word index
- σ is a stack of word indexes, its purpose is the same as the stack in TBP.
- H is the sequence of transitions that have been predicted till now.

The set of all configurations for text T is noted $\mathcal{C}_T$.

An *initial configuration* for a text T is defined as follows: $(s_0, T, 0, \beta, 0, [], [])$, where all tapes in β are empty.

An *accept configuration* is defined as $(s \in F, T, n_c, \beta, n_w, [], H)$, where n_c and n_w are respectively the number of characters and words in T.

3.3 Classifier

The classifiers that constitute the set $\mathcal{K}$ are functions that map a configuration to actions and scores.

The classifiers are independent of each other but they all take as input a configuration which contains all aspects of the current state of the RM, in particular, the content of all the tapes of the RM. The tapes contain all predictions already realized. Each classifier defines its own *Feature Function* which extracts from the input configuration all features considered useful for the type of prediction it realizes. We will not delve into the set of all possible features, let us just mention that most of them allow to access the content of a specific cell of a specific tape.

4 Training the RM

The training process of a RM is close to TBP training. It starts with a dependency tree that is decomposed into a sequence of (*state*, *configuration*, *action*) triples, by a static oracle. The difference with TBP is that the set of actions is considerably larger since it encompasses actions for all six tasks. This sequence is used to train the classifiers: every classifier receives examples corresponding to the states it is related to. The RM is trained using only correct examples, predicted by the oracle. In order to increase the robustness to error propagation, we use a dynamic oracle (Goldberg and Nivre, 2012) to extract a new set of training examples where the actions applied were the one predicted by the network.[3] The RM is therefore trained to predict the next action given potentially incorrect configurations.

Four epochs are devoted to the first part of the training process, followed by 26 more epochs in dynamic oracle regime.[4] At each epoch, the machine is used to decode the development set, and is saved if its score (mean score across all 6 levels) is the best so far. We used cross entropy as a loss function and Adagrad (Duchi et al., 2011) for optimization.

The classifiers used to predict the actions can be decomposed into three parts: the first part is devoted to feature extraction, it is composed of several encoders applied to different parts of the RM configuration. The output of these encoders are then concatenated yielding a dense vector representation of the current configuration, to which we apply a dropout of 0.5 and feed it into a Multi Layer Perceptron (MLP) composed of 2 hidden layers of respective sizes 3200 and 1600 with dropout 0.4 and ReLU activation. The output of the MLP is then fed into a decision layer, producting a probability distribution over the possible actions. The most probable action is predicted then applied to the configuration. A classifier can have up to 6 decision layers, one for every task. A schematic representation of the classifier structure can be found in

[3]Except for tokenization and sentence segmentation actions, because our dynamic oracle is not able to deal with incorrect segmentation.

[4]All hyper-parameters have been optimized for the development set described in section 6.

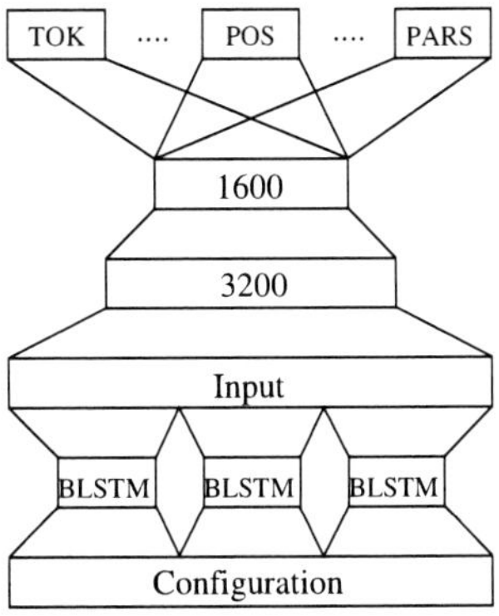

Figure 1: General structure of the classifiers of a RM. They take as input a configuration and predict an action for up to 6 tasks.

Figure 1.

The most complex part of the classifier is the transformation of the configuration into a vector: the input of the MLP. Depending of its feature function, the classifier extracts from the configuration elements that can be of different natures: the current state of the RM, tags or words read from the tapes, characters read from the input tape, previous action present in the history and words from the stack. All these elements are fed to specific Bi-LSTM that produce contextual representations, as in Kiperwasser and Goldberg (2016), that are in turn concatenated in the MLP input layer.

All feature values are represented by trainable embeddings of size 128. These embeddings are randomly initialized, except for word embeddings that are pretrained[5] exclusively on the train set, in order to produce an embedding for unknown words (using words occurring only once in the train set).

The Bi-LSTM that take sequences of these embeddings as input are made of only one layer of size 64.

5 Designing Reading Machines

The precise definition of RM, introduced in section 3, allows us to design a large number of machines. Every machine is defined by a large number of features and comparing machines is not always easy. In this section we define a more abstract description that is based on four high-level features, and define seven machines that are compared in section 6.

[5]Using GloVe (Pennington et al., 2014), implementation: https://github.com/stanfordnlp/GloVe.

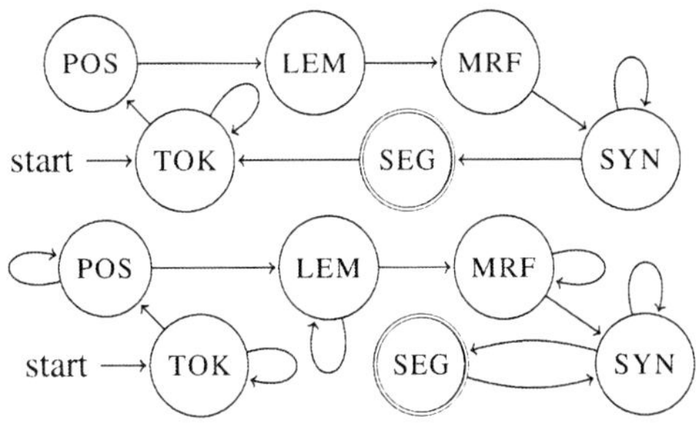

Figure 2: Two RM strategies that correspond to the order of predictions. Above, the INCR strategy and below the SEQ strategy.

We first describe the four high-level features then give a description of the machines.

5.1 Strategy

As mentioned in section 3, the strategy of a RM is the structure of the underlying automaton: its number of states and transition function. A strategy dictates the order in which the predictions are made. Two strategies: INCR and SEQ, are defined, they are represented in Figure 2. The actions that label the transitions have been omitted for readability reasons.

The main difference between the two strategies comes from the loops on all states of the SEQ strategy. These loops model the sequential behaviour of the RM: the whole text is processed at a given level before switching to the upper level. In contrast, the INCR strategy processes a word at a given level then performs a prediction at the next higher level for the same word. This difference can be illustrated in the way the matrix of Table 1 is filled: the SEQ machine fills it line by line, bottom-up, while the INCR machine fills it column by column, from left to right.

5.2 Feature Span

The *Feature Span* of a machine specifies the part of the tapes that are accessible to each classifier in order to make a prediction. Three feature spans have been defined, they are represented in Figure 3. Each of the three rectangles represents, schematically, the tapes of an RM, as in Table 1. The black square corresponds to the current prediction and the hatched area to the content of the tapes available for the current prediction. The past-low (PA-LO) feature span only sees the tapes content for the lower level past predictions. Future-low (FU-LO) sees the past, current and future predictions for lower levels.

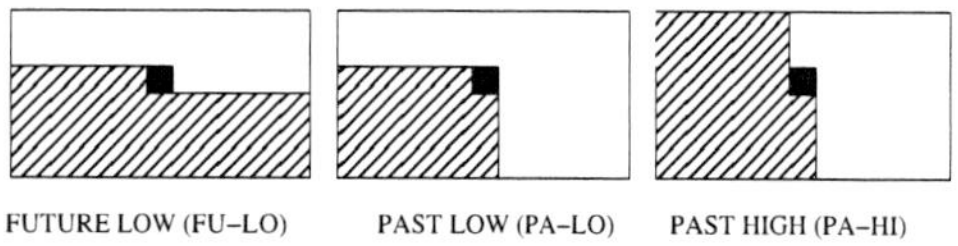

Figure 3: Three feature spans: the black square is the current prediction and the hatched area, the available features.

Past-high (PA-HI) have access to low, current and high-level predictions from the past.

In the PA-HI configuration, when the tagger, for example, has to select the POS tag of a word, it has access to the predictions made by all the modules, including the parser, for preceding words. The PA-HI feature span therefore offers an *explicit* way to model top down dependencies.

5.3 Number of Classifiers

As mentioned above, several states of a machine can share a single classifier to predict the actions associated to these states. The sharing of a single classifier by several states amounts to perform multi-task training, which "*uses the domain information contained in the training signals of related tasks as an inductive bias. It does this by learning tasks in parallel while using a shared representation; what is learned for each task can help other tasks be learned better*" (Caruana, 1997).

In our case, when a single classifier is used, for example, to perform both POS tagging and parsing, the representation of a configuration built by this classifier is obtained by optimizing both tasks. Decisions made by the parser can therefore *implicitly* influence the tagger. The Number of Classifiers is, with the Feature Span, the two ways that will be tested to take into account top down dependencies.

Two extreme choices have been made with respect to this dimension, in the first one, all states share a single classifier while in the second each state defines its own classifier, yielding two different values: 1 and 6.

5.4 Window Span

The *Window Span* of a machine is simply the span of the sliding window that gives access to the text. A window span is defined by a pair of integers that indicate how many characters, to the left and to the right of the character index, are accessible. The window span corresponds to the sliding window introduced by McConkie and Rayner (1975) used to model the perceptual span of a human reader.

Four different window spans have been defined: [-5,2], [-5, 5], [-5, 10] and [-5, 15]. We followed McConkie and Rayner (1976) in choosing asymmetric windows.

5.5 Seven Machines

Given the four dimensions defined above and the number of values per dimension, a total of 48 different machines can be defined. We have selected, among these, seven machines that can be grouped in four subsets, as shown in Table 3. Machines in a subset generally differ from one another for a single dimension, the exception are the two machines of the first subset. These four subsets correspond to the four experiments that are described in the following section. The letter in the first column of the table indicates identical machines. They have been given several names in order to ease the comparisons in section 6. The feature function of the classifiers of each of these machines can be found in table 4.

	RM	Strat.	F.Span	W.Span	NC
A	PA-HI	INCR	**PA-HI**	[-5,10]	6
	PA-LO	INCR	**PA-LO**	[-5,10]	6
B	C1	INCR	PA-HI	[-5,10]	**1**
A	C6	INCR	PA-HI	[-5,10]	**6**
B	INCR	**INCR**	**PA-HI**	[-5,10]	1
	SEQ	**SEQ**	**FU-LO**	[-5,10]	1
	[-5,2]	INCR	PA-HI	**[-5,2]**	6
	[-5,5]	INCR	PA-HI	**[-5,5]**	6
A	[-5,10]	INCR	PA-HI	**[-5,10]**	6
	[-5,15]	INCR	PA-HI	**[-5,15]**	6

Table 3: Definition of the machines used in the experiments. The letter in the first column indicates identical machines. NC stands for Number of Classifiers.

6 Experiments

The experiments presented in this section aim at exploring three directions. The first one is the modelling of top-down dependencies. We have introduced two means for taking into account such dependencies in a RM: joint prediction of several tasks, using a single classifier, and the feature span of the classifiers. The two first experiments aim at studying whether these two techniques allow to effectively model such dependencies. The second direction compares the sequential and the incremental strategies and measure how much information a parser gets from the knowledge of the next words

Machine	Features
C1 INCR	FORM,ID,POS,MRF,SYN: b.-3 b.-2 b.-1 b.0 s.0 s.1 s.2 b.0.0 s.0.0 s.0.-1 s.1.0 s.1.-1 s.2.0 s.2.-1 Prefix&Suffix of size 5: b.0 Raw text: [-5,10] around *character index* History: past 10 actions Split: list of applicable SPLIT actions Name: name of the current state Distances: from s.0 s.1 s.2 to b.0.
SEQ	Same as INCR with the addition of right context: b.1 b.2.
PA-HI C6 [-5,10]	Each of the 6 classifiers has the same features as C1.
PA-LO	Each of the 6 classifiers is different. The classifier corresponding to a given linguistic level will only have the features of PA-HI corresponding to this linguistic level and inferior levels. For example, the classifier corresponding to MRF will only access columns FORM,ID,POS,MRF for targets b.-3 b.-2 b.-1 b.0 and will not have the distance feature.
[-5,2]	Same as [-5,10] but with window [-5,2].
[-5,5]	Same as [-5,10] but with window [-5,5].
[-5,15]	Same as [-5,10] but with window [-5,15].

Table 4: Features used in our RM architecture. "b.i" stands for the word at position *word index*+i in the buffer and "s.i" for the ith topmost word on the stack. Additional suffixes ".0" and ".-1" refer respectively to the leftmost and rightmost dependent.

POS, lemma and morphological analysis. The third direction aims at measuring the effect of the window span on the performances of an incremental RM.

The machines realize six types of predictions: tokenization, part of speech tagging, lemmatization, morphological analysis, syntactic parsing and sentence segmentation. Each of these predictions are evaluated by a specific metric using the evaluation script of the CoNLL 2018 shared task (Zeman et al., 2018). Besides the task specific metrics, we report the Morphology-Aware Labeled Attachment Score (MLAS) which takes into account word segmentation, morphological and POS tagging as well as syntax, as described in Zeman et al. (2018). The MLAS allows us to compare the general performances of two machines, while the task specific metrics allow for a finer comparison of these machines.

Experiments have been conducted on French[6] data, using the GSD corpora of the Universal Dependencies collection (Zeman et al., 2019) version 2.7. In the official distribution of this corpus, the train/dev/test split is of respective sizes 364,349/36,775/10,298 words. In preliminary experiments, we found out that the test split was way too small to meaningfully compare machines. That's why we decided to use 10 fold cross-validation: we realized ten different 80%/10%/10% train/dev/test splits and trained ten copies of each of our machines on these splits. The ten test sets were then decoded by the corresponding copy of the machine and the predictions were concatenated. This technique allowed us to compare the machines on their predictions on a test set of 427,763 words. We tested the significance of our comparisons using paired bootstrap resampling[7] (Koehn, 2004), and reported in our tables the corresponding p-value, estimating the probability that in a pair of models, the model that appear to perform better is in reality a worse model. Unfortunately, the resampling script we used (the one used in the CoNLL 2018 shared task) is not able to produce p-values for the task of sentence segmentation, that is why the corresponding cells in tables 5,6 and 7 are empty.

6.1 Wide *vs* Narrow Feature Span

This experiment aims at studying if past high level predictions can help current low level predictions, which is the explicit means we have proposed to model top-down dependencies. In order to test this hypothesis, we compare machines PA-LO and PA-HI. Both machines differ on their Feature Span. PA-HI has access to past high-level predictions while PA-LO does not.

The results, displayed in Table 5, show that PA-HI yields lower results than PA-LO. This is true for the general MLAS measure, as well as sentence segmentation and morphological tagging. The differences obtained by the two machines on the other tasks are not significant. Contrary to what we expected, using past high level predictions does not seem to increase the performances of low-level modules. We do not have for the moment an explanation for this result. It could be explained by the errors made by PA-HI on earlier predictions which, in turn, provoke errors on current word predictions.

6.2 Multi Task *vs* Mono Task

The aim of our second experiment is to test the second means we have proposed to model top-down

[6]The same experiments can be replicated on any language of the UD collection. Comparing the respective merits of the different machines across languages is a very interesting but very resource demanding task (mainly for optimizing the hyper-parameters for each language) and we leave this for future work.

[7]Using implementation of Popel et al. (2017).

Task	PA-LO	PA-HI	p-value
MLAS	**77.70**	77.30	0.014
Seg	96.65	96.57	
LAS	86.88	86.77	0.193
UAS	89.13	89.03	0.183
Lemma	98.04	98.01	0.22
UFeats	**97.02**	96.87	0.003
UPOS	97.02	96.93	0.051
Words	99.60	**99.64**	0.02

Table 5: Wide *vs* Narrow Feature Span

dependencies: multi task prediction. Two machines are compared: C1 which uses a single classifier to predict all tasks and C6 which uses a specific classifier for every task. The results are reported in Table 6. The table shows that C1 outperforms C6 on the MLAS metric: on average, a multi-task setup performs better than a mono-task one. C1 is significantly better than C6 for parsing, morphological and POS tagging. While the two machines are equivalent on the other tasks. These results show that predictions based on representations of the machine configurations that are optimised for all tasks are beneficial for all tasks. It is tempting to conclude that multi task learning is an effective way to model top down dependencies. It is unfortunately premature to draw such a conclusion for multi task learning is a complex process that models a large number of dependencies in the data. More investigation using, for example, probing, is in order to give a definite answer to this question.

It is worth noting that C1 has six times less parameters than C6, because each classifier of C6 has as many parameter as the classifier of C1, another argument in favor of multi-task training.

Task	C1	C6	p-value
MLAS	**77.93**	77.29	0.001
Seg	96.40	96.57	
LAS	**87.08**	86.77	0.008
UAS	**89.33**	89.03	0.004
Lemma	98.02	98.01	0.39
UFeats	**97.01**	96.87	0.004
UPOS	96.99	96.93	0.135
Words	99.65	99.64	0.315

Table 6: Multi Task *vs* Mono Task

6.3 Sequential *vs* Incremental

In this experiment, two machines are compared, SEQ, a sequential machine that implements a pipeline architecture, and INCR that implements an incremental architecture. These two machines differ on two dimensions, their strategy as well as their feature span. The aim of this experiment is to measure to which extend the information given to a parser by the next words low level analysis (POS tagging, morphological tagging and lemmatization) help a parser. The SEQ machine implements a two words look-ahead: the parser has therefore access to the form, POS, lemma, and morphological analysis of the next two words.

The results of this experiment are reported in Table 7. As one can see, SEQ outperforms INCR on the MLAS metric: on average, SEQ gets better results than INCR. As was expected, it is the parser that takes advantage of the sequential strategy: both LAS and UAS are increased by around one point. The two architectures achieve equivalent performances on the low level tasks, meaning that early processing steps do not take advantage of the sequential architecture.

Task	INCR	SEQ	p-value
MLAS	77.93	**78.60**	0.000
Seg	**96.40**	95.96	
LAS	87.08	**87.56**	0.000
UAS	89.33	**89.89**	0.000
Lemma	98.02	98.01	0.403
UFeats	97.01	**97.16**	0.002
UPOS	96.99	**97.09**	0.036
Words	99.65	99.63	0.115

Table 7: Sequential *vs* Incremental

6.4 Window Span

Our last experiment aims to study the influence of the Window Span on the performances of an incremental machine. Four machines are compared: [-5,2], [-5,5], [-5,10], [-5,15].

The best MLAS results are obtained by machine [-5,10] which defines a look-ahead of 10 characters for its predictions. It is interesting to note that low values of look ahead has a dramatic effect on the performances. This is partly due to the metrics used in which tokenization errors provoke errors on higher level modules. As expected, we observe diminishing returns as we increase the Window Span to the right, and going to 15 characters slightly decreases performances. These results are in line with McConkie and Rayner (1975) who determined experimentally that the span of the window for humans is about four characters to the left of the current character and twelve characters to the right.

Task	[-5,2]	[-5,5]	[-5,10]	[-5,15]
MLAS	48.53	76.76	**77.29**	**77.19**
Seg	79.75	96.44	**96.57**	**96.68**
LAS	59.39	86.28	**86.77**	**86.69**
UAS	61.05	88.56	**89.02**	**88.96**
Lemma	83.67	97.89	**98.01**	**97.99**
UFeats	82.58	96.74	**96.87**	**96.83**
UPOS	82.46	96.71	**96.93**	**96.90**
Words	85.12	99.55	**99.64**	**99.65**

Table 8: Different values of Window Span

7 Conclusion and Future Work

This paper introduced a versatile parsing framework, called the Reading Machine, that allows us to compare incremental parsers that implement different parsing configurations. We illustrated this with two cases. In the first one, we compared different ways to take into account top down dependencies across six tasks. In the second, we compared the effect of the look-ahead on the parsing performances.

This work will be extended in several directions.

The first one concerns the analysis of the results obtained in our two first experiments. More investigation is needed to explain the reason why using past high level predictions cannot help low level current ones. Likewise, we would like to understand if the better results of multi task learning comes from the modelling of top down dependencies. Two means will be used in order to answer this question: probing and the development of (small) specialized test sets that focus on such phenomena.

The sequential machines that have been proposed are greedy: a local decision taken by a machine is never questioned even when contradicted by future events. This behaviour is not appealing from an NLP perspective nor from a psycholinguistic one. In order to tackle this problem, we will introduce in the Reading Machine a backtrack mechanism that can predict left movements leading to the re-analysis of a previously analyzed part of the text.

The third direction consists in evaluating the model against human experimental data. The Reading Machine has already been used to predict reading time. We will continue further in this direction and use the Reading Machine to predict saccades.

The strategies implemented in the RM described in this paper completely specify the order in which predictions are made. We plan to relax this constraint and let the RM learn strategies that optimize its performances. A RM would have the ability to decide the order in which to perform some tasks (specifically, POS tagging, lemmatization and morphological analysis).

8 Acknowledgments

This work was granted access to the HPC resources of IDRIS under the allocation 2020-AD011011708 made by GENCI.

References

Chris Alberti, David Weiss, Greg Coppola, and Slav Petrov. 2015. Improved transition-based parsing and tagging with neural networks. In *Proceedings of the 2015 Conference on Empirical Methods in Natural Language Processing*, pages 1354–1359.

Bernd Bohnet and Joakim Nivre. 2012. A transition-based system for joint part-of-speech tagging and labeled non-projective dependency parsing. In *Proceedings of the 2012 Joint Conference on Empirical Methods in Natural Language Processing and Computational Natural Language Learning*, pages 1455–1465. Association for Computational Linguistics.

Rich Caruana. 1997. Multitask learning. *Machine learning*, 28(1):41–75.

Matthieu Constant and Joakim Nivre. 2016. A transition-based system for joint lexical and syntactic analysis. In *Proceedings of the 54th Annual Meeting of the Association for Computational Linguistics (Volume 1: Long Papers)*, pages 161–171, Berlin, Germany. Association for Computational Linguistics.

Franck Dary, Abdellah Fourtassi, and Alexis Nasr. 2021a. On the role of low-level linguistic tasks for reading time prediction. In *Proceedings of the 43th Annual Meeting of the Cognitive Science Society*. In press.

Franck Dary, Alexis Nasr, and Abdellah Fourtassi. 2021b. TALEP at CMCL 2021 shared task: Non linear combination of low and high-level features for predicting eye-tracking data. In *Proceedings of the Workshop on Cognitive Modeling and Computational Linguistics*, pages 108–113, Online. Association for Computational Linguistics.

John Duchi, Elad Hazan, and Yoram Singer. 2011. Adaptive subgradient methods for online learning and stochastic optimization. *Journal of machine learning research*, 12(7).

Yoav Goldberg and Joakim Nivre. 2012. A dynamic oracle for arc-eager dependency parsing. In *Proceedings of COLING 2012*, pages 959–976.

John Hale. 2017. Models of human sentence comprehension in computational psycholinguistics.

Jun Hatori, Takuya Matsuzaki, Yusuke Miyao, and Jun'ichi Tsujii. 2012. Incremental joint approach to word segmentation, POS tagging, and dependency parsing in Chinese. In *Proceedings of the 50th Annual Meeting of the Association for Computational Linguistics (Volume 1: Long Papers)*, pages 1045–1053, Jeju Island, Korea. Association for Computational Linguistics.

Matthew Honnibal and Mark Johnson. 2014. Joint incremental disfluency detection and dependency parsing. *Transactions of the Association for Computational Linguistics*, 2:131–142.

Frank Keller. 2010. Cognitively plausible models of human language processing. In *Proceedings of the ACL 2010 Conference Short Papers*, pages 60–67. Association for Computational Linguistics.

Eliyahu Kiperwasser and Yoav Goldberg. 2016. Simple and accurate dependency parsing using bidirectional LSTM feature representations. *Transactions of the Association for Computational Linguistics*, 4:313–327.

Philipp Koehn. 2004. Statistical significance tests for machine translation evaluation. In *Proceedings of the 2004 Conference on Empirical Methods in Natural Language Processing*, pages 388–395, Barcelona, Spain. Association for Computational Linguistics.

Shuhei Kurita, Daisuke Kawahara, and Sadao Kurohashi. 2017. Neural joint model for transition-based Chinese syntactic analysis. In *Proceedings of the 55th Annual Meeting of the Association for Computational Linguistics (Volume 1: Long Papers)*, pages 1204–1214, Vancouver, Canada. Association for Computational Linguistics.

John SY Lee, Jason Naradowsky, and David A Smith. 2011. A discriminative model for joint morphological disambiguation and dependency parsing. In *Proceedings of the 49th Annual Meeting of the Association for Computational Linguistics: Human language technologies*, pages 885–894.

Zhenghua Li, Min Zhang, Wanxiang Che, Ting Liu, Wenliang Chen, and Haizhou Li. 2011. Joint models for Chinese POS tagging and dependency parsing. In *Proceedings of the 2011 Conference on Empirical Methods in Natural Language Processing*, pages 1180–1191, Edinburgh, Scotland, UK. Association for Computational Linguistics.

George W McConkie and Keith Rayner. 1975. The span of the effective stimulus during a fixation in reading. *Perception & Psychophysics*, 17(6):578–586.

George W McConkie and Keith Rayner. 1976. Asymmetry of the perceptual span in reading. *Bulletin of the psychonomic society*, 8(5):365–368.

Alexis Nasr, Carlos Ramisch, José Deulofeu, and André Valli. 2015. Joint dependency parsing and multiword expression tokenisation. In *Annual Meeting of the Association for Computational Linguistics*, pages 1116–1126.

Dat Quoc Nguyen and Karin Verspoor. 2018. An improved neural network model for joint POS tagging and dependency parsing. In *Proceedings of the CoNLL 2018 Shared Task: Multilingual Parsing from Raw Text to Universal Dependencies*, pages 81–91, Brussels, Belgium. Association for Computational Linguistics.

Joakim Nivre. 2003. An efficient algorithm for projective dependency parsing. In *Proceedings of the eighth international conference on parsing technologies*, pages 149–160.

Joakim Nivre. 2008. Algorithms for deterministic incremental dependency parsing. *Computational Linguistics*, 34(4):513–553.

Joakim Nivre. 2009. Non-projective dependency parsing in expected linear time. In *Proceedings of the Joint Conference of the 47th Annual Meeting of the ACL and the 4th International Joint Conference on Natural Language Processing of the AFNLP*, pages 351–359.

Jeffrey Pennington, Richard Socher, and Christopher D. Manning. 2014. Glove: Global vectors for word representation. In *Empirical Methods in Natural Language Processing (EMNLP)*, pages 1532–1543.

Martin Popel, Zdeněk Žabokrtský, and Martin Vojtek. 2017. Udapi: Universal api for universal dependencies. In *Proceedings of the NoDaLiDa 2017 Workshop on Universal Dependencies (UDW 2017)*, pages 96–101.

Hui Wan, Tahira Naseem, Young-Suk Lee, Vittorio Castelli, and Miguel Ballesteros. 2018. Ibm research at the conll 2018 shared task on multilingual parsing. In *Proceedings of the CoNLL 2018 Shared Task: Multilingual Parsing from Raw Text to Universal Dependencies*, pages 92–102.

Hiroyasu Yamada and Yuji Matsumoto. 2003. Statistical dependency analysis with support vector machines. In *Proceedings of IWPT*, volume 3, pages 195–206. Nancy, France.

Hang Yan, Xipeng Qiu, and Xuanjing Huang. 2020. A Graph-based Model for Joint Chinese Word Segmentation and Dependency Parsing. *Transactions of the Association for Computational Linguistics*, 8:78–92.

Masashi Yoshikawa, Hiroyuki Shindo, and Yuji Matsumoto. 2016. Joint transition-based dependency parsing and disfluency detection for automatic speech recognition texts. In *Proceedings of the 2016 Conference on Empirical Methods in Natural Language Processing*, pages 1036–1041, Austin, Texas. Association for Computational Linguistics.

Daniel Zeman, Jan Hajič, Martin Popel, Martin Potthast, Milan Straka, Filip Ginter, Joakim Nivre, and Slav Petrov. 2018. CoNLL 2018 shared task: Multilingual parsing from raw text to universal dependencies. In *Proceedings of the CoNLL 2018 Shared Task: Multilingual Parsing from Raw Text to Universal Dependencies*, pages 1–21, Brussels, Belgium. Association for Computational Linguistics.

Daniel Zeman et al. 2019. Universal dependencies 2.5. LINDAT/CLARIAH-CZ digital library at the Institute of Formal and Applied Linguistics (ÚFAL), Faculty of Mathematics and Physics, Charles University.

Yuan Zhang, Chengtao Li, Regina Barzilay, and Kareem Darwish. 2015. Randomized greedy inference for joint segmentation, POS tagging and dependency parsing. In *Proceedings of the 2015 Conference of the North American Chapter of the Association for Computational Linguistics: Human Language Technologies*, pages 42–52, Denver, Colorado. Association for Computational Linguistics.

Semi-Automatic Construction of Text-to-SQL Data for Domain Transfer

Tianyi Li[⋆], **Sujian Li**[†] and **Mark Steedman**[⋆]

[⋆]University of Edinburgh
[†]MOE Key Lab of Computational Linguistics, School of EECS, Peking University
tianyi.li@ed.ac.uk, lisujian@pku.edu.cn, steedman@inf.ed.ac.uk

Abstract

Strong and affordable in-domain data is a desirable asset when transferring trained semantic parsers to novel domains. As previous methods for semi-automatically constructing such data cannot handle the complexity of realistic SQL queries, we propose to construct SQL queries via context-dependent sampling, and introduce the concept of *topic*. Along with our SQL query construction method, we propose a novel pipeline of semi-automatic Text-to-SQL dataset construction that covers the broad space of SQL queries. We show that the created dataset is comparable with expert annotation along multiple dimensions, and is capable of improving domain transfer performance for SOTA semantic parsers.

1 Introduction

Due to the broad use of SQL in real-world databases, the task of mapping natural language questions to SQL queries (Text-to-SQL) has drawn considerable attention. Several large-scale cross-domain Text-to-SQL datasets have been manually constructed and advanced the development of Text-to-SQL semantic parsing (Zhong et al., 2017; Yu et al., 2018).

While these datasets are built for domain-general semantic parsing, current state-of-the-art (SOTA) semantic parsers still suffer sharp performance drop when generalising to unseen domains (Wang et al., 2020; Guo et al., 2019; Zhang et al., 2019).

This could be attributed to the observation that the mapping of Text-to-SQL vary vastly across different domains, particularly in terms of the expressions of predicates[1]. It is very difficult for models to generalize to those variations in a zero-shot fashion. Thus, additional in-domain data is desirable when applying semantic parsers to novel domains.

[1]An example illustrating such difference is presented in Appendix A

Unfortunately, the cost and scarcity of supervised data have been a major barrier for the wider application of the Text-to-SQL task, as creating pairs of natural language questions and SQL queries is a complex task demanding expertise in both SQL language and the specific domains. Take the SPIDER dataset (Yu et al., 2018) for example, 10,181 Text-SQL pairs in 200 databases (from 138 domains) required 11 computer science graduates to invest 1,000 human hours.

In semantic parsing, some semi-automatic dataset construction methods have been proposed. Wang et al. (2015) built logical forms compositionally, converted them to rigid pseudo natural language (Pseudo-NL) questions with rules, then crowd-sourced those Pseudo-NL questions into NL questions. Cheng et al. (2018) further broke down the pseudo-NL questions into question sequences to make them more digestible for crowd workers.

While these approaches shed light on the methodology of semi-automatic construction of semantic parsing datasets, applying them to collect broad-coverage Text-to-SQL data for domain transfer is not trivial. Firstly, SQL language has a much larger variety of realistic queries than Lambda-DCS logical forms (Liang, 2013), which were the focus of earlier work. Blind enumeration-up-to-a-certain-depth from a CFG is therefore intractable in size. Secondly, Herzig and Berant (2019) have discovered a mismatch between semi-automatically constructed queries and real-world queries, in terms of the distribution of logical form and the style of natural language expressions. As achieving accuracy gains in domain transfer demands high quality for the in-domain data, narrowing these mismatches is crucial.

In this paper, we propose a novel semi-automatic pipeline for robust construction of Text-SQL pairs as training data in novel domains, with broad semantic coverage, from databases only. Following

Proceedings of the 17th International Conference on Parsing Technologies (IWPT 2021), pages 38–49
Bangkok, Thailand (online), August 6, 2021.

Wang et al. (2015), our pipeline consists of three parts: automatic SQL query construction, SQL-to-PseudoNL conversion and PseudoNL-to-NL paraphrasing. In SQL query construction, we use a context-dependent probabilistic approach: first, we choose a topic of interest, a random n-tuple of tables in the novel domain, such as *Concerts and Stadiums*; then, we sample from a set of grammar rules, at each step pruning the generation space based on decision history. In SQL-to-PseudoNL conversion, we follow Cheng et al. (2018) in breaking down constructed SQL queries with templates, but also assign a "dominant concept" to topics to simplify Pseudo-NL questions. In PseudoNL-to-NL paraphrasing, we do crowd annotation, and provide crowd workers with various annotation scaffolds to collect quality NL questions. An example through our pipeline is shown in Figure 1.

We show that by using schema-inspired *topic* and context-dependent sampling instead of blind enumeration, SQL queries analogous to real-world queries can be constructed, and effective fine-tune datasets for domain transfer can be built. Our experiment shows that even a modest amount of our data facilitates domain transfer across a range of semantic parsers, raising accuracy in novel domains by up to 1%[2].

2 Related Work

Alternative Supervision To resolve the difficulty in gathering supervised data for semantic parsing, various methods have been proposed from different perspectives.

Numerous approaches have explored distant supervision to bypass the use of expensive annotated data. Kwiatkowski et al. (2013); Berant et al. (2013); Yao and Van Durme (2014); Berant and Liang (2014) used question-answer pairs as supervision instead of logical form annotations; Reddy et al. (2014) used web-scale corpora of descriptive sentences, formalizing semantic parsing as a graph matching problem. These methods perform well on factoid questions; however, for more complex questions, it is harder to infer the underlying queries from the answers alone.

Later on, semi-automatic data collection methods, which reduce the cost of annotation, have been given considerable attention. Wang et al.

[2]Our code and data will be released at `https://github.com/Teddy-Li/SemiAuto_Data_Text_SQL`

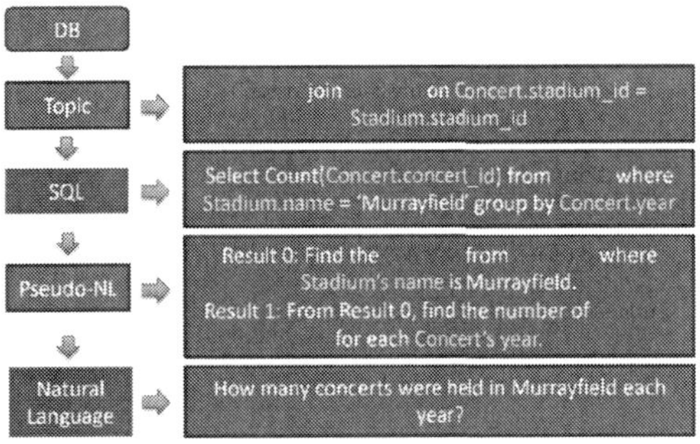

Figure 1: A example of the data construction pipeline, from the topic of "concerts and stadiums" to the final results: the SQL query and the paired natural language question.

(2015) propose to compose logical forms by combining sub-components through a grammar, and translate the resulting trees into NL questions via rigid Pseudo-NL questions and crowd-paraphrasing. Cheng et al. (2018) further replace the Pseudo-NL questions with question sequences to simplify the annotation for individual sentences.

While those approaches pioneered semi-automatic data collection, the query construction method based on exhaustive enumeration has its weaknesses. Herzig and Berant (2019) showed that there exists a significant mismatch between the distributions of created logical forms and real query logical forms, and between the language style of paraphrases and real questions.

Text-to-SQL Text-to-SQL as a semantic parsing task, has attracted increasing interest, where multiple large-scale datasets have been released. Zhong et al. (2017) created a large single-table Text-to-SQL dataset, WikiSQL, from Wikipedia entries, upon which many semantic parsers have been trained, achieving high accuracies surpassing 80% (Chang et al., 2020; Lyu et al., 2020; Wang et al., 2018; Hwang et al., 2019; He et al., 2019). Yu et al. (2018) proposed SPIDER, another large-scale text-to-SQL dataset with multi-table databases, much wider grammar coverage, and more complex queries. It involves features including GROUP-BY aggregation, ORDER-BY, nested queries. This has made SPIDER a more realistic, and also more challenging parsing task, with SOTA semantic parsers achieving accuracies of above 60%. (Guo et al., 2019; Wang et al., 2020).

Although SPIDER is considered a domain-general semantic parsing dataset, semantic parsers trained on it still suffer a sharp performance drop when generalizing to unseen domains[3].

Thus, additional resource for domain transfer is appealing. However, in this more complex multi-table Text-to-SQL task, previous semi-automatic dataset construction methods face an even greater challenge. With multi-table SQL queries with more complex clauses, exhaustive enumeration is intractable in size and prone to mismatches.

More recently, various methods of Text-to-SQL dataset construction have been proposed (Yu et al., 2020; Zhong et al., 2020; Zhang et al., 2021), further automating the SQL-to-NL step with neural question generation. However, for query construction, they either do vanilla grammar-based SQL query sampling (Zhang et al., 2021) or use template sketches from existing datasets (Zhong et al., 2020; Yu et al., 2020). On the other hand, we focus instead on the context-dependent construction of SQL queries that both generalize beyond existing datasets and remain realistic.

```
Z ::= Q intersect Q | Q union Q | Q except Q | Q
Q ::= Topic Filter Group Select Sort
Topic ::= PREDEFINED_TOPIC
Filter ::= and Filter Filter | or Filter Filter |
        > A V | > A Q | < A V | < A Q | > = A V |
        > = A Q | = A V | = A Q | like A V |
        between A V | not like A V | in A Q |
        not in A Q | ε
Group ::= Col_keys Filter | ε
Select ::= A Select | A        (with a limit of 5)
Sort ::= Order Col_keys | ε
Col_keys ::= C | C C
Order ::= most | least | asc Limit | desc Limit
A ::= C | max C | min C | sum C | avg C | count C |
        distinct_count C | count(*)
C ::= column
V ::= value
Limit ::= number | ε
```

Figure 2: The grammar for generating SQL queries, listed iteratively. *PREDEFINED_TOPIC* is the topic set with method in section 3.1; terminal nodes are in red, non-terminal nodes are in blue.

3 Method

Our pipeline takes database schema as input, and outputs a set of aligned pairs of NL questions and SQL queries. We start by selecting a topic of interest from the schema, followed by sampling production rules from a concise SQL query grammar as in figure 2, resulting in a created SQL query. We then convert the query into a sequence of pseudo-NL questions, and finally crowd-paraphrase the sequence into a fluent NL question.

Specifically, we highlight two key features in our SQL query construction algorithm, asserting control to the process of sampling:

- We set the topic, namely the attended subset of tables in database with an algorithm based on Pagerank and Prim's MST algorithm;
- At each step of sampling, we prune the space of candidates by conditioning the distribution of production rules heuristically on the decision history, namely ancestor nodes, left siblings and left siblings' descendants.

3.1 Setting the Topic

For each valid NL question, there is one topic referring to a concrete concept; similarly, for each real SQL query, however complex, there is one topic, the set of entities it attends to, typically specified in the 'FROM' clause, that should reflect some concrete concepts. For queries involving one table, the topic is simply the table itself; for queries involving multiple tables, which is an iconic feature of SPIDER, it is crucial to identify which tables should be bound together and how.

Our approach here, which is a novel contribution in this paper, takes inspiration from observations in existing datasets. In SPIDER, 93.9% of 'join-on' clauses are between columns with foreign-key relations, an additional 4.2% share the same name[4]. This is consistent with our intuition about SQL language, where join-on clauses are most closely related to foreign-key relations. The popularity of columns sharing the same name apart from foreign-keys is partly a result of missing foreign-key relations and partly a reflection of the fact that columns with the same names are likely relevant.

We therefore set up a table relation graph for each database to model the probabilities that a topic defined by join-on clauses is meaningful. When two columns have a foreign key relation or share the same name, we add an edge between their corresponding tables (foreign-key relations are given higher weights for frequency). Multiple edges between pairs of tables are reduced by sum. To maintain the completeness of grammar space, we assign a small 'background radiation' weight be-

[3] https://yale-lily.github.io/spider

[4] for examples of join-on relations with foreign-key and same-name, please refer to Table 5 in Appendix

tween each pair of tables.

The topic for each SQL query can then be modelled as a sub-graph of this table relation graph, and the transition distribution given previously chosen tables can be modelled with a stochastic version of Prim's MST algorithm (Prim, 1957), formalized as:

$$p(t_k|\Phi) = \frac{\sum_{e \in edge(t_k, \Phi)} e.w * e.To.w}{\sum_{e \in edge(\Phi^c, \Phi)} e.w * e.To.w} \quad (1)$$

where $\Phi = t_1, ..., t_{k-1}$ is the set of previously chosen tables, $e.To$ is the candidate table, and $e.w$ are edges' weight and $e.To.w$ are Pagerank weights of candidate tables.

With these transition probabilities, the problem has been reduced to choosing the first table. To do this, we need a prior distribution among all tables. Again, we use Pagerank for this purpose: first, each table is assigned an initial importance according to their columns, then we do Pagerank on the table relation graph with random-jump probability of 0.2 to get a context-aware importance among tables, which is then normalized to a distribution. Note that we turn edges to the reverse direction so that weights would accumulate from the primary side to the foreign side of foreign-key relations and the foreign sides would be more likely chosen as the first table, as we would hope.

In sum, as the first step of constructing an SQL query from scratch, we settle its topic. We first sample an 'initial table' from a prior distribution of tables, which is 'Concert' in the case of our example in Figure 1; then we iteratively expand to other tables until halting after a random number of steps[5], which in the case of our example, results in the value of *Topic* row in Figure 1.

3.2 Context-dependent Sampling

After sampling a topic from the table relation graph, we move on to sampling the whole SQL query from a concise SQL query grammar as in Figure 2. We start from a root node Z and recursively dive down until all branches have hit terminal nodes (colored red in Figure 2). An example is shown in Figure 3.

We follow depth-first traversal order, and, to create SQL query sets analogous to the queries in real world, we use decision history as condition of candidate distributions at each step. Namely, we

[5]in practice the maximum number of tables is limited to 4 following statistical observations.

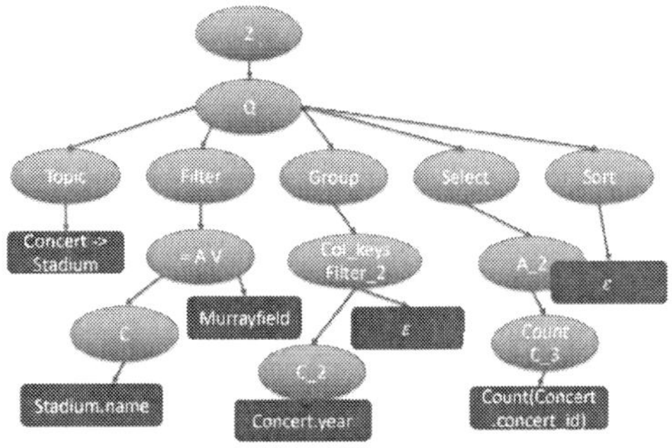

Figure 3: An Example of Created SQL query "Select Count(Concert.concert_id) from Concert join Stadium on Concert.stadium_id = Stadium.id where Stadium.name = 'Murrayfield' group by Concert.year" with tree structure.

assign a larger probability mass to relevant candidates, avoid contradictory or redundant candidates, thereby asserting control to clause structures.

On one hand, we want the resulting SQL queries to make sense in the real world; on the other hand, we don't want their distribution to over-fit to existing domains. Thus, in practice we employ a conservative heuristic approach, set up rules by collecting patterns of 'bad' queries and other domain-agnostic patterns from trials, and prune the space by tuning distributions toward 'good' combinations and against 'bad' ones.

For example, the following rule "A column is more likely chosen to 'where' clause if it has been chosen in the last 'where' clause", tunes probabilities against queries like *select editors' names from journal committees and their corresponding journals and editors, whose age is smaller than 50 and journal's sales is larger than 1600*, in favour of those like *select editors' names whose age is larger than 40 and smaller than 50*.

Additionally, to reduce redundancy, we validate all candidate clauses at each step by executing them against the databases and collecting responses. We compare query response before and after adding a candidate clause, and screen out clauses that either make no difference or result in empty responses. We present the full set of rules in Appendix B.

3.3 From SQL to Pseudo-NL

Following previous work, to translate SQL queries to NL questions, we first use a template-based approach to convert them to pseudo-NL questions. Similarly to Cheng et al. (2018), we deterministically convert complex SQL queries into sequences of pseudo-NL questions to make annotation easier. In practice, with the more complex SQL clause structures, we find it not ideal to split questions into sequences as granular as Cheng et al. (2018), because annotators again get lost in the labyrinth of coreferences between questions in the same sequence. Thus we re-balance the trade-off between the number of sentences and individual complexity towards longer but fewer sentences, so it's not too hard for crowd workers to follow[6].

Notably, while generally speaking SQL language looks similar to natural language, its FROM clauses with table-joining are very unnatural, and when involving many tables, can make their literal translations impenetrable. Unlike in NL questions where there is an integrated topic, in SQL language the topic defined by 'FROM' clause could be long and confusing. Take the example in Figure 1, its topic *'Concerts and Stadiums'* in the form of SQL query becomes *'Concert join Stadium on Concert.stadium_id = Stadium.id'*. Worse still, multiple tables also make the meaning of wildcard column '*' confusing in clauses such as *'select count(*)'*.

Luckily, we have observed that for a pair of tables joined by foreign key relations, we can always consider the foreign side as the 'main' table of the pair, since it is the one from which the primary side is extended. Therefore, we define this directionality for a topic sub-graph of the table relation graph: primary $\rightarrow$ foreign as root-wise and foreign $\rightarrow$ primary as leaf-wise; for table pairs linked by same-name relation, an edge is kept on both directions.

Then, for multi-table queries, we assume that the table(s) at the root-most position is the "dominant concept" of the topic. Since sub-graphs are predominantly trees, mostly there is one dominant concept for each query. Whenever possible, we replace all pseudo-NL phrases for the table joining, such as the above, with expressions like *'Concerts and their corresponding Stadiums'*, and replace all phrases for wildcard column *'count(*)'* with expressions like *'the number of Concerts'*. This way pseudo-NL questions are simplified, and the annotation burden is eased.

3.4 From Pseudo-NL to NL

The last part of our pipeline involves crowd-paraphrasing these pseudo-NL question sequences into fluent NL questions. We recruit workers on the Amazon Mechanical Turk (AMT) platform, present tasks to AMT workers randomly and pay \$0.25 for each task completed.

In each task, we present the workers with a pseudo-NL question sequence paired with examples from DB response. In pilot trials, we found that annotators tend to keep fragments from the pseudo-NL questions even when they're clearly rigid. We hypothesize that this is an exposure effect, that annotators' exposure to the pseudo-NL questions influenced their own style of expression.

As another of our novel contributions, we pose a countermeasure to this exposure effect. First, we engage annotators in the context of helping their foreign friends sound local. Further, we present a personalized example specific to each generated SQL query. These personalized examples are taken from expert annotated datasets in other domains, but can give crowd workers a general idea of what level of naturalness is expected and in which way.

Each personalized example involves a pseudo-NL question sequence, an expert-annotated NL question and an example DB response. To provide the most relevant hint, we retrieve from existing data the most similar entries to each created SQL query, where similarity is measured as the cosine similarity regarding an engineered feature vector[7]. We retrieve the top 10 example queries with smallest distances in the above terms. We then randomly pick one as the personalized example to display.

We employed only the English speaking AMT workers with 95%+ acceptance rate and 50+ acceptance history to restrict this paraphrasing task to a set of competent workers. However, empirically we still found a considerable number of workers submitting nonsensical paraphrases, apparently not understanding the task or giving up on the complex input. Thus, we restricted the access to only the trusted workers who had previously performed well in our task.

4 Our Experimental Corpus

4.1 Corpus Construction Details

We experiment on the basis of the SPIDER dataset, with data split details described in Table 1. Because the databases and Text-SQL pairs for SPIDER test set domains are not released, we re-split the 20 SPIDER development (dev) set domains equally

[6]For a flowchart with details please see Figure 4 in Appendix.

[7]For details of feature vector please refer to Appendix C.

Data Split	Domains	SQL Construction	SQL-to-NL	Data Size
seen-domain-train-set	166 train domains	Gold	Gold	7000
novel-domain-test-set	10 novel dev domains	Gold	Gold	440
seen-domain-dev-set	10 seen dev domains	Gold	Gold	594
novel-domain-ours-set	**10 novel dev domains**	**Ours**	**Ours**	**543**
novel-domain-oracle-set	**10 novel dev domains**	**Gold**	**Ours**	**466**
seen-domain-small-set	166 train domains	Gold	Gold	543
Zhang et al. (2021)	20 dev domains	-	-	58691

Table 1: Data splits involved in our experiment. **Ours** SQL construction refers to method in section 3.1, 3.2, while **Ours** SQL-to-NL refers to 3.3, 3.4. Zhang et al. (2021) is a SOTA data augmentation system described in 5.1.

into **seen** domains and **novel** domains[8]. Accordingly, we define the seen-domain-dev-set and novel-domain-test-set from the SPIDER dev set, along with the SPIDER train set renamed seen-domain-train-set.

Additionally, we collect two data sets in the novel domains, novel-domain-ours-set and novel-domain-oracle-set. Novel-domain-ours-set is our target dataset with entries constructed from scratch with only the databases and our full pipeline. Novel-domain-oracle-set entries start from the novel domain gold SQL queries, annotated with our SQL-to-NL method. Moreover, we create a new data split called seen-domain-small-set, which has the same size as novel-domain-ours-set, but is randomly sampled from the expert-annotated seen-domain-train-set.

We use a linear regression to derive the number of SQL queries to construct for each database, w.r.t the number of TABLES, COLUMNS and FOREIGN-KEY relations. Each created SQL query is paraphrased into natural language by 2 annotators as in SPIDER, paraphrases too short or too long are filtered out. The resulting data sizes are illustrated in Table 1.

In total, the paraphrasing and human evaluation (to be elaborated below) cost us $349.34.

4.2 Human Evaluation

To test the effectiveness of our SQL query construction and SQL-to-NL conversion method respectively, we conduct two experiments of human evaluation with participants recruited on AMT.

To evaluate the constructed SQL queries, we use the corresponding computer-generated pseudo-NL as a proxy for SQL queries to involve crowd-

[8]The 10 selected novel domains are: *orchestra, singer, real_estate_properties, tvshow, battle_death, voter_1, student_transcripts_tracking, concert_singer, world_1,* and *course_teach.*

Queries considered having following properties (in %)	ours	expert
Succinct	75.51	74.46
Sensible	95.95	89.49
Relevant	83.06	76.82
Complex	55.80	37.98

Table 2: Human evaluation results between ours and expert SQL queries.

sourcing. We present each participant with a Pseudo-NL question, ask them to indicate whether the Pseudo-NL is succinct, sensible, relevant and complex. Each question is randomly chosen either from our created novel-domain-ours-set or from expert-annotated SQL queries in novel-domain-oracle-set, where the choice is hidden from participant workers. We evaluate on all entries in the 10 novel domains, with results presented in Table 2.

As shown, compared to expert-annotated ones, participants considered a larger proportion of our queries complex, but also a larger proportion concise, sensible and relevant. Although human evaluation scores are subjective and could fluctuate across individuals, this at least shows that from the annotators' point of view, our created SQL queries are comparable to expert annotated ones on some dimensions.

To evaluate our SQL-to-NL conversion method, we compare our crowd-sourced questions from novel-domain-oracle-set with expert annotated NL questions from novel-domain-test-set. Since both are aligned to the same set of gold SQL queries, we show participants pairs of NL questions referring to the same SQL query. We ask the participants how similar the question pairs are, and which of them is smoother in language.

With crowd workers as judges, we cannot directly measure how rigorous our NL questions are in preserving the semantics of SQL queries. However, by taking expert-annotated questions as the gold standard of query semantics, and inspecting the similarity between ours and expert-annotated questions for the same gold-standard SQL queries, we can indirectly measure the level of rigorousness that our conversion method is capable of.

Results show that the average similarity between our questions and gold questions is scored 3.78 out of 1 to 5, indicating a good alignment between the meanings of the question pairs. As for preference, 45% of times our question is preferred, while 39% of times gold question is preferred and 16% of times the two are considered equally smooth in expression. This result verifies the validity of our SQL-to-NL conversion method.

5 Evaluation by Domain Transfer

5.1 Evaluation Setting

To further evaluate our pipeline's effectiveness, we do an extrinsic evaluation in the context of domain transfer. Namely, we test the capability of our created data to help semantic parsers generalize to novel domains. Below we first define 4 dataset settings and 2 training scenarios:

Dataset Settings

- PRETRAIN Trains on seen-domain-train-set[9], validates on seen-domain-dev-set, tests on novel-domain-test-set. This reflects the process of training a model on seen domains then applying the trained model to novel domains;
- OURS Trains on novel-domain-ours-set, tests on novel-domain-test-set. This is our target setting, which reflects training with our semi-automatically constructed in-domain data then test on real-world queries in the same domains;
- GOLD Trains on half (220 entries) of the novel-domain-test-set, tests on the other half. This setting approximates a theoretical upper bound, reflecting how much accuracy gain can be achieved with gold in-domain data;
- TRAIN(SMALL) Trains on novel-domain-small-set, tests on novel-domain-test-set. This setting is an out-of-domain expert-annotated baseline for OURS setting in RANDOM-INIT scenario, and answers the question "how powerful is our created, in-domain data compared to the expert-annotated but out-of-domain data, in terms of training models from random initialization".

Training Scenarios

- RANDOM-INIT Start training from randomly initialized model parameters. For models with BERT, initialize BERT parameters with pre-trained checkpoints[10];
- FINETUNE Start training from model checkpoints acquired from RANDOM-INIT training on PRETRAIN data.

We conducted experiments with 3 popular recent Text-to-SQL semantic parsers: lang2logic (Dong and Lapata, 2016), IRNet-BERT (Guo et al., 2019), and RAT-SQL-BERT (Wang et al., 2020). lang2logic is the first semantic parser to employ Seq2Seq paradigm, IRNet-BERT is the first practically effective semantic parser on SPIDER challenge, and RAT-SQL-BERT is the latest reproducible SOTA when using BERT-Large encoder. The lang2logic models were originally written in Lua and are re-implemented with PyTorch; to serve as a vanilla baseline, seq2seq setting is used instead of the more complex seq2tree setting. For RAT-SQL-BERT models, due to memory limits of our 1080 TI GPUs and for a fair comparison with IRNet-BERT, we use the bert-base-uncased version as in IRNet-BERT, instead of the bert-large-whole-word-masking version in the original implementation.

For each parser, we first train them under the RANDOM-INIT scenario with PRETRAIN data; then FINETUNE the pretrained model saperately, with OURS and GOLD data. Additionally, we train each parser under RANDOM-INIT scenario with OURS and TRAIN(SMALL) data respectively, to evaluate our data outside the scope of domain transfer.

For all RANDOM-INIT models we use the same set of hyper-parameters as in their original settings; for FINETUNE models, following the intuition that fine-tuning should have learning rates no larger than pretrain, we do log-uniform sampling through 1/3, 1/10, 1/30 and 1/100 of the original learning rates as well as the original learning rates themselves; for models with BERT encoders, we further grid-search both having the BERT learning rates fixed and aligned with other parameters.

We have attempted to compare with previous work on semi-automatic dataset construction. How-

[9]For definitions of data splits, please refer to Table 1

[10]https://huggingface.co/transformers/pretrained_models.html

Accuracy (%)	lang2logic	IRNet-BERT	RAT-SQL-BERT
pretrain	3.87	65.60	59.77
finetune-ours	**5.00***	**66.74**†	60.00$^{\diamond}$
finetune-gold	8.06	71.07	61.13
random-init-ours	1.14	21.79	19.19
random-init-train(small)	1.82	42.66	14.55

Table 3: Exact Match accuracy in percentage points. $\star$ means at learning rate of 1e-4, $\dagger$ means at 3e-4, $\diamond$ means at 1e-5. To faithfully reproduce a domain transfer setting, the accuracies of PRETRAIN models are reported on novel-domain-test-set. Therefore, reported accuracies may vary from the ones reported on the development set of SPIDER.

ever, the method of Wang et al. (2015) is restricted to LambdaDCS logical forms and not applicable to our setting of multi-table SQL queries; the data construction method of Cheng et al. (2018) is not contained in their open-source codebase, and the first author was unfortunately not reachable for that implementation.

Nonetheless, we discuss Zhang et al. (2021) for comparison, a recent work on large-scale Text-to-SQL data augmentation, with context-free sampling of SQL queries and hierarchical neural automatic NL generation without human intervention.

5.2 Results and Discussions

Evaluation results are shown in Table 3. Accuracies are evaluated on the novel-domain-test-set of SPIDER. As shown, extra in-domain data collected with our pipeline improves novel domain accuracy by more than 1% for both lang2logic and IRNet-BERT models.

We also tried applying the same fine-tuning to the IRNet and RAT-SQL parsers without BERT. However, that did not increase the accuracy. We attribute this difference to the fact that while our additional data provides information on the novel domain, its language style is not the same as SPIDER train set. Our crowd-paraphrased questions are bound to be different in style to expert-annotated questions. The conventional recurrent encoders, trained only on the SPIDER train set, fail to capture the meaning of questions in our fine-tune dataset. On the other hand, with BERT contextualizers, which had been trained on texts at the magnitude of billions, the language of our questions looks more familiar to models, and they can more successfully absorb the domain-related information encoded in our data. As BERT-Large models are bigger and more powerful, we would expect the accuracy gain to be larger with RAT-SQL-BERT-Large, and expect the same trend for other semantic parsers in general.

The finetune-gold result provides an approximate upper bound, from expert-annotated data pairs at the same magnitude of our size. It is encouraging that we are able to correct roughly 20% of the correctable errors by this standard. Further gains could reasonably be expected from increasing scale.

Comparisons between models trained from RANDOM-INIT scenario also show interesting findings. Since with both *random-init-ours* and *random-init-train(small)*, the data sizes are a magnitude smaller than the SPIDER training set used for PRETRAIN, parsers trained under these two settings perform less competitively than their FINETUNE counterparts. But among themselves, training from RANDOM-INIT with OURS data is generally comparable to that of expert-annotated TRAIN(SMALL) setting of the same size, and in the case of RAT-SQL-BERT it even exceeds that of TRAIN(SMALL).

The results in Table 3 are for the best fine-tuned model checkpoint on our test data, the novel-domain-test-set. This choice reflects the scenario of our chosen task: we start with novel domains, having only the databases available for use. We semi-automatically create an in-domain fine-tune dataset and train semantic parsers with it. We envisage deploying the fine-tuned models to arrive at the best model checkpoint by the use of feedback from users, for which optimizing on the novel-domain-test-set is used as a proxy.

We are nevertheless interested in knowing if we can choose the best model checkpoint independently of our test. In terms of our hypothetical scenario, it reflects whether we can achieve good performance with real queries, by assuming access to a fixed development set, and choosing the best model checkpoint according to performance on that fixed set.

The standard practice here is to validate on a

set-aside development set, then report the accuracy on the test set. However, the 440 entries of novel-domain-test-set is all the expert-annotated data that we have for our novel domains. In response to this dilemma, we split the novel-domain-test-set in half, into two subsets A and B. We then do cross-validation between them: we use one subset for picking the model checkpoint with highest accuracy, assessing its accuracy on the other (and vice versa). Under this setting, we still achieve an accuracy gain of 0.74% with IRNet-BERT and 1.25% with lang2logic.

Contemporary with our work, Zhang et al. (2021) generated a much larger set of 50,000+ synthetic training data (which they were able to do by not involving human judges). Under the same evaluation strategy as us in Table 3, and starting from a different IRNet-BERT pretrained baseline of 59.5%[11], they report an augmented accuracy of 61.7% on the SPIDER development set, obtaining an increase of 2.2%. However, we achieve half of that increase with only around 1% their amount of data. In the absence of access to their code, we have been unable to determine the performance that Zhang et al. (2021) would obtain from a comparably small dataset, but we feel confident that gains comparable to their full dataset could be obtained from our method with more modest increases in scale.

6 Conclusion

We have presented a novel approach to construct in-domain Text-to-SQL data, following the three-step paradigm of Wang et al. (2015). We randomly select a topic of interest from a table relation graph prior to building the actual query, and sample query clauses in a context-dependent manner. We identify "dominant concept" of the topics to simplify the converted Pseudo-NL, and retrieve personalised examples as annotation scaffold for crowd-paraphrasing. Our experiments show that our in-domain data is comparable with expert-annotated data, and capable of increasing the accuracy of SOTA IRNet-BERT semantic parser by up to 1%.

For future work, we plan to explore more sophisticated probabilistic models to control SQL query construction, and pair our query construction method with recent work on SQL-to-NL translation, so as to bring our method to larger scale.

[11] which is mainly due to their use of SPIDER development set and our use of novel-domain-test-set.

Acknowledgements

We thank Yantao Jia and Jeff Pan for helpful comments and feedbacks, we'd also like to thank the three anonymous reviewers for their valuable comments. This work was supported partly by a Mozilla PhD scholarship at Informatics Graduate School, by the University of Edinburgh Huawei Laboratory, and by National Natural Science Foundation of China (No. 61876009).

References

Jonathan Berant, A. Chou, Roy Frostig, and Percy Liang. 2013. Semantic parsing on Freebase from question-answer pairs. In *EMNLP*.

Jonathan Berant and Percy Liang. 2014. Semantic parsing via paraphrasing. In *Proceedings of the 52nd Annual Meeting of the Association for Computational Linguistics (Volume 1: Long Papers)*, pages 1415–1425, Baltimore, Maryland. Association for Computational Linguistics.

Shuaichen Chang, Pengfei Liu, Yun Tang, Jing Huang, Xiaodong He, and Bowen Zhou. 2020. Zero-shot Text-to-SQL learning with auxiliary task. In *AAAI*.

Jianpeng Cheng, Siva Reddy, and Mirella Lapata. 2018. Building a neural semantic parser from a domain ontology. *CoRR*, abs/1812.10037.

Li Dong and Mirella Lapata. 2016. Language to logical form with neural attention. In *Proceedings of the 54th Annual Meeting of the Association for Computational Linguistics (Volume 1: Long Papers)*, pages 33–43, Berlin, Germany. Association for Computational Linguistics.

Jiaqi Guo, Zecheng Zhan, Yan Gao, Yan Xiao, Jian-Guang Lou, Ting Liu, and Dongmei Zhang. 2019. Towards complex Text-to-SQL in cross-domain database with intermediate representation. In *Proceedings of the 57th Annual Meeting of the Association for Computational Linguistics*, pages 4524–4535, Florence, Italy. Association for Computational Linguistics.

Pengcheng He, Yi Mao, Kaushik Chakrabarti, and Weizhu Chen. 2019. X-SQL: reinforce schema representation with context. *arXiv preprint arXiv:1908.08113*.

Jonathan Herzig and Jonathan Berant. 2019. Don't paraphrase, detect! rapid and effective data collection for semantic parsing. In *Proceedings of the 2019 Conference on Empirical Methods in Natural Language Processing and the 9th International Joint Conference on Natural Language Processing (EMNLP-IJCNLP)*, pages 3810–3820, Hong Kong, China. Association for Computational Linguistics.

Wonseok Hwang, Jinyeong Yim, Seunghyun Park, and Minjoon Seo. 2019. A comprehensive exploration on WikiSQL with table-aware word contextualization. *arXiv preprint arXiv:1902.01069*.

Tom Kwiatkowski, Eunsol Choi, Yoav Artzi, and Luke Zettlemoyer. 2013. Scaling semantic parsers with on-the-fly ontology matching. In *Proceedings of the 2013 Conference on Empirical Methods in Natural Language Processing*, pages 1545–1556, Seattle, Washington, USA. Association for Computational Linguistics.

Percy Liang. 2013. Lambda dependency-based compositional semantics. *CoRR*, abs/1309.4408.

Qin Lyu, Kaushik Chakrabarti, Shobhit Hathi, Souvik Kundu, Jianwen Zhang, and Zheng Chen. 2020. Hybrid ranking network for Text-to-SQL. Technical Report MSR-TR-2020-7, Microsoft Dynamics 365 AI.

Robert Clay Prim. 1957. Shortest connection networks and some generalizations. *The Bell System Technical Journal*, 36(6):1389–1401.

Siva Reddy, Mirella Lapata, and Mark Steedman. 2014. Large-scale semantic parsing without question-answer pairs. *Transactions of the Association for Computational Linguistics*, 2:377–392.

Bailin Wang, Richard Shin, Xiaodong Liu, Oleksandr Polozov, and Matthew Richardson. 2020. RAT-SQL: Relation-aware schema encoding and linking for text-to-SQL parsers. In *Proceedings of the 58th Annual Meeting of the Association for Computational Linguistics*, pages 7567–7578, Online. Association for Computational Linguistics.

Chenglong Wang, Kedar Tatwawadi, Marc Brockschmidt, Po-Sen Huang, Yi Mao, Oleksandr Polozov, and Rishabh Singh. 2018. Robust text-to-sql generation with execution-guided decoding. *arXiv preprint arXiv:1807.03100*.

Yushi Wang, Jonathan Berant, and Percy Liang. 2015. Building a semantic parser overnight. In *Proceedings of the 53rd Annual Meeting of the Association for Computational Linguistics and the 7th International Joint Conference on Natural Language Processing (Volume 1: Long Papers)*, pages 1332–1342, Beijing, China. Association for Computational Linguistics.

Xuchen Yao and Benjamin Van Durme. 2014. Information extraction over structured data: Question answering with Freebase. In *Proceedings of the 52nd Annual Meeting of the Association for Computational Linguistics (Volume 1: Long Papers)*, pages 956–966, Baltimore, Maryland. Association for Computational Linguistics.

Tao Yu, Chien Sheng Wu, Xi Victoria Lin, Bailin Wang, Yi Chern Tan, Xinyi Yang, Dragomir Radev, Richard Socher, and Caiming Xiong. 2020. Grappa: Grammar-augmented pre-training for table semantic parsing.

Tao Yu, Rui Zhang, Kai Yang, Michihiro Yasunaga, Dongxu Wang, Zifan Li, James Ma, Irene Li, Qingning Yao, Shanelle Roman, Zilin Zhang, and Dragomir Radev. 2018. Spider: A large-scale human-labeled dataset for complex and cross-domain semantic parsing and Text-to-SQL task. In *Proceedings of the 2018 Conference on Empirical Methods in Natural Language Processing*, pages 3911–3921, Brussels, Belgium. Association for Computational Linguistics.

Ao Zhang, Kun Wu, Lijie Wang, Zhenghua Li, Xinyan Xiao, Hua Wu, Min Zhang, and Haifeng Wang. 2021. Data augmentation with hierarchical SQL-to-question generation for cross-domain Text-to-SQL parsing.

Rui Zhang, Tao Yu, Heyang Er, Sungrok Shim, Eric Xue, Xi Victoria Lin, Tianze Shi, Caiming Xiong, Richard Socher, and Dragomir Radev. 2019. Editing-based SQL query generation for cross-domain context-dependent questions. In *Proceedings of the 2019 Conference on Empirical Methods in Natural Language Processing and the 9th International Joint Conference on Natural Language Processing (EMNLP-IJCNLP)*, pages 5338–5349, Hong Kong, China. Association for Computational Linguistics.

Victor Zhong, Mike Lewis, Sida I. Wang, and Luke Zettlemoyer. 2020. Grounded adaptation for zero-shot executable semantic parsing. In *Proceedings of the 2020 Conference on Empirical Methods in Natural Language Processing (EMNLP)*, pages 6869–6882, Online. Association for Computational Linguistics.

Victor Zhong, Caiming Xiong, and Richard Socher. 2017. Seq2SQL: Generating structured queries from natural language using reinforcement learning. *CoRR*, abs/1709.00103.

A Cross-Domain Differences

The expression for query semantics can vary significantly across domains, SQL queries of similar structure can be mapped to fundamentally different questions.

For example, the two SQL queries in Table 4 look similar in their sketch, differing only in their schema tokens. However, their corresponding questions, when expressed in natural English, are very different even from the structures. For instance, the similar 'where' clause is a modifier of the subject 'brand' in one domain, and an adjunct of the predicate 'held' in the other.

B Set of Major Heuristic Rules

- Every table in topic is involved in at least one clause

Domain: Car Makers
SQL: Select Brand.car_maker, Count(Brands.brand_id) from Brands JOIN Country ON Brands.country_id = Country.country_id where Country. name = 'Germany' group by Brand.car_maker
Question: How many German brands does each car maker own?

Domain: Singers and Concerts
SQL: Select Concert.year, Count(Concert.concert_id) from Concert JOIN Stadium ON Concert.stadium_id = Stadium.id where Stadium.name = 'Murrayfield' group by Concert.year
Question: How many concerts were held in Murrayfield each year?

Table 4: An example pair of SQL queries with similar structures in different domains, the corresponding natural language questions that map to them have very different structures.

- A column is more likely chosen to 'WHERE' clause if it has been chosen in the previous 'WHERE' clause
- A sub-query nested in 'WHERE' clause likely returns the same column as the subject column in that 'WHERE' clause or is related to it via foreign-key relation
- Columns present in equality conditions are likely not chosen in 'GROUP BY' clauses.
- Subject columns in 'GROUP BY' clauses are likely to be selected.
- 'GROUP BY' clauses always take effect either by aggregating 'SELECT' columns, 'HAVING' conditions or 'ORDER BY' clauses.
- Columns present in 'SELECT' are likely also present in 'ORDER BY'
- When two queries are linked together via an 'UNION', 'EXCEPT' or 'INTERSECT', it is likely that the two queries share similar structure, only with one or two different structures such as 'WHERE' conditions.

Example: Foreign key
Select avg(T1.killed) from perpetrator as T1 join people as T2 on T1.people_id == T2.id where T2.height < 1.8m
How many people were killed by perpetrators shorter than 1.8m on average?
Example: Same Name
SELECT T1.id FROM trip AS T1 JOIN weather AS T2 ON T1.zip_code = T2.zip_code GROUP BY T2.zip_code HAVING avg(T2.mean_temperature_f) > 60
Give me ids for all the trip that took place in a zip code area with average mean temperature above 60.

Table 5: Examples of Foreign-Key and Same-Name conditions, with SQL queries in the first line and paired questions in the second.

C Feature Vector for Personalized Examples

In retrieving the personalized examples, the feature vectors for measuring similarity between SQL queries involve the following feature values. Features related to "SELECT", "FROM", "WHERE", "GROUP BY", "ORDER BY" and Set Operation clauses are listed in Table 6, 7, 8, 9, 10, 11 respectively.

Feature about "SELECT"	Weight
Number of "SELECT" clauses	1.0
Wildcard "*" in column	4.0
MAX in column	2.0
MIN in column	2.0
COUNT in column	2.0
SUM in column	2.0
AVG in column	2.0

Table 6: Feature vector values regarding the column clauses, with weights specified to the right of each feature.

Feature about "FROM"	Weight
Number of tables in "FROM"	1.0
All tables connected by "JOIN ON"	2.0

Table 7: Feature vector values regarding the "FROM" clauses, with weights specified to the right of each feature.

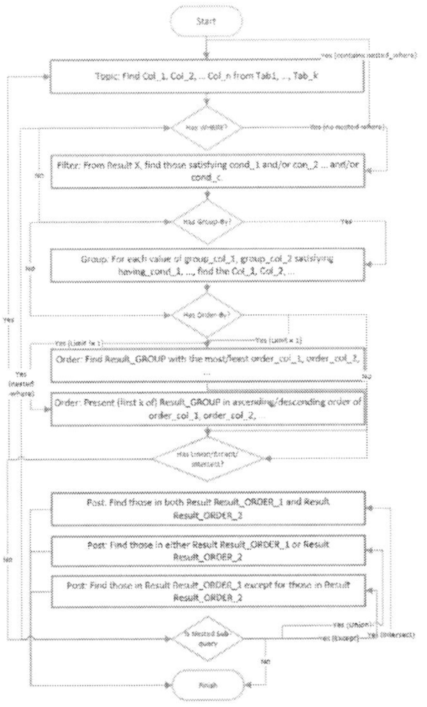

Figure 4: Flowchart illustration of how SQL queries are split into sequences of computer-generated questions. Triangle boxes and connection lines indicate the sequential relationship between these templates, in rectangle boxes are individual templates. In these templates, colored red are the slots to fill in. To build a sequence of Pseudo-NL questions, a program walks through the chart from start to finish, and lists the resulting instantiated templates iteratively as output.

Feature about "WHERE"	Weight
Empty "WHERE" clause	2.0
Number of "WHERE" clauses	1.0
"*" in column	4.0
MAX in column	1.0
MIN in column	1.0
COUNT in column	1.0
SUM in column	1.0
AVG in column	1.0
Sub-query in clauses	4.0
Column-valued clauses	4.0
'between' as operator	1.0
'equal' as operator	1.0
'larger than' as operator	1.0
'smaller than' as operator	1.0
'not larger than' as operator	1.0
'not smaller than' as operator	1.0
'not equal' as operator	1.0
'in' as operator	1.0
'like' as operator	1.0

Table 8: Feature vector values regarding the "WHERE" clauses, with weights specified to the right of each feature.

Feature about "GROUP BY"	Weight
Number of "GROUP BY" clauses	1.0
Involves "HAVING" clause	2.0
Involves "HAVING" with Sub-query	2.0

Table 9: Feature vector values regarding the "GROUP BY" clauses, with weights specified to the right of each feature.

Feature about "ORDER BY"	Weight
Number of "ORDER BY" clauses	1.0
Ascending / Descending order	1.0
Involves "LIMIT" clause	1.0
Involves "LIMIT 1"	2.0

Table 10: Feature vector values regarding the "ORDER BY" clauses, with weights specified to the right of each feature.

Feature about Set Operations	Weight
Involves "UNION" clause	4.0
Involves "EXCEPT" clause	4.0
Involves "INTERSECT" clause	4.0

Table 11: Feature vector values regarding the Set Operation clauses, with weights specified to the right of each feature.

Levi Graph AMR Parser using Heterogeneous Attention

Han He
Computer Science
Emory University
Atlanta GA 30322, USA
han.he@emory.edu

Jinho D. Choi
Computer Science
Emory University
Atlanta GA 30322, USA
jinho.choi@emory.edu

Abstract

Coupled with biaffine decoders, transformers have been effectively adapted to text-to-graph transduction and achieved state-of-the-art performance on AMR parsing. Many prior works, however, rely on the biaffine decoder for either or both arc and label predictions although most features used by the decoder may be learned by the transformer already. This paper presents a novel approach to AMR parsing by combining heterogeneous data (tokens, concepts, labels) as one input to a transformer to learn attention, and use only attention matrices from the transformer to predict all elements in AMR graphs (concepts, arcs, labels). Although our models [1] use significantly fewer parameters than the previous state-of-the-art graph parser, they show similar or better accuracy on AMR 2.0 and 3.0.

1 Introduction

Abstract Meaning Representation (AMR) has recently gained lots of interests due to its capability in capturing abstract concepts (Banarescu et al., 2013). In the form of directed acyclic graphs (DAGs), an AMR graph consists of nodes as concepts and edges as labeled relations. To build such a graph from plain text, a parser needs to predict concepts and relations in concord.

While significant research efforts have been conducted to improve concept and arc predictions, label prediction has been relatively stagnated. Most previous models have adapted the biaffine decoder for label prediction (Lyu and Titov, 2018; Zhang et al., 2019a; Cai and Lam, 2019; Zhou et al., 2020; Lindemann et al., 2020). These models assign labels from the biaffine decoder to arcs predicted by another decoder, which can be misled by incorrect arc predictions during decoding.

The enhancement of message passing between decoders for arc and label predictions has shown to be effective. Among these works, Cai and Lam (2020) emerge with an iterative method to exchange embeddings between concept and arc predictions and feed the enhanced embeddings to the biaffine decoder for label prediction. While this approach greatly improves accuracy, it complicates the network architecture without structurally avoiding the error propagation from the arc prediction.

This paper presents an efficient transformer-based (Vaswani et al., 2017) approach that takes a mixture of tokens, concepts, and labels as inputs, and performs concept generation, arc prediction, and label prediction jointly using only attentions from the transformer without using a biaffine decoder. Its compact structure (§3.3) enables cross-attention between heterogeneous inputs, providing a complete view of the partially built graph and a better representation of the current parsing state. A novel Levi graph decoder (§3.4) is also proposed that reduces the number of decoder parameters by 45% (from 5.5 million to 3.0 million) yet gives similar or better performance. To the best of our knowledge, this is the first text-to-AMR graph parser that operates on the heterogeneous data and adapts no biaffine decoder.

2 Related Work

Recent AMR parsing approaches can be categorized into four classes: (i) transition-based parsing which casts the parsing process into a sequence of transitions defined on an abstract machine (e.g., a transition system using a buffer and a stack) (Wang et al., 2016; Damonte et al., 2017; Ballesteros and Al-Onaizan, 2017; Peng et al., 2017; Guo and Lu, 2018; Liu et al., 2018; Naseem et al., 2019; Fernandez Astudillo et al., 2020; Lee et al.,

[1] Resources are publicly available at https://github.com/emorynlp/levi-graph-amr-parser.

Proceedings of the 17th International Conference on Parsing Technologies (IWPT 2021), pages 50–57
Bangkok, Thailand (online), August 6, 2021.

2020), (ii) seq2seq-based parsing [2] which transduces raw sentences into linearized AMR graphs in text form (Barzdins and Gosko, 2016; Konstas et al., 2017; van Noord and Bos, 2017; Peng et al., 2018; Xu et al., 2020; Bevilacqua et al., 2021), (iii) seq2graph-based parsing which incrementally and directly builds a semantic graph via expanding graph nodes without resorting to any transition system (Cai and Lam, 2019; Zhang et al., 2019b; Lyu et al., 2020). (iv) graph algebra parsing which translates an intermediate grammar structure into AMR (Artzi et al., 2015; Groschwitz et al., 2018; Lindemann et al., 2019, 2020).

Our work is most closely related to seq2graph paradigm while we extend the definition of node to accommodate relation labels in a Levi graph. We generate a Levi graph which is a linearized form originally used in seq2seq models for AMR-to-text (Beck et al., 2018; Guo et al., 2019; Ribeiro et al., 2019). Our Levi graph approach differs from seq2seq approaches in its attention based arc prediction, where arc is directly predicted by attention heads instead of brackets in the target sequence.

3 Approach

3.1 Text-to-Graph Transducer

Figure 1 shows the overview of our Text-to-Graph Transduction model. Let $W = \{w_0, w_1, \ldots, w_n\}$ be the input sequence where w_0 is a special token representing the target node and w_i is the i'th token. W is fed into a *Text Encoder* creating embeddings $\{e^w_0, e^w_1, \ldots, e^w_n\}$. In parallel, *NLP Tools* produce several features for w_i and pass them to a *Feature Encoder* to generate $\{e^f_0, e^f_1, \ldots, e^f_n\}$. Embeddings $\{e^w_i \oplus e^f_i : i \in [0, n]\}$ are put to a *Text Transformer*, which generates $E^t = \{e^t_0, e^t_1, \ldots, e^t_n\}$.[3]
Let $V = \{v_0, v_1, \ldots, v_m\}$ be the output sequence where v_0 is a special token representing the root and v_i is the i'th predicted node. V is fed into a *Graph Encoder* to create $E^v = \{e^v_0, e^v_1, \ldots, e^v_m\}$. Finally,

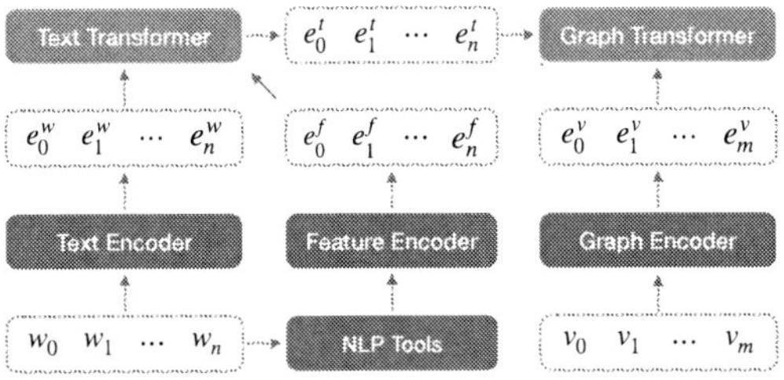

Figure 1: Overview of our Text-to-Graph Transducer.

E^t and E^v are fed into a *Graph Transformer* that predicts the target node as well as its relations to all nodes in V. The target node predicted by the *Graph Transformer* gets appended to V afterwards.[4]

3.2 Concept + Arc-Biaffine + Rel-Biaffine

Our first graph transformer generates $\{v_1, \ldots, v_m\}$ where v_i is a concept in the target graph, and predicts both arcs and labels using a biaffine decoder. Given E^t and E^v (§3.1), three matrices are created, $\mathcal{Q} = e^t_0 \in \mathbb{R}^{1 \times d}, \mathcal{K}|\mathcal{V} = [e^t_1, .., e^t_n, e^v_0, e^v_1, .., e^v_m] \in \mathbb{R}^{k \times d}$ $(k = n{+}m{+}1)$. These matrices are put to multiple layers of multi-head attention (MHA) producing $\{\alpha^i : i \in [1, h]\}$ and $\{\beta^i : i \in [1, h]\}$ from the last layer, where h is the total number of heads in MHA ($\mathrm{W}^{\mathcal{Q}|\mathcal{K}|\mathcal{V}}_i \in \mathbb{R}^{d \times d}, \mathrm{W}^{\oplus} \in \mathbb{R}^{(h \cdot d) \times d}$):

$$\alpha^i = \text{softmax}(\frac{(\mathcal{Q}\mathrm{W}^{\mathcal{Q}}_i)(\mathcal{K}\mathrm{W}^{\mathcal{K}}_i)^\top}{\sqrt{d}}) \quad \in \mathbb{R}^{1 \times k}$$
$$\beta^i = \alpha^i \cdot \mathcal{V} \cdot \mathrm{W}^{\mathcal{V}}_i \quad \in \mathbb{R}^{1 \times d}$$
$$\alpha^{\oslash} = [\alpha^1_j : j \in [1, n]] \quad \in \mathbb{R}^{1 \times n}$$
$$\beta^{\oplus} = (\beta^1 \oplus \ldots \oplus \beta^h) \cdot \mathrm{W}^{\oplus} \quad \in \mathbb{R}^{1 \times d}$$

$\alpha^{\oslash}_j$ indicates the probability of w_j being aligned to the target node, and $\beta^{\oplus}$ is the embedding representing the node. Let C be the list of all concepts in training data and L be the list of lemmas for tokens in W such that $|W| = |L|$. Given $X = C^\frown W^\frown L$, $\alpha^{\oslash}$ and $\beta^{\oplus}$ are fed into a *Node Decoder* estimating the score of each $x_i \in X$ being the target node:

$$g(C|W|L) = \text{softmax}(\beta^{\oplus} \cdot \mathrm{W}^{C|W|L})$$
$$p(x_i) = g(C) \cdot [\text{softmax}(\beta^{\oplus} \cdot \mathrm{W}^{G})]_i + g(W) \sum_{j \in W(x_i)} \alpha^{\oslash}_j + g(L) \sum_{j \in L(x_i)} \alpha^{\oslash}_j$$

$g(C|W|L)$ is the gate probability of the target node being in $C|W|L$, respectively ($\mathrm{W}^{C|W|L} \in \mathbb{R}^{d \times 1}$).

[2]Seq2seq-based parsing is sometimes categorized into "translation-based methods" (Koller et al., 2019) possibly due to the prevalence of seq2seq model in Neural Machine Translation, while we believe that translation refers more to the transduction between languages while AMR is neither a language nor an interlingua.

[3]In our case, BERT (Devlin et al., 2019) is used as the *Text Encoder* and $\forall_i.e^f_i = e^{\text{LEMMA}}_i \oplus e^{\text{POS}}_i \oplus e^{\text{NER}}_i \oplus e^{\text{CHAR}}_i$ is created by the *Feature Encoder* using predictions (lemmas, part-of-speech tags and named-entities) from the *NLP Tools* and character level features from a Convolutional Neural Network. In this work, we use CoreNLP (Manning et al., 2014) for a fair comparison with existing approaches.

[4]*Graph Encoder* creates $\forall_i.e^v_i = \text{transformer}(e^{\text{NODE}}_i \oplus e^{\text{CHAR}}_i)$.

$p(x_i)$ is estimated by measuring the probabilities of x_i being the target if $x_i \in C$ ($\mathrm{W}^G \in \mathbb{R}^{d\times|C|}$), and if $x_i \in W|L$ where $W|L(x_i) = \{j : (x_i = y_j) \wedge y_j \in W|L\}$, respectively. Finally, the output layer $o^{\text{node}} = [p(x_i) : x_i \in X] \in \mathbb{R}^{1\times(|C|+|W|+|L|)}$ gets created and $\arg\max_{x_i}(o^{\text{node}})$ is taken as the target.

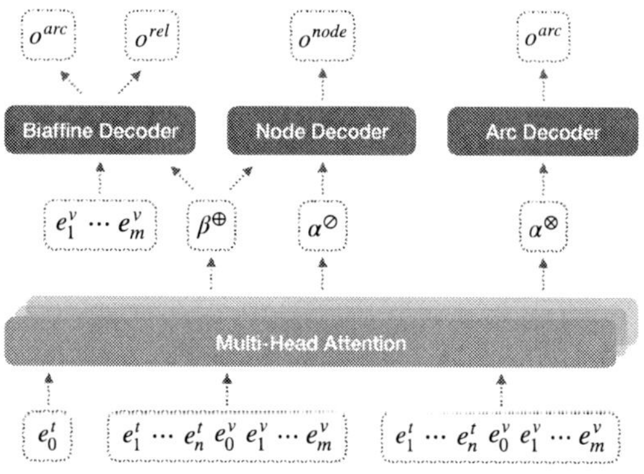

Figure 2: Overview of our Graph Transformer models. ND/BD/AD: node/biaffine/arc decoder. §3.2: ND for concept generation and BD for arc and label predictions; §3.3: ND for concept generation, AD for arc prediction, and BD for label prediction; §3.4: ND for concept and label generations and AD for arc prediction.

For arc and label predictions, the target embedding $\beta^{\oplus}$ is used to represent a head and the embeddings of previously predicted nodes, $\{e_1^v, \ldots, e_m^v\}$, are used to represent dependents in a *Biaffine Decoder*, which creates two output layers, $o^{\text{arc}} \in \mathbb{R}^{1\times m}$ and $o^{\text{rel}} \in \mathbb{R}^{1\times m\times|R|}$, to predict the target node being a head of the other nodes, where $|R|$ is the list of all labels in training data (Dozat and Manning, 2017).

3.3 Concept + Arc-Attention + Rel-Biaffine

Our second graph transformer is similar to the one in §3.2 except that it uses an *Arc Decoder* instead of the *Biaffine Decoder* for arc prediction. Given $A = \{\alpha^1, \ldots, \alpha^h\}$ in §3.2, $\alpha^{\otimes} \in \mathbb{R}^{1\times(m+1)}$ is created by first applying dimension-wise maxpooling to A and slicing the last $m+1$ dimensions as follows:

$$\alpha^{\otimes} = [\max(\alpha_j^1, \ldots, \alpha_j^h) : j \in [n+1, n+m+1]]$$

Notice that values in $\alpha^{\otimes}$ are derived from multiple heads; thus, they are not normalized. Each head is expected to learn different types of arcs. During decoding, any $v_i \in V$ whose $\alpha_i^{\otimes} \geq 0.5$ is predicted to be a dependent of the target node. During training, the negative log-likelihood of $\alpha^{\otimes}$ is optimized.[5]

The target node, say v_t, may need to be predicted as a dependent of v_i, in which case, the dependency is reversed (so v_t becomes the head of v_i), and the label is concatenated with the special tag _R (e.g., ARG0(v_i, v_t) becomes ARG0_R(v_t, v_i)).

3.4 Levi Graph + Arc-Attention

Our last graph transformer uses the *Node Decoder* for both concept and label generations and the *Arc Decoder* for arc prediction. In this model, $v_i \in V'$ can be either a concept or a label such that the original AMR graph is transformed into the Levi graph (Levi, 1942; Beck et al., 2018) (Figure 3).

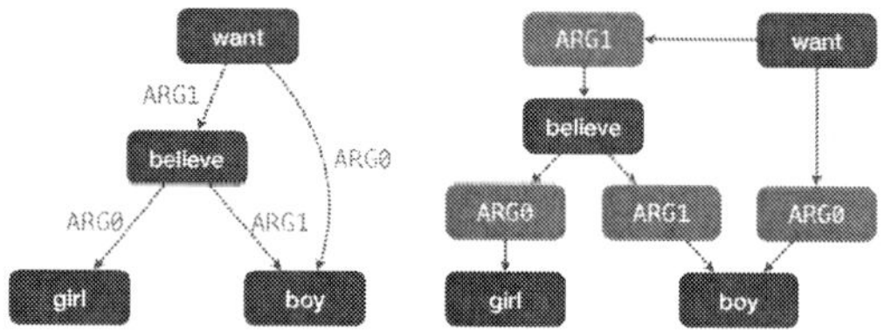

(a) AMR graph (b) Levi graph

Figure 3: AMR and Levi graphs for the input, "*The boy wants the girl to believe him*".

Unlike the node sequence containing only concepts in the AMR graph ordered by breadth-first traverse, used as the output sequence for the models in §3.2 and §3.3, the node sequence in this model is derived by inserting the label of each edge after head concept during training. This concepts-labels alternation has two advantages over a strict topological order: (i) it can handle erroneous cyclic graphs, (ii) it is easier to restore relations as each label is connected to its closest concept. The heterogeneous nature of node sequences from Levi graphs allows our Graph Transformer to learn attentions among 3 types of input, tokens, concepts, and labels, leading to more informed predictions.

Let V' be the output sequence consisting of both predicted concepts and labels. Let C' be the set of all concepts and labels in training data. Compared to V and C in §3.2, V' is about twice larger than V because every concept has one or more associated labels that indicate relations to its heads. However, C' is not so much larger than C because the addition from the labels is insignificant to the number of concepts that are already in C. By replacing $V|C$ with $V'|C'$ respectively, the *Node Decoder* in §3.2 can generate both concepts and labels. $\alpha^{\otimes}$ in §3.3 then gives attention scores among concepts and labels that can be used by the *Arc Decoder* to find arcs among them.

[5]This model still uses the *Biaffine Decoder* for label prediction.

	SMATCH		Fine-grained Evaluation						
	Labeled	Unlabeled	No WSD	Concept	SRL	Reent.	Neg.	NER	Wiki
Lindemann et al. (2019)	75.3	-	-	-	-	-	-	-	-
Naseem et al. (2019)	75.5	80	76	86	72	56	67	83	80
Zhang et al. (2019a)	76.3	79.0	76.8	84.8	69.7	60.0	75.2	77.9	85.8
Zhang et al. (2019b)	77.0	80	78	86	71	61	77	79	86
Cai and Lam (2020)	80.2	82.8	80.8	88.1	74.2	64.6	78.9	81.1	86.3
Xu et al. (2020)†	80.2	83.7	80.8	87.4	78.9	66.5	71.5	85.4	75.1
Lee et al. (2020)‡	81.3	85.3	81.8	88.7	88.7	66.3	79.2	71.9	79.4
Bevilacqua et al. (2021)§	84.5	86.7	84.9	89.6	79.7	72.3	79.9	83.7	87.3
CL20	**80.0**±0.2	82.5±0.3	**80.5**±0.3	88.0±0.1	73.7±0.4	63.8±0.7	79.2±0.3	**81.1**±0.3	**86.2**±0.1
ND + BD + BD	79.4±0.1	82.3±0.1	80.0±0.2	87.9±0.2	73.1±0.2	62.5±0.2	**79.8**±0.3	80.7±1.0	85.8±0.5
ND + AD + BD	**80.0**±0.1	**82.6**±0.1	**80.5**±0.1	**88.2**±0.1	73.6±0.4	63.3±0.4	79.4±1.0	80.8±0.8	**86.2**±0.3
ND + AD + LV	**80.0**±0.1	82.2±0.2	**80.5**±0.1	87.7±0.2	**74.5**±0.2	**64.1**±0.3	78.4±1.0	80.5±0.8	**86.2**±0.3

(a) Results on AMR 2.0 results. Supervised†/unsupervised§ pre-training and self-learning‡ are orthogonal to our work.

	SMATCH		Fine-grained Evaluation						
	Labeled	Unlabeled	No WSD	Concept	SRL	Reent.	Neg.	NER	Wiki
Lyu et al. (2020)	75.8	-	-	**88.0**	72.6	-	-	-	-
CL20	76.8±0.2	79.9±0.2	77.3±0.2	86.3±0.2	73.2±0.2	63.4±0.2	72.3±1.4	73.0±0.5	79.5±0.2
ND + BD + BD	75.8±0.2	79.0±0.1	76.2±0.1	84.6±0.2	72.1±0.3	61.7±0.4	72.6±0.7	71.6±0.3	78.7±0.2
ND + AD + BD	76.8±0.1	**80.1±0.1**	77.3±0.1	86.5±0.2	73.1±0.2	**63.6±0.2**	**73.2±0.9**	73.0±0.2	**79.6±0.1**
ND + AD + LV	**77.0±0.2**	79.8±0.2	**77.5±0.2**	86.1±0.1	**73.6±0.3**	62.6±0.6	71.3±0.4	**73.3±0.7**	79.5±0.3

(b) Results on AMR 3.0.

Table 1: Averages ± standard deviations on AMR 2.0 and 3.0 . CL20: results by running the original implementation of Cai and Lam (2020) 3 times, ND+BD+BD: §3.2, ND+AD+BD: §3.3, ND+AD+LV: §3.4.

4 Experiments

4.1 Experimental Setup

All models are experimented on both the AMR 2.0 (LDC2017T10) and 3.0 datasets (LDC2020T02). AMR 2.0 has been well-explored by recent work, while AMR 3.0 is the latest release about 1.5 times larger than 2.0 that has not yet been explored much. The detailed data statistics are shown in Table A.1.2. The training, development, and test sets provided in the datasets are used, and performance is evaluated with the SMATCH (F1) (Cai and Knight, 2013) as well as fine-grained metrics (Damonte et al., 2017). The same pre- and post-processing suggested by Cai and Lam (2020) are adapted. Section A.2 gives the hyper-parameter configuration of our models.

4.2 Results

All our models are run three times and their averages and standard deviations are reported in Table 1. Compared to CL20 using 2 transformers to decode arcs & concepts then apply attention across them, our models use 1 transformer for the *Node Decoder* achieving both objectives simultaneously. All models except for ND+BD reaches the same SMATCH score of 80% on AMR 2.0. ND+AD+LV shows a slight improvement over the others on AMR 3.0, indicating that it has a greater potential to be robust with a larger dataset. Considering that this model uses about 3M fewer parameters than CL20, these results are promising. ND+BD+BD consistently shows the lowest scores, implying the significance of modeling concept generation and arc prediction coherently for structure learning. ND+AD+LV shows higher scores for SRL and Reent whereas the other models show advantage on Concept and NER on AMR 2.0, although the trend is not as noticeable on AMR 3.0, implying that the Levi graph helps parsing relations but not necessarily tagging concepts.

Case Study We study the effect of our proposed two improvements: heterogeneous Graph Transformer and Levi graph, from the view of attention in Figure 4. Figure 4a shows that the core verb "*wants*" is heavily attended by every token, suggesting that our Graph Transformer successfully grasps the core idea. Figure 4b presents the soft alignment between nodes and tokens, which surprisingly overweights " *boy*", "*girl*" and "*believe*" possibly due to their dominance of semantics. Figure 4c illustrates the arc prediction, which is a lower triangular matrix obtained by zeroing out the upper triangle of stacked $\alpha^{\otimes}$. Its diagonal suggests that self-loop is crucial for representing each node.

5 Conclusion

We presented two effective approaches which achieve comparable (or better) performance comparing with the state-of-the-art parsers with significantly fewer parameters. Our text-to-graph trans-

(a) Token⇆token (b) Node⇆token (c) Node⇆node

Figure 4: Self- and cross-attention for tokens "*The boy wants the girl to believe him*" and nodes "*want believe* `ARG1` *boy* `ARG1` `ARG0` *girl* `ARG0`".

ducer enables self- and cross-attention in one transformer, improving both concept and arc prediction. With a novel Levi graph formalism, our parser demostrates its advantage on relation labeling. An interesting future work is to preserve benefits from both approaches in one model. It is also noteworthy that our Levi graph parser can be applied to a broad range of labeled graph parsing tasks including dependency trees and many others.

References

Yoav Artzi, Kenton Lee, and Luke Zettlemoyer. 2015. Broad-coverage CCG semantic parsing with AMR. In *Proceedings of the 2015 Conference on Empirical Methods in Natural Language Processing*, pages 1699–1710, Lisbon, Portugal. Association for Computational Linguistics.

Miguel Ballesteros and Yaser Al-Onaizan. 2017. AMR parsing using stack-LSTMs. In *Proceedings of the 2017 Conference on Empirical Methods in Natural Language Processing*, pages 1269–1275, Copenhagen, Denmark. Association for Computational Linguistics.

Laura Banarescu, Claire Bonial, Shu Cai, Madalina Georgescu, Kira Griffitt, Ulf Hermjakob, Kevin Knight, Philipp Koehn, Martha Palmer, and Nathan Schneider. 2013. Abstract meaning representation for sembanking. In *Proceedings of the 7th linguistic annotation workshop and interoperability with discourse*, pages 178–186.

Guntis Barzdins and Didzis Gosko. 2016. RIGA at SemEval-2016 task 8: Impact of Smatch extensions and character-level neural translation on AMR parsing accuracy. In *Proceedings of the 10th International Workshop on Semantic Evaluation (SemEval-2016)*, pages 1143–1147, San Diego, California. Association for Computational Linguistics.

Daniel Beck, Gholamreza Haffari, and Trevor Cohn. 2018. Graph-to-sequence learning using gated graph neural networks. In *Proceedings of the 56th Annual Meeting of the Association for Computational Linguistics (Volume 1: Long Papers)*, pages 273–283, Melbourne, Australia. Association for Computational Linguistics.

Michele Bevilacqua, Rexhina Blloshmi, and Roberto Navigli. 2021. One SPRING to rule them both: Symmetric AMR semantic parsing and generation without a complex pipeline. In *Proceedings of AAAI*.

Deng Cai and Wai Lam. 2019. Core semantic first: A top-down approach for AMR parsing. In *Proceedings of the 2019 Conference on Empirical Methods in Natural Language Processing and the 9th International Joint Conference on Natural Language Processing (EMNLP-IJCNLP)*, pages 3799–3809, Hong Kong, China. Association for Computational Linguistics.

Deng Cai and Wai Lam. 2020. AMR parsing via graph-sequence iterative inference. In *Proceedings of the 58th Annual Meeting of the Association for Computational Linguistics*, pages 1290–1301, Online. Association for Computational Linguistics.

Shu Cai and Kevin Knight. 2013. Smatch: an evaluation metric for semantic feature structures. In *Proceedings of the 51st Annual Meeting of the Association for Computational Linguistics (Volume 2: Short Papers)*, pages 748–752.

Joachim Daiber, Max Jakob, Chris Hokamp, and Pablo N. Mendes. 2013. Improving efficiency and accuracy in multilingual entity extraction. In *Proceedings of the 9th International Conference on Semantic Systems (I-Semantics)*.

Marco Damonte, Shay B. Cohen, and Giorgio Satta. 2017. An incremental parser for Abstract Meaning Representation. In *Proceedings of the 15th Conference of the European Chapter of the Association for Computational Linguistics: Volume 1, Long Papers*, pages 536–546, Valencia, Spain. Association for Computational Linguistics.

Jacob Devlin, Ming-Wei Chang, Kenton Lee, and Kristina Toutanova. 2019. BERT: Pre-training of deep bidirectional transformers for language understanding. In *Proceedings of the 2019 Conference of the North American Chapter of the Association for Computational Linguistics: Human Language Technologies, Volume 1 (Long and Short Papers)*, pages 4171–4186, Minneapolis, Minnesota. Association for Computational Linguistics.

Timothy Dozat and Christopher D. Manning. 2017. Deep Biaffine Attention for Neural Dependency Parsing. In *Proceedings of the 5th International Conference on Learning Representations*, ICLR'17.

Ramón Fernandez Astudillo, Miguel Ballesteros, Tahira Naseem, Austin Blodgett, and Radu Florian. 2020. Transition-based parsing with stack-transformers. In *Findings of the Association for Computational Linguistics: EMNLP 2020*, pages 1001–1007, Online. Association for Computational Linguistics.

Jonas Groschwitz, Matthias Lindemann, Meaghan Fowlie, Mark Johnson, and Alexander Koller. 2018. AMR dependency parsing with a typed semantic algebra. In *Proceedings of the 56th Annual Meeting of the Association for Computational Linguistics (Volume 1: Long Papers)*, pages 1831–1841, Melbourne, Australia. Association for Computational Linguistics.

Zhijiang Guo and Wei Lu. 2018. Better transition-based AMR parsing with a refined search space. In *Proceedings of the 2018 Conference on Empirical Methods in Natural Language Processing*, pages 1712–1722, Brussels, Belgium. Association for Computational Linguistics.

Zhijiang Guo, Yan Zhang, Zhiyang Teng, and Wei Lu. 2019. Densely connected graph convolutional networks for graph-to-sequence learning. *Transactions of the Association for Computational Linguistics*, 7:297–312.

Alexander Koller, Stephan Oepen, and Weiwei Sun. 2019. Graph-based meaning representations: Design and processing. In *Proceedings of the 57th Annual Meeting of the Association for Computational Linguistics: Tutorial Abstracts*, pages 6–11, Florence, Italy. Association for Computational Linguistics.

Ioannis Konstas, Srinivasan Iyer, Mark Yatskar, Yejin Choi, and Luke Zettlemoyer. 2017. Neural AMR: Sequence-to-sequence models for parsing and generation. In *Proceedings of the 55th Annual Meeting of the Association for Computational Linguistics (Volume 1: Long Papers)*, pages 146–157, Vancouver, Canada. Association for Computational Linguistics.

Young-Suk Lee, Ramón Fernandez Astudillo, Tahira Naseem, Revanth Gangi Reddy, Radu Florian, and Salim Roukos. 2020. Pushing the limits of AMR parsing with self-learning. In *Findings of the Association for Computational Linguistics: EMNLP 2020*, pages 3208–3214, Online. Association for Computational Linguistics.

Friedrich Wilhelm Levi. 1942. *Finite geometrical systems: six public lectues delivered in February, 1940, at the University of Calcutta*. University of Calcutta.

Matthias Lindemann, Jonas Groschwitz, and Alexander Koller. 2019. Compositional semantic parsing across graphbanks. In *Proceedings of the 57th Annual Meeting of the Association for Computational Linguistics*, pages 4576–4585, Florence, Italy. Association for Computational Linguistics.

Matthias Lindemann, Jonas Groschwitz, and Alexander Koller. 2020. Fast semantic parsing with well-typedness guarantees. In *Proceedings of the 2020 Conference on Empirical Methods in Natural Language Processing (EMNLP)*, pages 3929–3951, Online. Association for Computational Linguistics.

Yijia Liu, Wanxiang Che, Bo Zheng, Bing Qin, and Ting Liu. 2018. An AMR aligner tuned by transition-based parser. In *Proceedings of the 2018 Conference on Empirical Methods in Natural Language Processing*, pages 2422–2430, Brussels, Belgium. Association for Computational Linguistics.

Chunchuan Lyu, Shay B Cohen, and Ivan Titov. 2020. A differentiable relaxation of graph segmentation and alignment for amr parsing. *arXiv preprint arXiv:2010.12676*.

Chunchuan Lyu and Ivan Titov. 2018. AMR parsing as graph prediction with latent alignment. In *Proceedings of the 56th Annual Meeting of the Association for Computational Linguistics (Volume 1: Long Papers)*, pages 397–407, Melbourne, Australia. Association for Computational Linguistics.

Christopher D Manning, Mihai Surdeanu, John Bauer, Jenny Rose Finkel, Steven Bethard, and David McClosky. 2014. The stanford corenlp natural language processing toolkit. In *Proceedings of 52nd annual meeting of the association for computational linguistics: system demonstrations*, pages 55–60.

Tahira Naseem, Abhishek Shah, Hui Wan, Radu Florian, Salim Roukos, and Miguel Ballesteros. 2019. Rewarding Smatch: Transition-based AMR parsing with reinforcement learning. In *Proceedings of the 57th Annual Meeting of the Association for Computational Linguistics*, pages 4586–4592, Florence, Italy. Association for Computational Linguistics.

Rik van Noord and Johan Bos. 2017. Neural semantic parsing by character-based translation: Experiments with abstract meaning representations. *Computational Linguistics in the Netherlands Journal*, 7:93–108.

Xiaochang Peng, Linfeng Song, Daniel Gildea, and Giorgio Satta. 2018. Sequence-to-sequence models for cache transition systems. In *Proceedings of the 56th Annual Meeting of the Association for Computational Linguistics (Volume 1: Long Papers)*, pages 1842–1852, Melbourne, Australia. Association for Computational Linguistics.

Xiaochang Peng, Chuan Wang, Daniel Gildea, and Nianwen Xue. 2017. Addressing the data sparsity issue in neural AMR parsing. In *Proceedings of the 15th Conference of the European Chapter of the Association for Computational Linguistics: Volume 1, Long Papers*, pages 366–375, Valencia, Spain. Association for Computational Linguistics.

Leonardo F. R. Ribeiro, Claire Gardent, and Iryna Gurevych. 2019. Enhancing AMR-to-text generation with dual graph representations. In *Proceedings of the 2019 Conference on Empirical Methods in Natural Language Processing and the 9th International Joint Conference on Natural Language Processing (EMNLP-IJCNLP)*, pages 3183–3194, Hong Kong, China. Association for Computational Linguistics.

Ashish Vaswani, Noam Shazeer, Niki Parmar, Jakob Uszkoreit, Llion Jones, Aidan N Gomez, Łukasz Kaiser, and Illia Polosukhin. 2017. Attention is all you need. In *Advances in neural information processing systems*, pages 5998–6008.

Chuan Wang, Sameer Pradhan, Xiaoman Pan, Heng Ji, and Nianwen Xue. 2016. CAMR at SemEval-2016 task 8: An extended transition-based AMR parser. In *Proceedings of the 10th International Workshop on Semantic Evaluation (SemEval-2016)*, pages 1173–1178, San Diego, California. Association for Computational Linguistics.

Dongqin Xu, Junhui Li, Muhua Zhu, Min Zhang, and Guodong Zhou. 2020. Improving AMR parsing with sequence-to-sequence pre-training. In *Proceedings of the 2020 Conference on Empirical Methods in Natural Language Processing (EMNLP)*, pages 2501–2511, Online. Association for Computational Linguistics.

Sheng Zhang, Xutai Ma, Kevin Duh, and Benjamin Van Durme. 2019a. AMR parsing as sequence-to-graph transduction. In *Proceedings of the 57th Annual Meeting of the Association for Computational Linguistics*, pages 80–94, Florence, Italy. Association for Computational Linguistics.

Sheng Zhang, Xutai Ma, Kevin Duh, and Benjamin Van Durme. 2019b. Broad-coverage semantic parsing as transduction. In *Proceedings of the 2019 Conference on Empirical Methods in Natural Language Processing and the 9th International Joint Conference on Natural Language Processing (EMNLP-IJCNLP)*, pages 3786–3798, Hong Kong, China. Association for Computational Linguistics.

Qiji Zhou, Yue Zhang, Donghong Ji, and Hao Tang. 2020. AMR parsing with latent structural information. In *Proceedings of the 58th Annual Meeting of the Association for Computational Linguistics*, pages 4306–4319, Online. Association for Computational Linguistics.

A Appendix

A.1 Datasets and Pre/Post-Processing

Table 2 describes statistics of the AMR 2.0[6] and the AMR 3.0[7] datasets used in our experiments.

	Sentences	Tokens	Concepts	Relations
TRN	36,521	624,750	422,655	426,712
DEV	1,368	27,713	19,890	20,111
TST	1,371	28,279	26,513	27,175

(a) AMR 2.0.

	Sentences	Tokens	Concepts	Relations
TRN	55,635	965,468	656,123	667,577
DEV	1,722	34,696	25,171	25,568
TST	1,898	37,225	34,903	35,572

(b) AMR 3.0.

Table 2: Statistics of AMR 2.0 and 3.0. TRN/DEV/TST: training/development/evaluation set.

Tokenization, lemmatization, part-of-speech and named entity annotations are generated by the Stanford CoreNLP tool (Manning et al., 2014). Most frequent word senses are removed and restored during pre- and post-processing. The same graph recategorization is performed to assign specific subgraphs to a single node as in Cai and Lam (2020). Wikification is done using the DBpedia Spotlight (Daiber et al., 2013) during post-processing.

A.2 Hyper-Parameter Configuration

The hyper-parameters used in our models are described in Table 3.

Embeddings	
lemma	300
POS tag	32
NER tag	16
concept	300
char	32
Char-level CNN	
#filters	256
ngram filter size	[3]
output size	128
Text Encoder	
#transformer layers	4
Graph Encoder	
#transformer layers	2
Transformer Layer	
#heads	8
hidden size	512
feed-forward hidden size	1024
Graph Transformer	
feed-forward hidden size	1024
Biaffine	
hidden size	100

Table 3: Hyper-parameters settings.

[6]AMR 2.0: https://catalog.ldc.upenn.edu/LDC2017T10

[7]AMR 3.0: https://catalog.ldc.upenn.edu/LDC2020T02

Translate, *then* Parse! A strong baseline for Cross-Lingual AMR Parsing

Sarah Uhrig* **Yoalli Rezepka García*** **Juri Opitz** **Anette Frank**
Dept. of Computational Linguistics
Heidelberg University
69120 Heidelberg
⟨surname⟩@cl.uni-heidelberg.de

Abstract

In cross-lingual Abstract Meaning Representation (AMR) parsing, researchers develop models that project sentences from various languages onto their AMRs to capture their essential semantic structures: given a sentence in any language, we aim to capture its core semantic content through concepts connected by manifold types of semantic relations. Methods typically leverage large silver training data to learn a single model that is able to project non-English sentences to AMRs. However, we find that a simple baseline tends to be overlooked: translating the sentences to English and projecting their AMR with a monolingual AMR parser (`translate+parse`, `T+P`). In this paper, we revisit this simple two-step baseline, and enhance it with a strong NMT system and a strong AMR parser. Our experiments show that `T+P` outperforms a recent state-of-the-art system across all tested languages: German, Italian, Spanish and Mandarin with +14.6, +12.6, +14.3 and +16.0 Smatch points.

1 Introduction

Abstract Meaning Representation (AMR), introduced by Banarescu et al. (2013), aims at representing the meaning of a sentence in a semantic graph format. Nodes represent entities, events and concepts, while (typed) edges express their relations.

AMR itself, as of now, is English-focused, e.g., predicate frames are linked to English PropBank (Kingsbury and Palmer, 2002). However, the abstract nature of AMR, and the fact that they are not explicitly linked to syntactic structure, make it appealing for extracting semantic structure of sentences in various languages. This insight led to the recent interest in a new task: **cross-lingual AMR parsing** (Damonte and Cohen, 2018). Here, researchers develop models to project sentences from different languages onto AMR graphs. Models that have recently been proposed are typically trained on large-scale silver data and learn to directly project the non-English sentences onto their AMR graphs (see Figure 1) (Damonte and Cohen, 2018; Blloshmi et al., 2020). However, there is an intuitive baseline that we argue has so-far received too little attention: `translate+parse`, `T+P`. It first translates a sentence to a pivot language and applies a mono-lingual parser for that language. In light of the rapid progress of both NMT and AMR parsing models for English, our hypothesis is that this baseline has become more effective and thus more realistic. Moreover, we argue that it could be beneficial to disentangle two key latent representations involved in the process of cross-lingual AMR parsing: i) one that translates between two natural languages and ii) one that translates between a natural language and a meaning representation. This way, the cross-lingual AMR construction process is more transparent and can be better analyzed.

In our work we test these hypotheses by translating the source language sentences into English with a strong NMT system, and parse the resulting English sentences using a strong AMR parser. We show that our baseline delivers strong performance in cross-lingual AMR parsing across all considered languages, outperforming task-focused state-of-the-art models in all settings. We also discuss **fairer evaluation of cross-lingual AMR parsing** and **relevant implications** of this work for research into cross-lingual AMR parsing.

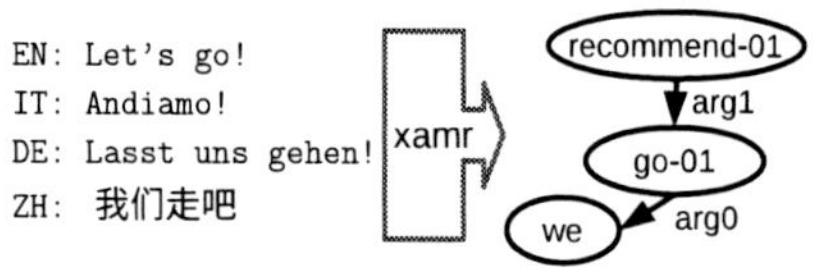

Figure 1: Cross-lingual AMR parsing as introduced by Damonte and Cohen (2018).

*Equal contribution.

Proceedings of the 17th International Conference on Parsing Technologies (IWPT 2021), pages 58–64
Bangkok, Thailand (online), August 6, 2021. ©2021 Association for Computational Linguistics

We will release all code under public license.[1]

2 Related work

Cross-lingual AMR parsing Cross-lingual AMR parsing was introduced by Damonte and Cohen (2018). They trained an alignment-based AMR parser model that leverages large amounts of parallel silver AMR data obtained through annotation projection from a curated parallel corpus. The authors also discussed `translate+parse` (`T+P`) as a baseline using either the NMT systems Google translate and Nematus (Sennrich et al., 2017), or the SMT system Moses (Koehn et al., 2007), together with a mono-lingual transition-based parser (Damonte et al., 2017). However, their best `T+P` approach was Google Translate (GT) – which cannot be fully replicated by other researchers since both training data and model structure are hidden. Given the recent advances in NMT (Barrault et al., 2019, 2020) and mono-lingual AMR parsing (Xu et al., 2020), where parsers now achieve scores on par with human IAA assessments (c.f. Banarescu et al. (2013)), we show that time is ripe to put more spotlight on `T+P`.

Blloshmi et al. (2020) address the problem from complementary perspectives: i) they train a system that projects AMR graphs from parsed English sentences to target sentences via a parallel corpus, yielding *gold non-English sentences* and *silver AMRs*. Conversely, ii) they train a system that employs an NMT system to translate English sentences from a human-annotated AMR dataset to another language, yielding pairs of *silver non-English sentences* and *gold AMRs*. This alleviates the dependency on external AMR aligners.

(Mono-lingual) AMR parsing Mono-lingual AMR parsing equally made big strides in recent years, so that today AMR parsers deliver benchmark scores that are on-par with measured human IAA. The latest step forward was achieved with neural sequence-to-sequence models pre-trained on large-scale MT benchmark data (Roberts et al., 2020; Xu et al., 2020) or are fine-tuning self-supervised seq-to-seq language models such as T5 or BART (Lewis et al., 2019; Bevilacqua et al., 2021). Previou models perform parsing based on different techniques, e.g., predicting latent alignments jointly with nodes (Lyu and Titov, 2018), or via an iterative BFS writing traversal (Cai and Lam, 2019, 2020).

3 Translate, then parse!

Our pipeline model contains two components:

Sent-to-Sent: NMT system We use Helsinki-NLP's *Opus-MT models* (Tiedemann and Thottingal, 2020) to translate the sentences to English. The models are freely accessible[2] and provide high scores on public evaluation benchmarks.[3]

Sent-to-AMR: AMR parser For parsing English target sentences to AMR, we use the parser from *amrlib*[4], which consists of a T5 language model (Roberts et al., 2020) that has been fine-tuned on English sentences and their AMRs.

4 Experiments

Data We employ the cross-lingual AMR parsing benchmark *LDC2020T07*. It was built from the test split of the English mono-lingual LDC2017T10 data by translating its sentences to four languages: German, Spanish, Italian and Mandarin Chinese. This amounts to a total of 5,484 AMR-sentence pairs, or 1,371 AMR-sentence pairs per language.

Baselines For all languages (German, Spanish, Italian and Mandarin Chinese), we compare against i) AMREAGER (Damonte and Cohen, 2018), and ii) XL-AMR (Blloshmi et al., 2020).

Evaluation metrics Our main evaluation metric is Smatch F1 (Cai and Knight, 2013). The Smatch metric aligns the predicted graph with the gold graph and computes an F1 score that measures normalized triple overlap. Additionally, we calculate F1 scores for finer-grained core semantic sub-tasks Damonte et al. (2017).[5] In our analyses (§4.2), we also study results with S2MATCH (Opitz et al., 2020), that offers a potentially fairer evaluation in cross-lingual AMR parsing, since it does not penalize allowed paraphrases that may emerge, e.g., due

[1] `https://github.com/Heidelberg-NLP/simple-xamr`

[2] They are implemented in *EasyNMT*, a SOTA NMT package: `https://github.com/UKPLab/EasyNMT`

[3] See `https://huggingface.co/Helsinki-NLP` for scores on benchmarks.

[4] `https://github.com/bjascob/amrlib`

[5] i) Unlabeled: score without node labels, ii) No WSD: score w/o predicate sense disambiguation; iii) Reentrancies: score on re-entrant nodes (coreference); iv) Concepts: score on concept nodes; v) Named Ent.: indicating NER performance; vi) negation: polarity detection performance; vii) SRL: semantic role labeling performance.

to the non-monotonous nature of translation (e.g., *huckleberry* $\rightarrow$ *Heidelbeere* (DE) $\rightarrow$ *blueberry*).

4.1 Main results

Results are displayed in Table 1. Overall, our `translate+parse` baseline outperforms previous work by large margins. In all assessed semantic categories, `T+P` outperforms XL-AMR models by more than 10 Smatch points. The smallest improvement obtained is achieved in IT with +12.6 points.

In some key semantic categories, the differences are extreme. For negation detection we obtain performance improvements that range from +26.5 points (IT) to +37.3 (DE). The named entity recognition improves by +20.3 points for German, +20.4 points for Spanish, +17.6 points for Italian.

4.2 Studies

Using a graded metric for evaluation When evaluating predicted AMRs against reference AMRs in cross-lingual AMR parsing, we are essentially comparing AMRs from sentences that are not exactly the same. This means that predicted concepts that are valid may get erroneously penalized by the evaluation metric. For instance, consider a German source sentence that contains *Heidelbeere*, and our cross-lingual AMR system predicts i) *huckleberry* or ii) *blueberry*. Depending on which concept is mentioned in the reference AMR graph (based on the unseen sentence from which the human SemBank annotator created this graph), only one of the two options will be viewed as correct, which results in unfair evaluation. To mitigate this, we propose to conduct the cross-lingual AMR evaluation using S2MATCH (Opitz et al., 2020), a metric that admits graded concept similarity. S2MATCH has a hyper-parameter τ that sets a threshold for sufficiently similar concept nodes across AMRs, using cosine-similarity. The alignment of similar concepts can increase the final score. The default τ is 0.5, but we also try 0.0 which is less strict and fosters dense alignment.

The results are displayed in Table 2. Interestingly, most score improvements are obtained for German (+3.9 points) and Mandarin Chinese (+5.2 points). We conjecture that this is because there is slightly less variety in EN-{ES, IT} translations, than for EN-DE, and especially for EN-ZH. This is also visible from the results of our baseline XL-AMR, which we reevaluate using S2MATCH: Most gains are obtained for Mandarin Chinese with an improvement of more than 7 points F1

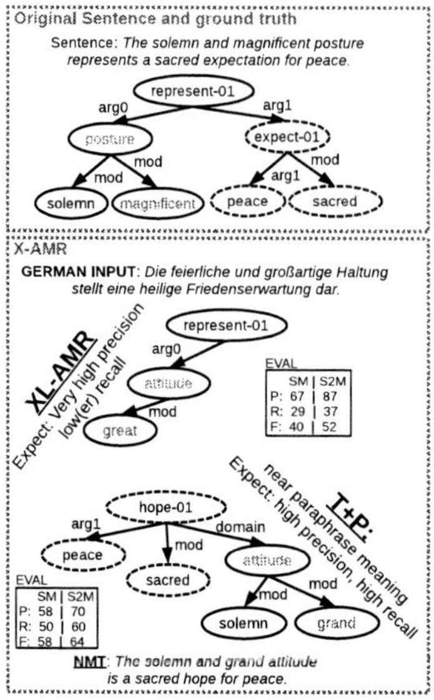

Figure 2: Evaluation example.

score. Inspecting test cases manually, we find many cases were S2MATCH made the evaluation fairer. For instance, the following *gold-pred (DE: [German word])* concept tuples are ignored by SMATCH but considered by S2MATCH: *pledge-promise (DE: 'versprechen'); write-compose (DE: 'verfasst') strong-resolute (DE: 'deutlich'); spirit-ghost (DE: 'Geist')*, etc. In all these cases the cross-lingual AMR system predicted the correct concept, but was penalized by SMATCH. A concrete example case, with lexical (see colored nodes) and structural (see dotted nodes) meaning-preserving divergences, is shown in Fig. 2.

For future work that applies cross-lingual AMR parsing evaluation, we recommend additional evaluation assessment with S2MATCH.

NMT quality The quality of our automatic translations is evaluated with two metrics: i) BLEU score (Papineni et al., 2002) and ii) S(entence-)BERT (Reimers and Gurevych, 2019), in order to assess surface-oriented as well as semantic similarity. For SBERT, we create sentence embeddings for both our translations and the English reference sentences and compute pair-wise cosine similarity.

Looking at the quality of our MT outputs (Table 4), we see that translation quality is generally quite high. The moderate BLEU scores seem to result more from variation in surface form than from incorrect translations, which is backed by the high cosine similarity scores across languages (and also

	AMREAGER				XL-AMR				`translate+parse`			
Metric	DE	ES	IT	ZH	DE	ES	IT	ZH	DE	ES	IT	ZH
SMATCH	39.1	42.1	43.2	34.6	53.0	58.0	58.1	43.1	**67.6**	**72.3**	**70.7**	**59.1**
Unlabeled	45.0	46.6	48.5	41.1	57.7	63.0	63.4	48.9	**71.9**	**76.5**	**75.1**	**65.4**
No WSD	39.2	42.2	42.5	34.7	53.2	58.4	58.4	43.2	**67.9**	**72.7**	**71.1**	**60.4**
Reentrancies	18.6	27.2	25.7	15.9	39.9	46.6	46.1	34.7	**55.8**	**60.9**	**58.2**	**47.5**
Concepts	44.9	53.3	52.3	39.9	58.0	65.9	64.7	48.0	**71.4**	**78.1**	**75.6**	**63.3**
Named Ent.	63.1	65.7	67.7	67.9	66.0	66.2	70.0	60.6	**86.3**	**86.6**	**87.6**	**84.2**
Negation	18.6	19.8	22.3	6.8	11.7	23.4	29.2	12.8	**49.0**	**59.5**	**55.7**	**38.5**
SRL	29.4	35.9	34.3	27.2	47.9	55.2	54.7	41.3	**61.7**	**68.0**	**65.8**	**54.1**

Table 1: F1 Smatch for two baselines and `T+P`. Best results in **bold**. Improvements > 20 points are underlined.

	Metric	XL-AMR DE	ES	IT	ZH	`translate+parse` DE	ES	IT	ZH
$\tau=\frac{1}{2}$	S2M P	59.7(4.3)	63.9(+3.9)	64.7(**+4.7**)	49.2(**+4.7**)	74.1(+3.1)	78.3(+2.5)	77.0(+2.8)	65.8 (**+4.0**)
	S2M R	54.8(+4.0)	59.9(+3.7)	59.4(+3.7)	47.3(**+5.0**)	67.3(+2.9)	71.5(+2.4)	70.0(+2.5)	60.4 (**+3.7**)
	S2M F1	57.1 (+4.1)	61.8(+3.1)	62.0(+3.9)	48.2(**+5.1**)	70.5(+2.9)	74.7(+2.4)	73.4(+2.7)	63.0 (**+3.9**)
τ=0.0	S2M P	61.5(+6.1)	65.4(+5.4)	66.2(+6.2)	51.3(**+6.6**)	75.2(+4.2)	79.1(+3.3)	77.9(+3.7)	67.1 (**+5.3**)
	S2M R	56.4(+5.6)	61.2(+5.0)	60.8(+5.1)	49.4(**+7.1**)	68.2(+3.8)	72.1(+3.0)	70.8(+3.3)	61.6 (**+4.9**)
	S2M F1	58.9(+5.9)	63.2(+5.2)	63.4(+5.3)	50.4(**+7.3**)	71.5(+3.9)	75.4(+3.1)	74.2(+3.5)	64.3 (**+5.2**)

Table 2: Evaluation using a graded metric. **Bold**: Largest improvement of a parser using fairer graded evaluation.

	XL-AMR D-ES	D-I	D-Z	ES-I	ES-Z	I-Z	`translate+parse` D-ES	D-I	D-Z	ES-I	ES-Z	I-Z
SMATCH	52.3	52.2	*40.9*	**58.5**	42.7	42.8	74.3	73.7	*61.6*	**79.0**	63.7	63.1
S2MATCH	58.7	58.6	*48.7*	**63.9**	50.2	50.4	77.7	77.2	*66.7*	**81.8**	68.6	68.0
Unl.	57.0	57.2	*46.6*	**63.3**	48.0	48.7	77.0	76.7	*65.7*	**81.6**	67.8	67.1
NoWSD	52.3	52.4	*41.0*	**58.7**	42.7	42.8	74.4	73.8	*61.7*	**79.0**	63.8	63.1
Conc.	57.7	56.8	*45.0*	**65.4**	47.7	47.4	75.1	74.2	*63.1*	**80.0**	65.6	64.8
NER	63.9	64.3	*56.6*	**68.2**	*56.6*	57.9	90.1	90.1	*83.8*	**91.2**	84.0	84.2
Neg.	7.6	9.7	*6.6*	**44.0**	12.8	11.6	61.3	55.4	*42.3*	**69.4**	46.2	47.8
Reent.	40.7	41.5	*34.6*	**49.8**	36.7	37.2	64.2	63.2	*50.4*	**69.6**	51.8	51.0
SRL	47.4	47.5	*39.5*	**55.8**	41.7	41.7	69.7	68.9	*56.5*	**75.0**	58.3	57.6

Table 3: Semantic consistency over language pairs measured with SMATCH, S2MATCH (τ=0). **Bold**/*italics* : highest/lowest score for language pairs.

	DE	ES	IT	ZH	mean
BLEU	0.41	0.49	0.46	0.23	0.40
SBERT (cosim)	0.93	0.95	0.94	0.88	0.92

Table 4: BLEU and SBERT MT quality assessment.

highlights the need for a fairer and graded AMR evaluation as proposed above.[6] Finally, comparing the different source languages, there seems to be a higher quality in the translations from German, Spanish, and Italian, compared to Mandarin Chinese. This is not only reflected in the BLEU scores, but also in the SBERT cosine scores, which suggest a higher semantic similarity between our translations from DE, ES, IT and the reference sentences.

Semantic cross-lingual consistency of cross-lingual AMR systems A cross-lingual AMR system should be expected to deliver the same or highly similar AMRs for two sentences from different languages, if the sentences carry the same meaning. We may say that a system is *semantically consistent* if it complies to this expectation.

To measure the degree of consistency, we evaluate system outputs of a cross-lingual AMR system for input language X against the outputs of the same system when fed sentences in language Y, from a *parallel* dataset (X,Y) of sentences in languages X and Y. In the standard evaluation, we computed $EVAL(system(X), A)$ and $EVAL(system(Y), A)$, where A are target AMRs. In this experiment, we instead calculate $EVAL(system(X), system(Y))$, assessing the degree of consistency of a $system$.

The results are provided in Table 3, where we see a very clear picture that holds true both for our joint baseline (XL-AMR) and our `T+P` approach and all examined semantic categories: the highest consistency is achieved for Spanish-Italian (ES-I, XL-AMR: 63.9 S2MATCH; `T+P`: 81.8 S2MATCH), while the lowest consistency is achieved for German and Mandarin Chinese (D-Z, XL-AMR: 48.7 S2MATCH; `T+P`: 66.7 S2MATCH). When directly comparing the parsing systems, overall `T+P` appears to offer better consistency in all categories, especially negation. However, the substantial variance between languages may indicate that either i) there is a great necessity for making cross-lingual parsers more robust or, ii), that AMR representations, as constructed from English, may be better prepared to represent (besides English) Spanish and Italian language, than, e.g, German or Chinese.

[6] This is also supported by a manual analysis of samples.

5 Discussion

We believe that the surprising effectiveness of `translate+parse` touches upon a key question: **to what degree can AMR be considered an interlingua**? On one hand, Banarescu et al. (2013) explicitly state that AMR 'is not designed as an interlingua'. Indeed, AMRs created for English sentences do have a flavour of English, since they are partially grounded in English PropBank (Kingsbury and Palmer, 2002). But linking AMRs to a PropBank of another language, e.g., Brazilian (Duran and Aluísio, 2012) or Arabic (Palmer et al., 2008), and parsing non-English sentences into corresponding AMRs, would not solve, but only displace the problem of being tied to a specific language's lexical semantic inventory.[7] On the other hand, AMR *does* contain abstract meaning components that represent language phenomena we may consider as universals: negation, occurrence of named entities, semantic events and their related participants, as well as semantic relations such as Possession, Purpose or Instrument.[8] We argue that this abstract structure again pushes AMR more towards an interlingua. Hence, the emergent interest in cross-lingual (A)MR (Oepen et al., 2020; Fan and Gardent, 2020; Sheth et al., 2021; Sherborne and Lapata, 2021) is well justified. However, even if AMR's *inventory* may favor an interlingual representation, we cannot, in general, expect a homomorphism of AMRs constructed from semantically equivalent sentences in various languages, given wide-spread phenomena that can preclude a uniform AMR representation, such as constructions involving head-switching phenomena or differences in lexical meaning.

Such a middle-ground is indicated by our results: (Too) much divergence may be involved when mapping non-English sentences to original EN-AMRs *directly*, which is penalized by the strict(er) SMATCH metric. We show that evaluation with the softer S2MATCH metric admits small deviations in the conceptual inventory of different languages. The fact that our *indirect* two-step approach T+P shows very strong performance also strengthens the view that AMR is not fully an interlingua. The better performance of T+P may in part be due to a capacity of strong NMT systems to neutralize some amount of inter-lingual divergence, so that evaluation against EN-AMRs can yield better results in this setting.

Note that in our T+P approach two important intermediate (latent) representations are clearly separated: one in the NMT model (that builds a bridge between two natural languages) and one in the parser (that builds a bridge between English and a language of meaning with a flavor of English). By analyzing divergences between source and target in the T step, we can uncover aspects of semantic representations that are *not* isomorphic between languages, and which – by transfer via translation – may be neutralized to match the pivot-flavored AMR structure. Hence, the T+P approach offers an ideal framework for studying interlingual similarities and divergences in cross-lingual AMR parsing, by comparing the structural-semantic divergences of non-English sentences and their translated English counterparts (aka translational divergences), with the aim of identifying structural-semantic differences between languages that can affect the cross-lingual mapping of sentences into a uniform interlingual AMR.[9]

6 Conclusion

We revisited `translate+parse`, an intuitive baseline for cross-lingual AMR parsing. Equipped with a recent NMT system and a monolingual AMR parser, T+P outperforms other approaches by large margins across all evaluation settings. We propose to employ a graded metric for fairer evaluation of cross-lingual AMR parsing. Our work can serve as a strong baseline for future development of cross-lingual AMR parsers. Finally, the T+P approach provides an ideal platform for deeper assessment, analysis, and break-down of potential interlingual aspects of AMR.

Acknowledgments

This work has been partially funded by the DFG within the project ACCEPT as part of the Priority Program "Robust Argumentation Machines" (SPP-1999). We thank our anonymous reviewers for constructive comments and valuable feedback.

[7] Potentially, this may be mitigated in the future by linking AMR to x-lingual PropBanks (Akbik et al., 2015)

[8] C.f. Xue et al. (2014).

[9] For example, we may train a system to parse Non-EN sentences to EN-(flavored)AMR graphs, and compare them to AMRs we obtain from *translated EN sentences* targeting the same EN-AMRs. Divergences we find between AMRs predicted in these settings can indicate phenomena leading to non-isomorphic AMRs that require attention when aiming for a true interlingual AMR formalism.

References

Alan Akbik, Laura Chiticariu, Marina Danilevsky, Yunyao Li, Shivakumar Vaithyanathan, and Huaiyu Zhu. 2015. Generating high quality proposition Banks for multilingual semantic role labeling. In *Proceedings of the 53rd Annual Meeting of the Association for Computational Linguistics and the 7th International Joint Conference on Natural Language Processing (Volume 1: Long Papers)*, pages 397–407, Beijing, China. Association for Computational Linguistics.

Laura Banarescu, Claire Bonial, Shu Cai, Madalina Georgescu, Kira Griffitt, Ulf Hermjakob, Kevin Knight, Philipp Koehn, Martha Palmer, and Nathan Schneider. 2013. Abstract Meaning Representation for sembanking. In *Proceedings of the 7th Linguistic Annotation Workshop and Interoperability with Discourse*, pages 178–186, Sofia, Bulgaria. Association for Computational Linguistics.

Loïc Barrault, Magdalena Biesialska, Ondřej Bojar, Marta R. Costa-jussà, Christian Federmann, Yvette Graham, Roman Grundkiewicz, Barry Haddow, Matthias Huck, Eric Joanis, Tom Kocmi, Philipp Koehn, Chi-kiu Lo, Nikola Ljubešić, Christof Monz, Makoto Morishita, Masaaki Nagata, Toshiaki Nakazawa, Santanu Pal, Matt Post, and Marcos Zampieri. 2020. Findings of the 2020 conference on machine translation (WMT20). In *Proceedings of the Fifth Conference on Machine Translation*, pages 1–55, Online. Association for Computational Linguistics.

Loïc Barrault, Ondřej Bojar, Marta R. Costa-jussà, Christian Federmann, Mark Fishel, Yvette Graham, Barry Haddow, Matthias Huck, Philipp Koehn, Shervin Malmasi, Christof Monz, Mathias Müller, Santanu Pal, Matt Post, and Marcos Zampieri. 2019. Findings of the 2019 conference on machine translation (WMT19). In *Proceedings of the Fourth Conference on Machine Translation (Volume 2: Shared Task Papers, Day 1)*, pages 1–61, Florence, Italy. Association for Computational Linguistics.

Michele Bevilacqua, Rexhina Blloshmi, and Roberto Navigli. 2021. One SPRING to Rule Them Both: Symmetric AMR Semantic Parsing and Generation without a Complex Pipeline. *AAAI*.

Rexhina Blloshmi, Rocco Tripodi, and Roberto Navigli. 2020. XL-AMR: Enabling cross-lingual AMR parsing with transfer learning techniques. In *Proceedings of the 2020 Conference on Empirical Methods in Natural Language Processing (EMNLP)*, pages 2487–2500, Online. Association for Computational Linguistics.

Deng Cai and Wai Lam. 2019. Core semantic first: A top-down approach for AMR parsing. In *Proceedings of the 2019 Conference on Empirical Methods in Natural Language Processing and the 9th International Joint Conference on Natural Language Processing (EMNLP-IJCNLP)*, pages 3799–3809, Hong Kong, China. Association for Computational Linguistics.

Deng Cai and Wai Lam. 2020. AMR parsing via graph-sequence iterative inference. In *Proceedings of the 58th Annual Meeting of the Association for Computational Linguistics*, pages 1290–1301, Online. Association for Computational Linguistics.

Shu Cai and Kevin Knight. 2013. Smatch: an evaluation metric for semantic feature structures. In *Proceedings of the 51st Annual Meeting of the Association for Computational Linguistics (Volume 2: Short Papers)*, pages 748–752, Sofia, Bulgaria. Association for Computational Linguistics.

Marco Damonte and Shay B. Cohen. 2018. Cross-lingual Abstract Meaning Representation parsing. In *Proceedings of the 2018 Conference of the North American Chapter of the Association for Computational Linguistics: Human Language Technologies, Volume 1 (Long Papers)*, pages 1146–1155, New Orleans, Louisiana. Association for Computational Linguistics.

Marco Damonte, Shay B. Cohen, and Giorgio Satta. 2017. An incremental parser for Abstract Meaning Representation. In *Proceedings of the 15th Conference of the European Chapter of the Association for Computational Linguistics: Volume 1, Long Papers*, pages 536–546, Valencia, Spain. Association for Computational Linguistics.

Magali Sanches Duran and Sandra Maria Aluísio. 2012. Propbank-br: a Brazilian treebank annotated with semantic role labels. In *Proceedings of the Eighth International Conference on Language Resources and Evaluation (LREC'12)*, pages 1862–1867, Istanbul, Turkey. European Language Resources Association (ELRA).

Angela Fan and Claire Gardent. 2020. Multilingual AMR-to-text generation. In *Proceedings of the 2020 Conference on Empirical Methods in Natural Language Processing (EMNLP)*, pages 2889–2901, Online. Association for Computational Linguistics.

Paul Kingsbury and Martha Palmer. 2002. From TreeBank to PropBank. In *Proceedings of the Third International Conference on Language Resources and Evaluation (LREC'02)*, Las Palmas, Canary Islands - Spain. European Language Resources Association (ELRA).

Philipp Koehn, Hieu Hoang, Alexandra Birch, Chris Callison-Burch, Marcello Federico, Nicola Bertoldi, Brooke Cowan, Wade Shen, Christine Moran, Richard Zens, Chris Dyer, Ondřej Bojar, Alexandra Constantin, and Evan Herbst. 2007. Moses: Open source toolkit for statistical machine translation. In *Proceedings of the 45th Annual Meeting of the Association for Computational Linguistics Companion Volume Proceedings of the Demo and Poster Sessions*, pages 177–180, Prague, Czech Republic. Association for Computational Linguistics.

Mike Lewis, Yinhan Liu, Naman Goyal, Marjan Ghazvininejad, Abdelrahman Mohamed, Omer

Levy, Ves Stoyanov, and Luke Zettlemoyer. 2019. Bart: Denoising sequence-to-sequence pre-training for natural language generation, translation, and comprehension. *arXiv preprint arXiv:1910.13461*.

Chunchuan Lyu and Ivan Titov. 2018. AMR parsing as graph prediction with latent alignment. In *Proceedings of the 56th Annual Meeting of the Association for Computational Linguistics (Volume 1: Long Papers)*, pages 397–407, Melbourne, Australia. Association for Computational Linguistics.

Stephan Oepen, Omri Abend, Lasha Abzianidze, Johan Bos, Jan Hajic, Daniel Hershcovich, Bin Li, Tim O'Gorman, Nianwen Xue, and Daniel Zeman. 2020. MRP 2020: The second shared task on cross-framework and cross-lingual meaning representation parsing. In *Proceedings of the CoNLL 2020 Shared Task: Cross-Framework Meaning Representation Parsing*, pages 1–22, Online. Association for Computational Linguistics.

Juri Opitz, Letitia Parcalabescu, and Anette Frank. 2020. AMR similarity metrics from principles. *Transactions of the Association for Computational Linguistics*, 8:522–538.

Martha Palmer, Olga Babko-Malaya, Ann Bies, Mona T Diab, Mohamed Maamouri, Aous Mansouri, and Wajdi Zaghouani. 2008. A pilot arabic propbank. In *LREC*.

Kishore Papineni, Salim Roukos, Todd Ward, and Wei-Jing Zhu. 2002. Bleu: a method for automatic evaluation of machine translation. In *Proceedings of the 40th Annual Meeting of the Association for Computational Linguistics*, pages 311–318, Philadelphia, Pennsylvania, USA. Association for Computational Linguistics.

Nils Reimers and Iryna Gurevych. 2019. Sentence-BERT: Sentence embeddings using Siamese BERT-networks. In *Proceedings of the 2019 Conference on Empirical Methods in Natural Language Processing and the 9th International Joint Conference on Natural Language Processing (EMNLP-IJCNLP)*, pages 3982–3992, Hong Kong, China. Association for Computational Linguistics.

Adam Roberts, Colin Raffel, and Noam Shazeer. 2020. How much knowledge can you pack into the parameters of a language model? *arXiv preprint arXiv:2002.08910*.

Rico Sennrich, Orhan Firat, Kyunghyun Cho, Alexandra Birch, Barry Haddow, Julian Hitschler, Marcin Junczys-Dowmunt, Samuel Läubli, Antonio Valerio Miceli Barone, Jozef Mokry, et al. 2017. Nematus: a toolkit for neural machine translation. *arXiv preprint arXiv:1703.04357*.

Tom Sherborne and Mirella Lapata. 2021. Zero-shot cross-lingual semantic parsing.

Janaki Sheth, Young-Suk Lee, Ramón Fernandez Astudillo, Tahira Naseem, Radu Florian, Salim Roukos, and Todd Ward. 2021. Bootstrapping multilingual AMR with contextual word alignments. In *Proceedings of the 16th Conference of the European Chapter of the Association for Computational Linguistics: Main Volume*, pages 394–404, Online. Association for Computational Linguistics.

Jörg Tiedemann and Santhosh Thottingal. 2020. Opus-mt–building open translation services for the world. In *Proceedings of the 22nd Annual Conference of the European Association for Machine Translation*, pages 479–480.

Dongqin Xu, Junhui Li, Muhua Zhu, Min Zhang, and Guodong Zhou. 2020. Improving AMR parsing with sequence-to-sequence pre-training. In *Proceedings of the 2020 Conference on Empirical Methods in Natural Language Processing (EMNLP)*, pages 2501–2511, Online. Association for Computational Linguistics.

Nianwen Xue, Ondřej Bojar, Jan Hajič, Martha Palmer, Zdeňka Urešová, and Xiuhong Zhang. 2014. Not an interlingua, but close: Comparison of English AMRs to Chinese and Czech. In *Proceedings of the Ninth International Conference on Language Resources and Evaluation (LREC'14)*, pages 1765–1772, Reykjavik, Iceland. European Language Resources Association (ELRA).

Great Service! Fine-grained Parsing of Implicit Arguments

Ruixiang Cui and **Daniel Hershcovich**
Department of Computer Science
University of Copenhagen
{rc, dh}@di.ku.dk

Abstract

Broad-coverage meaning representations in NLP mostly focus on explicitly expressed content. More importantly, the scarcity of datasets annotating diverse implicit roles limits empirical studies into their linguistic nuances. For example, in the web review "Great service!", the provider and consumer are implicit arguments of different types. We examine an annotated corpus of fine-grained implicit arguments (Cui and Hershcovich, 2020) by carefully re-annotating it, resolving several inconsistencies. Subsequently, we present the first transition-based neural parser that can handle implicit arguments dynamically, and experiment with two different transition systems on the improved dataset. We find that certain types of implicit arguments are more difficult to parse than others and that the simpler system is more accurate in recovering implicit arguments, despite having a lower overall parsing score, attesting current reasoning limitations of NLP models. This work will facilitate a better understanding of implicit and underspecified language, by incorporating it holistically into meaning representations.

1 Introduction

Studies of form and meaning, the dual perspectives of the language sign, can be traced back to modern linguistics since de Saussure (1916, 1978). They are relevant to modern NLP, as even current large neural language models cannot intrinsically achieve a human-analogous understanding of natural language (Žabokrtský et al., 2020; Bender and Koller, 2020). Computational linguists attempt to capture syntactic and semantic features by means of constructing meaning representation frameworks, such as PTG (Böhmová et al., 2003), EDS (Oepen and Lønning, 2006), AMR (Banarescu et al., 2013) and UCCA (Abend and Rappoport, 2013). Through such frameworks,

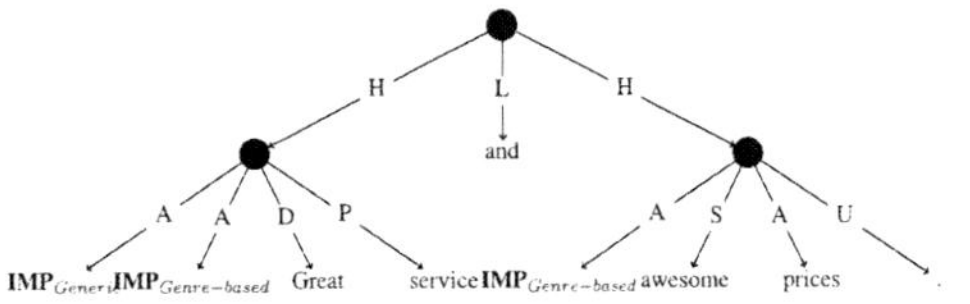

Figure 1: Example of a UCCA graph with fine-grained implicit arguments.

Participant	A	Linker	L
Center	C	Connector	N
Adverbial	D	Process	P
Elaborator	E	Quantifier	Q
Function	F	Relator	R
Ground	G	State	S
Parellel Scene	H	Time	T
Deictic		Generic	
Genre-based		Type-identifiable	
Non-specific		Iterated-set	

Table 1: UCCA Foundational Layer categories (above) and Implicit Participant Refinement Layer categories (below).

researchers have been exploring linguistic phenomena such as quantification (Pustejovsky et al., 2019), coreference (Prange et al., 2019), and word sense (Schneider et al., 2018).

In recent years, a few studies have been dedicated to annotating and modelling implicit and underspecified language (Roesiger et al., 2018; Elazar and Goldberg, 2019; McMahan and Stone, 2020). For example, in the online review "there is no delivery", two of the omitted elements are the business agent and delivered items. However, previous works focus on specific phenomena requiring linguistic and collaborative reasoning, e.g., bridging resolution, numeric fused-heads identification and referential communication. Such datasets overexpose models to limited linguistic expressions, without leveraging the complete syntactic and semantic features of the context, regardless of the diversity of implicit roles.

O'Gorman (2019) and Cui and Hershcovich

Proceedings of the 17th International Conference on Parsing Technologies (IWPT 2021), pages 65–77
Bangkok, Thailand (online), August 6, 2021. ©2021 Association for Computational Linguistics

(2020) present works on fine-grained implicit role typology, incorporating it into the meaning representation frameworks AMR and UCCA, respectively. They lay a foundation for the interpretation of idiosyncratic behaviours of implicit arguments from a linguistic and cognitive perspective. Nevertheless, neither provided a dataset ready for computational studies of such implicit arguments.

We take the latter as a starting point, addressing several theoretical inconsistencies, and evaluate its applicability by carefully re-annotating their pilot dataset and providing inter-annotator agreement. Our categorisation set, consisting of six implicit role types, is compatible with UCCA's semantic notion of Scene rather than specific linguistic phenomena. Furthermore, as opposed to previous work, it tackles only essential implicit arguments, salient in cognitive processing.

We design the first semantic parser, with two different transition systems, that has the ability to parse fine-grained implicit arguments for meaning representations and evaluate its performance on the revisited dataset. To conclude, we reflect on this work's objectives and the challenges to face in future research on implicit arguments[1].

2 Revisiting Implicit Argument Refinement

Universal Conceptual Cognitive Annotation (UCCA; Abend and Rappoport, 2013), a typologically-motivated meaning representation framework, has been targeted by several parsing shared tasks (Hershcovich et al., 2019b; Oepen et al., 2019, 2020). It uses directed acyclic graphs (DAG) anchored in surface tokens, where labelled edges represent semantic relations. In the *foundational layer*, these are based on the notion of Scenes (States and Processes), their Participants and modifiers. UCCA distinguishes *primary* edges, corresponding to explicit content, from *remote* edges, allowing cross-Scene relations. Additionally, *Implicit* units represent entities of importance to the interpretation of a Scene that are not explicitly anchored in the text. Several refinement layers have been proposed beyond the foundational layer, adding distinctions important for semantic roles and coreference (Shalev et al., 2019; Prange et al., 2019).

[1]Revisited Implicit EWT dataset is available on `https://github.com/ruixiangcui/UCCA-Refined-Implicit-EWT_English`. The code for the implicit parser is on `https://github.com/ruixiangcui/implicit_parser`

2.1 Fine-grained Implicit Argument Refinement for UCCA

Cui and Hershcovich (2020) proposed a fine-grained implicit argument typology implemented as a refinement layer of Participants for UCCA, centering around the semantic notion of Scene. Their proposed categorisation set consisting of six types, listed in Table 1, is argued to have low annotation complexity and ambiguity, thus requiring relatively low cognitive load for annotation than other fine-grained implicit argument typologies (O'Gorman, 2019).

For example, the online review "Great service and awesome price!" is annotated as follows and visualised as Figure 1:

(1) [Great$_D$ service$_P$ $IMP_{Generic}$ $IMP_{Genre-based}$]$_H$ and$_L$ [awesome$_S$ prices$_A$ $IMP_{Genre-based}$]$_H$!

There are two Scenes invoked in the sentence. "Great service" with "service" as a Process, and "awesome prices" with "awesome" as a State. Who is serving, who is being served and what is priced are distinct implicit arguments (*IMP*), which require reasoning to resolve.

Genre-based roles refer to conventional omission in the genre (Ruppenhofer and Michaelis, 2010). The corpus is based on online reviews, where reviewers typically do not mention what is under review. Therefore, an implicit argument in each Scene is marked as Genre-based referring to the reviewee. *Generic* roles denote "people in general" (Lambrecht and Lemoine, 2005). In the example, the recipient could be anyone, rather than a specific person.

2.2 Revisiting Inconsistencies

Despite the general soundness of Cui and Hershcovich (2020)'s typology, we find multiple inconsistencies in it: prominently, the treatment of Process and State Scenes and of nominalisation, and some borderline cases. We propose to revisit these cases and introduce consistent implicit argument refinement guidelines.

2.2.1 State Scenes and Process Scenes

UCCA differentiates Scenes according to their persistency in time (Abend and Rappoport, 2013): stative Scenes are temporally persistent states, while processual Scenes are evolving events. Cui and Hershcovich (2020) did not annotate implicit arguments in State Scenes, although they are essentially similar. We, therefore, categorise them using the same guidelines. This phenomenon is rather pervasive in the dataset, as in Example 1 and 2:

(2) Very$_D$ friendly$_S$ [[even$_E$ at$_C$]$_R$ weekends$_C$]$_T$ $IMP_{Genre-based}$.

2.2.2 The Definition of Prominent Elements

While UCCA only annotates implicit units when they are "prominent in the interpretation of the Scene" (Abend and Rappoport, 2013), it is not always clear what should be regarded as such: the level of uniqueness plays an essential role in recognising the prominence of an argument. For example, even distinguishing definite and indefinite articles may pose a challenge to semantic analysis (Carlson and Sussman, 2005). There are some linguistic tests for testing whether an argument is semantically mandatory (Goldberg, 2001; Hajič et al., 2012). As for UCCA, we posit that time, location and instrument modifiers, as a rule, are ubiquitous to such an extent that no implicit argument should be annotated unless a Process or State warrants it. In Example 3 (visualised as the upper graph in Figure 2a), in the Scene "you leave," the departing action demands that the implicit source location is vital for understanding, unlike the location element in Example 1 or 2, where they are of low prominence.

(3) [(*You*)$_A$ have$_D$ [[a$_F$... mechanic$_C$] real$_D$]$_{P/A}$ check$_P$ $IMP_{Non-specific}$]$_H$ before$_L$ [you$_A$ leave$_P$ $IMP_{Non-specific}$]$_H$.

2.2.3 Nominalisation as Agent Nouns

An Agent noun derives from another word denoting an action, and that identifies an entity that perform that action. In UCCA, such an expression is annotated as a single unit with both the Process and Participant categories. As in Example 3, "a real mechanic" is marked P/A. Like time or location, it is subjective whether and how many implicit arguments should be annotated given the possible list of involved receivers, instruments, etc.

For a profession like "mechanic", whatever is being repaired, as well as the repair tools, can be omitted. While an agent noun can invoke a Scene, they could also simply serve as a title. Such cases, e.g. "doctor," "professor" and "chairman," are common. To facilitate consistent annotation, we decide never to annotate implicit Participants in Scenes licensed by agent nouns. This means that there is just one Participant, the person themselves.

2.2.4 Indefinite Deictic Participant

Deictic arguments refer to the implicit speaker or addressee. They may be confused with Generic roles when it is ambiguous whether the speaker or addressee participates in the Scene. As a rule, we posit that an implicit Participant ought to be Generic unless it evidently refers to the speaker or addressee. Example 4 shows an ambiguous case.

(4) [The$_F$ experience$_C$]$_P$ $IMP_{Generic}$ [with$_R$ every$_Q$ department$_C$]$_A$ has$_F$ been$_F$ great$_D$.

3 Fine-grained Implicit Argument Corpus

As a pilot annotation experiment, Cui and Hershcovich (2020) reviewed and refined 116 randomly selected passages from an UCCA-annotated dataset of web reviews (UCCA EWT; Hershcovich et al., 2019a). The dataset was annotated by only one annotator. With our revisited guidelines, we ask two annotators[2] to revisit the original dataset, adding or modifying implicit arguments, and subsequently refining their categories, using UCCAApp (Abend et al., 2017).

3.1 Evaluation of Implicit Argument Annotation

Standard UCCA evaluation compares two graphs (e.g., created by different annotators, or one being the gold annotation and the other predicted by a parser), providing an F1 score by matching the edges by their terminal span and category (Hershcovich et al., 2019b). However, the standard evaluation completely ignores implicit argument annotation. To quantify inter-annotator agreement and later parser performance (§6), we provide an evaluation metric taking these units into account.

To compare a graph G_1 with implicit units I_1 to a graph G_2 with implicit units I_2 over the same sequence of terminals $W = w_1, \ldots, w_n$, for each implicit node i, we identify its parent node $p(i)$, denoting the set of terminals spanned by it as the yield $y(p(i)) \subseteq W$, and its category as the label $\ell(p(i), i)$. Define the set of mutual implicit units between G_1 and G_2:

$$M(G_1, I_1, G_2, I_2) = \left\{ (i,j) \in I_1 \times I_2 \;\middle|\; \begin{array}{l} y_1(p_1(i)) = y_2(p_2(j)) \wedge \\ \ell_1(p_1(i), i) = \ell_2(p_2(j), j) \end{array} \right\}$$

[2]The annotators have a background in linguistics and cognitive science. One has experience in annotating UCCA's Foundational Layer. Training for the other took ~10 hours.

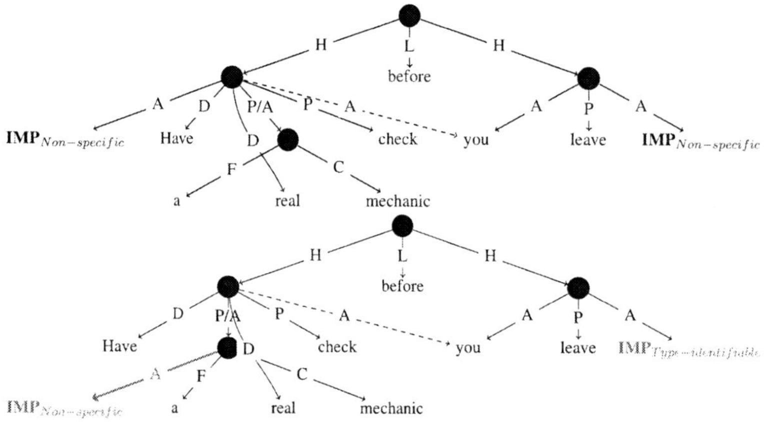

(a) In the predicted graph, a mismatched and a mislabelled implicit node are shown in red.

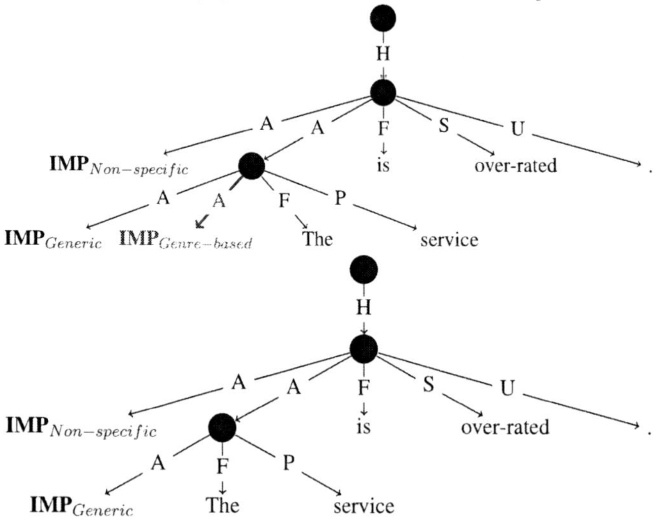

(b) In the gold graph, one implicit node is marked in blue, indicating it is not matched in the predicted graph.

Figure 2: Evaluation examples. Above: gold graphs. Below: predicted graphs.

The F-score is the harmonic mean of labelled precision and recall, defined by dividing $|M(G_1, I_1, G_2, I_2)|$ by $|I_1|$ and $|I_2|$, respectively.

In labelled evaluation, it is worth noting that we require a full match of the two sets of labels/categories rather than just intersection, which suffices in standard UCCA evaluation (of non-implicit units). That is, if there are two or more implicit nodes under one parent, it is only considered a correct match when both the numbers of implicit nodes and their labels are equal. We also introduce unlabelled evaluation, which only requires that parents' spans match.

For example, in Figure 2a, the reference graph has two implicit arguments. The first implicit unit's parent spans {have, a, real, mechanic, check} and the second's {you, leave}. In the predicted graph, two implicit units are predicted. The first implicit unit's parent spans {a, real, mechanic} while the second one spans the same terminals as the reference graph. We can see that the spans of the first implicit unit do not match—the second matches but with the wrong label. Therefore, in labelled and unlabelled implicit unit evaluation, the precision, recall, and F1 scores are all 0 and 0.5, respectively.

In Figure 2b, the reference graph has three implicit units, labelled Non-specific, Generic and Genre-based. One spans {The, service, is, over-rated} while two span {The, service}. Although the predicted graph has two implicit units with correct labels (Non-specific and Generic), it misses both implicit units under the second parent span,

	Deictic	Generic	Genre-based	Type-identifiable	Non-specific	Iterated-set	*Total Implicit Arguments*
Cui and Hershcovich (2020)	66	65	103	39	100	12	*385*
Our dataset	107	86	147	6	36	9	*391*

Table 2: Statistics of Revisited Implicit Corpus compared to the pilot annotation.

viz. the two sets merely intersect but are not equal. Therefore, the triplet precision, recall and F1 score for labelled evaluation are all 0.5 and the triplet for unlabelled evaluation are 1.

3.2 Inter-annotator Agreement

The two annotators separately reviewed and refined 15 out of the 116 passages (taken from the original test split). Using the evaluation metric proposed in §3.1, the labelled and unlabelled F1 scores are 73.8% and 91.3% respectively (see Appendix A). Annotators have a Cohen's κ (Cohen, 1960) of 69.3% on the six-type fine-grained classification of the implicit arguments whose parents' spans match. For comparison, on the FiGref scheme, O'Gorman (2019) report a Cohen's κ of 55.2% on a 14-way classification and of 58.1% on a four-way classification. Gerber and Chai (2010) proposed a relevant task to annotate implicit arguments for instances of nominal predicates in sentences, which has a Cohen's κ of 67%. While we maintain a comprehensive fine-grained typology, we still see an improvement in agreement over other corpora.

3.3 Statistics of Revisited Implicit Corpus

Finally, one annotator reviewed and refined all 116 passages. The second reviewed their annotation after completion. The full revisited dataset contains 393 passages, 3700 tokens and 5475 nodes. Table 2 compares our revisited dataset to the unreviewed dataset of Cui and Hershcovich (2020).

We see a major decline in Non-specific and Type-identifiable implicit arguments, because of the clearer definition of prominent elements and cases of agent nouns. Deictic, Generic and Genre-based increase their amount thanks to incorporating implicit arguments in State Scenes rather than only Process Scenes. The number of Iterated-set remains small due to the rareness of aspectual morphology and habitual/iterative constructions in English and in the corpus. However, it is still necessary to keep the category and separate out its instances rather than lump into another category or even ignore them. Since implicit arguments of such kind could be more common in morphologically rich languages, we want to keep a clean mapping of habitual/iterative constructions so as to facilitate the studies of implicit roles' diverse behaviours in languages other than English.

4 Two Transition Systems for Parsing Implicit Arguments

We build the first neural parser that supports parsing implicit arguments dynamically in meaning representations, with two different transition systems. We design a transition-based parser, modelled upon Nivre (2003): a stack $S = (\dots, s_1, s_0)$ holds processed words. $B = (b_0, b_1, \dots)$ is a buffer containing tokens or nodes to be processed. V is a set of nodes, and E is a set of labelled edges. We denote s_0 as the first element on S and b_0 as the first element on B. Given a sentence composed by a sequence of tokens t_1, t_2, ..., t_n, the parser is initialized to have a Root node on S, and all surface tokens in B. The parser will at each step deterministically choose the most probable transition based on its current parsing state. Oracle action sequences are generated for training on gold-standard annotations.

We propose two transition systems, IMPLICIT-EAGER and IMPLICIT-STANDARD, to deal with implicit arguments over the architecture of HIT-SCIR 2019 (Che et al., 2019), which ranked first in UCCA parsing in the MRP 2019 shared task (Oepen et al., 2019). The transition system incorporates all nine transitions, namely, LEFT-EDGE, RIGHT-EDGE, SHIFT, REDUCE, NODE, SWAP, LEFT-REMOTE, RIGHT-REMOTE and FINISH.

SHIFT, together with REDUCE, are standard transitions. SHIFT moves b_0 to S, while REDUCE pops s_0 from S (when it should not be attached to any element in B).

Following transition-based constituent parsing, NODE$_X$ creates a new non-terminal node (Sagae and Lavie, 2005). Such node will be created on the buffer, as a parent of s_0 with an X-labelled edge.

LEFT-EDGE$_X$ and RIGHT-EDGE$_X$ add an X-labelled primary edge between the first two elements on S. When the first element is the parent of the second element on S, LEFT-EDGE$_X$ is executed; in reverse, RIGHT-EDGE$_X$ will be chosen when the second element has the first element as its child. The left/right direction is the same as

Before Transition				Transition	After Transition					Condition
Stack	Buffer	Nodes	Edges		Stack	Buffer	Nodes	Edges	Terminal?	
S	$x \mid B$	V	E	SHIFT	$S \mid x$	B	V	E	–	
$S \mid x$	B	V	E	REDUCE	S	B	V	E	–	
$S \mid x$	B	V	E	NODE$_X$	$S \mid x$	$y \mid B$	$V \cup \{y\}$	$E \mid (y, x)_X$	–	$x \neq$ root
$S \mid x$	B	V	E	NODE	$S \mid x$	$y \mid B$	$V \cup \{y\}$	E	–	
$S \mid x$	B	V	E	IMPLICIT$_X$	$S \mid x$	$y \mid B$	$V \cup \{y\}$	$E \mid (x, y)^{\#}_X$	–	
$S \mid y, x$	B	V	E	LEFT-EDGE$_X$	$S \mid y, x$	B	V	$E \mid (x, y)_X$	–	
$S \mid x, y$	B	V	E	RIGHT-EDGE$_X$	$S \mid x, y$	B	V	$E \mid (x, y)_X$	–	$\begin{cases} x \notin w_{1:n}, \\ y \neq \text{ root }, \\ y \not\leadsto_G x \end{cases}$
$S \mid y, x$	B	V	E	LEFT-REMOTE$_X$	$S \mid y, x$	B	V	$E \mid (x, y)^*_X$	–	
$S \mid x, y$	B	V	E	RIGHT-REMOTE$_X$	$S \mid x, y$	B	V	$E \mid (x, y)^*_X$	–	
$S \mid x, y$	B	V	E	SWAP	$S \mid y$	$x \mid B$	V	E	–	$i(x) < i(y)$
[root]	$\emptyset$	V	E	FINISH	$\emptyset$	$\emptyset$	V	E	+	

Table 3: The transition sets of two implicit transition systems. Actions marked in red are for IMPLICIT-EAGER, blue for IMPLICIT-STANDARD. We write the **stack** with its top to the right and the **buffer** with its head to the left. $(\cdot,\cdot)_X$ denotes a X-labelled edge, $(\cdot,\cdot)^*_X$ a remote X-labelled edge, and $(\cdot,\cdot)^{\#}_X$ an X-labelled edge to an implicit node. $i(x)$ is a running index for the created nodes. The prospective child of the EDGE action cannot have a primary parent. The newly generated node by IMPLICIT$_X$ action is prohibited from having any descendant. NODE generates a concept node on the buffer, but deos not produce an arc. This table is adapted from Hershcovich et al. (2017).

where the arc points to. LEFT-REMOTE$_X$ and RIGHT-REMOTE$_X$ are similar to LEFT-EDGE$_X$ and RIGHT-EDGE$_X$, yet these two transitions create remote edges, creating reentrencies. The X-labelled edge will be assigned a Remote attribute.

SWAP deals with non-planar graphs (a generalisation of non-projective trees), in other words, discontinuous constituents. It pops the second node on S and adds it to the top of B. FINISH is the terminal transition, which pops the Root node and marks the transition state as terminal.

In IMPLICIT-EAGER, we introduce a new transition IMPLICIT$_X$ adding an implicit node to the buffer and attaching it with a labelled edge in one step. In IMPLICIT-STANDARD, we simplify the existing NODE transition to only create a node without attaching it, with the purpose of treating implicit units like primary ones and generating them dynamically. We elaborate their designs in Section 4.1 and Section 4.2. Table 3 shows the transition set.

4.1 IMPLICIT-EAGER

Besides the nine transitions described above, IMPLICIT-EAGER introduces the IMPLICIT$_X$ transition, which creates a new unit on B as the child of s_0, with an X-labelled edge. The IMPLICIT action is different from the NODE action of IMPLICIT-STANDARD in the sense that the integrally generated edge makes the new node a child of s_0 rather than its parent, as in NODE$_X$. Equally importantly, the new node is prohibited to have any child in contrast to the *primary* nodes that the NODE$_X$ action generates.

4.2 IMPLICIT-STANDARD

IMPLICIT-STANDARD adopts a more modular approach. Rather than complicating the transition systems, it treats primary non-terminal nodes and implicit nodes equally by simplifying the NODE$_X$ action, making it generate a new unit on the buffer without attaching it with any (labelled) edge. We assume primary non-terminal nodes and implicit nodes are identical in essence, thus handling them without discrimination. Whenever an ungenerated child or parent of s_0 is found, NODE is executed so that a concept node will be created on B. This action does not cope with edge generation; the work is left to LEFT-EDGE$_X$ or RIGHT-EDGE$_X$. In the oracle, we can tell whether the node is primary or implicit by observing its relations. If the newly created node is the child of s_0 and does not have any descendants, it is an implicit node; otherwise, a primary node.

5 Experiments

5.1 Data Preprocessing

We convert UCCA XML data to MRP format using the open-source `mtool` software.[3] As the UCCA data provided in MRP 2019 shared task did not contain implicit information, HIT-SCIR 2019 is not designed to read this information in our dataset. We modify the parser to read node properties, and to

[3] `https://github.com/cfmrp/mtool`

Data	# Sentences	# Tokens	# Nodes	# Edges	# Deictic	# Generic	# Genre-based	# Type-i	# Non-s	# Iterated-s	# Implicit sum
EWT Train	2723	44751	59654	97561							
EWT Dev	554	5394	7534	11987							
EWT Eval	535	5381	7431	11907							
Overall					not refined	not refined	not refined	not refined	not refined	not refined	153
IMP Train	285	2671	3936	6146	87	59	103	3	18	4	274
IMP Dev	59	540	781	1217	11	15	19	1	10	0	56
IMP Eval	49	489	709	1106	9	12	25	2	8	5	61
Overall					107	86	147	6	36	9	391

Table 4: Statistics of train, dev and evaluation set in Original EWT and Revisited Implicit EWT. For each set, number of sentences, number of tokens, number of nodes, number of instances of 6 implicit categories and their sum are listed.

	Primary			Remote			**Implicit**					
	LP	**LR**	**LF**	**LP**	**LR**	**LF**	**LP**	**LR**	**LF**	**UP**	**UR**	**UF**
Baseline	0.495	0.467	0.480	0.538	0.304	0.389	1	0	0	1	0	0
IMPLICIT-EAGER	0.503	0.472	0.487	0.333	0.100	0.154	0.333 (7/21)	0.140 (7/50)	0.197	0.428 (9/21)	0.180 (9/50)	0.254
IMPLICIT-STANDARD	0.474	0.431	0.451	0.438	0.280	0.341	**0.409** (9/22)	**0.180** (9/50)	**0.250**	**0.500** (11/22)	**0.220** (11/50)	**0.306**

Table 5: Experiment results on Revisited Implicit EWT in percents. For primary edges, remote edges, and implicit prediction, listed are Labelled Precision(LP), Labelled Recall (LR) and Labelled F-score (LF). In addition, Unlabelled precision (UL), Unlabelled Recall (UR) and Unlabelled F-score are also listed for implicit evaluation.

convert UCCA data from and to MRP format. The updated version of `mtool` is available on GitHub.[4]

5.2 Experimental Setup

Our parsers use stack LSTM to stabilize gradient descent process and speed up training; we enrich contextual information by employing the pretrained language model BERT as a feature input (Graves, 2013; Devlin et al., 2018). The model is implemented in AllenNLP (Gardner et al., 2018). We use the HIT-SCIR 2019 parser as the baseline for comparison. We keep the same hyperparameters as Che et al. (2019) except batch size, adjusted from 8 to 4 due to resource constraints. We do not tune hyperparameters on either the original or revisited dataset.[5]

We use the train, validation and evaluation split from Hershcovich et al. (2019b), which was originally from UD EWT, with the ratio of 0.75, 0.125 and 0.125. The evaluation set has been validated as the gold standard. Table 4 shows detailed statistics of train, dev and eval set of both the original and revisited dataset, on which we trained the baseline parser, IMPLICIT-EAGER and IMPLICIT-STANDARD.[6]

6 Results

Table 5 presents experimental results on Revisited Implicit EWT by three parsers, the baseline HIT-SCIR 2019 parser, IMPLICIT-EAGER and IMPLICIT-STANDARD on Revisited Implicit EWT. Regarding performance on the dataset, the baseline is not able to predict implicit argument as expected. However, both IMPLICIT-EAGER and IMPLICIT-STANDARD managed to predict implicit arguments.

Based on the evaluation method mentioned in section 3.1, IMPLICIT-EAGER's labelled precision and labelled recall on Revisited Implicit EWT are 0.333 and 0.14; the unlabelled precision and unlabelled recall are 0.428 and 0.18. For the primary edge and remote edge evaluation, noticeably, IMPLICIT-EAGER also outperforms the baseline on primary edges by 0.007 in F-score on the revisited dataset.

Even though IMPLICIT-STANDARD has the worse results in terms of primary parsing, it gains boosted performance on all targets in implicit evaluation. Its unlabelled implicit precision, recall and F-score are 0.5, 0.22 and 0.306, defeating IMPLICIT-EAGER by 0.072, 0.04 and 0.052, respectively.

For labelled evaluation, IMPLICIT-STANDARD surpasses IMPLICIT-EAGER even further; the labelled precion, recall and F-score are 0.419, 0.180 and 0.250, respectively exceeding IMPLICIT-EAGER by 0.076, 0.04 and 0.053.

Table 6 presents the three parsers' performances on Original EWT. The baseline produced better results on primary edges and remote edges on Original EWT.

The reason why IMPLICIT-STANDARD outper-

[4] `https://github.com/ruixiangcui/mtool`

[5] Hyperparameter settings are listed in Appendix B.

[6] See training details in Appendix C.

	Primary			Remote		
	LP	**LR**	**LF**	**LP**	**LR**	**LF**
Baseline	0.710	0.701	0.706	0.547	0.365	0.438
IMPLICIT-EAGER	0.675	0.597	0.634	0.527	0.344	0.416
IMPLICIT-STANDARD	0.656	0.571	0.610	0.458	0.225	0.302

Table 6: Experiment results on Original EWT in percents. As there is no implicit argument in the dataset, only performances on primary edges and remote edges are listed.

forms IMPLICIT-EAGER on implicit evaluation but decrease in accuracy on primary evaluation might be attributed to its equal treatment of primary nodes and implicit nodes.

7 Discussion

As is indicated in Table 5, IMPLICIT-EAGER and IMPLICIT-STANDARD successfully predicted respectively seven and nine implicit arguments with the correct fine-grained implicit labels. In the unlabelled evaluation, nine and 11 implicit arguments were predicted each.

Table 7 shows the confusion matrix of the performances of IMPLICIT-EAGER and IMPLICIT-STANDARD on the evaluation set of Revisited Implicit EWT. Both parsers have predicted roughly the same amount of implicit arguments, 22 and 21, respectively.

Noticeably, IMPLICIT-EAGER has emitted 12 Deictic implicit arguments, accounting for 57.1% of all predictions, 14 and 66.7% if including partial matches as Deictic & Generic and Deictic & Genre-based. While IMPLICIT-STANDARD has a more uniform distribution over prediction categories. Deictic, Generic and Genre-based are the most predicted ones. Moreover, one Non-specific implicit argument, despite being wrongly labelled, is also predicted by IMPLICIT-STANDARD, while IMPLICIT-EAGER has never predicted labels other than Deictic, Generic and Genre-based, which have significantly more instances in the training set.

Both implicit parsers have predicted correctly four Deictic and three Generic & Genre-based implicit arguments. Besides, IMPLICIT-STANDARD managed to predict two more correct Genre-based while IMPLICIT-EAGER has never predicted successfully stand-alone Genre-based implicit argument. IMPLICIT-STANDARD has a remarkably higher labelled precision of 66.7% in Deictic than IMPLICIT-EAGER of 33.3%, while the latter has a higher precision of 75% in Generic & Genre-based than IMPLICIT-STANDARD of 50%. Lamentably,

IMPLICIT-EAGER	UNMATCHED	Non-specific	Non-specific & Generic	Non-specific & Type-identifiable	Deictic	Deictic & Iterated-set	Generic	Generic & Genre-based	Genre-based	Iterated-set	Type-identifiable	P	*Total*
UNMATCHED	0	5	1	1	4	1	1	7	14	4	1	2	*41*
Deictic	6	1	0	0	**4**	0	0	0	1	0	0	0	*12*
Deictic & Generic	1	0	0	0	0	0	0	0	0	0	0	0	*1*
Deictic & Genre-based	1	0	0	0	0	0	0	0	0	0	0	0	*1*
Generic & Genre-based	1	0	0	0	0	0	0	**3**	0	0	0	0	*4*
Genre-based	3	0	0	0	0	0	0	0	0	0	0	0	*3*
IMPLICIT-STANDARD													
UNMATCHED	0	6	1	1	4	1	1	6	12	4	1	2	*39*
Non-specific	1	0	0	0	0	0	0	0	0	0	0	0	*1*
Deictic	2	0	0	0	**4**	0	0	0	0	0	0	0	*6*
Deictic & Genre-based	0	0	0	0	0	0	0	1	0	0	0	0	*1*
Generic	2	0	0	0	0	0	0	0	0	0	0	0	*2*
Generic & Genre-based	3	0	0	0	0	0	0	**3**	0	0	0	0	*6*
Genre-based	3	0	0	0	0	0	0	0	**2**	0	0	0	*5*
Genre-based & P	0	0	0	0	0	0	0	0	1	0	0	0	*1*

Table 7: Confusion matrix on the Revisited Implicit EWT evaluation set: The column is the predicted labels while the row is the actual labels. Noticeably, the parsers are able to predict implicit elements of other categories in theory, such as Process (P). If not clarified otherwise, the fine-grained implicit categories are Participant by default.

neither of the implicit parsers has emitted prediction for Type-identifiable nor Iterated-set. It is necessarily expected as both categories have less than five instances in the training set.

Although this paper focuses on fine-grained implicit Participants, there are already some implicit arguments of other categories annotated in the foundational layer, especially Process and Center. Interestingly, in the sentence "Fresh and excellent quality," IMPLICIT-STANDARD generated two implicit arguments, Genre-based and Process in the Scene "Fresh." It means not only that it infers the Scene misses a Genre-based Participant, but also a Process, i.e., the main relation that evolves in time.

8 Related Work

Parsing implicit argument was introduced into NLP by Ruppenhofer et al. (2009); Gerber and Chai (2010, 2012), but has been coarse-grained and annotated within Nombank (Meyers et al., 2004), limited to ten nominal predicates.

Bender et al. (2011) identified ten relevant linguistic phenomena, ran several parsers and associated their output with target dependencies. Roth and Frank (2015) used a rule-based method for identifying implicit arguments, which depends on semantic role labelling and coreference resolution. Similarly, Silberer and Frank (2012); Chiarcos and

Schenk (2015); Schenk and Chiarcos (2016) proposed parsing methods for SemEval 2010 data, but they are only able to parse implicit arguments on a coarse level as well. Cheng and Erk (2018) built a narrative cloze model and evaluated it on Gerber and Chai (2010)'s dataset.

9 Conclusion

Implicit arguments are pervasive in the text but have not been well studied from a general perspective in NLP. In this work, we revisited a recently proposed fine-grained implicit argument typology by addressing its current deficiencies. We annotated a corpus based on the revised guidelines and designed an evaluation metric for measuring implicit argument parsing performance, demonstrating the annotation's reliability with a superior inter-annotator agreement comparing to other fine-grained implicit argument studies. The dataset will be available to facilitate relevant research.

We introduced the first semantic parser, with two different transition systems, that can handle and predict implicit nodes dynamically, and label them with promising accuracy as part of the meaning representations. We evaluated it on the new dataset and found that some types of implicit arguments are harder to parse than others and that a simpler transition system performs better on parsing implicit arguments at the cost of primary parsing. The fine-grained implicit argument task is challenging and calls for further research.

In future work, we plan to create a large resource of implicit arguments by automatically extracting them from various linguistic constructions in unlabelled text, use it for pre-training of language models, and evaluate them on our and other datasets to gain more insights into this linguistic phenomenon. A post-processing baseline to find implicit arguments after parsing the whole graph would also be interesting for future investigation.

10 Acknowledgments

The authors thank Miryam de Lhoneux and the anonymous reviewers for their helpful feedback.

References

Omri Abend and Ari Rappoport. 2013. Universal Conceptual Cognitive Annotation (UCCA). In *Proceedings of the 51st Annual Meeting of the Association for Computational Linguistics (Volume 1: Long Papers)*, pages 228–238, Sofia, Bulgaria. Association for Computational Linguistics.

Omri Abend, Shai Yerushalmi, and Ari Rappoport. 2017. UCCAApp: Web-application for syntactic and semantic phrase-based annotation. In *Proceedings of ACL 2017, System Demonstrations*, pages 109–114, Vancouver, Canada. Association for Computational Linguistics.

Laura Banarescu, Claire Bonial, Shu Cai, Madalina Georgescu, Kira Griffitt, Ulf Hermjakob, Kevin Knight, Philipp Koehn, Martha Palmer, and Nathan Schneider. 2013. Abstract Meaning Representation for sembanking. In *Proceedings of the 7th Linguistic Annotation Workshop and Interoperability with Discourse*, pages 178–186, Sofia, Bulgaria. Association for Computational Linguistics.

Emily M. Bender, Dan Flickinger, Stephan Oepen, and Yi Zhang. 2011. Parser evaluation over local and non-local deep dependencies in a large corpus. In *Proceedings of the 2011 Conference on Empirical Methods in Natural Language Processing*, pages 397–408, Edinburgh, Scotland, UK. Association for Computational Linguistics.

Emily M. Bender and Alexander Koller. 2020. Climbing towards NLU: On meaning, form, and understanding in the age of data. In *Proceedings of the 58th Annual Meeting of the Association for Computational Linguistics*, pages 5185–5198, Online. Association for Computational Linguistics.

Alena Böhmová, Jan Hajič, Eva Hajičová, and Barbora Hladká. 2003. The Prague dependency treebank. In *Treebanks*, pages 103–127. Springer.

Greg Carlson and Rachel Shirley Sussman. 2005. *Seemingly Indefinite Definites*, pages 71 – 86. De Gruyter Mouton, Berlin, Boston.

Wanxiang Che, Longxu Dou, Yang Xu, Yuxuan Wang, Yijia Liu, and Ting Liu. 2019. HIT-SCIR at MRP 2019: A unified pipeline for meaning representation parsing via efficient training and effective encoding. In *Proceedings of the Shared Task on Cross-Framework Meaning Representation Parsing at the 2019 Conference on Natural Language Learning*, pages 76–85, Hong Kong. Association for Computational Linguistics.

Pengxiang Cheng and Katrin Erk. 2018. Implicit argument prediction with event knowledge. In *Proceedings of the 2018 Conference of the North American Chapter of the Association for Computational Linguistics: Human Language Technologies, Volume 1 (Long Papers)*, pages 831–840, New Orleans, Louisiana. Association for Computational Linguistics.

Christian Chiarcos and Niko Schenk. 2015. Memory-based acquisition of argument structures and its application to implicit role detection. In *Proceedings of the 16th Annual Meeting of the Special Interest*

Group on Discourse and Dialogue, pages 178–187, Prague, Czech Republic. Association for Computational Linguistics.

Jacob Cohen. 1960. A coefficient of agreement for nominal scales. *Educational and Psychological Measurement*, 20(1):37–46.

Ruixiang Cui and Daniel Hershcovich. 2020. Refining implicit argument annotation for UCCA. In *Proceedings of the Second International Workshop on Designing Meaning Representations*, pages 41–52, Barcelona Spain (online). Association for Computational Linguistics.

Jacob Devlin, Ming-Wei Chang, Kenton Lee, and Kristina Toutanova. 2018. Bert: Pre-training of deep bidirectional transformers for language understanding. *arXiv preprint arXiv:1810.04805*.

Yanai Elazar and Yoav Goldberg. 2019. Where's my head? Definition, data set, and models for numeric fused-head identification and resolution. *Transactions of the Association for Computational Linguistics*, 7:519–535.

Matt Gardner, Joel Grus, Mark Neumann, Oyvind Tafjord, Pradeep Dasigi, Nelson F Liu, Matthew Peters, Michael Schmitz, and Luke Zettlemoyer. 2018. Allennlp: A deep semantic natural language processing platform. In *Proceedings of Workshop for NLP Open Source Software (NLP-OSS)*, pages 1–6.

Matthew Gerber and Joyce Chai. 2010. Beyond NomBank: A study of implicit arguments for nominal predicates. In *Proceedings of the 48th Annual Meeting of the Association for Computational Linguistics*, pages 1583–1592, Uppsala, Sweden. Association for Computational Linguistics.

Matthew Gerber and Joyce Y. Chai. 2012. Semantic role labeling of implicit arguments for nominal predicates. *Computational Linguistics*, 38(4):755–798.

Adele E Goldberg. 2001. Patient arguments of causative verbs can be omitted: The role of information structure in argument distribution. *Language sciences*, 23(4-5):503–524.

Alex Graves. 2013. Generating sequences with recurrent neural networks. *arXiv preprint arXiv:1308.0850*.

Jan Hajič, Eva Hajičová, Jarmila Panevová, Petr Sgall, Ondřej Bojar, Silvie Cinková, Eva Fučíková, Marie Mikulová, Petr Pajas, Jan Popelka, Jiří Semecký, Jana Šindlerová, Jan Štěpánek, Josef Toman, Zdeňka Urešová, and Zdeněk Žabokrtský. 2012. Announcing Prague Czech-English Dependency Treebank 2.0. In *Proceedings of the Eighth International Conference on Language Resources and Evaluation (LREC'12)*, pages 3153–3160, Istanbul, Turkey. European Language Resources Association (ELRA).

Daniel Hershcovich, Omri Abend, and Ari Rappoport. 2017. A transition-based directed acyclic graph parser for UCCA. In *Proceedings of the 55th Annual Meeting of the Association for Computational Linguistics (Volume 1: Long Papers)*, pages 1127–1138, Vancouver, Canada. Association for Computational Linguistics.

Daniel Hershcovich, Omri Abend, and Ari Rappoport. 2019a. Content differences in syntactic and semantic representation. In *Proceedings of the 2019 Conference of the North American Chapter of the Association for Computational Linguistics: Human Language Technologies, Volume 1 (Long and Short Papers)*, pages 478–488, Minneapolis, Minnesota. Association for Computational Linguistics.

Daniel Hershcovich, Zohar Aizenbud, Leshem Choshen, Elior Sulem, Ari Rappoport, and Omri Abend. 2019b. SemEval-2019 task 1: Cross-lingual semantic parsing with UCCA. In *Proceedings of the 13th International Workshop on Semantic Evaluation*, pages 1–10, Minneapolis, Minnesota, USA. Association for Computational Linguistics.

Knud Lambrecht and Kevin Lemoine. 2005. Definite null objects in (spoken) french. *Grammatical constructions: Back to the roots*, 4:13.

Brian McMahan and Matthew Stone. 2020. Analyzing speaker strategy in referential communication. In *Proceedings of the 21th Annual Meeting of the Special Interest Group on Discourse and Dialogue*, pages 175–185, 1st virtual meeting. Association for Computational Linguistics.

Adam Meyers, Ruth Reeves, Catherine Macleod, Rachel Szekely, Veronika Zielinska, Brian Young, and Ralph Grishman. 2004. The NomBank project: An interim report. In *Proceedings of the Workshop Frontiers in Corpus Annotation at HLT-NAACL 2004*, pages 24–31, Boston, Massachusetts, USA. Association for Computational Linguistics.

Joakim Nivre. 2003. An efficient algorithm for projective dependency parsing. In *Proceedings of the Eighth International Conference on Parsing Technologies*, pages 149–160.

Stephan Oepen, Omri Abend, Lasha Abzianidze, Johan Bos, Jan Hajic, Daniel Hershcovich, Bin Li, Tim O'Gorman, Nianwen Xue, and Daniel Zeman. 2020. MRP 2020: The second shared task on cross-framework and cross-lingual meaning representation parsing. In *Proceedings of the CoNLL 2020 Shared Task: Cross-Framework Meaning Representation Parsing*, pages 1–22, Online. Association for Computational Linguistics.

Stephan Oepen, Omri Abend, Jan Hajic, Daniel Hershcovich, Marco Kuhlmann, Tim O'Gorman, Nianwen Xue, Jayeol Chun, Milan Straka, and Zdenka Uresova. 2019. MRP 2019: Cross-framework meaning representation parsing. In *Proceedings of the Shared Task on Cross-Framework Meaning Representation Parsing at the 2019 Conference on Natural*

Language Learning, pages 1–27, Hong Kong. Association for Computational Linguistics.

Stephan Oepen and Jan Tore Lønning. 2006. Discriminant-based MRS banking. In *Proceedings of the Fifth International Conference on Language Resources and Evaluation (LREC'06)*, Genoa, Italy. European Language Resources Association (ELRA).

Timothy J O'Gorman. 2019. *Bringing Together Computational and Linguistic Models of Implicit Role Interpretation*. Ph.D. thesis, University of Colorado at Boulder.

Jakob Prange, Nathan Schneider, and Omri Abend. 2019. Semantically constrained multilayer annotation: The case of coreference. In *Proceedings of the First International Workshop on Designing Meaning Representations*, pages 164–176, Florence, Italy. Association for Computational Linguistics.

James Pustejovsky, Ken Lai, and Nianwen Xue. 2019. Modeling quantification and scope in Abstract Meaning Representations. In *Proceedings of the First International Workshop on Designing Meaning Representations*, pages 28–33, Florence, Italy. Association for Computational Linguistics.

Ina Roesiger, Arndt Riester, and Jonas Kuhn. 2018. Bridging resolution: Task definition, corpus resources and rule-based experiments. In *Proceedings of the 27th International Conference on Computational Linguistics*, pages 3516–3528, Santa Fe, New Mexico, USA. Association for Computational Linguistics.

Michael Roth and Anette Frank. 2015. Inducing implicit arguments from comparable texts: A framework and its applications. *Computational Linguistics*, 41(4):625–664.

Josef Ruppenhofer and Laura A Michaelis. 2010. A constructional account of genre-based argument omissions. *Constructions and Frames*, 2(2):158–184.

Josef Ruppenhofer, Caroline Sporleder, Roser Morante, Collin Baker, and Martha Palmer. 2009. SemEval-2010 task 10: Linking events and their participants in discourse. In *Proceedings of the Workshop on Semantic Evaluations: Recent Achievements and Future Directions (SEW-2009)*, pages 106–111, Boulder, Colorado. Association for Computational Linguistics.

Kenji Sagae and Alon Lavie. 2005. A classifier-based parser with linear run-time complexity. In *Proceedings of the Ninth International Workshop on Parsing Technology*, pages 125–132, Vancouver, British Columbia. Association for Computational Linguistics.

Ferdinand de Saussure. 1916. Cours de linguistique générale. *Paris: Payot. edited posthumously by C. Bally and A. Riedlinger.*

Ferdinand de Saussure. 1978. Cours de linguistique générale. *Paris: Payot. edited posthumously by C. Bally and A. Riedlinger.*

Niko Schenk and Christian Chiarcos. 2016. Unsupervised learning of prototypical fillers for implicit semantic role labeling. In *Proceedings of the 2016 Conference of the North American Chapter of the Association for Computational Linguistics: Human Language Technologies*, pages 1473–1479, San Diego, California. Association for Computational Linguistics.

Nathan Schneider, Jena D. Hwang, Vivek Srikumar, Jakob Prange, Austin Blodgett, Sarah R. Moeller, Aviram Stern, Adi Bitan, and Omri Abend. 2018. Comprehensive supersense disambiguation of English prepositions and possessives. In *Proceedings of the 56th Annual Meeting of the Association for Computational Linguistics (Volume 1: Long Papers)*, pages 185–196, Melbourne, Australia. Association for Computational Linguistics.

Adi Shalev, Jena D. Hwang, Nathan Schneider, Vivek Srikumar, Omri Abend, and Ari Rappoport. 2019. Preparing SNACS for subjects and objects. In *Proceedings of the First International Workshop on Designing Meaning Representations*, pages 141–147, Florence, Italy. Association for Computational Linguistics.

Carina Silberer and Anette Frank. 2012. Casting implicit role linking as an anaphora resolution task. In **SEM 2012: The First Joint Conference on Lexical and Computational Semantics – Volume 1: Proceedings of the main conference and the shared task, and Volume 2: Proceedings of the Sixth International Workshop on Semantic Evaluation (SemEval 2012)*, pages 1–10, Montréal, Canada. Association for Computational Linguistics.

Zdeněk Žabokrtský, Daniel Zeman, and Magda Ševčíková. 2020. Sentence meaning representations across languages: What can we learn from existing frameworks? *Computational Linguistics*, pages 1–61.

Appendices

A Inter-annotator Confusion Matrix

Tabel 8 shows the confusion matrix for measuring inter-annotator agreement on the evaluation set. The unlabelled F-score is 91.3%, and the labelled F1-score is 73.8%. The Cohen's κ between two annotators is 69.3%.

	UNMATCHED	Nonspecific	Nonspecific|Generic	Nonspecific|Type-identifiable	Deictic	Deictic|Iterated-set	Generic	Generic|Genre-based	Genre-based	Iterated/repeated/set	Type-identifiable	P
UNMATCHED	0	1	0	0	0	0	1	0	1	1	1	0
Nonspecific	0	4	0	0	0	0	0	0	4	0	0	0
Nonspecific|Deictic	0	0	0	0	0	1	0	0	0	0	0	0
Nonspecific|Generic	0	0	1	0	0	0	0	0	0	0	0	0
Nonspecific|Genre-based	0	0	0	0	0	0	0	1	0	0	0	0
Nonspecific|Type-identifiable	0	0	0	1	0	0	0	0	0	0	0	0
Deictic	2	0	0	0	8	0	0	0	0	0	0	0
Deictic|Genre-based	0	0	0	0	0	0	0	1	0	0	0	0
Generic|Genre-based	0	0	0	0	0	0	0	8	0	0	0	0
Genre-based	0	2	0	0	0	0	0	0	11	0	0	0
Type-identifiable	1	0	0	0	0	0	0	0	0	0	0	0
Iterated-set	1	0	0	0	0	0	0	0	0	3	0	0
P	0	0	0	0	0	0	0	0	0	0	0	2

Table 8: Confusion matrix of the evaluation set for measuring inter-annotator agreement

B Hyperparameter Settings

Our parsers use stack LSTM to stabilize gradient descent process and speed up training; we enrich contextual information by employing the pre-trained language model BERT as a feature input. We keep the same hyperparameter setting for all three parsers, the baseline parser HIT-SCIR 2019, IMPLICIT-EAGER and IMPLICIT-STANDARD. The setting is shown as the Table 9.

Hyperparameter	Value
Hidden dimension	20
Action dimension	50
Optimizer	Adam
β_1, β_2	0.9, 0.99
Dropout	0.5
Layer dropout	0.2
Recurrent dropout	0.2
Input dropout	0.2
Batch size	4
Epochs	50
Base learning rate	1×10^{-3}
BERT learning rate	5×10^{-5}
Gradient clipping	5.0
Gradient norm	5.0
Learning rate scheduler	slanted triangular
Gradual Unfreezing	True
Cut Frac	0.1
Ratio	32

Table 9: Implicit Parser hyperparameters.

C Training Details

As Table 10 shows, the training time is 2 days 22 hours for the baseline on Original UCCA EWT (50 epochs). Best epoch is 3rd; 3 hours for the baseline on Revisted Implicit EWT (30 epochs). Best epoch is 22nd; 1 day 8 hours and 1 day 19 hours for IMPLICIT-EAGER and IMPLICIT-STANDARD on Original UCCA EWT (10 epochs, 13 epochs), respectively, with the best epoch being the 3rd and 2nd; And finally, 6 hours and 8 hours for IMPLICIT-EAGER and IMPLICIT-STANDARD on Revisited Implicit EWT (50 epochs). The best epoch is 21st and 37th, respectively. One can see that all parsers achieved the best performance at an early stage on Original UCCA EWT. However, both implicit parsers took longer time to train on Original UCCA EWT than the baseline.

	Original Full UCCA EWT			Revisited Implicit Dataset		
	Training time	# Epochs	# Best Epoch	Training time	# Epochs	# Best Epoch
Baseline	2 days 22 h	50	3	3 h	30	22
IMPLICIT-EAGER	1 day 8 h	10	3	6 h	50	21
IMPLICIT-STANDARD	1 day 19 h	13	2	8 h	50	37

Table 10: Training details of the baseline, IMPLICIT-EAGER and IMPLICIT-STANDARD on orignial UCCA EWT and Revisited Implicit EWT., including training times, the number of best epoch and total epochs.

*A Falta de Pan, Buenas Son Tortas:**
The Efficacy of Predicted UPOS Tags for Low Resource UD Parsing

Mark Anderson
Universidade da Coruña, CITIC
Department of CS & IT
m.anderson@udc

Mathieu Dehouck
LaTTiCe, CNRS, ENS
Université Sorbonne Nouvelle
mathieu.dehouck@udc.es

Carlos Gómez-Rodríguez
Universidade da Coruña, CITIC
Department of CS & IT
carlos.gomez@udc.es

Abstract

We evaluate the efficacy of predicted UPOS tags as input features for dependency parsers in lower resource settings to evaluate how treebank size affects the impact tagging accuracy has on parsing performance. We do this for real low resource universal dependency treebanks, artificially low resource data with varying treebank sizes, and for very small treebanks with varying amounts of augmented data. We find that predicted UPOS tags are somewhat helpful for low resource treebanks, especially when fewer fully-annotated trees are available. We also find that this positive impact diminishes as the amount of data increases.

1 Introduction

Low resource parsing is a long-standing problem in NLP and many techniques have been introduced to tackle it (Hwa et al., 2005; Zeman and Resnik, 2008; Ganchev et al., 2009; McDonald et al., 2011; Agić et al., 2016). For an extensive review and comparison of techniques see Vania et al. (2019). Here we focus on the utility of part-of-speech (POS) tags as features for low resource dependency parsers.

POS tags are a common feature for dependency parsers. Tiedemann (2015) highlighted the unrealistic performance of low resource parsers when using gold POS tags in a simulated low resource setting. The performance difference was stark despite using fairly accurate taggers, which is not a reasonable assumption for low resource languages. Tagging performance in low resource settings is still very weak even when utilising cross-lingual techniques and other forms of weak supervision (Kann et al., 2020). Even when more annotated data is available, it isn't clear how useful POS tags are for neural dependency parsers, especially when utilising character embeddings (Ballesteros et al., 2015; de Lhoneux et al., 2017). Work investigating the utility of POS tags typically observe a small increase in performance or no impact when used as features for neural dependency parsers. Smith et al. (2018) found that universal POS (UPOS) tags offer a marginal improvement for their transition based parser for multi-lingual universal dependency (UD) parsing. Dozat et al. (2017) also observed an improvement in parsing performance for graph-based parsers when the predicted UPOS tags came from sufficiently accurate taggers.

Zhang et al. (2020) only found POS tags to be useful for English and Chinese when utilising them as an auxiliary task in a multi-task system. Anderson and Gómez-Rodríguez (2020) found that a prohibitively high accuracy was needed to utilise predicted UPOS tags for both graph- and transition-based parsers for UD parsing. They also obtained results that suggested smaller treebanks might be able to directly utilise less accurate UPOS tags. We evaluate this further by analysing the impact of tagging accuracy on UD parsing in low resource contexts, with regards to the amount of data available to train taggers and parsers.

2 Methodology

We performed three experiments. The first is an evaluation of predicted tags as features for biaffine parsers for real low resource treebanks. It also includes parsers trained with UPOS tagging as an auxiliary task similar to the experiments in Zhang et al. (2020). The second experiment evaluates the impact of different tagging accuracies on different dataset sizes using artificial low resource treebanks by sampling from high resource treebanks. The last experiment utilises a data augmentation technique to investigate the efficacy of predicted UPOS tags for very small treebanks (~20 sentences) when

**Lacking yeast-proven bread, a flatbread alternative will suffice*, i.e. if you can't get more fully-annotated dependency trees, annotating UPOS tags can still be helpful.

Proceedings of the 17th International Conference on Parsing Technologies (IWPT 2021), pages 78–83
Bangkok, Thailand (online), August 6, 2021. ©2021 Association for Computational Linguistics

augmented with varying amounts of data.

Low resource data We take all UD v2.6 treebanks (Zeman et al., 2020) with less than 750 sentences in both its training dataset and development dataset. We cluster these treebanks into two groups, very low with less than 50 sentences and low with less than 750. The very low resource treebanks consist of Buryat BDT (bxr), Kazakh KTB (kk), Kurmanji MG (kmr), Livvi KKPP (olo), and Upper Sorbian UFAL (hsb). The low resource set is made up of Belarusian HSE (be), Galician TreeGal (gl), Lithuanian HSE (lt), Marathi UFAL (mr), Old Russian RNC (orv), Tamil TTB (ta), and Welsh CCG (cy). We combined the training and development data (when available) to then split them 80|20. The statistics for the resulting splits are shown in Table 1. We use the original test data for analysis.

Artificial low resource data We use Indonesian GSD (id), Irish IDT (ga), Japanese GSD (ja), and Wolof WTB (wo) to create artificially low resource treebanks. We take a sample of 100, 232, and 541 sentences from the training and development data. These are then split 80|20 for training and development data. We do this three times for each treebank size so we have multiple samples to verify our results. We use the original test data for analysis.

Augmented data For the experiment using augmented data we use a subset of the smallest treebanks, namely Kazakh, Kurmanji, and Upper Sorbian. We then generate data using the subtree swapping data augmentation technique of Dehouck and Gómez-Rodríguez (2020). We generate 10, 25, and 50 trees for each and we then split them 80|20. We do this three times for each number of generated trees. We use the original test data for analysis.

Subtree swapping We gather all the sub-trees with a continuous span which has a `NOUN`, `VERB`, `ADJ` or `PROPN` as its root node. Other UPOS tags are not used due the likelihood of generating ungrammatical structures. With regards to the permitted relation of the root nodes, we consider all core arguments, all nominal dependents, and most non-core dependents (excluding `discourse`, `expl` and `dislocated`). Then given a tree, we swap one of its sub-trees with one from another tree given that their respective roots have the same UPOS tag, dependency relation and morphological features and given that the sub-trees are lexically different. We repeat the process a second time using a third tree. During this second swap, we do not allow the previously swapped subtree to be altered again so as to avoid redundancy. For a more detailed description of this process see Dehouck and Gómez-Rodríguez (2020). We create all possible trees generated from the three original trees given the constraints described above, repeat this for each triplet of trees, and finally take a sample from this set of augmented data.

	Train		Dev	
	sents	tokens	sents	tokens
bxr	15	120	4	33
kk	24	395	7	134
kmr	16	192	4	50
olo	15	114	4	30
hsb	18	310	5	150
be	307	6,441	77	1,449
gl	480	12,317	120	3,119
lt	166	3,444	42	852
mr	335	2,751	84	686
orv	256	8,253	64	1903
ta	383	6,082	96	1,254
cy	491	10,719	123	2,616

Table 1: Number of trees in training and development splits as used for low resource UD treebanks.

Controlling UPOS accuracy For each treebank size and split for the artificial low resource treebanks we trained taggers with varying accuracies (60, 66, 72, 78, 85, 89). We allowed a small window around the accuracy for each bin of ± 0.25. Following a similar methodology to Anderson and Gómez-Rodríguez (2020) to obtain taggers with varying accuracies, we train the taggers as normal and save models when they reach a desired accuracy. We then train parsers using predicted tags from each of the taggers and use predicted tags at inference. For the data augmentation experiment we used accuracy bins of 41, 44, 48, and 51.

Network details Both the taggers and parsers use word embeddings and character embeddings. The parsers use UPOS tag embeddings except for the MTL setup and the baseline models without tags. The embeddings are randomly initialised. The parsers consist of the embedding layer followed by BiLSTM layers and then a biaffine mechanism (Dozat and Manning, 2017). The taggers are similar but with an MLP following the BiLSTMs instead. We ran a hyperparameter search evaluated on the development data of Irish and Wolof. This resulted in 3 BiLSTM layers with 200 nodes, 100 dimensions for each embedding type with 100 dimensions for input to the character LSTM. The arc

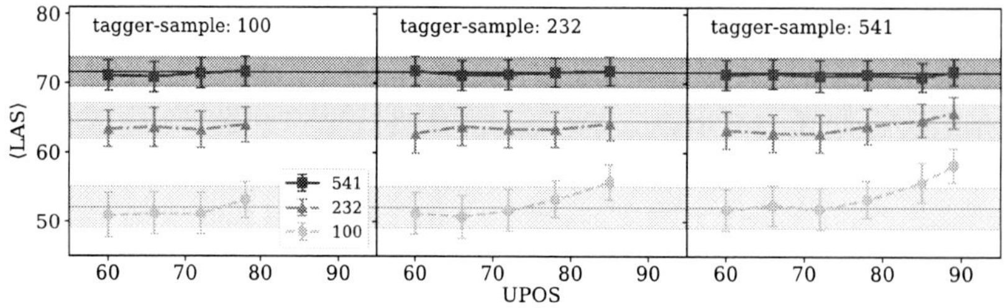

Figure 1: Impact of tagging accuracy for varying amounts of data for both taggers and parsers using artificial low resource data. The standard error of UPOS accuracy is not shown as it is very small ($< 0.1\%$ relative error for all bins). Horizontal lines and corresponding shaded area show the mean parsing performance and the standard error for the baseline parsers trained without UPOS tags.

MLP of the biaffine structure has 100 dimensions, whereas the relation MLP has 50.

3 Results and discussion

Table 2 shows the real low resource treebank results. Table 2a shows the results for the treebanks with less than 50 sentences. The performance is very low across the board so it is difficult to draw any substantial conclusions, however, using gold tags has a large impact over not using any, almost doubling the labeled attachment score. Also, using predicted tags does result in an increase on average, but Kazakh and Kurmanji lose almost a point. Further those two treebanks and also Buryat have reasonable gains when using the multi-task framework. The average multi-task score is strongly affected by the large drop seen for Upper Sorbian, which also suffers with respect to tagging accuracy when using the multi-task setup.

Table 2b shows the results for the low resource treebanks with less than 750 sentences. On average using predicted UPOS tags achieves a sizeable increase over not using any tags of about 1.2, despite the average tagging accuracy only being 85.89%. This suggests that in a lower resource setting the tagging accuracy doesn't have to be quite so high as is needed for high resource settings. Increases in performance are seen for all treebanks except Lithuanian and Tamil. While Lithuanian has the second lowest tagging score, Tamil has a fairly high score, so it seems that the accuracy needed is somewhat language-specific or at the very least data-dependent. The difference for the treebanks in Table 2b is almost 9 points higher for using gold tags. The multi-task performance is about 1.4 points less than using predicted tags on average. However, Lithuanian and Tamil obtain an increase in performance using the multi-task system in comparison to using predicted tags.

Figure 1 shows the average LAS performance for the parsers trained with the artificial low resource data. When the parsers have sufficient data, using UPOS tags doesn't offer any improvement in performance. For the parsers trained with 232 samples, there is a slight upward trend when using tags predicted from taggers trained with 541 samples. The improvement increases with respect to UPOS tag accuracy and exceeds the performance of the parsers trained with no UPOS tags. The most no-

	UPOS		LAS			
	Single	Multi	None	Pred	Gold	Multi
bxr	48.72	48.34	10.45	12.36	20.31	14.41
kk	53.37	52.14	22.48	21.63	36.66	23.50
kmr	50.56	53.73	19.16	18.31	35.54	21.58
olo	37.84	37.37	9.74	10.89	17.54	7.59
hsb	53.44	47.28	18.36	20.03	41.88	14.66
avg	48.79	47.77	16.04	16.64	30.39	16.25

(a) Very low resource: less than 50 sentences.

	UPOS		LAS			
	Single	Multi	None	Pred	Gold	Multi
be	92.82	87.29	61.82	64.91	68.87	62.28
gl	93.54	88.56	70.60	72.73	79.06	70.54
lt	79.25	71.51	37.17	35.94	48.30	38.96
mr	80.58	76.46	57.04	58.74	64.32	56.31
orv	87.77	81.60	49.53	51.34	60.24	50.33
ta	86.88	79.23	63.85	62.75	74.31	63.15
cy	91.77	86.41	72.10	72.93	80.71	73.00
avg	85.89	77.77	55.24	56.52	64.13	55.10

(b) Low resource: less than 750 sentences.

Table 2: Performance of different low resource parsers: using predicted UPOS tags as features (Pred), multi-task system where tagging is an auxiliary task to parsing (Multi), using gold UPOS tags as features (Gold), and without using UPOS tags as features (None). The accuracies of the predicted UPOS tags (Single) and that of the multi-task (Multi) are also reported.

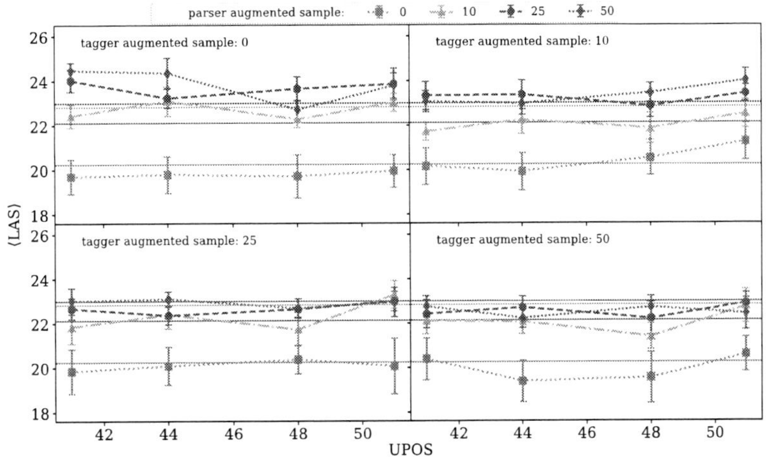

Figure 2: Impact of tagging accuracy for varying amounts of data for both taggers and parsers using augmented data (0, 10, 25, and 50 augmented trees) on top of the original gold data. The standard error of UPOS accuracy is not shown as it is very small ($< 0.1\%$ relative error for all bins). Horizontal lines show the mean parsing performance for the baseline parsers trained without UPOS tags (standard error not shown due to too much overlap between augmented data sample sizes).

ticeable improvement is for the parsers trained with only 100 samples. The impact of UPOS accuracy is clearer as the tagger sample size increases as higher accuracies can be obtained. The best performance is with the most accurate taggers (89%).

This is a potentially useful finding if annotators have little time, as annotating UPOS tags is much less time-sensitive and can help improve parsing performance if a limited number of tree-annotated sentences are available. However, taking parsers using only 100 fully-annotated training sentences as a baseline, the average performance using 232 parsed sentences without UPOS tags is over 10 points higher, whereas the increase gained training the taggers with 541 tagged sentences is only 5 points. So it is clear that if time permits such that annotators can increase the number of tree annotations, they will likely prove to be more useful. But UPOS tags could be obtained using projection methods and/or active learning techniques (Baldridge and Palmer, 2009; Das and Petrov, 2011; Garrette et al., 2013; Täckström et al., 2013). Also, multilingual projection methods could be used, but they typically generate trees as well as POS tags (Agić et al., 2016; Johannsen et al., 2016).

Figure 2 shows the impact of predicted UPOS accuracy when using data generated with subtree swapping augmentation. The first result worth noting is that the augmented data increases performance in this very low resource context. Across the board, the best performing parsers using augmented data outperform the parsers trained only on gold data by 3-6 points which corroborates the findings in previous work. However, it appears that there is a limit to how much augmented data helps as the performance of the parsers which use 25 and 50 augmented instances is similar.

It also appears that this upper limit is even lower for training taggers with the best performance coming when using predicted tags from taggers utilising only 10 augmented samples or none at all. Using more invariably hurts performance no matter what accuracy the taggers obtained, as can be seen in the subplots showing the performance for parsers trained with predicted tags from taggers using 25 and 50 augmented samples. Also, there is no clear trend showing the impact of UPOS accuracy in this very low resource context.

4 Conclusion

We have presented results which suggest that lower accuracy taggers can still be beneficial when little data is available for training parsers, but this requires a high ratio of UPOS annotated data to tree annotated data. Experiments using artificial low resource treebanks highlight that this utility diminishes if the number of samples reaches a fairly small amount. We have also shown that very small treebanks can benefit from augmented data and utilise predicted UPOS tags even when they come from taggers with very low accuracy. Our experiments haven't considered pretrained multilingual language models (LMs) which could potentially offset the small benefits of using POS tags. It would be interesting to develop this analysis further by testing whether the implicit information encoded in these LMs are more useful than explicit but potentially erroneous POS tag information. Finally, as one reviewer highlighted, the set of POS tags in the UD framework might just not be sufficiently informative in this setting. While this might be true, the greater contributing factor is surely the low accuracy of the taggers.

Acknowledgments

This work has received funding from the European Research Council (ERC), under the European Union's Horizon 2020 research and innovation programme (FASTPARSE, grant agreement No 714150), from ERDF/MICINN-AEI (ANSWER-ASAP, TIN2017-85160-C2-1-R), from Xunta de Galicia (ED431C 2020/11), and from Centro de Investigación de Galicia "CITIC", funded by Xunta de Galicia and the European Union (ERDF - Galicia 2014-2020 Program), by grant ED431G 2019/01.

References

Željko Agić, Anders Johannsen, Barbara Plank, Héctor Martínez Alonso, Natalie Schluter, and Anders Søgaard. 2016. Multilingual projection for parsing truly low-resource languages. *Transactions of the Association for Computational Linguistics*, 4:301–312.

Mark Anderson and Carlos Gómez-Rodríguez. 2020. On the frailty of universal POS tags for neural UD parsers. In *Proceeding of the 24th SIGNLL Conference on Computational Natural Language Learning*, Online.

Jason Baldridge and Alexis Palmer. 2009. How well does active learning actually work? time-based evaluation of cost-reduction strategies for language documentation. In *Proceedings of the 2009 Conference on Empirical Methods in Natural Language Processing*, pages 296–305.

Miguel Ballesteros, Chris Dyer, and Noah A Smith. 2015. Improved transition-based parsing by modeling characters instead of words with LSTMs. *arXiv preprint arXiv:1508.00657*.

Dipanjan Das and Slav Petrov. 2011. Unsupervised part-of-speech tagging with bilingual graph-based projections. In *Proceedings of the 49th Annual Meeting of the Association for Computational Linguistics: Human Language Technologies*, pages 600–609.

Miryam de Lhoneux, Yan Shao, Ali Basirat, Eliyahu Kiperwasser, Sara Stymne, Yoav Goldberg, and Joakim Nivre. 2017. From raw text to universal dependencies-look, no tags! In *Proceedings of the CoNLL 2017 Shared Task: Multilingual Parsing from Raw Text to Universal Dependencies*, pages 207–217.

Mathieu Dehouck and Carlos Gómez-Rodríguez. 2020. Data augmentation via subtree swapping for dependency parsing of low-resource languages. In *to appear in the 28th International Conference on Computational Linguistics (COLING 2020)*, online.

Timothy Dozat and Christopher D Manning. 2017. Deep biaffine attention for neural dependency parsing. *Proceedings of the 5th International Conference on Learning Representations*.

Timothy Dozat, Peng Qi, and Christopher D Manning. 2017. Stanford's graph-based neural dependency parser at the CoNLL 2017 shared task. In *Proceedings of the CoNLL 2017 Shared Task: Multilingual Parsing from Raw Text to Universal Dependencies*, pages 20–30.

Kuzman Ganchev, Jennifer Gillenwater, and Ben Taskar. 2009. Dependency grammar induction via bitext projection constraints. In *Proceedings of the Joint Conference of the 47th Annual Meeting of the ACL and the 4th International Joint Conference on Natural Language Processing of the AFNLP*, pages 369–377.

Dan Garrette, Jason Mielens, and Jason Baldridge. 2013. Real-world semi-supervised learning of pos-taggers for low-resource languages. In *Proceedings of the 51st Annual Meeting of the Association for Computational Linguistics (Volume 1: Long Papers)*, pages 583–592.

Rebecca Hwa, Philip Resnik, Amy Weinberg, Clara Cabezas, and Okan Kolak. 2005. Bootstrapping parsers via syntactic projection across parallel texts. *Natural Language Engineering*, 11(3):311–325.

Anders Johannsen, Željko Agić, and Anders Søgaard. 2016. Joint part-of-speech and dependency projection from multiple sources. In *Proceedings of the 54th Annual Meeting of the Association for Computational Linguistics (Volume 2: Short Papers)*, pages 561–566.

Katharina Kann, Ophélie Lacroix, and Anders Søgaard. 2020. Weakly supervised POS taggers perform poorly on truly low-resource languages. *Proceedings of the AAAI Conference on Artificial Intelligence*, 34(5):8066–8073.

Ryan McDonald, Slav Petrov, and Keith Hall. 2011. Multi-source transfer of delexicalized dependency parsers. In *Proceedings of the 2011 Conference on Empirical Methods in Natural Language Processing*, pages 62–72.

Aaron Smith, Miryam de Lhoneux, Sara Stymne, and Joakim Nivre. 2018. An investigation of the interactions between pre-trained word embeddings, character models and POS tags in dependency parsing. *arXiv preprint arXiv:1808.09060*.

Oscar Täckström, Dipanjan Das, Slav Petrov, Ryan McDonald, and Joakim Nivre. 2013. Token and type constraints for cross-lingual part-of-speech tagging. *Transactions of the Association for Computational Linguistics*, 1:1–12.

Jörg Tiedemann. 2015. Cross-lingual dependency parsing with universal dependencies and predicted pos labels. *Proceedings of the Third International Conference on Dependency Linguistics (Depling 2015)*, pages 340–349.

Clara Vania, Yova Kementchedjhieva, Anders Søgaard, and Adam Lopez. 2019. A systematic comparison of methods for low-resource dependency parsing on genuinely low-resource languages. In *Proceedings of the 2019 Conference on Empirical Methods in Natural Language Processing and the 9th International Joint Conference on Natural Language Processing (EMNLP-IJCNLP)*, pages 1105–1116.

Daniel Zeman, Joakim Nivre, et al. 2020. Universal Dependencies 2.6. LINDAT/CLARIAH-CZ digital library at the Institute of Formal and Applied Linguistics (ÚFAL), Faculty of Mathematics and Physics, Charles University.

Daniel Zeman and Philip Resnik. 2008. Cross-language parser adaptation between related languages. In *Proceedings of the IJCNLP-08 Workshop on NLP for Less Privileged Languages*, pages 35–42.

Yu Zhang, Zhenghua Li, Houquan Zhou, and Min Zhang. 2020. Is POS tagging necessary or even helpful for neural dependency parsing? *arXiv preprint arXiv:2003.03204*.

Multilingual Dependency Parsing for Low-Resource African Languages: Case Studies on Bambara, Wolof, and Yoruba

Cheikh Bamba Dione
University of Bergen / Sydnesplassen 7, 5007 Bergen
dione.bamba@uib.no

Abstract

This paper describes a methodology for syntactic knowledge transfer between high-resource languages to extremely low-resource languages. The methodology consists in leveraging multilingual BERT self-attention model pretrained on large datasets to develop a multilingual multi-task model that can predict Universal Dependencies annotations for three African low-resource languages. The UD annotations include universal part-of-speech, morphological features, lemmas, and dependency trees. In our experiments, we used multilingual word embeddings and a total of 11 Universal Dependencies treebanks drawn from three high-resource languages (English, French, Norwegian) and three low-resource languages (Bambara, Wolof and Yoruba). We developed various models to test specific language combinations involving contemporary contact languages or genetically related languages. The results of the experiments show that multilingual models that involve high-resource languages and low-resource languages with contemporary contact between each other can provide better results than combinations that only include unrelated languages. As far as genetic relationships are concerned, we could not draw any conclusion regarding the impact of language combinations involving the selected low-resource languages, namely Wolof and Yoruba.

1 Introduction

Treebanks constitute valuable resources for many Natural Language Processing (NLP) applications. They can be used as training and testing data for a wide range of NLP algorithms as well as to induce robust parsing models (Manning and Schütze, 1999). Unfortunately, developing treebanks in form of large annotated data used to be a very time- and resource-consuming task. As a consequence, annotated data (in particular the type required for parsing) is lacking for most languages, especially for low-resource languages.

To help speed up the treebank development process, various supervised learning techniques (Weiss et al., 2015; Straka and Straková, 2017; Straka, 2018) have been developed in recent past. The supervised monolingual approach based on syntactically annotated corpora has long been the most common approach to parsing. However, thanks to recent developments involving feature representation methods and neural network models, the idea of combining treebanks for multilingual UD parsing has become a more common approach. Multilingual modeling constitute a very attractive approach to circumvent the low-resource limitation, as it allows one to create models that can parse the language's text quite accurately in the absence of annotated data for the given language. This occurs through syntactic knowledge transfer across multiple languages. The multilingual approach has yielded encouraging results for both low-resource (Guo et al., 2015) as well as for high-resource (Ammar et al., 2016) languages.

The idea of combining treebanks for transfer learning was first introduced in Vilares et al. (2016), which train bilingual parsers on pairs of UD treebanks, showing similar improvements. Subsequently, in the CoNLL 2018 Shared Task, Smith et al. (2018) presented the Uppsala system, which follows the same idea. That system combines treebanks of one language or closely related languages together over 82 treebanks and parses all UD annotations in a multi-task pipeline architecture for a total of 34 models. This approach provides two main advantages. First, it reduces the number of models required to parse each language. Second, it can provide results that are no worse than training on each treebank individually, and in especially low-resource cases, significantly improved. In the same spirit, Kondratyuk and Straka (2019) con-

Proceedings of the 17th International Conference on Parsing Technologies (IWPT 2021), pages 84–92
Bangkok, Thailand (online), August 6, 2021.

ducted a multilingual multi-task parsing study for 124 Universal Dependencies (Nivre et al., 2016) treebanks across 75 languages, and demonstrated that a multilingual model can yield better results than monolingual models for different languages.

In this paper, we use the approach described by Kondratyuk and Straka (2019) to produce a cross-lingual transfer model that can predict UD annotations for three extremely low-resource African languages by using knowledge from medium- to high-resource European languages. The UD annotations include universal part-of-speech (UPOS), morphological features (FEATS), lemmas (LEM), and dependency trees (DEPS).

The structure of the paper is as follows. Section 2 first provides a brief description of the low-resource languages used as case studies in this research work. Section 3 provides an overview of our approach, and section 4 details the neural network-based parsing model. Section 5 describes a series of experiments conducted on high-resource and low-resource languages to verify our assumptions. Section 6 presents an analysis of our results. Section 7 concludes the discussion.

2 Languages used as our case studies

The low-resource languages selected for this study are Bambara, Wolof and Yoruba. Bambara is spoken in Mali, Ivory Coast, Upper Guinea, in the western part of Burkina Faso and in eastern Senegal. Wolof is spoken in Senegal, in The Gambia and in Mauritania. Yoruba is spoken in West Africa, most prominently in Southwestern Nigeria.

These West African languages belong to two different subgroups of the larger Niger-Congo family of languages. Bambara is part of the Mande subgroup, while Wolof and Yoruba are Atlantic-Congo languages. While the ultimate genetic unity of Atlantic-Congo languages is widely accepted, the internal cladistic structure is not well established (Dixon et al., 1997), especially with respect to the connection of the Mande languages, which has never been demonstrated. For instance, the Mande languages lack the noun-class morphology that is the primary identifying feature of the Atlantic-Congo languages. Wolof and Yoruba are genetically related to each other, but not closely related to Bambara. Interestingly, while Wolof does not have much language contact with Yoruba (if any), it actually may share areal features with Bambara, since their common geographic location allowed for a long history of contact between these two languages.

Bambara is highly isolating and has a very strict word order: Subject AUX / TAM (tense-aspect-mood markers) Object Verb (Creissels, 2007). It is a tone language, with two tones: high and low. Wolof is an agglutinative language with an SVO and head-modifier basic word order (Robert, 2018). Unlike many other languages of the Niger-Congo family, Wolof is not a tonal language. Yoruba is a highly isolating language and the sentence structure follows Subject Verb Object (Adelani et al., 2021). In addition, Yoruba is a tonal language with three tones: low, middle (optional) and high.

The three low-resource languages are fairly well documented. For Bambara, there exist hundreds of linguistic papers and few recent reference grammars published about that language (Dumestre, 2003; Vydrin, 2019). There are also some dictionaries available, including the Bamadaba online dictionary[1] and a 15k print dictionary (Dumestre, 2011). Likewise, Wolof has several descriptive grammars and few dictionaries, e.g. the French-Wolof print dictionaries (Diouf, 2003; Cisse, 1998) and an online Wolof dictionary.[2] Similarly, for Yoruba, there are many literary texts, newspapers, religious kinds of literature, and some blogs in the language. There are also academic papers, print dictionaries, e.g. the Yoruba-English dictionary by Odoje (2019), and online dictionary[3] published in the language.

Although these languages are well-documented, until very recently, they did not or still do not really have a Universal Dependency corpus. Bambara has a 12k tokens UD treebank (Aplonova and Tyers, 2017). Yoruba has a 8k tokens UD treebank.[4] For these two languages, only test set data are available (no training data), making them good candidates for zero-shot learning. Wolof has a 44k tokens UD treebank (Dione, 2019) that consists of a training, a development and a test set. As these numbers show, the sizes of these UD treebanks are extremely small. This alone does not make them low-resource languages, but they are poorly equipped with regard to NLP tools as well. For instance, while Yoruba and Bambara are documented with huge written corpora,[5] these are mostly not achieved for research

[1] http://cormand.huma-num.fr/bamadaba.html

[2] https://www.lexilogos.com/wolof_dictionnaire.htm

[3] https://www.lexilogos.com/english/yoruba_dictionary.htm

[4] `https://universaldependencies.org/treebanks/yo_ytb/index.html`

[5] For instance, Bambara has an 11 million corpus of writ-

and NLP purposes. For Wolof, resources and tools have only very recently begun to emerge, including a finite-state morphological analyzer (Dione, 2012), a small treebank (Dione, 2014) and computational grammar/parser (Dione, 2020) based on the Lexical-Functional Grammar (LFG) framework (Bresnan, 2001; Dalrymple, 2001). We chose to focus on three languages due to the availability of UD treebanks for these languages, even though for two of these languages only test data are available.

3 Approach

Our approach consists in developing several multilingual parsing models using different language combinations of medium- to high-resource languages (English, French, Norwegian) and low-resource languages (Bambara, Wolof, Yoruba) that have had some contemporary language contact. The languages used for training the models have been selected with the assumption that contemporary contact languages, at least in certain scenarios, share (structural) similarities with the low-resource languages in question. English has a long history of contact with Yoruba, leading to a variety of morphosyntactic changes and lexical borrowings in the latter language (Ogundepo, 2015). Our expectation is that the match rate between English and Yoruba should be somewhat high. Likewise, we expect to see similar patterns between French and the Bambara and Wolof languages with which it has had a long contact. For instance, through French influence there exists two varieties of Wolof: urban Wolof, used especially in cities, and Kajoor Wolof (also referred to as 'pure' Wolof), which is spoken mostly in rural areas (Ngom, 2003). In addition, we include Norwegian as a control language with no direct contact or genetic relation with any of the selected low-resource languages.

Recents studies, including (Lim et al., 2018) conducted similar experiments to explore the impact of using contemporary contact languages or genetically related languages (e.g. Finnish) in multilingual parsing scenarios involving low-resource languages (e.g. North Saami and Komi-Zyrian). Their findings showed that specific language combinations of contemporary contact languages or genetically related languages may enable improved dependency parsing.

ten texts: `http://cormand.huma-num.fr/index.html`

4 Method

Parsing approaches can be divided into two main types: transition-based (Nivre, 2004) vs. graph-based (McDonald et al., 2005) models. In transition-based dependency parsing, the parser starts in an initial configuration and, at each step, asks a guide to choose between one of several transitions (actions) into new configurations. The parser stops if it reaches a terminal configuration, returning the dependency tree associated with that configuration. In relatively recent past, transition-based dependency parsing using neural networks has enjoyed increasing success, starting with the fast and accurate parser presented by Chen and Manning (2014). Subsequently, many other neural network transition-based models have been developed using different techniques, including stack LSTM (Dyer et al., 2015), biaffine attention (Dozat and Manning, 2016), and recurrent neural networks (Kuncoro et al., 2017).

The basic idea of graph-based dependency parsing is to produce a dependency tree in form of a directed graph with some constraints by first generating all possible candidate dependency graphs for a given sentence. Subsequently, each tree is scored and the parser picks the one with the highest score. During training, the parser induces a model for scoring an entire dependency graph for a sentence. During parsing, it finds the highest scoring dependency graph, given the induced model. More recently, graph-based approaches have shown to outperform transition-based approaches when it comes to UD-type corpora, notably with the neural graph-based parser of Dozat et al. (2017), who won the CoNLL 2017 UD Shared Task by a wide margin.

In this study, we chose UDify (Kondratyuk and Straka, 2019), a neural model which uses the graph-based biaffine attention parser developed by Dozat and Manning (2016); Dozat et al. (2017). UDify is a single multitask model that produces UD annotations (UPOS, FEATS, LEM, DEPS) jointly. In a first step, UDify generates contextual embeddings for any input sentence by using the cased[6] pre-trained multilingual BERT network (Devlin et al., 2018), a self-attention (Vaswani et al., 2017) network of 12 layers, 12 attention heads per layer, and hidden dimensions of 768. The BERT model was trained by predicting randomly masked input

[6]https://github.com/google-research/bert/blob/master/multilingual.md

words on the entirety of the top 104 languages with the largest Wikipedias, including two African languages: Swahili and Yoruba. BERT segments texts into (unnormalized) sub-word units using the wordpiece tokenizer (Wu et al., 2016). In a second step, the UDify model integrates task-specific layer-wise attention similar to ELMo (Peters et al., 2018). Finally, each UD task is decoded simultaneously using softmax classifiers. During training, various regularization techniques are applied to the BERT network, including input masking, increased dropout, weight freezing, discriminative fine-tuning, and layer dropout.

5 Experiments

We conducted a series of experiments on Bambara, Wolof and Yoruba. For these languages, we tested different language combinations for the cross-lingual model.

The dataset used in our experiments are provided in Table 1. This consist of a total of 11 UD v2.3 treebanks drawn from three medium- to high-resource languages (English, French, Norwegian) and three low-resource languages (Bambara, Wolof, Yoruba). Table 1 shows the selected treebank(s) used for each language. For English and French, we used several treebanks. For Norwegian, we only selected the Bokmål treebank, leaving out the Nynorsk one in order to reduce computational expenses.[7]

The percentage distribution of the individual languages in our training corpus is shown in Figure 1. As can be seen, ca. 95,5% of the data used in our experiments are drawn from the high-resource languages' treebanks.

Table 2 displays information about the vocabulary of the combined treebanks, including the total number of tokens, BERT wordpieces, UPOS, XPOS, UD Features, lemmas and dependency relations (Deps). To tackle the issue related to a ballooning vocabulary, we use BERT's wordpiece tokenizer directly for all inputs.

For multilingual training with UDify, the 11 UD treebanks are concatenated into a single treebank, similar to McDonald et al. (2011); Kondratyuk and Straka (2019). This single treebank consists of a training, a development and a test set. For each epoch, sample input sentences were drawn randomly from the training data and fed to the neural network in form of mixed batches, i.e. each batch may contain sentences from any language or treebank. The sentences are shuffled and bundled into batches of 8 sentences each. We employ a base learning rate of $1e^{-3}$ that is kept constant until we unfreeze BERT in the second epoch. We then linearly warm up the learning rate for the next 1,000 batches. Next, we apply inverse square root learning rate decay for the remaining epochs. Following Kondratyuk and Straka (2019), training was done for a total of 80 epochs (ca. 3 days) on a single GPU (RTX 2080). The hyperparameters used for our model are given in Table 3.

6 Results and analysis

For comparison, we show in Table 4 UDify scores obtained for Bambara and Yoruba as reported by Kondratyuk and Straka (2019). These scores are obtained by evaluating UDify on 124 treebanks with the official CoNLL 2018 Shared Task evaluation script.

The experiments reported by Kondratyuk and Straka (2019) did not include Wolof, since no UD treebank was available for that language at that time. For this purpose, we trained a customized monolingual UDify model on the Wolof training data and applied that model on the Wolof test set. The results of this monolingual training are shown in Table 5. These scores are used as a baseline to compare the impact of the monolingual and the multilingual models.

For multilingual dependency parsing, we run several experiments in which we keep the settings described in section 5, excluding only one language at a time. In an initial experiment, we used all the treebanks presented in section 5 for which training data are available. This consists of a total of 9 out of the 11 UD treebanks.[8] Then, the created multilingual model has been used to parse the test data of the selected low-resource languages. The results are given in Table 6 and indicate an improvement of ca. 5% and 4,38% in terms of UAS and LAS, respectively for Bambara. Likewise, a significant increase of 11,37% and 12,34% in UAS and LAS, respectively, has been observed for Yoruba. Also, for Wolof, we compared the scores displayed in Table 5 (i.e. monolingual model) with those presented in Table 6 (i.e. multilingual model). Such a comparison reveals that parsing quality increases by 2.23%

[7]In fact, we have tried to include the Nynorsk treebank as well, but this led to quite computationally expensive costs when training the multilingual model.

[8]Recall that the Bambara and Yoruba treebanks contain only test data.

Language	Treebank Name	# Tokens	# Sentences
Bambara	Bambara CRB	13.82k	1.03k
English	UD_English_EWT	254.83k	16.62k
	UD_English-GUM	80.18k	4.40k
	UD_English-ParTUT	49.62k	2.09k
French	UD_French-FTB	556.06k	18.53k
	UD_French-ParTUT	27.67k	1.02k
	UD_French-Sequoia	68.64k	3.10k
	UD_French-Spoken	34.98k	2.79k
Norwegian	UD_Norwegian-Bokmaal	310.22k	20.04k
Wolof	Wolof WTB	42.83k	2.11k
Yoruba	Yoruba YTB	2.67k	0.10k

Table 1: UD treebanks used in the experiments

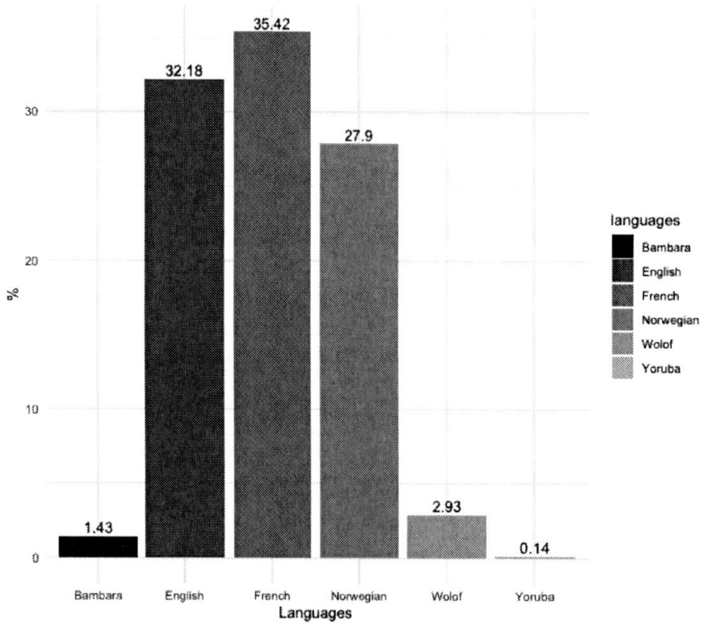

Figure 1

TOKEN	VOCAB SIZE
Word Form	178,214
BERT Wordpieces	119,547
UPOS	17
XPOS	206
UFeats	1300
Lemmas (tags)	3,834
Deps	86

Table 2: Vocabulary sizes of words and tags over the 11 UD v2.3 treebanks

hyperparameter	
Dependency tag dimension	256
Dependency arc dimension	768
Optimizer	Adam
β_1, β_2	0.9, 0.99
Weight decay	0.01
Label Smoothing	0.03
Dropout	0.5
BERT dropout	0.2
Mask probability	0.2
Layer dropout	0.1
Batch size	8
Epochs	80
Base learning rate	$1e^{-3}$
BERT learning rate	$5e{-5}$
Learning rate warmup steps	1000
Gradient clipping	5.0

Table 3: Our model hyperparameters.

Treebank	UPOS	FEATS	LEM	UAS	LAS
Bambara	30.86	57.96	20.42	30.28	8.60
Yoruba	50.86	78.32	85.56	37.62	19.09

Table 4: The full test results on Bambara and Yoruba when training UDify on the **124** UD treebanks (Kondratyuk and Straka, 2019).

Language	UPOS	FEATS	LEM	UAS	LAS
Wolof	87.90	69.97	87.86	73.48	63.84

Table 5: The test results on Wolof when training UDify on monolingual Wolof data.

and 3.19% in terms of UAS and LAS, respectively. This provides a good indication that a transfer learning approach in a multilingual dependency parsing context seems to have positive impact (at least for Wolof), outperforming the monolingual model.

To assess the impact of some language combinations, we run several additional experiments where we keep the same setting and language data as described above, excluding only one language at a time. Accordingly, we run a similar experiment as the previous one, excluding the English treebanks from the training. The results of this experiment are displayed in Table 7. For Bambara, excluding the English treebank did cause a very slight drop of parsing quality. In contrast, for Yoruba, we could observe a substantial decrease of 3.8% and 2.9% UAS and LAS, respectively. Interestingly, for Wolof, this actually led to a slight improvement in UAS (0.43%) and LAS (0.83%).

In the same way, we run a similar experiment where we exclude only the French treebanks to assess their impact on the overal results for the selected low-resource African languages. The results of this experiment are shown in Table 8. For Bambara, this caused a decrease of 3.78% and 2.85% UAS and LAS, respectively. Parsing quality also drops for Wolof in terms of UAS (-2.28%) and LAS (-1.74%). For Yoruba, no real impact on parsing quality could be observed.

Treebank	UPOS	FEATS	LEM	UAS	LAS
Bambara	36.29	45.18	23.89	34.28	12.98
Wolof	89.64	75.06	89.95	75.71	67.03
Yoruba	60.73	60.43	93.59	48.99	31.43

Table 6: The full test results on Bambara, Wolof and Yoruba when training UDify on the **9** UD treebanks (the Bambara and Yoruba treebanks are only used for testing).

Treebank	UPOS	FEATS	LEM	UAS	LAS
Bambara	35.05	44.32	23.84	33.83	12.94
Wolof	90.49	77.25	90.82	76.14	67.86
Yoruba	59.19	60.18	93.21	45.19	28.53

Table 7: The full test results on Bambara, Wolof and Yoruba when training UDify on the **8** UD treebanks, **excluding the English treebanks**.

Treebank	UPOS	FEATS	LEM	UAS	LAS
Bambara	33.89	42.86	23.66	30.50	10.13
Wolof	89.61	82.33	91.53	73.43	65.29
Yoruba	60.32	55.78	91.19	48.69	30.87

Table 8: The full test results on Bambara, Wolof and Yoruba when training UDify on the **7** UD treebanks, **excluding the French treebanks**.

As mentioned above, we used Norwegian as a control language to verify our assumption with re-

Treebank	UPOS	FEATS	LEM	UAS	LAS
Bambara	36.02	45.08	23.87	33.94	11.94
Wolof	90.76	83.55	90.91	75.35	67.25
Yoruba	59.94	58.68	88.30	48.09	30.87

Table 9: The full test results on Bambara, Wolof and Yoruba when training UDify on the **10** UD treebanks, **excluding the Norwegian treebank**.

Treebank	UPOS	FEATS	LEM	UAS	LAS
Bambara	29.44	69.08	13.36	30.91	11.21
Wolof	23.02	45.78	65.95	27.51	10.15
Yoruba	67.44	59.26	78.39	52.74	33.80

Table 10: The full test results on Bambara, Wolof and Yoruba when training UDify on the **10** UD treebanks, **excluding the Wolof training treebank**.

spect to the impact of using genetic or geographical relation. Norwegian is selected, as it is a language with no direct contact or genetic relation with any of the studied low-resource languages. To verify our assumption, we run an additional experiment where we removed the Norwegian data from the training, keeping the remaining 10 UD treebanks as before. The results of this experiment are provided in Table 9. This operation does not seem to have a substantial impact on parsing quality for any of the three low-resource languages. For instance, for both Bambara and Yoruba, a slight drop in UAS and LAS could be observe, but the decrease is less than 1% in all these cases. For Wolof, even a slight improvement could be observed of ca. 0.22% in LAS only (compared with -0.36% drop in UAS).

In a final experiment, we wanted to test the impact of not using the Wolof data during training. Thus, we trained a model using the 10 treebanks, excluding the Wolof UD training set and applied the model to the three test sets of the studied low-resource languages (this means that we evaluated Wolof for zero-shot learning). The results of this experiment are given in Table 10. Interestingly, for Bambara, this operation caused a decrease of parsing quality of 3.37% UAS and 1.77% LAS. For Wolof, as expected, we noted parsing accuracy dropped drastically by 48.2% UAS and 56.88% LAS. This large drop in parsing result can be explained by the fact that the Wolof test set is relatively large (e.g. compared to the test sets for Bambara and Yoruba). Surprisingly, for Yoruba, removing the Wolof data in the training had a positive impact. Parsing quality for Yoruba increased by ca. 3.75% UAS and 2.37% LAS. At first glance, this seems to contradict our expectation that genetically related languages may enable improved dependency parsing, at least for our case study. But a crucial question to consider is whether the genetic relationship between these two languages is just a classification issue and that, from the language characteristics, these two languages are not so closely related as the classification would suggest. Based on our data and experiments, we could not draw any conclusion as to whether the obtained results emerge from an issue related to the data used or to the language classification or to something else. This might need further investigation.

7 Conclusion

In this paper, we have presented a multilingual approach to parsing that is effective for languages with few resources and no syntactically annotated corpora available for training. We have shown that specific language combinations involving contemporary contact languages can provide better results than combinations that only include unrelated languages. We should note, however, that for Wolof and Yoruba, which are supposed to be genetically related languages, we rather observed a decrease of parsing results from the Yoruba side when using the Wolof training data. It remains a question for further study whether this decrease observed here are actually attributable to a lack of real genetic relationship between the language or to the lack of (large) training data for Yoruba.

References

David Ifeoluwa Adelani, Jade Abbott, Graham Neubig, Daniel D'souza, Julia Kreutzer, Constantine Lignos, Chester Palen-Michel, Happy Buzaaba, Shruti Rijhwani, Sebastian Ruder, et al. 2021. Masakhaner: Named entity recognition for african languages. *arXiv preprint arXiv:2103.11811*.

Waleed Ammar, George Mulcaire, Miguel Ballesteros, Chris Dyer, and Noah A. Smith. 2016. Many languages, one parser. *Transactions of the Association for Computational Linguistics*, 4:431–444.

Ekaterina Aplonova and Francis M. Tyers. 2017. Towards a dependency-annotated treebank for Bambara. In *Proceedings of the 16th International Workshop on Treebanks and Linguistic Theories*, pages 138–145, Prague, Czech Republic.

Joan Bresnan. 2001. *Lexical-Functional Syntax*. Blackwell, Oxford.

Danqi Chen and Christopher Manning. 2014. A fast and accurate dependency parser using neural networks. In *Proceedings of the 2014 Conference on Empirical Methods in Natural Language Processing (EMNLP)*, pages 740–750, Doha, Qatar. Association for Computational Linguistics.

Mamadou Cisse. 1998. *Dictionnaire wolof-français*. Editions Karthala, 75013 Paris.

Denis Creissels. 2007. A sketch of bambara argument structure. In *Workshop on Grammar and Processing of Verbal Arguments. Leipzig*, pages 20–21.

Mary Dalrymple. 2001. *Lexical-Functional Grammar (Syntax and Semantics, Volume 34) (Syntax and Semantics)*. Academic Press.

Jacob Devlin, Ming-Wei Chang, Kenton Lee, and Kristina Toutanova. 2018. Bert: Pre-training of deep bidirectional transformers for language understanding. *arXiv preprint arXiv:1810.04805*.

Cheikh Bamba Dione. 2019. Developing universal dependencies for wolof. In *Proceedings of the Third Workshop on Universal Dependencies (UDW, SyntaxFest 2019)*, pages 12–23, Paris, France. Association for Computational Linguistics.

Cheikh M. Bamba Dione. 2012. A Morphological Analyzer For Wolof Using Finite-State Techniques. In *Proceedings of the Eigth International Conference on Language Resources and Evaluation (LREC'12)*, Istanbul, Turkey. ELRA.

Cheikh M Bamba Dione. 2014. LFG parse disambiguation for Wolof. *Journal of Language Modelling*, 2(1):105–165.

Cheikh M. Bamba Dione. 2020. Implementation and evaluation of an LFG-based parser for Wolof. In *Proceedings of the 12th Language Resources and Evaluation Conference*, pages 5128–5136, Marseille, France. European Language Resources Association.

Jean-Léopold Diouf. 2003. *Dictionnaire wolof-français et français-wolof*. Editions Karthala, Paris.

Robert MW Dixon, Robert MW Dixon, and Dixon Robert Malcolm Ward. 1997. *The rise and fall of languages*. Cambridge University Press.

Timothy Dozat and Christopher D. Manning. 2016. Deep biaffine attention for neural dependency parsing. *CoRR*, abs/1611.01734.

Timothy Dozat, Peng Qi, and Christopher D. Manning. 2017. Stanford's graph-based neural dependency parser at the CoNLL 2017 shared task. In *Proceedings of the CoNLL 2017 Shared Task: Multilingual Parsing from Raw Text to Universal Dependencies*, pages 20–30, Vancouver, Canada. Association for Computational Linguistics.

Gérard Dumestre. 2003. *Grammaire fondamentale du bambara*. KARTHALA Editions.

Gérard Dumestre. 2011. *Dictionnaire bambara-français, suivi d'un index abrégé français-bambara*. KARTHALA Editions.

Chris Dyer, Miguel Ballesteros, Wang Ling, Austin Matthews, and Noah A. Smith. 2015. Transition-based dependency parsing with stack long short-term memory. In *Proceedings of the 53rd Annual Meeting of the Association for Computational Linguistics and the 7th International Joint Conference on Natural Language Processing (Volume 1: Long Papers)*, pages 334–343, Beijing, China. Association for Computational Linguistics.

Jiang Guo, Wanxiang Che, David Yarowsky, Haifeng Wang, and Ting Liu. 2015. Cross-lingual dependency parsing based on distributed representations. In *Proceedings of the 53rd Annual Meeting of the Association for Computational Linguistics and the 7th International Joint Conference on Natural Language Processing (Volume 1: Long Papers)*, pages 1234–1244, Beijing, China. Association for Computational Linguistics.

Dan Kondratyuk and Milan Straka. 2019. 75 Languages, 1 Model: Parsing Universal Dependencies Universally. In *Proceedings of the 2019 Conference on Empirical Methods in Natural Language Processing and the 9th International Joint Conference on Natural Language Processing (EMNLP-IJCNLP)*, pages 2779–2795, Hong Kong, China. Association for Computational Linguistics.

Adhiguna Kuncoro, Miguel Ballesteros, Lingpeng Kong, Chris Dyer, Graham Neubig, and Noah A. Smith. 2017. What do recurrent neural network grammars learn about syntax? In *Proceedings of the 15th Conference of the European Chapter of the Association for Computational Linguistics: Volume 1, Long Papers*, pages 1249–1258, Valencia, Spain. Association for Computational Linguistics.

KyungTae Lim, Niko Partanen, and Thierry Poibeau. 2018. Multilingual dependency parsing for low-resource languages: Case studies on north saami and Komi-Zyrian. In *Proceedings of the Eleventh International Conference on Language Resources and Evaluation (LREC 2018)*, Miyazaki, Japan. European Language Resources Association (ELRA).

Christopher D Manning and Hinrich Schütze. 1999. *Foundations of Statistical Natural Language Processing*. MIT Press, Cambridge, MA.

Ryan McDonald, Fernando Pereira, Kiril Ribarov, and Jan Hajič. 2005. Non-projective dependency parsing using spanning tree algorithms. In *Proceedings of Human Language Technology Conference and Conference on Empirical Methods in Natural Language Processing*, pages 523–530, Vancouver, British Columbia, Canada. Association for Computational Linguistics.

Ryan McDonald, Slav Petrov, and Keith Hall. 2011. Multi-source transfer of delexicalized dependency parsers. In *Proceedings of the 2011 Conference on Empirical Methods in Natural Language Processing*, pages 62–72, Edinburgh, Scotland, UK. Association for Computational Linguistics.

Fallou Ngom. 2003. The social status of arabic, french, and english in the senegalese speech community. *Language Variation and Change*, 15(3):351.

Joakim Nivre. 2004. Incrementality in deterministic dependency parsing. In *Proceedings of the Workshop on Incremental Parsing: Bringing Engineering and Cognition Together*, pages 50–57, Barcelona, Spain. Association for Computational Linguistics.

Joakim Nivre, Marie-Catherine de Marneffe, Filip Ginter, Yoav Goldberg, Jan Hajic, Christopher D. Manning, Ryan McDonald, Slav Petrov, Sampo Pyysalo, Natalia Silveira, Reut Tsarfaty, and Daniel Zeman. 2016. Universal Dependencies v1: A Multilingual Treebank Collection. In *Proceedings of the Tenth International Conference on Language Resources and Evaluation (LREC 2016)*, Paris, France. European Language Resources Association (ELRA).

Clement Odoje. 2019. *Yoruba-English/ English-Yoruba Dictionary & Phrasebook* . Hippocrene Books.

Abimbola O Ogundepo. 2015. Contrastive study of english and yoruba morphological systems–implications for nigerian teachers and learners of english. *International Journal of English Language and Linguistics Research*, 3(4):1–8.

Matthew E Peters, Mark Neumann, Mohit Iyyer, Matt Gardner, Christopher Clark, Kenton Lee, and Luke Zettlemoyer. 2018. Deep contextualized word representations. *arXiv preprint arXiv:1802.05365*.

Stéphane Robert. 2018. Wolof: a grammatical sketch. In Friederike Lüpke, editor, *The Oxford guide to the Atlantic languages of West Afric*. Oxford University Press.

Aaron Smith, Bernd Bohnet, Miryam de Lhoneux, Joakim Nivre, Yan Shao, and Sara Stymne. 2018. 82 treebanks, 34 models: Universal Dependency parsing with multi-treebank models. In *Proceedings of the CoNLL 2018 Shared Task: Multilingual Parsing from Raw Text to Universal Dependencies*, pages 113–123, Brussels, Belgium. Association for Computational Linguistics.

Milan Straka. 2018. UDPipe 2.0 prototype at CoNLL 2018 UD shared task. In *Proceedings of the CoNLL 2018 Shared Task: Multilingual Parsing from Raw Text to Universal Dependencies*, pages 197–207, Brussels, Belgium. Association for Computational Linguistics.

Milan Straka and Jana Straková. 2017. Tokenizing, pos tagging, lemmatizing and parsing ud 2.0 with udpipe. In *Proceedings of the CoNLL 2017 Shared Task: Multilingual Parsing from Raw Text to Universal Dependencies*, pages 88–99, Vancouver, Canada. Association for Computational Linguistics.

Ashish Vaswani, Noam Shazeer, Niki Parmar, Jakob Uszkoreit, Llion Jones, Aidan N. Gomez, Lukasz Kaiser, and Illia Polosukhin. 2017. Attention is all you need.

David Vilares, Carlos Gómez-Rodríguez, and Miguel A. Alonso. 2016. One model, two languages: training bilingual parsers with harmonized treebanks. In *Proceedings of the 54th Annual Meeting of the Association for Computational Linguistics (Volume 2: Short Papers)*, pages 425–431, Berlin, Germany. Association for Computational Linguistics.

Valentin Vydrin. 2019. *Cours de grammaire bambara*. Inalco presses.

David Weiss, Chris Alberti, Michael Collins, and Slav Petrov. 2015. Structured training for neural network transition-based parsing. *arXiv preprint arXiv:1506.06158*.

Yonghui Wu, Mike Schuster, Zhifeng Chen, Quoc V. Le, Mohammad Norouzi, Wolfgang Macherey, Maxim Krikun, Yuan Cao, Qin Gao, Klaus Macherey, Jeff Klingner, Apurva Shah, Melvin Johnson, Xiaobing Liu, Lukasz Kaiser, Stephan Gouws, Yoshikiyo Kato, Taku Kudo, Hideto Kazawa, Keith Stevens, George Kurian, Nishant Patil, Wei Wang, Cliff Young, Jason Smith, Jason Riesa, Alex Rudnick, Oriol Vinyals, Greg Corrado, Macduff Hughes, and Jeffrey Dean. 2016. Google's neural machine translation system: Bridging the gap between human and machine translation. *CoRR*, abs/1609.08144.

Bidirectional Domain Adaptation Using Weighted Multi-Task Learning

Daniel Dakota
Uppsala University
ddakota@lingfil.uu.se

Zeeshan Ali Sayyed
Indiana University
zasayyed@iu.edu

Sandra Kübler
Indiana University
skuebler@indiana.edu

Abstract

Domain adaption in syntactic parsing is still a significant challenge. We address the issue of data imbalance between the in-domain and out-of-domain treebank typically used for the problem. We define domain adaptation as a Multi-task learning (MTL) problem, which allows us to train two parsers, one for each domain. Our results show that the MTL approach is beneficial for the smaller treebank. For the larger treebank, we need to use loss weighting in order to avoid a decrease in performance below the single task. In order to determine to what degree the data imbalance between two domains and the domain differences affect results, we also carry out an experiment with two imbalanced in-domain treebanks and show that loss weighting also improves performance in an in-domain setting. Given loss weighting in MTL, we can improve results for *both* parsers.

1 Introduction

Domain adaption in syntactic parsing is still a significant challenge. While recent work has shown steady improvements, we have not necessarily achieved proportionally better results as expected with neural models (Fried et al., 2019). One simple reason can be attributed to the fact that we have severe limitations in terms of existing data, data sizes, and the imbalance between the two treebanks typically present in domain adaptation settings.

Multi-task learning (MTL; Caruana, 1997) allows for joint learning, which can help facilitate cross information sharing between tasks. This has proven particularly beneficial for tasks that have large data imbalances, with the smaller data tasks benefiting substantially more (Johansson, 2013; Benton et al., 2017; Ruder et al., 2019), and should thus also be useful in domain adaptation.

We define domain adaptation as an MTL problem where the two tasks correspond to training on two treebanks from different domains. Note that in this setting, we do not have a primary and a secondary task, but instead we can interpret both tasks as primary.

One of the inherent difficulties we face in cross-domain parsing are large discrepancies in the size of the treebanks. This creates a default training scenario of imbalance across the domains that should benefit the smaller domain, but it may inversely impact the larger domain, resulting in a degradation in performance due to negative transfer in a multi-task learning model, compared to their single task (STL) baselines. We investigate here whether it is possible to control the negative impact of the smaller domain on the larger one, and how the imbalance factor impacts this balance. This means that in all cases, we evaluate on *both* domains.

More specifically, we investigate the following questions:

1. How does the MTL parser handle different levels of data imbalance? This assumes that in a domain adaptation setting, normally a small in-domain treebank is combined with a large out-of-domain treebank.

2. How effective is loss weighting in addressing the data imbalance? Can we optimize both MTL tasks given the data imbalance?

3. Is it more important to address the data imbalance or the differences between domains for successful domain adaptation?

2 Related Work

2.1 MTL in Parsing

MTL inherently allows for the joint learning of tasks. Learning related tasks, such as POS tagging and dependency parsing, has been shown to be beneficial (Bohnet and Nivre, 2012; Zhang and Weiss,

Proceedings of the 17th International Conference on Parsing Technologies (IWPT 2021), pages 93–105
Bangkok, Thailand (online), August 6, 2021.

2016). A practical assumption is that there is shared information that can be beneficial, particularly if the tasks are closely related.

Neural networks have increased the ability and ease by which models can exploit information sharing. Much recent parsing research has examined the impact of parameter sharing across treebanks and languages (Ammar et al., 2016; Kitaev et al., 2019), though often not explicitly within an MTL setup, where different treebanks/languages are treated as multiple tasks. Soft sharing of parameters has proven effective on treebanks of the same annotation style in lower resource settings (Duong et al., 2015) as well as for multiple treebanks of the same language when hard sharing all other parameters (Stymne et al., 2018). However, sharing too many parameters between unrelated languages has been shown not to be beneficial (de Lhoneux et al., 2018).

More explicit MTL settings with treebanks representing different individual tasks have proven successful in array of settings across languages and architectures (Guo et al., 2016; Johansson and Adesam, 2020; Kankanampati et al., 2020).

2.2 MTL in Domain Adaptation

Much recent work has resulted in significant gains in domain adaptation across several languages via the direct or indirect transfer of parameters and embeddings for languages such as Chinese (Li et al., 2019, 2020), English (Joshi et al., 2018; Fried et al., 2019), Finnish (Virtanen et al., 2019), and French (Martin et al., 2020).

More explicit MTL work by Søgaard and Goldberg (2016) found that lower level tasks are best kept at lower layers, as the shared representations benefit from the sequence of information learned, with the approach demonstrating success in domain adaption for chunking for English. Using hyperlinks as a form of weak supervision was used by Søgaard (2017) to improve several NLP tasks both in-domain and out-of-domain, including chunking, for both English and Quechua. Peng and Dredze (2017) use an MTL setting to leverage Chinese word segmentation and NER across two domains, news and social media. They share lower levels but retain domain specific projection layers with task specific models. Results outperform disjoint adaption methods and suffer less from diminishing returns as training sizes increase.

2.3 MTL Performance

While MTL has resulted in improvements across many tasks and settings, an STL can still outperform an MTL model (Martínez Alonso and Plank, 2017; Bingel and Søgaard, 2017; Liang et al., 2020). Reasons for such a lack of increase or even degradation in performance for a certain task may be found in negative transfer as tasks may learn at different rates, and a single task may dominate the learning (Lee et al., 2016), or poor scheduling may result in catastrophic forgetting (French, 1999).

Another key fact is the correct choice of tasks. However, it is not clear how to best select tasks. Auxiliary task label distributions (Martínez Alonso and Plank, 2017), the learning curve of the primary task (Bingel and Søgaard, 2017), the difficulty of the auxiliary task (Liebel and Körner, 2018), the relationship between the data of the tasks in terms of size (Luong et al., 2015; Benton et al., 2017; Augenstein and Søgaard, 2017; Schulz et al., 2018) and properties (Wu et al., 2020), among other findings[1], have all shown to influence the effectiveness of MTL.

One way to mitigate the negative transfer is to give different weights to the tasks, helping to maximize the contributions for the more pertinent tasks and lessen the impact of sub-optimal tasks (Lee et al., 2016, 2018). Such strategies have shown promise in computer vision, where optimal loss weights can allow an MTL model to improve over a corresponding STL when it would otherwise show a degradation in performance (Kendall et al., 2018).

Winata et al. (2018) weighted losses for language modeling and POS tagging in an MTL setting, finding a lower weight to language modeling yielded a reduction in perplexity in modeling code-switching between Chinese and English. A multi-task supervised pretraining adaption strategy using a hierarchical architecture that learns multiple tasks on a source domain before fine-tuning them on the target was implemented by Meftah et al. (2020). By using different weights for the different level tasks, starting with higher weights for lower tasks before incrementally increasing weights to higher level tasks during training, they achieve a noticeable error reduction in POS tagging, dependency parsing, and chunking.

Our experiments focus on improving parsing in a domain adaptation setting using MTL plus separate

[1] See (Søgaard and Goldberg, 2016; Guo et al., 2019; Schröder and Biemann, 2020) for more discussion.

		Train	Dev	Test
German	GSD	13 814	799	977
	tweeDe	1 000	150	151
Italian	ISDT	13 121	564	482
	TWITTIRÒ	1 000	144	142
	PoSTWITA	1 000	150	150
	ParTUT	1 000	150	150

Table 1: Treebank sizes (number of sentences).

loss weighting to improve both tasks.

3 Methodology

3.1 Treebanks

For our experiments, we focus on German and Italian, since both languages have smaller treebanks based on Twitter data, which will allow us to avoid domain differences in the smaller domain. We use treebanks annotated with Universal Dependencies V2.7 (Nivre et al., 2020). For German, we use GSD, which is based on news, reviews, and Wikipedia pages, and tweeDe (Rehbein et al., 2019) as the Twitter treebank. For Italian, we use ISDT and ParTUT, which consist of legal, news, and Wikipedia texts, plus TWITTIRÒ (Cignarella et al., 2019) and PoSTWITA (Sanguinetti et al., 2018) as the Twitter treebanks.

Table 1 shows the sizes of the treebanks used in our experiments. For tweeDe we used the first 1 000 sentences for train, and the following 150 and 151 sentences for dev and test respectively. In order to account for treebank size variations of the Twitter treebanks, we limit the maximal sizes of train and dev for TWITTIRÒ and PoSTWITA to the first 1 000 train sentences and 150 dev and test sentences respectively, but we do not reduce the GSD or ISDT treebanks. For the in-domain experiments in section 6, we also use the ParTUT treebank, since it covers domains similar to ISDT. We reduce the treebank size in the manner in which we reduce the Twitter treebanks.

3.2 Parser

We use the graph-based neural dependency parser by Dozat and Manning (2017) as our base parser and extend it to an MTL architecture using hard parameter sharing. Our MTL parser treats the parsing of each treebank as a separate MTL task, where the tasks share the BiLSTM layers which encode the input embeddings, which are calculated by concatenating all the different types of embeddings that are used. These BiLSTM encodings are then passed through a dimension-reducing Multi-layered Perceptrons (MLP) to strip away arc and relationship information deemed irrelevant for the task at hand. We implement two MLP schemes, one in which we share the MLP layers across tasks (shared-MLP; left part of Figure 1) and the other in which each task has its own MLP layers (unshared; right part of Figure 1). Finally, in order for the model to learn task specific information, we apply task-specific biaffine attention layers to the MLP output to produce scores for both arcs and labels. A more detailed description of the parser architecture can be found in Sayyed and Dakota (2021).

Hyperparameters	Value
Embedding Dimensions	300
POS Tag Embedding Dimension	100
Bert Mapping Dimenstion	100
Number of BERT Layers Used	4
Number of LSTM Layers	3
LSTM Hidden Layer Dimension	400
Optimizer	Adam
Patience	50
Batch Size	20k tokens
Learning Rate	2e-3

Table 2: Hyperparameter settings for MTL parser.

We modify the PyTorch (Paszke et al., 2019) implementation of the biaffine parser provided by Zhang et al. (2020)[2], to implement our MTL parser[3]. We retain many of the default hyperparameters used in the original base parser. Table 2 lists the parameters which we have changed. Word and POS embeddings are initialized randomly. For the BERT embeddings (Devlin et al., 2019), a scalar mixture of the last four layers of BERT is passed through a linear layer to produce BERT embeddings of the specified dimension.

3.3 Loss Weighting

We train the MTL parser by having a different objective function for each task, and we optimize for each task separately. We do this by randomly choosing a task from the given tasks and then randomly choosing a batch of sentences along with their annotations from that task before calculating the loss for that batch, backpropagating the errors, and updating all the model parameters (shared and

[2]https://github.com/yzhangcs/parser

[3]Our code is available from https://github.com/zeeshansayyed/multiparser

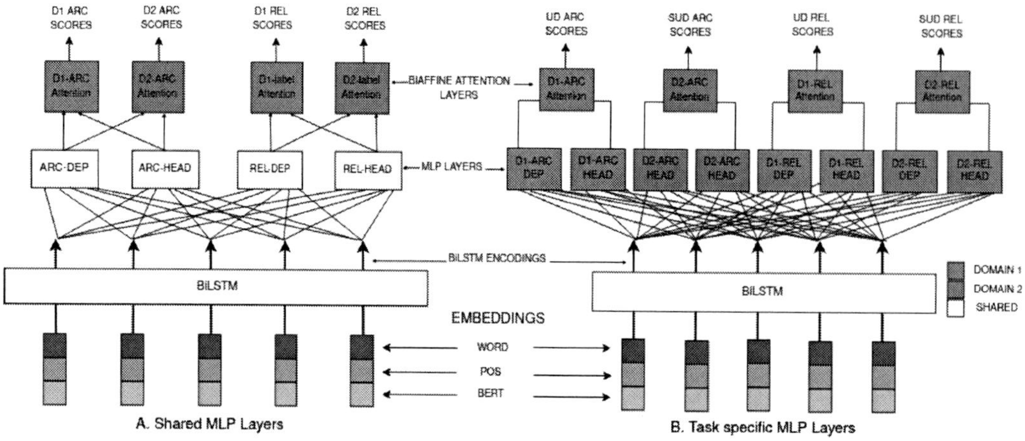

Figure 1: Multi-task model architecture.

unshared). In a given epoch, we chose sentences without replacement.

The task specific objective function is given by:

$$\mathcal{L}_t(X_t; \Theta) = \mathcal{L}_a(X_t; \Theta) + \mathcal{L}_l(X_t; \Theta) \quad (1)$$

where t is the task number, X_t represents the input batch for task t, Θ denotes all model parameters, $\mathcal{L}_a$ and $\mathcal{L}_l$ represent the cross entropy losses for arc and label scores in batch X_t respectively.

In the loss weighting experiments in section 5, in order to compensate for the varying difficulty of tasks, we weigh each objective function differently and then optimize for it, as follows:

$$\mathcal{L}_t(X_t; \Theta) = w_t \cdot (\mathcal{L}_a(X_t; \Theta) + \mathcal{L}_l(X_t; \Theta)) \quad (2)$$

where w_t is the weight for task t and $\sum w_t = 1$.

3.4 Experimental Setup

Our focus is on comparing the performance of the MTL parser against that of an STL baseline. This means that we need a better understanding of the interactions between treebank sizes, learning curves, and weighting. For this reason, we show learning curves comparing corresponding MTL and STL models or different MTL weight settings.

For the learning curves, we start with 1 000 sentences from each treebank and then double the training size for the large treebank until the max. size is reached, while the Twitter treebanks remain fixed.

We experiment with three different input embeddings: We train word and POS embeddings (using gold POS tags as input). We then use the word embeddings, POS embeddings, and the combination of word and POS embeddings plus BERT embeddings (Devlin et al., 2019). For the BERT embeddings, German and Italian language specific BERT embeddings are used[4].

We report the average LAS score over three seeds (10, 20, 30)[5] using the CoNLL 2018 shared task scorer (Zeman et al., 2018). All reported experiments are on the development set unless otherwise stated.

4 STL vs. MTL Learning Curves

Our first set of experiments concerns the question how different levels of size imbalance in the training data from the two domains affect an MTL parser.

Figure 2 presents learning curves comparing the German treebanks, Figures 3 and 4 compare the two Italian Twitter treebanks to ISDT. Across all settings, we see that using only word embeddings gives the lowest results, followed by word plus POS tag embeddings, with word plus POS tag plus BERT embeddings resulting in the highest LAS. $\mathcal{L}_t(X_t; \Theta) = w_t \cdot (\mathcal{L}_{a;t} + \mathcal{L}_{l;t})$

Also across all experiments, we see that sharing the MLP layers (in green) is slightly more beneficial to the smaller Twitter treebanks than having separate layers (in blue). The differences between the shared and unshared model are even smaller for

[4]`https://github.com/stefan-it/fine-tuned-berts-seq`

[5]For a small number of settings, one of the seeds produced results that were >30 points lower than for the other seeds. For those cases, we used seed 40 as a replacement.

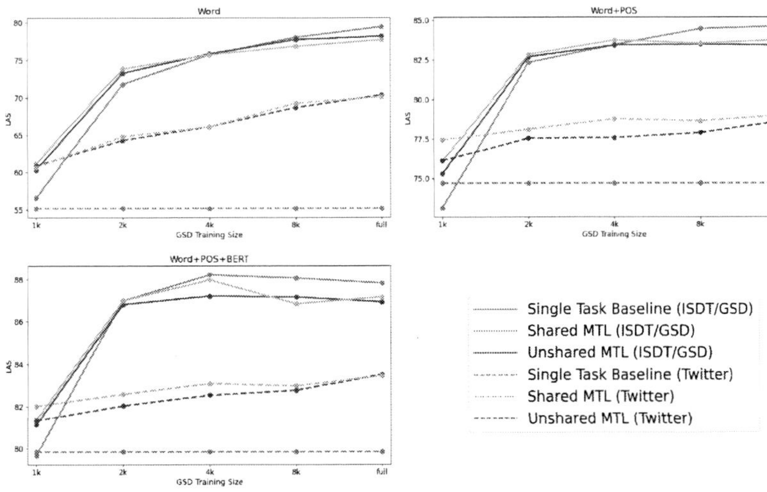

Figure 2: Results on German (GSD and tweeDe) when adding GSD training sentences (using word, word+POS, and word+POS+BERT embeddings respectively).

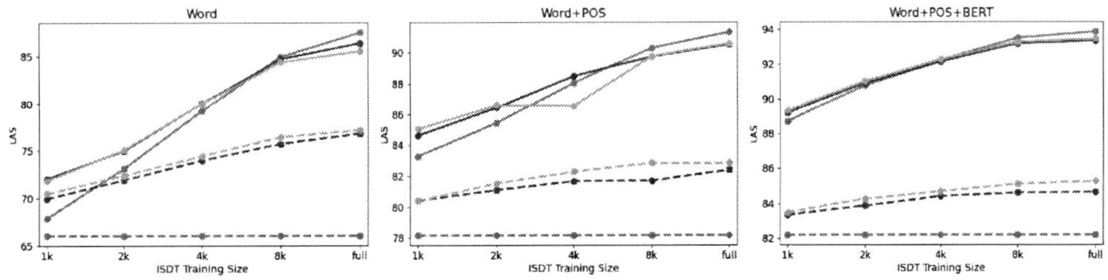

Figure 3: Results on Italian TWITTIRÒ when adding ISDT training sentences (word, word+POS, and word+POS+BERT embeddings). For legend, see Figure 2.

the large treebanks.

The two German treebanks have very similar performance at 1k while there is a considerable difference between the Italian trebanks, with the Twitter treebanks being more difficult to parse than ISDT.

When looking at the results on German in Figure 2, we see that in all settings, the MTL setup is beneficial for the tweeDe treebank, independent of the amount of out of domain training data. The same holds initially for the GSD treebank.

However, as more GSD data becomes available, the MTL setup starts to be detrimental for the GSD parser, and the results stay below the STL baseline. Additionally, the type of embeddings plays a factor in the overall improvement: While the curves flatten out quickly for word+POS and word+POS+BERT embeddings, the curve for word embeddings indicates that adding the full set still results in gains. It is also concerning that for the word+POS and word+POS+BERT embeddings, the results on GSD start decreasing after 4k GSD sentences. We attribute this to negative transfer, i.e., the MTL setting is more focused on finding an optimal solution between the non-Twitter and the Twitter task, resulting in a degradation in performance of the non-Twitter task from the equally prioritized Twitter signals. Note that while this makes sense from a MTL point of view, it is counter-intuitive from a domain adaptation perspective: For the GSD task, this means that adding more in-domain data results in lower in-domain performance.

The results for the Italian treebanks in Figures 3 and 4 exhibit similar, but not identical trends to the German experiments. One noticeable difference is that the ISDT improvements tend to be far more linear, where we only begin to see a flattening of the curve at the full training size. Another more interesting difference concerns the point where the STL on the large treebank (GSD or ISDT) improves

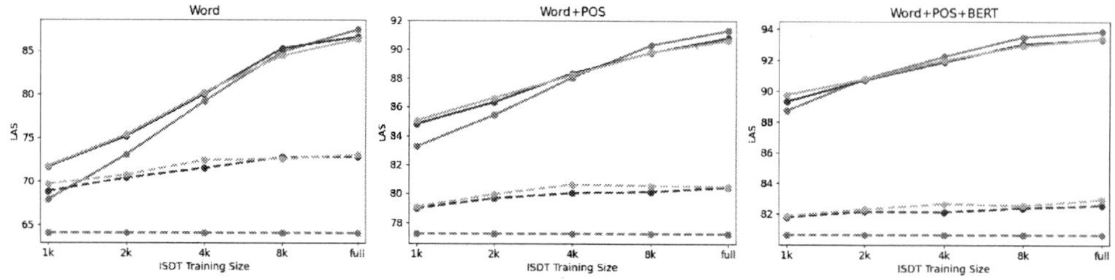

Figure 4: Results on Italian PoSTWITA when adding ISDT training sentences (word, word+POS, and word+POS+BERT embeddings). For legend, see Figure 2.

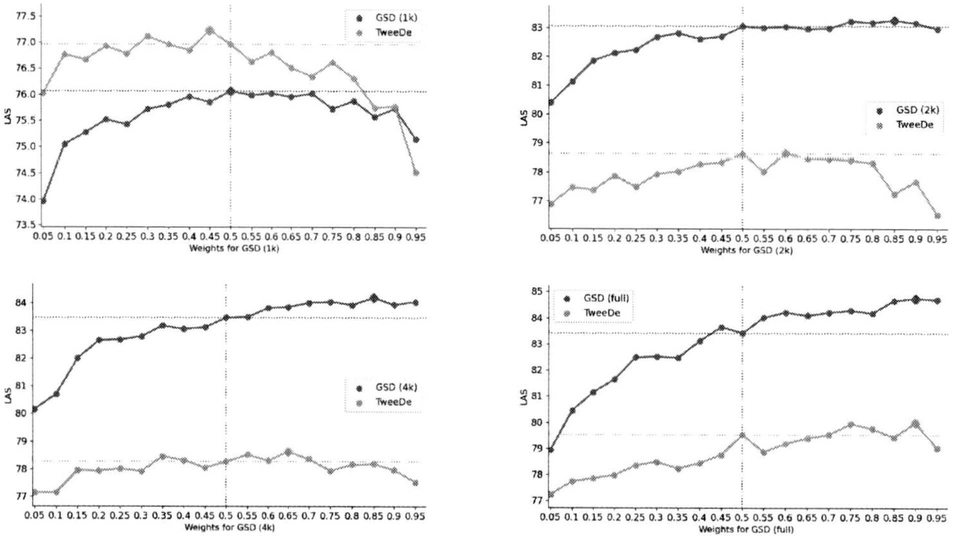

Figure 5: Effect of loss weighting in German; all experiments use 1k tweeDe and range from 1k, 2k (upper), 4k to all GSD data (lower) for training.

over the MTL model: For German, this happens systematically at 4k, for Italian, it ranges from 4-8k for TWITTIRÒ and 2-8k for PoSTWITA depending on the type of embeddings. We see that for word+POS+BERT, the STL is already on par with the MTL model at 2k, but the word embeddings model needs closer to 8k.

5 Loss Weighting

We now turn to the question of loss weighing, i.e., can we address the data imbalance problem if we assign higher weights to one or the other task in the loss function? Using loss weighting would give us a principled way of handling the data imbalance. For a description of the weighting scheme, see section 3.3. For the experiments in this section, all MTL tasks are learned using the shared MLP setting (as it performed better in most settings of section 4) and word+POS embeddings (as it performed better than word-only embeddings but does not require pretraining on external sources, such as BERT), and we vary the training size of the large treebank between 1k, 2k, 4k, and all available training data.

Figure 5 shows the results for the German treebanks, Figure 6 shows the combination of the Italian ISDT and TWITTIRÒ, and Figure 7 the combination of ISDT and PoSTWITA. Each graph shows the results for the two tasks per setting.

All experiments in section 4 are based on standard alternating loss for both tasks, i.e., the loss for each task is used as is, which is equivalent to having a weight of 1. For the experiments here, the X-axis denotes the weights applied to the large treebank task, ranging from 0 to 1. The corresponding weight applied to the second task is $1 - x$, i.e., it

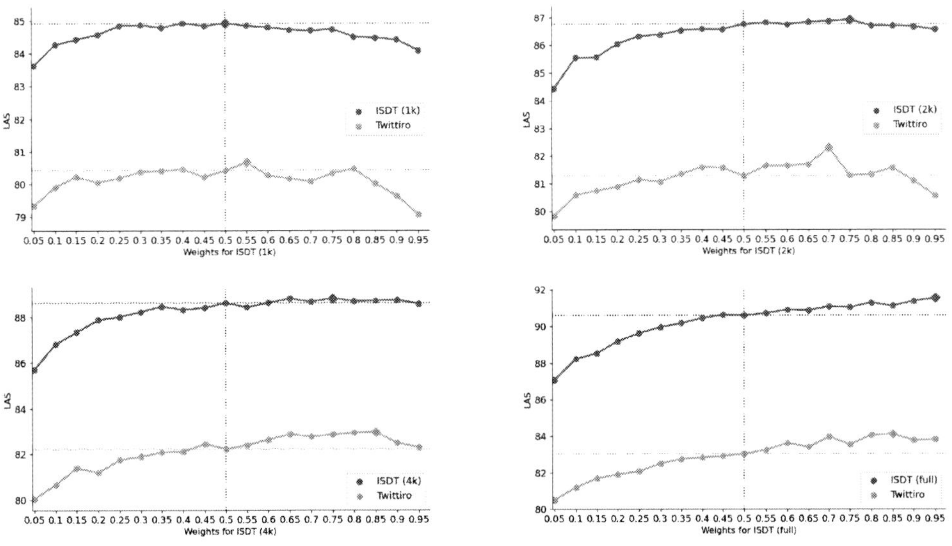

Figure 6: Effect of loss weighting in Italian; all experiments use 1k TWITTIRÒ and range from 1k, 2k (upper), 4k to all ISDT data (lower) for training.

decreases from 1 to 0. For each weight, we report the LAS for either task, blue denoting the large treebank and orange the Twitter treebank. The vertical dotted lines mark the 0.5 weight setting, where both tasks are weighted equally, and the horizontal dotted lines denote the performance of the MTL parser in this setting. The diamond markers in each line denote the best performance achieved by weighted MTL parser for that task.

Looking at the German results in Figure 5, we see that in the 1k setting, the optimal performance for GSD is reached when each task is assigned a weight of 0.5. For tweeDe, the optimal performance is reached in the same area, namely for a weight setting of 0.45:0.55 for GSD:tweeDe. In the 2k setting, even though the optimal performance shifts towards higher weights for the large treebank (0.85 for GSD and 0.4 for tweeDe), the actual increase in performance is minimal compared to the balanced weight setting. This trend continues as we add more data to GSD (for 4k and full settings): The optimal weights move closer to the maximal weight for the large treebank. This shows that as the treebank sizes become more imbalanced, the optimal performance is reached by applying a higher weight to the large treebank and consequently a lower weight to the small Twitter treebank.

It is also interesting to see that for the 1k setting, the tweeDe results surpass the GSD results. This suggests that the tweeDe data are syntactically easier than the GSD ones. We also see that the performance for tweeDe starts plateauing once it reaches the 0.5 weight setting for imbalanced scenarios (2k, 4k and full). Hence, for tweeDe, the performance gain in the optimal setting beyond 0.5 is smaller than for GSD. Moreover, while the MTL models using balanced weights (section 4) do not always improve over the STL baselines, weighted MTL improves in all settings and all tasks. For GSD, the highest gain over the STL occurs in the 1k setting. The more data we add, the smaller the improvement. For the full GSD set, the improvement is minimal.

The results for the two Italian experiments, in Figure 6 for the combination of ISDT and TWITTIRÒ, and in Figure 7 for the combination of ISDT and PoSTWITA, show similar trends with some differences. For both experiments, the Twitter task shows slightly concave curves for 1k and 2k respectively. Starting from 4k, we see an upward trend for ISDT as the weight for the large task increases. For German, this only occurs with the full GSD training set.

These results show that for smaller data sizes, i.e., when the two treebanks are closer to balanced, weighting does not matter that much: For most settings, the optimal results are close to a 0.5 weight. As the data imbalance increases, it becomes more important to slide the weights towards the larger task in order to avoid negative transfer.

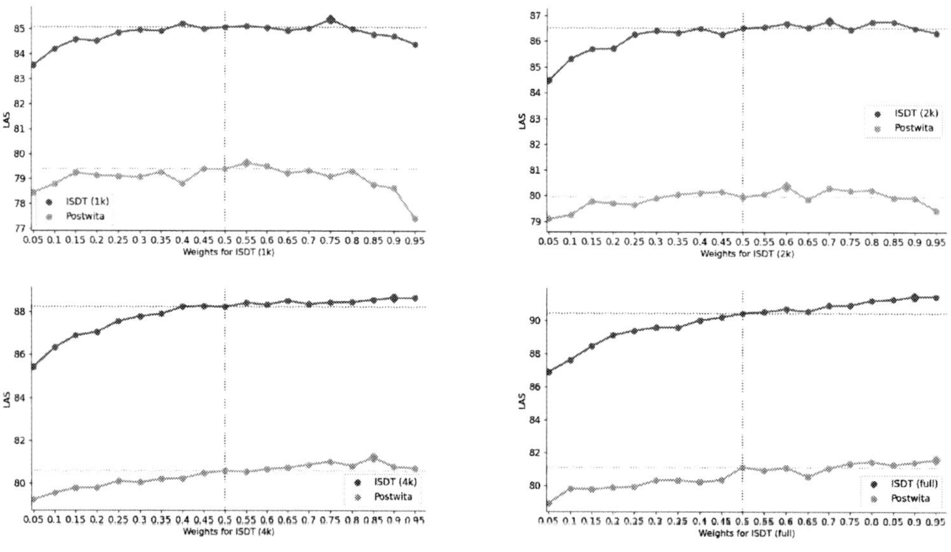

Figure 7: Effect of loss weighting in Italian; all experiments use 1k PoSTWITA and range from 1k, 2k (upper), 4k to all ISDT data (lower) for training.

The weighted MTL models allow us to use the maximum data for the larger treebank and even reach a slight gain in performance over the STL. The Twitter treebanks show even more improvement than in the standard MTL setup, suggesting that they benefit from a reduction of their own signal along with a more powerful signal from the large treebank.

Weighting the different losses is akin to having different learning rates for each task (i.e., treebank), impacting the contribution each has on the step sizes derived from the loss in finding an optimal solution (Sébastien et al., 2018). When the data sizes of the two domains are closer, the steps taken by each benefit each other. As the non-Twitter data increases however, the Twitter data have too much influence on the step sizes, resulting in a degradation on the non-Twitter treebank since standard MTL optimizes both equally. While MTL is thought to help overcome local optima that can occur in an STL (Bingel and Søgaard, 2017), in our case, we assume that the weights have a similar effect: They help both the non-Twitter and Twitter models overcome local optima encountered in a standard MTL setup.

6 Controlling Data Imbalance Vs. Domain Differences

So far, we have treated domain adaptation as a data imbalance problem. This is certainly a factor since we mostly use a large scale out-of-domain treebank to improve results in-domain. However, there are also genuine differences between the domains, and it is unclear to what degree they individually contribute to the difficulty. For this reason we conduct two additional experiments on Italian, in which we pair a larger treebank with its smaller counterpart from the same domain. In other words, we now focus on an in-domain comparison of a small and a large treebank. The more these results deviate from the previous results, the more influence the domain differences have on parser performance.

In the first experiment, we compare Twitter treebanks, i.e., we pair the smaller TWITTIRÒ treebank with the larger PoSTWITA treebank. In the second experiment, we compare the more general treebanks, i.e., we pair the smaller ParTUT treebank with the larger ISDT. For the Twitter in-domain experiments, we simply double the PoSTWITA data as we did with the ISDT reaching the full size (at about 5.3k sentences). For ISDT and ParTUT we follow the same methodology.

Figure 8 shows non-weighted MTL curves for Twitter and non-Twitter in-domain data sets respectively. The curves in both settings exhibit similar trends to the trends in Figure 3 in that the STL system begins to outperform the MTL system at the end of the curves, but that the small in-domain treebanks reach a very similar performance to their larger counterparts. This suggests that while do-

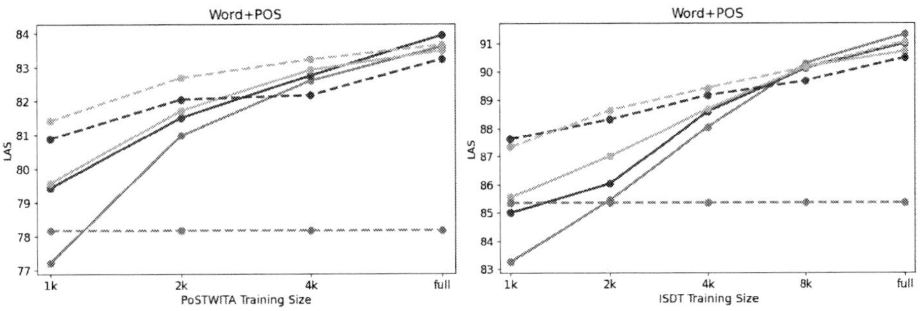

Figure 8: Results on Italian TWITTIRÒ when adding PoSTWITA training sentences on left and Italian ParTUT when adding ISDT on the right, both using word+POS.

	STL	MTL	weighted MTL	wMTL weights
PoSTWITA	83.60	83.46	**83.66**	0.65
TWITTIRÒ	78.17	83.65	**84.14**	0.35
ISDT	91.31	90.71	91.27	0.90
ParTUT	85.35	91.05	**91.34**	0.10

Table 3: LAS Results Word+POS for STL, shared MTL, and weighted shared MTL using the full data sets. ISDT paired with ParTUT.

main differences play a role in negative transfer, they appear to be less important than the data imbalance between treebanks, thus validating our decision to approach domain adaptation as an MTL task.

We conduct a single weighted experiment, using the best weights from Figures 5-7 and the best results reported in section 7. The results are shown in Table 3. We see a similar trend as in the out-of-domain experiments where the MTL setting shows a degradation for ISDT compared to its STL setting while ParTUT shows an increase at higher imbalances. For the Twitter treebanks, the differences are minimal. The weighted MTL increases the performance on ISDT over the MTL setting but does not quite match the STL setting, while the weighted MTL setting further increases the performance of the ParTUT treebank. The weighted MTL for PoSTWITA shows a slight increase over the STL and over the non-weighted MTL setting for TWITTIRÒ. Such findings suggest that even in-domain data imbalances can benefit from weighting, but may not benefit as much as treebank pairs in a domain adaptation setting.

7 Best Results

In Table 4, we show the highest LAS scores for the STL and shared MTL models, on dev and test using Word+POS embeddings. While the unweighted MTL settings result in noticeable lower LAS for both large treebanks, we see slight gains in the weighted MTL experiments, when given upwards of 0.9 loss weights. For all Twitter treebanks, the MTL setting shows considerable gains between 3-5% absolute. The weighted MTL setting improves over MTL by another 1-1.5%. We see the same developments across the dev and test sets.

8 Conclusion & Future Work

We have investigated the use of MTL for domain adaptation in parsing to address the data imbalance. The effectiveness of MTL depends on many interacting factors as laid out in section 2.3. Important factors we directly examine in our experiments are data size imbalances, difficulty of tasks, and task learning rates. Our learning curves for German and Italian show that MTL underperforms an STL when the data size imbalances become too great, due to negative transfer in optimizing for two tasks. Additionally, both our out-of-domain and in-domain experiments demonstrate that task learning difficulty affects both setups, even with balanced data. By using loss weighting, we are able to influence the learning rates of individual tasks, which helps reduce the negative transfer caused by both the data size imbalances and tasks difficulties. This allows us to train weighted MTL models where *both parsers are able to outperform both STL*

Test	Lg.	Treebank	STL	MTL	weighted MTL	wMTL weights
dev	German	GSD	84.63	83.76	**84.74**	0.90
		tweeDe	74.69	79.01	**79.99**	0.10
	Italian	ISDT	91.31	T: 90.59; P: 90.31	T: **91.54**; P: **91.45**	0.95; 0.90
		TWITTIRÒ	78.17	82.83	**84.11**	0.15
		PoSTWITA	77.22	80.48	**81.58**	0.05
test	German	GSD	81.35	80.70	**81.56**	0.90
		tweeDe	76.18	81.77	**82.52**	0.10
	Italian	ISDT	91.80	T: 91.18; P:90.92	T: **92.07**; P: 91.79	0.95; 0.90
		TWITTIRÒ	78.07	81.64	**82.28**	0.15
		PoSTWITA	75.46	78.57	**79.24**	0.05

Table 4: LAS Results Word+POS for STL, shared MTL, and weighted shared MTL using the full data sets. T: paired with TWITTIRÒ, P: with PoSTWITA.

and non-weighted MTL models on both treebanks at the same time, even when highly imbalanced, for in-domain and out-of-domain experiments for both German and Italian. We conclude that while domain differences certainly play a factor, data imbalance appears to have more influence on parser performance.

In the future, our experiments need to be extended to a wider range of languages and target domains. Additionally, we will investigate strategies for dynamic learning of weights (Guo et al., 2019; Liu et al., 2019; Ming et al., 2019; Yim and Kim, 2020) for determining optimal loss weighting automatically, as well as more complex scheduling approaches (Kiperwasser and Ballesteros, 2018; Guo et al., 2018; Sébastien et al., 2018) to further improve performance.

Acknowledgements

The authors would like to thank Ines Rehbein for providing the tweeDe treebank, members of the Uppsala Parsing Group: Artur Kulmizev, Joakim Nivre, and Sara Stymne for their feedback, as well as the anonymous reviewers for their comments. This research was supported in part by Lilly Endowment, Inc., through its support for the Indiana University Pervasive Technology Institute. The first author is supported by the Swedish strategic research programme eSSENCE.

References

Waleed Ammar, George Mulcaire, Miguel Ballesteros, Chris Dyer, and Noah A. Smith. 2016. Many languages, one parser. *Transactions of the Association for Computational Linguistics*, 4:431–444.

Isabelle Augenstein and Anders Søgaard. 2017. Multitask learning of keyphrase boundary classification. In *Proceedings of the 55th Annual Meeting of the Association for Computational Linguistics (ACL)*, pages 341–346, Vancouver, Canada.

Adrian Benton, Margaret Mitchell, and Dirk Hovy. 2017. Multitask learning for mental health conditions with limited social media data. In *Proceedings of the 15th Conference of the European Chapter of the Association for Computational Linguistics (EACL)*, pages 152–162, Valencia, Spain.

Joachim Bingel and Anders Søgaard. 2017. Identifying beneficial task relations for multi-task learning in deep neural networks. In *Proceedings of the 15th Conference of the European Chapter of the Association for Computational Linguistics (EACL)*, pages 164–169, Valencia, Spain.

Bernd Bohnet and Joakim Nivre. 2012. A transition-based system for joint part-of-speech tagging and labeled non-projective dependency parsing. In *Proceedings of the 2012 Joint Conference on Empirical Methods in Natural Language Processing and Computational Natural Language Learning*, pages 1455–1465, Jeju Island, Korea.

Rich Caruana. 1997. Multitask learning. *Machine Learning*, 28(1):41–75.

Alessandra Teresa Cignarella, Cristina Bosco, and Paolo Rosso. 2019. Presenting TWITTIRÒ-UD: An Italian Twitter treebank in Universal Dependencies. In *Proceedings of the Fifth International Conference on Dependency Linguistics (Depling, SyntaxFest 2019)*, pages 190–197, Paris, France.

Jacob Devlin, Ming-Wei Chang, Kenton Lee, and Kristina Toutanova. 2019. BERT: Pre-training of deep bidirectional transformers for language understanding. In *Proceedings of the 2019 Conference of the North American Chapter of the Association for Computational Linguistics: Human Language Technologies (NAACL-HLT)*, pages 4171–4186, Minneapolis, MN.

Timothy Dozat and Christopher Manning. 2017. Deep biaffine attention for neural dependency parsing. In

5h International Conference on Learning Representations (ICLR 2017)*, Toulon, France.

Long Duong, Trevor Cohn, Steven Bird, and Paul Cook. 2015. Low resource dependency parsing: Cross-lingual parameter sharing in a neural network parser. In *Proceedings of the 53rd Annual Meeting of the Association for Computational Linguistics and the 7th International Joint Conference on Natural Language Processing (ACL-IJCNLP)*, pages 845–850, Beijing, China.

Robert French. 1999. Catastrophic forgetting in connectionist networks. *Trends in Cognitive Sciences*, 3:128–135.

Daniel Fried, Nikita Kitaev, and Dan Klein. 2019. Cross-domain generalization of neural constituency parsers. In *Proceedings of the 57th Annual Meeting of the Association for Computational Linguistics (ACL)*, pages 323–330, Florence, Italy.

Han Guo, Ramakanth Pasunuru, and Mohit Bansal. 2019. AutoSeM: Automatic task selection and mixing in multi-task learning. In *Proceedings of the 2019 Conference of the North American Chapter of the Association for Computational Linguistics: Human Language Technologies (NAACL-HLT)*, pages 3520–3531, Minneapolis, MN.

Jiang Guo, Wanxiang Che, Haifeng Wang, and Ting Liu. 2016. A universal framework for inductive transfer parsing across multi-typed treebanks. In *Proceedings of COLING 2016, the 26th International Conference on Computational Linguistics*, pages 12–22, Osaka, Japan.

Michelle Guo, Albert Haque, De-An Huang, Serena Yeung, and Li Fei-Fei. 2018. Dynamic task prioritization for multitask learning. In *Computer Vision – ECCV 2018*, pages 282–299, Munich, Germany.

Richard Johansson. 2013. Training parsers on incompatible treebanks. In *Proceedings of the 2013 Conference of the North American Chapter of the Association for Computational Linguistics: Human Language Technologies (NAACL-HLT)*, pages 127–137, Atlanta, GA.

Richard Johansson and Yvonne Adesam. 2020. Training a Swedish constituency parser on six incompatible treebanks. In *Proceedings of the 12th Language Resources and Evaluation Conference (LREC)*, pages 5219–5224, Marseille, France.

Vidur Joshi, Matthew Peters, and Mark Hopkins. 2018. Extending a parser to distant domains using a few dozen partially annotated examples. In *Proceedings of the 56th Annual Meeting of the Association for Computational Linguistics (ACL)*, pages 1190–1199, Melbourne, Australia.

Yash Kankanampati, Joseph Le Roux, Nadi Tomeh, Dima Taji, and Nizar Habash. 2020. Multitask easy-first dependency parsing: Exploiting complementarities of different dependency representations. In *Proceedings of the 28th International Conference on Computational Linguistics (COLING)*, pages 2497–2508, Barcelona, Spain (Online).

Alex Kendall, Yarin Gal, and Roberto Cipolla. 2018. Multi-task learning using uncertainty to weigh losses for scene geometry and semantics. In *Proceedings of the IEEE Conference on Computer Vision and Pattern Recognition (CVPR)*, pages 7482–7491, Salt Lake City, UT.

Eliyahu Kiperwasser and Miguel Ballesteros. 2018. Scheduled multi-task learning: From syntax to translation. *Transactions of the Association for Computational Linguistics*, 6:225–240.

Nikita Kitaev, Steven Cao, and Dan Klein. 2019. Multilingual constituency parsing with self-attention and pre-training. In *Proceedings of the 57th Annual Meeting of the Association for Computational Linguistics (ACL)*, pages 3499–3505, Florence, Italy.

Giwoong Lee, Eunho Yang, and Sung Ju Hwang. 2016. Asymmetric multi-task learning based on task relatedness and loss. In *Proceedings of the 33rd International Conference on International Conference on Machine Learning (ICML)*, page 230–238, New York, NY.

Hae Beom Lee, Eunho Yang, and Sung Ju Hwang. 2018. Deep asymmetric multi-task feature learning. In *Proceedings of the 35th International Conference on Machine Learning (ICML)*, pages 2956–2964, Stockholm, Sweden.

Miryam de Lhoneux, Johannes Bjerva, Isabelle Augenstein, and Anders Søgaard. 2018. Parameter sharing between dependency parsers for related languages. In *Proceedings of the Conference on Empirical Methods in Natural Language Processing (EMNLP)*, pages 4992–4997, Brussels, Belgium.

Ying Li, Zhenghua Li, and Min Zhang. 2020. Semi-supervised domain adaptation for dependency parsing via improved contextualized word representations. In *Proceedings of the 28th International Conference on Computational Linguistics (COLING)*, pages 3806–3817, Barcelona, Spain (Online).

Zhenghua Li, Xue Peng, Min Zhang, Rui Wang, and Luo Si. 2019. Semi-supervised domain adaptation for dependency parsing. In *Proceedings of the 57th Annual Meeting of the Association for Computational Linguistics (ACL)*, pages 2386–2395, Florence, Italy.

Jian Liang, Ziqi Liu, Jiayu Zhou, Xiaoqian Jiang, Changshui Zhang, and Fei Wang. 2020. Model-protected multi-task learning. *IEEE Transactions on Pattern Analysis and Machine Intelligence*.

Lukas Liebel and Marco Körner. 2018. Auxiliary tasks in multi-task learning. arXiv:1805.06334v2.

Shengchao Liu, Yingyu Liang, and Anthony Gitter. 2019. Loss-balanced task weighting to reduce negative transfer in multi-task learning. *Proceedings of the AAAI Conference on Artificial Intelligence*, 33(01):9977–9978.

Minh-Thang Luong, Quoc Le, Ilya Sutskever, Oriol Vinyals, and Lukasz Kaiser. 2015. Multi-task sequence to sequence learning. In *Proceedings of ICLR*, San Juan, Puerto Rico.

Louis Martin, Benjamin Muller, Pedro Javier Ortiz Suárez, Yoann Dupont, Laurent Romary, Éric de la Clergerie, Djamé Seddah, and Benoît Sagot. 2020. CamemBERT: A tasty French language model. In *Proceedings of the 58th Annual Meeting of the Association for Computational Linguistics (ACL)*, pages 7203–7219, Online.

Héctor Martínez Alonso and Barbara Plank. 2017. When is multitask learning effective? semantic sequence prediction under varying data conditions. In *Proceedings of the 15th Conference of the European Chapter of the Association for Computational Linguistics (EACL)*, pages 44–53, Valencia, Spain.

Sara Meftah, Nasredine Semmar, Mohamed-Ayoub Tahiri, Youssef Tamaazousti, Hassane Essafi, and Fatiha Sadat. 2020. Multi-task supervised pretraining for neural domain adaptation. In *Proceedings of the Eighth International Workshop on Natural Language Processing for Social Media*, pages 61–71, Online.

Zuheng Ming, Junshi Xia, Muhammad Muzzamil Luqman, Jean-Christophe Burie, and Kaixing Zhao. 2019. Dynamic multi-task learning for face recognition with facial expression. arXiv:1911.03281.

Joakim Nivre, Marie-Catherine de Marneffe, Filip Ginter, Jan Hajič, Christopher D. Manning, Sampo Pyysalo, Sebastian Schuster, Francis Tyers, and Daniel Zeman. 2020. Universal Dependencies v2: An evergrowing multilingual treebank collection. In *Proceedings of the 12th Language Resources and Evaluation Conference (LREC)*, pages 4034–4043, Marseille, France.

Adam Paszke, Sam Gross, Francisco Massa, Adam Lerer, James Bradbury, Gregory Chanan, Trevor Killeen, Zeming Lin, Natalia Gimelshein, Luca Antiga, et al. 2019. Pytorch: An imperative style, high-performance deep learning library. arXiv:1912.01703.

Nanyun Peng and Mark Dredze. 2017. Multi-task domain adaptation for sequence tagging. In *Proceedings of the 2nd Workshop on Representation Learning for NLP*, pages 91–100, Vancouver, Canada.

Ines Rehbein, Josef Ruppenhofer, and Bich-Ngoc Do. 2019. tweeDe – a Universal Dependencies treebank for German tweets. In *Proceedings of the 18th International Workshop on Treebanks and Linguistic Theories (TLT, SyntaxFest 2019)*, pages 100–108, Paris, France.

Sebastian Ruder, Joachim Bingel, Isabelle Augenstein, and Anders Søgaard. 2019. Latent multi-task architecture learning. *Proceedings of the AAAI Conference on Artificial Intelligence*, 33(01):4822–4829.

Manuela Sanguinetti, Cristina Bosco, Alberto Lavelli, Alessandro Mazzei, Oronzo Antonelli, and Fabio Tamburini. 2018. PoSTWITA-UD: an Italian Twitter treebank in Universal Dependencies. In *Proceedings of the Eleventh International Conference on Language Resources and Evaluation (LREC)*, Miyazaki, Japan.

Zeeshan Ali Sayyed and Daniel Dakota. 2021. Annotations matter: Leveraging multi-task learning to parse UD and SUD. In *Findings of the ACL: ACL-IJCNLP 2021*, Online.

Fynn Schröder and Chris Biemann. 2020. Estimating the influence of auxiliary tasks for multi-task learning of sequence tagging tasks. In *Proceedings of the 58th Annual Meeting of the Association for Computational Linguistics (ACL)*, pages 2971–2985, Online.

Claudia Schulz, Steffen Eger, Johannes Daxenberger, Tobias Kahse, and Iryna Gurevych. 2018. Multi-task learning for argumentation mining in low-resource settings. In *Proceedings of the 2018 Conference of the North American Chapter of the Association for Computational Linguistics: Human Language Technologies (NAACL-HLT)*, pages 35–41, New Orleans, LA.

Jean Sébastien, Orhan Firat, and Melvin Johnson. 2018. Adaptive scheduling for multi-task learning. In *Proceedings of the Continual Learning Workshop at 32nd Conference on Neural Information Processing Systems (NeurIPS)*, Montréal, Canada.

Anders Søgaard. 2017. Using hyperlinks to improve multilingual partial parsers. In *Proceedings of the 15th International Conference on Parsing Technologies*, pages 67–71, Pisa, Italy.

Anders Søgaard and Yoav Goldberg. 2016. Deep multi-task learning with low level tasks supervised at lower layers. In *Proceedings of the 54th Annual Meeting of the Association for Computational Linguistics (ACL)*, pages 231–235, Berlin, Germany.

Sara Stymne, Miryam de Lhoneux, Aaron Smith, and Joakim Nivre. 2018. Parser training with heterogeneous treebanks. In *Proceedings of the 56th Annual Meeting of the Association for Computational Linguistics (ACL)*, pages 619–625, Melbourne, Australia.

Antti Virtanen, Jenna Kanerva, Rami Ilo, Jouni Luoma, Juhani Luotolahti, Tapio Salakoski, Filip Ginter, and Sampo Pyysalo. 2019. Multilingual is not enough: BERT for Finnish. arXiv:1912.07076.

Genta Indra Winata, Andrea Madotto, Chien-Sheng Wu, and Pascale Fung. 2018. Code-switching language modeling using syntax-aware multi-task learning. In *Proceedings of the Third Workshop on Computational Approaches to Linguistic Code-Switching*, pages 62–67, Melbourne, Australia.

Sen Wu, Hongyang R. Zhang, and Christopher Ré. 2020. Understanding and improving information transfer in multi-task learning. In *8th International Conference on Learning Representations*, Online.

Jonghwa Yim and Sang Hwan Kim. 2020. Learning boost by exploiting the auxiliary task in multi-task domain. arXiv:2008.02043.

Daniel Zeman, Jan Hajič, Martin Popel, Martin Potthast, Milan Straka, Filip Ginter, Joakim Nivre, and Slav Petrov. 2018. CoNLL 2018 shared task: Multilingual parsing from raw text to Universal Dependencies. In *Proceedings of the CoNLL 2018 Shared Task: Multilingual Parsing from Raw Text to Universal Dependencies*, pages 1–21, Brussels, Belgium.

Yu Zhang, Zhenghua Li, and Min Zhang. 2020. Efficient second-order TreeCRF for neural dependency parsing. In *Proceedings of the 58th Annual Meeting of the Association for Computational Linguistics (ACL)*, pages 3295–3305, Online.

Yuan Zhang and David Weiss. 2016. Stack-propagation: Improved representation learning for syntax. In *Proceedings of the 54th Annual Meeting of the Association for Computational Linguistics (ACL)*, pages 1557–1566, Berlin, Germany.

Strength in Numbers: Averaging and Clustering Effects in Mixture of Experts for Graph-Based Dependency Parsing

Xudong Zhang, Joseph Le Roux, Thierry Charnois
Laboratoire d'Informatique de Paris Nord,
Université Sorbonne Paris Nord – CNRS UMR 7030,
F-93430, Villetaneuse, France
{xudong.zhang, leroux, thierry.charnois}@lipn.fr

Abstract

We review two features of *mixture of experts* (MoE) models which we call *averaging* and *clustering* effects in the context of graph-based dependency parsers learned in a supervised probabilistic framework. *Averaging* corresponds to the ensemble combination of parsers and is responsible for variance reduction which helps stabilizing and improving parsing accuracy. *Clustering* describes the capacity of MoE models to *give more credit* to experts believed to be more accurate given an input. Although promising, this is difficult to achieve, especially without additional data.

We design an experimental set-up to study the impact of these effects.Whereas averaging is always beneficial, clustering requires good initialization and stabilization techniques, but its advantages over mere averaging seem to eventually vanish when enough experts are present.

As a by product, we show how this leads to state-of-the-art results on the PTB and the CoNLL09 Chinese treebank, with low variance across experiments.

1 Introduction

Combinations of elementary parsers are known to improve accuracy. Sometimes called *joint systems*, they often use different representations, *i.e.* lexicalized constituents and dependencies (Rush et al., 2010; Green and Žabokrtský, 2012; Le Roux et al., 2019; Zhou et al., 2020). These approaches have been devised to join the strengths and overcome the weaknesses of elementary systems.

In this work, however, we follow another line of research consisting of mixtures and products of similar experts (Jacobs et al., 1991; Brown and Hinton, 2001), instantiated for parsing in (Petrov et al., 2006; Petrov, 2010) and especially appealing when individual experts have high variance, typically when training involves neural networks. Indeed Petrov (2010) used products of experts trained via Expectation-Maximization (a non-convex function minimization) converging to local minima.

In this work we propose to study the combination of parsers, from a probabilistic point of view, as a mixture model, *i.e.* a learnable convex interpolation of probabilities. This has previously been studied in (Petrov et al., 2006) for PCFGs with the goal of overcoming the locality assumptions, and we want to see if neural graph-based dependency parsers, with non-markovian feature extractors, can also benefit from this framework. It has several advantages: it is conceptually simple and easy to implement, it is not restricted to projective dependency parsing (although we only experiment this case), and while the time and space complexity increases with the number of systems, this is hardly a problem in practice thanks to GPU parallelization.

Simple averaging models, or ensembles, can also be framed as mixture models where mixture coefficients are equal. We are able to quantify the variance reduction, both theoretically and empirically and show that this simple model of graph-based parser combinations perform better on average, and achieve a higher accuracy than single systems.

While the full mixture model is appealing, since it could in principle both decrease variance and find the optimal interpolation weights to better combine parser predictions, the non-convexity of the learning objective is a major issue that, when added to the non-convexity of potential functions, can prevent parameterization to converge to a good solution. By trying to specialize parsers to specific input, the variance is not decreased. More importantly, experiments indicate that useful data, that is data with an effect on parameterization, becomes too scarce to train the clustering device.

Another drawback of finite mixture models is that inference, *i.e.* finding the optimal tree, becomes intractable. We tackle this issue by using an alternative objective similar to Minimal Bayes-

Proceedings of the 17th International Conference on Parsing Technologies (IWPT 2021), pages 106–118
Bangkok, Thailand (online), August 6, 2021. ©2021 Association for Computational Linguistics

Risk (Goel and Byrne, 2000) and PCFG-LA combination (Petrov, 2010) for which decoding is exact.

Our contribution can be summarized as follows:

- We frame dependency parser combinations as finite mixture models (§2) and discuss two properties: averaging and clustering. We derive an efficient decoder (LMBR) merging predictions at the arc level (§3).
- When isolating the averaging effect, we show that resulting systems exhibit an empirical variance reduction which corroborates theoretical predictions, and are more accurate (§4).
- We study the causes of instability in mixture learning, outline why simple regularization is unhelpful and give an EM-inspired learning method preventing detrimental over-specialization (§5). Still, improvement over mere averaging is difficult to achieve.
- These methods obtain state-of-the-art results on two standard datasets, the PTB and the CoNLL09 Chinese dataset (§6), with low variance making it robust to initial conditions.

2 Mixture of Experts

2.1 Notations

We write a sentence as $x = x_0, x_1, \ldots, x_n$, with x_0 a dummy root symbol, and otherwise x_i the ith word, and n the number of words. For $h, d \in [n]$ with $[n] = \{0, \ldots, n\}$, (h, d) is the directed arc from head x_h to dependent x_d. We note the set of all parse trees (arborescences) for x as $\mathcal{Y}(x)$ and the elements in this set as $y \in \mathcal{Y}(x)$, with $(h, d) \in y$ if (h, d) is an arc in y. $\mathcal{L}$ stands for the set of arc labels. The vector of arc labels in tree y is noted as $l(y) \in \mathcal{L}^n$. We note $l(y)_{hd}$ the label for arc (h, d) in y, or l_{hd} when y is clear from the context.

2.2 Parsers as Experts

Experts can be any probabilistic graph-based dependency parser, provided that we can efficiently compute the energy of a parse tree, the global energy of a sentence (the sum of all parse tree energies, called the partition function) and the marginal probability of an arc in a sentence. In the remaining we focus on projective first- and second-order parsers, where these quantities are computed via tabular methods or backpropagation[1].

[1] Matrix-tree theorem could be used to adapt this work to non-projective first-order models (Smith and Smith, 2007)

Tree structure For a graph-based dependency parser, the tree probability is defined as:

$$p(y|x) = \frac{\exp(s(x, y))}{Z(x) \equiv \sum_{y' \in \mathcal{Y}(x)} \exp(s(x, y'))}$$

with $s(x, y)$ the tree energy giving the correctness of y for x, and $Z(x)$ the partition function.

In first-order models (Eisner, 1996), tree scores are sums of arc scores:

$$s(x, y) = \sum_{(h,d) \in y} s(h, d)$$

Eisner (1997) generalizes scores to the second-order by considering pairs of adjacent siblings:

$$s(x, y) = \sum_{(h,d) \in y} s(h, d) + \sum_{\substack{(h,d_1) \\ (h,d_2) \in y}} s(h, d_1, d_2)$$

with $h < d_1 < d_2$ or $d_2 < d_1 < h$. For projective first- or second-order models, $Z(x)$ and $p(y|x)$ are efficiently calculated (Zhang et al., 2020b). Moreover marginal arc probability $p\big((h, d)|x\big)$ can be efficiently calculated from the partition function by applying backpropagation from $\log Z(x)$ to $s(h, d)$, see (Eisner, 2016; Zmigrod et al., 2020; Zhang et al., 2020a):

$$p((h, d)|x) = \sum_{\substack{y \in \mathcal{Y}(x) \\ (h,d) \in y}} p(y|x) = \frac{\partial \log Z(x)}{\partial s(h, d)}$$

Tree Labelling The labelling model is also a Boltzmann distribution:

$$p(l|(h, d), x) = \frac{\exp(s(l, h, d))}{\sum_{l' \in \mathcal{L}} \exp(s(l', h, d))}$$

where $s(l, h, d)$ is the score for label l on (h, d).

Following (Dozat and Manning, 2017; Zhang et al., 2020a), label predictions are independent:

$$p(l(y)|y, x) = \prod_{(h,d) \in y} p(l_{hd}|(h, d), x) \quad (1)$$

Parse Probability Given the structure y and its labelling $l(y)$, the parse probability is:

$$p\big(l(y), y|x\big) = p(y|x) \times p\big(l(y)|y, x\big) \quad (2)$$

Learning Potential functions s can be implemented by feed-forward neural networks or biaffine functions (Dozat and Manning, 2017), and parameterized by maximizing a log-likelihood.

2.3 Mixture and Averaging

For arborescence probabilities a finite mixture model (MoE) is a weighted sum of the probabilities given by all experts:

$$p(y|x) = \sum_{k=1}^{K} \omega_k(x) p_k(y|x) \tag{3}$$

where mixture weights verify $\forall x, \omega_k(x) \geq 0$ and $\sum_{k=1}^{K} \omega_k(x) = 1$ and can be adjusted by a gating network (Jacobs et al., 1991). We can interpret ω as a device whose role is to *cluster* input in K categories and assign each category to an expert.

By forcing $\omega_k(x) = \frac{1}{K}, \forall x$, we have a simpler averaging model, sometimes called *ensemble*:

$$p(y|x) = \frac{1}{K} \sum_{k=1}^{K} p_k(y|x)$$

Note that MoEs combine elementary probabilities, not tree scores: each expert energy is first normalized before the combination.

A similar mixture is applied to labelling, *i.e.*:

$$p(l(y)|y, x) = \sum_{k=1}^{K} \lambda_k(x) p_k(l(y)|y, x)$$

3 Decoding with a Mixture Model

Learning MoEs will be covered in Section 5 and we first turn to the problem of finding an appropriate tree, for instance the most probable parse tree:

$$y^* = \underset{y \in \mathcal{Y}(x)}{\operatorname{argmax}}\, p(y|x) = \underset{y \in \mathcal{Y}(x)}{\operatorname{argmax}} \sum_{k=1}^{K} \omega_k(x) p_k(y|x)$$

This maximization is difficult, even in the absence of labels, since this isn't a log-linear function of the arc scores anymore: y^* cannot be searched in the log-space among unnormalized arc scores.

3.1 MBR Decoding

In this case, a more attractive alternative is Minimum Bayesian Risk (MBR) decoding (Smith and Smith, 2007), because it decomposes error in a way similar to the metrics used in dependency parsing (UAS/LAS) and is tractable. MBR requires to compute marginal arc probabilities which are the weighted sums of elementary marginals:

$$p\big((h, d)|x\big) = \sum_{k=1}^{K} \omega_k(x) p_k\big((h, d)|x\big)$$

The intuition behind MBR is that instead of maximizing the probability of the parse tree, we try to minimize the risk of choosing wrong arcs, *i.e.* to maximize the arc marginals in the parse tree:

$$y^* = \underset{y \in \mathcal{Y}(x)}{\operatorname{argmax}} \prod_{(h,d) \in y} p\big((h, d)|x\big) = \mathrm{MBR}(x)$$

Once computed marginal log-probabilities, Eisner algorithm (Eisner, 1996), (Eisner, 1997) or Chu-Liu-Edmonds (McDonald et al., 2005) can be applied to solve MBR.

3.2 MBR Decoding with Labels

In many dependency parsing models, decoding of arcs and labels is pipelined, see for instance (Dozat and Manning, 2017; Zhang et al., 2020a; Fossum and Knight, 2009): first arcs are decoded and then, with the decoded arcs, maximization is performed over labels:

$$y^* = \underset{y \in \mathcal{Y}(x)}{\operatorname{argmax}}\, p(y|x) \text{ then } l^* = \underset{l = l(y^*)}{\operatorname{argmax}}\, p(l|y^*, x)$$

However, solutions found this way are not the maximizers for $p(l, y|x)$, as defined in Eq. 2. The problem is that the effect of labelling is not considered in arc decoding: a high probability arc can get picked up even with a low label score.

First we remark that each label in l^* is the most probable label l for a pair (h, d), denoted by $L_{hd} = \operatorname{argmax}_{l \in \mathcal{L}} p(l|(h, d), x)$. Decoding becomes:

$$y^* = \underset{y}{\operatorname{argmax}}\, p(y|x) \prod_{(h,d) \in y} p(L_{hd}|(h, d), x)$$

This way l^* is deterministic wrt to y^* and (y^*, l^*) are maximizers for Eq. 2. We note labelling $L(y)$ where $l(y)_{hd} = L_{hd}, \forall (h, d) \in y$. This can be combined with MBR without changing decoding algorithms, and we call this variant LMBR:

$$y^* = \underset{(y, l = L(y))}{\operatorname{argmax}} \prod_{(h,d) \in y} p\big((h, d)|x\big) p\big(L_{hd}|(h, d), x\big)$$

i.e. we can apply MBR with arc probabilities reparameterized with label probabilities. Experiments show that LMBR exhibits a small but consistent accuracy increase over MBR.

4 Averaging and Variance Reduction

In this section we assume all experts to be equally weighted. We define the variance of the system on $\mathcal{T}$ as the average variance of marginal arc probability:

$$\sigma^2 = \frac{\sum_{(x,y)\in\mathcal{T}} \sum_{(h,d)\in y} \sigma^2\Big(p\big((h,d)|x\big)\Big)}{\sum_{(x,y)\in\mathcal{T}} |y|}$$

with $\sigma^2(p((h,d)|x))$ the variance of the marginal probability.

We show how the variance of the MoE is smaller than the variance of experts. We focus on structure prediction $p(y|x)$, but definitions are applicable to the labelling model as well. This is an already known result for mixture models in general, but the proof is here instantiated for a mixture of graph-based parsers. Moreover, we will recover this result experimentally in Section 6.

Assuming we have a mixture of K elementary systems, we will estimate the marginal probability variance with:

$$\sigma^2\Big(p\big((h,d)|x\big)\Big) = \frac{1}{K}\sum_{k=1}^{K}(\pi(k) - \bar{\pi})^2$$

with $\pi(k)$ the probability $p_k\big((h,d)|x\big)$ given by the kth elementary system and average $\bar{\pi} = \frac{1}{K}\sum_{k=1}^{K}\pi(k)$

Increasing the number of experts in the MoE will decrease variance of the system. To see this, we assume that the marginal probability for a well trained expert, over a fixed sentence and a fixed arc, is a measurable function $f_{(h,d),x} : \mathbb{R} \to \mathbb{R}$ of a random seed $S_k \in \mathbb{R}$, which represents the fact that p_k is the result of a learning process with many sources of randomization[2] (initialization, stochastic batches, dropout...):

$$p_k((h,d)|x) = f_{(h,d),x}(S_k)$$

with $S_k \in \mathbb{R}$ a random seed assigned to k^{th} expert at the beginning of training, assumed to be independent for different experts.

Since in practice a pseudo-random generator is used, the value of marginal probability for particular sentence and arc is deterministic when the random seed is fixed. Thus, it is sufficient to use a deterministic function to represent $p_k((h,d),x)$, with random seed S_k as input. Moreover, we just need the function to be measurable.

We can now view $f_{(h,d),x}(S)$ as a random variable and we note its variance as $\sigma^2_{(h,d),x}$. It is in fact the variance of the marginal arc probability given by this expert, for (h,d) given x. For an averaging MoE, the marginal probability becomes:

$$p((h,d)|x) = \frac{1}{K}\sum_{k=1}^{K} f_{(h,d),x}(S_k)$$

with K number of experts in the mixture model.

If random variables $\{S_k\}_{k\in K}$ are independent, $\{f_{(h,d),x}((S_k)\}_{k\in K}$ also are independent (Baldi, 2017). Thus, the variance of the mixture model for particular sentence and arc should be $\frac{1}{K}$ times the variance of experts:

$$\Sigma^2_{(h,d),x} = \frac{\sigma^2_{(h,d),x}}{K} \tag{4}$$

with Σ the variance of the mixture model. In other words, the log-variance of a mixture model decreases linearly with $\log K$, with slope -1, *i.e.*:

$$\log \Sigma^2_{(h,d),x} = \log \sigma^2_{(h,d),x} - \log K$$

Experiments in Section 6 Figure 1 show that the estimated log-variance of the averaging system decreases when the number of experts increases and that this relation is close to linear with a slope approaching -1, comforting our independence assumption.

5 Training with Clustering

When mixture weights are adjustable, MoE models are able to give more credit to experts believed to perform better on specific input. This can be exploited during parameterization. The role of ω is thus to learn how to cluster input into K categories, each category being assigned to an expert.[3]

For input sentence x and corresponding tree y, assuming parameterization is performed by maximizing the log-likelihood of the training set via SGD, the objective of mixture model learning with gating network ω can be written as:

$$L(\phi,\theta) = \log\sum_{k=1}^{K}\omega_k(x;\phi)p_k(y|x;\theta_k) \tag{5}$$

[2] f should also be indexed by the training set, but we omit this for the sake of readability.

[3] We note that averaging MoE models do not require a specific training: experts can be trained separately and the ensemble is gathered at decoding time only.

where ϕ are the parameters of the gating network, and θ_k are the parameters of the kth expert.

Partial derivatives to the gating network are:

$$\frac{\partial L(\phi,\theta)}{\partial \phi} = \sum_{k=1}^{K} \frac{\omega_k(\phi)p_k(\theta_k)}{\sum_{k'=1}^{K} \omega_{k'}(\phi)p_{k'}(\theta_{k'})} \frac{\partial \log \omega_k(\phi)}{\partial \phi} \tag{6}$$

while for expert parameters we have:

$$\frac{\partial L(\phi,\theta)}{\partial \theta_k} = \frac{\omega_k(\phi)p_k(\theta_k)}{\sum_{k'=1}^{K} \omega_{k'}(\phi)p_{k'}(\theta_{k'})} \frac{\partial \log p_k(\theta_k)}{\partial \theta_k}. \tag{7}$$

We found that optimizing directly with equations (6) and (7) causes degeneration, *i.e.* one ω_k approaches 1 while the other $\omega_{k'}$ decrease to almost 0. Indeed, gradient ascent with (6) will increase ω_k for an expert k that gives high weight to training samples while gradient ascent with (7) will generate increased gradient, and in turn increased probabilities, for experts with high value of ω_k. The two processes re-enforce each other and result quickly in an extreme partition between experts.

One may think that the degeneration problem can be alleviated with a smoothing prior or regularization. In practice, we tried entropy as regularization to force towards a uniform distribution on ω_k. We found that a heavy entropy penalization is required to avoid the degeneration problem, which makes ω_k too uniform to be an accurate clustering device.

Avoid Extreme Partition Thus, to alleviate the degeneration problem without forcing a strong smoothing constraint, we propose to modify Eq. (6) into:

$$\frac{\partial L'(\phi,\theta)}{\partial \phi} = \sum_{k=1}^{K} \frac{p_k(\theta_k)}{\sum_{k'=1}^{K} p_{k'}(\theta_{k'})} \frac{\partial \log \omega_k(\phi)}{\partial \phi} \tag{8}$$

i.e. we force the weight update to be proportional to the relative probability. The advantage of Eq. (8) is that gradient are weighted by a more objective quantity $\frac{p_k(\theta_k)}{\sum_{k'=1}^{K} p_{k'}(\theta_{k'})}$. For an example where $p_k(x)$ is close to uniform, we can benefit from the averaging effect, while for an example which shows strong preference for a particular expert, we can also learn the partition coefficients proportional to their correctness.

Stabilize Training Neuron dropout (Srivastava et al., 2014) is a common technique to avoid overfitting which unfortunately proved difficult in this setting. The problem is that $s_k(x, y)$ gives very different results with or without dropout which reflects on $p_k(y|x)$ causing drastic changes from one evaluation to the other. To mitigate this problem, we use probabilities without dropout (noted as $\tilde{p}_k(\theta)$) to calculate the weighted coefficients of gradient.

The final optimization process can be separated into two alternate parts, *(i)* optimization of the gating parameters:

$$\frac{\partial L'(\phi,\theta)}{\partial \phi} = \sum_{k=1}^{K} \frac{\tilde{p}_k(\theta_k)}{\sum_{k'=1}^{K} \tilde{p}_{k'}(\theta_{k'})} \frac{\partial \log \omega_k(\phi)}{\partial \phi}$$

and *(ii)* optimization of experts:

$$\frac{\partial L(\phi,\theta)}{\partial \theta_k} = \sum_{k=1}^{K} \frac{\omega(\phi)\tilde{p}_k(\theta_k)}{\sum_{k'=1}^{K} \omega_{k'}\tilde{p}_{k'}(\theta_{k'})} \frac{\partial \log p_k(\theta_k)}{\partial \theta_k}$$

In practice, this permitted reaching a lower loss value after training.

6 Experiments

Data We run experiments over two datasets for projective dependency parsing: The English Penn Treebank (PTB) data with Stanford Dependencies (Marcus et al., 1993) and CoNLL09 Chinese data (Hajič et al., 2009). We use standard train/dev/test splits and evaluate with UAS/LAS metrics. Customarily, punctuation is ignored on PTB evaluation.

Experts We run tests with first-order (FOP) and second-order parsers (SOP) as mixture model experts, with re-implemented versions of the CRF and CRF2o parsers of Zhang et al. (2020a).[4] For decoding, we use the LMBR decoding presented in Section 3.2, which guarantees a small but consistent improvement over pipeline MBR decoding.

For each input word, these systems use 3 embeddings: the first is a fixed pretrained vector[5], the second is trainable and looked-up in a table, and the third is computed by a BiLSTM at the character level (CharLSTM). The first two embeddings are summed and concatenated with the char sequence embedding. For FOP and SOP, contextual lexical features are the results of 3-layer BiLSTMs applied to word embedding sequences. The scoring of arcs is then similar to (Dozat and Manning, 2017): lexical features are transformed for head or modifier roles by two feed-forward networks and combined to score arcs via a biaffine transformation.

[4] `https://github.com/kidlestar/MOE.git`.

[5] For English we used Glove embeddings (Pennington et al., 2014), while for Chinese we extracted pretrained embeddings from the publicly available model of Zhang et al. (2020b).

On PTB, in order to compare with recent parsing results, we set up BFOP and BSOP (B for Bert), variants of the FOP and SOP settings: we follow Fonseca and Martins (2020) and concatenate an additional BERT embedding (Devlin et al., 2019) (the average of the 4 last layers of the *bert-base-uncased* model) to the embedding vector fed to the BiLSTM layers.

Gating (mixture weights ω) is implemented by a K-class softmax over a feed-forward network whose input are the concatenation of initial and final contextual lexical feature vectors returned by the 3-layer BiLSTM. Hyper-parameters are set similarly to Zhang et al. (2020a), with the exception of the learning rate decreased to 10^{-4} and patience (that is the maximum number of epochs without LAS increase on the development set) set to 20.

We train 12 independent models for each expert type, with random seed set to system time.

6.1 Averaging Effect Analysis

The experimental procedure is shown in Experimental Setup 1, with $M_1, \ldots, M_{12}$ denoting the trained experts, K number of experts in the mixture model and r the number of repetitions.

Models: $M_1, \ldots, M_{12}$;
Initialization: K, r;
repeat r **times**
1. Shuffle the order of $M_1, \ldots, M_{12}$;
2. Combine sequentially every K models together, creating $12/K$ mixture averaging models;
3. Compute UAS, LAS of models;
4. Calculate system variance for models;

end
Experimental Setup 1: Averaging Effect

We set K from 1 to 6 with r always set to 5. We show results for PTB and CoNLL09 Chinese on dev data for each type of mixture of experts, and different number of experts in Table 1 and Table 3. For UAS and LAS, each entry is given as:

$$\text{Average}_{\text{min}}^{\text{max}} \pm \text{std}$$

where average is the *average* score for all trials in this setting and *max* (resp. *min*) is the highest (resp. *lowest*) score obtained by an experiment in this setting. We also give standard deviation *std* as a way to see the effects of variance reduction.

Finally the last row gives the average relative error reduction (R.E.R) from single expert mode ($K = 1$) to ensemble mode with $K = 6$.

6.2 Clustering Effect Analysis

We conduct clustering effect analysis over the mixture model with 6 experts. Preliminary experiments showed that, like in most non-convex problems, good initialization is very important. For that reason we use already trained experts as starting points[6] although the mixture could benefit from more diversely trained experts. We leave this for future work. The procedure is described in Experimental Setup 2 and this whole procedure is repeated 5 times to compute average performance.

Models: $M_1, \ldots M_{12}$;
Initialization: $K = 6$;
repeat r **times**
1. Select randomly K models, creating mixture models;
2. Do fine tuning of mixture models with gating network;
3. Calculating UAS, LAS of mixture model after fine tuning;

end
Experimental Setup 2: Clustering Effect

Scores on development set before and after fine tuning are shown in Table 4. Note that because shuffling might give different candidate sets than in the averaging experiments UAS and LAS results are not exactly the same as $K = 6$ results in Table 1, Table 2 and Table 3.

6.3 Discussion

Averaging Tables 1 to 3 show that UAS and LAS generally increase on average with the number of models in the mixture model, and that ensemble performs often on average better than the best single systems in each category (notable exceptions: UAS for FOP and models with BERT on PTB).

Averaging generally decreases the standard deviation, which is evident for (B)FOP. For (B)SOP the decrease trend is less clear. However, we still found that the smallest standard deviation is usually given by high number of experts ($K = 5, 6$).

[6] We tried deterministic annealing with both randomly initialized experts and already trained experts. While it helped in the former case, the latter was more accurate, but still less accurate than systems trained without.

K	FOP		SOP	
	UAS	LAS	UAS	LAS
1	$95.83^{\mathbf{96.04}}_{95.72} \pm 0.08$	$94.06^{94.24}_{93.91} \pm 0.08$	$95.87^{95.94}_{95.77} \pm 0.06$	$94.07^{94.16}_{93.97} \pm 0.05$
2	$95.88^{\mathbf{96.04}}_{95.76} \pm 0.06$	$94.15^{94.32}_{94.05} \pm 0.07$	$95.92^{96.05}_{95.85} \pm 0.05$	$94.15^{94.27}_{94.08} \pm 0.04$
3	$95.93^{96.03}_{95.84} \pm 0.05$	$94.22^{94.32}_{94.11} \pm 0.05$	$95.94^{96.04}_{95.85} \pm 0.06$	$94.18^{94.27}_{94.08} \pm 0.06$
4	$\mathbf{95.95}^{\mathbf{96.04}}_{95.90} \pm 0.04$	$\mathbf{94.24}^{\mathbf{94.35}}_{94.16} \pm 0.05$	$\mathbf{95.98}^{\mathbf{96.07}}_{95.91} \pm 0.05$	$94.22^{\mathbf{94.31}}_{94.15} \pm 0.04$
5	$95.93^{96.00}_{95.84} \pm 0.04$	$\mathbf{94.24}^{94.33}_{94.14} \pm 0.05$	$\mathbf{95.98}^{96.04}_{95.92} \pm 0.04$	$\mathbf{94.24}^{94.29}_{\mathbf{94.18}} \pm 0.03$
6	$\mathbf{95.95}^{95.98}_{\mathbf{95.91}} \pm 0.02$	$\mathbf{94.24}^{94.30}_{\mathbf{94.21}} \pm 0.03$	$\mathbf{95.98}^{96.01}_{\mathbf{95.94}} \pm 0.02$	$\mathbf{94.24}^{94.28}_{\mathbf{94.18}} \pm 0.03$
R.E.R.	2.88%	3.03%	2.66%	2.87%

Table 1: PTB dev results, with First-Order (FOP) and Second-Order (SOP) parsers as experts.

K	BFOP		BSOP	
	UAS	LAS	UAS	LAS
1	$96.31^{96.46}_{96.23} \pm 0.06$	$94.60^{94.77}_{94.53} \pm 0.06$	$96.35^{96.42}_{96.23} \pm 0.04$	$94.63^{94.68}_{94.55} \pm 0.04$
2	$96.37^{96.48}_{96.26} \pm 0.05$	$94.69^{94.79}_{94.61} \pm 0.05$	$96.38^{96.51}_{96.26} \pm 0.06$	$94.71^{94.79}_{95.60} \pm 0.05$
3	$96.40^{96.49}_{96.33} \pm 0.04$	$94.74^{94.82}_{94.68} \pm 0.04$	$96.39^{96.50}_{96.29} \pm 0.06$	$94.71^{94.79}_{94.61} \pm 0.04$
4	$96.43^{\mathbf{96.53}}_{96.38} \pm 0.04$	$94.77^{\mathbf{94.89}}_{94.72} \pm 0.04$	$96.38^{96.47}_{96.28} \pm 0.05$	$94.72^{94.79}_{94.62} \pm 0.05$
5	$\mathbf{96.45}^{96.51}_{96.38} \pm 0.04$	$\mathbf{94.79}^{94.85}_{\mathbf{94.74}} \pm 0.04$	$\mathbf{96.41}^{\mathbf{96.52}}_{96.29} \pm 0.06$	$\mathbf{94.73}^{\mathbf{94.82}}_{94.65} \pm 0.05$
6	$96.44^{96.51}_{\mathbf{96.40}} \pm 0.03$	$\mathbf{94.79}^{94.85}_{\mathbf{94.74}} \pm 0.03$	$96.39^{96.46}_{\mathbf{96.32}} \pm 0.04$	$\mathbf{94.73}^{\mathbf{94.82}}_{\mathbf{94.67}} \pm 0.04$
R.E.R.	3.52%	3.52%	1.64%	1.86%

Table 2: PTB dev results, with Bert-First-Order (BFOP) and Bert-Second-Order (BSOP) parsers as experts.

K	FOP		SOP	
	UAS	LAS	UAS	LAS
1	$89.20^{89.42}_{89.04} \pm 0.12$	$86.28^{86.49}_{86.10} \pm 0.12$	$89.40^{89.48}_{89.31} \pm 0.06$	$86.45^{86.52}_{86.28} \pm 0.07$
2	$89.44^{89.60}_{89.32} \pm 0.08$	$86.59^{86.74}_{86.45} \pm 0.08$	$89.65^{89.78}_{89.51} \pm 0.07$	$86.76^{86.89}_{86.57} \pm 0.07$
3	$89.55^{89.66}_{89.39} \pm 0.07$	$86.71^{86.82}_{86.54} \pm 0.07$	$89.74^{89.86}_{89.62} \pm 0.07$	$86.86^{86.98}_{86.72} \pm 0.08$
4	$89.62^{89.68}_{89.52} \pm 0.04$	$86.80^{86.87}_{86.70} \pm 0.05$	$89.83^{89.94}_{89.70} \pm 0.08$	$86.96^{87.08}_{86.86} \pm 0.07$
5	$\mathbf{89.66}^{89.71}_{89.57} \pm 0.04$	$86.83^{86.89}_{86.75} \pm 0.04$	$\mathbf{89.87}^{\mathbf{89.98}}_{89.75} \pm 0.07$	$\mathbf{87.00}^{\mathbf{87.11}}_{86.87} \pm 0.07$
6	$\mathbf{89.66}^{\mathbf{89.77}}_{\mathbf{89.61}} \pm 0.05$	$\mathbf{86.85}^{\mathbf{86.93}}_{\mathbf{86.81}} \pm 0.04$	$\mathbf{89.87}^{89.93}_{\mathbf{89.79}} \pm 0.05$	$\mathbf{87.00}^{87.08}_{\mathbf{86.92}} \pm 0.04$
R.E.R.	4.26%	4.15%	4.43%	4.06%

Table 3: CoNLL09 dev results, with First-Order (FOP) and Second-Order (SOP) parsers as experts.

Method	PTB		CoNLL09 Chinese	
	UAS	LAS	UAS	LAS
FOP	$95.94^{95.96}_{95.91} \pm 0.02$	$94.23^{94.26}_{94.21} \pm 0.02$	$89.67^{89.71}_{89.62} \pm 0.03$	$\mathbf{86.86}^{86.91}_{86.81} \pm 0.04$
CFOP	$\mathbf{95.98}^{96.00}_{95.94} \pm 0.02$	$\mathbf{94.29}^{94.31}_{94.27} \pm 0.02$	$\mathbf{89.68}^{89.72}_{89.62} \pm 0.04$	$\mathbf{86.86}^{86.90}_{86.80} \pm 0.04$
SOP	$95.98^{96.00}_{95.95} \pm 0.02$	$94.23^{94.28}_{94.20} \pm 0.03$	$89.85^{89.92}_{89.81} \pm 0.04$	$86.98^{87.06}_{86.93} \pm 0.06$
CSOP	$\mathbf{95.99}^{96.01}_{95.97} \pm 0.01$	$\mathbf{94.25}^{94.28}_{94.22} \pm 0.02$	$\mathbf{89.89}^{89.95}_{89.82} \pm 0.04$	$\mathbf{87.03}^{87.12}_{86.95} \pm 0.06$
BFOP	$\mathbf{96.43}^{96.46}_{96.42} \pm 0.02$	$\mathbf{94.79}^{94.82}_{94.76} \pm 0.02$	-	-
CBFOP	$96.42^{96.46}_{96.39} \pm 0.03$	$94.78^{94.81}_{94.72} \pm 0.03$	-	-
BSOP	$96.41^{96.46}_{96.37} \pm 0.04$	$94.75^{94.82}_{94.67} \pm 0.05$	-	-
CBSOP	$\mathbf{96.42}^{96.46}_{96.38} \pm 0.04$	$\mathbf{94.76}^{94.82}_{94.70} \pm 0.05$	-	-

Table 4: Clustering Effect with $K = 6$ on dev, where CFOP, CSOP, CBSOP represent models after training

We remark that on PTB similar performance on dev was achieved by FOP and SOP, with a slightly better UAS for SOP, which is expected by the capacity of the model to better represent structures. This corroborates findings of (Falenska and Kuhn, 2019). But this contradicts results for CoNLL09 where SOP always gives best results, in line with observations of Fonseca and Martins (2020). For BERT experiments on PTB, BSOP achieves better performance than BFOP with one or two experts. However, when the number of experts increases, BFOP outperforms BSOP.

We complement our discussion with Figure 1[7] which depicts variance reduction by the number of

[7]For CoNLL09, we found similar results. The figure is not shown for space limitation.

experts in log-scale: almost linear of for all models, as predicted by our independence assumption.

We note that UAS and LAS improves little or not at all from $K = 5$ to $K = 6$. This is in accordance with the variance analysis for that the decrease of variance will become smaller when number of experts becomes higher. Indeed, applying Eq. (4), the decrease of variance from $K = 1$ to $K = 2$ is $\frac{1}{2}\sigma^2_{(h,d),x}$, while from $K = 5$ to $K = 6$ it is only $\frac{1}{30}\sigma^2_{(h,d),x}$, 15 times lower. This correponds to the observation the improvements of UAS and LAS tend to decrease with the number of experts until it reaches a plateau.

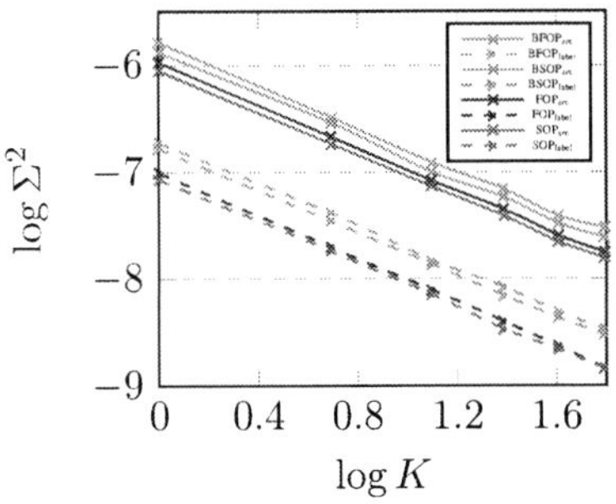

Figure 1: Variance by experts on PTB Dev Data.

Clustering We found that a modest improvement on UAS and LAS (0.01%-0.06% absolute) can be achieved by clustering (except for FOP on CoNLL09 Chinese). The average performance benefits generally from clustering while a tiny decrease (0.01%) is observed for BFOP on PTB.

Since FOP, SOP, BFOP and BSOP are all strong learners for PTB and CoNLL09 Chinese, *i.e.* UAS and LAS approaches 99% for both PTB and CoNLL09 on training data for all models, we can assume that an expert belonging to one of these models can learn efficiently most of the training data, as opposed to just a portion of it. Thus, only a a few of training instances can significantly be better covered by clustering. Moreover, as averaging has already achieved a considerable improvement (around 0.2%-0.6% absolute), a biased ω_k obtained from clustering may harm the gain from averaging.

6.4 Results on Test

Tables 5 and 6 show test results on PTB and CoNLL09, comparisons with recent models. We show test results of SOP and CSOP with 6 experts for PTB and CoNLL09. Additionally for PTB, we show BFOP, CBFOP, BSOP and CBSOP with 6 experts to make comparison with recent parsers, often more sophisticated than our approach, with BERT. We give the results with the same typographical system as Zhang et al. (2020a) Please note that, while average results keep the same semantics, *max* and *min* give test results of the LAS highest- and lowest- (resp.) scoring systems *on the development set*. We note that results of Zhang et al. (2020a) would correspond our model with $K = 1$.

For averaging models, we apply significance t-tests (Dror et al., 2018) with level $\alpha = 0.05$ to FOP, BFOP, SOP, BSOP with $K = 6$ against $K = 1$. For PTB and CoNLL09, p-value is always smaller than 0.005. We note that for parsers without BERT, averaging can achieve a considerable improvement with SOP and gives new SOTA. We also point out that, if FOP and SOP could find equivalently good models on dev, SOP models seem to better generalize. For parsers with BERT, with a simple averaging of BSOP, we achieve comparable performances (or even better in case of LAS) when comparing to more involved methods such as (Li et al., 2020; Mohammadshahi and Henderson, 2021). It remains to be seen whether they can also benefit from MoEs.

Regarding clustering, even if we obtained an average improvement on dev, test data hardly benefits from it. Still, we note a small improvement of UAS on SOP CoNLL09. Finally we stress that best performing settings on PTB test, namely BSOP and CBSOP, were not better performing than BFOP and CBFOP on development data on average (although max systems were similar): second-order models seem to slightly better handle unseen data.

6.5 Parallel Training and Decoding

Training averaging ensembles can be paralleled with sufficient GPUs, since each expert is trained independently. For fine tuning with clustering, most of the training could in principle be paralleled as well, although for the sake of simplicity we didn't implement such a training procedure: the training time of clustering model increases linearly with number of experts. As we only need a few epochs for fine tuning, the overall training time is comparable to training a single expert.

For decoding, calculations are performed in parallel as well. First marginal probabilities for arcs and labels are computed for every expert in parallel. Then they are combined either as a simple average or as a weighted sum. Finally, we apply the decoding algorithm (LMBR) *once* over the combined

Method	PTB		CoNLL09 Chinese	
	UAS	LAS	UAS	LAS
(Dozat and Manning, 2017)	95.74	94.08	88.90	85.38
(Li et al., 2019)	95.93	94.19	88.77	85.58
(Ji et al., 2019)	95.97	94.31	-	-
(Zhang et al., 2020a)	96.14	94.49	89.63	86.52
FOP, $K = 6$	$96.20^{96.19}_{96.20} \pm 0.02$	$94.64^{94.63}_{94.64} \pm 0.02$	$89.91^{89.84}_{89.99} \pm 0.06$	$87.00^{86.94}_{87.09} \pm 0.07$
CFOP, $K = 6$	$96.20^{96.18}_{96.18} \pm 0.02$	$94.65^{94.62}_{94.63} \pm 0.02$	$89.94^{89.92}_{89.93} \pm 0.04$	$87.03^{87.02}_{87.00} \pm 0.04$
SOP, $K = 6$	$\mathbf{96.29}^{96.30}_{96.29} \pm 0.02$	$\mathbf{94.71}^{94.72}_{94.73} \pm 0.02$	$90.06^{90.14}_{89.97} \pm 0.07$	$\mathbf{87.12}^{87.19}_{87.00} \pm 0.07$
CSOP, $K = 6$	$96.27^{96.27}_{96.32} \pm 0.03$	$94.69^{94.70}_{94.72} \pm 0.03$	$\mathbf{90.07}^{90.00}_{89.99} \pm 0.08$	$\mathbf{87.12}^{87.24}_{87.02} \pm 0.09$

Table 5: Comparison on test sets without BERT.

Method	PTB	
	UAS	LAS
(Li et al., 2020)	96.44	94.63
(Mohammadshahi and Henderson, 2021)	**96.66**	95.01
BFOP, $K = 6$	$96.58^{96.60}_{96.57} \pm 0.02$	$95.06^{95.07}_{95.02} \pm 0.02$
CBFOP, $K = 6$	$96.58^{96.59}_{96.54} \pm 0.02$	$95.06^{95.07}_{95.02} \pm 0.02$
BSOP, $K = 6$	$96.64^{\mathbf{96.66}}_{96.58} \pm 0.02$	$\mathbf{95.09}^{95.11}_{95.12} \pm 0.03$
CBSOP, $K = 6$	$96.62^{\mathbf{96.66}}_{96.64} \pm 0.03$	$95.07^{\mathbf{95.12}}_{95.07} \pm 0.03$

Table 6: Comparison of BERT models on PTB test set.

probability. The overhead is thus quite limited, for instance with $K = 6$ the overall decoding time is only around 10% higher than with a single expert.

7 Related Work

Ensembling parsers showed good results in shared tasks (Che et al., 2018)[8] and were framed as a combination of experts in (Petrov, 2010). In this work we show how this is related to mixtures and distinguish averaging and clustering effects.

The use of mixture model for syntactic parsing was introduced in (Petrov et al., 2006) for PCFG models, where it provided an access to non-local features unreachable to mere PCFGs. However, now that powerful non-Markovian feature extractors (*i.e.* BiLSTMs or Transformers) are widely used, the expected gain is more difficult to characterize, but we hypothesize that it is related to the softmax bottleneck (Yang et al., 2018) implied by using different exponential models in all predictions, even when richly parameterized.

We modelled parser combinations with finite mixture models, but more sophisticated parsing models (Kim et al., 2019) use infinite mixture models. In this case it might be more difficult to discriminate between averaging and clustering. Our mixture is essentially a latent variable model where the latent variables range over experts. Although inspired from EM with neural networks, similarly to (Nishida and Nakayama, 2020), other methods based on ELBo and sampling could also be utilized (Corro and Titov, 2019; Zhu et al., 2020).

8 Conclusion

We framed dependency parser combination as a finite mixture model, showed that this model presents two distinct properties –an averaging effect and a clustering effect– and devised an efficient decoding method. Moreover, we studied the impact of the averaging effect, namely variance reduction during training, and consequently better accuracy. We investigated the reasons of instability when learning mixture models, and proposed an EM-inspired method to avoid over-specialization. When used as fine-tuning, this method may improve accuracy over averaging. As a by-product, this method gives state-of-the-art results when combined with first-order and second-order projective parsers on two standard datasets.

This work can be further expanded in future research: the increase of parameters can be seen as overparameterization, and many parameters must be redundant. A potentially fruitful avenue of research could be the investigation of the subnetwork hypothesis, *i.e.* whether distillation could give a smaller network with similar performance.

Acknowledgments

This work is partially supported by a public grantoverseen by the French National Research Agency (ANR) as part of the program Investissements d'Avenir (ANR-10-LABX-0083). It contributes to the IdEx Université de Paris (ANR-18-IDEX-0001). This work is partially supported by a public grant overseen by the French ANR (ANR-16-CE33-0021).

[8]Ensembling is widely used in Machine Translation shared tasks, such as WMT.

References

Paolo Baldi. 2017. Stochastic calculus. In *Stochastic Calculus*, pages 1–14. Springer.

Andrew D. Brown and Geoffrey E. Hinton. 2001. Products of hidden markov models. In *Proceedings of the Eighth International Workshop on Artificial Intelligence and Statistics, AISTATS 2001, Key West, Florida, USA, January 4-7, 2001*. Society for Artificial Intelligence and Statistics.

Wanxiang Che, Yijia Liu, Yuxuan Wang, Bo Zheng, and Ting Liu. 2018. Towards better UD parsing: Deep contextualized word embeddings, ensemble, and treebank concatenation. In *Proceedings of the CoNLL 2018 Shared Task: Multilingual Parsing from Raw Text to Universal Dependencies*, pages 55–64, Brussels, Belgium. Association for Computational Linguistics.

Caio Corro and Ivan Titov. 2019. Differentiable perturb-and-parse: Semi-supervised parsing with a structured variational autoencoder. In *7th International Conference on Learning Representations, ICLR 2019, New Orleans, LA, USA, May 6-9, 2019*. OpenReview.net.

Jacob Devlin, Ming-Wei Chang, Kenton Lee, and Kristina Toutanova. 2019. BERT: Pre-training of deep bidirectional transformers for language understanding. In *Proceedings of the 2019 Conference of the North American Chapter of the Association for Computational Linguistics: Human Language Technologies, Volume 1 (Long and Short Papers)*, pages 4171–4186, Minneapolis, Minnesota. Association for Computational Linguistics.

Timothy Dozat and Christopher D. Manning. 2017. Deep biaffine attention for neural dependency parsing. In *5th International Conference on Learning Representations, ICLR 2017, Toulon, France, April 24-26, 2017, Conference Track Proceedings*. OpenReview.net.

Rotem Dror, Gili Baumer, Segev Shlomov, and Roi Reichart. 2018. The hitchhiker's guide to testing statistical significance in natural language processing. In *Proceedings of the 56th Annual Meeting of the Association for Computational Linguistics (Volume 1: Long Papers)*, pages 1383–1392, Melbourne, Australia. Association for Computational Linguistics.

Jason Eisner. 1996. Efficient normal-form parsing for Combinatory Categorial Grammar. In *34th Annual Meeting of the Association for Computational Linguistics*, pages 79–86, Santa Cruz, California, USA. Association for Computational Linguistics.

Jason Eisner. 1997. Bilexical grammars and a cubic-time probabilistic parser. In *Proceedings of the Fifth International Workshop on Parsing Technologies*, pages 54–65, Boston/Cambridge, Massachusetts, USA. Association for Computational Linguistics.

Jason Eisner. 2016. Inside-outside and forward-backward algorithms are just backprop (tutorial paper). In *Proceedings of the Workshop on Structured Prediction for NLP*, pages 1–17, Austin, TX. Association for Computational Linguistics.

Agnieszka Falenska and Jonas Kuhn. 2019. The (non-)utility of structural features in BiLSTM-based dependency parsers. In *Proceedings of the 57th Annual Meeting of the Association for Computational Linguistics*, pages 117–128, Florence, Italy. Association for Computational Linguistics.

Erick Fonseca and André F. T. Martins. 2020. Revisiting higher-order dependency parsers. In *Proceedings of the 58th Annual Meeting of the Association for Computational Linguistics*, pages 8795–8800, Online. Association for Computational Linguistics.

Victoria Fossum and Kevin Knight. 2009. Combining constituent parsers. In *Proceedings of Human Language Technologies: The 2009 Annual Conference of the North American Chapter of the Association for Computational Linguistics, Companion Volume: Short Papers*, pages 253–256, Boulder, Colorado. Association for Computational Linguistics.

Vaibhava Goel and William J. Byrne. 2000. Minimum bayes-risk automatic speech recognition. *Comput. Speech Lang.*, 14(2):115–135.

Nathan Green and Zdeněk Žabokrtský. 2012. Hybrid combination of constituency and dependency trees into an ensemble dependency parser. In *Proceedings of the Workshop on Innovative Hybrid Approaches to the Processing of Textual Data*, pages 19–26, Avignon, France. Association for Computational Linguistics.

Jan Hajič, Massimiliano Ciaramita, Richard Johansson, Daisuke Kawahara, Maria Antònia Martí, Lluís Màrquez, Adam Meyers, Joakim Nivre, Sebastian Padó, Jan Štěpánek, Pavel Straňák, Mihai Surdeanu, Nianwen Xue, and Yi Zhang. 2009. The CoNLL-2009 shared task: Syntactic and semantic dependencies in multiple languages. In *Proceedings of the Thirteenth Conference on Computational Natural Language Learning (CoNLL 2009): Shared Task*, pages 1–18, Boulder, Colorado. Association for Computational Linguistics.

Sepp Hochreiter and Jürgen Schmidhuber. 1997. Long short-term memory. *Neural computation*, 9(8):1735–1780.

Robert A Jacobs, Michael I Jordan, Steven J Nowlan, and Geoffrey E Hinton. 1991. Adaptive mixtures of local experts. *Neural computation*, 3(1):79–87.

Tao Ji, Yuanbin Wu, and Man Lan. 2019. Graph-based dependency parsing with graph neural networks. In *Proceedings of the 57th Annual Meeting of the Association for Computational Linguistics*, pages 2475–2485, Florence, Italy. Association for Computational Linguistics.

Yoon Kim, Chris Dyer, and Alexander Rush. 2019. Compound probabilistic context-free grammars for grammar induction. In *Proceedings of the 57th Annual Meeting of the Association for Computational Linguistics*, pages 2369–2385, Florence, Italy. Association for Computational Linguistics.

Guillaume Lample, Miguel Ballesteros, Sandeep Subramanian, Kazuya Kawakami, and Chris Dyer. 2016. Neural architectures for named entity recognition. In *Proceedings of the 2016 Conference of the North American Chapter of the Association for Computational Linguistics: Human Language Technologies*, pages 260–270, San Diego, California. Association for Computational Linguistics.

Joseph Le Roux, Antoine Rozenknop, and Mathieu Lacroix. 2019. Representation learning and dynamic programming for arc-hybrid parsing. In *Proceedings of the 23rd Conference on Computational Natural Language Learning (CoNLL)*, pages 238–248, Hong Kong, China. Association for Computational Linguistics.

Ying Li, Zhenghua Li, Min Zhang, Rui Wang, Sheng Li, and Luo Si. 2019. Self-attentive biaffine dependency parsing. In *IJCAI*, pages 5067–5073.

Zuchao Li, Hai Zhao, and Kevin Parnow. 2020. Global greedy dependency parsing. In *Proceedings of the AAAI Conference on Artificial Intelligence*, volume 34, pages 8319–8326.

Mitchell P. Marcus, Beatrice Santorini, and Mary Ann Marcinkiewicz. 1993. Building a large annotated corpus of English: The Penn Treebank. *Computational Linguistics*, 19(2):313–330.

Ryan McDonald, Fernando Pereira, Kiril Ribarov, and Jan Hajič. 2005. Non-projective dependency parsing using spanning tree algorithms. In *Proceedings of Human Language Technology Conference and Conference on Empirical Methods in Natural Language Processing*, pages 523–530, Vancouver, British Columbia, Canada. Association for Computational Linguistics.

Alireza Mohammadshahi and James Henderson. 2021. Recursive Non-Autoregressive Graph-to-Graph Transformer for Dependency Parsing with Iterative Refinement. *Transactions of the Association for Computational Linguistics*, 9:120–138.

Noriki Nishida and Hideki Nakayama. 2020. Unsupervised discourse constituency parsing using Viterbi EM. *Transactions of the Association for Computational Linguistics*, 8:215–230.

Jeffrey Pennington, Richard Socher, and Christopher Manning. 2014. GloVe: Global vectors for word representation. In *Proceedings of the 2014 Conference on Empirical Methods in Natural Language Processing (EMNLP)*, pages 1532–1543, Doha, Qatar. Association for Computational Linguistics.

Slav Petrov. 2010. Products of random latent variable grammars. In *Human Language Technologies: The 2010 Annual Conference of the North American Chapter of the Association for Computational Linguistics*, pages 19–27, Los Angeles, California. Association for Computational Linguistics.

Slav Petrov, Leon Barrett, and Dan Klein. 2006. Non-local modeling with a mixture of PCFGs. In *Proceedings of the Tenth Conference on Computational Natural Language Learning (CoNLL-X)*, pages 14–20, New York City. Association for Computational Linguistics.

Sashank J. Reddi, Satyen Kale, and Sanjiv Kumar. 2018. On the convergence of adam and beyond. In *International Conference on Learning Representations*.

Alexander M. Rush, David Sontag, Michael Collins, and Tommi Jaakkola. 2010. On dual decomposition and linear programming relaxations for natural language processing. In *Proceedings of the 2010 Conference on Empirical Methods in Natural Language Processing*, pages 1–11, Cambridge, MA. Association for Computational Linguistics.

David A. Smith and Noah A. Smith. 2007. Probabilistic models of nonprojective dependency trees. In *Proceedings of the 2007 Joint Conference on Empirical Methods in Natural Language Processing and Computational Natural Language Learning (EMNLP-CoNLL)*, pages 132–140, Prague, Czech Republic. Association for Computational Linguistics.

Nitish Srivastava, Geoffrey Hinton, Alex Krizhevsky, Ilya Sutskever, and Ruslan Salakhutdinov. 2014. Dropout: a simple way to prevent neural networks from overfitting. *The journal of machine learning research*, 15(1):1929–1958.

Zhilin Yang, Zihang Dai, Ruslan Salakhutdinov, and William W. Cohen. 2018. Breaking the softmax bottleneck: A high-rank RNN language model. In *6th International Conference on Learning Representations, ICLR 2018, Vancouver, BC, Canada, April 30 - May 3, 2018, Conference Track Proceedings*. OpenReview.net.

Yu Zhang, Zhenghua Li, and Min Zhang. 2020a. Efficient second-order TreeCRF for neural dependency parsing. In *Proceedings of the 58th Annual Meeting of the Association for Computational Linguistics*, pages 3295–3305, Online. Association for Computational Linguistics.

Yu Zhang, Houquan Zhou, and Zhenghua Li. 2020b. Fast and accurate neural CRF constituency parsing. In *Proceedings of IJCAI*, pages 4046–4053.

Junru Zhou, Zuchao Li, and Hai Zhao. 2020. Parsing all: Syntax and semantics, dependencies and spans. In *Findings of the Association for Computational Linguistics: EMNLP 2020*, pages 4438–4449, Online. Association for Computational Linguistics.

Hao Zhu, Yonatan Bisk, and Graham Neubig. 2020. The return of lexical dependencies: Neural lexicalized pcfgs.

Ran Zmigrod, Tim Vieira, and Ryan Cotterell. 2020. Efficient computation of expectations under spanning tree distributions.

A Marginal Probability of Arc for Mixture Model

With Eq. (3). The marginal probability of mixture model can be written as:

$$p((h,d)|x) = \sum_{\substack{y\in\mathcal{Y}(x)\\(h,d)\in y}} \sum_{k=1}^{K} \omega_k p_k(y|x)$$

By changing the order of sum, we can have:

$$p((h,d)|x) = \sum_{k=1}^{K} \omega_k \sum_{\substack{y\in\mathcal{Y}(x)\\(h,d)\in y}} p_k(y|x)$$

The inner part is exactly $p_k((h,d)|x)$. Thus, we have:

$$p((h,d)|x) = \sum_{k=1}^{K} \omega_k p_k((h,d)|x)$$

B Quick Gradient Analysis of Gating Network

We start from Eq. (6).

For mixture model with well trained experts, most of the data are equivalent for all experts, which means $p_k(y|x)$ have similar value for all experts. To see quickly why gradient approaches 0 in this case, we assume further that $p_k(y|x)$ has the same value for equivalent data. Thus, Eq. (6) becomes:

$$\frac{\partial L(\phi,\theta)}{\partial \phi} = \sum_{k=1}^{K} \omega_k(\phi) \frac{\partial \log \omega_k(\phi)}{\partial \phi}$$

With a little more deduction, we have:

$$\begin{aligned}\frac{\partial L(\phi,\theta)}{\partial \phi} &= \sum_{k=1}^{K} \omega_k(\phi) \frac{1}{\omega_k(\phi)} \frac{\partial \omega_k(\phi)}{\partial \phi}\\ &= \sum_{k=1}^{K} \frac{\partial \omega_k(\phi)}{\partial \phi}\\ &= \frac{\partial \sum_{k=1}^{K} \omega_k(\phi)}{\partial \phi}\\ &= \frac{\partial 1}{\partial \phi}\\ &= 0\end{aligned}$$

As the function is continuous w.r.t. p_k, for data which provides similar value of probability on all experts, the gradient will approaches zero. Thus, for training with Eq. (6), only a small part of data, which shows strong preference of particular experts, is used to train the gating network.

For training with Eq. (8), all the data is useful for training the gating network. In fact, the gradient of Eq. (8) becomes zero when:

$$\omega_k(\phi) = \frac{p_k(\theta_k)}{\sum_{k'=1}^{K} p_{k'}(\theta_{k'})}$$

Thus for data which are equivalent for all experts, a uniform weight will be learnt while for data with strong preference of particular experts, a biased weight proportional to the probability correctness on each expert can also be learnt.

C Gating Network Structure, hyper-parameters of training

The gating network structure is similar to the structure of parse model.

Embedding Word embedding for word x_i is an concatenation of two parts: normal word embedding and CharLSTM embedding:

$$e_i = \text{emb}(x_i) \bigoplus \text{CharLSTM}(x_i)$$

when there is pre-trained embedding, the first item is the sum of word embedding calculated by neural network, and the exterior pretrained embedding:

$$\text{emb}(x_i) = \text{WordEMB}(x_i) + \text{PreEMB}(x_i)$$

We suppose that PreEMB has the same size as WordEMB

BiLSTM The embedding vectors are then passed to 3 layers of BiLSTM, with the output at position i is noted as h_i.

Coefficient Extractor The coefficient extractor part is constructed of one layer of LSTM (Hochreiter and Schmidhuber, 1997) and one layer of MLP. The last hidden state of LSTM is passed to MLP, which compress the vector size to the number of experts in the mixture model. Two groups of coefficient extractor are used to calculate separately the weight of combination for arc and label. We note the output of MLP as $\mathbf{C} \in \mathbb{R}^K$, with:

$$\mathbf{C}_{\text{arc}} = \text{MLP}_{\text{arc}}(\text{LSTM}_{\text{arc}}(h_0, ..., h_n))$$

$$\mathbf{C}_{\text{label}} = \text{MLP}_{\text{label}}(\text{LSTM}_{\text{label}}(h_0, ..., h_n))$$

The output of MLP is passed to Softmax to calculate the weight for each expert:

$$[\omega_1, ..., \omega_K] = \text{Softmax}(\mathbf{C}_{\text{arc}})$$

$$[\omega_1^l, ..., \omega_K^l] = \text{Softmax}(\mathbf{C}_{\text{label}})$$

Model hyper-parameters of fine tuning is shown in Table 7. We use also Adam (Reddi et al., 2018) for training, with learning rate set to $2e^{-4}$ (10 times smaller than learning rate used for training experts). The patience is set to 20 instead of the original value 100. For fine tuning, we found that best score is usually achieved in less than 20 epochs and does not increase later.

Param	Value	Param	Value
WordEMB size	100	Embedding dropout	0.33
CharLSTM size	50	CharLSTM dropout	0.00
BiLSTM size	400	BiLSTM dropout	0.33
LSTM_{arc} size	400	LSTM_{arc} dropout	0.00
$\text{LSTM}_{\text{label}}$ size	400	$\text{LSTM}_{\text{label}}$ dropout	0.00
MLP_{arc} size	K	MLP_{arc} dropout	0.00
$\text{MLP}_{\text{label}}$ size	K	$\text{MLP}_{\text{label}}$ dropout	0.00
Learning Rate	$\mathbf{2e^{-4}}$	β_1, β_2	0.90
Annealing	$0.75^{\frac{t}{5000}}$	Patience	**20**

Table 7: Hyper-parameters of Fine Tuning

D Implementation Differences

We implement Zhang et al. (2020a) CRF model and CRF2o model with two tiny technical differences.

The first one is that the CharLSTM (Lample et al., 2016) part in Zhang et al. (2020a) treats the beginning of the sentence <bos> (the special token to represent the beginning of the sentence) as five separate characters: <, b, o, s, >.

Our implementation treats the beginning of sentence as one special character for CharLSTM.

Another difference is that Zhang et al. (2020a) treats the lengths of every sentence as $n + 2$ by considering two special tokens <bos> and <eos> (although in practice, only <bos> was added to every sentence). In our implementation, we keep the length of sentence as the number of words n. This is because the log probability of arc and label only considers the words in the sentence without special tokens. Thus our batch size should be a little bit higher than Zhang et al. (2020a).

One final difference is that for MBR decoding, (Zhang et al., 2020a) maximizes the sum of marginal arc probability. While in our implementation of MBR, we maximize the product of marginal arc probability.

E Variance Reduction on CoNLL09

We note that the label variance for FOP and SOP are quite similar that they overlap together for CoNLL09 Chinese.

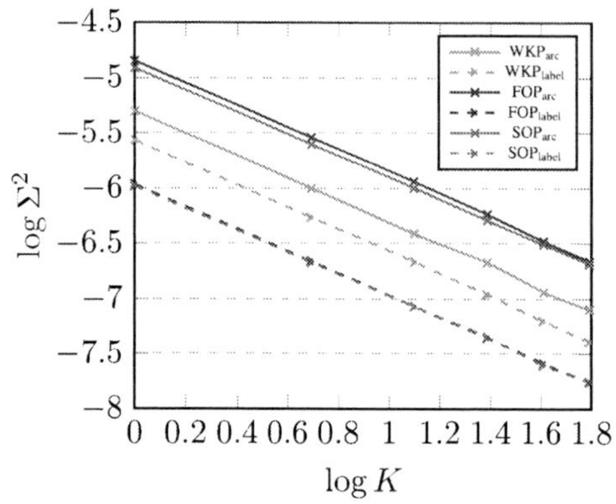

Figure 2: Variance of System to CoNLL09 Chinese

A Modest Pareto Optimisation Analysis of Dependency Parsers in 2021

Mark Anderson
Universidade da Coruña, CITIC
Department of CS & IT
m.anderson@udc

Carlos Gómez-Rodríguez
Universidade da Coruña, CITIC
Department of CS & IT
carlos.gomez@udc.es

Abstract

We evaluate three leading dependency parser systems from different paradigms on a small yet diverse subset of languages in terms of their accuracy-efficiency Pareto front. As we are interested in efficiency, we evaluate core parsers without pretrained language models (as these are typically huge networks and would constitute most of the compute time) or other augmentations that can be transversally applied to any of them. Biaffine parsing emerges as a well-balanced default choice, with sequence-labelling parsing being preferable if inference speed (but not training energy cost) is the priority.

1 Introduction

The inefficiency of modern NLP systems has recently come under scrutiny, especially regarding their large energy consumption (Strubell et al., 2019). This hasn't started a revolution, but there is some NLP work where efficiency is considered. Zhang and Duh (2020) studied different settings for neural machine translation systems, evaluating not only accuracy but also certain costs such as inference time, training time, and model size. Zhou et al. (2021) analysed the fine-tuning and inference time for pretrained LMs, and estimated the cost of pretraining. Jacobsen et al. (2021) presented a Pareto optimisation analysis for POS taggers, considering accuracy and model size.

In parsing in particular, Strzyz et al. (2019) evaluated dependency parsing as sequence labelling specifically to increase inference efficiency and also undertook a Pareto optimisation analysis. Others used model compression via distillation to increase inference speed of neural parsers with a mixed bag of results (Dehouck et al., 2020; Anderson and Gómez-Rodríguez, 2020a). Dehouck et al. (2020) also took into consideration the training energy costs of distilling models, which highlighted the high energy cost of this technique.

We present a Pareto optimisation analysis on modern dependency parsing systems. We cover three systems which are broadly representative of current approaches. We analyse their efficiency with respect to inference speed and also their training cost, measured in energy consumption.

Contribution: A simple, modest analysis on the merits of different parser systems that cover three current paradigms. Our goal is not to provide surprising results, but a realistic snapshot of the current state of affairs of a representative sample of modern parsing systems on linguistically diverse data. This analysis runs the systems in a consistent way with respect to software, hardware, and network settings. We also offer a brief overview of self-reported performance on PTB for systems that have a published speed. We add to this measurements for a subset of these systems which we ran locally for a more consistent comparison, i.e. something of a reproducibility effort.

Disclaimer We make a practical comparison for practitioners, so we focus on publicly available systems on typical hardware that doesn't require a huge budget. We are not making general claims that technique X is always more efficient than technique Y in the abstract or that this will hold in any hardware. Also, the extent to which an implementation has been engineered will impact performance, so we have referenced the original repositories used.[1]

2 PTB performance

For historical reasons, it is common practice for parsers to report performance results on the English Penn Treebank (PTB) (Marcus and Marcinkiewicz, 1993). While such results at best provide a partial picture on a single language, they are by far the

[1]The moderately edited code is available at `http://www.grupolys.org/software/iwpt2021/parsers-code.zip`.

Proceedings of the 17th International Conference on Parsing Technologies (IWPT 2021), pages 119–130
Bangkok, Thailand (online), August 6, 2021.

	speed (sent/s)			
	GPU	CPU	UAS	LAS
HPSG (Zhou and Zhao, 2019)	159*	-	96.09*	94.68*
Biaffine w CRF (Zhang et al., 2020a)	400*		96.14*	94.49*
Pointer-LR (Fernández-González and Gómez-Rodríguez, 2019)	23*	-	96.04*	94.43*
GNN (Ji et al., 2019)	416*	-	95.97*	94.31*
Pointer-TD (Ma et al., 2018)	10.2†	-	95.87*	94.19*
Biaffine (Dozat and Manning, 2017)	411*	-	95.74*	94.08*
Distilled-Ensemble (Kuncoro et al., 2016)	-	20*	94.26*	92.06*
BIST - Transition (Kiperwasser and Goldberg, 2016)	-	76±1‡	93.9*	91.9*
SeqLab (Strzyz et al., 2019)	648±20*	101±2*	93.67*	91.72*
BIST - Graph (Kiperwasser and Goldberg, 2016)	-	80±0‡	93.1*	91.0*
CM (Chen and Manning, 2014)	-	654*	91.80*	89.60*
Pointer-LR	95±1	8±0	96.02	94.47
Biaffine (PyTorch)	1003±3	53±0	95.74	94.07
UUParser (Smith et al., 2018)	-	42±1	94.63	92.77
Distilled-Biaffine (Anderson and Gómez-Rodríguez, 2020a)	1153±3	96±0	94.59	92.64
SeqLab	1064±13	99±1	93.46	91.49
MaltParser 1.9.2 w/ Stack lazy (Nivre et al., 2007)	-	473±11	89.29	86.95

Table 1: Performance for current leading parsers for the English PTB with POS tags predicted from the Stanford POS tagger. $*$ denotes values taken from the original paper, † from Fernández-González and Gómez-Rodríguez (2019), and ‡ from Strzyz et al. (2019). Values with no superscript are from running the models on our system locally (speeds averaged over 5 runs) and with a batch size of 256 (excluding UUParser which doesn't support batching) with GloVe 100 dimension embeddings. Table is extended from one in Anderson and Gómez-Rodríguez (2020a).

most comprehensive source of results provided in the literature under a consistent context (at least in terms of data and splits, although not hardware), so they are useful to see high-level trends and as a starting point to choose parsers for our experiment.

In Table 1 we report performance of modern parsing systems for which speeds have been reported. We couldn't find a reported speed of Clark et al. (2018) which currently has the highest reported performance on PTB (UAS 96.61 and LAS 95.02) when not using BERT. However, its main contribution is semi-supervised augmentations that could be utilised by any parsing system, with their core parser being the Biaffine parser. Zhou and Zhao (2019)'s system leverages constituency and dependency parsing and when not using training data with both constituency and dependency annotations (often not available) the system achieves UAS 95.82 LAS 94.43 (i.e. very similar in LAS to the other top-performing sytems). Zhang et al. (2020a) use a Biaffine parser but with a moderate beam search, which is obviously less efficient than the original. It results in a small increase in performance. Ji et al. (2019) use graph neural networks to learn enriched high-order information from partial parses. It again only gains small increases over Biaffine, but is more computationally complex and code is not available.

We report results for UUParser of Smith et al. (2018) that we ran locally (refreshingly the original paper didn't use PTB). While the results show a reasonable speed-accuracy trade-off, we opted not to use this for the current analysis as the original code is implemented in DyNet which doesn't properly support CUDA, and is a different framework from that of the other parsers we opted to choose.

Based on this, we opted to use the basic Biaffine parser to represent graph-based parsers, the Pointer-LR network as the representative of transition-based algorithms,[2] and the sequence-labelling parser to represent SL systems. They all have the added benefit of working under the same software and having code available.

Note that, as we make emphasis on efficiency, we focus on reasonably bare-bones versions of the parsers. The impact of pretrained language models, or other augmentations that are transversal to the parsing system, is outside the scope of this paper.

3 Pareto optimisation analysis

Here we detail the parsing systems, the data we used, and how model structures were altered.

3.1 Parsers

All the parsers use BiLSTMs, but have additional structures which set them apart from one another

[2]Some might argue that it isn't a clear cut case of a transition-based parser, but it transitions from state to state like more traditonal algorithms.

and use one of three paradigms broadly speaking: one is a transition-based parser, one is a sequence-labelling parser, and the last is a graph-based parser. For space reasons, we only very briefly outline them here, but give more details in Appendix A.

Left-to-right pointer network (L2R). One of the current top-performing parsers on PTB, it uses a left-to-right transition-based algorithm that builds a number of attachments equal to sentence length using a pointer network (Ma et al., 2018; Fernández-González and Gómez-Rodríguez, 2019).[3]

Deep biaffine (BIAFFINE) (Dozat and Manning, 2017) is an edge-factored graph-based parser that produces a matrix of scores giving a probability distribution on arcs, where the Chu-Liu-Edmonds algorithm (Chu and Liu, 1965; Edmonds, 1967) is then applied to obtain a tree.

Sequence labelling parser (SEQLAB) encodes trees as a sequence of labels, so that a direct one-to-one prediction can be made for each token in a sentence (Spoustová and Spousta, 2010; Li et al., 2018b; Strzyz et al., 2019).[4] We implement it using the Biaffine system described above (for uniformity) editing it to be a sequence-labelling system.

3.2 Data

In our choice of treebanks, we balance three factors: the need to use a small number of treebanks (as our detailed Pareto analysis implies training a large number of models per treebank), linguistic diversity and treebank quality. This leads us to choose 4 high-quality (manually annotated or corrected, and relatively large) treebanks covering 3 different language families and 4 subfamilies: UD-Hindi-HDTB, UD-Polish-PDB, UD-Korean-Kaist and the Chinese Penn Treebank. More details of each treebank, justifying their diversity and adequacy for the analysis are given in Appendix C.

3.3 Methodology

We vary the size of the BiLSTM component of the networks by their number of layers and nodes. Each parser has randomly-initialised character embeddings and pretrained word embeddings as only inputs. We use pretrained FastText embeddings (Grave et al., 2018). Except for Chinese, as the FastText embeddings are in the traditional script, so we use the embeddings from Li et al. (2018a).[5] The embeddings are reduced to 100 dimensions using PCA. The structure of the networks are very similar. The L2R system uses a biaffine transformation to score the transitions at each step similar to the BIAFFINE parser, and we use the same sizes for the layers. The SEQLAB system is altered from the BIAFFINE implementation and is exactly the same except the layers needed for the biaffine transformation are replaced by two MLPs which predict the labels for each token. The only major difference in the networks is that L2R uses a CNN to create the character embeddings and the other two use BiLSTMs. We didn't change this in order to avoid modifications to the systems. The network hyperparameters are shown in Table 2 in Appendix B. Models were trained on GPU, but we report the energy used by both the GPU and CPU.

We could have altered other aspects of the network, but the main computational cost comes from the BiLSTM layer. The other main contender to alter would be the embedding layers. For example, we could have altered the size of the character BiLSTM/CNN, but certain experiments show that it has a limited impact on accuracy (Smith et al., 2018; Anderson and Gómez-Rodríguez, 2020b).

We measured the speed of each system on each treebank by running them 5 times using a single CPU core, both for speeds measured running on GPU and CPU, so that we get a reasonably accurate measure of the speed for each treebank. We then report macro averaged speeds across treebanks.

We use the `energyusage` package for measuring training energy.[6] It measures the power usage of the GPU and CPU while a process is running (having taken a measure of the background usage). We minimised the use of the system when training these models to obtain accurate measurements, but they aren't overly precise. This isn't a major issue as the measurements are over long periods of time and so unless there were massive fluctuations when training a given model, comparison is fine. We use joules (or kJ and MJ) as they are the SI units for energy (BIPM, 2019) and, unlike carbon emissions, they are independent of external factors like regional electricity generation grids.

Hardware: Intel Core i7-7700 and Nvidia GeForce GTX 1080.

Software: Python 3.7.0, PyTorch 1.0.0, and CUDA 8.0.

[3]https://github.com/danifg/SyntacticPointer.

[4]We use refactored encoding/decoding functions from https://github.com/mstrise/dep2label.

[5]`https://jima.me/open/cwv/`

[6]`https://pypi.org/project/energyusage`

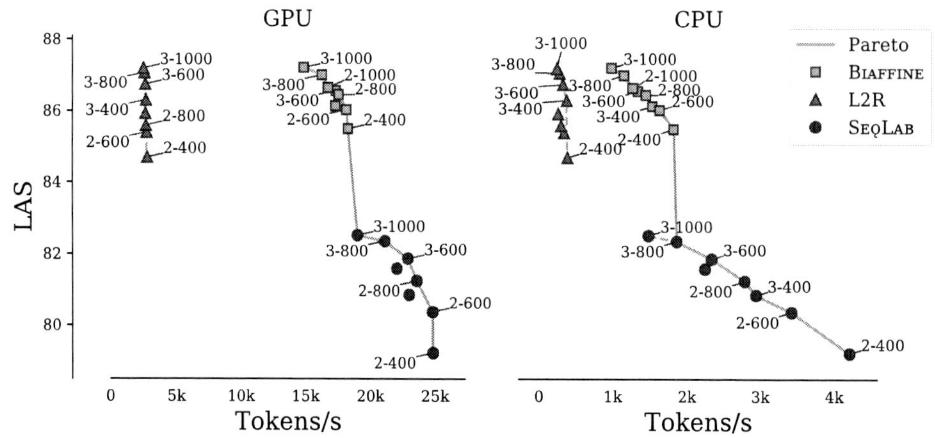

Figure 1: Pareto fronts for L2R, BIAFFINE, and SEQLAB for the development data.

3.4 Pareto fronts: inference speed

Figure 1 shows LAS versus parsing speed for the development data (we also present the same for the test data in Figure 7 in the Appendix that echoes the visualisation seen here). The individual Pareto front for each parser is shown (light grey, dashed) As expected, models with larger networks are more accurate but slower. More interestingly, the overall Pareto front is exclusively constructed of BIAFFINE and SEQLAB systems. While L2R does achieve similar accuracy scores as BIAFFINE, it is considerably slower. SEQLAB is the fastest option by a clear margin (especially smaller networks on CPU). So the practical advice to draw from this aspect or the Pareto optimisation would be to use BIAFFINE if accuracy is the main concern, or SEQLAB if inference time is important.

3.5 Pareto fronts: training energy

Figure 2 shows LAS against the average energy (across treebanks) consumed during training (in training, we always use the GPU). There is no clear link between the energy consumed and the accuracy of a system. However, this visualisation highlights that SEQLAB is nowhere near optimal with respect to training efficiency.

The amount of energy consumed during training is basically dependent on the time it takes each system to converge as can be seen in Figure 3. In this figure, we show individual models (i.e. not averaged over treebanks). The relation for BIAFFINE and SEQLAB is very clearly linear between energy and training time, suggesting that there is nothing intrinsically more energy consuming between these systems beyond convergence time. For L2R, this relation seems to hold broadly, but is less clear. It appears that L2R is more sensitive to the nature of

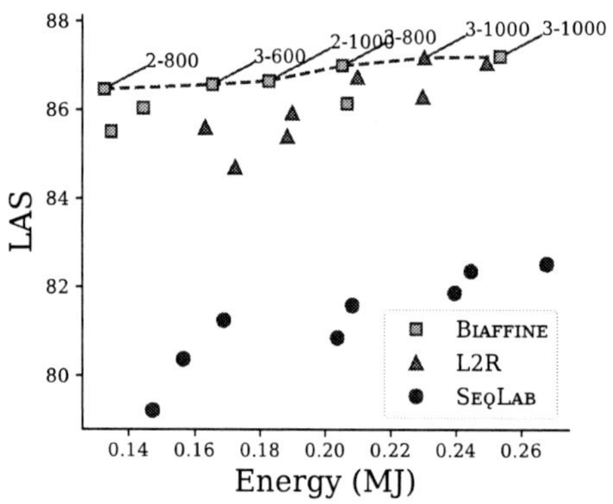

Figure 2: Pareto fronts for L2R, BIAFFINE, and SEQLAB for training energy.

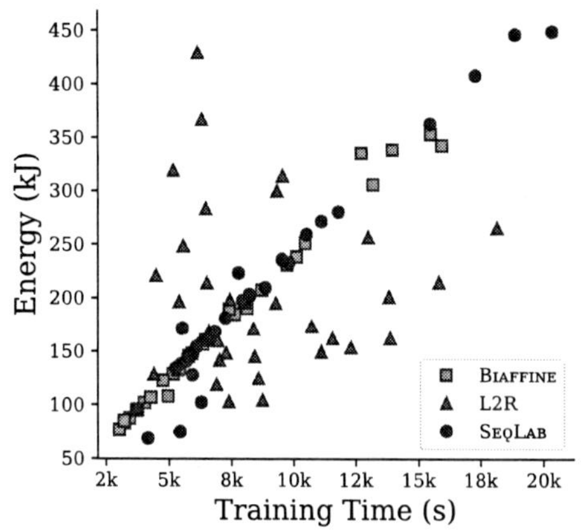

Figure 3: Training energy consumption with respect to training time.

the data, which we expand on in Appendix F.

4 Limitations of analysis

While our analysis is not ground-breaking or particularly expansive in nature, we do think it is useful in practice and acts as mini-review of the current state of affairs in dependency parsing. However, there are a number of limitations in this study. First, we only look at the parameters associated with the BiLSTMs. We feel this is fairly justified, but it is obviously feasible that varying these parameters and not the others could have different effects for each parsing system even if that is fairly unlikely. While we do look at a very diverse set of languages with diverse linguistic features, it is still a fairly small sample. We were somewhat limited by having to train many models and felt it would be better to focus on a sample of diverse languages with quality data than many languages and less model settings. Of course, this analysis could be extended to use more languages, but we expect this would further corroborate the results presented here. Also by using a small set of treebanks, we don't cover a wide array of domains (the data is mainly fiction and news).

Another potential limitation is only using one dependency annotation scheme (the scheme used for CTB was a precursor to UD), but in lieu of a theoretical reason that the parsers would behave differently using a different scheme (e.g. surface syntactic UD (SUD) treebanks containing much more non-projectivity (Gerdes et al., 2018)) this feels like a light limitation.

A slightly more pressing limitation is the absence of a feature analysis because certain systems could potentially benefit from different features. Work has been presented in this direction and has shown that predicted POS tags aren't wonderfully useful (Smith et al., 2018; Anderson and Gómez-Rodríguez, 2020b; Zhang et al., 2020b). However, these analyses didn't include SEQLAB parsers at all and the transition-based system used was a lower-performing system, UUParser. So it is feasible that L2R and SEQLAB would benefit from predicted POS tags. That can be left open for the future.

Another limitation is that we only trained one model for each BiLSTM setting. While training a model for each treebank somewhat offset this, it is still possible that with different initialisation, these parsers would behave slightly differently. However, it is unlikely to cause material differences in the performance and as mentioned, this is quite strongly offset by training on varying treebanks.

And finally, we focused on parsers trained on fairly large amounts of annotated data. We leave the analysis of different parsing systems in a low-resource setting for others, but we point out that when training on very little data, training costs aren't much of a concern and on truly low-resource languages, data parsed at production is also going to be scarce so inference speed won't be the bottleneck.

5 Conclusion

We have presented a simple Pareto optimisation analysis for a representative sample of modern dependency parsers. We evaluated efficiency in two ways. We evaluated the trade-off between accuracy and parsing speed and the trade-off between accuracy and training energy consumption. The BIAFFINE and SEQLAB occupied the speed Pareto front with the former being slower and more accurate and the latter being faster and less accurate. We didn't observe any real trade-off with regards to training energy and performance, but it was clear that SEQLAB is not particularly efficient in this regard. Typically training energy varied based on how long a model took to converge, with L2R being somewhat sensitive to the different treebanks. Overall, for most scenarios, BIAFFINE emerged as a well-balanced practical solution. For the sake of candour, we offer a brief discussion of the limitations of this analysis in Appendix 4.

Acknowledgments

This work has received funding from the European Research Council (ERC), under the European Union's Horizon 2020 research and innovation programme (FASTPARSE, grant agreement No 714150), from ERDF/MICINN-AEI (ANSWER-ASAP, TIN2017-85160-C2-1-R), from Xunta de Galicia (ED431C 2020/11), and from Centro de Investigación de Galicia "CITIC", funded by Xunta de Galicia and the European Union (ERDF - Galicia 2014-2020 Program), by grant ED431G 2019/01.

References

Mark Anderson and Carlos Gómez-Rodríguez. 2020a. Distilling neural networks for greener and faster dependency parsing. In *Proceedings of the 16th International Conference on Parsing Technologies and the IWPT 2020 Shared Task on Parsing into Enhanced Universal Dependencies*, pages 2–13, Online. Association for Computational Linguistics.

Mark Anderson and Carlos Gómez-Rodríguez. 2020b. On the frailty of universal POS tags for neural UD parsers. In *Proceedings of the 24th Conference on Computational Natural Language Learning*, pages 69–96, Online. Association for Computational Linguistics.

Riyaz Ahmad Bhat, Rajesh Bhatt, Annahita Farudi, Prescott Klassen, Bhuvana Narasimhan, Martha Palmer, Owen Rambow, Dipti Misra Sharma, Ashwini Vaidya, Sri Ramagurumurthy Vishnu, et al. 2017. The hindi/urdu treebank project. In *Handbook of Linguistic Annotation*, pages 659–697. Springer.

Dana Bielec. 1998. *Polish: An Essential Grammar*. Routledge, London.

BIPM. 2019. *Le Système international d'unités / The International System of Units ('The SI Brochure')*, ninth edition. Bureau international des poids et mesures.

Lucien Brown. 2015. Honorifics and politeness. *The handbook of Korean linguistics*, pages 303–319.

Suk-Jin Chang. 1996. *Korean*. John Benjamins, Philadelphia.

Danqi Chen and Christopher Manning. 2014. A fast and accurate dependency parser using neural networks. In *Proceedings of the 2014 Conference on Empirical Methods in Natural Language Processing (EMNLP)*, pages 740–750, Doha, Qatar. Association for Computational Linguistics.

Key-Sun Choi, Young S Han, Young G Han, and Oh W Kwon. 1994. Kaist tree bank project for korean: Present and future development. In *Proceedings of the International Workshop on Sharable Natural Language Resources*, pages 7–14. Citeseer.

Yoeng-Jin Chu and Tseng-Hong Liu. 1965. On the shortest arborescence of a directed graph. *Scientia Sinica*, 14:1396–1400.

Jayeol Chun, Na-Rae Han, Jena D Hwang, and Jinho D Choi. 2018. Building universal dependency treebanks in korean. In *Proceedings of the Eleventh International Conference on Language Resources and Evaluation (LREC 2018)*.

Kevin Clark, Minh-Thang Luong, Christopher D. Manning, and Quoc Le. 2018. Semi-supervised sequence modeling with cross-view training. In *Proceedings of the 2018 Conference on Empirical Methods in Natural Language Processing*, pages 1914–1925, Brussels, Belgium. Association for Computational Linguistics.

Federica Cognola and Jan Casalicchio. 2018. On the null-subject phenomenon. *Null subjects in Generative Grammar. A Synchronic and Diachronic Perspective*, pages 1–28.

Bernard Comrie. 1978. Ergativity. In Winfred P. Lehmann, editor, *Syntactic Typology: Studies in the Phenomenology of Language*, pages 329–394. University of Texas Press, Austin.

Mathieu Dehouck, Mark Anderson, and Carlos Gómez-Rodríguez. 2020. Efficient EUD parsing. In *Proceedings of the 16th International Conference on Parsing Technologies and the IWPT 2020 Shared Task on Parsing into Enhanced Universal Dependencies*, pages 192–205, Online. Association for Computational Linguistics.

Timothy Dozat and Christopher D Manning. 2017. Deep biaffine attention for neural dependency parsing. *Proceedings of the 5th International Conference on Learning Representations*.

Jack Edmonds. 1967. Optimum branchings. *Journal of Research of the national Bureau of Standards B*, 71(4):233–240.

Ronald F Feldstein. 2001. *A concise Polish grammar*. Citeseer.

Daniel Fernández-González and Carlos Gómez-Rodríguez. 2019. Left-to-right dependency parsing with pointer networks. In *Proceedings of NAACL-HLT*, pages 710–716.

Kim Gerdes, Bruno Guillaume, Sylvain Kahane, and Guy Perrier. 2018. SUD or surface-syntactic Universal Dependencies: An annotation scheme near-isomorphic to UD. In *Proceedings of the Second Workshop on Universal Dependencies (UDW 2018)*, pages 66–74, Brussels, Belgium. Association for Computational Linguistics.

Edouard Grave, Piotr Bojanowski, Prakhar Gupta, Armand Joulin, and Tomas Mikolov. 2018. Learning word vectors for 157 languages. In *Proceedings of the International Conference on Language Resources and Evaluation (LREC 2018)*.

One-Soon Her and Chen-Tien Hsieh. 2010. On the semantic distinction between classifiers and measure words in chinese. *Language and linguistics*, 11(3):527–551.

Magnus Jacobsen, Mikkel H. Sørensen, and Leon Derczynski. 2021. Optimal size-performance tradeoffs: Weighing pos tagger models.

Tao Ji, Yuanbin Wu, and Man Lan. 2019. Graph-based dependency parsing with graph neural networks. In *Proceedings of the 57th Annual Meeting of the Association for Computational Linguistics*, pages 2475–2485, Florence, Italy. Association for Computational Linguistics.

Eliyahu Kiperwasser and Yoav Goldberg. 2016. Simple and accurate dependency parsing using bidirectional LSTM feature representations. *Transactions of the Association for Computational Linguistics*, 4:313–327.

HE Klockmann. 2012. Polish numerals and quantifiers: A syntactic analysis of subject-verb agreement mismatches. Master's thesis, Utrecht University.

Adhiguna Kuncoro, Miguel Ballesteros, Lingpeng Kong, Chris Dyer, and Noah A. Smith. 2016. Distilling an ensemble of greedy dependency parsers into one MST parser. In *Proceedings of the 2016 Conference on Empirical Methods in Natural Language Processing*, pages 1744–1753, Austin, Texas. Association for Computational Linguistics.

Iksop Lee and Robert Ramsey. 2000. *The Korean Language*. State University of New York Press, New York.

Charles N. Li and Sandra A. Thompson. 1981. *Mandarin Chinese: a Functional Reference Grammar*. University of California Press, Berkeley.

Shen Li, Zhe Zhao, Renfen Hu, Wensi Li, Tao Liu, and Xiaoyong Du. 2018a. Analogical reasoning on chinese morphological and semantic relations. In *Proceedings of the 56th Annual Meeting of the Association for Computational Linguistics (Volume 2: Short Papers)*, pages 138–143. Association for Computational Linguistics.

Zuchao Li, Jiaxun Cai, Shexia He, and Hai Zhao. 2018b. Seq2seq dependency parsing. In *Proceedings of the 27th International Conference on Computational Linguistics*, pages 3203–3214, Santa Fe, New Mexico, USA. Association for Computational Linguistics.

Meichun Liu. 2015. Tense and aspect in mandarin chinese. *The Oxford Handbook of Chinese Linguistics*, pages 274–289.

Xuezhe Ma, Zecong Hu, Jingzhou Liu, Nanyun Peng, Graham Neubig, and Eduard Hovy. 2018. Stack-pointer networks for dependency parsing. In *Proceedings of the 56th Annual Meeting of the Association for Computational Linguistics (Volume 1: Long Papers)*, pages 1403–1414.

Mitchell P Marcus and Mary Ann Marcinkiewicz. 1993. Building a large annotated corpus of English: The Penn Treebank. *Computational Linguistics*, 19(2).

R. S. McGregor. 1977. *Outline of Hindi Grammar*. Oxford University Press, Delhi. 2nd edition.

Joakim Nivre, Johan Hall, Jens Nilsson, Atanas Chanev, Gülşen Eryigit, Sandra Kübler, Svetoslav Marinov, and Erwin Marsi. 2007. MaltParser: A language-independent system for data-driven dependency parsing. *Natural Language Engineering*, 13(2):95–135.

Martha Palmer, Rajesh Bhatt, Bhuvana Narasimhan, Owen Rambow, Dipti Misra Sharma, and Fei Xia. 2009. Hindi syntax: Annotating dependency, lexical predicate-argument structure, and phrase structure. In *The 7th International Conference on Natural Language Processing*, pages 14–17.

Waltraud Paul. 2008. The serial verb construction in chinese: A tenacious myth and a gordian knot. *Linguistic Review - LINGUIST REV*, 25:367–411.

G. J. Ramstedt. 1968. *A Korean Grammar*, volume 82 of *Memoirs of the Finno-Ugric Society*. Anthropological Publications, Oosterhout, The Netherlands.

James Robertson. 2006. *The Testament of Gideon Mack*. Penguin Books Ltd.

Anna Siewierska. 1993. Syntactic weight vs. information structure and word order variation in polish. *Journal of Linguistics*, 29:233–265.

Aaron Smith, Bernd Bohnet, Miryam de Lhoneux, Joakim Nivre, Yan Shao, and Sara Stymne. 2018. 82 treebanks, 34 models: Universal Dependency parsing with multi-treebank models. In *Proceedings of the CoNLL 2018 Shared Task: Multilingual Parsing from Raw Text to Universal Dependencies*, pages 113–123, Brussels, Belgium. Association for Computational Linguistics.

Aaron Smith, Miryam de Lhoneux, Sara Stymne, and Joakim Nivre. 2018. An investigation of the interactions between pre-trained word embeddings, character models and POS tags in dependency parsing. In *EMNLP 2018: 2018 Conference on Empirical Methods in Natural Language Processing*, pages 2711–2720.

R. Snell and S. Weightman. 1989. *Teach yourself Hindi*. Hodder and Stoughton, London.

Ho-Min Sohn. 1999. *The Korean Language*. Cambridge University Press, Cambridge.

Seok Choong Song. 1988. *Explorations in Korean Syntax and Semantics*. Institute of East Asian Studies, University of California Berkeley, Berkeley.

Drahomíra Johanka Spoustová and Miroslav Spousta. 2010. Dependency parsing as a sequence labeling task. *The Prague Bulletin of Mathematical Linguistics*, 94(2010):7–14.

Emma Strubell, Ananya Ganesh, and Andrew McCallum. 2019. Energy and policy considerations for deep learning in NLP. *Proceedings of the 56th Annual Meeting of the Association for Computational Linguistics*.

Michalina Strzyz, David Vilares, and Carlos Gómez-Rodríguez. 2019. Viable dependency parsing as sequence labeling. In *Proceedings of the 2019 Conference of the North American Chapter of the Association for Computational Linguistics: Human Language Technologies, Volume 1 (Long and Short Papers)*, pages 717–723, Minneapolis, Minnesota. Association for Computational Linguistics.

Michalina Strzyz, David Vilares, and Carlos Gómez-Rodríguez. 2020. Bracketing encodings for 2-planar dependency parsing. In *Proceedings of the 28th International Conference on Computational Linguistics*, pages 2472–2484.

Bernd Wiese. 2011. Optimal specifications: On case marking in polish. *Syntax and morphology multidimensional*, 24:101.

Alina Wróblewska. 2018. Extended and enhanced polish dependency bank in universal dependencies format. In *Proceedings of the Second Workshop on Universal Dependencies (UDW 2018)*, pages 173–182.

Naiwen Xue, Fei Xia, Fu-Dong Chiou, and Marta Palmer. 2005. The Penn Chinese treebank: Phrase structure annotation of a large corpus. *Natural language engineering*, 11(2):207.

Nianwen Xue, Fu-Dong Chiou, and Martha Palmer. 2002. Building a large-scale annotated chinese corpus. In *COLING 2002: The 19th International Conference on Computational Linguistics*.

Xuan Zhang and Kevin Duh. 2020. Reproducible and efficient benchmarks for hyperparameter optimization of neural machine translation systems. *Transactions of the Association for Computational Linguistics*, 8:393–408.

Yu Zhang, Zhenghua Li, and Min Zhang. 2020a. Efficient second-order TreeCRF for neural dependency parsing. In *Proceedings of the 58th Annual Meeting of the Association for Computational Linguistics*, pages 3295–3305, Online. Association for Computational Linguistics.

Yu Zhang, Zhenghua Li, Houquan Zhou, and Min Zhang. 2020b. Is POS tagging necessary or even helpful for neural dependency parsing? *arXiv preprint arXiv:2003.03204*.

Junru Zhou and Hai Zhao. 2019. Head-driven phrase structure grammar parsing on Penn Treebank. In *Proceedings of the 57th Annual Meeting of the Association for Computational Linguistics*, pages 2396–2408.

Xiyou Zhou, Zhiyu Chen, Xiaoyong Jin, and William Yang Wang. 2021. HULK: An energy efficiency benchmark platform for responsible natural language processing. In *Proceedings of the 16th Conference of the European Chapter of the Association for Computational Linguistics: System Demonstrations*, pages 329–336, Online. Association for Computational Linguistics.

Appendix A Parsers

Left-to-right pointer network (L2R) is a parser which uses a left to right transition-based algorithm that builds a number of attachments equal to the length of a given sentence together with a

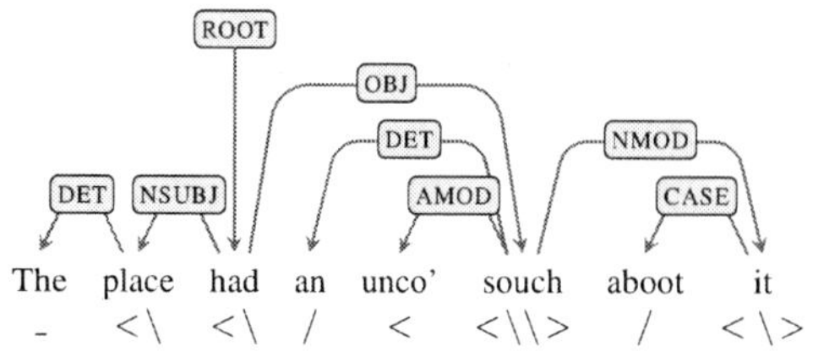

Figure 4: The bracketing encoding from Strzyz et al. (2019). Text is an extract from Robertson (2006).

pointer network which can point to a given position in the sentence for each token (Ma et al., 2018; Fernández-González and Gómez-Rodríguez, 2019).[7] It is one of the current top performing parsers. We use the implementation as is, except we make moderate alterations to overcome hard-coded filepaths and the like. Otherwise, the only hyperparameter we change is the number of encoder layers and the number of nodes in the encoder and decoder layers.

Sequence labelling parser (SEQLAB) is a parsing system that first encodes trees as a set of labels, so that a direct one-to-one prediction can be made for each token in a sentence (Spoustová and Spousta, 2010; Li et al., 2018b; Strzyz et al., 2019).[8] We use the original bracketing encoding from Strzyz et al. (2019) as it doesn't require UPOS tags to decode (as the other leading encoding does), it performs closely to a more recent bracketing encoding that covers more non-projectivity (Strzyz et al., 2020), and the latter encoding wasn't publicly available when this work commenced. It casts a tree as series of tags which are made up of left and right brackets and forward and backwards slashes which encode the incoming and outgoing arcs for each respective node. The encoding for each token is based on edges associated with the preceding tokens and the direction of the edges. More formally, the encoding for w_i is given by:

$$
\begin{array}{ll}
<- & \text{if } \epsilon_{j(i-1)} \in \mathcal{E} \wedge j > i-1 \\
\backslash - & \times k \mid k = \sum\limits_{w_j \in S} \begin{cases} 1 & \text{if } j < i \wedge \epsilon_{ij} \in \mathcal{E} \\ 0 & \text{otherwise} \end{cases} \\
/- & \times k \mid k = \sum\limits_{w_j \in S} \begin{cases} 1 & \text{if } i-1 < j \wedge \epsilon_{(i-1)j} \in \mathcal{E} \\ 0 & \text{otherwise} \end{cases} \\
>- & \text{if } \epsilon_{ji} \wedge j < i
\end{array}
$$

[7] https://github.com/danifg/SyntacticPointer

[8] We use refactored encoding/decoding functions from https://github.com/mstrise/dep2label.

We use the biaffine implementation described below and edit it to be a simple sequence-labelling system, i.e. an embedding layer, followed by a number of BiLSTM layers, and MLPs one for predicting the bracket tags and one for predicting the edge labels. We use the same hyperparameters as used for the biaffine parser.

Deep biaffine (BIAFFINE) is a graph-based parser that creates two representations of each token from the hidden representations from BiLSTMs, hypothesised to be a representation of each token as dependents and as heads (Dozat and Manning, 2017).[9] An affine transformation is applied to the head representation and then this and the dependent one are then combined via a second affine transformation (hence biaffine) to give a matrix of scores, which gives a probability distribution for each node representing the probability any other node is that node's head. A well-formed tree is then enforced using the Chu–Liu/Edmonds' algorithm (Chu and Liu, 1965; Edmonds, 1967). The edge labels are then predicted based on the predicted edges. We use the standard hyperparameters for this system except where we match them to better correspond to the L2R parser and then only alter the hyperparameters associated with the BiLSTMs.

Appendix B Network hyperparameters

Hyperparameter	Value
Word embedding dimensions	100
Character embedding in (¬ L2R)	32
Character embedding out (¬ L2R)	100
Character dimension (if L2R)	100
Embedding dropout	0.33
Arc MLP dimensions (¬ SEQLAB)	512
Label MLP dimensions (¬ SEQLAB)	128
MLP layers	1
Epochs	200
Patience	10
Training batch size	32

Table 2: Hyperparameters for all models. L2R uses a CNN char. embedding layer and SEQLAB doesn't have a biaffine layer. Other parameters are as in the original (except SEQLAB which uses those of BIAFFINE).

Appendix C Data

We use a small sample of treebanks covering languages from 3 different language families and 4 sub-families and which represent different syntactic systems covering analytic, fusional, and agglutinative languages and all are written in different scripts. We offer a brief description of the treebanks used and some of the salient features of their respective languages. The treebanks were chosen to represent varying syntactic features, but also because of their high quality from being either manually annotated or manually corrected. We also chose relatively large treebanks. The statistics for each treebank are shown in Table 3.

UD Hindi-HDTB (Hindi) is a UD treebank for Hindi based on manually annotated news data (Palmer et al., 2009; Bhat et al., 2017). Hindi is a lightly fusional language with some degree of verbal inflection and noun declension but also makes extensive use of postpositions (McGregor, 1977). It is a split-ergative language meaning in certain cases it uses a nominative-accusative structure but in others it uses an ablative-ergative syntax where the subject of an intransitive verb behaves like the object of a transitive one (Comrie, 1978). It also exhibits tripartite behaviour in certain clauses, where the subject of intransitive verbs, the object of transitive verbs, and the subject of transitive verbs all have different case markings (Comrie, 1978). It is a SOV language, but it has a fairly free word order (Snell and Weightman, 1989). It is Indo-Iranian and is written in the Devanagari script.

UD Polish-PDB (Polish) is a UD treebank manually annotated on fiction, non-fiction, and news data (Wróblewska, 2018). Polish is a highly fusional language with a high degree of verbal inflection (Feldstein, 2001) and 7 case-markings (Wiese, 2011). It is a null-subject language (Cognola and Casalicchio, 2018) with a nominal SVO order but has relatively free word order (Siewierska, 1993). Like most Slavic languages it doesn't make use of articles (Bielec, 1998) but it does have a complex system of numeral and quantifiers that result in agreement mistmatches (Klockmann, 2012). It is a Balto-Slavic language written in the Latin script.

UD Korean Kaist (Korean) is a large treebank generated from a constituency treebank which was semi-automatically annotated with manual corrections based on academic, fiction, and news data (Choi et al., 1994; Chun et al., 2018). Korean is a strongly suffixing agglutinative language (Ramstedt, 1968; Sohn, 1999). This results in a large number of cases and a high degree of verbal inflection (Chang, 1996; Song, 1988; Lee and Ramsey,

[9] The original repository (`https://github.com/zysite/biaffine-parser`) redirects to a larger set of biaffine based parsers, but is largerly the same.

	Training					Development					Test				
	Sents.	Tokens	Avg. Len.	NP	Chars.	Sents.	Tokens	Avg. Len.	NP	Chars.	Sents.	Tokens	Avg. Len.	NP	Chars.
Chinese	15K	408K	28.2	0.0	4.9	2K	51K	28.0	0.0	4.9	2K	49K	27.3	0.0	4.9
Hindi	13K	281K	22.1	2.6	11.4	2K	35K	22.2	2.4	11.5	2K	35K	22.2	2.4	11.3
Korean	23K	296K	13.9	4.5	8.2	2K	25K	13.2	4.7	8.6	2K	28K	13.4	4.0	8.3
Polish	18K	282K	16.9	1.4	5.4	2K	35K	16.7	1.5	5.4	2K	34K	16.2	1.4	5.4

Table 3: Treebank statistics: number of sentences (Sents.), number of tokens (Tokens), average sentence length (Avg. Len.), percentage for non-projective arcs (NP), average word length (Chars.).

2000). It is technically a SOV ordered languae but it has a highly flexible word order (Ramstedt, 1968; Sohn, 1999). Korean also uses honorifics and speech levels, the former encoding the social relationship between the speaker and the referents in a discussion and the latter the speaker and the person/people being spoken to (Brown, 2015). It is a Koreanic language written in the Hangul script.

Chinese Penn Treebank (Chinese) is large manually annotated treebank for Mandarin based on news data (Xue et al., 2002, 2005). It is an analytic, isolating language with a SVO dominant word order and is a pro-drop language (Li and Thompson, 1981). Chinese has no grammatical tense markers so relies on context or temporal expressions, but aspect is expressed via the use of particles (Liu, 2015). Classifiers and measure words must be used when a noun is preceded by a number, a demonstrative pronoun, or certain quantifiers which are particles that appear between these qualifiers and their respective nouns (Her and Hsieh, 2010). Chinese is said to be a verb stacking language, where more than one verb or verb phrases are stacked together in the same clause, but there is some disagreement if the way verbs are combined actually constitutes verb stacking (Li and Thompson, 1981; Paul, 2008). It is a Sino-Tibetan language written in simplified Hanzi. We re-split the data because the standard split has tiny development and test sets. The resulting sizes are shown Table 3.

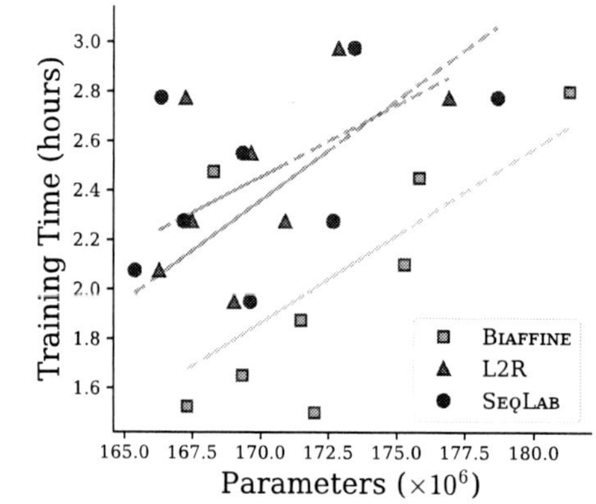

Figure 5: Average training time against total network parameters.

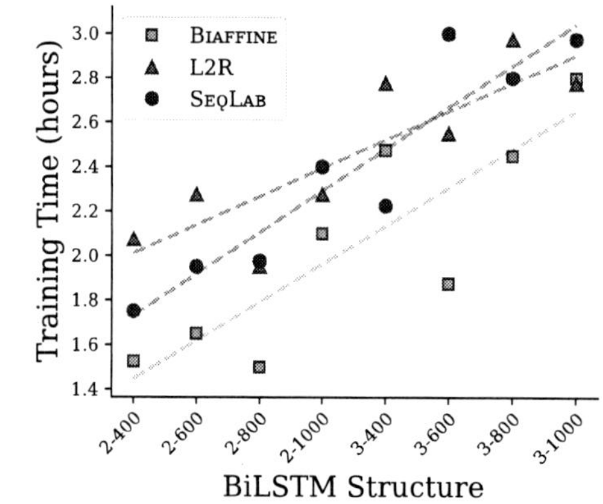

Figure 6: Average training time against BiLSTM structure.

Appendix D Training time

Figure 6 shows the average training time (across treebanks) for each parser against the BiLSTM structure. There is a clear linear relation as the complexity of the BiLSTM increases. That is considering a BiLSTM with 2 layers and 1000 nodes to be less complex than one with 3 layers and 400 nodes. We also show a similar plot in the Figure 5, but against the total number of parameters in the network, which shows a similar but less clear trend.

Appendix E Full data

Table 4 shows the full LAS scores for each system for each treebank with different BiLSTM configurations on the development data. Similarly, Table 5 shows the results for the test data. Figure 7 shows LAS against inference speed for the test data and echoes what was observed for the development data in Figure 1. Table 6 shows the total training energy cost, total training time, and the parameters for each parser and for each BiLSTM configuration.

BiLSTM Layers	Nodes	BIAFFINE zh	hi	ko	pl	avg	SEQLAB zh	hi	ko	pl	avg	L2R zh	hi	ko	pl	avg
2	400	80.59	89.83	85.35	86.22	85.50	71.35	85.18	80.47	79.88	79.22	79.68	89.99	83.81	85.32	84.70
	600	81.33	90.48	85.43	86.88	86.03	72.76	86.11	81.05	81.55	80.37	80.62	90.31	84.11	86.54	85.40
	800	81.81	90.61	86.02	87.38	86.45	74.27	86.48	81.63	82.60	81.24	81.59	90.03	83.97	86.77	85.59
	1000	82.15	90.56	85.91	87.95	86.64	74.82	87.06	81.55	82.91	81.58	81.66	90.54	84.06	87.45	85.93
3	400	81.71	90.55	85.45	86.83	86.13	73.62	86.42	81.23	82.15	80.85	82.50	90.85	84.67	87.16	86.29
	600	81.93	90.62	86.04	87.66	86.56	75.46	87.32	81.64	83.03	81.86	83.25	91.13	84.75	87.83	86.74
	800	82.65	91.06	85.94	88.35	87.00	76.20	87.65	81.66	83.90	82.35	83.57	91.00	84.99	88.66	87.06
	1000	82.98	91.16	86.03	88.64	87.20	76.74	87.50	81.61	84.21	82.51	83.41	91.20	85.28	88.84	87.18

Table 4: Full LAS results on the development data.

BiLSTM Layers	Nodes	BIAFFINE zh	hi	ko	pl	avg	SEQLAB zh	hi	ko	pl	avg	L2R zh	hi	ko	pl	avg
2	400	81.03	89.74	84.58	86.76	85.53	72.92	86.66	80.11	82.68	80.59	79.95	90.27	83.13	85.39	84.69
	600	81.82	90.39	84.89	87.38	86.12	74.43	87.59	80.84	83.84	81.68	80.74	90.43	83.77	86.68	85.41
	800	82.27	90.60	85.10	88.20	86.55	75.27	87.74	80.93	84.43	82.09	81.73	90.27	83.57	86.76	85.58
	1000	82.70	90.71	84.83	88.44	86.67	76.44	87.71	80.40	85.07	82.41	81.86	90.35	83.73	87.42	85.84
3	400	81.93	90.42	84.51	87.49	86.09	76.14	88.21	81.40	85.58	82.83	82.63	90.98	84.57	87.59	86.44
	600	82.27	90.23	85.45	88.39	86.59	78.13	88.77	81.96	86.69	83.89	83.69	91.22	84.10	88.09	86.78
	800	83.11	91.08	85.46	88.78	87.11	78.67	88.61	81.75	86.88	83.98	83.72	90.93	84.43	89.18	87.06
	1000	83.47	90.94	85.56	88.86	87.21	78.91	89.26	81.68	87.20	84.26	83.65	91.18	84.47	89.34	87.16

Table 5: Full LAS results on the test data.

BiLSTM Layers	Nodes	Total Energy (MJ) BIAFFINE	SEQLAB	L2R	Total Time (hours) BIAFFINE	SEQLAB	L2R	Avg. Parameters ($\times 10^6$) BIAFFINE	SEQLAB	L2R
2	400	0.54	0.59	0.69	6.1	7.0	8.3	167.3	165.4	166.3
	600	0.58	0.63	0.75	6.6	7.8	9.1	169.3	167.2	167.5
	800	0.53	0.68	0.65	6.0	7.9	7.8	172.0	169.6	169.0
	1000	0.73	0.83	0.76	8.4	9.6	9.1	175.3	172.7	170.9
3	400	0.83	0.81	0.92	9.9	8.9	11.1	168.3	166.3	167.2
	600	0.66	0.96	0.84	7.5	12.0	10.2	171.5	169.3	169.6
	800	0.82	0.98	1.00	9.8	11.2	11.9	175.8	173.4	172.9
	1000	1.01	1.07	0.92	11.2	11.9	11.1	181.3	178.7	176.9

Table 6: Total energy consumed during training, total training time, and average parameters for each parser system for different BiLSTM configurations.

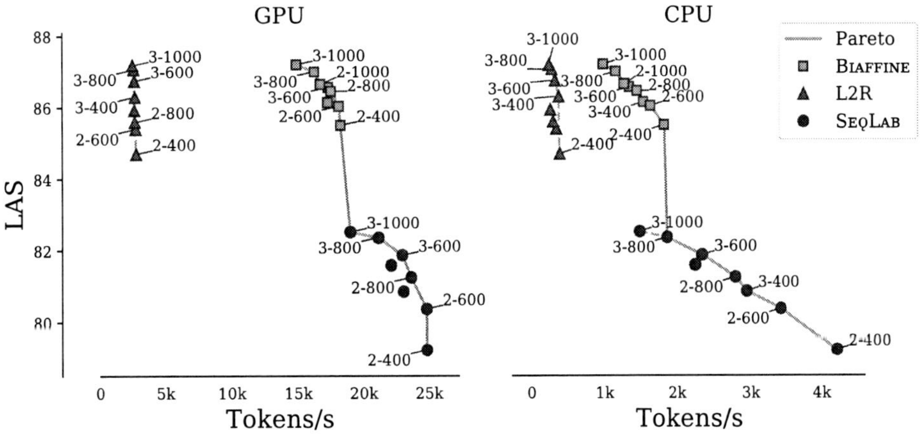

Figure 7: Pareto fronts for L2R, BIAFFINE, and SEQLAB on the test data.

Appendix F L2R training efficiency

Figure 8 shows training energy against training time for L2R for each treebank used. Clearly, the points associated with each treebank cluster. It is clear training the parser on the Korean data is much more energy consuming compared to the others (which form a linear dispersion). It isn't particularly clear why this would be the case based on the statistics in Table 3, except that Korean has the largest number of instances.

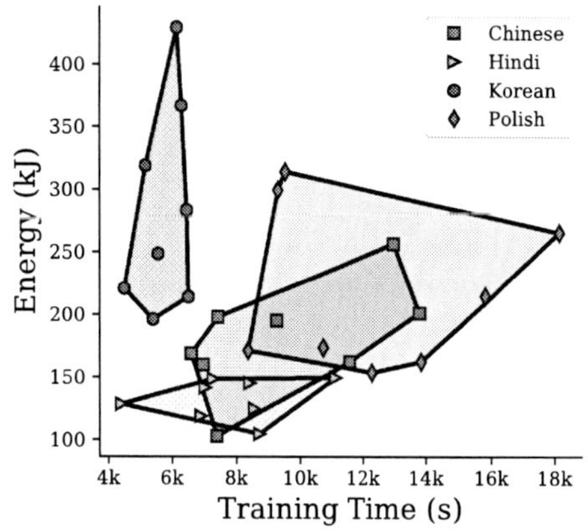

Figure 8: Energy against training time for L2R systems. L2R is more impacted by different data.

Applying Occam's Razor to Transformer-Based Dependency Parsing: What Works, What Doesn't, and What is Really Necessary

Stefan Grünewald[★◆] Annemarie Friedrich[◆] Jonas Kuhn[★]

[★]Institut für Maschinelle Sprachverarbeitung, University of Stuttgart

[◆]Bosch Center for Artificial Intelligence, Renningen, Germany

stefan.gruenewald|annemarie.friedrich@de.bosch.com

jonas.kuhn@ims.uni-stuttgart.de

Abstract

The introduction of pre-trained transformer-based contextualized word embeddings has led to considerable improvements in the accuracy of graph-based parsers for frameworks such as Universal Dependencies (UD). However, previous works differ in various dimensions, including their choice of pre-trained language models and whether they use LSTM layers. With the aims of disentangling the effects of these choices and identifying a simple yet widely applicable architecture, we introduce STEPS, a new modular graph-based dependency parser. Using STEPS, we perform a series of analyses on the UD corpora of a diverse set of languages. We find that the choice of pre-trained embeddings has by far the greatest impact on parser performance and identify XLM-R as a robust choice across the languages in our study. Adding LSTM layers provides no benefits when using transformer-based embeddings. A multi-task training setup outputting additional UD features may contort results. Taking these insights together, we propose a simple but widely applicable parser architecture and configuration, achieving new state-of-the-art results (in terms of LAS) for 10 out of 12 diverse languages.[1]

1 Introduction

Recent years have seen considerable improvements in the performance of syntactic dependency parsers for frameworks such as Universal Dependencies (UD; de Marneffe et al., 2014). For graph-based parsers, these improvements can in large part be attributed to two developments: (1) the introduction of deep biaffine classifiers (Dozat and Manning, 2017), which now constitute the de-facto standard approach for graph-based dependency parsing, and

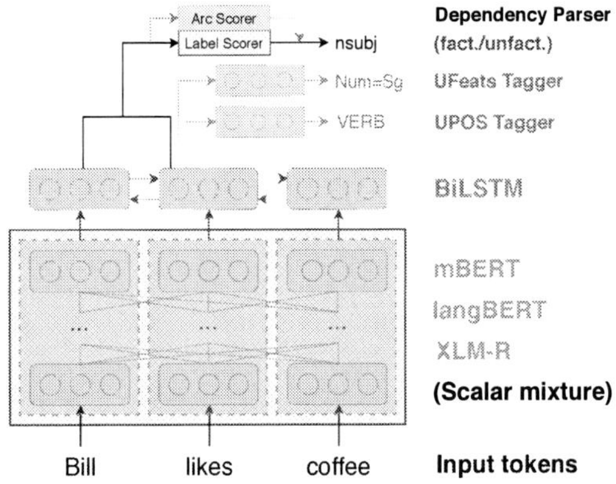

Figure 1: Modular architecture of the STEPS parser. Dotted lines denote optional components.

(2) the rise of pre-trained distributed word representations, particularly transformer-based contextualized embeddings such as BERT (Devlin et al., 2019) or RoBERTa (Liu et al., 2019). Both characteristics are present in recent top-performing systems (Che et al., 2018; Straka et al., 2019; Kondratyuk and Straka, 2019; Kanerva et al., 2018, 2020; Che et al., 2018).

However, there remain a considerable number of implementation and configuration choices whose impact on parser performance is less well understood. This is evidenced by the many different model configurations (see Table 1) present in parsers that have achieved top results in recent shared tasks addressing UD parsing (Zeman et al., 2017, 2018; Bouma et al., 2020). The choices include (a) the particular pre-trained word embeddings or language model to use, (b) whether to utilize an LSTM in addition to (fine-tuned) contextualized word embeddings; and (c) whether to use a multi-task training setup simultaneously predicting additional UD features (such as morphology or parts of speech) during parsing.

[1]We release our code and pre-trained models on github.com/boschresearch/steps-parser.

Proceedings of the 17th International Conference on Parsing Technologies (IWPT 2021), pages 131–144
Bangkok, Thailand (online), August 6, 2021. ©2021 Association for Computational Linguistics

The aim of this paper is to disentangle the effects of the above factors and determine their impact on parser performance. We appeal to the concept of Occam's razor by ways of avoiding architectural elements that do not bring about a testable advantage. With this idea in mind, we introduce STEPS (the **S**tuttgart **T**ransformer-based **E**xtensible **P**arsing **S**ystem), a modular graph-based dependency parser which implements commonly used modules such as biaffine scorers (Dozat et al., 2017; Kondratyuk and Straka, 2019) or LSTM layers (Straka, 2018) (see Figure 1). Using STEPS, we perform a series of experiments on the UD treebanks of a diverse set of languages. Our setup facilitates estimating the impact of the various architectures and configuration decisions in a comparable way.

Our most important insight is that a relatively simple architecture using biaffine heads on top of fine-tuned XLM-R (Conneau et al., 2020) leads to the highest parsing accuracy for almost all languages in our study, outperforming prior systems on most languages. Our analysis indicates that LSTM layers do not lead to benefits. Simplifying the architecture even further by using a single scorer for edge and label prediction results in similar performance but on average leads to longer training times. Our contributions are as follows:

(1) We introduce STEPS, a new implementation of a graph-based dependency parser designed to be modular and easily extensible. STEPS achieves new state-of-the-art UD parsing performance (in terms of LAS) for 10 out of the 12 typologically diverse languages in our study. We will make our code and pre-trained models for 12 languages publicly available.

(2) We conduct a detailed experimental study, identifying components of parser architecture that are really necessary to obtain a strongly performing system that is applicable across a wide range of languages. The final system uses XLM-R, no LSTM layer, and a factorized edge and label scoring architecture.

(3) We show that multi-task setups predicting additional features as commonly employed in UD parsing may confound results for parsing for individual languages; we hence propose to compare parsing accuracy in unified evaluation settings in future work.

(4) We show that our parser can be easily adapted to Enhanced UD parsing, also resulting in state-of-the-art performance(in terms of ELAS) for 5 out of 7 evaluated languages.

Parser	**Pre-trained embed.**	**LSTM**	**MTL**
StanfordNLP	word2vec, fastText	yes	no
UDPipe 2.0	word2vec, fastText	yes	yes
HIT-SCIR	fastText, ELMo	yes	no
UDify	mBERT	no	yes
Trankit	XLM-R	no	yes

Table 1: Settings for a number of previously state-of-the-art graph-based dependency parsers. "LSTM" states whether the parser makes use of an LSTM, and "MTL" states whether the parser is also trained to simultaneously predict other UD properties such as POS tags or morphological features.

This paper is structured as follows. Sec. 2 gives the necessary background on relevant state-of-the-art neural graph-based dependency parsers as well as related work on analysing and comparing parsers. Sec. 3 describes the architecture and configuration options for our new STEPS parser, at the same time introducing the various factors studied in our experiments (Sec. 4). Sec. 5 presents the adaption of our system to Enhanced UD. Finally, we discuss implications for parser choice and future parser design (Sec. 6).

2 Related Work

This section provides a brief outline of the use of contextualized word embeddings in syntactic parsers, recently developed graph-based dependency parsers, and related work on dependency parser analysis.

Contextualized Word Embeddings in Dependency Parsing. Like in other sub-fields of natural language processing, using contextualized word embeddings has become the de-facto standard when building syntactic parsers. Dyer et al. (2015) use LSTM-based contextual representations for the stack and buffer in transition-based parsing, while Kiperwasser and Goldberg (2016) use BiLSTM-based feature representations for individual tokens in both graph-based and transition-based parsing. In both of these cases, the underlying LSTM is trained simultaneously with the target task. In contrast, recently the predominant approach towards contextualized word representations has been to pre-train systems on large-scale language modeling objectives, then taking their representations as input for a target task, optionally while continuing to fine-tune them. This approach was initially proposed using an LSTM-based system (ELMo; Peters et al., 2018) and has since been transferred to transformers (e.g., BERT; Devlin et al., 2019). Transformer-based pre-trained language models have proven wildly successful and have become a standard method for a wide range of NLP tasks, including syntactic dependency parsing.

Recent Graph-based Parsers. Table 1 shows the configurations of three parsers that were among the best-performing systems in the CoNLL 2017 and CoNLL 2018 Shared Tasks on UD parsing, as well as the more recent UDify and Trankit parsers.

StanfordNLP (Dozat et al., 2017) was one of the first systems to apply the biaffine graph-based parser architecture to Universal Dependency parsing. Its token representations make use of pre-trained word2vec (Mikolov et al., 2013) embeddings that are contextualized using a BiLSTM. **UDPipe 2.0** (Straka, 2018) uses a multi-task setup in which POS and feature tagging, lemmatization, and dependency parsing share layers. The system was later extended (Straka et al., 2019, henceforth **UDPipe+**) by incorporating multilingual BERT (mBERT; Devlin et al., 2019) in its token representations. **HIT-SCIR** (Che et al., 2018) was one of the first UD parsers to make use of contextualized pre-trained word embeddings (in the form of ELMo; Peters et al., 2018). The model does not make use of a multi-task training setup. **UDify** (Kondratyuk and Straka, 2019) differs from previous UD parsers in two ways. First, it does not use an LSTM layer for token representation, instead using a learned scalar mixture of mBERT layers and fine-tuning mBERT during training. This is in contrast to the three aforementioned parsers, which do not fine-tune their pre-trained token embeddings. Second, UDify learns a single model for all languages, concatenating all UD 2.5 training sets. **Trankit** (Nguyen et al., 2021) is a recently released end-to-end UD parsing system built on the XLM-R language model. In contrast to UDify and our own STEPS parser, it does not fine-tune the entire language model, but instead inserts Adapter layers (Pfeiffer et al., 2020a,b) to efficiently create language-specific models for 56 languages.

Multi-Purpose Parsers. Other parsers with modular or extensible architectures include **Alto** (Gontrum et al., 2017), a prototyping tool for new grammar formalisms based on Interpreted Regular Tree Grammars (IRTGs), and **PanParser** (Aufrant and Wisniewski, 2018), a modular framework for transition-based dependency parsing. In contrast to these two, STEPS is a graph-based dependency parser that focuses on easy configuration of different transformer-based language models and neural architecture variants.

Parser Analyses and Comparisons. Recent years have seen a wide range of studies comparing different language models for dependency parsing (e.g., Kanerva et al., 2018; Pyysalo et al., 2020; Smith et al., 2018). Additionally, several studies have investigated the amount of implicit syntactic information captured in pre-trained LMs such as ELMo and BERT (Tenney et al., 2019a,b; Hewitt and Manning, 2019). Conversely, several studies have investigated the utility of structural features for dependency parsing in the presence of LSTMs and/or contextualized word embeddings, generally finding that their impact is diminished in the presence of contextual information (Falenska and Kuhn, 2019; Fonseca and Martins, 2020).

Kulmizev et al. (2019) compare the effect of deep contextualized word embeddings on transition-based and graph-based dependency parsers, showing that their inclusion makes the two approaches virtually equivalent in terms of parsing accuracy. Our work is similar to theirs in the sense that we also evaluate several very different dimensions of parser architecture at the same time, utilizing the same underlying backbone and thus ensuring comparability across experiments.

3 STEPS: A Modular Graph-Based Dependency Parser

In this section, we describe our modular dependency parser STEPS (**S**tuttgart **T**ransformer-based **E**xtensible **P**arsing **S**ystem). Each subsection focuses on a particular aspect of the parser setup, providing background on its usage and its potential impact on parser performance.

3.1 Input Token Representation

STEPS provides a number of different options for input token representation. As Table 1 shows, parsers have made use of a variety of pre-trained embeddings, with transformer-based language models having become the predominant current approach. We hence focus on the latter and compare multilingual BERT (**mBERT**; Devlin et al.,

2019), language-specific BERTs (**langBERT**), and the multilingual **XLM-R-large** model (Conneau et al., 2020). XLM-R utilizes the pre-training optimizations first proposed for RoBERTa (Liu et al., 2019), which includes training on a considerably larger amount of data. A detailed overview of all transformer models used in our experiments is provided in the second column of Table 2.

STEPS represents each token i using a vector $\mathbf{r}_i$ corresponding to the embedding of its first wordpiece token. Following Kondratyuk and Straka (2019), we compute token embeddings as weighted sums of the representations of the respective tokens given by the internal transformer encoder layers, resulting in either 768- oder 1024-dimensional embeddings depending on the transformer model used. Coefficients for this sum are learned during training, and layer dropout is applied in order to prevent the model from focusing on particular layers. Our model learns a different set of these coefficients of for each output task (see Sec. 3.2 and Sec. 3.3 below). In addition to the above described **transformer-only** setting, we also compute another version of token embeddings by feeding the embeddings computed by the sum operations into a multi-layer bidirectional **LSTM** (BiLSTM), whose per-token output then constitutes $\mathbf{r}_i$.

3.2 Biaffine Classifier Architecture

STEPS makes use of biaffine classifiers as proposed by Dozat and Manning (2017), which have become the de-facto standard method for graph-based dependency parsing. In a first step, a head representation $\mathbf{h}_i^{head}$ and a dependent representation $\mathbf{h}_i^{dep}$ are created for each input token i represented as embedding vector $\mathbf{r}_i$ via two single-layer feedforward neural networks:

$$\mathbf{h}_i^{head} = \text{FNN}^{head}(\mathbf{r}_i) \tag{1}$$

$$\mathbf{h}_i^{dep} = \text{FNN}^{dep}(\mathbf{r}_i) \tag{2}$$

These representations are then fed into the biaffine function, which maps head–dependent pairs (i, j) onto vectors $\mathbf{s}_{i,j}$ of arbitrary size:

$$\mathbf{s}_{i,j} = \text{Biaff}(\mathbf{h}_i^{head}, \mathbf{h}_j^{dep}) \tag{3}$$

$$\text{Biaff}(\mathbf{x}_1, \mathbf{x}_2) = \mathbf{x}_1^\top \mathbf{U}\mathbf{x}_2 + W(\mathbf{x}_1 \oplus \mathbf{x}_2) + \mathbf{b} \tag{4}$$

$\mathbf{U}$, W and $\mathbf{b}$ are learned parameters; $\oplus$ denotes the concatenation operation. The scores $s_{i,j}$ can now be leveraged in different ways to construct an output tree or graph; this will be described next.

First, the **factorized** approach (Dozat and Manning, 2017) uses two instances of biaffine classifiers. The first classifier (the "arc scorer") is responsible for predicting which (unlabeled) edges exist in the output structure. It predicts, for each token, a probability distribution over potential syntactic heads (i.e., all other tokens in the sentence). We then feed the log-probabilities to the Chu-Liu/Edmonds maximum spanning tree algorithm (Chu and Liu, 1965; Edmonds, 1967) and label the resulting tree using the label scorer. The second classifier (the "label scorer") then assigns dependency labels to edges predicted in the first step.

The **unfactorized** approach, proposed by Dozat and Manning (2018) for semantic graph parsing, uses only a single biaffine classifier (namely the label scorer). Non-existence of dependencies is encoded using simply another label ($\varnothing$). We adapt this approach to tree parsing by discarding the arc scorer and computing the edge weights for the Chu-Liu/Edmonds MST algorithm as $\log(1 - P(\varnothing))$ in order to extract a labeled dependency tree directly. To the best of our knowledge, this is the first time that the unfactorized architecture has been applied to the parsing of dependency tree structures.

3.3 Multi-Task Training

We study the effects of a multi-task training setup by implementing two approaches to training our parser: (a) **dep-only**, in which the model is trained only on syntactic dependencies; and (b) multi-task learning (**MTL**), in which the model additionally predicts universal part-of-speech tags (UPOS) and morphological features (UFeats). We follow Kondratyuk and Straka (2019) by learning different coefficients for the transformer layers for these tagging tasks (see Sec. 3.1) and then using a single-layer feed-forward neural network to extract logit vectors over the respective label vocabularies. By default, the loss for the entire system is computed as the sum of losses for the individual output modules (UPOS tagger, UFeats tagger, and dependency parser). However, we also add the option of scaling the loss of the individual output modules in order to prevent individual tasks from overwhelming the system as a whole (see Sec. 4.6).

4 Experiments

This section describes our experimental setup and reports the results of our experiments on pre-trained embeddings (Sec. 4.3), factorized vs. unfactor-

Language	Transformer LM	UD Treebank
Arabic	ArabicBERT-large (Safaya et al., 2020)	PADT (Smrž et al., 2008)
Chinese	Chinese BERT (Devlin et al., 2019)	GSD
Czech	Slavic-BERT (Arkhipov et al., 2019)	PDT (Bejček et al., 2012)
English	RoBERTa-large (Liu et al., 2019)	EWT (Silveira et al., 2014)
Finnish	FinBERT (Virtanen et al., 2019)	TDT
German	German BERT (github.com/dbmdz/berts)	GSD (McDonald et al., 2013)
Hindi	WikiBERT-Hindi (Pyysalo et al., 2020)	HDTB (Bhat et al.; Palmer et al., 2009)
Italian	Italian BERT-XXL (github.com/dbmdz/berts)	ISDT
Japanese	WikiBERT-Japanese (Pyysalo et al., 2020)	GSD
Korean	KR-BERT (Lee et al., 2020)	Kaist (Chun et al., 2018)
Latvian	WikiBERT-Latvian (Pyysalo et al., 2020)	LVTB
Russian	RuBERT (Kuratov and Arkhipov, 2019)	SynTagRus (Droganova et al., 2018)
Multilingual	mBERT (Devlin et al., 2019)	–
Multilingual	XLM-R (Conneau et al., 2020)	–

Table 2: Language models and UD treebanks used in our experiments. Citations for treebanks are given where provided in treebank repository documentation.

ized parser architecture (Sec. 4.5), LSTM usage (Sec. 4.4), and multi-task training (Sec. 4.6).

4.1 Experimental Setup

Languages and treebanks. We select 12 languages, covering a diverse range of language families and writing systems, by applying linguistic criteria similar to those outlined by de Lhoneux et al. (2017). For each language, we select the largest available treebank from UD 2.6 for which token data is freely available. These treebanks are listed in the third column of Table 2. In all of our experiments, we use gold tokens and train language-specific models, testing on the test set of the respective treebank.

Evaluation metrics. We compute UAS and LAS using the official evaluation script for the CoNLL 2018 Shared Task.[2] UAS (Unlabeled Attachment Score) computes the fraction of tokens that have been assigned the correct syntactic head. LAS (Labeled Attachment Score) records the fraction of tokens that have been assigned the correct syntactic head with the correct edge label.

4.2 Implementation

Our parser is implemented in Python, using PyTorch (Paszke et al., 2019) and the Huggingface Transformers library (Wolf et al., 2019). Training is performed on a single nVidia Tesla V100 GPU.

Hyperparameters. We aim to obtain a simple yet high-performing hyperparameter configuration. To do so, we start out with the configuration of UDify, which is architecturally quite similar to STEPS, and tune parameters using grid search in ca. 40 runs on a small development set (consisting of English, Arabic, and Korean data), aiming at a simplified setup that achieves good results across these diverse languages. The hyperparameters examined by us were

- Hidden size of the biaffine classifier (256 / 512 / 768 / 1024)
- Batch size (16 / 32)
- Base learning rate ($7e^{-6}$ to $5e^{-5}$)
- Early stopping patience (10 / 15 / 20 epochs)
- Learning rate schedule (constant LR / warmup only / cosine annealing / Noam)

In large part, our final settings are identical to UDify's values with the following differences. We use the AdamW optimizer (Loshchilov and Hutter, 2019) instead of Adam; we perform neither label smoothing nor gradient clipping; and we do not use differential learning rates. In addition, we do not train for a fixed number of epochs, but instead stop once performance on the validation set does not increase for 15 epochs, or after at most 24 hours.

For model variants involving LSTMs, we tuned the hyperparameters involved in these layers (number of layers; hidden size; dropout; learning rate) in a second round of optimization consisting of 15 trials of random search on the English data. We then picked the two best-performing models and ran them on the other languages, finding that one of them performed best on all languages.

[2] https://universaldependencies.org/conll18/conll18_ud_eval.py

Transformer LM	
Token mask probability	0.15
Layer dropout	0.1
Hidden dropout	0.2
Attention dropout	0.2
Output dropout	0.5
Biaffine classifier	
Arc scorer dimension	768 or 1024[a]
Label scorer dimension	256 or 768/1024[b]
Dropout	0.33
LSTM	
Hidden size	330
Number of layers	3
Dropout	0.5
LSTM learning rate	$5e^{-4}$
Optimization	
Optimizer	AdamW
β_1, β_2	0.9, 0.999
Weight decay	0
Batch size	32
Base learning rate	$4e^{-5}$
LR schedule	Noam
LR warmup	1 epoch

Table 3: Hyperparameter values. [a]Identical to hidden size of the transformer encoder. [b]256 in factorized models, hidden size of transformer encoder in unfactorized models.

All of our final hyperparameter settings can be found in Table 3.

4.3 Impact of Pre-Trained Word Embeddings

We first evaluate how parsing performance differs when varying the underlying pre-trained language model. We here do not include an LSTM layer and perform only dependency parsing. Table 4 shows results for all 12 treebanks used in this study. UDPipe+ refers to the version of UDPipe enhanced with BERT and Flair embeddings proposed by Straka et al. (2019) and described in Sec. 2. UDify refers to the original system trained on all UD languages without treebank-specific fine-tuning. As multilingual training usually results in improved performance for low-resource languages at the cost of lowering scores for high-resource languages (Üstün et al., 2020), for meaningful comparison, we train UDify$_{\text{mono}}$ on single treebanks. Trankit$_{\text{large}}$ refers to the version of Trankit which uses XLM-R-large as the underlying language model, same as STEPS$_{\text{XLM-R}}$.

STEPS$_{\text{mBERT}}$ roughly corresponds to UDify$_{\text{mono}}$, and indeed the models overall perform similarly. We attribute differences to slightly different training setups. While UDify is trained for 80 epochs, STEPS employs early stopping after 15 epochs without improvement. Moreover, we did not disable multi-task learning for parallel UD feature prediction in UDify$_{\text{mono}}$, and this may be an explanation why STEPS$_{\text{mBERT}}$ does much better on Finnish, Czech and Russian, where morphological features may be harder to predict. (For a principled comparison of multi-task setups, see Sec. 4.6.) By contrast, UDPipe+ often outperforms UDify, UDify$_{\text{mono}}$, and STEPS$_{\text{mBERT}}$, which is likely due to the fact that it trains its own word embeddings in addition to mBERT and additionally makes use of character-level representations via GRUs.

Parsing accuracy of STEPS is very high across the board, with new state-of-the-art results being achieved on all languages except Japanese and German. For most languages, the best results are achieved using STEPS$_{\text{XLM-R}}$, with STEPS$_{\text{langBERT}}$ coming in second. In contrast, using mBERT is not the best option on any treebank. In fact, the only languages for which mBERT achieves better results than langBERT in our experiments are Latvian and Hindi.[3] While using langBERT usually yields worse parsing accuracy than XLM-R, results are roughly on par for Arabic and English. We note that the language-specific models we chose for these treebanks (ArabicBERT-large and RoBERTa-large, respectively) are the only ones with a number of trainable parameters similar to XLM-R, while all others have a considerably smaller number of parameters. This highlights the importance of model size in pre-trained word embeddings.

STEPS$_{\text{XLM-R}}$ and Trankit$_{\text{large}}$ show rather similar performance overall, which is to be expected given the fact that both are built on the same underlying language model (XLM-R-large). The slight advantage for STEPS$_{\text{XLM-R}}$ observed on most languages may stem from the fact that it fine-tunes the entire transformer model instead of merely adding Adapter layers, and that it does not use a multi-task training setup (cf. Sec. 4.6). Interestingly, on Finnish and Latvian, both systems outperform other existing parsers by very large margins (around 4.9 and 6.5 LAS, respectively). We assume that there are two main reasons for this. First, XLM-R is pre-trained on CommonCrawl data (Conneau et al., 2020; Wenzek et al., 2020) as opposed to Wikipedia dumps, which results not only in several orders

[3]In a similar study comparing mBERT- and langBERT-based parsers, Kanerva et al. (2020) also found Latvian to be one of the few languages for which mBERT outperformed the language-specific (WikiBERT) version. Both the Latvian and the Hindi Wikipedias are rather small, consisting of only 21M and 35M tokens, respectively (Pyysalo et al., 2020).

	ar PADT	cs PDT	de GSD	en EWT	fi TDT	hi HDTB	it ISDT	ja GSD	ko Kaist	lv LVTB	ru STR	zh GSD
UDPipe+	84.62	92.56	84.06	90.40	89.49	92.50	93.38	**94.27**	87.54	84.50	93.68	86.74
UDify	82.88	92.88	83.59	88.50	82.03	91.46	93.69	92.08	84.52	85.09	93.13	83.75
$\text{UDify}_{\text{mono}}$	83.34	91.58	84.28	89.52	86.74	91.44	93.14	92.14	86.45	85.45	92.32	82.95
$\text{Trankit}_{\text{large}}$	86.51	93.11	**86.27**	91.64	94.31	93.17	94.63	78.14	40.76	91.76	95.16	87.38
$\text{STEPS}_{\text{mBERT}}$	83.80	92.69	84.08	89.16	88.91	91.30	93.13	92.22	24.49	85.05	93.74	84.94
$\text{STEPS}_{\text{langBERT}}$	**86.60**	92.99	85.87	**91.98**	93.57	91.16	94.25	92.98	84.56	82.61	94.44	86.20
$\text{STEPS}_{\text{XLM-R}}$	86.55	**94.58**	86.07	91.91	**94.36**	**93.34**	**94.86**	94.10	**89.93**	**91.93**	**95.30**	**87.75**
$\text{STEPS}_{\text{XLM-R-LSTM}}$	86.41	94.52	86.20	91.58	93.92	93.28	94.57	94.01	89.91	91.61	95.27	86.96
$\text{STEPS}_{\text{XLM-R-unfact}}$	86.32	94.38	86.19	91.57	94.11	93.21	94.58	93.58	89.86	91.76	95.17	87.47

Table 4: Labeled Attachment Score (LAS) for **basic dependency parsing** varying input embeddings and architecture. STEPS scores are averages of three runs.

of magnitude more training data (over 1 billion tokens for both languages), but also presumably more heterogenous data, which may provide better generalizations for the domains in our test data.[4] Second, XLM-R has a much larger vocabulary size than mBERT (250k vs. 100k), which means it may account better for the rich morphology of these languages. On average, a Finnish (Latvian) token is split up into 2.4 (2.1) word pieces when using mBERT, but only 1.9 (1.8) word pieces when using XLM-R.

Finally, we note that $\text{STEPS}_{\text{mBERT}}$ and $\text{Trankit}_{\text{large}}$ perform extremely poorly on Korean (24.49/40.76 LAS on average), indicating that the models do not properly learn from the data. We assume that this may be a tokenization or character encoding issue unique to the Korean-Kaist treebank.[5] However, a similar pattern is not observed for any of the other parser models, and we were unfortunately unable to identify the exact cause despite our best efforts.

4.4 Impact of LSTM Layer

We evaluate the performance of a system identical to $\text{STEPS}_{\text{XLM-R}}$ described above, but with 3 additional BiLSTM layers added on top of the language model ($\text{STEPS}_{\text{XLM-R-LSTM}}$ in Table 4). Changes in performance are generally small. With the exception of German, including LSTM layers actually decreases parsing accuracy slightly. The LSTM model contains more trainable parameters and also makes use of differential learning rates, yet, we did not find any meaningful differences in convergence speed and training times. Hence, we conclude that when fine-tuning an underlying transformer-based language model, adding LSTM layers on top is not necessary. However, results may differ for systems that additionally train their own token embeddings or make use of character-based representations, both of which we do not address in our experiments.

4.5 Impact of Factorization

Dozat and Manning (2018) show that for semantic dependency graph parsing, a simplified parser architecture predicting edge presence and edge labels from the same scoring matrix achieves largely identical results compared to a model using two separate classifiers for arcs and labels. We here dive into the question whether such an unfactorized approach is also able to achieve competitive results in syntactic tree parsing. We do so by implementing a version of $\text{STEPS}_{\text{XLM-R}}$ that makes use of the unfactorized approach as descibed in Sec. 3.2.

Results of our experiments can be found in the row labeled $\text{STEPS}_{\text{XLM-R-unfact}}$ in Table 4. Overall, performance of the unfactorized approach is very close to the factorized version, but slightly lower. While this shows that the unfactorized approach is indeed viable for tree parsing, analysis of the training times reveals an increase by ca. 30 % on average when using the unfactorized model, indicating that the shared scorer takes a longer time to converge.

In light of these results, we propose to stick with the factorized version for syntactic tree parsing. At least in a research setting, shorter training times allow for a larger set of experiments and thus ultimately in using fewer resources. When applying

[4]Both fi-TDT and lv-LVTB contain, among others, "non-standard" data such as blog entries, legal texts, and spoken language (Haverinen et al., 2014; Pretkalniņa et al., 2018).

[5]As pointed out by an anonymous reviewer, Korean-Kaist uses a rather different tokenization strategy than other UD treebanks, with tokens corresponding to larger chunks. Relying on just the first word pieces for token embeddings may be problematic in this context.

the parser, differences in model size and parsing time are negligible.

4.6 Impact of Multi-Task Approach

Finally, we analyze how performance changes when predicting UPOS and UFeats in addition to dependencies. For these experiments, we use XLM-R as input embeddings and a factorized architecture. For UFeats, we follow UDify's approach and consider each possible combination of morphological features a unique label. As shown in Table 5, $\text{STEPS}_{\text{MTL}}$ achieves very high accuracies for UPOS and UFeats, performing on par with or only slightly worse than the previous state of the art ($\text{Trankit}_{\text{large}}$) for most languages. However, we find that compared to the dependency-only system, parsing accuracy drops considerably in the multi-task setting (up to over 1 LAS for Finnish).

During training of $\text{STEPS}_{\text{MTL}}$, accuracy on the validation set increased very rapidly for the tagging tasks and reached levels close to the final values after only a few epochs, while accuracy for the parsing task increased much slower. This suggests that the loss for the tagging tasks might overwhelm the system as a whole, causing the parser modules to underfit. We therefore also test $\text{STEPS}_{\text{MTLscale}}$, in which the loss for UPOS and UFeats is scaled down to 5% during training. $\text{STEPS}_{\text{MTLscale}}$ performs close to $\text{STEPS}_{\text{MTL}}$, even outperforming it in the case of Hindi. In turn, however, accuracy for UPOS and particularly UFeats drops considerably.

To sum up, our experiments indicate that multi-task setups as commonly employed in UD parsing have a non-negligible effect on parsing performance. Hence, when comparing parser performance, it is crucial to take potential multi-task setups into account. If the respective setups differ, ignoring them may result in misleading interpretations of parsing performance of model architectures (unless the variable of interest is the multi-task setup itself).

4.7 Summary

Our experimental findings can be summarized as follows: (a) Choice of pre-trained embeddings has the greatest impact on parser performance, with XLM-R yielding the best results in most cases; (b) adding LSTM layers is not necessary when working with a large fine-tuned language model; (c) a factorized parser architecture is preferable due to faster training; (d) when using a multi-task approach incorporating UPOS and UFeats prediction, there is a tradeoff between tagging and parsing accuracy, and conclusions regarding architecture should be drawn by comparing experiments performed in the same setting. Crucially, one of the simplest parsers in our evaluation ($\text{STEPS}_{\text{XLM-R}}$) achieves the best results overall, often surpassing more complex previous work.

5 Enhanced UD Parsing with STEPS

In order to determine whether our conclusions also hold for the related graph parsing task of Enhanced UD (Schuster and Manning, 2016), we run an additional batch of experiments on 7 treebanks from the IWPT 2020 Shared Task (Bouma et al., 2020).

Modifications to STEPS. We modify STEPS to generate dependency graphs using a factorized approach as proposed by Dozat and Manning (2018) for semantic dependency parsing, weighting the losses of the edge and label scorers:

$$\ell = \lambda_{edge}\ell_{edge} + \lambda_{label}\ell_{label}. \qquad (5)$$

After tuning on English in a set of preliminary experiments, we set the hyperparameters λ_{edge} to 1.0 and λ_{label} to 0.05. For comparison, we also evaluate the unfactorized version of our parser.

While enhanced UD does not require output graphs to be trees, it imposes the constraint that every node must be reachable from the root. We use the heuristic proposed by Grünewald and Friedrich (2020) for graph post-processing, which greedily adds the highest-scoring edge from a node that is reachable from the root to a node that is unreachable from the root until the condition is fulfilled.

Furthermore, for certain relations such as *nmod* or *obl*, enhanced UD allows for the inclusion of lexical material (such as prepositions) in dependency labels. To avoid data sparsity issues resulting from the increase in the number of dependency labels, we follow the label de- and re-lexicalization strategy proposed by Grünewald and Friedrich (2020), replacing lexical materials in labels with with placeholders such as *obl:[case]*. At prediction time, lexicalized parts of the labels can be retrieved from the respective child nodes in the graph. We apply this strategy for all languages in our study except Finnish and Russian (which do not have lexicalized labels) and Arabic (for which we additionally look up lemmas of the lexical material using a simple majority baseline method).

TREEBANK	MODEL	UPOS	UFEATS	UAS	LAS
Arabic (ar_padt)	Trankit$_{large}$	95.47	**95.54**	90.90	86.51
	STEPS$_{dep-only}$	–	–	**90.96**	**86.55**
	STEPS$_{MTL}$	**97.24**	94.89	90.34	86.01
	STEPS$_{MTLscale}$	96.47	87.74	90.80	86.41
Czech PDT (cs_pdt)	Trankit$_{large}$	99.37	**98.23**	95.51	93.11
	STEPS$_{dep-only}$	–	–	**95.89**	**94.58**
	STEPS$_{MTL}$	**99.41**	98.06	95.59	94.19
	STEPS$_{MTLscale}$	98.97	94.20	95.85	94.52
German (de_gsd)	Trankit$_{large}$	**95.48**	**91.91**	**90.11**	**86.27**
	STEPS$_{dep-only}$	–	–	90.02	86.07
	STEPS$_{MTL}$	95.40	**91.91**	89.53	85.46
	STEPS$_{MTLscale}$	94.65	83.33	89.74	85.80
English (en_ewt)	Trankit$_{large}$	**97.91**	**98.04**	93.59	91.64
	STEPS$_{dep-only}$	–	–	**93.90**	**91.91**
	STEPS$_{MTL}$	97.84	98.02	93.47	91.50
	STEPS$_{MTLscale}$	96.58	96.49	93.80	91.78
Finnish TDT (fi_tdt)	Trankit$_{large}$	**98.72**	**97.07**	95.55	94.31
	STEPS$_{dep-only}$	–	–	**95.69**	**94.36**
	STEPS$_{MTL}$	98.52	96.75	94.62	93.11
	STEPS$_{MTLscale}$	98.19	88.70	95.59	94.26
Hindi (hi_hdtb)	Trankit$_{large}$	**98.12**	93.98	96.16	93.17
	STEPS$_{dep-only}$	–	–	96.11	93.34
	STEPS$_{MTL}$	98.09	**94.49**	95.96	93.03
	STEPS$_{MTLscale}$	97.51	88.60	**96.18**	**93.39**
Italian (it_isdt)	Trankit$_{large}$	98.80	98.43	95.93	94.63
	STEPS$_{dep-only}$	–	–	**96.25**	**94.86**
	STEPS$_{MTL}$	**98.81**	**98.58**	95.80	94.36
	STEPS$_{MTLscale}$	98.43	94.28	96.09	94.69
Japanese (ja_gsd)	Trankit$_{large}$	92.57	97.58	86.62	78.14
	STEPS$_{dep-only}$	–	–	**95.62**	**94.10**
	STEPS$_{MTL}$	**98.21**	**99.98**	95.38	93.78
	STEPS$_{MTLscale}$	96.94	99.91	95.53	94.00
Korean (ko_kaist)	Trankit$_{large}$	69.86	98.95	67.96	40.76
	STEPS$_{dep-only}$	–	–	**91.71**	**89.93**
	STEPS$_{MTL}$	**96.41**	**100.00**	91.48	89.73
	STEPS$_{MTLscale}$	93.90	**100.00**	91.53	89.77
Latvian (lv_lvtb)	Trankit$_{large}$	**97.83**	**95.38**	94.19	91.76
	STEPS$_{dep-only}$	–	–	**94.32**	**91.93**
	STEPS$_{MTL}$	97.73	94.79	93.44	90.99
	STEPS$_{MTLscale}$	96.72	81.42	93.97	91.61
Russian (ru_syntagrus)	Trankit$_{large}$	**99.34**	**98.47**	96.18	95.16
	STEPS$_{dep-only}$	–	–	**96.32**	**95.30**
	STEPS$_{MTL}$	99.27	98.34	95.94	94.88
	STEPS$_{MTLscale}$	98.99	95.91	96.19	95.20
Chinese (zh_gsd)	Trankit$_{large}$	96.83	99.48	90.03	87.38
	STEPS$_{dep-only}$	–	–	**90.72**	**87.75**
	STEPS$_{MTL}$	**97.20**	**99.50**	89.70	86.86
	STEPS$_{MTLscale}$	95.21	98.53	90.31	87.39

Table 5: Results for **basic dependency parsing** vs. **parsing and feature prediction (multi-task)** for STEPS$_{XLM-R}$. Scorres are averages of three runs. For UPOS and UFeats, we report accuracy.

Experimental Results. We compare our results against **TurkuNLP**, a modified version of UDify which scored 1st in the official evaluation of the IWPT 2020 Shared Task, and **ShanghaiTech**, which scored 1st in the unofficial post-evaluation.

We evaluate in terms of ELAS (Enhanced LAS, i.e., F1 score over the set of enhanced dependencies in the system output and the gold standard) using the official evaluation script for the IWPT 2020 Shared Task[6] and report per-treebank results for TurkuNLP and ShanghaiTech as submitted.[7] To ensure comparability with previous work, we compute our results using raw text as input and using Stanza (Qi et al., 2020) for tokenization and sentence segmentation. Table 6 reports our results. Our parser achieves very high accuracy, outperforming TurkuNLP and ShanghaiTech on all evaluated languages except Arabic and Czech. Notably, the latter system also uses XLM-R embeddings, but with a more complex parser architecture.

Unlike in tree parsing, the unfactorized system actually slightly outperforms the factorized system on a number of languages, with the largest margins

	Turku-NLP	Shanghai-Tech	STEPS$_{XLM-R}$ fact	unfact
ar-PADT	**77.83**	77.73	77.42	77.68
cs-PDT	88.17	**90.63**	89.49	89.43
en-EWT	86.14	86.30	87.11	**87.28**
fi-TDT	89.24	89.97	**91.53**	91.51
it-ISDT	91.54	91.49	92.35	**92.39**
lv-LVTB	84.94	87.64	**89.04**	88.95
ru-STR	90.69	92.31	93.68	**93.75**

Table 6: Results (ELAS) for **enhanced dependency parsing**. Scores are averages of three runs.

on Arabic and English. Taken together, these results show that (a) our best approach is not only robust across languages, but also across (syntactic) parsing tasks, and (b) the unfactorized approach may be well-suited to graph parsing tasks, which is in line with the results of Dozat and Manning (2018).

6 Discussion and Conclusion

In this paper, we have performed a detailed and principled analysis on a variety of decisions arising during dependency parser design. **What works?** We have identified an architecture based on fine-tuned XLM-R embeddings and factorized scoring

[6] `https://universaldependencies.org/iwpt20/iwpt20_xud_eval.py`

[7] `https://universaldependencies.org/iwpt20/Results.html`

that lead to new state-of-the-art performance for 11 out of 12 diverse language in our study on basic UD parsing, and for 5 out of 7 lanugages for enhanced UD parsing. **What doesn't?** Adding LSTM layers on top of the transformer leads to a decrease in accuracy in most cases. We have also shown that multi-task setups predicting UPOS and UFeats often degrade parsing performance. **What is really necessary?** For current state-of-the-art UD parsers, we recommend making sure that the pre-trained language model covers the intended domain well. In addition, keeping a factorized approach is a good idea for tree parsing, while in graph parsing, a single scorer module may suffice.

In this paper, we have addressed a high- to medium-resource scenario, assuming that we know the application language of a parser and thus training a single parser per language. Future work may address multilingual approaches such as the training setup used by UDify or the recently proposed UDapter (Üstün et al., 2020), which aims at boosting performance of low-resource languages while keeping performance of high-resource languages high. Furthermore, it would be interesting to see if our results about biaffine achitectures also hold for non-syntactic tasks that have recently been framed as dependency parsing tasks, such as Named Entity Recognition (Yu et al., 2020), negation scope detection (Kurtz et al., 2020) or Semantic Role Labeling (Shi et al., 2020).

To sum up, in this paper we have applied "Occam's razor" to graph-based dependency parsing. We believe that the insights from our study will foster further research on dependency parsing and on framing other tasks as dependency parsing, taking our simplified but robustly performing STEPS parser as a starting point.

Acknowledgments

We thank Agnieszka Falenska, Heike Adel, Lukas Lange, Hendrik Schuff, Jannik Strötgen, as well as the anonymous reviewers for their valuable comments with regard to this work.

References

Mikhail Arkhipov, Maria Trofimova, Yuri Kuratov, and Alexey Sorokin. 2019. Tuning multilingual transformers for language-specific named entity recognition. In *Proceedings of the 7th Workshop on Balto-Slavic Natural Language Processing*, pages 89–93, Florence, Italy. Association for Computational Linguistics.

Lauriane Aufrant and Guillaume Wisniewski. 2018. Panparser: a modular implementation for efficient transition-based dependency parsing. *The Prague Bulletin of Mathematical Linguistics*, 111(1):57–86.

Eduard Bejček, Jarmila Panevová, Jan Popelka, Pavel Straňák, Magda Ševčíková, Jan Štěpánek, and Zdeněk Žabokrtský. 2012. Prague Dependency Treebank 2.5 – a revisited version of PDT 2.0. In *Proceedings of COLING 2012*, pages 231–246, Mumbai, India. The COLING 2012 Organizing Committee.

Riyaz Ahmad Bhat, Rajesh Bhatt, Annahita Farudi, Prescott Klassen, Bhuvana Narasimhan, Martha Palmer, Owen Rambow, Dipti Misra Sharma, Ashwini Vaidya, Sri Ramagurumurthy Vishnu, et al. The hindi/urdu treebank project. In *Handbook of Linguistic Annotation*. Springer Press.

Gosse Bouma, Djamé Seddah, and Daniel Zeman. 2020. Overview of the IWPT 2020 shared task on parsing into enhanced Universal Dependencies. In *Proceedings of the 16th International Conference on Parsing Technologies and the IWPT 2020 Shared Task on Parsing into Enhanced Universal Dependencies*, pages 151–161, Online. Association for Computational Linguistics.

Wanxiang Che, Yijia Liu, Yuxuan Wang, Bo Zheng, and Ting Liu. 2018. Towards better UD parsing: Deep contextualized word embeddings, ensemble, and treebank concatenation. In *Proceedings of the CoNLL 2018 Shared Task: Multilingual Parsing from Raw Text to Universal Dependencies*, pages 55–64, Brussels, Belgium. Association for Computational Linguistics.

Yoeng-Jin Chu and Tseng-Hong Liu. 1965. On the shortest arborescence of a directed graph. *Scientia Sinica*, 14:1396–1400.

Jayeol Chun, Na-Rae Han, Jena D. Hwang, and Jinho D. Choi. 2018. Building Universal Dependency treebanks in Korean. In *Proceedings of the Eleventh International Conference on Language Resources and Evaluation (LREC 2018)*, Miyazaki, Japan. European Language Resources Association (ELRA).

Alexis Conneau, Kartikay Khandelwal, Naman Goyal, Vishrav Chaudhary, Guillaume Wenzek, Francisco Guzmán, Edouard Grave, Myle Ott, Luke Zettlemoyer, and Veselin Stoyanov. 2020. Unsupervised cross-lingual representation learning at scale. pages 8440–8451.

Jacob Devlin, Ming-Wei Chang, Kenton Lee, and Kristina Toutanova. 2019. BERT: Pre-training of deep bidirectional transformers for language understanding. In *Proceedings of the 2019 Conference of the North American Chapter of the Association for Computational Linguistics: Human Language Technologies, Volume 1 (Long and Short Papers)*, pages 4171–4186, Minneapolis, Minnesota. Association for Computational Linguistics.

Timothy Dozat and Christopher D. Manning. 2017. Deep biaffine attention for neural dependency parsing. In *5th International Conference on Learning Representations, ICLR 2017, Toulon, France, April 24-26, 2017, Conference Track Proceedings*. OpenReview.net.

Timothy Dozat and Christopher D. Manning. 2018. Simpler but more accurate semantic dependency parsing. In *Proceedings of the 56th Annual Meeting of the Association for Computational Linguistics (Volume 2: Short Papers)*, pages 484–490, Melbourne, Australia. Association for Computational Linguistics.

Timothy Dozat, Peng Qi, and Christopher D. Manning. 2017. Stanford's graph-based neural dependency parser at the CoNLL 2017 shared task. In *Proceedings of the CoNLL 2017 Shared Task: Multilingual Parsing from Raw Text to Universal Dependencies*, pages 20–30, Vancouver, Canada. Association for Computational Linguistics.

Kira Droganova, Olga Lyashevskaya, and Daniel Zeman. 2018. Data conversion and consistency of monolingual corpora: Russian ud treebanks. In *Proceedings of the 17th International Workshop on Treebanks and Linguistic Theories (TLT 2018), December 13–14, 2018, Oslo University, Norway*, 155, pages 52–65. Linköping University Electronic Press.

Chris Dyer, Miguel Ballesteros, Wang Ling, Austin Matthews, and Noah A. Smith. 2015. Transition-based dependency parsing with stack long short-term memory. In *Proceedings of the 53rd Annual Meeting of the Association for Computational Linguistics and the 7th International Joint Conference on Natural Language Processing (Volume 1: Long Papers)*, pages 334–343, Beijing, China. Association for Computational Linguistics.

Jack Edmonds. 1967. Optimum branchings. *Journal of Research of the national Bureau of Standards B*, 71(4):233–240.

Agnieszka Falenska and Jonas Kuhn. 2019. The (non-)utility of structural features in BiLSTM-based dependency parsers. In *Proceedings of the 57th Annual Meeting of the Association for Computational Linguistics*, pages 117–128, Florence, Italy. Association for Computational Linguistics.

Erick Fonseca and André F. T. Martins. 2020. Revisiting higher-order dependency parsers. In *Proceedings of the 58th Annual Meeting of the Association for Computational Linguistics*, pages 8795–8800, Online. Association for Computational Linguistics.

Johannes Gontrum, Jonas Groschwitz, Alexander Koller, and Christoph Teichmann. 2017. Alto: Rapid prototyping for parsing and translation. In *Proceedings of the Software Demonstrations of the 15th Conference of the European Chapter of the Association for Computational Linguistics*, pages 29–32, Valencia, Spain. Association for Computational Linguistics.

Stefan Grünewald and Annemarie Friedrich. 2020. RobertNLP at the IWPT 2020 shared task: Surprisingly simple enhanced UD parsing for English. In *Proceedings of the 16th International Conference on Parsing Technologies and the IWPT 2020 Shared Task on Parsing into Enhanced Universal Dependencies*, pages 245–252, Online. Association for Computational Linguistics.

Katri Haverinen, Jenna Nyblom, Timo Viljanen, Veronika Laippala, Samuel Kohonen, Anna Missilä, Stina Ojala, Tapio Salakoski, and Filip Ginter. 2014. Building the essential resources for finnish: the turku dependency treebank. *Language Resources and Evaluation*, 48(3):493–531.

John Hewitt and Christopher D. Manning. 2019. A structural probe for finding syntax in word representations. In *Proceedings of the 2019 Conference of the North American Chapter of the Association for Computational Linguistics: Human Language Technologies, Volume 1 (Long and Short Papers)*, pages 4129–4138, Minneapolis, Minnesota. Association for Computational Linguistics.

Jenna Kanerva, Filip Ginter, Niko Miekka, Akseli Leino, and Tapio Salakoski. 2018. Turku neural parser pipeline: An end-to-end system for the CoNLL 2018 shared task. In *Proceedings of the CoNLL 2018 Shared Task: Multilingual Parsing from Raw Text to Universal Dependencies*, pages 133–142, Brussels, Belgium. Association for Computational Linguistics.

Jenna Kanerva, Filip Ginter, and Sampo Pyysalo. 2020. Turku enhanced parser pipeline: From raw text to enhanced graphs in the IWPT 2020 shared task. In *Proceedings of the 16th International Conference on Parsing Technologies and the IWPT 2020 Shared Task on Parsing into Enhanced Universal Dependencies*, pages 162–173, Online. Association for Computational Linguistics.

Eliyahu Kiperwasser and Yoav Goldberg. 2016. Simple and accurate dependency parsing using bidirectional lstm feature representations. *Transactions of the Association for Computational Linguistics*, 4:313–327.

Dan Kondratyuk and Milan Straka. 2019. 75 languages, 1 model: Parsing universal dependencies universally. In *Proceedings of the 2019 Conference on Empirical Methods in Natural Language Processing and the 9th International Joint Conference on Natural Language Processing (EMNLP-IJCNLP)*, pages 2779–2795, Hong Kong, China. Association for Computational Linguistics.

Artur Kulmizev, Miryam de Lhoneux, Johannes Gontrum, Elena Fano, and Joakim Nivre. 2019. Deep contextualized word embeddings in transition-based and graph-based dependency parsing - a tale of two parsers revisited. In *Proceedings of the 2019 Conference on Empirical Methods in Natural Language Processing and the 9th International Joint Conference on Natural Language Processing (EMNLP-IJCNLP)*, pages 2755–2768, Hong Kong, China. Association for Computational Linguistics.

Yuri Kuratov and Mikhail Arkhipov. 2019. Adaptation of deep bidirectional multilingual transformers for russian language. *arXiv preprint arXiv:1905.07213*.

Robin Kurtz, Stephan Oepen, and Marco Kuhlmann. 2020. End-to-end negation resolution as graph parsing. In *Proceedings of the 16th International Conference on Parsing Technologies and the IWPT 2020 Shared Task on Parsing into Enhanced Universal Dependencies*, pages 14–24, Online. Association for Computational Linguistics.

Sangah Lee, Hansol Jang, Yunmee Baik, Suzi Park, and Hyopil Shin. 2020. Kr-bert: A small-scale korean-specific language model. *arXiv preprint arXiv:2008.03979*.

Miryam de Lhoneux, Sara Stymne, and Joakim Nivre. 2017. Old school vs. new school: Comparing transition-based parsers with and without neural network enhancement. In *The 15th Treebanks and Linguistic Theories Workshop (TLT)*, pages 99–110.

Yinhan Liu, Myle Ott, Naman Goyal, Jingfei Du, Mandar Joshi, Danqi Chen, Omer Levy, Mike Lewis, Luke Zettlemoyer, and Veselin Stoyanov. 2019. Roberta: A robustly optimized bert pretraining approach. *arXiv preprint arXiv:1907.11692*.

Ilya Loshchilov and Frank Hutter. 2019. Decoupled weight decay regularization. In *International Conference on Learning Representations*.

Marie-Catherine de Marneffe, Timothy Dozat, Natalia Silveira, Katri Haverinen, Filip Ginter, Joakim Nivre, and Christopher D. Manning. 2014. Universal Stanford dependencies: A cross-linguistic typology. In *Proceedings of the Ninth International Conference on Language Resources and Evaluation (LREC'14)*, pages 4585–4592, Reykjavik, Iceland. European Language Resources Association (ELRA).

Ryan McDonald, Joakim Nivre, Yvonne Quirmbach-Brundage, Yoav Goldberg, Dipanjan Das, Kuzman Ganchev, Keith Hall, Slav Petrov, Hao Zhang, Oscar Täckström, Claudia Bedini, Núria Bertomeu Castelló, and Jungmee Lee. 2013. Universal Dependency annotation for multilingual parsing. In *Proceedings of the 51st Annual Meeting of the Association for Computational Linguistics (Volume 2: Short Papers)*, pages 92–97, Sofia, Bulgaria. Association for Computational Linguistics.

Tomas Mikolov, Kai Chen, Greg Corrado, and Jeffrey Dean. 2013. Efficient estimation of word representations in vector space. In *1st International Conference on Learning Representations, ICLR 2013, Scottsdale, Arizona, USA, May 2-4, 2013, Workshop Track Proceedings*.

Minh Van Nguyen, Viet Dac Lai, Amir Pouran Ben Veyseh, and Thien Huu Nguyen. 2021. Trankit: A light-weight transformer-based toolkit for multilingual natural language processing. In *Proceedings of the 16th Conference of the European Chapter of the Association for Computational Linguistics: System Demonstrations*, pages 80–90, Online. Association for Computational Linguistics.

Martha Palmer, Rajesh Bhatt, Bhuvana Narasimhan, Owen Rambow, Dipti Misra Sharma, and Fei Xia. 2009. Hindi syntax: Annotating dependency, lexical predicate-argument structure, and phrase structure. In *The 7th International Conference on Natural Language Processing*, pages 14–17.

Adam Paszke, Sam Gross, Francisco Massa, Adam Lerer, James Bradbury, Gregory Chanan, Trevor Killeen, Zeming Lin, Natalia Gimelshein, Luca Antiga, Alban Desmaison, Andreas Kopf, Edward Yang, Zachary DeVito, Martin Raison, Alykhan Tejani, Sasank Chilamkurthy, Benoit Steiner, Lu Fang, Junjie Bai, and Soumith Chintala. 2019. Pytorch: An imperative style, high-performance deep learning library. In H. Wallach, H. Larochelle, A. Beygelzimer, F. d' Alché-Buc, E. Fox, and R. Garnett, editors, *Advances in Neural Information Processing Systems 32*, pages 8024–8035. Curran Associates, Inc.

Matthew Peters, Mark Neumann, Mohit Iyyer, Matt Gardner, Christopher Clark, Kenton Lee, and Luke Zettlemoyer. 2018. Deep contextualized word representations. In *Proceedings of the 2018 Conference of the North American Chapter of the Association for Computational Linguistics: Human Language Technologies, Volume 1 (Long Papers)*, pages 2227–2237, New Orleans, Louisiana. Association for Computational Linguistics.

Jonas Pfeiffer, Andreas Rücklé, Clifton Poth, Aishwarya Kamath, Ivan Vulić, Sebastian Ruder, Kyunghyun Cho, and Iryna Gurevych. 2020a. AdapterHub: A framework for adapting transformers. In *Proceedings of the 2020 Conference on Empirical Methods in Natural Language Processing: System Demonstrations*, pages 46–54, Online. Association for Computational Linguistics.

Jonas Pfeiffer, Ivan Vulić, Iryna Gurevych, and Sebastian Ruder. 2020b. MAD-X: An Adapter-Based Framework for Multi-Task Cross-Lingual Transfer. In *Proceedings of the 2020 Conference on Empirical Methods in Natural Language Processing (EMNLP)*, pages 7654–7673, Online. Association for Computational Linguistics.

Lauma Pretkalniņa, Laura Rituma, and Baiba Saulīte. 2018. Deriving enhanced universal dependencies from a hybrid dependency-constituency treebank. In *International Conference on Text, Speech, and Dialogue*, pages 95–105. Springer.

Sampo Pyysalo, Jenna Kanerva, Antti Virtanen, and Filip Ginter. 2020. Wikibert models: deep transfer learning for many languages. *arXiv preprint arXiv:2006.01538*.

Peng Qi, Yuhao Zhang, Yuhui Zhang, Jason Bolton, and Christopher D. Manning. 2020. Stanza: A Python natural language processing toolkit for many human languages. In *Proceedings of the 58th Annual Meeting of the Association for Computational Linguistics: System Demonstrations*.

Ali Safaya, Moutasem Abdullatif, and Deniz Yuret. 2020. Kuisail at semeval-2020 task 12: Bert-cnn for offensive speech identification in social media.

Sebastian Schuster and Christopher D. Manning. 2016. Enhanced English Universal Dependencies: An improved representation for natural language understanding tasks. In *Proceedings of the Tenth International Conference on Language Resources and Evaluation (LREC'16)*, pages 2371–2378, Portorož, Slovenia. European Language Resources Association (ELRA).

Tianze Shi, Igor Malioutov, and Ozan Irsoy. 2020. Semantic role labeling as syntactic dependency parsing. In *Proceedings of the 2020 Conference on Empirical Methods in Natural Language Processing (EMNLP)*, pages 7551–7571, Online. Association for Computational Linguistics.

Natalia Silveira, Timothy Dozat, Marie-Catherine de Marneffe, Samuel Bowman, Miriam Connor, John Bauer, and Christopher D. Manning. 2014. A gold standard dependency corpus for English. In *Proceedings of the Ninth International Conference on Language Resources and Evaluation (LREC-2014)*.

Aaron Smith, Miryam de Lhoneux, Sara Stymne, and Joakim Nivre. 2018. An investigation of the interactions between pre-trained word embeddings, character models and POS tags in dependency parsing. In *Proceedings of the 2018 Conference on Empirical Methods in Natural Language Processing*, pages 2711–2720, Brussels, Belgium. Association for Computational Linguistics.

Otakar Smrž, Viktor Bielický, Iveta Kouřilová, Jakub Kráčmar, Jan Hajič, and Petr Zemánek. 2008. Prague arabic dependency treebank: A word on the million words. In *Proceedings of the Workshop on Arabic and Local Languages (LREC 2008)*, pages 16–23, Marrakech, Morocco.

Milan Straka. 2018. UDPipe 2.0 prototype at CoNLL 2018 UD shared task. In *Proceedings of the CoNLL 2018 Shared Task: Multilingual Parsing from Raw Text to Universal Dependencies*, pages 197–207, Brussels, Belgium. Association for Computational Linguistics.

Milan Straka, Jana Straková, and Jan Hajič. 2019. Evaluating contextualized embeddings on 54 languages in pos tagging, lemmatization and dependency parsing. *arXiv preprint arXiv:1908.07448*.

Ian Tenney, Dipanjan Das, and Ellie Pavlick. 2019a. BERT rediscovers the classical NLP pipeline. In *Proceedings of the 57th Annual Meeting of the Association for Computational Linguistics*, pages 4593–4601, Florence, Italy. Association for Computational Linguistics.

Ian Tenney, Patrick Xia, Berlin Chen, Alex Wang, Adam Poliak, R Thomas McCoy, Najoung Kim, Benjamin Van Durme, Sam Bowman, Dipanjan Das, and Ellie Pavlick. 2019b. What do you learn from context? probing for sentence structure in contextualized word representations. In *International Conference on Learning Representations*.

Ahmet Üstün, Arianna Bisazza, Gosse Bouma, and Gertjan van Noord. 2020. UDapter: Language adaptation for truly Universal Dependency parsing. In *Proceedings of the 2020 Conference on Empirical Methods in Natural Language Processing (EMNLP)*, pages 2302–2315, Online. Association for Computational Linguistics.

Antti Virtanen, Jenna Kanerva, Rami Ilo, Jouni Luoma, Juhani Luotolahti, Tapio Salakoski, Filip Ginter, and Sampo Pyysalo. 2019. Multilingual is not enough: Bert for finnish. *arXiv preprint arXiv:1912.07076*.

Guillaume Wenzek, Marie-Anne Lachaux, Alexis Conneau, Vishrav Chaudhary, Francisco Guzmán, Armand Joulin, and Edouard Grave. 2020. CCNet: Extracting high quality monolingual datasets from web crawl data. In *Proceedings of the 12th Language Resources and Evaluation Conference*, pages 4003–4012, Marseille, France. European Language Resources Association.

Thomas Wolf, Lysandre Debut, Victor Sanh, Julien Chaumond, Clement Delangue, Anthony Moi, Pierric Cistac, Tim Rault, Rémi Louf, Morgan Funtowicz, Joe Davison, Sam Shleifer, Patrick von Platen, Clara Ma, Yacine Jernite, Julien Plu, Canwen Xu, Teven Le Scao, Sylvain Gugger, Mariama Drame, Quentin Lhoest, and Alexander M. Rush. 2019. Huggingface's transformers: State-of-the-art natural language processing. *ArXiv*, abs/1910.03771.

Juntao Yu, Bernd Bohnet, and Massimo Poesio. 2020. Named entity recognition as dependency parsing. In *Proceedings of the 58th Annual Meeting of the Association for Computational Linguistics*, pages 6470–6476, Online. Association for Computational Linguistics.

Daniel Zeman, Jan Hajič, Martin Popel, Martin Potthast, Milan Straka, Filip Ginter, Joakim Nivre, and

Slav Petrov. 2018. CoNLL 2018 shared task: Multilingual parsing from raw text to Universal Dependencies. In *Proceedings of the CoNLL 2018 Shared Task: Multilingual Parsing from Raw Text to Universal Dependencies*, pages 1–21, Brussels, Belgium. Association for Computational Linguistics.

Daniel Zeman, Martin Popel, Milan Straka, Jan Hajič, Joakim Nivre, Filip Ginter, Juhani Luotolahti, Sampo Pyysalo, Slav Petrov, Martin Potthast, Francis Tyers, Elena Badmaeva, Memduh Gokirmak, Anna Nedoluzhko, Silvie Cinková, Jan Hajič jr., Jaroslava Hlaváčová, Václava Kettnerová, Zdeňka Urešová, Jenna Kanerva, Stina Ojala, Anna Missilä, Christopher D. Manning, Sebastian Schuster, Siva Reddy, Dima Taji, Nizar Habash, Herman Leung, Marie-Catherine de Marneffe, Manuela Sanguinetti, Maria Simi, Hiroshi Kanayama, Valeria de Paiva, Kira Droganova, Héctor Martínez Alonso, Çağrı Çöltekin, Umut Sulubacak, Hans Uszkoreit, Vivien Macketanz, Aljoscha Burchardt, Kim Harris, Katrin Marheinecke, Georg Rehm, Tolga Kayadelen, Mohammed Attia, Ali Elkahky, Zhuoran Yu, Emily Pitler, Saran Lertpradit, Michael Mandl, Jesse Kirchner, Hector Fernandez Alcalde, Jana Strnadová, Esha Banerjee, Ruli Manurung, Antonio Stella, Atsuko Shimada, Sookyoung Kwak, Gustavo Mendonça, Tatiana Lando, Rattima Nitisaroj, and Josie Li. 2017. CoNLL 2017 shared task: Multilingual parsing from raw text to Universal Dependencies. In *Proceedings of the CoNLL 2017 Shared Task: Multilingual Parsing from Raw Text to Universal Dependencies*, pages 1–19, Vancouver, Canada. Association for Computational Linguistics.

Incorporating Compositionality and Morphology into End-to-End Models

Emily Pitler
Google Research
epitler@google.com

Abstract

Many neural end-to-end systems today do not rely on syntactic parse trees, as much of the information that parse trees provide is encoded in the parameters of pretrained models. Lessons learned from parsing technologies and from taking a multilingual perspective, however, are still relevant even for end-to-end models.

This talk will describe work that relies on compositionality in semantic parsing and in reading comprehension requiring numerical reasoning. We'll then describe a new dataset that requires advances in multilingual modeling, and some approaches designed to better model morphology than off-the-shelf subword models that make some progress on these challenges.

Proceedings of the 17th International Conference on Parsing Technologies (IWPT 2021), page 145
Bangkok, Thailand (online), August 6, 2021.

From Raw Text to Enhanced Universal Dependencies: the Parsing Shared Task at IWPT 2021

Gosse Bouma* **Djamé Seddah**† **Daniel Zeman**°

*University of Groningen, Centre for Language and Cognition
†INRIA Paris
°Charles University in Prague, Faculty of Mathematics and Physics, ÚFAL
g.bouma@rug.nl, djame.seddah@inria.fr
zeman@ufal.mff.cuni.cz

Abstract

We describe the second IWPT task on end-to-end parsing from raw text to Enhanced Universal Dependencies. We provide details about the evaluation metrics and the datasets used for training and evaluation. We compare the approaches taken by participating teams and discuss the results of the shared task, also in comparison with the first edition of this task.

1 Introduction

Universal Dependencies (UD) (Nivre et al., 2020) is a framework for cross-linguistically consistent treebank annotation that has so far been applied to 114 languages. UD defines two levels of annotation, the basic trees and the enhanced graphs (EUD) (Schuster and Manning, 2016).

There are several good parsers that can predict the basic trees (including tokenization and morphology) for previously unseen text (Straka et al., 2016; Qi et al., 2020). Two large shared tasks on basic UD parsing were organized at CoNLL (Zeman et al., 2017, 2018). Enhanced UD parsing attracted comparatively less attention until the shared task organized at IWPT 2020 (Bouma et al., 2020). The present paper describes a second instance of that task, organized as a part of the 17th International Conference on Parsing Technologies[1] (IWPT), collocated with ACL-IJCNLP 2021. Like in the previous year, the evaluation was done on datasets covering 17 languages from four language familiies.

This paper is a follow-up of the overview paper of the previous instance of the shared task (Bouma et al., 2020). To make the paper self-contained, we include updated versions of some sections of that paper, in particular describing the enhanced annotation format, the task, and the evaluation metric. The data section now documents the modifications we made to the data from UD release 2.7.

2 Motivation

The basic dependency annotation in the Universal Dependencies format introduces labeled edges between nodes that represent tokens in the input string, where each node is a dependent of exactly one other node, with the exception of the node token. While this tree structure supports many downstream tasks, there are also phenomena that are hard to capture using single-parent edges only. The enhanced dependency layer therefore supports richer annotation where nodes may have more than one parent, and where additional 'empty' nodes represent elided material that is not overtly expressed in the input string. The enhanced level can be used to account for a range of linguistic phenomena (see Section 3) and to support downstream applications that rely on the semantic interpretation of the input.

There are now a number of treebanks that include enhanced dependency annotation. Furthermore, the recent shared tasks on dependency parsing and subsequent work have shown that considerable progress has been made in multilingual dependency parsing. For enhanced dependency parsing, there are additional challenges. The enhanced representation is a connected directed graph, possibly containing cycles, while the bulk of dependency parsing work still focuses on rooted trees. The set of labels to be predicted is also much larger, as some enhanced dependency labels incorporate the lemma of certain dependents.

On the other hand, it has been shown that much of the enhanced annotation can be predicted on the basis of the basic UD annotation (Nyblom et al., 2013; Schuster et al., 2017; Nivre et al., 2018). Moreover, most state-of-the-art work in dependency parsing uses a graph-based approach, where

[1] https://iwpt21.sigparse.org

Proceedings of the 17th International Conference on Parsing Technologies (IWPT 2021), pages 146–157
Bangkok, Thailand (online), August 6, 2021.

the assumption that the output must form a tree is only used in the final step from predicted links to final output. And finally, work on deep-syntax and semantic parsing has shown that accurate mapping of strings into rich graph representations is possible (Oepen et al., 2014, 2015, 2019, 2020) and could even lead to state-of-the-art performance for downstream applications as shown by the results of the Extrinsic Parsing Evaluation shared task (Oepen et al., 2017).

The previous IWPT shared task (Bouma et al., 2020) reflected this development quite well: some submissions took the way of direct text-to-graph mapping, some of them predicted a rooted tree and then employed heuristics to enhance it; and one submission encoded graphs as trees, then used a tree parser to predict them. Since it was the first task of its kind on large scale multilingual Enhanced Dependencies parsing and some teams may not have been able to successfully implement all their ideas in time (or new ideas may have occurred after seeing what other teams had done), a second round of the task is a natural next step to see whether we can do even better.

3 Enhanced Universal Dependencies

UD version 2[2] states that apart from the morphological and basic dependency annotation layers, strings may be annotated with an additional, enhanced, dependency layer, where the following phenomena can be captured:

- Gapping. To support a linguistically more satisfying treatment of ellipsis, empty nodes can be introduced to represent missing predicates in gapping constructions.

- Parent of coordination. Incoming relations are propagated from the parent of the coordination structure to each conjunct.

- Shared dependent of coordination. Outgoing relations are propagated from each conjunct to a shared dependent, e.g., a shared subject or object of coordinate verbs.

- Control and raising constructions. The external subject of `xcomp` dependents, if present, can be explicitly marked.

- Relative clauses. The antecedent noun of a relative clause is annotated as a dependent of a node within the relative clause (thus introducing a cycle) and the relative pronoun is annotated as a `ref` dependent of the antecedent noun.

- Case information. Selected dependents (in particular `obl` and `nmod`), if they are marked by morphological case and/or by an adpositional case dependent, can now be labeled as `obl:marker` or `nmod:marker` where `marker` is the lemma of the case dependent and/or the value of the morphological feature `Case`.

All enhancements are optional, so a UD treebank may contain enhanced graphs with one type of enhancement and still lack the other types.

4 Data

The evaluation was done on 17 languages from 4 language families: Arabic, Bulgarian, Czech, Dutch, English, Estonian, Finnish, French, Italian, Latvian, Lithuanian, Polish, Russian, Slovak, Swedish, Tamil, Ukrainian. The language selection is driven simply by the fact that at least partial enhanced representation is available for the given language.

Training and development data were based on the UD release 2.7 (Zeman et al., 2020) but for several treebanks the enhanced annotation is richer than in UD 2.7. Besides improvements in the officially released versions of the individual treebanks, a few other things have changed in comparison to the IWPT 2020 task. The English data now includes the GUM treebank (its enhanced annotation was not present in UD 2.7 but it was being prepared for UD 2.8 and it was ready in time for the shared task). As in 2020, we include two French treebanks whose enhanced annotation is still not included in the official UD releases, but the annotation is more conservative this year, omitting the extra labels for diathesis neutralization (Candito et al., 2017) and surface vs deep syntax markers. Still, some enhancements in French go slightly beyond the official UD guidelines (see below for details). In Polish, we now harmonize the relation subtypes in the three treebanks so that merging them into one dataset is no longer an issue. Finally, we omit the Chukchi treebank, which is new in UD 2.7 and has enhanced graphs, but the graphs are there only

[2] https://universaldependencies.org/u/overview/enhanced-syntax.html

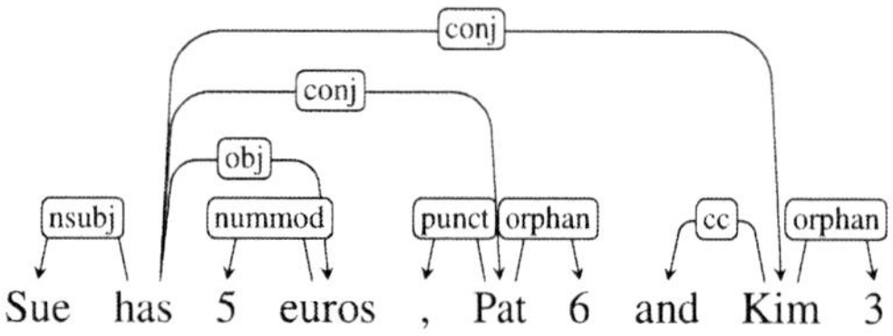

Figure 1: A basic tree of a gapping structure.

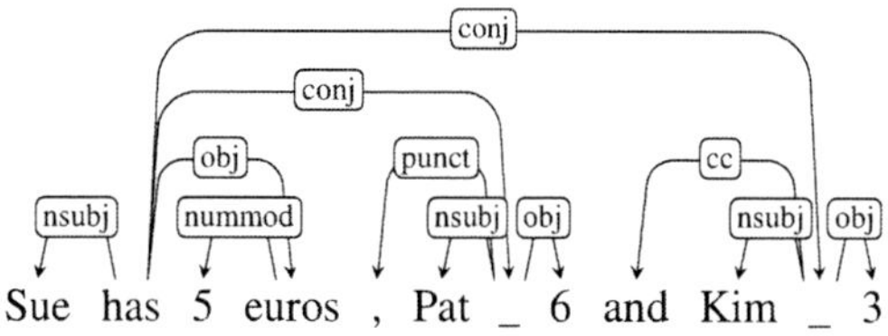

Figure 2: The correct enhanced graph of the gapping structure from Figure 1. "_" are empty nodes.

to provide empty nodes to capture incorporated modifiers (rather than gapping); furthermore, the treebank is too small and has no training data.

There are 13 treebanks of 7 languages in UD 2.7 that contain all types of enhancements: Czech (CAC, FicTree, PDT, and PUD), Dutch (Alpino and LassySmall), English (EWT and PUD), Italian (ISDT), Lithuanian (ALKSNIS), Slovak (SNK), and Swedish (Talbanken and PUD). For the remaining languages, we applied simple heuristics and added at least some enhancements for the purpose of the shared task, but these annotations are not yet part of the regular UD releases. We only applied our heuristics to the missing enhancement types; we did not attempt to modify the enhancements provided by the data providers. Table 1 gives an overview of enhancements in individual treebanks.

Treebank	UD 2.7	Task
Arabic PADT	GPS RC	GPS RC
Bulgarian BTB	PSXRC	PSXRC
Czech CAC	GPSXRC	GPSXRC
Czech FicTree	GPSXRC	GPSXRC
Czech PDT	GPSXRC	GPSXRC
Czech PUD	GPSXRC	GP XRC
Dutch Alpino	GPSXRC	GPSXRC
Dutch LassySmall	GPSXRC	GPSXRC
English EWT	GPSXRC	GPSXRC
English GUM		GPSXRC
English PUD	GPSXRC	GPSXRC
Estonian EDT	GPS R	GPS RC
Estonian EWT	G	GP RC
Finnish PUD	GP	GP RC
Finnish TDT	GPSX	GPSXRC
French FQB		PSXR
French Sequoia		PSXR
Italian ISDT	GPSXRC	GPSXRC
Latvian LVTB	GPSX C	GPSXRC
Lithuanian ALKS.	GPSXRC	GPSXRC
Polish LFG	PSX C	PSXRC
Polish PDB	PS	GPSXRC
Polish PUD	PS	GPSXRC
Russian SynTagRus	G	GP XRC
Slovak SNK	GPSXRC	GPSXRC
Swedish PUD	GPSXRC	GPSXRC
Swedish Talbanken	GPSXRC	GPSXRC
Tamil TTB	PS	PS RC
Ukrainian IU	GPSXR	GPSXRC

Table 1: New annotation for the shared task. Abbreviations: G = gapping; P = parent of coordination; S = shared dependent of coordination; X = external subject of controlled verb; R = relative clause; C = case-enhanced relation label.

The enhancements differ in how easily and accurately they can be inferred from the basic UD annotation:

- Enhancing relation labels with case information is deterministic. We apply it to the relations `obl`, `nmod`, `advcl` and `acl`. If they have a `case` or `mark` dependent, we add its lowercased lemma (for fixed multiword expressions or for multiple `case`/`mark` dependents we glue the lemmas with the "_" character). For `obl` and `nmod` we further examine the `Case` feature and add its lowercased value, if present.
- Linking the parent of coordination to all conjuncts is deterministic.
- Recognizing and transforming relative clauses is easy if relative pronouns can be recognized. This can be tricky in languages where the same pronouns can be used relatively (Figure 3) and interrogatively (Figure 4). We cannot recognize all instances of the latter case reliably; fortunately they do not seem to be too frequent.
- External subjects of `xcomp` clauses are subjects, objects or oblique dependents of the matrix clause. To find them, we need to know whether the governing verb has subject or ob-

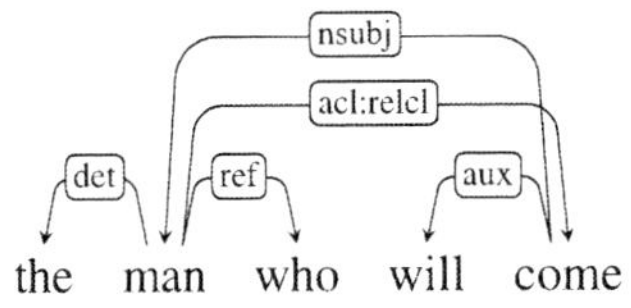

Figure 3: Enhanced graph of a relative clause.

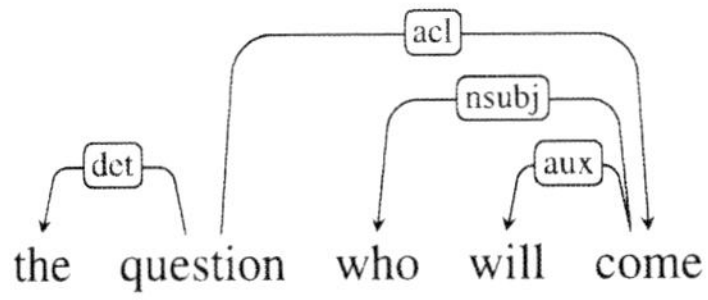

Figure 4: Enhanced graph of an interrogative clause.

ject control. We use language-specific verb lists, which can resolve many cases, but not all. If a verb is not on any list, we skip it.

- Gapping can be easily identified by the presence of the `orphan` relation in the basic tree, insertion of empty nodes is thus trivial. However, we do not know the type of the relation between the empty node and the orphaned dependents. Figure 2 shows a graph where each empty node has one `nsubj` and one `obj` dependent. We cannot infer these labels from the basic tree (Figure 1), so we use `dep` instead.

- Linking conjuncts to shared dependents cannot be done reliably because we cannot know whether a dependent should be shared (this may be sometimes difficult even for a human annotator!) Therefore we do not attempt to add this enhancement to the datasets that do not have it.

Although the UD releases distinguish several different treebanks for some languages, for the purpose of the shared task evaluation we merged all test sets of each language. We wanted to promote robust parsers that are not tightly tied to one particular dataset. Merging treebanks of one language was possible because for almost all languages it holds that treebanks participating in the present task are maintained by the same team, hence no significant treebank-specific annotation decisions are expected. The exceptions are English and Polish but there should not be any significant divergence in these languages either. In English, the GUM corpus is maintained by other people than EWT and PUD; nevertheless, the corpora use the same set of relations, and there are ongoing efforts to harmonize the way the relations are used. In Polish, the LFG treebank uses a different set of relation subtypes than PDB and PUD; however, this year we removed the subtypes that are not used in all three treebanks, so it should be possible to train a parser on one treebank and successfully apply it to another.

Treebank	basic	lab	add	rem
Arabic PADT	301399	27	7	1
Bulgarian BTB	156151	12	4	1
Czech CAC	494383	18	13	2
Czech FicTree	167056	13	11	2
Czech PDT	1506484	17	10	2
Czech PUD	18610	17	8	2
Dutch Alpino	208540	13	5	1
Dutch LassySmall	98044	14	5	1
English EWT	254829	13	6	1
English GUM	134476	14	6	1
English PUD	21176	15	6	1
Estonian EDT	437769	22	2	1
Estonian EWT	56399	18	8	1
Finnish PUD	15813	19	3	1
Finnish TDT	202291	18	10	1
French FQB	24135	0	2	0
French Sequoia	70567	0	5	0
Italian ISDT	298344	17	6	1
Latvian LVTB	219955	16	11	2
Lithuanian ALKSNIS	70047	23	12	1
Polish LFG	130968	9	3	0
Polish PDB	350036	16	9	1
Polish PUD	18389	18	9	1
Russian SynTagRus	1106296	17	7	1
Slovak SNK	106097	15	7	1
Swedish PUD	19076	16	7	1
Swedish Talbanken	96819	15	8	1
Tamil TTB	9581	27	3	0
Ukrainian IU	122094	16	10	1
total	6696809	17	8	1

Table 2: Comparing the impact of enhancements in the shared task treebanks where 'basic' is the number of basic dependencies (i.e., the number of words in the treebank) and the rest is given as a percentage of 'basic': 'lab' are enhanced dependencies that differ from a basic dependency only in label; 'add' are new enhanced dependencies (not only label but also the parent node differs from basic); 'rem' are basic dependencies that were removed from the enhanced graph.

Table 2 shows that the effect of enhancements

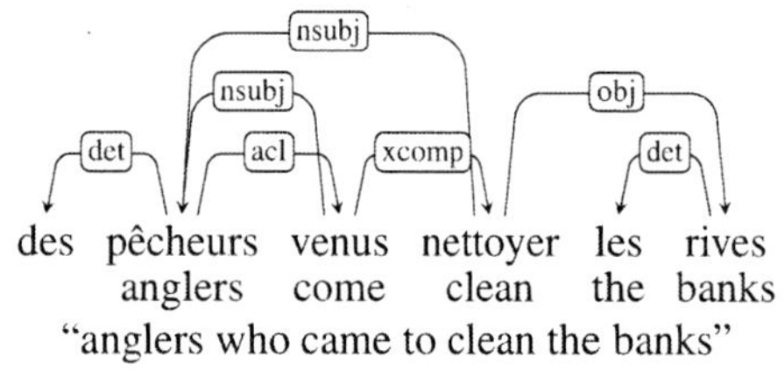

Figure 5: Participial adnominal clauses in French are treated similarly to relative clauses: The modified noun is attached as a subject of the participle (and here also of the `xcomp` infinitive controlled by the participle).

differs quite a bit between the various languages. For instance, the percentage of basic dependencies that have a different label in the enhanced graph (mostly because of adding the case information to `obl` and other relations), ranges from 0 to 27%. Enhanced dependencies that introduce truly novel edges are rarer. In the table they are again expressed relatively to the number of basic dependencies, and the figure varies between 2 and 13%. Up to 2% basic edges are omitted in the enhanced graph.

There are slight differences in how individual languages implement particular enhancement types. Some languages follow earlier proposals for enhanced relation subtypes that are not supported by the current UD guidelines, e.g., external subjects are labeled `nsubj:xsubj`, antecedents of relative clauses are `nsubj:relsubj` or `obj:relobj`, the "case" information is extended to showing conjunction lemma with conjuncts (`conj:and`, `conj:or` etc.) Empty nodes are occasionally used for other ellipsis types than gapping or stripping. The adding of relations from relative clauses to modified nouns is further extended in French to infinitival and participial adnominal clauses, as in Figure 5.[3]

Upon completion of the shared task, the data has been made publicly available at the permanent address `http://hdl.handle.net/11234/1-3728`.

5 Task

As in the previous dependency parsing shared tasks, participants were expected to go from raw, untokenized strings to full dependency annotation. The evaluation focused on the enhanced annotation layer, but the participants were encouraged to predict all annotation layers, and the evaluation of the other layers is available on the shared task website.[4] The task was open, in the sense that participants were allowed to use any additional resources they deemed fit (with the exception of UD 2.7 test data) as long as this was announced in advance and the additional resource was freely available to everybody.

The submitted system outputs had to be valid CoNLL-U files; if a file was invalid, its score would be zero.[5] The official UD validation script[6] was used to check validity, although only at 'level 2', which means that only basic file format was checked and not the annotation guidelines (e.g., an unknown relation label would not render the file invalid). Constraints that have to be met at this level are that there must be at least one root node and every node must be reachable via a directed path from at least one root node (*rootedness* and *connectedness*), that the enhanced graph can contain cycles, but not self-loops (a node depending on itself), and that dependency labels can only contain characters from a limited set.

In addition to CoNLL-U validity, we also required that systems do not alter any non-whitespace characters when processing the input. This is a pre-requisite for the evaluation, where system-predicted tokens must be aligned with gold-standard tokens; files with modified word forms would be rejected.

6 Evaluation Metrics

The main evaluation metric is ELAS (*labeled attachment score on enhanced dependencies*), where ELAS is defined as F_1-score over the set of enhanced dependencies in the system output and the gold standard. Complete edge labels are taken into account, i.e. `obl:on` differs from `obl`. A second metric is EULAS, which differs from ELAS in that only the universal part of the dependency relation label is taken into account. Relation subtypes are ignored, i.e., `obl:on`, `obl:auf`, and `obl` are treated as identical.

Another issue we address is the evaluation of empty nodes. A consequence of the treatment of gapping and ellipsis is that some sentences contain

[3]See (Candito et al., 2017) for details of the other enhancements they added (controlled-adjectives, causative constructions, etc.)

[4]`https://universaldependencies.org/iwpt21/`

[5]`https://universaldependencies.org/format.html`

[6]`https://universaldependencies.org/release_checklist.html#validation`

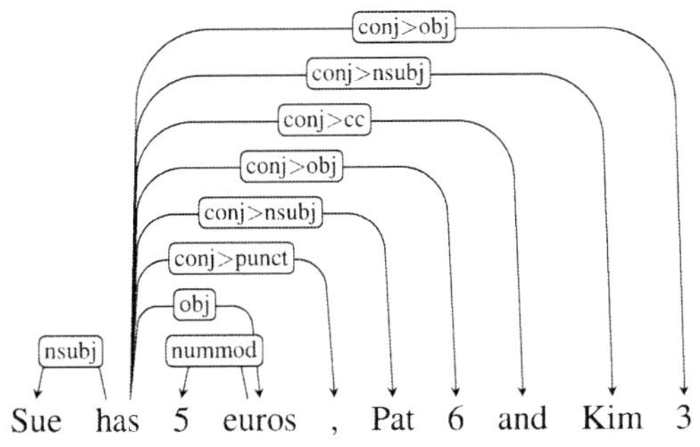

Figure 6: The enhanced graph from Figure 2 after collapsing empty nodes and reflecting the paths in dependency labels.

additional nodes (numbered 1.1 etc.). It is not guaranteed that gold and system agree on the position in the string where these should appear, but the information encoded by these additional nodes might nevertheless be identical. Thus, such empty nodes should be considered equal even if their string index differs. To ensure that this is the case, we have opted for a solution that basically compiles the information expressed by empty nodes into the dependency label of its dependents. I.e. if a dependent with dependency label `L2` has an empty node `i2.1` as parent which itself is an `L1` dependent of `i1`, its dependency label will be expanded into a path `i1:L1>L2`. This preserves the information that the dependent was an `L2` dependent of 'something' that was itself an `L1` dependent of `i1`, while at the same time removing the potentially conflicting `i2.1` (Figure 6).[7]

Finally, to analyze results, we computed ELAS scores per phenomenon. This should be seen as a diagnostic only, and is intended to gain further insights into the capability of various systems to deal with challenging phenomena, such as the proper analysis of phenomena occurring in the context of coordination and ellipsis.

7 Approaches

The predominant approach to obtaining the enhanced dependency graph is to use a biaffine function, i.e., predicting for each pair of nodes how likely it is that they are in a parent-child relation. There is wide variety in the way the final annotation graph is obtained, and ensuring that the result is valid (i.e. connected). GREW (Guillaume and Perrier, 2021) uses manually constructed rewrite rules to map basic UD into EUD, while FASTPARSE (Anderson and Gómez-Rodríguez, 2021) and NUIG (Choudhary and O'riordan, 2021) reformulate the task as a sequence-labeling task.

For the initial stages of the analysis (sentence splitting, tokenization, lemmatization, POS-tagging) most teams use Stanza (Qi et al., 2020) or Trankit (Van Nguyen et al., 2021) or similar methods. In a post-evaluation experiment, the DCU-EPFL team (Barry et al., 2021) obtained improved scores using Trankit instead of Stanza, while the TGIF team (Shi and Lee, 2021) uses a variation of the Trankit and Stanza systems to obtain the best pre-processing results, especially for sentence-splitting.

A wide variety of monolingual and multilingual pre-trained language models is used, with XML-R (Conneau et al., 2020) being the most popular. The ShanghaiTech system (Wang et al., 2021) learns an input representation from a combination of pre-trained language models where the various representations are concatenated into a single vector and masking is used to learn a weighting for various components of the combined vector. Both COMBO (Klimaszewski and Wróblewska, 2021) and UNIPI (Attardi et al., 2021) use a method that learns weights for the scores obtained from various layers of the BERT model to be used as input for the biaffine parser.

Most teams reduce the number of edge labels during training by de-lexicalizing edge labels. Dependency paths involving an empty node are usually also replaced by concatenating the path labels into a single path, as is also done in the evaluation script, thereby removing the need to predict empty nodes.

8 Results

Table 3 gives scores for LAS, EULAS, and ELAS macro-averaged over languages.[8] The 'baseline' is simply copying the UD annotation to EUD, but note that this is a strong baseline as it assumes perfect UD input, something that clearly is not the case for automated systems. Nevertheless, most systems perform well above the baseline for ELAS.

[7] If there are multiple empty nodes in the sentence, we lose the information which orphans were siblings and which were not. On the other hand, multiple empty nodes in one sentence are extremely rare.

[8] More detailed results (per language and treebank, unofficial results) are available on the website of the shared task, `https://universaldependencies.org/iwpt21/Results.html`

The NUIG submission was incomplete, in that the results for some languages were missing. The submissions of TGIF and ShanghaiTech contain dummy annotations for all annotation layers except EUD, so no LAS is provided.

LAS and ELAS correlate strongly, with ELAS generally being 3-4% lower than LAS, except for DCU-EPFL, whose ELAS beats LAS. The best system in the first edition of this shared task (Bouma et al., 2020) obtained a ELAS of 84.50, while the current highest scoring system obtains an ELAS of 89.24. The average of ELAS of the top-5 was 78.75 for the first edition, while the current top-5 has an average of 86.14. The higher scores are most likely both due to more uniform annotations across treebanks as described in section 4 and improvements in approaches.

Team	LAS	EULAS	ELAS
baseline	100.00	96.28	79.87
TGIF	n/a	90.16	89.24
ShanghaiTech	n/a	88.49	87.07
RobertNLP	89.18	88.00	86.97
Combo	87.84	85.20	83.79
Unipi	87.25	85.24	83.64
DCU-EPFL	82.65	84.47	83.57
Grew	85.77	84.07	81.58
Fastparse	71.72	68.78	65.81
Nuig	39.78	31.63	30.03

Table 3: Evaluation results on the test data, macro-averaged over languages. LAS is the evaluation of the basic dependency annotation, while EULAS and ELAS evaluate the enhanced graph.

Table 4 gives the highest ELAS per language. Again, we see considerable improvements for all languages compared to the best ELAS for that language in the first edition of the shared task. The only exception is English, but it should be noted that for English the GUM treebank was added to this years data, so that results are not really comparable.

For the first edition of this task (Bouma et al., 2020) we provided a qualitative evaluation, where scores were computed per treebank, while taking into account that some treebanks do not include all enhancements stated in the guidelines in their enhanced layer. This year, as the annotation is considerable more uniform across treebanks, we decided to concentrate on performance per enhancement type. We used a script that labeled each edge in

Language	**2020**	**2021**
Arabic	77.82	82.26
Bulgarian	90.73	93.63
Czech	87.51	92.24
Dutch	85.14	91.78
English[1]	88.94	88.19
Estonian	84.54	88.38
Finnish	89.49	91.75
French[2]	86.23	91.73
Italian	91.54	93.31
Latvian	84.94	90.23
Lithuanian	77.64	86.06
Polish	84.64	91.46
Russian	90.69	94.01
Slovak	88.56	94.96
Swedish	85.64	89.90
Tamil	64.23	65.58
Ukrainian	87.22	92.78

Table 4: Best ELAS per language for 2020 and 2021. All best scores for 2021 were obtained by TGIF except for Arabic (ShanghaiTech). [1]*: English compares the score for the EWT and PUD treebanks (2020) with EWT+PUD+GUM (2021).* [2]*: French compares the scores between the 2021 more simple annotation scheme and the 2020 more complex original proposal.*

the enhanced annotation as belonging to one of the phenomena or enhancement types listed in Table 5. ELAS per phenomenon are given in Table 6. Note that the classification script assumes that basic UD annotation is also provided. For systems that only provide dummy labels and relations in their basic annotation (TGIF and ShanghaiTech), scores for some of the phenomena can therefore not be computed in a meaningful way and we replaced the score with 'n/a'. Table 6 illustrates that some systems do not take gapping (G) and treatment of orphans (O) into account. Also, scores for coordination (P and S), controlled subjects (X) and relatives (R) differ quite a bit among systems. While some of the phenomena are relatively rare in the data, it seems that to do well on the task, a system needs to perform reasonably well on all the phenomena listed here.

9 Conclusions

The second edition of the shared task for parsing into enhanced universal dependencies shows improvements at various levels. First of all, the same set of languages was included as for the first edition,

B	basic	this enhanced edge is identical to an edge in the basic tree (including the label)
C	cased	case-enhanced relation (the relation with the shorter label may or may not exist in the basic tree)
L	relabeled	the same two nodes are also connected in the basic tree but the label is different and the difference does not look like a case enhancement
G	gapping	the parent or the child is an empty node; the edge was added because of gapping
O	orphan	basic relation missing from enhanced graph because it was replaced by a relation to/from an empty node (the basic edge is not necessarily labeled `orphan`)
P	coparent	shared parent of coordination, relation propagated to a non-first conjunct
S	codepend	shared dependent of coordination, relation propagated from a non-first conjunct
X	xsubj	relation between a controlled predicate and its external subject
R	relcl	relation between a node in a relative clause and the modified nominal; also the `ref` relation between the modified nominal and the coreferential relative pronoun
W	relpron	basic relation incoming to a relative pronoun is missing from enhanced graph because it was replaced by the `ref` relation
M	missing	basic relation is missing from the enhanced graph but none of the above reasons applies
E	enhanced	this enhanced edge does not exist in the basic tree and none of the above reasons applies

Table 5: Classification of enhanced dependencies according to phenomenon and enhancement type.

Phenom'n	Combo	DCU_EPFL	Fastparse	Grew	RobertNLP	ShanghaiTech	TGIF	Unipi
B	90.86	89.13	78.32	88.00	91.56	n/a	n/a	90.19
C	83.28	80.17	61.03	76.79	83.10	n/a	n/a	82.30
L	0.00	0.02	0.00	0.00	0.03	0.01	0.00	0.05
G	21.81	0.00	0.00	12.57	0.00	56.55	58.39	0.00
O	29.84	0.00	0.00	15.81	0.00	n/a	n/a	0.00
P	60.63	73.48	26.39	62.09	64.78	75.91	79.61	61.24
S	38.02	59.07	0.71	40.92	64.19	65.40	69.22	57.64
X	64.29	84.41	3.37	71.00	86.82	85.96	88.09	84.75
R	64.73	84.42	1.53	65.21	85.38	85.67	85.08	82.42
W	88.17	87.06	0.00	81.50	90.63	n/a	n/a	90.76
M	0.00	0.01	0.00	0.00	0.00	0.00	0.00	0.00
E	0.51	0.51	0.02	0.00	0.00	0.09	0.09	1.77

Table 6: ELAS per phenomenon. Scores are micro-averaged, i.e. computed for the concatenation of all treebanks. Note that for systems that only provide dummy annotations for basic UD, some of the scores cannot be computed in a meaningful way. The NUIG system was not included as it lacked results for some languages.

but now we were using treebanks of UD release 2.7 (Zeman et al., 2020). This EUD annotation of this release is more consistent and according to guidelines than the data of release 2.5, but we still had to harmonize some of the annotations so that differences in annotation would not have a negative effect on system performance.

Second, the requirement that submitted annotations should be minimally valid according to the guidelines, was now more easily met by all participating teams. Teams ensured that graphs would be connected, for instance, by applying several heuristics that introduce the minimal amount of additional edges to meet connectedness.

Third, while the best performing system in the first shared task used a method that pre-compiled the enhanced annotation graph into a tree, compatible with basic UD, and used a standard dependency parsing algorithm for learning to produce such annotations, almost all systems in this years shared task went for a graph-based approach. There still is quite a bit of variation in the way the graph is constructed though, with some systems first producing a tree, and then adding additional edges, where others try to produce the graph directly. At the same time, most systems do apply some form of pre-compilation to make the data more suitable for learning. In particular, case-enhanced dependency labels are replaced by de-lexicalized labels that can be easily reconstructed in postprocessing.

Similarly, most teams adopt a method that removes 'empty' nodes and instead expresses the information in incoming and outgoing edges from these nodes in the form of complex dependency labels (as is done in the evaluation script as well).

Finally, a very positive outcome of this evaluation is that scores have increased considerably, not only for the top performing system, but also for the top-5 systems. In particular, lower performance now seems to be restricted to languages for which very limited amounts of data is available, and, as Table 4 shows, the best system obtains an ELAS of over 90% for 11 of the 17 languages included in the evaluation.

Acknowledgments

We heartily thank everyone involved in the development of the Enhanced UD treebanks and who made this shared task possible.

This work has been partially supported by the LUSyD project, grant 20-16819X of the Czech Science Foundation (GAČR). The second author was partly funded by two French National Research Agency projects, PARSITI (ANR-16-CE33-0021) and SoSweet (ANR-15-CE38-0011).

References

Mark Anderson and Carlos Gómez-Rodríguez. 2021. Splitting EUD graphs into trees: A quick and clatty approach. In *Proceedings of the 17th International Conference on Parsing Technologies and the IWPT 2021 Shared Task on Parsing into Enhanced Universal Dependencies*.

Giuseppe Attardi, Daniele Sartiano, and Maria Simi. 2021. Biaffine dependency and semantic graph parsing for enhanced universal dependencies. In *Proceedings of the 17th International Conference on Parsing Technologies and the IWPT 2021 Shared Task on Parsing into Enhanced Universal Dependencies*.

James Barry, Alireza Mohammadshahi, Joachim Wagner, Jennifer Foster, and James Henderson. 2021. The dcu-epfl enhanced dependency parser at the iwpt 2021 shared task. In *Proceedings of the 17th International Conference on Parsing Technologies and the IWPT 2021 Shared Task on Parsing into Enhanced Universal Dependencies*.

Gosse Bouma, Djamé Seddah, and Daniel Zeman. 2020. Overview of the IWPT 2020 Shared Task on Parsing into Enhanced Universal Dependencies. In *Proceedings of the 16th International Conference on Parsing Technologies and the IWPT 2020 Shared Task on Parsing into Enhanced Universal Dependencies*, pages 151–161, Stroudsburg, PA, USA. Association for Computational Linguistics.

Marie Candito, Bruno Guillaume, Guy Perrier, and Djamé Seddah. 2017. Enhanced UD dependencies with neutralized diathesis alternation. In *Proceedings of the Fourth International Conference on Dependency Linguistics (Depling 2017)*, pages 42–53, Pisa, Italy.

Chinmay Choudhary and Colm O'riordan. 2021. End-to-end mbert based seq2seq enhanced dependency parser with linguistic typology knowledge. In *Proceedings of the 17th International Conference on Parsing Technologies and the IWPT 2021 Shared Task on Parsing into Enhanced Universal Dependencies (IWPT 2021)*, pages 225–232, Bangkok, Thailand (online). Association for Computational Linguistics.

Alexis Conneau, Kartikay Khandelwal, Naman Goyal, Vishrav Chaudhary, Guillaume Wenzek, Francisco Guzmán, Edouard Grave, Myle Ott, Luke Zettlemoyer, and Veselin Stoyanov. 2020. Unsupervised cross-lingual representation learning at scale. In *Proceedings of the 58th Annual Meeting of the Association for Computational Linguistics*, page 8440–8451.

Bruno Guillaume and Guy Perrier. 2021. Graph Rewriting for Enhanced Universal Dependencies. In *Proceedings of the 17th International Conference on Parsing Technologies and the IWPT 2021 Shared Task on Parsing into Enhanced Universal Dependencies*.

Mateusz Klimaszewski and Alina Wróblewska. 2021. Combo: a new module for EUD parsing. In *Proceedings of the 17th International Conference on Parsing Technologies and the IWPT 2021 Shared Task on Parsing into Enhanced Universal Dependencies*.

Joakim Nivre, Marie-Catherine de Marneffe, Filip Ginter, Jan Hajič, Christopher D. Manning, Sampo Pyysalo, Sebastian Schuster, Francis Tyers, and Daniel Zeman. 2020. Universal Dependencies v2: An evergrowing multilingual treebank collection. In *Proceedings of the Twelfth International Conference on Language Resources and Evaluation (LREC 2020)*, pages 4027–4036, Paris, France. European Language Resources Association.

Joakim Nivre, Paola Marongiu, Filip Ginter, Jenna Kanerva, Simonetta Montemagni, Sebastian Schuster, and Maria Simi. 2018. Enhancing universal dependency treebanks: A case study. In *Proceedings of the Second Workshop on Universal Dependencies (UDW 2018)*, pages 102–107.

Jenna Nyblom, Samuel Kohonen, Katri Haverinen, Tapio Salakoski, and Filip Ginter. 2013. Predicting conjunct propagation and other extended Stanford Dependencies. In *Proceedings of the Second International Conference on Dependency Linguistics*

(DepLing 2013), pages 252–261, Praha, Czechia. Matfyzpress.

Stephan Oepen, Omri Abend, Lasha Abzianidze, Johan Bos, Jan Hajič, Daniel Hershcovich, Bin Li, Tim O'Gorman, Nianwen Xue, and Daniel Zeman. 2020. MRP 2020: The Second Shared Task on Cross-framework and Cross-Lingual Meaning Representation Parsing. In *Proceedings of the CoNLL 2020 Shared Task: Cross-Framework Meaning Representation Parsing*, pages 1–22, Online.

Stephan Oepen, Omri Abend, Jan Hajič, Daniel Hershcovich, Marco Kuhlmann, Tim O'Gorman, Nianwen Xue, Jayeol Chun, Milan Straka, and Zdeňka Urešová. 2019. MRP 2019: Cross-framework meaning representation parsing. In *Proceedings of the Shared Task on Cross-Framework Meaning Representation Parsing at the 2019 Conference on Natural Language Learning*, pages 1–27, Hong Kong. Association for Computational Linguistics.

Stephan Oepen, Jari Björne, Richard Johansson, Emanuele Lapponi, Filip Ginter, Erik Velldal, and Lilja Øvrelid. 2017. The 2017 Shared Task on Extrinsic Parser Evaluation (EPE 2017).

Stephan Oepen, Marco Kuhlmann, Yusuke Miyao, Daniel Zeman, Silvie Cinková, Dan Flickinger, Jan Hajič, and Zdeňka Urešová. 2015. SemEval 2015 task 18: Broad-coverage semantic dependency parsing. In *Proceedings of the 9th International Workshop on Semantic Evaluation (SemEval 2015)*. Association for Computational Linguistics.

Stephan Oepen, Marco Kuhlmann, Yusuke Miyao, Daniel Zeman, Dan Flickinger, Jan Hajič, Angelina Ivanova, and Yi Zhang. 2014. Semeval 2014 task 8: Broad-coverage semantic dependency parsing. In *Proceedings of the 8th International Workshop on Semantic Evaluation (SemEval 2014)*, pages 63–72.

Peng Qi, Yuhao Zhang, Yuhui Zhang, Jason Bolton, and Christopher D Manning. 2020. Stanza: A Python natural language processing toolkit for many human languages. In *Proceedings of the 58th Annual Meeting of the Association for Computational Linguistics: System Demonstrations*, page 101–108, Seattle, WA, USA.

Sebastian Schuster, Eric De La Clergerie, Marie Candito, Benoît Sagot, Christopher D. Manning, and Djamé Seddah. 2017. Paris and Stanford at EPE 2017: Downstream evaluation of graph-based dependency representations.

Sebastian Schuster and Christopher D. Manning. 2016. Enhanced English Universal Dependencies: An Improved Representation for Natural Language Understanding Tasks. In *Proceedings of the 10th International Conference on Language Resources and Evaluation (LREC 2016)*, Paris, France. European Language Resources Association.

Tianze Shi and Lillian Lee. 2021. TGIF: Tree-Graph Integrated-Format Parser for Enhanced UD with Two-Stage Generic- to Individual-Language Finetuning. In *Proceedings of the 17th International Conference on Parsing Technologies and the IWPT 2021 Shared Task on Parsing into Enhanced Universal Dependencies*.

Milan Straka, Jan Hajič, and Jana Straková. 2016. Udpipe: trainable pipeline for processing conll-u files performing tokenization, morphological analysis, pos tagging and parsing. In *Proceedings of the Tenth International Conference on Language Resources and Evaluation (LREC'16)*, pages 4290–4297.

Minh Van Nguyen, Viet Lai, Amir Pouran Ben Veyseh, and Thien Huu Nguyen. 2021. Trankit: A light-weight transformer-based toolkit for multilingual natural language processing. In *Proceedings of the 16th Conference of the European Chapter of the Association for Computational Linguistics: System Demonstrations*, page 80–90.

Xinyu Wang, Zixia Jia, Yong Jiang, and Kewei Tu. 2021. Enhanced universal dependency parsing with automated concatenation of embeddings. In *Proceedings of the 17th International Conference on Parsing Technologies and the IWPT 2021 Shared Task on Parsing into Enhanced Universal Dependencies*.

Daniel Zeman, Jan Hajič, Martin Popel, Martin Potthast, Milan Straka, Filip Ginter, Joakim Nivre, and Slav Petrov. 2018. CoNLL 2018 shared task: Multilingual parsing from raw text to universal dependencies. In *Proceedings of the CoNLL 2018 Shared Task: Multilingual Parsing from Raw Text to Universal Dependencies*, pages 1–21, Brussels, Belgium. Association for Computational Linguistics.

Daniel Zeman, Joakim Nivre, Mitchell Abrams, Elia Ackermann, Noëmi Aepli, Hamid Aghaei, Željko Agić, Amir Ahmadi, Lars Ahrenberg, Chika Kennedy Ajede, Gabrielė Aleksandravičiūtė, Ika Alfina, Lene Antonsen, Katya Aplonova, Angelina Aquino, Carolina Aragon, Maria Jesus Aranzabe, Hórunn Arnardóttir, Gashaw Arutie, Jessica Naraiswari Arwidarasti, Masayuki Asahara, Luma Ateyah, Furkan Atmaca, Mohammed Attia, Aitziber Atutxa, Liesbeth Augustinus, Elena Badmaeva, Keerthana Balasubramani, Miguel Ballesteros, Esha Banerjee, Sebastian Bank, Verginica Barbu Mititelu, Victoria Basmov, Colin Batchelor, John Bauer, Seyyit Talha Bedir, Kepa Bengoetxea, Gözde Berk, Yevgeni Berzak, Irshad Ahmad Bhat, Riyaz Ahmad Bhat, Erica Biagetti, Eckhard Bick, Agnė Bielinskienė, Kristín Bjarnadóttir, Rogier Blokland, Victoria Bobicev, Loïc Boizou, Emanuel Borges Völker, Carl Börstell, Cristina Bosco, Gosse Bouma, Sam Bowman, Adriane Boyd, Kristina Brokaitė, Aljoscha Burchardt, Marie Candito, Bernard Caron, Gauthier Caron, Tatiana Cavalcanti, Gülşen Cebiroğlu Eryiğit, Flavio Massimiliano Cecchini, Giuseppe G. A. Celano, Slavomír Čéplö, Savas Cetin, Özlem Çetinoğlu, Fabricio Chalub, Ethan Chi, Yongseok Cho, Jinho Choi, Jayeol Chun, Alessandra T. Cignarella, Silvie Cinková, Aurélie Collomb, Çağrı Çöltekin, Miriam Connor, Marine Courtin, Elizabeth Davidson, Marie-Catherine de Marneffe, Valeria de Paiva, Mehmet Oguz Derin, Elvis de Souza, Arantza Diaz de Ilarraza, Carly Dickerson, Arawinda Dinakaramani, Bamba Dione, Peter Dirix, Kaja Dobrovoljc, Timothy Dozat, Kira Droganova, Puneet Dwivedi, Hanne Eckhoff, Marhaba Eli, Ali Elkahky, Binyam Ephrem, Olga Erina, Tomaž Erjavec, Aline Etienne, Wograine Evelyn, Sidney Facundes, Richárd Farkas, Marília Fernanda, Hector Fernandez Alcalde, Jennifer Foster, Cláudia Freitas, Kazunori Fujita, Katarína Gajdošová, Daniel Galbraith, Marcos Garcia, Moa Gärdenfors, Sebastian Garza, Fabrício Ferraz Gerardi, Kim Gerdes, Filip Ginter, Iakes Goenaga, Koldo Gojenola, Memduh Gökırmak, Yoav Goldberg, Xavier Gómez Guinovart, Berta González Saavedra, Bernadeta Griciūtė, Matias Grioni, Loïc Grobol, Normunds Grūzītis, Bruno Guillaume, Céline Guillot-Barbance, Tunga Güngör, Nizar Habash, Hinrik Hafsteinsson, Jan Hajič, Jan Hajič jr., Mika Hämäläinen, Linh Hà Mỹ, Na-Rae Han, Muhammad Yudistira Hanifmuti, Sam Hardwick, Kim Harris, Dag Haug, Johannes Heinecke, Oliver Hellwig, Felix Hennig, Barbora Hladká, Jaroslava Hlaváčová, Florinel Hociung, Petter Hohle, Eva Huber, Jena Hwang, Takumi Ikeda, Anton Karl Ingason, Radu Ion, Elena Irimia, Ọlájídé Ishola, Tomáš Jelínek, Anders Johannsen, Hildur Jónsdóttir, Fredrik Jørgensen, Markus Juutinen, Sarveswaran K, Hüner Kaşıkara, Andre Kaasen, Nadezhda Kabaeva, Sylvain Kahane, Hiroshi Kanayama, Jenna Kanerva, Boris Katz, Tolga Kayadelen, Jessica Kenney, Václava Kettnerová, Jesse Kirchner, Elena Klementieva, Arne Köhn, Abdullatif Köksal, Kamil Kopacewicz, Timo Korkiakangas, Natalia Kotsyba, Jolanta Kovalevskaitė, Simon Krek, Parameswari Krishnamurthy, Sookyoung Kwak, Veronika Laippala, Lucia Lam, Lorenzo Lambertino, Tatiana Lando, Septina Dian Larasati, Alexei Lavrentiev, John Lee, Phương Lê Hồng, Alessandro Lenci, Saran Lertpradit, Herman Leung, Maria Levina, Cheuk Ying Li, Josie Li, Keying Li, Yuan Li, KyungTae Lim, Krister Lindén, Nikola Ljubešić, Olga Loginova, Andry Luthfi, Mikko Luukko, Olga Lyashevskaya, Teresa Lynn, Vivien Macketanz, Aibek Makazhanov, Michael Mandl, Christopher Manning, Ruli Manurung, Cătălina Mărănduc, David Mareček, Katrin Marheinecke, Héctor Martínez Alonso, André Martins, Jan Mašek, Hiroshi Matsuda, Yuji Matsumoto, Ryan McDonald, Sarah McGuinness, Gustavo Mendonça, Niko Miekka, Karina Mischenkova, Margarita Misirpashayeva, Anna Missilä, Cătălin Mititelu, Maria Mitrofan, Yusuke Miyao, AmirHossein Mojiri Foroushani, Amirsaeid Moloodi, Simonetta Montemagni, Amir More, Laura Moreno Romero, Keiko Sophie Mori, Shinsuke Mori, Tomohiko Morioka, Shigeki Moro, Bjartur Mortensen, Bohdan Moskalevskyi, Kadri Muischnek, Robert Munro, Yugo Murawaki, Kaili Müürisep, Pinkey Nainwani, Mariam Nakhlé, Juan Ignacio Navarro Horñiacek, Anna Nedoluzhko, Gunta Nešpore-Bērzkalne, Lương Nguyễn Thị, Huyền Nguyễn Thị Minh, Yoshihiro Nikaido, Vitaly Nikolaev, Rattima Nitisaroj, Alireza Nourian, Hanna Nurmi, Stina Ojala, Atul Kr. Ojha, Adéday`ọ Olúòkun, Mai Omura, Emeka Onwuegbuzia, Petya Osenova, Robert Östling, Lilja Øvrelid, Şaziye Betül Özateş, Arzucan Özgür, Balkız Öztürk Başaran, Niko Partanen, Elena Pascual, Marco Passarotti, Agnieszka Patejuk, Guilherme Paulino-Passos, Angelika Peljak-Łapińska, Siyao Peng, Cenel-Augusto Perez, Natalia Perkova, Guy Perrier, Slav Petrov, Daria Petrova, Jason Phelan, Jussi Piitulainen, Tommi A Pirinen, Emily Pitler, Barbara Plank, Thierry Poibeau, Larisa Ponomareva, Martin Popel, Lauma Pretkalniņa, Sophie Prévost, Prokopis Prokopidis, Adam Przepiórkowski, Tiina Puolakainen, Sampo Pyysalo, Peng Qi, Andriela Rääbis, Alexandre Rademaker, Taraka Rama, Loganathan Ramasamy, Carlos Ramisch, Fam Rashel, Mohammad Sadegh Rasooli, Vinit Ravishankar, Livy Real, Petru Rebeja, Siva Reddy, Georg Rehm, Ivan Riabov, Michael Rießler, Erika Rimkutė, Larissa Rinaldi, Laura Rituma, Luisa Rocha, Eiríkur Rögnvaldsson, Mykhailo Romanenko, Rudolf Rosa, Valentin Roșca, Davide Rovati, Olga Rudina, Jack Rueter, Kristján Rúnarsson, Shoval Sadde, Pegah Safari, Benoît Sagot, Aleksi Sahala, Shadi Saleh, Alessio Salomoni, Tanja Samardžić, Stephanie Samson, Manuela Sanguinetti, Dage Särg, Baiba Saulīte, Yanin Sawanakunanon, Kevin Scannell, Salvatore Scarlata, Nathan Schneider, Sebastian Schuster, Djamé Seddah, Wolfgang Seeker, Mojgan Seraji, Mo Shen, Atsuko Shimada, Hiroyuki Shirasu, Muh Shohibussirri, Dmitry Sichinava, Einar Freyr Sigurðsson, Aline Silveira, Natalia Silveira, Maria Simi, Radu Simionescu, Katalin Simkó, Mária Šimková, Kiril Simov, Maria Skachedubova, Aaron Smith, Isabela Soares-Bastos, Carolyn Spadine, Steinhór Steingrímsson, Antonio Stella, Milan Straka, Emmett Strickland, Jana Strnadová, Alane Suhr, Yogi Lesmana Sulestio, Umut Sulubacak, Shingo Suzuki, Zsolt Szántó, Dima Taji, Yuta Takahashi, Fabio Tamburini, Mary Ann C. Tan, Takaaki Tanaka, Samson Tella, Isabelle Tellier, Guillaume Thomas, Liisi Torga, Marsida Toska, Trond Trosterud, Anna Trukhina, Reut Tsarfaty, Utku Türk, Francis Tyers, Sumire Uematsu, Roman Untilov, Zdeňka Urešová, Larraitz Uria, Hans Uszkoreit, Andrius Utka, Sowmya Vajjala, Daniel van Niekerk, Gertjan van Noord, Viktor Varga, Eric Villemonte de la Clergerie, Veronika Vincze, Aya Wakasa, Joel C. Wallenberg, Lars Wallin, Abigail Walsh, Jing Xian Wang, Jonathan North Washington, Maximilan Wendt, Paul Widmer, Seyi Williams, Mats Wirén, Christian Wittern, Tsegay Woldemariam, Tak-sum Wong, Alina Wróblewska, Mary Yako, Kayo Yamashita, Naoki Yamazaki, Chunxiao Yan, Koichi Yasuoka, Marat M. Yavrumyan, Zhuoran Yu, Zdeněk Žabokrtský, Shorouq Zahra, Amir Zeldes, Hanzhi Zhu, and Anna Zhuravleva. 2020. Universal dependencies 2.7.

LINDAT/CLARIAH-CZ digital library at the Institute of Formal and Applied Linguistics (ÚFAL), Faculty of Mathematics and Physics, Charles University.

Daniel Zeman, Martin Popel, Milan Straka, Jan Hajič, Joakim Nivre, Filip Ginter, Juhani Luotolahti, Sampo Pyysalo, Slav Petrov, Martin Potthast, Francis Tyers, Elena Badmaeva, Memduh Gökırmak, Anna Nedoluzhko, Silvie Cinková, Jan Hajič jr., Jaroslava Hlaváčová, Václava Kettnerová, Zdeňka Urešová, Jenna Kanerva, Stina Ojala, Anna Missilä, Christopher D. Manning, Sebastian Schuster, Siva Reddy, Dima Taji, Nizar Habash, Herman Leung, Marie-Catherine de Marneffe, Manuela Sanguinetti, Maria Simi, Hiroshi Kanayama, Valeria de Paiva, Kira Droganova, Héctor Martínez Alonso, Çağrı Çöltekin, Umut Sulubacak, Hans Uszkoreit, Vivien Macketanz, Aljoscha Burchardt, Kim Harris, Katrin Marheinecke, Georg Rehm, Tolga Kayadelen, Mohammed Attia, Ali Elkahky, Zhuoran Yu, Emily Pitler, Saran Lertpradit, Michael Mandl, Jesse Kirchner, Hector Fernandez Alcalde, Jana Strnadová, Esha Banerjee, Ruli Manurung, Antonio Stella, Atsuko Shimada, Sookyoung Kwak, Gustavo Mendonca, Tatiana Lando, Rattima Nitisaroj, and Josie Li. 2017. Conll 2017 shared task: Multilingual parsing from raw text to universal dependencies. In *Proceedings of the CoNLL 2017 Shared Task: Multilingual Parsing from Raw Text to Universal Dependencies*, pages 1–19, Vancouver, Canada. Association for Computational Linguistics.

COMBO: a new module for EUD parsing

Mateusz Klimaszewski[1,2] **Alina Wróblewska**[2]
[1]Warsaw University of Technology
[2]Institute of Computer Science, Polish Academy of Sciences
m.klimaszewski@ii.pw.edu.pl
alina@ipipan.waw.pl

Abstract

We introduce the COMBO-based approach for EUD parsing and its implementation, which took part in the IWPT 2021 EUD shared task. The goal of this task is to parse raw texts in 17 languages into Enhanced Universal Dependencies (EUD). The proposed approach uses COMBO to predict UD trees and EUD graphs. These structures are then merged into the final EUD graphs. Some EUD edge labels are extended with case information using a single language-independent expansion rule. In the official evaluation, the solution ranked fourth, achieving an average ELAS of 83.79%. The source code is available at https://gitlab.clarin-pl.eu/syntactic-tools/combo.

1 Introduction

Data-driven dependency parsers achieve high parsing performance for languages representing different language families. The state-of-the-art dependency parsers are trained with supervised learning methods on large correctly annotated treebanks, e.g. from Universal Dependencies (UD, Nivre et al., 2020). UD is an international initiative aimed at developing a cross-linguistically consistent annotation schema and at building a large multilingual collection of dependency treebanks annotated according to this schema. A relatively small subset of UD treebanks is annotated with higher-order syntactic-semantic representations that encode various linguistic phenomena and are called Enhanced Universal Dependencies (EUD).

Dependency treebanks, especially the uniformly annotated UD treebanks, are used for multilingual system development, e.g. within multiple shared tasks on dependency parsing (Buchholz and Marsi, 2006; Nivre et al., 2007; Seddah et al., 2013, 2014; Zeman et al., 2017, 2018). In particular, the IWPT 2020 shared task on Parsing into Enhanced Universal Dependencies (Bouma et al., 2020) is worth mentioning, because it is the predecessor of the current IWPT 2021 shared task (Bouma et al., 2021). All shared tasks contributed to rapid advancement of language parsing technology, inter alia, the formulation of groundbreaking parsing algorithms and their publicly available implementations (e.g. Nivre et al., 2006; McDonald et al., 2006; Straka and Straková, 2017; Dozat et al., 2017; Rybak and Wróblewska, 2018; He and Choi, 2020).

Dependency parsing is an important issue in various sophisticated downstream tasks, including but not limited to sentiment analysis (Sun et al., 2019), relation extraction (Zhang et al., 2018; Vashishth et al., 2018; Guo et al., 2019), semantic role labelling (Wang et al., 2019), or question answering (Khashabi et al., 2018). On the other hand, even if EUD parsing aims at predicting semantically informed structures, which seem to be appropriate in advanced NLP tasks, it is not yet used in solving these tasks. An obstacle can be the availability of the state-of-the-art EUD parsers, e.g. two top systems at the IWPT 2020 EUD shared task (i.e. Kanerva et al., 2020; Heinecke, 2020) are not publicly available and therefore difficult to integrate into NLU systems without having to implement them from scratch. Meeting the potential expectations of NLU system architects, the source code of COMBO with the new EUD parsing module and the pre-trained models developed as part of our solution submitted to this shared task are publicly available.

The proposed solution to EUD parsing is based on (1) Stanza tokeniser (Qi et al., 2020), (2) COMBO (Klimaszewski and Wróblewska, 2021), a data-driven language-independent system for morphosyntactic prediction, i.e. part-of-speech tagging, morphological analysis, lemmatisation, dependency parsing, and EUD parsing (see Section

Proceedings of the 17th International Conference on Parsing Technologies (IWPT 2021), pages 158–166
Bangkok, Thailand (online), August 6, 2021.

3.3), (3) an algorithm that merges predicted labelled dependency arcs and predicted EUD arcs, and builds the final EUD graphs (see Section 3.4), and (4) two linguistically motivated language-independent rules that improve the final EUD graphs (see Section 3.5). The first expansion rule adds case information sublabels to EUD modifiers, and the second one amends enhanced arcs coming into the function words. These two rules are integrated into the proposed EUD parsing system.

In the official evaluation, our EUD parser ranked 4th, obtaining an average ELAS of 83.79% and EULAS of 85.20%.[1] It is worth emphasising that COMBO predicts labelled dependency trees with an average LAS of 88.91%, only being slightly outperformed by the ROBERTNLP system.

2 Shared task description

The IWPT 2021 EUD shared task consists in evaluating systems for parsing raw texts into Enhanced Universal Dependencies. The systems are trained and evaluated on data supplied by the organisers.

Data The shared task dataset includes treebanks for 17 languages from 4 language families. The largest group in this collection is constituted by Indo-European languages, i.e. Bulgarian, Czech, Polish, Russian, Slovak, Ukrainian (Slavic), Dutch, English, Swedish (Germanic), French, Italian (Romance), and Latvian, Lithuanian (Baltic). There are also representatives of the Uralic (Finnic) languages, i.e. Estonian and Finnish, the Afro-Asiatic (Semitic) languages – Arabic, and the Southern Dravidian languages – Tamil. The datasets vary in size and type of enhancements.

Enhancement types Various linguistic phenomena are encoded in EUD graphs:

- propagation of conjuncts in coordination constructions (see Figure 1),
- null nodes encoding elided predicates in coordination constructions (see Figure 2),
- additional subject relations in control and raising constructions (see Figure 3),
- coreference relations in relative clause constructions (see Figure 4),
- detailed case information sublabels of the modifiers (see Figure 5).

[1] https://universaldependencies.org/iwpt21/results_official_coarse.html

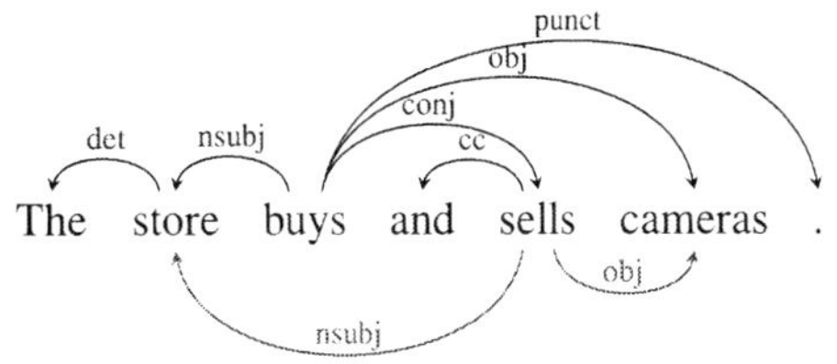

Figure 1: The EUD graph with the conjoined predicate; the conjoined verbs (*buys* and *sells*) share the subject (*the store*) and the object (*cameras*), and the propagated relations are indicated with the bottom blue enhanced edges.

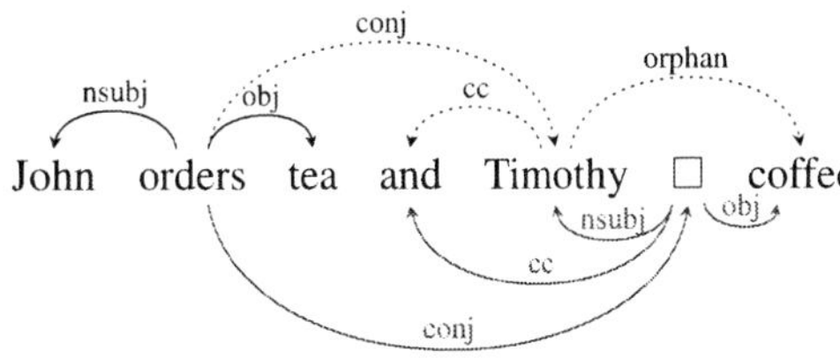

Figure 2: The EUD graph with an empty node □ and the bottom blue enhanced edges. The tree edges removed from the EUD graph are dotted.

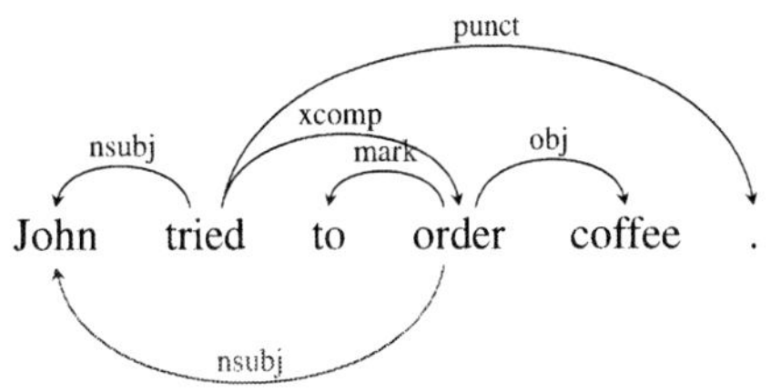

Figure 3: The EUD graph with the bottom blue enhanced edge encoding subject control with the control predicate *try*.

3 System overview

The EUD parsing system is built of the following components: a data encoder boosted with a contextual language model (see Section 3.1), morphosyntactic predictors (see Section 3.2), an EUD predictor (see Section 3.3), an algorithm merging predicted labelled dependency arcs and enhanced dependency arcs (see Section 3.4), and a post-processing module (see Section 3.5).

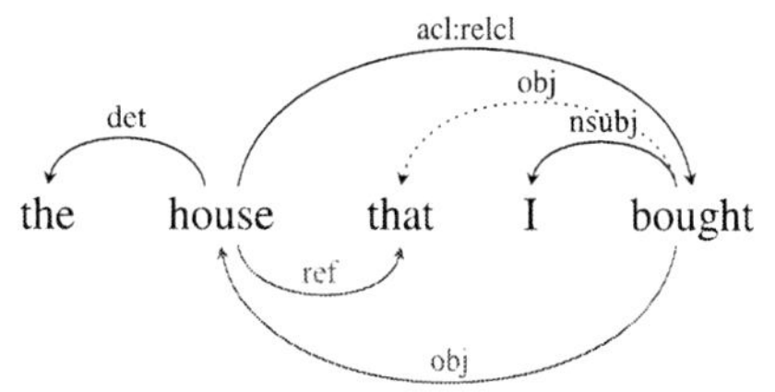

Figure 4: The EUD graph representing a relative clause modifying the noun *house*. The enhanced edges are marked with the bottom blue arcs and the tree edge removed from the EUD graph is dotted.

3.1 Data encoder

The encoder vectorises the tokenised input data. The input tokens are first represented as a concatenation of a character-based word embedding estimated during system training with a dilated convolutional neural network (Yu and Koltun, 2016), and a BERT-based embedding estimated as follows. BERT-based language models (LM, Devlin et al., 2019; Conneau et al., 2020) are not fine-tuned during system training. Instead, we apply the scalar mix technique based on Peters et al. (2018) to produce an embedding (h) for a word i as a weighted sum of embeddings from all layers:

$$h_i = \gamma \sum_{j=1}^{L} s_j h_{ij} \qquad (1)$$

Parameters γ and s_j are learnable weights, additionally s_j are softmax-normalised. L is the number of transformer layers. At the point of using LM, the data is already tokenised. If LM intra-tokeniser splits a word into multiple subwords, the embeddings h are estimated for these subwords and averaged. The vectors of words or averaged vectors of subwords are finally transformed with one fully connected (FC) layer.

The encoder with two BiLSTM layers (Hochreiter and Schmidhuber, 1997; Graves and Schmidhuber, 2005) transforms the concatenations of the character-based word embeddings and the transformed BERT-based embeddings into token vectors. The BiLSTM-transformed token embeddings are used as input to morphosyntactic predictors and the EUD parsing module.

3.2 Morphosyntactic predictors

The proposed approach is based on various morphosyntactic predictions. Part-of-speech tags, morphological features, and lemmata are used in the post-processing step to extract case information expanding enhanced sublabels of modifiers (see Section 3.5). The merge algorithm (see Section 3.4), in turn, combines labelled dependency arcs with enhanced dependency arcs predicted by EUD parsing module.

3.3 EUD predictor

The EUD parsing module consists of an enhanced arc classifier and an enhanced label classifier. The arc classifier utilises two single FC layers that transform encoded token vectors into head and dependent embeddings. These embeddings are used to calculate an adjacency matrix (A) of an enhanced graph. A is a $n \times n$ matrix, where n is the number of tokens in a sentence (plus the ROOT node). The matrix element A_{ij} corresponds to the dot product of the i-th dependent embedding and the j-th head embedding. The dot product indicates the certainty of the edge between two tokens. The sigmoid function, applied to each element of A, allows the network to predict many heads for a given dependent, i.e. EUD graphs are built.
The enhanced label classifier also applies two fully connected layers to estimate head (e_i) and dependent (e_j) embeddings (they differ from embeddings estimated in the enhanced arc prediction). Enhanced dependency labels are predicted by a fully connected layer with the softmax activation function which is given the dependent embedding concatenated with the head embedding.

$$e_{head} = FC(e_i) \qquad (2)$$

$$e_{dep} = FC(e_j) \qquad (3)$$

$$label = argmax(FC(e_{head}, e_{dep})) \qquad (4)$$

The loss function is only propagated for those pairs (i, j) that belong to ground truth (i.e. arcs existing in the enhanced dependency graph).

3.4 Merge algorithm

The predicted enhanced graphs could be used without further processing. However, their quality could definitely be improved if they exploited information from the predicted dependency trees. Enhanced dependency graphs appear to be heavily tree-based (see the example EUD graphs in Section 2). The EUD graphs include some additional edges, empty nodes, and extended labels of modifiers (and conjuncts in some languages), or their structure is slightly transformed. We therefore decided to merge the predicted trees and the predicted enhanced graphs.

Algorithm 1: The merge algorithm

```
Input: T := (V, E_T) : tree
       G := (V, E_G) : graph
Output: EUD : the final EUD graph
E_EUD = {};
for e in E_T do
    if label(e) ≠ acl:relcl then
        E_EUD := E_EUD + e;
for e in E_G do
    if e ∉ E_EUD and
      has_no_cycle(E_EUD + e) then
        E_EUD := E_EUD + e;
for e in E_T do
    if label(e) = acl:relcl then
        E_EUD := E_EUD + e;
EUD := (V, E_EUD);
```

The merge algorithm (see Algorithm 1) successively adds the predicted tree and graph edges to the set of EUD edges, and then composes the final EUD graph of these edges. It starts by selecting all tree edges except for edges with the *acl:relcl* label. The EUD graphs representing relative clauses contain cycles (see Figure 4). Refraining from adding the *acl:relcl* relations in this step, we attempt to avoid the cycle problem thereafter. In the second step, consecutive graph edges are added to the EUD set as long as they do not form a cycle or there are no edges with the same or a different label in the EUD set (i.e. we eliminate duplicate edges). In the last step, the *acl:relcl* relations are added to the EUD set which is then used to compose a final EUD graph.

We are aware that UD relations selected in the first merging step do not contain case information, e.g. the *obl* relation is transferred to the EUD set, although this relation should be de facto labelled *obl:because_of*, *obl:for*, or *obl:outside*. However, our preliminary experiments indicated that the anticipated enhanced labels often had erroneous case extensions, which could not even come from a sentence. Correcting labels with accidental case extensions would require defining a large number of relabelling rules that would have to be adapted to a particular language. Extending the modifier labels rather than correcting them seems to be a more transparent and simple procedure. We thus define one rule that derives case information from automatically predicted morphological features and lemmata (see Rule 1 in Section 3.5). The rule is utilised in the post-processing step, which is the last step of building the EUD graphs.

3.5 Post-processing

We define two rules that improve the automatically predicted EUD graphs.

Rule 1 The first rule specifies case information of the following modifiers: *nmod* (nominal modifier), *obl* (oblique nominal), *acl* (clasual modifier of nouns), *advcl* (adverbial clause modifier), and of conjuncts (*conj*). The case information (lemma) is derived from *case*/*mark* or *cc* dependents of a modifier or a conjunct, respectively, and from the modifier's morphological attribute *Case*. Figure 5 exemplifies extending UD labels with case information.[2]

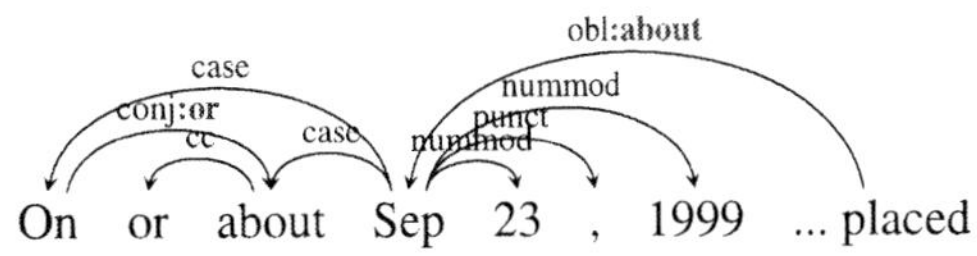

Figure 5: The EUD graph with blue, bolded sublabels representing case information. The text excerpt comes from the sentence "On or about September 23, 1999 a request for service was placed by the above referenced counterparty.".

The rule is language-independent and UD-based. However, as not all treebanks attribute case information to their modifiers or conjuncts, the rule applies only to predefined languages, e.g. the conjunct extension is only valid in English, Italian, Dutch, and Swedish.

Rule 2 The second rule corrects enhanced edges coming into the function words that are labelled *mark*, *punct*, *root*, *case*, *det*, *cc*, *cop*, *aux* and *ref*. They should not be assigned other dependency relation types in EUD graphs. If a token *and* is assigned the *cc* grammatical function in a dependency tree, and thus also in the corresponding EUD graph (the first merge step), it cannot be simultaneously a subject (*nsubj*), for example. If such an erroneous *nsubj* relation exists, it is removed from the EUD graph in line with the second rule.

[2]This sentence originates from the English dev set. As the case extension of the *obl* label is derived from the structure coordinating two prepositions (i.e. *on* and *about*), we wonder about correctness of selecting only *about* as the case extension.

Language	Model name	Reference
Arabic	bert-base-arabertv2	Antoun et al. (2020)
English	bert-base-cased	Devlin et al. (2019)
French	camembert-base	Martin et al. (2020)
Finnish	bert-base-finnish-cased-v1	Virtanen et al. (2019)
Polish	herbert-large-cased	Mroczkowski et al. (2021)
Others	xlm-roberta-large	Conneau et al. (2020)

Table 1: Language models used in the experiments. Names refer to Transformers library (Wolf et al., 2020).

4 Experimental setup

4.1 Segmentation and preprocessing

Stanza tokeniser (Qi et al., 2020) is used to split raw text into sentences, split sentences into tokens, and optionally to expand multi-words. We train a new segmentation model for each language on the training data provided in the shared task.[3] Whenever there are several UD treebanks for a language, we train the segmentation model on the concatenation of all training datasets available for that language. Multi-word expansion involves only two languages, i.e. Arabic and Tamil, because it does not cause substantial gains in parsing other languages.

In order to collapse empty nodes, training data are preprocessed with the official UD script.[4] Dependents of the collapsed empty nodes are assigned new labels, corresponding to the empty node label and the dependent label joined with the special symbol $>$. During prediction, the collapsed labels are expanded and empty nodes are added at the end of a sentence, following He and Choi (2020). This design decision is motivated by the fact that (1) it is difficult to find a proper position of elided tokens or phrases, especially in free word order languages, and (2) the evaluation procedure does not take an empty node position into account, i.e. appending an empty node at the end of a sentence does not downgrade the score. It is important to note that designing a heuristic that identifies proper positions of elided elements remains an open issue, and appending empty nodes at the end of a sentence is only a makeshift solution.

[3] It is not allowed to use versions of UD other than 2.7 in the IWPT 2021 shared task (see `https://universaldependencies.org/iwpt21/task_and_evaluation.html`). As the publicly available Stanza models are trained on UD 2.5, we have to train new models on UD 2.7.

[4] `https://github.com/UniversalDependencies/tools/blob/master/enhanced_collapse_empty_nodes.pl`

Input data are encoded using BERT-based language models. Depending on the language, either language-specific BERT (Devlin et al., 2019) or multilingual XLM-R (Conneau et al., 2020) is used (see Table 1).

4.2 Morphosyntactic prediction

COMBO system (Klimaszewski and Wróblewska, 2021) is used to predict part-of-speech tags, morphological features, lemmata, and dependency trees. For the purpose of this task, we also implement a new EUD parsing module (see Section 3.3) and integrate it with COMBO. Similarly to segmentation models, we train one COMBO model for a language on all treebanks provided for this language in the shared task data using the default training parameters (see Table 2).[5]

Hyperparameter	Value
Optimiser	Adam (Kingma and Ba, 2015)
Learning rate	0.002
β_1 and β_2	0.9
Number of epochs	400
BiLSTM layers	2
BiLSTM dropout rate	0.33
LSTM hidden size	512
Arc projection size	512
Label projection size	128

Table 2: COMBO training parameters (the upper entries) and model parameters (the bottom entries).

5 Results

The shared task submissions are evaluated with two evaluation metrics: ELAS – LAS[6] on enhanced de-

[5] All models are trained and tested on a single NVIDIA V100 card.

[6] LAS (labelled attachment score) is the proportion of tokens that are assigned the correct head and dependency label

pendencies, and EULAS – LAS on enhanced dependencies where labels are restricted to the UD relation types, i.e. sublabels are ignored. COMBO ranks 4th, achieving 84.71% ELAS in the qualitative evaluation (an average over treebanks), and 83.79% ELAS in the coarse evaluation (an average over languages). In terms of EULAS, it ranks 4th achieving 86.30% in the qualitative evaluation, and 5th achieving 85.20% in the coarse evaluation. In addition to ELAS and EULAS metrics, the systems are also compared in terms of quality of predicting labelled dependency trees measured with LAS (the secondary evaluation measure). In the LAS ranking, COMBO takes second place achieving 88.91% in the qualitative evaluation, and 87.84% in the coarse evaluation, being slightly overcome by the ROBERTNLP system (89.25% in the qualitative evaluation, and 89.18% in the coarse evaluation). Table 3 presents the official results of COMBO models per language.

Language	LAS	EULAS	ELAS
Arabic	81.04	78.35	76.39
Bulgarian	89.52	87.41	86.67
Czech	93.30	90.57	89.08
Dutch	90.93	88.90	87.07
English	87.22	85.27	84.09
Estonian	87.53	85.56	84.02
Finnish	92.28	88.79	87.28
French	89.29	88.10	87.32
Italian	93.27	91.16	90.40
Latvian	90.25	86.22	84.57
Lithuanian	84.75	81.28	79.75
Polish	92.75	90.22	87.65
Russian	94.29	91.76	90.73
Slovak	91.72	88.53	87.04
Swedish	87.82	85.26	83.20
Tamil	56.28	53.49	52.27
Ukrainian	90.96	87.60	86.92
Average	**87.84**	**85.20**	**83.79**

Table 3: The official evaluation results per language.

Post-processing impact We measure the impact of the post-processing step (i.e. extending graph labels with case information and correcting edges coming into the function words) on the development data per language (see Table 4). Following the training approach, we concatenate the datasets

according to the gold standard.

Language	Before		After	
	EULAS	ELAS	EULAS	ELAS
Arabic	77.46	57.32	77.89	76.40
Bulgarian	89.50	78.97	90.29	89.30
Czech	89.93	74.96	91.28	89.91
Dutch	87.96	76.22	88.94	87.64
English	85.13	74.40	85.49	84.30
Estonian	86.27	68.73	86.92	85.45
Finnish	86.98	72.08	87.92	86.44
French	90.48	89.99	91.10	90.62
Italian	89.84	75.47	91.10	90.31
Latvian	85.65	73.72	86.44	84.88
Lithuanian	82.37	63.56	83.41	82.32
Polish	90.08	77.97	90.64	87.64
Russian	90.43	75.93	91.03	90.10
Slovak	87.89	71.71	89.39	87.90
Swedish	85.62	73.59	86.09	84.07
Tamil	54.35	40.48	54.84	53.38
Ukrainian	88.30	73.51	89.13	88.52

Table 4: Impact of the post-processing step.

Language	Sentences		Tokens	
	TGIF	Stanza	TGIF	Stanza
Arabic	96.87	79.92	99.99	99.97
Dutch	94.32	83.82	99.90	99.89
Lithuanian	96.22	87.74	99.99	99.81
Swedish	99.03	93.64	99.86	99.44

Table 5: The quality of TGIF and Stanza segmentation in the selected languages.

if a language has multiple treebanks. The second rule modifies the graph structure. However, as the EULAS scores are almost negligible, using this rule seems questionable. The first rule, in turn, does not modify the structure of EUD graphs, but only their edge labels, and its impact on improving ELAS scores is significant.

Segmentation drawback The official evaluation results show significant discrepancies in the quality of tokenisation and sentence segmentation. The highest differences in sentence segmentation between TGIF, the winner of the shared task, and Stanza used in our approach are shown in Table 5. For example, there is a loss of more than 15 percentage points in sentence segmentation of the Arabic texts. We therefore decide to investigate the impact of the quality of sentence segmentation and tokenisation on the final results. For this purpose,

Language	LAS	EULAS	ELAS
Arabic	81.04 (+4.51)	78.35 (+4.3)	76.39 (+4.24)
Dutch	90.93 (+1.52)	88.90 (+1.61)	87.07 (+1.59)
Lithuanian	84.75 (+1.35)	81.28 (+1.34)	79.75 (+1.31)
Swedish	87.82 (+1.24)	85.26 (+1.21)	83.20 (+1.17)

Table 6: Performance gain in predicting UD trees and EUD graphs of gold-standard tokanised test sentences from the languages with the worst segmentation quality. The values in brackets show the improvement over the baseline (i.e. Stanza tokenisation).

we conduct an additional experiment consisting in predicting EUD graphs on the test data with gold-standard tokenisation and sentence segmentation. The results of this experiment show a gain of around 1.5 pp for all tested languages except Arabic with the gain over 4 pp (see Table 6).

6 Conclusion

We presented the COMBO-based solution to EUD parsing which took part in the IWPT 2021 EUD shared task. The proposed approach is hybrid, i.e. based on machine learning and rule-based algorithms. First, UD trees and EUD graphs (and also morphosyntactic features of tokens, i.e. parts of speech, morphological features, and lemmata) are automatically predicted with the data-driven COMBO system. Then, the predicted structures are combined into the EUD graphs using the developed rule-based merge algorithm. Finally, the labels of modifiers and conjuncts in the merged EUD graphs are extended with case information using an expansion rule. The proposed solution is simple and language-independent. We recognise that we could still improve the results, e.g. by defining language-specific correction rules. However, our objective was to build an easy-to-use system for predicting EUD graphs that is publicly available and can be efficiently use to solve sophisticated NLU tasks.

Acknowledgments

The research presented in this paper was founded by the Polish Ministry of Education and Science as part of the investment in the CLARIN-PL research infrastructure. The computing was performed at Poznań Supercomputing and Networking Center.

References

Wissam Antoun, Fady Baly, and Hazem Hajj. 2020. AraBERT: Transformer-based model for Arabic language understanding. In *Proceedings of the 4th Workshop on Open-Source Arabic Corpora and Processing Tools, with a Shared Task on Offensive Language Detection*, pages 9–15, Marseille, France. European Language Resource Association.

Gosse Bouma, Djamé Seddah, and Daniel Zeman. 2020. Overview of the IWPT 2020 shared task on parsing into enhanced Universal Dependencies. In *Proceedings of the 16th International Conference on Parsing Technologies and the IWPT 2020 Shared Task on Parsing into Enhanced Universal Dependencies*, pages 151–161, Online. Association for Computational Linguistics.

Gosse Bouma, Djamé Seddah, and Daniel Zeman. 2021. From raw text to enhanced universal dependencies: The parsing shared task at iwpt 2021. In *Proceedings of the 17th International Conference on Parsing Technologies (IWPT 2021)*, pages 146–157, Bangkok, Thailand (online). Association for Computational Linguistics.

Sabine Buchholz and Erwin Marsi. 2006. CoNLL-X shared task on multilingual dependency parsing. In *Proceedings of the Tenth Conference on Computational Natural Language Learning (CoNLL-X)*, pages 149–164, New York City. Association for Computational Linguistics.

Alexis Conneau, Kartikay Khandelwal, Naman Goyal, Vishrav Chaudhary, Guillaume Wenzek, Francisco Guzmán, Edouard Grave, Myle Ott, Luke Zettlemoyer, and Veselin Stoyanov. 2020. Unsupervised cross-lingual representation learning at scale. In *Proceedings of the 58th Annual Meeting of the Association for Computational Linguistics*, pages 8440–8451, Online. Association for Computational Linguistics.

Jacob Devlin, Ming-Wei Chang, Kenton Lee, and Kristina Toutanova. 2019. BERT: Pre-training of deep bidirectional transformers for language understanding. In *Proceedings of the 2019 Conference of the North American Chapter of the Association for Computational Linguistics: Human Language Technologies, Volume 1 (Long and Short Papers)*, pages 4171–4186, Minneapolis, Minnesota. Association for Computational Linguistics.

Timothy Dozat, Peng Qi, and Christopher D. Manning. 2017. Stanford's graph-based neural dependency parser at the CoNLL 2017 shared task. In *Proceedings of the CoNLL 2017 Shared Task: Multilingual Parsing from Raw Text to Universal Dependencies*, pages 20–30, Vancouver, Canada. Association for Computational Linguistics.

Alex Graves and Jürgen Schmidhuber. 2005. Framewise Phoneme Classification with Bidirectional LSTM and Other Neural Network Architectures. *Neural Networks*, 18(5):602–610.

Zhijiang Guo, Yan Zhang, and Wei Lu. 2019. Attention guided graph convolutional networks for relation extraction. In *Proceedings of the 57th Annual Meeting of the Association for Computational Linguistics*, pages 241–251, Florence, Italy. Association for Computational Linguistics.

Han He and Jinho D. Choi. 2020. Adaptation of multilingual transformer encoder for robust enhanced Universal Dependency parsing. In *Proceedings of the 16th International Conference on Parsing Technologies and the IWPT 2020 Shared Task on Parsing into Enhanced Universal Dependencies*, pages 181–191. Association for Computational Linguistics.

Johannes Heinecke. 2020. Hybrid enhanced Universal Dependencies parsing. In *Proceedings of the 16th International Conference on Parsing Technologies and the IWPT 2020 Shared Task on Parsing into Enhanced Universal Dependencies*, pages 174–180, Online. Association for Computational Linguistics.

Sepp Hochreiter and Jürgen Schmidhuber. 1997. Long short-term memory. *Neural Computation*, 9(8):1735–1780.

Jenna Kanerva, Filip Ginter, and Sampo Pyysalo. 2020. Turku enhanced parser pipeline: From raw text to enhanced graphs in the IWPT 2020 shared task. In *Proceedings of the 16th International Conference on Parsing Technologies and the IWPT 2020 Shared Task on Parsing into Enhanced Universal Dependencies*, pages 162–173, Online. Association for Computational Linguistics.

Daniel Khashabi, Tushar Khot, Ashish Sabharwal, and Dan Roth. 2018. Question answering as global reasoning over semantic abstractions.

Diederik P. Kingma and Jimmy Ba. 2015. Adam: A method for stochastic optimization. In *3rd International Conference on Learning Representations, ICLR 2015, San Diego, CA, USA, May 7-9, 2015, Conference Track Proceedings*.

Mateusz Klimaszewski and Alina Wróblewska. 2021. The COMBO package [online]. Available: `https://gitlab.clarin-pl.eu/syntactic-tools/combo`, Institute of Computer Science, PAS, Accessed on: June 2, 2021.

Louis Martin, Benjamin Muller, Pedro Javier Ortiz Suárez, Yoann Dupont, Laurent Romary, Éric de la Clergerie, Djamé Seddah, and Benoît Sagot. 2020. CamemBERT: a tasty French language model. In *Proceedings of the 58th Annual Meeting of the Association for Computational Linguistics*, pages 7203–7219, Online. Association for Computational Linguistics.

Ryan McDonald, Kevin Lerman, and Fernando Pereira. 2006. Multilingual dependency analysis with a two-stage discriminative parser. In *Proceedings of the Tenth Conference on Computational Natural Language Learning (CoNLL-X)*, pages 216–220. Association for Computational Linguistics.

Robert Mroczkowski, Piotr Rybak, Alina Wróblewska, and Ireneusz Gawlik. 2021. HerBERT: Efficiently pretrained transformer-based language model for Polish. In *Proceedings of the 8th Workshop on Balto-Slavic Natural Language Processing*, pages 1–10, Kiyv, Ukraine. Association for Computational Linguistics.

Joakim Nivre, Johan Hall, Sandra Kübler, Ryan McDonald, Jens Nilsson, Sebastian Riedel, and Deniz Yuret. 2007. The CoNLL 2007 shared task on dependency parsing. In *Proceedings of the 2007 Joint Conference on Empirical Methods in Natural Language Processing and Computational Natural Language Learning (EMNLP-CoNLL)*, pages 915–932, Prague, Czech Republic. Association for Computational Linguistics.

Joakim Nivre, Johan Hall, Jens Nilsson, Gülşen Eryiğit, and Svetoslav Marinov. 2006. Labeled pseudo-projective dependency parsing with support vector machines. In *Proceedings of the Tenth Conference on Computational Natural Language Learning (CoNLL-X)*, pages 221–225, New York City. Association for Computational Linguistics.

Joakim Nivre, Marie-Catherine de Marneffe, Filip Ginter, Jan Hajič, Christopher D. Manning, Sampo Pyysalo, Sebastian Schuster, Francis Tyers, and Daniel Zeman. 2020. Universal Dependencies v2: An evergrowing multilingual treebank collection. In *Proceedings of the 12th Language Resources and Evaluation Conference*, pages 4034–4043, Marseille, France. European Language Resources Association.

Matthew Peters, Mark Neumann, Mohit Iyyer, Matt Gardner, Christopher Clark, Kenton Lee, and Luke Zettlemoyer. 2018. Deep contextualized word representations. In *Proceedings of the 2018 Conference of the North American Chapter of the Association for Computational Linguistics: Human Language Technologies, Volume 1 (Long Papers)*, pages 2227–2237, New Orleans, Louisiana. Association for Computational Linguistics.

Peng Qi, Yuhao Zhang, Yuhui Zhang, Jason Bolton, and Christopher D. Manning. 2020. Stanza: A python natural language processing toolkit for many human languages. In *Proceedings of the 58th Annual Meeting of the Association for Computational Linguistics: System Demonstrations*, pages 101–108, Online. Association for Computational Linguistics.

Piotr Rybak and Alina Wróblewska. 2018. Semi-supervised neural system for tagging, parsing and lematization. In *Proceedings of the CoNLL 2018 Shared Task: Multilingual Parsing from Raw Text to Universal Dependencies*, pages 45–54. Association for Computational Linguistics.

Djamé Seddah, Sandra Kübler, and Reut Tsarfaty. 2014. Introducing the SPMRL 2014 shared task on parsing morphologically-rich languages. In *Proceedings of the First Joint Workshop on Statistical Parsing of Morphologically Rich Languages and Syntactic Analysis of Non-Canonical Languages*, pages 103–109, Dublin, Ireland. Dublin City University.

Djamé Seddah, Reut Tsarfaty, Sandra Kübler, Marie Candito, Jinho D. Choi, Richárd Farkas, Jennifer Foster, Iakes Goenaga, Koldo Gojenola Galletebeitia, Yoav Goldberg, Spence Green, Nizar Habash, Marco Kuhlmann, Wolfgang Maier, Joakim Nivre, Adam Przepiórkowski, Ryan Roth, Wolfgang Seeker, Yannick Versley, Veronika Vincze, Marcin Woliński, Alina Wróblewska, and Eric Villemonte de la Clergerie. 2013. Overview of the SPMRL 2013 shared task: A cross-framework evaluation of parsing morphologically rich languages. In *Proceedings of the Fourth Workshop on Statistical Parsing of Morphologically-Rich Languages*, pages 146–182, Seattle, Washington, USA. Association for Computational Linguistics.

Milan Straka and Jana Straková. 2017. Tokenizing, POS tagging, lemmatizing and parsing UD 2.0 with UDPipe. In *Proceedings of the CoNLL 2017 Shared Task: Multilingual Parsing from Raw Text to Universal Dependencies*, pages 88–99, Vancouver, Canada. Association for Computational Linguistics.

Kai Sun, Richong Zhang, Samuel Mensah, Yongyi Mao, and Xudong Liu. 2019. Aspect-level sentiment analysis via convolution over dependency tree. In *Proceedings of the 2019 Conference on Empirical Methods in Natural Language Processing and the 9th International Joint Conference on Natural Language Processing (EMNLP-IJCNLP)*, pages 5679–5688, Hong Kong, China. Association for Computational Linguistics.

Shikhar Vashishth, Rishabh Joshi, Sai Suman Prayaga, Chiranjib Bhattacharyya, and Partha Talukdar. 2018. RESIDE: Improving distantly-supervised neural relation extraction using side information. In *Proceedings of the 2018 Conference on Empirical Methods in Natural Language Processing*, pages 1257–1266. Association for Computational Linguistics.

Antti Virtanen, Jenna Kanerva, Rami Ilo, Jouni Luoma, Juhani Luotolahti, Tapio Salakoski, Filip Ginter, and Sampo Pyysalo. 2019. Multilingual is not enough: BERT for finnish. *CoRR*, abs/1912.07076.

Yufei Wang, Mark Johnson, Stephen Wan, Yifang Sun, and Wei Wang. 2019. How to best use syntax in semantic role labelling. In *Proceedings of the 57th Annual Meeting of the Association for Computational Linguistics*, pages 5338–5343, Florence, Italy. Association for Computational Linguistics.

Thomas Wolf, Lysandre Debut, Victor Sanh, Julien Chaumond, Clement Delangue, Anthony Moi, Pierric Cistac, Tim Rault, Remi Louf, Morgan Funtowicz, Joe Davison, Sam Shleifer, Patrick von Platen, Clara Ma, Yacine Jernite, Julien Plu, Canwen Xu, Teven Le Scao, Sylvain Gugger, Mariama Drame, Quentin Lhoest, and Alexander Rush. 2020. Transformers: State-of-the-art natural language processing. In *Proceedings of the 2020 Conference on Empirical Methods in Natural Language Processing: System Demonstrations*, pages 38–45, Online. Association for Computational Linguistics.

Fisher Yu and Vladlen Koltun. 2016. Multi-Scale Context Aggregation by Dilated Convolutions. *CoRR*, abs/1511.07122.

Daniel Zeman, Jan Hajič, Martin Popel, Martin Potthast, Milan Straka, Filip Ginter, Joakim Nivre, and Slav Petrov. 2018. CoNLL 2018 shared task: Multilingual parsing from raw text to Universal Dependencies. In *Proceedings of the CoNLL 2018 Shared Task: Multilingual Parsing from Raw Text to Universal Dependencies*, pages 1–21, Brussels, Belgium. Association for Computational Linguistics.

Daniel Zeman, Martin Popel, Milan Straka, Jan Hajič, Joakim Nivre, Filip Ginter, Juhani Luotolahti, Sampo Pyysalo, Slav Petrov, Martin Potthast, Francis Tyers, Elena Badmaeva, Memduh Gokirmak, Anna Nedoluzhko, Silvie Cinková, Jan Hajič jr., Jaroslava Hlaváčová, Václava Kettnerová, Zdeňka Urešová, Jenna Kanerva, Stina Ojala, Anna Missilä, Christopher D. Manning, Sebastian Schuster, Siva Reddy, Dima Taji, Nizar Habash, Herman Leung, Marie-Catherine de Marneffe, Manuela Sanguinetti, Maria Simi, Hiroshi Kanayama, Valeria de Paiva, Kira Droganova, Héctor Martínez Alonso, Çağrı Çöltekin, Umut Sulubacak, Hans Uszkoreit, Vivien Macketanz, Aljoscha Burchardt, Kim Harris, Katrin Marheinecke, Georg Rehm, Tolga Kayadelen, Mohammed Attia, Ali Elkahky, Zhuoran Yu, Emily Pitler, Saran Lertpradit, Michael Mandl, Jesse Kirchner, Hector Fernandez Alcalde, Jana Strnadová, Esha Banerjee, Ruli Manurung, Antonio Stella, Atsuko Shimada, Sookyoung Kwak, Gustavo Mendonça, Tatiana Lando, Rattima Nitisaroj, and Josie Li. 2017. CoNLL 2017 shared task: Multilingual parsing from raw text to Universal Dependencies. In *Proceedings of the CoNLL 2017 Shared Task: Multilingual Parsing from Raw Text to Universal Dependencies*, pages 1–19, Vancouver, Canada. Association for Computational Linguistics.

Yuhao Zhang, Peng Qi, and Christopher D. Manning. 2018. Graph convolution over pruned dependency trees improves relation extraction. In *Proceedings of the 2018 Conference on Empirical Methods in Natural Language Processing*, pages 2205–2215. Association for Computational Linguistics.

Splitting EUD graphs into trees: A quick and clatty approach

Mark Anderson **Carlos Gómez-Rodríguez**
Universidade da Coruña, CITIC
FASTPARSE Lab, LyS Research Group,
Departamento de Ciencias de la Computación y Tecnologías de la Información
{m.anderson,carlos.gomez}@udc.es

Abstract

We present the system submission from the FASTPARSE team for the EUD Shared Task at IWPT 2021. We engaged in the task last year by focusing on efficiency. This year we have focused on experimenting with new ideas on a limited time budget. Our system is based on splitting the EUD graph into several trees, based on linguistic criteria. We predict these trees using a sequence-labelling parser and combine them into an EUD graph. The results were relatively poor, although not a total disaster and could probably be improved with some polishing of the system's rough edges.

1 Introduction

In our group's submission to the IWPT 2020 shared task on EUD parsing (Dehouck et al., 2020), we focused on efficiency by applying distillation and training set reduction together with a rule-based approach to convert EUD graphs to UD trees that could be processed by an off-the-shelf parser. Here we describe our entry to the 2021 edition (Bouma et al., 2021), where we keep the focus on algorithmic simplification of graphs, as well as a prioritisation of efficiency over raw accuracy, but we take the chance to explore different questions that we deem interesting in the context of a breadth-first exploration of the search space of parsing techniques, even if they are not (at least in their current form) competitive in terms of pushing speed or accuracy metrics.

In particular, we wanted to experiment with the application of sequence labelling parsing (Strzyz et al., 2019b) to the problem, which we apply to graph parsing for the first time. And more in particular, with the use of a linguistics-oriented approach (à la Dehouck et al. (2020)) to guide the parsing process by splitting the EUD graphs into coherent components that can be then parsed by a multitask learning system.

Sequence labelling, the task of assigning one discrete label to each token of a sequence, has long been used for various natural language processing tasks whose output can naturally be represented in this form, such as PoS tagging or named entity recognition. In the case of syntactic parsing, sequence labelling can be applied after defining an encoding that casts each possible syntactic tree for a sentence of length n as a sequence of n labels. While an early attempt to apply it to dependency parsing (Spoustová and Spousta, 2010) yielded subpar accuracy, the advances in machine learning architectures in the last decade have made this kind of approaches practically viable both for constituency (Gómez-Rodríguez and Vilares, 2018) and dependency parsing (Strzyz et al., 2019b). However, to our knowledge, sequence labelling approaches have not previously been tried for any sort of graph parsing.

One possible way of extending the search space of a parsing approach is to apply the approach to parse a constant amount of subgraphs (typically, two) whose union provides the final output. This has been applied to go beyond noncrossing dependency trees in transition-based dependency parsing by splitting trees into two subsets of arcs (planes) such that there cannot be crossings within each of them, but their union (the final output) can have crossing arcs (Gómez-Rodríguez and Nivre, 2010; Gómez-Rodríguez and Nivre, 2013; Fernández-González and Gómez-Rodríguez, 2018). In semantic parsing, it has also be used to extend the search space from noncrossing graphs to pagenumber-2 graphs by Sun et al. (2017), who use graph-based parsing to obtain two noncrossing graphs that are combined by Lagrangian relaxation. In the context of sequence labeling, this approach was recently applied by Strzyz et al. (2020) with similar goals and methods as the transition-based parsers above.

Proceedings of the 17th International Conference on Parsing Technologies (IWPT 2021), pages 167–174
Bangkok, Thailand (online), August 6, 2021.

While all these approaches split the output with the goal of relaxing noncrossing constraints, the same can be applied to relax single-head constraints, i.e., go from tree to graph parsing. For example, any graph with in-degree at most 2 can trivially be expressed as the union of two trees. Here we apply that idea in the context of sequence labeling parsing, i.e., we try to generate several sequences of labels (via multitask learning), each of which represents a tree, and which together form an EUD graph.

However, all these splitting approaches share an underlying question: which of the (exponentially many) possible splits is more adequate for the model to adequately learn the parsing problem? The work cited above applies purely algorithmic criteria to choose a canonical split: lazy criteria to minimise the number of plane (subset) switches (Gómez-Rodríguez and Nivre, 2010) or the number of arcs assigned to the second plane (Strzyz et al., 2020), or systematic algorithms that assign crossing arcs to alternating planes (Sun et al., 2017). These provide splits that are related to the full parse by systemantic structural criteria, but not by linguistic criteria. Since it has been repeatedly shown that it is possible to jointly learn different kinds of dependencies in such a way that they complement each other (e.g. with syntactic and semantic dependencies, as in (Henderson et al., 2013; Zhou et al., 2020)) and sequence labeling parsing can benefit from integrating several linguistic representations using multitask learning (Strzyz et al., 2019a), what if we try to split parses in a linguistically meaningful way, yielding subsets of dependencies with a distinct meaning that can then be jointly learned? Here we evaluate such an approach.

2 Splitting graphs

The vast majority of nodes in a EUD graph only has one incoming edge. If we were to only use one edge per node, we would cover 94.15% of the edges. Only allowing a maximum of two incoming edges covers 99.53 % edges, three covers 99.88%, and four covers 99.95%. Figure 2 shows how many nodes have different numbers of incoming edges. Note the logarithmic scale used for the number of nodes. We believe that our graph splitting process results in covering a maximum of two edges, although we have not checked it formally. We attempted to split the trees in a linguistically grounded way. We first create what call the basic tree which most closely corresponds to the relative UD tree. We then create a relative, control, and conjunct tree. It is worth noting that, contrary to the work cited in the introduction where parses are split into two disjoint subgraphs, here we have four trees and all these trees can (and usually) overlap. We now describe the different trees into which we split the graph, as well as the collating procedure to combine output trees again into an EUD graph.

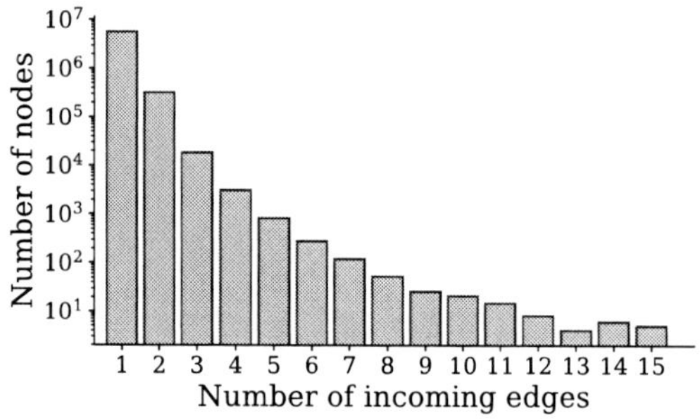

Figure 2: Counts of nodes with x number of incoming edges.

Basic tree This tree is made up of the EUD edges that correspond directly to the UD edges. With one exception for case marking. We add a relative position for the lemma (rather than the lemma itself). This means multi-word case marking is not covered. If no such edge exists we set

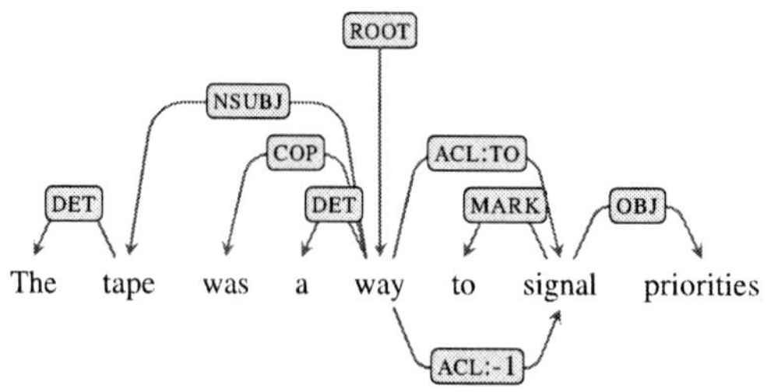

Figure 1: **Basic** tree split. Only ACL:TO changes to ACL:-1 for the relative lemma encoding.

the edge to (0, root). Although there should be no way this introduces cycles, we check for them anywhere and if any are found we use the Chu-Liu-Edmonds algorithm (CLE) (Chu and Liu, 1965; Edmonds, 1967), setting scores for expected edges to a sufficiently high value so that they are prioritised, while the others are set very low. If the MST tree has a different edge than in the basic tree, we set that edge to (0, root). If the CLE algorithm changes the ref edge, we change the incoming edge to its head to (0, root). An example is shown in Figure 1.

Relative clause tree We take the basic tree of a graph and replace incoming edges to nodes with `ref` edges. Again we check for cycles. This tree type was based on an error. We thought that the relative pronoun had two incoming edges: one from the head of the relative clause and one from the referent. This meant we unnecessarily split the basic and relative trees. An example of this is shown in Figure 3.

Conjunct tree We start from the basic tree. When an edge is "conj" we replace it with the edge in the EUD column that has the same rel as the conj head edge. We use the same cycle check as for the previous trees. An example is shown in Figure 4.

Control tree We take the basic tree again and this time replace the original nsubj edges of a node when its head has an incoming xcomp or ccomp edge with the other nsubj edge in the EUD graph for the node. We handle potential cycles as usual. An example is shown in Figure 5. Another error is introduced here, where we don't swap in the `ccomp` edges.

Cycles Only Arabic-PADT has issues with acyclicity after running CLE. So we just collapse the edges that have been changed (this accounts for three instances in the training data).

Collating trees into graphs As we operated on a limited time budget, the collating method is egregiously simple. For each node, we take the set of unique edges from all the predicted edges across all trees. When an edge exists between w_i and w_j in more than one tree, we use the label from the first occurrence which is typically that of the basic tree.

Table 1 shows the EULAS and ELAS when splitting the gold graphs and collating them again. We clearly can cover most of the graph edges with this procedure with Arabic enhanced labels being very low. We believe that this is a bug, but it could be due to some inherent unexpected characteristic of our basic splitting procedure.

	EULAS	ELAS
ar-padt	94.04	81.91
bg-btb	97.09	97.06
cs-cac	94.72	93.18
cs-fictree	94.21	91.75
cs-pdt	94.41	92.36
en-ewt	97.44	97.44
en-gum	97.09	97.09
et-edt	95.61	92.35
et-ewt	95.75	91.27
fi-tdt	92.73	87.13
fr-sequoia	96.22	96.22
it-isdt	96.32	95.98
lt-alksnis	94.08	87.35
lv-lvtb	93.77	93.77
nl-alpino	98.07	98.01
nl-lassysmall	97.34	97.30
pl-lfg	99.02	99.02
pl-pdb	96.37	96.19
ru-syntagrus	97.97	97.68
sk-snk	96.23	94.18
sv-talbanken	96.31	96.31
ta-ttb	97.62	93.39
uk-iu	96.35	95.97

Table 1: Graphs formed from splitting the gold annotated development trees and subsequently collating them again.

3 Parser

We use a BiLSTM network which has word and character embeddings as input. We use a sequence-labelling parser so the edges are predicted as separate labels for each token. Similarly, the edge labels are predicted separetly. But both label predictions are jointly trained with a hard-sharing multi-task architecture with equal weighted loss contributions. UDPipe 2.0 was used for tokenization, lemmatization, and tagging. FastText word embeddings were used but limit vocab space to 50k tokens for memory constraints (Bojanowski et al., 2017). We then train 4 parsers for each treebank which are trained on the data generated by splitting the graph, i.e. there is one parser for the basic trees, one for the relative trees, and so on. Then the parsers are used to predict their respective tree type and these are all collated to create the predicted graphs for each treebank.

Sequence labelling parser (SeqLab) is a parsing approach based on encoding trees as a se-

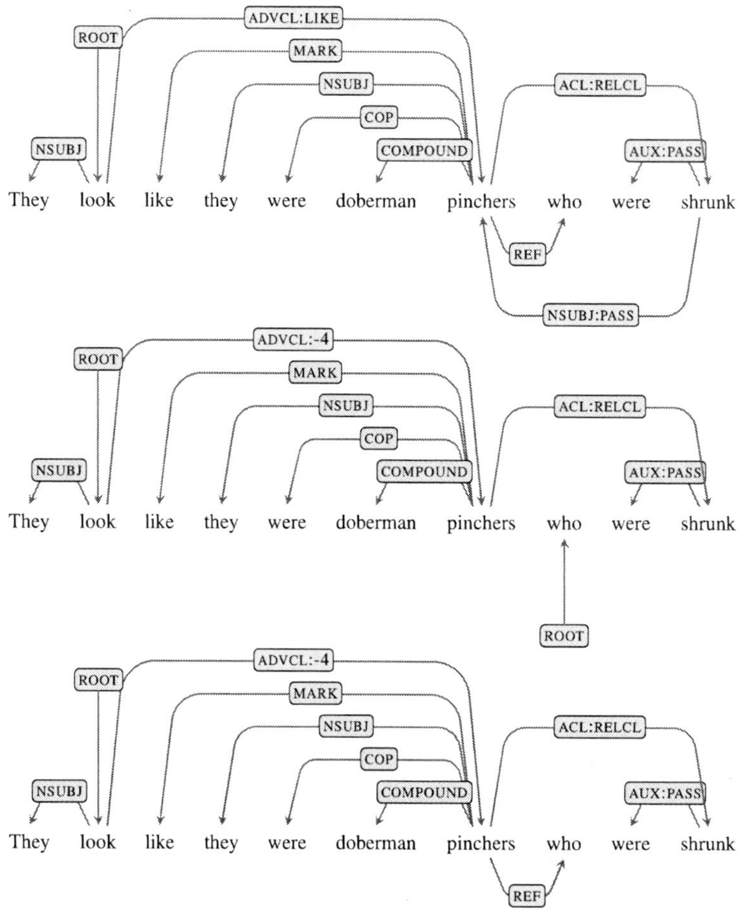

Figure 3: **Relative** tree split. Top full EUD graph, middle basic tree, bottom relative tree.

quence of one label per token in a sentence, so parsing is reduced to a standard sequence labelling problem (Spoustová and Spousta, 2010; Li et al., 2018; Strzyz et al., 2019b).[1] We choose to use the original bracketing encoding from Strzyz et al. (2019b), as it does not require UPOS tags on decoding (the other leading encoding does). While there is a more recent bracketing encoding that covers more non-projectivity (Strzyz et al., 2020), this also involves splitting trees which we assumed would add too much complexity on top of our linguistic-based splitting. Our chosen encoding represents a tree as sequence of tags composed of left and right brackets representing each word's incoming and outgoing arcs. Namely, the encoding for w_i is based on:

$$
\begin{aligned}
<\!- \quad & \text{if } \epsilon_{j(i-1)} \in \mathcal{E} \wedge j > i-1 \\
\backslash\!- \quad & \times k \mid k = \sum_{w_j \in S} \begin{cases} 1 & \text{if } j < i \wedge \epsilon_{ij} \in \mathcal{E} \\ 0 & \text{otherwise} \end{cases} \\
/\!- \quad & \times k \mid k = \sum_{w_j \in S} \begin{cases} 1 & \text{if } i-1 < j \wedge \epsilon_{(i-1)j} \in \mathcal{E} \\ 0 & \text{otherwise} \end{cases} \\
>\!- \quad & \text{if } \epsilon_{ji} \wedge j < i
\end{aligned}
$$

We repurposed a PyTorch biaffine implementation and edit it to be a simple sequence-labelling system, i.e. embedding layers, followed by a number of BiLSTM layers, and one MLP for predicting bracket tags and another for edge labels. The hyperparameters are shown in Table 2. The original code for the biaffine is no longer available but a similar version is still available.[2] More details of the system can be found in Anderson and Gómez-Rodríguez (2021).

[1] We use refactored encoding/decoding functions from https://github.com/mstrise/dep2label.

[2] https://github.com/yzhangcs/parser

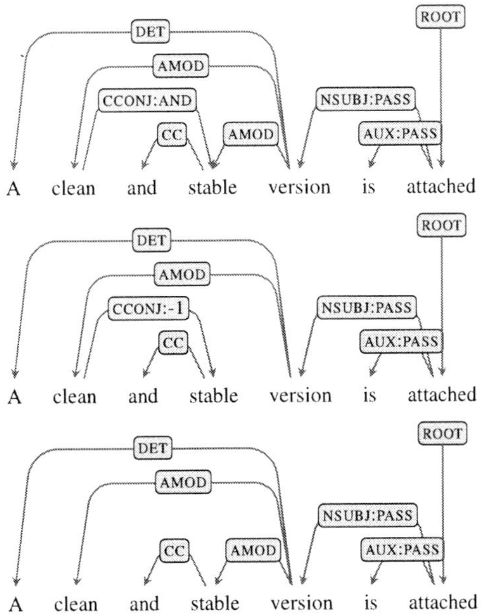

Figure 4: **Conjunct** tree split. Top full EUD graph, middle basic tree, bottom conjunct tree.

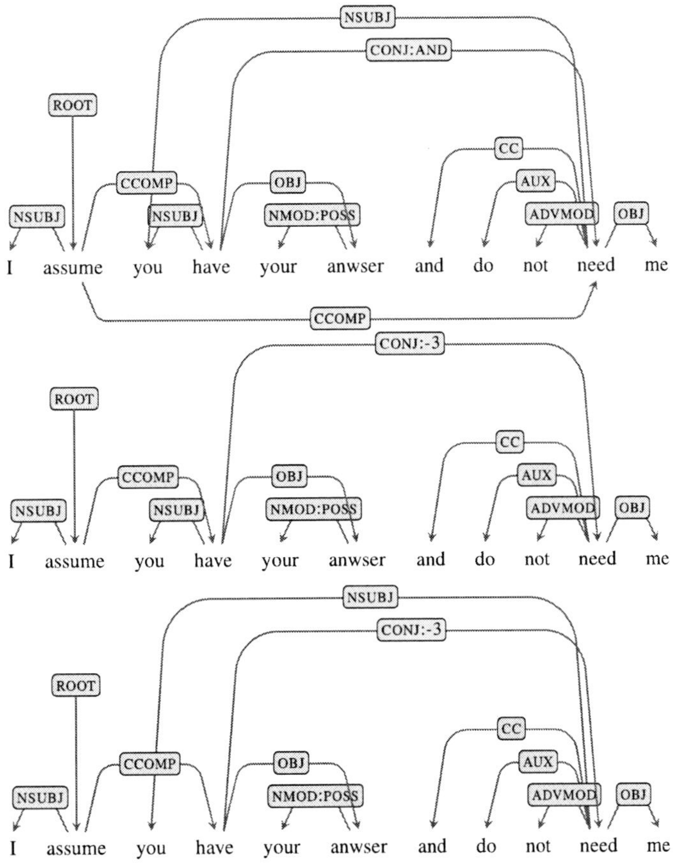

Figure 5: **Control** tree split. Top full EUD graph, middle basic tree, bottom control tree.

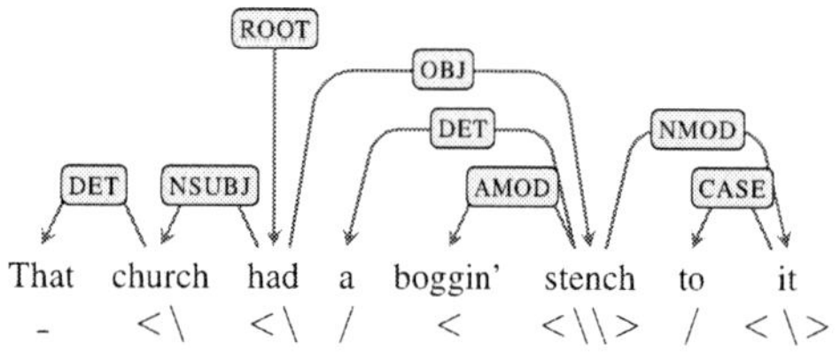

Figure 6: The bracketing encoding introduced by Strzyz et al. (2019b).

Hyperparameter	Value
Word embedding dimensions	300
Char embedding dimensions	100
Char BiLSTM dimensions	100
Embedding dropout	0.33
BiLSTM dimensions	500
BiLSTM layers	3
BiLSTM dropout	0.33
MLP layers	1
Learning rate	0.02
MLP dropout	0.33
Momentum	0.9
L2 norm λ	0.9
Annealing	$0.75^\wedge(^t/_{5000})$
ϵ	1×10^{-12}
Optimiser	Adam
Loss function	cross entropy
Epochs	200
Min vocab freq.	1
Batch size	32
Patience	10

Table 2: Network hyperparameters.

4 Results

The results were rather underwhelming, but our system wasn't an abject failure. Figure 7 shows the average performance of the parsers trained on each tree type. The performance is pretty stable across each type which is not surprising as the overall structure doesn't vary greatly. But the average performance on the collated trees is quite a bit less as shown in Table 3. We decided to include EUAS which measures the unlabelled graph structure. This shows that the parser does learn the graph structure fairly well, but really struggles with labelling the edges. This could be due to appending the labels with the relative positioning of lemmas used for case marking making it harder to predict even the basic label type. Figure 8 shows the breakdown of the three metrics for each treebank. It is clear that for each treebank a fairly accurate prediction of the graph structure is achieved, but the labelled versions perform much worse. Table 4 shows the full results of out system on the test data. The performance across the board is fairly weak and resulted in the worst system which submitted predictions for the full treebank set (and was second last overall).

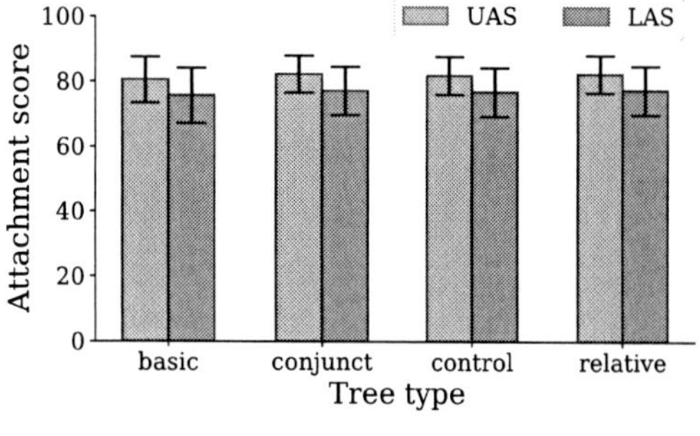

Figure 7: Average performance of parser on each tree type

EUAS	86.66
EULAS	72.02
ELAS	69.21

Table 3: Average scores over all treebanks.

5 Discussion and conclusion

The relative tree split was based on a mistake. We should have left the REF edges in the basic tree and added the NSUBJ label variant to the referent in the relative tree. The way it is implemented, we lose those edges. Despite this error, we can still reconstruct most of the edges in the graphs. Beyond this, we can't capture higher-order edges with this method. We did try using a SWEEP tree, to capture certain 3rd degree edges. But it seemed as the parser struggled to make sensible predictions and subsequently time ran out before we could test this thoroughly.

The collator is very naive. A major issue is introducing extra dummy root edges due to the nature of the split. Another thing we could have tried would have been to collate edges from trees that are only associated with the specific phenomenon of a given tree (i.e. conjunct trees only propagating conjunct edges.)

Also, looking at the difference in performance between EUAS and ELAS, it seems the labelling is bad. And the difference between EULAS and ELAS suggests this isn't just a matter of the case marking messing things up. However, the use of relative positional encoding of the case marking might make it harder to learn the labels. Although, the LAS for each tree type isn't that low. So it

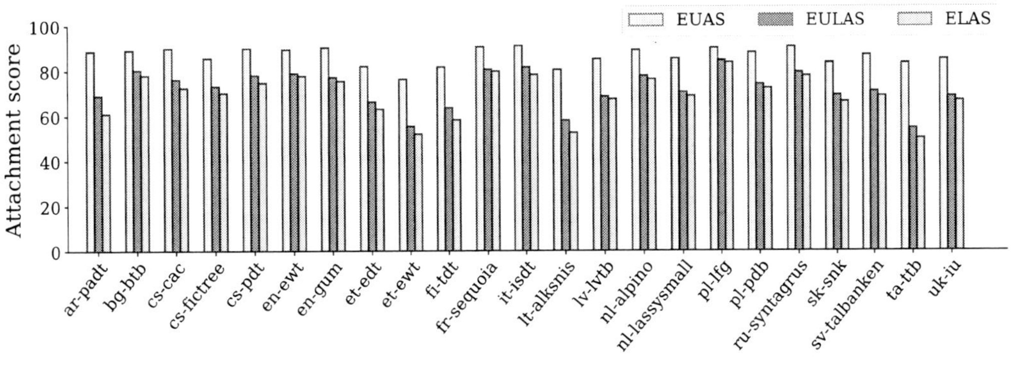

Figure 8: Performance of parser on each treebank.

Language	Tokens	Words	Sentences	UPOS	XPOS	UFeats	AllTags	Lemmas	UAS	LAS	CLAS	MLAS	BLEX	EULAS	ELAS
Arabic	99.98	94.58	82.09	91.68	88.96	89.14	88.65	90.37	69.84	64.88	59.10	54.18	56.33	61.13	53.74
Bulgarian	99.91	99.91	94.17	99.15	97.19	97.95	96.84	97.97	87.85	83.39	78.08	74.62	75.91	80.65	78.73
Czech	99.88	99.88	93.18	98.86	95.83	96.01	94.98	98.77	83.75	79.16	74.58	69.89	73.73	76.15	72.85
Dutch	99.74	99.74	69.26	96.79	95.29	96.44	94.61	97.06	79.85	74.37	65.23	60.10	63.06	70.49	68.89
English	98.38	99.06	88.92	95.85	95.30	94.16	91.39	96.04	82.36	77.99	73.46	64.94	70.55	74.51	73.00
Estonian	99.58	99.58	85.60	96.89	97.65	95.78	94.24	94.90	71.70	64.50	59.25	54.75	56.38	63.48	60.05
Finnish	99.70	99.68	88.65	97.84	56.14	96.44	54.29	92.11	69.06	62.46	55.58	51.73	51.40	63.20	57.71
French	99.65	99.23	94.35	97.05	99.23	91.11	90.28	97.45	84.03	77.14	67.40	57.56	65.57	74.65	73.18
Italian	99.93	99.84	98.76	98.52	98.44	98.23	97.66	98.66	88.16	84.92	77.15	73.97	75.79	82.11	78.32
Latvian	99.33	99.33	98.74	96.28	89.64	93.79	88.84	95.81	78.37	72.03	67.81	60.47	65.26	67.62	66.43
Lithuanian	99.91	99.91	87.87	95.97	90.37	91.07	89.41	93.61	61.39	53.55	47.68	41.70	44.66	52.52	48.27
Polish	99.40	99.83	97.52	98.50	93.04	90.80	87.70	97.87	84.32	78.28	73.23	63.04	71.69	74.62	71.52
Russian	99.60	99.60	98.80	98.86	99.60	88.97	88.76	98.33	87.09	83.23	79.62	66.43	78.39	80.13	78.56
Slovak	100.00	99.99	85.15	97.67	90.14	93.42	89.19	96.47	78.23	71.71	66.18	59.41	63.54	67.09	64.28
Swedish	99.18	99.18	93.54	97.25	95.57	88.82	87.63	93.60	78.88	73.11	68.64	56.05	63.96	69.37	67.26
Tamil	99.16	94.26	97.52	84.19	82.67	82.27	75.64	88.95	59.80	47.66	42.60	34.50	40.15	46.18	42.53
Ukrainian	99.85	99.81	96.61	97.89	94.22	94.18	93.13	97.39	76.26	70.79	65.07	59.24	63.42	65.41	63.42
Average	99.60	99.02	91.22	96.43	91.72	92.86	88.43	95.61	77.70	71.72	65.92	58.98	63.52	68.78	65.81

Table 4: Full results on test data per language.

could potentially be an issue about the way the trees are collated. Perhaps a first step would be to separate the relative case marking from the relation labels and treat it as a separate task in the MTL system.

We have presented a simple technique that can easily be extended (and implemented better) but manages to predict relatively accurate unlabelled graphs. It also isn't an utter failure when considering labelled edges, but it seems curious that the performance drops so much compared to the unlabelled performance.

Acknowledgments

This work has received funding from the European Research Council (ERC), under the European Union's Horizon 2020 research and innovation programme (FASTPARSE, grant agreement No 714150), from ERDF/MICINN-AEI (ANSWER-ASAP, TIN2017-85160-C2-1-R), from Xunta de Galicia (ED431C 2020/11), and from Centro de Investigación de Galicia "CITIC", funded by Xunta de Galicia and the European Union (ERDF - Galicia 2014-2020 Program), by grant ED431G 2019/01.

References

Mark Anderson and Carlos Gómez-Rodríguez. 2021. A modest Pareto optimisation analysis of dependency parsers in 2021. In *Proceedings of the 17th International Conference on Parsing Technologies and the IWPT 2021 Shared Task on Parsing into Enhanced Universal Dependencies*, Online. Association for Computational Linguistics.

Piotr Bojanowski, Edouard Grave, Armand Joulin, and Tomas Mikolov. 2017. Enriching word vectors with subword information. *Transactions of the Association for Computational Linguistics*, 5:135–146.

Gosse Bouma, Djamé Seddah, and Daniel Zeman. 2021. From raw text to Enhanced Universal Dependencies: The parsing shared task at IWPT 2021. In *Proceedings of the 17th International Conference on Parsing Technologies (IWPT 2021)*, pages 146–157, Bangkok, Thailand (online). Association for Computational Linguistics.

Yoeng-Jin Chu and Tseng-Hong Liu. 1965. On the shortest arborescence of a directed graph. *Scientia Sinica*, 14:1396–1400.

Mathieu Dehouck, Mark Anderson, and Carlos Gómez-Rodríguez. 2020. Efficient EUD parsing. In *Proceedings of the 16th International Conference on Parsing Technologies and the IWPT 2020 Shared Task on Parsing into Enhanced Universal Dependencies*, pages 192–205, Online. Association for Computational Linguistics.

Jack Edmonds. 1967. Optimum branchings. *Journal of Research of the national Bureau of Standards B*, 71(4):233–240.

Daniel Fernández-González and Carlos Gómez-Rodríguez. 2018. A dynamic oracle for linear-time 2-planar dependency parsing. In *Proceedings of the 2018 Conference of the North American Chapter of the Association for Computational Linguistics: Human Language Technologies, Volume 2 (Short Papers)*, pages 386–392. Association for Computational Linguistics.

Carlos Gómez-Rodríguez and Joakim Nivre. 2010. A transition-based parser for 2-planar dependency structures. In *Proceedings of the 48th Annual Meeting of the Association for Computational Linguistics (ACL 2010)*, pages 1492–1501. Association for Computational Linguistics.

Carlos Gómez-Rodríguez and Joakim Nivre. 2013. Divisible transition systems and multiplanar dependency parsing. *Comput. Linguist.*, 39(4):799–845.

Carlos Gómez-Rodríguez and David Vilares. 2018. Constituent parsing as sequence labeling. In *Proceedings of the 2018 Conference on Empirical Methods in Natural Language Processing*, pages 1314–1324. Association for Computational Linguistics.

James Henderson, Paola Merlo, Ivan Titov, and Gabriele Musillo. 2013. Multilingual Joint Parsing of Syntactic and Semantic Dependencies with a Latent Variable Model. *Computational Linguistics*, 39(4):949–998.

Zuchao Li, Jiaxun Cai, Shexia He, and Hai Zhao. 2018. Seq2seq dependency parsing. In *Proceedings of the 27th International Conference on Computational Linguistics*, pages 3203–3214, Santa Fe, New Mexico, USA. Association for Computational Linguistics.

Drahomíra Johanka Spoustová and Miroslav Spousta. 2010. Dependency parsing as a sequence labeling task. *The Prague Bulletin of Mathematical Linguistics*, 94(2010):7–14.

Michalina Strzyz, David Vilares, and Carlos Gómez-Rodríguez. 2019a. Sequence labeling parsing by learning across representations. In *Proceedings of the 57th Annual Meeting of the Association for Computational Linguistics*, pages 5350–5357, Florence, Italy. Association for Computational Linguistics.

Michalina Strzyz, David Vilares, and Carlos Gómez-Rodríguez. 2019b. Viable dependency parsing as sequence labeling. In *Proceedings of NAACL-HLT*, pages 717–723.

Michalina Strzyz, David Vilares, and Carlos Gómez-Rodríguez. 2020. Bracketing encodings for 2-planar dependency parsing. In *Proceedings of the 28th International Conference on Computational Linguistics*, pages 2472–2484.

Weiwei Sun, Junjie Cao, and Xiaojun Wan. 2017. Semantic dependency parsing via book embedding. In *Proceedings of the 55th Annual Meeting of the Association for Computational Linguistics (Volume 1: Long Papers)*, pages 828–838, Vancouver, Canada. Association for Computational Linguistics.

Junru Zhou, Zuchao Li, and Hai Zhao. 2020. Parsing all: Syntax and semantics, dependencies and spans. In *Findings of the Association for Computational Linguistics: EMNLP 2020*, pages 4438–4449, Online. Association for Computational Linguistics.

Graph Rewriting for Enhanced Universal Dependencies

Bruno Guillaume
Université de Lorraine, CNRS,
Inria, LORIA, Nancy, France
bruno.guillaume@inria.fr

Guy Perrier
Université de Lorraine, CNRS,
Inria, LORIA, Nancy, France
guy.perrier@loria.fr

Abstract

This paper describes a system proposed for the IWPT 2021 Shared Task on Parsing into Enhanced Universal Dependencies (EUD). We propose a Graph Rewriting based system for computing Enhanced Universal Dependencies, given the Basic Universal Dependencies (UD).

1 Introduction

The IWPT 2021 Shared Task on Parsing into Enhanced Universal Dependencies (Bouma et al., 2021) is a second edition of an equivalent shared task in 2020 (Bouma et al., 2020). The goal of the shared task is to produce EUD (Schuster and Manning, 2016), with several new annotation layers expressed on top of UD annotations (Nivre et al., 2020).

In the previous shared task, there were two kinds of approaches: producing EUD annotation from raw text with machine learning methods or producing EUD from UD with a rule-based approach (with or without some learning to optimize rule usage). Like (Heinecke, 2020) or (Dehouck et al., 2020), our proposal corresponds to the second approach: we used an existing tool for producing UD annotations and work only on the conversion from UD to EUD. Unlike other rule-based approaches, we used GREW, a generic Graph Rewriting tool (Bonfante et al., 2018), in order to describe the rules for enhancement.

Another specificity of our work is that we primarily design our rules by following the guidelines. Even if, in a secondary step and in the context of the shared task, we adapt the system to the corpora which diverge from the guidelines (section 2.6), we can easily provide a system closer to the guidelines, adpatable to languages specificities.

Our system achieved 81.58 ELAS score on the task, starting from UDPIPE annotation with an LAS of 85.77. In the paper, we present the system, analyse the results and make some in-depth analysis on French and English of discrepancies between GOLD_{EUD} data and the output of our system starting GOLD_{UD} annotations.

2 Description of the system

2.1 Parsing to UD

For this shared-task, we used the UDPIPE2 (Straka et al., 2016) through the online service[1] to produce the UD annotation of the data. The models used for each language are trained in UD version 2.6 on the following corpora: Arabic-PADT, Bulgarian-BTB, Czech-PDT, English-EWT, Estonian-EDT, Finnish-TDT, French-GSD, Italian-ISDT, Lithuanian-ALKSNIS, Dutch-Alpino, Polish-PDB, Slovak-SNK, Swedish-Talbanken, Tamil-TTB, Ukrainian-IU[2].

2.2 GREW

The transformation UD to EUD is described with the graph rewriting tool GREW[3]. Each rule is defined by a pattern and a set of commands describing how to modify the graph. A dedicated strategy mechanism allows for controlling rules applications (in which order subsets of rules must be applied and how they must be iterated). A global transformation system (rules and strategies) is called a Graph Rewriting System (GRS).

2.3 Representation of EUD annotations

We use here the convention already adopted in the Deep-Sequoia project (Candito et al., 2014), in which dependencies are drawn in black when the

[1] https://lindat.mff.cuni.cz/services/udpipe/

[2] The only modification done was on the Czech output where 7 obvious errors on the lemmatisation makes the conversion producing non valid data.

[3] https://grew.fr/

Proceedings of the 17th International Conference on Parsing Technologies (IWPT 2021), pages 175–183
Bangkok, Thailand (online), August 6, 2021. ©2021 Association for Computational Linguistics

relation exists both in UD layer and EUD layer, in red when they are present in UD layer only and in blue (and below) when they are present in EUD layer only (see Figure 1). This prevents from having two relations when both layers are identical and make figures easier to read.

2.4 From UD to EUD

Our goal was to design a GRS, following the EUD guidelines, to convert the UD annotations into EUD annotations, but we observed that the conversion system has to be adapted to each language and to some particular annotation choices.

As the rules of a GRS are organized in strategies, this adaptation is done by activating or not the applications of subsets of rules in the definition of the main strategy of a generic GRS. The rules are freely available[4].

2.4.1 The six types of enhancement

The EUD guidelines identify 6 types of enhancements, and for each type, we have designed a subset of rules to achieve it. We briefly describe the main features of each subset.

Empty nodes for elided predicates Predicate elision is detected thanks to the presence of `orphan` dependencies. They are mainly found in coordinations and sometimes with parataxis relations. Figure 1 shows the UD annotation of a sentence with ellipsis[5].

First, a null node `N` is created and a dependency `N -obj→ trees` is introduced from `N` to the head of the second conjunct `trees`. The label `obj` is determined by a parallelism with the dependency `sold -obj→ strawberries` [6]. The dependency `trees -cc→ and` is also raised to `N`.

In a second stage, all `orphan` dependencies from the head of the second conjunct are transformed into dependencies from the null node. The labels of the new dependencies are determined from the context. In our example, the dependency `trees -orphan→ winter` is transformed into the dependency `N -obl→ winter`, because `N` is a verb, `winter` a noun with a `case` dependent.

Propagation of incoming dependencies to conjuncts The propagation of incoming dependencies to the conjuncts of a coordination is systematical. The only difficulty concerns modifiers: if a word `H` is modified by a coordination, the label of the dependency from `H` to the head of the first conjunct may need to be changed depending of the POS of the second conjunct. In Figure 2, the dependency `come -obl→ parents` has to be propagated to the head of the other conjunct, the adverb `separately`. Because of this POS, the label has to be changed and the dependency becomes `come -advmod→ separately`.

Many gold corpora of the task do not take into account differences of POS between the conjunct heads and propagate the incoming dependencies without changing their labels.

Propagation of outgoing dependencies from conjuncts The main problem for this enhancement comes from the ambiguity of the UD annotation schema. It is not possible to distinguish a left dependency on a coordination from a left dependency on the first conjunct of the coordination because both are attached to the head of the first conjunct.

But, it is necessary to remove the ambiguity in order to know if one should propagate a left dependency. This is more or less easy depending on the type of the dependency. In Figure 3, the `nsubj` and `cop` dependencies on the noun `acteur` must be propagated on the head of the second conjunct `protagoniste`. It is easy to design a specific rule for each type of dependency to perform the propagation, what we have done. But, if the dependency is an `advmod` dependency, there is no general criterion for removing the ambiguity. The dependency on `souvent` should be propagated, but not the dependencies on `n'` and `pas`. This depends on the modifier adverb but also on the context. This is a point where our rule-based approach marks its limits compared to learning approaches. Of course, the answer depends strongly on the language and we will see how to take into account the specificity of each language in subsection 2.5.

For right dependencies, there is no ambiguity, because a right dependent on the first conjunct that follow all conjuncts is necessarily a dependent on the coordination.

Additional subject relations for control and raising constructions Raising and control verbs take an infinitive as a `xcomp` dependent and the en-

[4] `https://gitlab.inria.fr/grew/udtoeud`

[5] All examples are extracted form the corpora used in the task. Due to lack of space, expressions in square brackets, which are not essential to our purpose, are skipped in the annotation.

[6] Even if the subject is also a candidate, we always favour the object in this case.

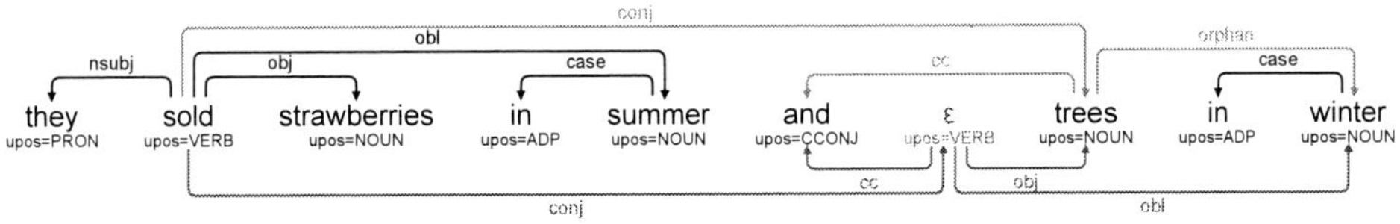

Figure 1: They sold strawberries in summer [,] and [Christmas] trees in [the] winter

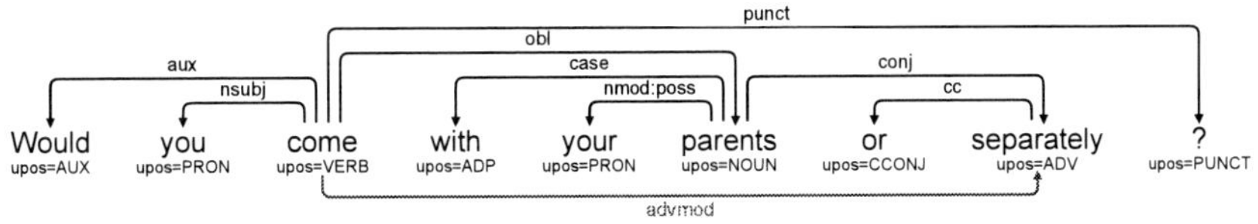

Figure 2: Would you come with your parents or separately ?

hanced subject of the infinitive is either the subject, the direct object or the indirect object of the main verb, if that argument exists. The choice between the three possibilities depends on the lexical information about the raising or control verbs. In our approach, this means that we need lexicons per language. Most often, we do not have such lexicons and choose the subject of the main verb as the subject of the infinitive, as this is the most likely.

Coreference in relative clause constructions The relative clause enhancement adds `ref` dependencies from the antecedent to the relative pronoun and all dependencies targeting the relative pronoun are moved to the antecedent.

In Figure 4, the sentence contains two relative pronouns, `dont` and `qui`. Let us focus on `qui`. First, rules make an upward path from the relative pronoun by following the dependencies until finding an `acl:relcl` dependency. In the example, this requires crossing a dependency `nsubj` and then `conj`. As soon as the dependency `acl:relcl` is reached, it is possible to add the `ref` dependency, because its source is known, it is the source of the dependency `acl:relcl` and the antecedent of the relative pronoun, and the target of the dependency as well, the relative pronoun, which is kept in memory. In a second stage, all dependencies targeting the relative pronoun are moved to the antecedent. In the example, the dependency `nécessite −nsubj→ qui` is transformed into the dependency `nécessite −nsubj→ entreprise`.

Modifier labels that contain the preposition or other case-marking information With regard to this enhancement, we strictly follow the guidelines: if a `case` or `mark` dependent on a modifier is a multiword expression, we add the form of the expression to the dependency representing the modification; if it is a single word, we add the lemma of the word.

The guidelines don't cover the case of several `case` or `mark` dependencies having the same source. In Figure 5, the conjunction `because` and the preposition `in` both depend on the same governor `zone` (dependencies in orange). We decide to add the outermost dependent lemma to the modifier dependency `feel −advcl→ zone` because it is related to this dependency, whereas `in` has no relationship to it.

If the two candidate dependents are consecutive, we consider them as a single multiword and add the concatenation of their lemmas to the modifier dependency.

2.4.2 Rule ordering

The six types of enhancements are not totally independent, some of them interact, so the order of application between the six corresponding subsets of rules is not neutral. Figure 1 shows an interaction between the subset implementing ellipsis processing and the subset implementing the propagation of outgoing dependencies of a coordination. If we apply the latter first, it is not possible to propagate the dependency `sold −nsubj→ they` to the second conjunct of the coordination because its verb is elided. We must apply first the subset creating a null node representing this verb.

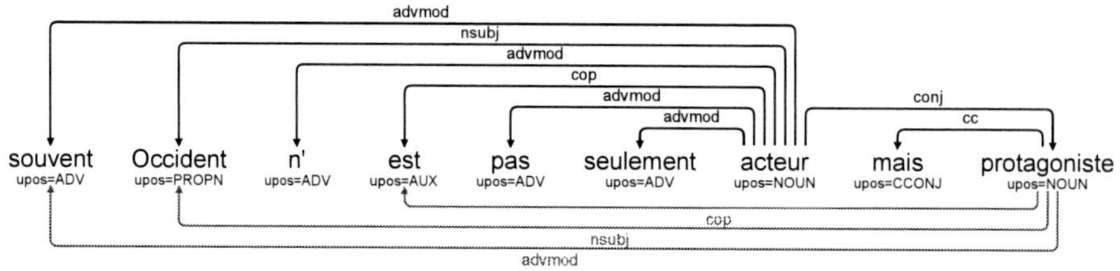

Figure 3: souvent [, l'] Occident n' est pas seulement [l'] acteur [,] mais [aussi le] protagoniste [des violations des droits de l' homme] (often[, the] West is not only [the] actor[,] but [also the] protagonist [of human rights violations])

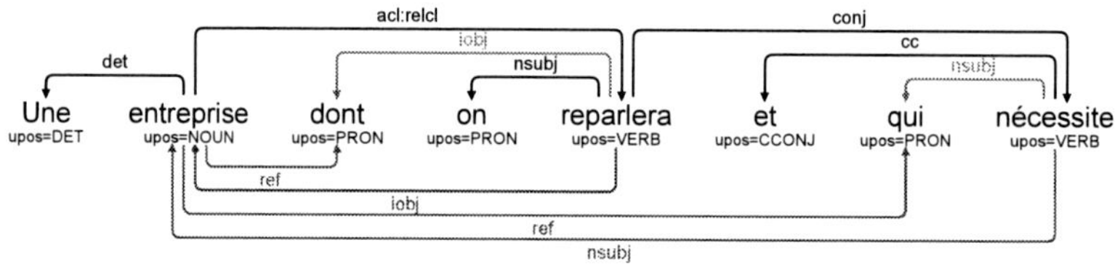

Figure 4: Une entreprise dont on reparlera et qui nécessite [un budget important] (A business that will be talked about again and that requires [a large budget])

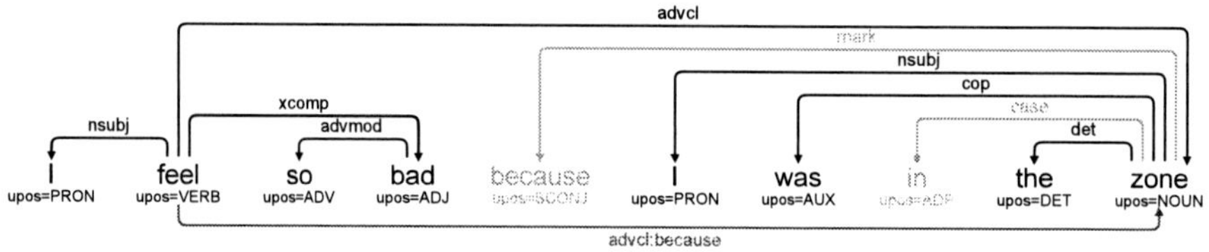

Figure 5: I feel so bad because I was [so] in the zone [that I didn't even get her name]

The subset of rules adding case or mark information to modifier dependencies must be applied at the end because it does not create any possibility to apply another subset later.

The order between the application of the five other subsets is relatively free. Figure 4 shows an example of interaction between the subset relating to relative clauses and the subset implementing the propagation of incoming dependencies of a coordination. We applied the former subset first and to apply the second subset, we only need to propagate the dependency `entreprise −acl:relcl→ reparlera` to the second conjunct of the coordination. But there is no problem to reverse the order between the two subsets.

Even if the order chosen between the 6 subsets aims at minimizing the number of rule applications, we cannot avoid applying some subsets a second time. Figure 6 shows an example of repetition in the subset application. To add the dependency `build −nsubj→ I`, we need first to apply the subset related to control verbs. We obtain the dependency `sell −nsubj→ I`. Then we apply the subset related to the propagation of outgoing dependencies of a coordination. We obtain the dependency `use −nsubj→ I`. Finally, we apply the subset relative to control verbs a second time and we obtain the last dependency `build −nsubj→ I`.

All rules presented in this subsection constitute the generic GRS used to convert the UD annotation into the EUD for the 17 languages.

2.5 Adaptation to the specificities of languages

Rule packages are added to the generic GRS to express specificities of language groups. In order to be applied, they are inserted in the strategy at carefully chosen positions in the generic strategy.

In this way, strategies can be designed adapted to particular languages, by activating or not these new packages.

Now, let us examine which types of rules can be added to express specificities of certain languages.

Null Subject Languages Arabic, Bulgarian, Czech, Estonian, Finnish, Italian, Polish, Russian, Slovak, Tamil and Ukrainian are null subject languages. Their grammar permits verbs to lack an explicit subject. This can be a problem for the propagation of subjects of coordinated verbs.

Consider the Polish sentence *"Moje gospodarstwo daje mi zabezpieczenie, mam gdzie wrócić (My farm gives me security, I have a place to come back to)"*. The general rules of subject propagation will propagate the subject *gospodarstwo* from the verb *daje* to the coordinated verb *mam*, which is incorrect because *mam* is at first person and does not require any explicit subject. In order to avoid the propagation, a specific rule marks all first and second person finite verbs, so that they cannot receive a subject dependency. For the third person, there is an ambiguity. In the Polish sentence *"Chłopiec wstaje, otwiera drzwi"*, there are two correct translations in English: *"The boy gets up, opens the door"* and *"The boy gets up, he opens the door"*, because one can propagate the subject *boy* or not. We chose to propagate the subject, which means that in this case, there is no difference between null subject languages and others.

Case addition to the dependency labels for modifiers For case-based languages, the labels of the dependencies targeting modifiers are augmented with their cases. The rule package implementing this enhancement is trivial.

Left dependents of a coordination We designed rules to propagate the left dependents of a coordination by dependency types. As we said before, a left dependent on the first conjunct of a coordination is ambiguous: it can depend on the whole coordination or only on the first conjunct. In order to determine, for a given language if a given type of dependency must be propagated or not, we tested the two alternatives on the dev corpus of the shared task and keep the alternative yielding the highest score.

This method has important limits because it depends on the annotation of the gold corpus. Moreover it is very coarse; for a given dependency type, not all dependencies have the same behaviour: some must be propagated, others not. It would be necessary to refine the conversion rules but for that, we need linguistic knowledge about the concerned language.

Raising and control verbs The default rule we use is to consider that the subject of the raised or controlled verb is the subject of the main verb but this is not always true. A language-specific lexicon should indicate for each of these verbs which argument of the main verb is the subject of the raised or controlled verb. From the training and development corpora available for the task, we have created lexicons for a five languages: Dutch, English, French,

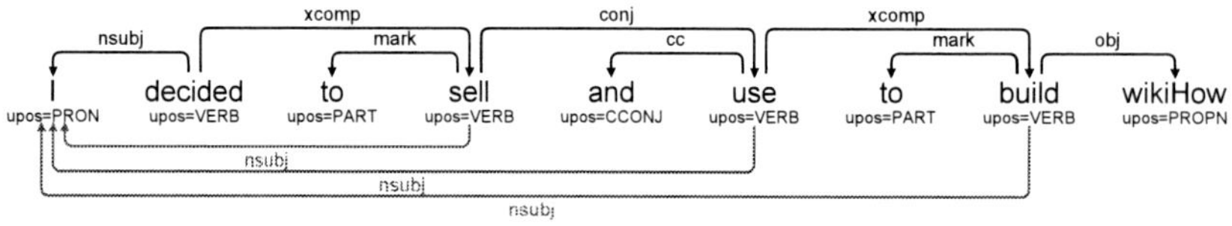

Figure 6: [So] I decided to sell [eHow] and use [the proceeds] to build wikiHow.

Italian and Polish.

2.6 Adaptation to annotation choices

Some annotators of the gold corpora do not strictly follow the guidelines. We have adapted our GRS to their choices on some very specific points.

Dependency label extension specific to one language In Dutch, enhancements for relative clauses distinguish antecedents of relative pronouns that play the deep role of subject and direct object in the relative clause with the extensions `relsubj` and `relobj`. We have designed specific rules to add this extension.

Enhancements partially taken into account We have taken into account the fact that enhancements are only partially achieved for Arabic, Bulgarian, Estonian, French, Russian and Tamil.

Coordinating conjunction raising For the Arabic, Dutch, English, Italian and Swedish treebanks, the names of coordinating conjunctions are added to the corresponding `conj` dependencies, in the same way as for prepositions and subordinating conjunction. We have taken this into account even though it is not indicated in the guidelines.

Propagation of `root` dependencies According to the guidelines, `root` incoming dependencies of a coordination should be propagated like all incoming dependencies, but some treebanks do not and we take this into account.

The French and the Polish treebanks, the latter partially, not only add subjects for raising and control verbs, as mentioned in the guidelines, but add deep subjects for modifier infinitive and participial clauses. Since this goes beyond the guidelines, we do not consider these enhancements.

Table 1 summarizes the three kinds of adaptation to the different languages.

3 Results

Data we submit to the task, called Grew(UDPipe), is the output of the application of a language specific GRS to the output of UDPipe. Figure 7 shows for each language, the LAS of UDPipe and the ELAS of Grew(UDPipe). We can observe that the final result highly depends on the UD annotation quality produced by UDPipe.

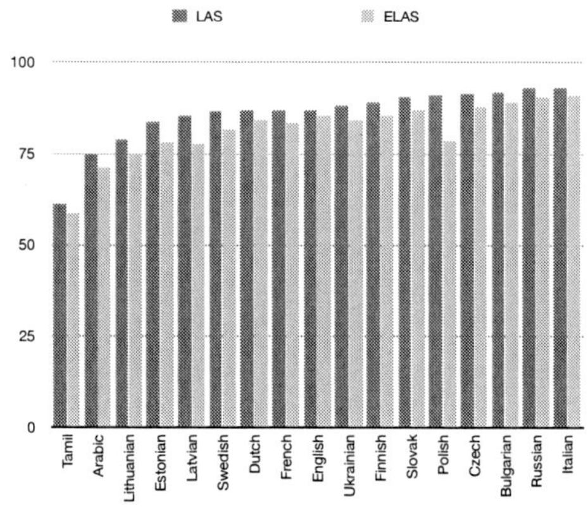

Figure 7: LAS of UDPipe and ELAS of Grew(UDPipe)

In addition to the results provided by the orgnanisers, we make complementary analysis, focusing on the UD to EUD transformation. In Table 2, we report the ELAS score obtained by our system applied on the gold UD annotation as input. We also recall the same measure reported last year by two others systems (Dehouck et al., 2020; Heinecke, 2020). The score of our system is in most of the case between the two other proposal, closed to Dehouck's system except for Estonian and Swedish.

4 Analysis of discrepancies with the gold annotation In French and English

In order to better understand the behaviour of our GRS, we made some manual inspection of the difference between the annotation Grew(GOLD$_{UD}$) and GOLD$_{EUD}$. We focused on the two languages for which we had the grammatical skills to analyze the discrepancies: French and English.

	ar	bg	cs	nl	en	et	fi	fr	it	lv	lt	pl	ru	sk	sv	ta	uk
null subject	X	X	X			X	X		X			X	X	X		X	X
left dep propag							X			X							
left aux dep propag												X					
left case dep propag										X		X					
left cop dep propag										X		X					
left mark dep propag										X		X					
case raising			X			X	X			X	X	X	X	X		X	X
subj control raising				X	X			X	X			X					
specific extens				X													
partial enhancement	X	X				X		X					X			X	
coord conj raising				X	X				X						X		
root propagation											X	X	X	X		X	X

Table 1: The three kinds of adaptation of the system. Top: adaptation to languages; middle: adding lexical information; bottom: adaptation to specific annotations observed in dev data.

Language Shared task	Dehouck 2020	Heinecke 2020	Our 2021
Arabic	98.8	95.2	98.5
Bulgarian	98.6	97.8	97.6
Czech	97.9	94.7	97.6
Dutch	98.9	94.4	97.6
English	99.5	98.0	99.0
Estonian	99.2	92.6	93.9
Finnish	97.3	94.4	96.9
French	98.9	96.4	99.0
Italian	99.5	98.4	98.8
Latvian	95.7	91.0	92.1
Lithuanian	98.8	94.6	98.2
Polish	94.9	91.1	95.2
Russian	98.6	95.4	98.2
Slovak	98.8	95.4	98.1
Swedish	98.8	96.1	94.7
Tamil	99.3	97.0	98.3
Ukrainian	95.8	94.6	95.9
Average	**98.2**	**95.1**	**97.0**

Table 2: Evalutation of the rule-based systems on Gold UD data: Dehouck (Dehouck et al., 2020), Heinecke (Heinecke, 2020) and our system

4.1 Discrepancies in French

For the French corpus, we observed 589 discrepancies[7] of the computed annotation with the gold annotation, and we manually analyzed the first 100. Table 3 details this analysis.

In order to explain mislabeling in the propagation of incoming dependencies of a coordination, let us return to the example in Figure 2. In propagating incoming dependencies of a coordination that is a modifier, we cannot automatically propagate the label related to the first conjunct to the other conjuncts, because we have to take into account the POS of the heads of these conjuncts. This was not taken into account for the two errors mentioned in the table.

In the table, we have also distinguished errors related to subject or object attributives from errors related to raising and control verbs, because of their particular property: the attributives may have other POS than verb. For exemple, consider the sentence *ils laissent les troupes de la KFOR en paix (they leave the KFOR troops in peace)*. The noun *peace* has an enhanced subject, which is *troops*. The gold annotation ignores this type of subject.

44 discrepancies come from the fact that the gold annotation implements enhancements that are not considered by the guidelines. Columns ¬**EUD** gives a detailed analysis of these enhancements with the number by type. Let us give an example to explain the last type of these non-standard enhancements. Consider the phrase *l'occasion également pour J.-P. Bruneau de présenter ses voeux (the occasion also for J.-P. Bruneau to present his wishes)*. The gold annotation indicates that *J.-P. Bruneau* is the enhanced subject of *present*, which is not

[7]Number of differences computed by the `diff` Unix tool: differences in consecutive lines are merged as one difference.

	EUD	UD	GRS	¬EUD
Total	**47**	**1**	**8**	**44**
Non-propagated incoming dependencies of a coordination	29			
Non-propagated left outgoing dependencies of a coordination	6			
Wrongly propagated left outgoing dependencies of a coordination			1	
Non-propagated right outgoing dependencies of a coordination	2			
Label errors in the propagation of incoming dependencies of a coordination	2			
Forgotten subject of controlled verb	3		1	
Verbs considered as control verbs by error			2	
Forgotten subjects of subject attributes	3			
Forgotten subjects of object attributes	2			
Grammaticaly ill-formed sentence			1	
Incorrect handling of light verb constructions			3	
Subjects of epithet participles				28
Subjects of modifier infinitive or participial clauses				14
Subjects of infinitives in constructions NOUN + PREP + NOUN + de + INF				2

Table 3: Manual inspection of the 100 first discrepancies in French between GOLD$_{EUD}$ and GREW(GOLD$_{UD}$). Columns are: errors in EUD gold annotation, errors in UD gold annotation, errors produced by our GRS, EUD gold annotations non described in guidelines.

considered by the guidelines.

4.2 Discrepancies in English

For the English test corpus, we observed 815 discrepancies of the computed annotation with the gold annotation, and we also manually inspected the first 100. Table 4 gives a detailed analysis of these errors with their number by type.

5 Conclusion

We have observed that many conversion problem arise with the CASEDEPREL layer. This layer is of course highly dependent of the language (because lexical information is used in relation definitions). This prevent the new relation to be universal and we believe that this is counterproductive in the objective of a universal description among a large set of languages.

In this paper, we have proposed a rule-based system for computing EUD annotation from UD. Our raw results are far behind the best systems of the task. This can be explained by the fact that we are dependent of the basic UD annotation provided by another tool. Moreover, the manual inspection we have made shows that, at least on English and French, the GOLD test data used in the task are not error-free and contains several annotations that are not described in the guidelines. We can suspect that this is in favour of the learning based approaches which are designed to adapt to the annotated data, completely ignoring the guidelines.

Despite its weakness, we believe that our system have several benefits:

- It has highlighted some places where the guidelines require precisions, like the presence of several `case` or `mark` on the same head;
- It can be used for improving the existing EUD data in the project by identiying annotation error in the current EUD annotations; using a different approach, we can guess that the errors reported will be complementary to the ones that can spotted with other methods;
- Thanks to the modular aspect of the GRS with rules packages adpated to language specificities, it is usable as a starting point for adding EUD annotation layer on languages where there is no such data and where learning based methods cannot be used.

References

Guillaume Bonfante, Bruno Guillaume, and Guy Perrier. 2018. *Application of Graph Rewriting to Natural Language Processing*, volume 1 of *Logic, Linguistics and Computer Science Set*. ISTE Wiley.

Gosse Bouma, Djamé Seddah, and Daniel Zeman. 2020. Overview of the IWPT 2020 shared task on parsing into enhanced Universal Dependencies. In *Proceedings of the 16th International Conference on Parsing Technologies and the IWPT 2020 Shared Task on Parsing into Enhanced Universal Dependencies*, pages 151–161, Online. Association for Computational Linguistics.

Gosse Bouma, Djamé Seddah, and Daniel Zeman. 2021. From raw text to enhanced universal dependencies:

	EUD	UD	GRS	Guidelines
Total	**54**	**17**	**10**	**19**
Non-propagated incoming dependencies of a coordination	9			
Non-propagated outgoing dependencies of a coordination	18		4	
Propagation of incoming dependencies of a coordination	7		1	
Verbs considered as control verbs by error	1			
Forgotten subjects of subject attributes	2			
Forgotten subjects of object attributes	1			
Wrongly processed relative clause constructions	2			
Errors in raising of single labels for case or mark dependencies	11		2	
Errors in raising of fixed labels for case or mark dependencies	3			
`Pos` extension forgotten in `nmod:pos` labels			1	
Wrongly processed ellipsis			2	
Relatives pronouns annotated as interrogative		17		
Two `case` / `mark` on the same source				15
Non alphabetic `ADP` (like "@")				4

Table 4: Manual inspection of the 100 first discrepancies in English between gold annotation and GRS applied on GOLD_{UD}. Columns are: errors in EUD gold annotation, errors in UD gold annotation, errors produced by our GRS, cases unspecified in the guidelines.

The parsing shared task at iwpt 2021. In *Proceedings of the 17th International Conference on Parsing Technologies (IWPT 2021)*, pages 146–157, Bangkok, Thailand (online). Association for Computational Linguistics.

Marie Candito, Guy Perrier, Bruno Guillaume, Corentin Ribeyre, Karën Fort, Djamé Seddah, and Éric de la Clergerie. 2014. Deep syntax annotation of the sequoia French treebank. In *Proceedings of the Ninth International Conference on Language Resources and Evaluation (LREC'14)*, pages 2298–2305, Reykjavik, Iceland. European Language Resources Association (ELRA).

Mathieu Dehouck, Mark Anderson, and Carlos Gómez-Rodríguez. 2020. Efficient EUD parsing. In *Proceedings of the 16th International Conference on Parsing Technologies and the IWPT 2020 Shared Task on Parsing into Enhanced Universal Dependencies*, pages 192–205, Online. Association for Computational Linguistics.

Johannes Heinecke. 2020. Hybrid enhanced Universal Dependencies parsing. In *Proceedings of the 16th International Conference on Parsing Technologies and the IWPT 2020 Shared Task on Parsing into Enhanced Universal Dependencies*, pages 174–180, Online. Association for Computational Linguistics.

Joakim Nivre, Marie-Catherine de Marneffe, Filip Ginter, Jan Hajič, Christopher D. Manning, Sampo Pyysalo, Sebastian Schuster, Francis Tyers, and Daniel Zeman. 2020. Universal Dependencies v2: An evergrowing multilingual treebank collection. In *Proceedings of the 12th Language Resources and Evaluation Conference*, pages 4034–4043, Marseille, France. European Language Resources Association.

Sebastian Schuster and Christopher D. Manning. 2016. Enhanced English Universal Dependencies: An improved representation for natural language understanding tasks. In *Proceedings of the Tenth International Conference on Language Resources and Evaluation (LREC'16)*, pages 2371–2378, Portorož, Slovenia. European Language Resources Association (ELRA).

Milan Straka, Jan Hajič, and Jana Straková. 2016. UDPipe: Trainable pipeline for processing CoNLL-U files performing tokenization, morphological analysis, POS tagging and parsing. In *Proceedings of the Tenth International Conference on Language Resources and Evaluation (LREC'16)*, pages 4290–4297, Portorož, Slovenia. European Language Resources Association (ELRA).

Biaffine Dependency and Semantic Graph Parsing for Enhanced Universal Dependencies

Giuseppe Attardi, Daniele Sartiano, Maria Simi
Dipartmento di Informatica,
University of Pisa
{attardi, sartiano, simi}@di.unipi.it

Abstract

This paper presents the system used in our submission to the *IWPT 2021 Shared Task*. This year the official evaluation metrics was ELAS, therefore dependency parsing might have been avoided as well as other pipeline stages like POS tagging and lemmatization. We nevertheless chose to deploy a combination of a dependency parser and a graph parser. The dependency parser is a biaffine parser, that uses transformers for representing input sentences, with no other feature. The graph parser is a semantic parser that exploits a similar architecture except for using a sigmoid crossentropy loss function to return multiple values for the predicted arcs. The final output is obtained by merging the output of the two parsers. The dependency parser achieves top or close to top LAS performance with respect to other systems that report results on such metrics, except on low resource languages (Tamil, Estonian, Latvian).

1 System Overview

The shared task 2021 aims specifically at performing enhanced dependency parsing, starting from raw text, in a multi-language setting consisting of seventeen languages Bouma et al. (2021).

We concentrate on the syntactic parsing and enhancement stages, by exploiting existing tools for tokenization, sentence splitting.

2 Syntactic parsing

State of the art dependency parsers currently often adopt the graph-based model, based on neural networks for the choice of arcs and labels.

In particular the Bi-LSTM-based deep biaffine neural dependency parser by Dozat and Manning (2017) has been quite popular and used in three out of five of the top submissions to the CoNLL 2018 Shared Task: Multilingual Parsing from Raw Text to Universal Dependencies (Zeman et al., 2018), in particular in the top non-ensemble submission (Kanerva et al., 2018).

We trained our own models for each language on the shared task treebanks using DiaParser, which uses the Stanza tokenizer and multi-word splitter.

2.1 DiaParser

DiaParser is a dependency parser derived from Supar[1], which exploits transformers to obtain contextualized word representations. Such representations are obtained by first applying the specific transformer tokenizer, splitting them into wordpieces, and then the embeddings for words is obtained as the average of the wordpiece embeddings.

The code for the parser is available on GitHub[2].

We exploit the idea to provide hints to the parser, obtained from structural syntax probes (Hewitt and Manning, 2019). We explored the idea to use a syntax probe to extract hints for the parser to estimate the most likely edges for the parse tree. Eventually a quite simple solution proved effective: to extract values from one of the attention layers of the transformer (typically layer 6) and add them to the score of the biaffine layer with a trainable weight $alpha$.

One may consider a transformer as computing three functions, the outputs $T_o : \mathbb{R}^{n\times d} \to \mathbb{R}^{n\times d}$, the hidden states $T_h : \mathbb{R}^{n\times d} \to \mathbb{R}^{L\times n\times d}$, and the attention weights $T_a : \mathbb{R}^{n\times d} \to \mathbb{R}^{H\times L\times n\times n}$ for H heads and for L layers.

Given a sentence with n words $\mathbf{w} = [w_1, w_2, ..., w_n]$, we feed the parser with $\mathbf{E} = [e_1, ..., e_n]$, where $e_i = mix_l(T_o(\mathbf{w}))_i$ is the scalar mix of the top l layers of the outputs of the transformer T applied to $\mathbf{w}$ (Liu et al., 2019a).

The attentive parser estimates the probability of

[1] https://github.com/yzhangcs/parser
[2] https://github.com/Unipisa/diaparser

Proceedings of the 17th International Conference on Parsing Technologies (IWPT 2021), pages 184–188
Bangkok, Thailand (online), August 6, 2021.

each possible arc for sentence $\mathbf{w}$ as follows:

$$\begin{aligned}\mathbf{v}_i^{(a\text{-}d)}, \mathbf{v}_i^{(a\text{-}h)} &= \mathrm{MLP}^{(a\text{-}d)}(\mathbf{e}_i), \mathrm{MLP}^{(a\text{-}h)}(\mathbf{e}_i),\\ A &= T_a(\mathbf{w})_l^{(h)}\\ S_{ij}^{(arc)} &= [\mathbf{v}_i^{(a\text{-}d)}, 1]^\top U^{arc}\mathbf{v}_i^{(a\text{-}h)}\\ &+ \alpha \cdot A_{ij}\\ P(y_{ij}^{(arc)}|\mathbf{w}) &= \mathrm{softmax}_j(S_i^{(arc)})\end{aligned} \tag{1}$$

where α is a learned weight and A are the attention weights of the transformer T for a given layer l and the given head h.

During prediction the syntactic parser applies the Chu-Liu-Edmonds algoritm (Chu, 1965; EDMONDS, 1967) to ensure the well-formedness of the parse tree, but only after a quick check that the arcs contain cycles.

The results we obtained with such an extension on the English development corpus where 92.21 UAS and 90.31 LAS, using Electra (Clark et al., 2020) as transformer as well as for attention, a small improvement with respect to 91.32 UAS and 89.33 LAS without using these features.

2.2 Semantic Graph Parser

The graph parser uses the approach of Dozat and Manning (2018).

The graph parser shares the same architecture as the biaffine dependency parser, except in for using a sigmoid cross entropy loss function instead of a softmax, to allow for multiple results. Those arcs with a logit value greater than zero are retained.

$$\begin{aligned}S_{ij}^{(arc)} &= \{s_{i,j} \geq 0\}\\ P(y_{ij}^{(arc)}|\mathbf{w}) &= \mathrm{argmax}_j(S_i^{(arc)})\end{aligned} \tag{2}$$

The scores of each pair of words in $\mathbf{w}$ can be decoded into a graph by keeping only edges that received a positive score. Labels are assigned to each such predicted edge, choosing the highest-scoring label for that edge.

The two losses of the edge and arc labels predictors are combined through an hyper-parameter $\lambda \in \{0, 1\}$:

$$\ell = \lambda\ell^{(label)} + (1-\lambda)\ell^{(edge)} \tag{3}$$

The methods does not ensure a fully connected graph, hence we merge it with the tree produced by the syntactic parser.

The final enhanced dependency arcs are obtained as the union of the arcs predicted by the syntactic and semantic parsers, with a check that no extra arcs to the root are introduced.

3 System Description

3.1 Tokenization

DiaParser exploits the Stanza tokenizer and multi-word splitter to perform sentence splitting, tokenization and multi-word splitting. It automatically downloads tokenizer models for each language from the Stanza repository. We trained a specific MWT model for Italian, trained on the Italian UD treebank Italian_ISST, augmented with a special list of sentences, representative of 75 categories of verb conjugations and of articled prepositions, which we contributed back to the official Stanza distribution.

3.2 Experiments

The syntactic and semantic parsers were trained separately on each language corpus, using language specific transformer models, where available. For languages with more than one corpus, they were just concatenated together into a single corpus.

We used the following transformers for sentence representations and attention weights:

Lang.	Model
ar	asafaya/bert-large-arabic
bg	DeepPavlov/bert-base-bg-cs-pl-ru-cased
cs	DeepPavlov/bert-base-bg-cs-pl-ru-cased
en	google/electra-base-discriminator
fi	TurkuNLP/bert-base-finnish-cased-v1
fr	dbmdz/bert-base-french-europeana-cased
it	dbmdz/electra-base-italian-xxl-cased-discriminator
nl	wietsedv/bert-base-dutch-cased
ro	DeepPavlov/rubert-base-cased
sv	KB/bert-base-swedish-cased
uk	dbmdz/electra-base-ukrainian-cased-discriminator

Table 1: Transformer models used for each language.

For all other languages we used `bert-base-multilingual-cased`.

4 Settings and Results

4.1 Experimental Settings

In training, we used the official train and gold development sets. We used the development set to select the model hyper-parameters based on LAS for the dependency parser and labeled F1 on enhanced dependencies for the semantic graph parser.

We use a batch size of 2000 tokens with the AdamW (Loshchilov and Hutter, 2019) optimizer. The hyper-parameters of our system are shown in

Parameter	Value
Arc hidden size	500
Rel hidden size	100
MLP dropout	33%
Transformer layers	4
Optimizer	AdamW
Learning rate	5e-5
Warmup	0.1
Loss interpolation (λ)	0.1
batch size	2000

Table 2: Hyper parameters used in the experiments.

Table 2, which are mostly adopted from previous work on dependency parsing.

4.2 Results

The official results are those labeled unipi-smax in our submission, obtained through merging the outputs of the dependency and semantic graph parser.

Table 3 shows our team official results obtained in tokenization, tagging, parsing and enhancement on the test sets.

5 Pretrained Multilingual Model

After the submission deadline, we experimented building a single model on the concatenation of the training corpora of all languages. The corpora was preprocessed to eliminate empty nodes, which represent implicit nodes, denoted with IDs such as 2.1 in the CoNLLU file format. We used the official script `enhanced_collapse_empty_nodes.pl`, which collapses graphs reducing such empty nodes into non-empty nodes and introducing new dependency labels.

We used the official script to collapse graphs through reducing such empty nodes into non-empty nodes and introducing new dependency labels. In the post-process, we add empty nodes according to the dependency labels. As the official evaluation only score the collapsed graphs, such a process does not impact the system performance.

Then the enhanced dependency labels in the training corpus were de-lexicalized, stripping lexical information from labels, like in (Grünewald and Friedrich, 2020), replacing them with placeholders (e.g. obl:[case]) indicating where in the dependency graph the lexical information is expected to be found. This process allowed us to reduce the total number of enhanced dependency labels from 6125 to 1282.

This also made it possible to fit the model to be trained into the 32GB of memory of our V100 GPU. We run the training in parallel on 4 such GPUs: each epoch took about 45 minutes and run for 29 epochs.

The model was trained using contextualized word embeddings from RoBERTa (Liu et al., 2019b), more precisely `xlm-roberta-large` from HuggingFace[3] using a scalar mixture of the top 4 hidden layers (Liu et al., 2019a).

Then the model was fine tuned on each language with its specific language corpus. The enhanced dependency labels in the output of the parser are converted back to their lexical notation using a heuristic processing similar to the one outlined in (Grünewald and Friedrich, 2020):

Furthermore, for languages that have case morphology, like Czech, the case is added to the label.

The multilingual model does provide significant improvements for languages with smaller corpora, in particular Latvian, Lithuanian and Tamil, as shown in Table 4:

Notably Lithuanian improves on EULAS by 6.75 points. The ELAS scores do not improve as much, possibly due to the ri-lexicalization algorithms that may need tuning to each language.

6 Conclusions

We experimented using two parsers with the same architecture to perform syntactic and semantic parsing. We first trained parser models on the specific corpus for each language. The final output is obtained by merging the outputs of the two parsers. This simple approach works reasonably well for languages with large enough corpora.

To address the difficulty in handling low resource languages, we explored building a single model trained on all corpora and fine tuning it on each specific corpora. Since enhanced dependency labels contain lexical parts and the number of such labels is quite large, we adopted a preprocessing step to de-lexicalize the labels. The approach gave promising results on some languages, but the back-convertion algorithm that introduces the lexical parts in the labels after parsing still needs to be improved.

Given the similarity of the architectures of the syntactic and semantic parsers, the prospect of performing joint training is promising and has been

[3]https://huggingface.co/xlm-roberta-large

Language	Tok	Sent	UAS	LAS	EULAS	ELAS
Arabic	99.96	80.83	86.19	81.97	79.79	77.17
Bulgarian	99.93	97.49	95.29	92.71	91.89	90.84
Czech	99.91	95.05	94.13	92.36	90.14	88.73
Dutch	99.82	70.55	90.12	87.69	84.92	84.14
English	98.36	91.34	90.64	88.47	87.75	87.11
Estonian	99.62	87.44	87.11	84.14	82.66	81.27
Finnish	99.60	91.90	94.25	92.76	90.61	89.62
French	99.78	96.44	93.47	90.30	88.91	87.43
Italian	99.77	98.75	95.03	93.65	92.52	91.81
Latvian	99.82	99.07	89.90	86.63	83.92	83.01
Lithuanian	99.84	88.11	82.75	78.31	74.61	71.31
Polish	99.41	98.35	94.93	92.71	90.94	88.31
Russian	99.59	99.03	94.51	93.32	91.49	90.90
Slovak	99.96	86.00	93.32	91.75	88.77	86.05
Swedish	99.45	93.53	90.86	88.53	86.61	84.91
Tamil	99.01	88.35	63.27	56.04	54.16	51.73
Ukrainian	99.85	96.75	93.68	91.92	89.41	87.51
Average	**99.63**	**91.70**	**89.97**	**87.25**	**85.24**	**83.64**

Table 3: UNIPI Official results on the test set.

Language	Tok	Sent	UAS	LAS	EULAS	ELAS
Latvian	99.82	99.07	89.90	86.63	87.54	84.78
Lithuanian	99.84	88.11	82.75	78.31	81.36	76.62
Slovak	99.96	86.00	93.32	91.75	91.47	81.17
Tamil	99.01	88.35	63.27	56.04	55.90	53.71

Table 4: Preliminary results with multi-language model.

considered but left for further research.

Acknowledgments

The experiments were run on a server with four NVIDIA Tesla V100 GPUs generously offered by prof. Marco Aldinucci of the University of Turin.

References

Gosse Bouma, Djamé Seddah, and Daniel Zeman. 2021. From raw text to enhanced universal dependencies: The parsing shared task at iwpt 2021. In *Proceedings of the 17th International Conference on Parsing Technologies (IWPT 2021)*, pages 146–157, Bangkok, Thailand (online). Association for Computational Linguistics.

Y. Chu. 1965. On the shortest arborescence of a directed graph. *Scientia Sinica*, 14:1396–1400.

Kevin Clark, Minh-Thang Luong, Quoc V Le, and Christopher D Manning. 2020. Electra: Pre-training text encoders as discriminators rather than generators. *arXiv preprint arXiv:2003.10555*.

Timothy Dozat and Christopher D. Manning. 2017. Deep biaffine attention for neural dependency parsing. In *5th International Conference on Learning Representations, ICLR 2017, Toulon, France, April 24-26, 2017, Conference Track Proceedings*. OpenReview.net.

Timothy Dozat and Christopher D. Manning. 2018. Simpler but more accurate semantic dependency parsing. In *Proceedings of the 56th Annual Meeting of the Association for Computational Linguistics (Volume 2: Short Papers)*, pages 484–490, Melbourne, Australia. Association for Computational Linguistics.

J. EDMONDS. 1967. Optimum branchings. *Journal of Research of the National Bureau of Standards, B*, 71:233–240.

Stefan Grünewald and Annemarie Friedrich. 2020. RobertNLP at the IWPT 2020 shared task: Surprisingly simple enhanced UD parsing for English. In *Proceedings of the 16th International Conference on Parsing Technologies and the IWPT 2020 Shared Task on Parsing into Enhanced Universal Dependencies*, pages 245–252, Online. Association for Computational Linguistics.

John Hewitt and Christopher D. Manning. 2019. A structural probe for finding syntax in word representations. In *Proceedings of the 2019 Conference of the North American Chapter of the Association for Computational Linguistics: Human Language Technologies, Volume 1 (Long and Short Papers)*, pages 4129–4138, Minneapolis, Minnesota. Association for Computational Linguistics.

Jenna Kanerva, Filip Ginter, Niko Miekka, Akseli Leino, and Tapio Salakoski. 2018. Turku neural parser pipeline: An end-to-end system for the CoNLL 2018 shared task. In *Proceedings of the CoNLL 2018 Shared Task: Multilingual Parsing from Raw Text to Universal Dependencies*, pages 133–142, Brussels, Belgium. Association for Computational Linguistics.

Nelson F. Liu, Matt Gardner, Yonatan Belinkov, Matthew E. Peters, and Noah A. Smith. 2019a. Linguistic knowledge and transferability of contextual representations. In *Proceedings of the 2019 Conference of the North American Chapter of the Association for Computational Linguistics: Human Language Technologies, Volume 1 (Long and Short Papers)*, pages 1073–1094, Minneapolis, Minnesota. Association for Computational Linguistics.

Yinhan Liu, Myle Ott, Naman Goyal, Jingfei Du, Mandar Joshi, Danqi Chen, Omer Levy, Mike Lewis, Luke Zettlemoyer, and Veselin Stoyanov. 2019b. Roberta: A robustly optimized bert pretraining approach.

Ilya Loshchilov and F. Hutter. 2019. Decoupled weight decay regularization. In *ICLR*.

Daniel Zeman, Jan Hajič, Martin Popel, Martin Potthast, Milan Straka, Filip Ginter, Joakim Nivre, and Slav Petrov. 2018. CoNLL 2018 shared task: Multilingual parsing from raw text to universal dependencies. In *Proceedings of the CoNLL 2018 Shared Task: Multilingual Parsing from Raw Text to Universal Dependencies*, pages 1–21, Brussels, Belgium. Association for Computational Linguistics.

Enhanced Universal Dependency Parsing with Automated Concatenation of Embeddings

Xinyu Wang[◇♠], **Zixia Jia**[◇♠], **Yong Jiang**[†], **Kewei Tu**[◇*]
[◇]School of Information Science and Technology, ShanghaiTech University
Shanghai Engineering Research Center of Intelligent Vision and Imaging
[†]DAMO Academy, Alibaba Group
{wangxy1,jiazx,tukw}@shanghaitech.edu.cn
{yongjiang.jy}@alibaba-inc.com

Abstract

This paper describes the system used in submission from SHANGHAITECH team to the *IWPT 2021 Shared Task*. Our system is a graph-based parser with the technique of Automated Concatenation of Embeddings (ACE). Because recent work found that better word representations can be obtained by concatenating different types of embeddings, we use ACE to automatically find the better concatenation of embeddings for the task of enhanced universal dependencies. According to official results averaged on 17 languages, our system ranks 2nd over 9 teams.

1 Introduction

Compared to the Universal Dependencies (UD) (Nivre et al., 2016), the Enhanced Universal Dependencies (EUD) (Bouma et al., 2020, 2021)[1] makes some of the implicit relations between words more explicit and augments some of the dependency labels to facilitate the disambiguation of types of arguments and modifiers. The representation of EUD is an enhanced graph with reentrancies, cycles, and empty nodes. Such representation can represent richer grammatical relations than rooted trees, but it is harder to learn. To make the learning process relatively easy, we transfer the enhanced graph to a bi-lexical structure like annotation of semantic dependency parsing (SDP) (Oepen et al., 2015) by reducing reentrancies and empty nodes into new labels. Therefore, many approaches for SDP can be adopted by EUD. Instead of the second-order parser that was used in previous work (Wang et al., 2019, 2020b; Wang and Tu, 2020), we apply the biaffine parser (Dozat and Manning, 2018) which is one of the state-of-the-art approaches of SDP for simplicity.

Recent developments on pre-trained contextualized embeddings have significantly improved the performance of structured prediction tasks in natural language processing. A lot of work has also shown that word representations based on the concatenation of multiple pre-trained contextualized embeddings and traditional non-contextualized embeddings (such as word2vec (Mikolov et al., 2013) and character embeddings (Santos and Zadrozny, 2014)) can further improve performance (Peters et al., 2018; Akbik et al., 2018; Straková et al., 2019; Wang et al., 2020a). Wang et al. (2021) proposed Automated Concatenation of Embeddings to automate the process of finding better concatenations of embeddings and further improved performance of many tasks. We utilize their method to find concatenations of pre-trained embeddings as the input of the biaffine parser for EUD. Because there are many contextualized embeddings, such as XLMR (Conneau et al., 2020a), BERT (Devlin et al., 2018) and Flair (Akbik et al., 2018), non-contextualized embeddings, such as word2vec (Mikolov et al., 2013), GloVe (Pennington et al., 2014), and fastText (Bojanowski et al., 2017), and character embeddings (Santos and Zadrozny, 2014). The search space of embeddings concatenation is large in size, besides, we need to train models of 17 languages respectively. Following Wang et al. (2021), we use reinforcement learning to efficiently find the better embeddings concatenation for each language. Experimental results averaged on 17 languages show the effectiveness of our approach. Our system is ranked 2nd over 9 teams in the official evaluation.

2 System Description

2.1 Data Pre-processing

We adopt the same data pre-processing method as Wang et al. (2020b) which transfers EUD graphs

♠: Equal contributions.
[1]https://universaldependencies.org/u/overview/enhanced-syntax.html

Proceedings of the 17th International Conference on Parsing Technologies (IWPT 2021), pages 189–195
Bangkok, Thailand (online), August 6, 2021.

to SDP graphs. For the reentrancies of the same head and dependent on different labels in the EUD graph, we combined these arcs into one and concatenate the labels of these arcs with a special symbol '+' representing the combination of two arcs. For the empty nodes in the EUD graph, there is an official script that can reduce such empty nodes into non-empty nodes with new dependency labels[2].

2.2 Approach

We follow the approach of Wang et al. (2021)[3] to build our system. Our system contains two parts: an ACE module to determine embedding concatenation as inputs, a biaffine parser to predict edges' existence and labels between each word pair. We introduce these two parts respectively.

ACE Given a sentence with n words $\mathbf{w} = [w_1, w_2, ..., w_n]$, we first get the input representations $\boldsymbol{V} = [\boldsymbol{v}_1; \cdots; \boldsymbol{v}_i; \cdots; \boldsymbol{v}_n]$, $\boldsymbol{V} \in \mathbb{R}^{d \times n}$ for the sentence, where $\boldsymbol{v}_i$ is word representation of i-th word and it is a concatenation of L types of word embeddings:

$$\boldsymbol{v}_i^l = \text{embed}_i^l(\boldsymbol{x}); \quad \boldsymbol{v}_i = [\boldsymbol{v}_i^1; \boldsymbol{v}_i^2; \ldots; \boldsymbol{v}_i^L]$$

where embed^l is the model of l-th embeddings, $\boldsymbol{v}_i \in \mathbb{R}^d$, $\boldsymbol{v}_i^l \in \mathbb{R}^{d^l}$. d^l is the hidden size of embed^l. Our ACE use a binary vector $\boldsymbol{a} = [a_1, \cdots, a_l, \cdots, a_L]$ as an mask to choose a subset of embeddings of L types and mask out the rest. Thus, the embeddings become:

$$\boldsymbol{v}_i = [\boldsymbol{v}_i^1 a_1; \ldots; \boldsymbol{v}_i^l a_l; \ldots; \boldsymbol{v}_i^L a_L]$$

where a_l is a binary variable.

To learn this mask (i.e., embeddings concatenation), we set a controller which interact with our EUD parser to iteratively generate the embedding mask from the search space. Defined the probability distribution of selecting an concatenation $\boldsymbol{a}$ as $P^{\text{ctrl}}(\boldsymbol{a}; \boldsymbol{\theta}) = \prod_{l=1}^{L} P_l^{\text{ctrl}}(a_l; \theta_l)$. Each element a_l of $\boldsymbol{a}$ is sampled independently from a Bernoulli distribution, which is defined as:

$$P_l^{\text{ctrl}}(a_l; \theta_l) = \begin{cases} \sigma(\theta_l) & a_l = 1 \\ 1 - P_l^{\text{ctrl}}(a_l = 1; \theta_l) & a_l = 0 \end{cases} \quad (1)$$

[2]For more details, please refer to https://universaldependencies.org/iwpt20/task_and_evaluation.html.

[3]https://github.com/Alibaba-NLP/ACE. Our code will be released here as well.

where σ is the sigmoid function.

We use reinforcement learning and take the accuracy on development set of our EUD parser as reward signal R. The controller's target is to maximize the expected reward $J(\boldsymbol{\theta}) = \mathbb{E}_{P^{\text{ctrl}}(\boldsymbol{a}; \boldsymbol{\theta})}[R]$ through the policy gradient method (Williams, 1992). We defined the reward function as:

$$\boldsymbol{r}^t = \sum_{i=1}^{t-1} (R_t - R_i) \gamma^{Hamm(\boldsymbol{a}^t, \boldsymbol{a}^i) - 1} |\boldsymbol{a}^t - \boldsymbol{a}^i| \quad (2)$$

Where $\gamma \in (0, 1)$. $|\boldsymbol{a}^t - \boldsymbol{a}^i|$ is a binary vector, representing the change between current embedding concatenation $\boldsymbol{a}^t$ at current time step t and $\boldsymbol{a}^i$ at previous time step i. R_t and R_i are the reward at time step t and i. $Hamm(\boldsymbol{a}^t, \boldsymbol{a}^i)$ is the Hamming distance of two concatenations.

Since calculating the exact expectation is intractable in our approach, the gradient of $J(\boldsymbol{\theta})$ is approximated by sampling only one selection following the distribution $P^{\text{ctrl}}(\boldsymbol{a}; \boldsymbol{\theta})$ at each step for training efficiency. With the reward function, the final formulation is:

$$\nabla_{\boldsymbol{\theta}} J_t(\boldsymbol{\theta}) \approx \sum_{l=1}^{L} \nabla_{\boldsymbol{\theta}} \log P_l^{\text{ctrl}}(a_l^t; \theta_l) r_l^t \quad (3)$$

EUD Parser After getting the representation $\boldsymbol{V}$ of the sentence $\boldsymbol{w}$, we use a three-layer BiLSTM taking the representation as input:

$$\boldsymbol{R} = \text{BiLSTM}(\boldsymbol{V})$$

Where $\boldsymbol{R} = [\boldsymbol{r}_1, \ldots, \boldsymbol{r}_n]$ represents the output from the BiLSTM. For the arc prediction and label prediction, we use two different feed-forward networks and biaffine functions:

$$s_{ij}^{(\text{arc})} = \text{FNN\_Biaffine}^{(\text{arc})}(\boldsymbol{r}_i, \boldsymbol{r}_j)$$
$$\mathbf{s}_{ij}^{(\text{label})} = \text{FNN\_Biaffine}^{(\text{label})}(\boldsymbol{r}_i, \boldsymbol{r}_j)$$

The arc probability distribution and the label probability distribution for each potential arc are:

$$P^{(\text{arc})}(y_{ij}^{(\text{arc})} | \text{w}) = \text{softmax}([s_{ij}^{(\text{arc})}; 0])$$
$$P^{(\text{label})}(y_{ij}^{(\text{label})} | \text{w}) = \text{softmax}(\mathbf{s}_{ij}^{(\text{label})})$$

According to $s_{ij}^{(\text{arc})}$, we first use MST (McDonald et al., 2005) algorithm to get a tree structure, then we additionally add arcs for the positions that $s_{ij}^{(\text{arc})} > 0$. Such method can get a EUD graph and ensure the connectivity of the graph. Wang

EMBEDDING (LANGUAGE)	RESOURCE	URL
fastText (all)	Bojanowski et al. (2017)	github.com/facebookresearch/fastText
M-BERT (all)	Devlin et al. (2019)	huggingface.co/bert-base-multilingual-cased
BERT (en, et, sk, ta, uk)	Devlin et al. (2019)	huggingface.co/bert-base-cased
BERT (ar)	Safaya et al. (2020)	huggingface.co/asafaya/bert-large-arabic
BERT (bg, cs, pl, ru)	Arkhipov et al. (2019)	huggingface.co/DeepPavlov/bert-base-bg-cs-pl-ru-cased
BERT (fi)	Virtanen et al. (2019)	huggingface.co/TurkuNLP/bert-base-finnish-cased-v1
BERT (fr)	Martin et al. (2020)	huggingface.co/camembert-base
BERT (it)	dbmdz	huggingface.co/dbmdz/bert-base-italian-cased
BERT (lt)	U&R(2020)	huggingface.co/EMBEDDIA/litlat-bert
BERT (lv)	U&R(2020)	huggingface.co/EMBEDDIA/litlat-bert
BERT (nl)	wietsedv	huggingface.co/wietsedv/bert-base-dutch-cased
BERT (sv)	Malmsten et al. (2020)	huggingface.co/KB/bert-base-swedish-cased
XLM-R (all)	Conneau et al. (2020b)	huggingface.co/xlm-roberta-large
RoBERTa (uk)	youscan	huggingface.co/youscan/ukr-roberta-base
RoBERTa (ru)	Blinov and Avetisian (2020)	huggingface.co/blinoff/roberta-base-russian-v0
RoBERTa (nl)	Delobelle et al. (2020)	huggingface.co/pdelobelle/robbert-v2-dutch-base
RoBERTa (others)	Liu et al. (2019)	huggingface.co/roberta-large
XLNet (en)	Yang et al. (2019)	huggingface.co/xlnet-large-cased

Table 1: The embeddings we used in our system. The URL is where we downloaded the embeddings. 'all' means we use the model for all the languages. 'other' means we use this RoBERTa model for all the languages except the uk, ru and nl.

et al. (2020b) shows that the non-projective tree algorithm (MST) is better than the projective tree algorithm (Eisner's) for the EUD task. We select the label with the highest score of each potential arc.

Given any labeled sentence $(\boldsymbol{w}, \boldsymbol{Y}^{\star})$, where $\boldsymbol{Y}^{\star}$ stands for a gold parse graph, to train the system, we follow the approach of Wang et al. (2019) with the cross entropy loss:

$$\mathcal{L}^{(\text{arc})}(\Lambda) = -\sum_{i,j} \log(P_{\Lambda}(y_{ij}^{\star(\text{arc})}|\boldsymbol{w}))$$

$$\mathcal{L}^{(\text{label})}(\Lambda) = -\sum_{i,j} \mathbb{1}(y_{ij}^{\star(\text{arc})}) \log(P_{\Lambda}(y_{ij}^{\star(\text{label})}|\boldsymbol{w}))$$

where Λ is the parameters of our system, $\mathbb{1}(y_{ij}^{\star(\text{arc})})$ denotes the indicator function and equals 1 when edge (i, j) exists in the gold parse and 0 otherwise, and i, j ranges over all the tokens $\boldsymbol{w}$ in the sentence. The two losses are combined by a weighted average.

$$\mathcal{L} = \lambda\mathcal{L}^{(label)} + (1-\lambda)\mathcal{L}^{(arc)}$$

Where λ is a hyper-parameter.

Language	Fine-tuned XLM-R	ACE
	ELAS	ELAS
Arabic	76.07	82.90
Bulgarian	87.92	91.46
Czech	91.64	92.95
Dutch	87.11	92.33
English	86.04	89.24
Estonian	87.13	89.37
Finnish	86.00	91.66
French	74.74	93.65
Italian	89.31	93.03
Latvian	84.83	90.11
Lithuanian	68.92	85.48
Polish	87.98	90.90
Russian	91.52	93.22
Slovak	85.26	90.92
Swedish	76.02	88.04
Tamil	38.66	69.84
Ukrainian	79.60	90.87
Average	81.10	87.98

Table 2: Compared ELAS scores on development set of fine-tuning single XLM-R embedding and ACE.

3 Settings and Results

3.1 Experimental Settings

In training, we use the official development set as the development set. We tune the hyper-parameters on the development set and determine the hyper-parameter values according to the labeled F1 score (LF1) which is the evaluation metric used in SDP. LF1 measures the correctness of each arc-label pair. We use a batch size of 2000 tokens with the Adam (Kingma and Ba, 2015) optimizer. We set 30 steps of reinforcement learning, and the time of each reinforcement learning step depends on the size of data set. The hyper-parameters of our biaffine parser are shown in Table 5, which are mostly adopted from previous work on dependency parsing. For the hyper-parameters of our ACE module, we follow the settings of Wang et al. (2021). We only use the tokenized words as the model input. For the sentence

Language	TGIF	Ours	ROBERTNLP	COMBO	Team Name UNIPI	DCU EPFL	GREW	FASTPARSE	NUIG
Arabic	81.23	**82.26**	81.58	76.39	77.17	71.01	71.13	53.74	0.00
Bulgarian	**93.63**	92.52	93.16	86.67	90.84	92.44	88.83	78.73	78.45
Czech	**92.24**	91.78	90.21	89.08	88.73	89.93	87.66	72.85	0.00
Dutch	**91.78**	88.64	88.37	87.07	84.14	81.89	84.09	68.89	0.00
English	**88.19**	87.27	87.88	84.09	87.11	85.70	85.49	73.00	65.40
Estonian	**88.38**	86.66	86.55	84.02	81.27	84.35	78.19	60.05	54.03
Finnish	**91.75**	90.81	91.01	87.28	89.62	89.02	85.20	57.71	0.00
French	**91.63**	88.40	88.51	87.32	87.43	86.68	83.33	73.18	0.00
Italian	**93.31**	92.88	93.28	90.40	91.81	92.41	90.98	78.32	0.00
Latvian	**90.23**	89.17	88.82	84.57	83.01	86.96	77.45	66.43	56.67
Lithuanian	**86.06**	80.87	80.76	79.75	71.31	78.04	74.62	48.27	59.13
Polish	**91.46**	90.66	89.78	87.65	88.31	89.17	78.20	71.52	0.00
Russian	**94.01**	93.59	92.64	90.73	90.90	92.83	90.56	78.56	66.33
Slovak	**94.96**	90.25	89.66	87.04	86.05	89.59	86.92	64.28	67.45
Swedish	**89.90**	86.62	88.03	83.20	84.91	85.20	81.54	67.26	63.12
Tamil	**65.58**	58.94	59.33	52.27	51.73	39.32	58.69	42.53	0.00
Ukrainian	**92.78**	88.94	88.86	86.92	87.51	86.09	83.90	63.42	0.00
Avg.	**89.24**	87.07	86.97	83.79	83.64	83.57	81.58	65.81	30.03

Table 3: Official results of all systems.

Language	**Stanza**				**Trankit**			
	Tokens	**Words**	**Sentences**	**ELAS**	**Tokens**	**Words**	**Sentences**	**ELAS**
Arabic	99.97	87.32	84.57	63.70	99.95	99.39	96.79	82.26
Bulgarian	99.93	99.93	97.49	92.59	99.78	99.78	98.79	92.52
Czech	99.92	99.92	95.03	91.50	99.93	99.92	97.56	91.78
Dutch	99.94	99.94	82.32	89.62	99.00	99.00	83.48	88.64
English	98.95	98.97	91.28	86.92	98.63	98.87	94.29	87.27
Estonian	99.68	99.68	90.26	86.44	99.39	99.39	94.85	86.66
Finnish	99.65	99.63	91.02	90.21	99.63	99.63	96.39	90.81
French	99.60	99.39	95.61	87.60	99.76	99.75	97.23	88.40
Italian	99.95	99.59	98.76	92.18	99.88	99.86	99.07	92.88
Latvian	99.78	99.78	98.85	89.26	99.74	99.74	98.69	89.17
Lithuanian	99.92	99.92	88.13	80.43	99.84	99.84	95.72	80.87
Polish	99.51	99.54	98.26	89.58	99.47	99.92	99.05	90.66
Russian	99.58	99.58	99.04	93.34	99.70	99.70	99.45	93.59
Slovak	99.96	99.96	86.27	89.01	99.95	99.94	95.31	90.25
Swedish	99.44	99.44	93.64	85.80	99.78	99.78	98.25	86.62
Tamil	99.92	86.95	98.76	46.70	98.33	94.19	100.00	58.94
Ukrainian	99.76	99.75	96.02	88.79	99.77	99.76	97.55	88.94
Average	99.73	98.19	93.25	84.92	99.56	99.32	96.62	87.07

Table 4: Comparison of different tokenization toolkits.

Hidden Layer	**Hidden Sizes**
BiLSTM LSTM	3*768
Arc/Label	500
Embedding/LSTM Dropouts	33%
Loss Interpolation (λ)	0.025
Adam β_1	0.9
Adam β_2	0.9
Learning rate	$2e^{-3}$
LR decay	0.5

Table 5: Hyper-parameters for our system.

and word segmentation, we used the pretrained large model of *trankit* (Nguyen et al., 2021). The embeddings we used in the ACE module for each language are shown in Table 1. For transformer-style embeddings, we only take the hidden states of the topmost layer and we only take the first piece subword representation as the multi-pieces word representation. We built our codes based on PyTorch (Paszke et al., 2019), and trained the model for each language on a single Tesla V100 GPU.

3.2 Main Results

Table 2 shows the ELAS scores (defined as F1-score over the set of enhanced dependencies in the system output and the gold standard) on development set of biaffine parser with fine-tuning single XLM-R embedding and with our ACE module. We can see that with ACE, the performance of most languages models is improved a lot.

Table 3 shows the results of official evaluations of all teams. We only show the ELAS in the results. We can see that our model gets the 1st on the Arabic language and gets the 2nd on averaged ELAS over 17 languages.

3.3 Tokenization Performances of Different Toolkits

In our experiments, we have tried two different tokenization toolkits. One is *stanza* (Qi et al., 2020) which is from Standford NLP Group, the others is *trankit* (Nguyen et al., 2021) which is a light-weight Transformer-based Python Toolkit for multilingual NLP. We use pretrained models of the two toolkits respectively. Furthermore, We train tokenization model of *stanza* for each language. Both settings of *stanza* are worse than *trankit* on sentence segmentation score. Table 4 shows the sentences and words segmentation scores of *stanza* trained on each language and pretrained *trankit*. We see that although *stanza* is better than *trankit* on segmentation score of tokens, there is a huge performance gap on segmentation score of sentences between *trankit* and *stanza*. Therefore, the final ELAS on test set tokenized by *trankit* is better than *stanza*.

4 Conclusion

Our system is a parser with automated embeddings concatenation and a biaffine encoder. Empirical results show the effectiveness of ACE to enhanced universal dependencies. Our system ranks 2nd over 9 teams according to the official ELAS.

References

Alan Akbik, Duncan Blythe, and Roland Vollgraf. 2018. Contextual string embeddings for sequence labeling. In *Proceedings of the 27th International Conference on Computational Linguistics*, pages 1638–1649, Santa Fe, New Mexico, USA. Association for Computational Linguistics.

Mikhail Arkhipov, Maria Trofimova, Yuri Kuratov, and Alexey Sorokin. 2019. Tuning multilingual transformers for language-specific named entity recognition. In *Proceedings of the 7th Workshop on Balto-Slavic Natural Language Processing*, pages 89–93, Florence, Italy. Association for Computational Linguistics.

Pavel Blinov and Manvel Avetisian. 2020. Transformer models for drug adverse effects detection from tweets. In *Proceedings of the Fifth Social Media Mining for Health Applications Workshop & Shared Task*, pages 110–112, Barcelona, Spain (Online). Association for Computational Linguistics.

Piotr Bojanowski, Edouard Grave, Armand Joulin, and Tomas Mikolov. 2017. Enriching word vectors with subword information. *Transactions of the Association for Computational Linguistics*, 5:135–146.

Gosse Bouma, Djamé Seddah, and Daniel Zeman. 2020. Overview of the IWPT 2020 Shared Task on Parsing into Enhanced Universal Dependencies. In *Proceedings of the 16th International Conference on Parsing Technologies and the IWPT 2020 Shared Task on Parsing into Enhanced Universal Dependencies*, Seattle, US. Association for Computational Linguistics.

Gosse Bouma, Djamé Seddah, and Daniel Zeman. 2021. From raw text to enhanced universal dependencies: The parsing shared task at iwpt 2021. In *Proceedings of the 17th International Conference on Parsing Technologies (IWPT 2021)*, pages 146–157, Bangkok, Thailand (online). Association for Computational Linguistics.

Alexis Conneau, Kartikay Khandelwal, Naman Goyal, Vishrav Chaudhary, Guillaume Wenzek, Francisco Guzmán, Edouard Grave, Myle Ott, Luke Zettlemoyer, and Veselin Stoyanov. 2020a. Unsupervised cross-lingual representation learning at scale. In *Proceedings of the 58th Annual Meeting of the Association for Computational Linguistics*, pages 8440–8451, Online. Association for Computational Linguistics.

Alexis Conneau, Kartikay Khandelwal, Naman Goyal, Vishrav Chaudhary, Guillaume Wenzek, Francisco Guzmán, Edouard Grave, Myle Ott, Luke Zettlemoyer, and Veselin Stoyanov. 2020b. Unsupervised cross-lingual representation learning at scale. In *Proceedings of the 58th Annual Meeting of the Association for Computational Linguistics*, pages 8440–8451, Online. Association for Computational Linguistics.

Pieter Delobelle, Thomas Winters, and Bettina Berendt. 2020. RobBERT: a Dutch RoBERTa-based Language Model. In *Findings of the Association for Computational Linguistics: EMNLP 2020*, pages 3255–3265, Online. Association for Computational Linguistics.

Jacob Devlin, Ming-Wei Chang, Kenton Lee, and Kristina Toutanova. 2018. Bert: Pre-training of deep bidirectional transformers for language understanding. *arXiv preprint arXiv:1810.04805*.

Jacob Devlin, Ming-Wei Chang, Kenton Lee, and Kristina Toutanova. 2019. BERT: Pre-training of deep bidirectional transformers for language understanding. In *Proceedings of the 2019 Conference of the North American Chapter of the Association for Computational Linguistics: Human Language Technologies, Volume 1 (Long and Short Papers)*, pages 4171–4186, Minneapolis, Minnesota. Association for Computational Linguistics.

Timothy Dozat and Christopher D Manning. 2018. Simpler but more accurate semantic dependency parsing. *arXiv preprint arXiv:1807.01396*.

Diederik P Kingma and Jimmy Ba. 2015. Adam: A method for stochastic optimization. In *International Conference on Learning Representations*.

Yinhan Liu, Myle Ott, Naman Goyal, Jingfei Du, Mandar Joshi, Danqi Chen, Omer Levy, Mike Lewis, Luke Zettlemoyer, and Veselin Stoyanov. 2019. Roberta: A robustly optimized bert pretraining approach. *arXiv preprint arXiv:1907.11692*.

Martin Malmsten, Love Börjeson, and Chris Haffenden. 2020. Playing with words at the national library of sweden – making a swedish bert.

Louis Martin, Benjamin Muller, Pedro Javier Ortiz Suárez, Yoann Dupont, Laurent Romary, Éric de la Clergerie, Djamé Seddah, and Benoît Sagot. 2020. CamemBERT: a tasty French language model. In *Proceedings of the 58th Annual Meeting of the Association for Computational Linguistics*, pages 7203–7219, Online. Association for Computational Linguistics.

Ryan McDonald, Koby Crammer, and Fernando Pereira. 2005. Online large-margin training of dependency parsers. In *Proceedings of the 43rd Annual Meeting of the Association for Computational Linguistics (ACL'05)*, pages 91–98.

Tomas Mikolov, Ilya Sutskever, Kai Chen, Greg S Corrado, and Jeff Dean. 2013. Distributed representations of words and phrases and their compositionality. In *Advances in neural information processing systems*, pages 3111–3119.

Minh Van Nguyen, Viet Lai, Amir Pouran Ben Veyseh, and Thien Huu Nguyen. 2021. Trankit: A light-weight transformer-based toolkit for multilingual natural language processing. In *Proceedings of the 16th Conference of the European Chapter of the Association for Computational Linguistics: System Demonstrations*.

Joakim Nivre, Marie-Catherine de Marneffe, Filip Ginter, Yoav Goldberg, Jan Hajič, Christopher D. Manning, Ryan McDonald, Slav Petrov, Sampo Pyysalo, Natalia Silveira, Reut Tsarfaty, and Daniel Zeman. 2016. Universal Dependencies v1: A multilingual treebank collection. In *Proceedings of the Tenth International Conference on Language Resources and Evaluation (LREC'16)*, pages 1659–1666, Portorož, Slovenia. European Language Resources Association (ELRA).

Stephan Oepen, Marco Kuhlmann, Yusuke Miyao, Daniel Zeman, Silvie Cinková, Dan Flickinger, Jan Hajic, and Zdenka Uresova. 2015. Semeval 2015 task 18: Broad-coverage semantic dependency parsing. In *Proceedings of the 9th International Workshop on Semantic Evaluation (SemEval 2015)*, pages 915–926.

Adam Paszke, Sam Gross, Francisco Massa, Adam Lerer, James Bradbury, Gregory Chanan, Trevor Killeen, Zeming Lin, Natalia Gimelshein, Luca Antiga, et al. 2019. Pytorch: An imperative style, high-performance deep learning library. In *Advances in Neural Information Processing Systems*, pages 8024–8035.

Jeffrey Pennington, Richard Socher, and Christopher Manning. 2014. Glove: Global vectors for word representation. In *Proceedings of the 2014 conference on empirical methods in natural language processing (EMNLP)*, pages 1532–1543.

Matthew Peters, Mark Neumann, Mohit Iyyer, Matt Gardner, Christopher Clark, Kenton Lee, and Luke Zettlemoyer. 2018. Deep contextualized word representations. In *Proceedings of the 2018 Conference of the North American Chapter of the Association for Computational Linguistics: Human Language Technologies, Volume 1 (Long Papers)*, pages 2227–2237, New Orleans, Louisiana. Association for Computational Linguistics.

Peng Qi, Yuhao Zhang, Yuhui Zhang, Jason Bolton, and Christopher D Manning. 2020. Stanza: A python natural language processing toolkit for many human languages. *arXiv preprint arXiv:2003.07082*.

Ali Safaya, Moutasem Abdullatif, and Deniz Yuret. 2020. KUISAIL at SemEval-2020 task 12: BERT-CNN for offensive speech identification in social media. In *Proceedings of the Fourteenth Workshop on Semantic Evaluation*, pages 2054–2059, Barcelona (online). International Committee for Computational Linguistics.

Cicero D Santos and Bianca Zadrozny. 2014. Learning character-level representations for part-of-speech tagging. In *Proceedings of the 31st international conference on machine learning (ICML-14)*, pages 1818–1826.

Jana Straková, Milan Straka, and Jan Hajic. 2019. Neural architectures for nested NER through linearization. In *Proceedings of the 57th Annual Meeting of the Association for Computational Linguistics*, pages 5326–5331, Florence, Italy. Association for Computational Linguistics.

Matej Ulčar and Marko Robnik-Šikonja. 2020. LitLat BERT. CLARIN-LT digital library in the Republic of Lithuania.

Antti Virtanen, Jenna Kanerva, Rami Ilo, Jouni Luoma, Juhani Luotolahti, Tapio Salakoski, Filip Ginter, and Sampo Pyysalo. 2019. Multilingual is not enough: BERT for finnish. *CoRR*, abs/1912.07076.

Xinyu Wang, Jingxian Huang, and Kewei Tu. 2019. Second-order semantic dependency parsing with end-to-end neural networks. In *Proceedings of the 57th Annual Meeting of the Association for Computational Linguistics*, pages 4609–4618, Florence, Italy. Association for Computational Linguistics.

Xinyu Wang, Yong Jiang, Nguyen Bach, Tao Wang, Zhongqiang Huang, Fei Huang, and Kewei Tu. 2021. Automated Concatenation of Embeddings for Structured Prediction. In *the Joint Conference of the 59th Annual Meeting of the Association for Computational Linguistics and the 11th International Joint Conference on Natural Language Processing (**ACL-IJCNLP 2021**)*. Association for Computational Linguistics.

Xinyu Wang, Yong Jiang, Nguyen Bach, Tao Wang, Huang Zhongqiang, Fei Huang, and Kewei Tu. 2020a. More embeddings, better sequence labelers? In *Findings of EMNLP*, Online.

Xinyu Wang, Yong Jiang, and Kewei Tu. 2020b. Enhanced Universal Dependency parsing with second-order inference and mixture of training data. In *Proceedings of the 16th International Conference on Parsing Technologies and the IWPT 2020 Shared Task on Parsing into Enhanced Universal Dependencies*, pages 215–220, Online. Association for Computational Linguistics.

Xinyu Wang and Kewei Tu. 2020. Second-order neural dependency parsing with message passing and end-to-end training. In *Proceedings of the 1st Conference of the Asia-Pacific Chapter of the Association for Computational Linguistics and the 10th International Joint Conference on Natural Language Processing*, pages 93–99, Suzhou, China. Association for Computational Linguistics.

Ronald J Williams. 1992. Simple statistical gradient-following algorithms for connectionist reinforcement learning. *Machine learning*, 8(3-4):229–256.

Zhilin Yang, Zihang Dai, Yiming Yang, Jaime Carbonell, Russ R Salakhutdinov, and Quoc V Le. 2019. Xlnet: Generalized autoregressive pretraining for language understanding. In *Advances in neural information processing systems*, pages 5753–5763.

RobertNLP at the IWPT 2021 Shared Task: Simple Enhanced UD Parsing for 17 Languages

Stefan Grünewald[★♦] **Frederik Oertel**[♦] **Annemarie Friedrich**[♦]
[★]Institut für Maschinelle Sprachverarbeitung, University of Stuttgart
[♦]Bosch Center for Artificial Intelligence, Renningen, Germany
stefan.gruenewald|frederiktobias.oertel|annemarie.friedrich
@de.bosch.com

Abstract

This paper presents our multilingual dependency parsing system as used in the *IWPT 2021 Shared Task on Parsing into Enhanced Universal Dependencies*. Our system consists of an unfactorized biaffine classifier that operates directly on fine-tuned XLM-R embeddings and generates enhanced UD graphs by predicting the best dependency label (or absence of a dependency) for each pair of tokens. To avoid sparsity issues resulting from lexicalized dependency labels, we replace lexical items in relations with placeholders at training and prediction time, later retrieving them from the parse via a hybrid rule-based/machine-learning system. In addition, we utilize model ensembling at prediction time. Our system achieves high parsing accuracy on the blind test data, ranking 3rd out of 9 with an average ELAS F1 score of 86.97.

Submission	Score
1. TGIF	**89.24**
2. ShanghaiTech	87.07
3. RobertNLP	86.97
Median	83.64

Table 1: Overview of IWPT 2021 results (avg. ELAS F1 score). Full results can be found at https://universaldependencies.org/iwpt21/results.html.

1 Introduction

Enhanced Universal Dependencies (Schuster and Manning, 2016) are an extension of the widely used Universal Dependencies (UD) framework for syntactic dependency annotation (de Marneffe et al., 2014). To better model linguistic phenomena such as coordination, raising/control, and relative clauses, enhanced UD extends basic UD trees by including additional dependencies between tokens in order to make relations between content words more explicit. While there is evidence for the utility of enhanced dependencies in downstream applications (Schuster et al., 2017), adding them means that dependency structures are not constrained to trees any more, which makes parsing them a different problem with its own set of challenges.

In the past, research on enhanced UD parsing has mostly focused on rule-based methods for extracting enhanced graphs from existing basic trees (Nyblom et al., 2013; Simi and Montemagni, 2018; Nivre et al., 2018). Furthermore, only a relatively small number of UD treebanks is annotated with enhanced dependencies. Recently, however, interest in enhanced UD has increased, most notably with the IWPT 2020 Shared Task (Bouma et al., 2020), which asked contestants to produce enhanced UD graphs from raw text for 17 languages.

For our submission to the 2021 edition of the Shared Task (Bouma et al., 2021), we adapt our English-only submission from last year (Grünewald and Friedrich, 2020) to all 17 languages that are part of the competition. The core principles of our system remain the same:

- We do not rely on basic dependencies for creating enhanced graphs. Instead, we directly parse from raw tokens into enhanced UD graphs.
- We use an unfactorized biaffine classifier architecture which predicts the most likely dependency label (or absence of a dependency) for each pair of tokens in the sentence, forming a dependency graph from the union of these predictions.
- Inputs to the biaffine classifier are extracted directly from a fine-tuned transformer-based language model.

Proceedings of the 17th International Conference on Parsing Technologies (IWPT 2021), pages 196–203
Bangkok, Thailand (online), August 6, 2021.

Instead of a strictly rule-based system as used by Grünewald and Friedrich (2020), we use a hybrid rule-based/machine-learning system to retrieve lexical material for dependency labels at prediction time (see Sec. 2.5). In order to further increase our parser's accuracy as well as its robustness across treebanks, we use model ensembling.

As shown in Table 1, our system achieves high parsing accuracy, ranking 3rd out of 9 with an average ELAS score of 86.97.

2 Our Model

This section describes the components of our parser as submitted to the Shared Task.

2.1 Pre-processing

For tokenization and sentence segmentation, we employ Trankit$_{\text{large}}$ (Nguyen et al., 2021), which achieves state-of-the-art (or near state-of-the-art) results for these tasks on the languages present in the Shared Task. We use the default model for each language.

2.2 Input Token Representation

We use the transformer-based, multilingual XLM-R$_{\text{large}}$ language model (Conneau et al., 2020) to generate contextualized word embeddings for the tokens of the input sentence, fine-tuning the model while training our parser. We create the wordpiece-tokenized input for XLM-R by feeding each token into the XLM-R tokenizer. In addition, we prepend a special *[root]* token to each sentence, which serves as an artificial head of the *root* relation that must be present in every sentence. This token receives a fixed, learned embedding instead of a contextualized XLM-R embedding, but with the same number of dimensions.

The final embedding $\mathbf{r}_i$ for a token at position i is extracted by forming a weighted sum of the internal XLM-R layers at the position corresponding to the first wordpiece of the original token. Following Kondratyuk and Straka (2019), coefficients for this weighted sum are learned during training, while randomly dropping layers to prevent the model from focusing on only a single layer.

2.3 Dependency Classification

Figure 1 shows an overview of our neural-network based dependency classifier, which predicts relation labels (or absence of a relation) between pairs of tokens.

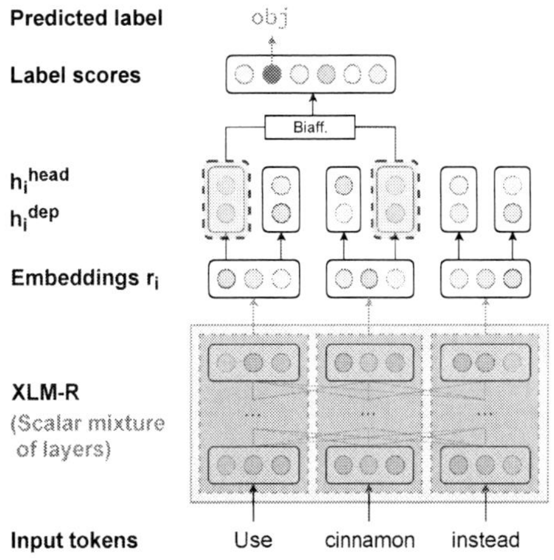

Figure 1: Architecture of neural network predicting dependency relations between pairs of tokens.

Classifier architecture. Our dependency classifier follows the architecture proposed by Dozat and Manning (2018), which is capable of producing general (bi-lexical) dependency graph structures. The approach works by creating, for each input token embedding $\mathbf{r}_i$, a head representation $\mathbf{h}_i^{head}$ and a dependent representation $\mathbf{h}_i^{dep}$ via two single-layer feedforward neural networks:

$$\mathbf{h}_i^{head} = \text{FNN}^{head}(\mathbf{r}_i) \quad (1)$$

$$\mathbf{h}_i^{dep} = \text{FNN}^{dep}(\mathbf{r}_i) \quad (2)$$

For each ordered pair (i, j) of tokens in the sentence, their respective head and dependent representations are then fed to a biaffine classifier (Eq. 3, Dozat and Manning, 2017), which outputs logits $\mathbf{s}_{i,j}$ over the possible dependency labels.[1]

We encode the absence of a dependency relation between two tokens as simply another label ($\varnothing$). This "unfactorized" approach is in contrast to a "factorized" approach that first predicts presence or absence of relations and then uses a second classifier to predict labels. Dozat and Manning (2018) found that the unfactorized approach performed on par with the factorized approach for *semantic* dependency parsing, and this finding has been shown to also apply to enhanced UD parsing (Grünewald et al., 2021).

Finally, we can extract a probability distribution

[1]Note that this means that each pair of tokens is fed to the classifier twice as an ordered pair, once with i as the potential head and j as the potential dependent, and once the other way around.

$P(y_{i,j})$ over dependency labels from the logits:

$$\text{Biaff}(\mathbf{x}_1, \mathbf{x}_2) = \mathbf{x}_1^\top \mathbf{U}\mathbf{x}_2 + W(\mathbf{x}_1 \oplus \mathbf{x}_2) + \mathbf{b} \quad (3)$$

$$\mathbf{s}_{i,j} = \text{Biaff}\big(\mathbf{h}_i^{head}, \mathbf{h}_j^{dep}\big) \quad (4)$$

$$P(y_{i,j}) = \text{softmax}(\mathbf{s}_{i,j}) \quad (5)$$

$\mathbf{U}$, W and $\mathbf{b}$ in (3) are learned parameters; $\oplus$ denotes the concatenation operation. The model is trained to minimize cross entropy loss w. r. t. the true dependency label between each pair of tokens.

De-lexicalizing dependency labels. Because enhanced UD adds lexical information to certain dependencies (e.g., *obl:instead_of*), the number of possible dependency labels is very large for most treebanks, with up to over 1100 for Arabic-PADT. Among the languages being part of the Shared Task, French is an exception as its treebanks do not make use of lexicalized labels. To avoid sparsity issues, we strip lexical information from labels during training, instead replacing them with placeholders (e.g., *obl:[case]*) indicating where in the dependency graph the lexical information is expected to be found (see Sec. 2.5 for a detailed description of the reconstruction process). This way, we can remove all lexicalized relations from the label vocabulary, instead adding only a much smaller number of placeholder labels. The basic relation types affected by this process are *nmod*, *obl*, *acl*, *advcl*, and *conj*. We keep all other, non-lexicalized subtype labels, including those that occur together with lexical material (e.g., *obl:järgi:gen* becomes *obl:[case]:gen*). Our procedure reduces label counts substantially, e.g., to 59 for Arabic.

2.4 Assembling the Dependency Graph

The outputs $P(y_{i,j})$ provided by the dependency classifier can be regarded as a 3-dimensional tensor, with one dimension corresponding to the tokens as heads, one dimension corresponding to the tokens as dependents, and the third dimension corresponding to the label set. Figure 2 gives a two-dimensional view of this tensor, with each cell containing the highest-scoring label for a head (row label) and dependent (column label) pair.

Ensembling. Instead of continuing directly with the predicted matrices as described above, we train multiple models with different initializations for each language and then ensemble them by averaging their output probabilities during prediction. In other words, we compute the probabilities of labels $P(y_{i,j})$ between two ordered tokens i and j as

$$P(y_{i,j}) = \frac{1}{m} \sum_{k=1}^{m} \text{softmax}(\mathbf{s}_{i,j}^{(k)}) \quad (6)$$

where m is the number of models and $\mathbf{s}_{i,j}^{(k)}$ is the unnormalized output vector of the k-th model for the token pair (i, j).

For languages for which more than one training treebank is available, we ensemble models trained on different treebanks. For more details on this procedure, see section Sec. 3.1.

Ensuring graph structure constraints. Using the output tensors created via ensembling, we can assemble a dependency graph by retrieving the highest-scoring dependency (or $\varnothing$, i.e., no relation) for each pair of tokens in the sentence and forming their union (omitting the diagonal as enhanced UD does not allow links starting and ending at the same node). Although enhanced UD eliminates the requirement that dependency graphs must be trees, it maintains the structural constraint that every token must be reachable from the root of the graph.[2] Although our system learns to produce graphs that obey this constraint in the vast majority of cases, there are cases where structurally invalid graphs are retrieved. To make these graphs structurally valid, we perform the following heuristic post-processing steps:

1. If the graph has more than one root, we remove all but the most confidently predicted *root* dependency.

2. If there are one or more nodes in the graph that are not reachable from the root, we select the most confidently predicted non-$\varnothing$ edge from a reachable to an unreachable node and add it to the graph. We repeat this step until every node is reachable from the root.

Removal of superfluous dependencies. UD contains several relations that empirically only appear on their own, i.e., whose dependent may have only one incoming edge of this type. These relations are *fixed*, *flat*, *goeswith*, *punct*, and *cc*. If our parser erroneously predicts several of these relations for a single token (e.g., punctuation being

[2]Graphs in enhanced UD may have more than one root, but empirically, the vast majority have only one root. Therefore, we assume exactly one root for each dependency graph for simplicity.

	[root]	Use	cinnamon	instead	of	sugar	or	sweetener
[root]	∅	*root*	∅	∅	∅	∅	∅	∅
Use	∅	∅	*obj*	∅	∅	*obl:[case]*	∅	*obl:[case]*
cinnamon	∅	∅	∅	∅	∅	∅	∅	∅
instead	∅	∅	∅	∅	*fixed*	∅	∅	∅
of	∅	∅	∅	∅	∅	∅	∅	∅
sugar	∅	∅	∅	*case*	∅	∅	∅	*conj:[cc]*
or	∅	∅	∅	∅	∅	∅	∅	∅
sweetener	∅	∅	∅	∅	∅	∅	*cc*	∅

Figure 2: Prediction matrix of the dependency classifier. Cell entries show the highest-scoring label for each ordered pair of tokens, with row/column labels indicating potential heads/dependents respectively.

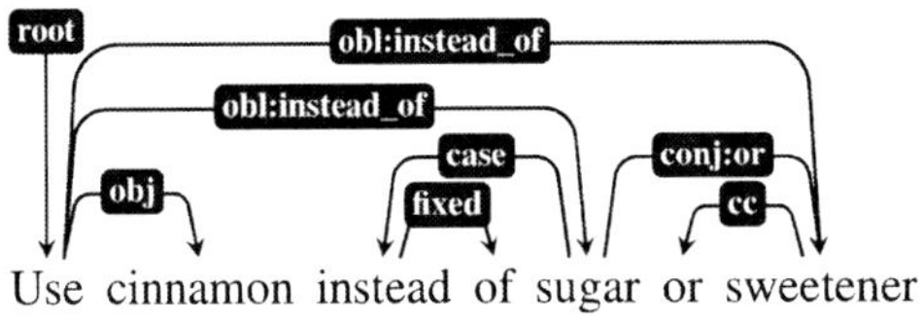

Figure 3: Dependency graph with lexicalized labels.

attached to several tokens at once), we remove all but the most confidently predicted dependency.

2.5 Label Lexicalization

As outlined in Sec. 2.3, lexical information is stripped from dependency labels during training, using the format *base:[placeholder]*. At prediction time, we re-lexicalize predicted placeholder labels using a two-step procedure. First, lexical material is retrieved from the dependency graph using a rule-based heuristic, and then a machine-learning classifier is run on the output to correct potential errors.

Re-lexicalization heuristic. The main rule of our re-lexicalization heuristic checks if the token has a dependent that is attached via the placeholder of the de-lexicalized relation in question. If so, we lexicalize the relation with the token of this dependent. For example, in Figure 3, our parser predicts *obl:[case]* and we hence re-lexicalize this relation with the token(s) of the *case* dependents of "sugar." (Multiword expressions, such as "instead of", are handled by concatenating word forms linked by the *fixed* relation.) In addition, there is a number of more fine-grained rules to handle lexicalization in the context of specific constructions such as coordination. More details are reported by Grünewald and Friedrich (2020).

Treebank	Heuristic	Hybrid
Arabic-PADT	93.4	97.5
Czech-PDT	90.9	99.2
English-EWT	98.4	98.8
Estonian-EDT	98.8	99.8
Latvian-LVTB	99.4	99.7
Polish-PDB	91.8	98.9
Slovak-SNK	93.0	98.0
Tamil-TTB	16.1	66.1

Table 2: Re-lexicalization accuracy (%) on a selection of gold development treebanks.

As can be seen in Table 2, the rule-based heuristic achieves good results in the case of English – the language that it was initially designed for – and for a number of other languages (e.g. Estonian and Latvian), with re-lexicalization accuracies greater than 98 % when evaluating on the gold development data. However, it performs markedly worse for some of the other languages in the Shared Task, such as Arabic, Czech and (especially) Tamil. The main reason for this is that the heuristic can only retrieve word forms directly from the raw sentence, whereas the lexical material in gold dependency labels is lemmatized.

Rule-based label transducer. To increase re-lexicalization accuracy, we perform a second step after running the heuristic on the initial parser output, automatically learning a "label transducer" for each language from treebank data. For each language, we train a RandomForest classifier (Breiman, 2001) that takes as input the lexicalized labels predicted by our heuristic as well as a representation of its sentential context. The label transducer then predicts a new label, which may differ from the initial prediction made by the heuristic. In other words, the label transducer functions as an ML-based error correction mechanism.

The input features for the classifier are (a) a one-hot encoding of the lexicalized label predicted by the heuristic, e.g., *conj:als*; and (b) a binary encoding of all tokens in the graph that are at most 1 dependency edge away from the endpoint of the relation in question. The output space is the set of lexicalized dependency labels as present in the gold training data.

In few cases, the label transducer predicts a different base relation type compared to the one given as input, i.e., it may transform an input of *conj:als* into an output of *nmod:in*. As we observed that

XLM-R embeddings	
Embeddings dimension	1024
Token mask probability	0.15
Layer dropout	0.1
Hidden dropout	0.2
Attention dropout	0.2
Output dropout	0.5
Biaffine classifier	
Hidden size	1024
Dropout	0.33
AdamW Optimizer	
Batch size	32
LR schedule	Noam
Warmup steps	1 epoch
Peak learning rate	$4e^{-5}$
β_1, β_2	0.9, 0.999
Weight decay	0.0

Table 3: Basic hyperparameter values used in training.

such predictions are almost always incorrect, we keep the heuristic's output in these cases.

On the gold development data, we find that including the ML-based transducer in the relexicalization process leads to moderate to large accuracy increases (see Table 2). This is the case particularly for languages where lexical material in dependencies often differs from the raw tokens in the graph (e.g., Arabic and Tamil).

3 Experiments

This section describes our main submission, as well as a number of additional experiments.

3.1 Experimental Settings

We use the provided training and development data for training and validation, respectively. During training, we use gold-segmented sentences and gold tokenization.

For hyperparameter settings, we mostly stick with the values of Grünewald and Friedrich (2020). The exceptions are parameters related to the training process itself, where we use a batch size of 32 in conjunction with an inverse square root ("Noam") learning rate schedule (Vaswani et al., 2017) that reaches a peak LR of $4e^{-5}$ after one epoch of training. We found this configuration to yield results comparable to our previous setup, but at noticeably higher training efficiency. Table 3 shows the full set of hyperparameters.

The above setup works robustly across languages, with Tamil being the only exception, reaching only ca. 54 ELAS F1 on the development data. For the low resource setting of parsing Tamil, we hence use a batch size of 1, a lower learning rate ($1e^{-5}$), as well as a longer warmup time (5 epochs) and higher early stopping patience (40 epochs).

Language	Ensemble composition
Czech	3xPDT, 1xCAC, 1xFictree
Dutch	3xAlpino, 2xLassySmall
English	3xEWT, 2xGUM
Estonian	4xEDT, 1xEWT
Polish	5xPDB

Table 4: Ensemble compositions for languages with more than one training treebank.

We train 5 models per language and ensemble these models for our final predictions (see Sec. 2.4). For languages with more than one training treebank, we train models on all treebanks provided, with more models trained on larger treebanks. The one exception to this is Polish, where we found ensembling of models trained on both the PDB and LFG treebanks to yield worse results than just training on PDB (likely due to systematic annotation differences). Table 4 shows the ensemble composition for all languages with multiple training treebanks.

Each model is trained using a single nVidia Tesla V100 GPU, stopping early when ELAS F1 score on the development set does not improve for 20 epochs, or after at most 24 hours. Training time varies substantially by treebank and correlates with treebank size, with training being fastest for Tamil-TTB (ca. 2 hours on average) and slowest for Russian-SynTagRus and Czech-PDT (both run into the 24-hour time limit).

3.2 Results of Submission

Table 5 shows the results (in terms of ELAS F1 score) on the blind test data for our main submission (rightmost column, ensemble$_{\mathsf{hyb}}$) as well as the 1st- and 2nd-scoring submissions of the Shared Task (TGIF and ShanghaiTech), as well as the median submission for each language. Our system achieves an average ELAS F1 score of 86.97 %, ranking 3rd with a margin of more than 3 points over the median.

The best results achieved by our system are for Bulgarian and Italian, each with ELAS F1 scores of over 93. In contrast, Tamil is the language that we perform by far the worst on, with an ELAS F1 score of around 59. In an extreme low-resource scenario such as parsing Tamil (where the training data consists of only 400 sentences), adaptions to our framework will be necessary.

Language	Other teams			RobertNLP		
	TGIF	Shanghai	*Median*	single	$\text{ensemble}_{\text{heur}}$	$\text{ensemble}_{\text{hyb}}$
Arabic	81.23	**82.26**	76.39	81.37	81.12	***81.58***
Bulgarian	**93.63**	92.52	90.84	92.94	92.91	***93.16***
Czech	**92.24**	91.78	89.08	89.99	89.51	***90.21***
Dutch	**91.78**	88.64	84.14	88.02	88.21	***88.37***
English	**88.19**	87.27	85.70	87.29	***87.89***	87.88
Estonian	**88.38**	86.66	84.02	86.10	86.52	***86.55***
Finnish	**91.75**	90.81	89.02	90.77	90.97	**91.01**
French	**91.63**	88.40	87.32	***88.59***	88.51	88.51
Italian	**93.31**	92.88	91.81	93.00	93.16	***93.28***
Latvian	**90.23**	89.17	84.57	88.68	88.80	***88.82***
Lithuanian	**86.06**	80.87	78.04	***80.98***	80.76	80.76
Polish	**91.46**	90.66	88.31	89.49	89.54	***89.78***
Russian	**94.01**	93.59	90.90	92.55	92.33	***92.64***
Slovak	**94.96**	90.25	87.04	89.60	89.29	***89.66***
Swedish	**89.90**	86.62	84.91	87.72	88.02	***88.03***
Tamil	**65.58**	58.94	52.27	58.24	59.00	***59.33***
Ukrainian	**92.78**	88.94	86.92	88.56	***88.86***	***88.86***
Average	**89.24**	87.07	83.64	86.70	86.78	***86.97***

Table 5: Parsing results (ELAS F1) on blind test data in the IWPT 2021 Shared Task. $\text{ensemble}_{\text{hyb}}$ is our main submission, using both the re-lexicalization heuristic and the label transducer.

3.3 Analysis of Results

To tease out the effects of re-lexicalization and ensembling, we submitted two more experiments on the blind test data after the official deadline.

Effect of re-lexicalization strategy. In a first experiment, we did not use our machine learning-based label transducer for re-lexicalization of labels, instead relying only on the rule-based heuristic. The results of this experiment can be found in the column labelled "$\text{ensemble}_{\text{heur}}$" in Table 5.

Using only the heuristic for label lexicalization results in a modest, but noticeable accuracy hit across languages, reducing the average ELAS F1 score by roughly 0.2. The languages most affected are Czech (-0.70), Arabic (-0.46), Slovak (-0.35), and Tamil (-0.33), in which differences between lexical material in the sentence and their lemmas included in lexicalized labels are frequent. In contrast, many languages see only small or no performance drops (e.g. Lithuanian, Swedish); for English, performance even increases very slightly when removing the label transducer.

These results indicate that while using our hybrid system is beneficial, good results for most languages can also be achieved when relying solely on our re-lexicalization heuristic. This makes it conceivable that in conjunction with a high-accuracy lemmatizer, a purely rule-based system may perform on par with a hybrid system, and we view this as an interesting avenue for future work.

Effect of ensembling. In a second experiment, we did not perform model ensembling for prediction, instead only using a single model for each language. The column labelled "single" in Table 5 reports the best results achieved for each language when using only the best single model.

As can be seen, utilizing only a single model per language results in a moderate average performance drop of 0.27 ELAS F1 points. With the exception of French and Lithuanian, all languages benefit from model ensembling, with Tamil (+1.09), English (+0.59), Estonian (+0.45), and Dutch (+0.35) showing the strongest improvements. As the latter three include data from different treebanks in their blind test sets, this indicates that ensembling may also help parser robustness when mixing models trained on different datasets.

However, although the overall effect of ensembling is notable, our parser nonetheless retains a relatively strong performance even without it, and still would have scored 3rd in the Shared Task if it was only using single models.

4 Conclusion

In this paper, we have described our submission to the IWPT 2021 Shared Task, which ranked 3rd out of 9 with an average ELAS F1 score of 86.97. Our model is an extension of the previously English-only system (Grünewald and Friedrich, 2020), demonstrating that the same approach is also yields very good results for other languages with only relatively minor modifications. In post-submission ablation experiments, we find that our parser benefits from model ensembling and a machine learning-assisted approach to label lexicalization.

A remaining issue of our parser is its rather poor performance in a low-resource setting (Tamil). Addressing this weakness, ideally while maintaining the parser's relatively simple core architecture, may be a promising avenue for future work.

References

Gosse Bouma, Djamé Seddah, and Daniel Zeman. 2021. From raw text to enhanced universal dependencies: The parsing shared task at iwpt 2021. In *Proceedings of the 17th International Conference on Parsing Technologies (IWPT 2021)*, pages 146–157, Bangkok, Thailand (online). Association for Computational Linguistics.

Gosse Bouma, Djamé Seddah, and Daniel Zeman. 2020. Overview of the IWPT 2020 shared task on parsing into enhanced Universal Dependencies. In *Proceedings of the 16th International Conference on Parsing Technologies and the IWPT 2020 Shared Task on Parsing into Enhanced Universal Dependencies*, pages 151–161, Online. Association for Computational Linguistics.

Leo Breiman. 2001. Random forests. *Machine learning*, 45(1):5–32.

Alexis Conneau, Kartikay Khandelwal, Naman Goyal, Vishrav Chaudhary, Guillaume Wenzek, Francisco Guzmán, Edouard Grave, Myle Ott, Luke Zettlemoyer, and Veselin Stoyanov. 2020. Unsupervised cross-lingual representation learning at scale. pages 8440–8451.

Timothy Dozat and Christopher D. Manning. 2017. Deep biaffine attention for neural dependency parsing. In *5th International Conference on Learning Representations, ICLR 2017, Toulon, France, April 24-26, 2017, Conference Track Proceedings*. OpenReview.net.

Timothy Dozat and Christopher D. Manning. 2018. Simpler but more accurate semantic dependency parsing. In *Proceedings of the 56th Annual Meeting of the Association for Computational Linguistics (Volume 2: Short Papers)*, pages 484–490, Melbourne, Australia. Association for Computational Linguistics.

Stefan Grünewald and Annemarie Friedrich. 2020. RobertNLP at the IWPT 2020 shared task: Surprisingly simple enhanced UD parsing for English. In *Proceedings of the 16th International Conference on Parsing Technologies and the IWPT 2020 Shared Task on Parsing into Enhanced Universal Dependencies*, pages 245–252, Online. Association for Computational Linguistics.

Stefan Grünewald, Annemarie Friedrich, and Jonas Kuhn. 2021. Applying Occam's razor to transformer-based dependency parsing: What works, what doesn't, and what is really necessary. In *Proceedings of the 17th International Conference on Parsing Technologies and the IWPT 2021 Shared Task on Parsing into Enhanced Universal Dependencies*, Online. Association for Computational Linguistics.

Dan Kondratyuk and Milan Straka. 2019. 75 languages, 1 model: Parsing universal dependencies universally. In *Proceedings of the 2019 Conference on Empirical Methods in Natural Language Processing and the 9th International Joint Conference on Natural Language Processing (EMNLP-IJCNLP)*, pages 2779–2795, Hong Kong, China. Association for Computational Linguistics.

Marie-Catherine de Marneffe, Timothy Dozat, Natalia Silveira, Katri Haverinen, Filip Ginter, Joakim Nivre, and Christopher D. Manning. 2014. Universal Stanford dependencies: A cross-linguistic typology. In *Proceedings of the Ninth International Conference on Language Resources and Evaluation (LREC'14)*, pages 4585–4592, Reykjavik, Iceland. European Language Resources Association (ELRA).

Minh Van Nguyen, Viet Dac Lai, Amir Pouran Ben Veyseh, and Thien Huu Nguyen. 2021. Trankit: A light-weight transformer-based toolkit for multilingual natural language processing. In *Proceedings of the 16th Conference of the European Chapter of the Association for Computational Linguistics: System Demonstrations*, pages 80–90, Online. Association for Computational Linguistics.

Joakim Nivre, Paola Marongiu, Filip Ginter, Jenna Kanerva, Simonetta Montemagni, Sebastian Schuster, and Maria Simi. 2018. Enhancing universal dependency treebanks: A case study. In *Proceedings of the Second Workshop on Universal Dependencies (UDW 2018)*, pages 102–107, Brussels, Belgium. Association for Computational Linguistics.

Jenna Nyblom, Samuel Kohonen, Katri Haverinen, Tapio Salakoski, and Filip Ginter. 2013. Predicting conjunct propagation and other extended Stanford dependencies. In *Proceedings of the Second International Conference on Dependency Linguistics (DepLing 2013)*, pages 252–261, Prague, Czech Republic. Charles University in Prague, Matfyzpress, Prague, Czech Republic.

Sebastian Schuster, Éric Villemonte de La Clergerie, Marie Candito, Benoît Sagot, Christopher Manning, and Djamé Seddah. 2017. Paris and Stanford at EPE 2017: Downstream evaluation of graph-based dependency representations. In *Proceedings of the 2017 Shared Task on Extrinsic Parser Evaluation (EPE 2017)*, pages 47–59.

Sebastian Schuster and Christopher D. Manning. 2016. Enhanced English Universal Dependencies: An improved representation for natural language understanding tasks. In *Proceedings of the Tenth International Conference on Language Resources and Evaluation (LREC'16)*, pages 2371–2378, Portorož, Slovenia. European Language Resources Association (ELRA).

Maria Simi and Simonetta Montemagni. 2018. Bootstrapping enhanced universal dependencies for Italian. In *5th Italian Conference on Computational Linguistics, CLiC-it 2018*, volume 2253. CEUR-WS.

Ashish Vaswani, Noam Shazeer, Niki Parmar, Jakob Uszkoreit, Llion Jones, Aidan N Gomez, Ł ukasz Kaiser, and Illia Polosukhin. 2017. Attention is all you need. In *Advances in Neural Information Processing Systems*, volume 30. Curran Associates, Inc.

The DCU-EPFL Enhanced Dependency Parser at the IWPT 2021 Shared Task

James Barry[1], Alireza Mohammadshahi[2,3], Joachim Wagner[1], Jennifer Foster[1], James Henderson[2]
[1] ADAPT Centre, School of Computing, Dublin City University
[2] Idiap Research Institute
[3] École Polytechnique Fédérale de Lausanne—EPFL
[1] {james.barry, joachim.wagner, jennifer.foster}@adaptcentre.ie
[2] {alireza.mohammadshahi, james.henderson}@idiap.ch

Abstract

We describe the *DCU-EPFL* submission to the IWPT 2021 Parsing Shared Task: *From Raw Text to Enhanced Universal Dependencies*. The task involves parsing Enhanced UD graphs, which are an extension of the basic dependency trees designed to be more facilitative towards representing semantic structure. Evaluation is carried out on 29 treebanks in 17 languages and participants are required to parse the data from each language starting from raw strings. Our approach uses the Stanza pipeline to preprocess the text files, XLM-RoBERTa to obtain contextualized token representations, and an edge-scoring and labeling model to predict the enhanced graph. Finally, we run a post-processing script to ensure all of our outputs are valid Enhanced UD graphs. Our system places 6th out of 9 participants with a coarse Enhanced Labeled Attachment Score (ELAS) of 83.57. We carry out additional post-deadline experiments which include using Trankit for pre-processing, XLM-RoBERTa$_{\text{LARGE}}$, treebank concatenation, and multitask learning between a basic and an enhanced dependency parser. All of these modifications improve our initial score and our final system has a coarse ELAS of 88.04.

1 Introduction

The IWPT 2021 Parsing Shared Task: *From Raw Text to Enhanced Universal Dependencies* (Bouma et al., 2021) is the second task involving the prediction of Enhanced Universal Dependencies (EUD) graphs[1] following the 2020 task (Bouma et al., 2020). EUD graphs are an extension of basic UD trees, designed to be more useful in shallow natural language understanding tasks (Schuster and Manning, 2016) and lend themselves more easily to the representation of semantic structure than strict surface structure dependency trees. In the shared task, the enhanced graphs must be predicted from raw text, i.e. participants must segment the input into sentences and tokens. Participants are encouraged to predict lemmas, Part-of-Speech (POS) tags, morphological features and basic dependency trees as well.

Our system, *DCU-EPFL*, uses a single multilingual Transformer (Vaswani et al., 2017) encoder, namely XLM-RoBERTa (XLM-R) (Conneau et al., 2020), which is a multilingual RoBERTa model (Liu et al., 2019), to obtain contextualized token encodings. These are then passed to the enhanced dependency parsing model. The system is straightforward to apply to new languages with enhanced UD annotations. In the official submission, we use the same hyper-parameters for all languages. Our parsing component can produce arbitrary graphs, including graph structures where words may have multiple heads and cyclic graphs. Our system uses the following three components:

1. Stanza (Qi et al., 2020) for sentence segmentation, tokenization and the prediction of all UD features apart from the enhanced graph.
2. A Transformer-based dependency parsing model to predict Enhanced UD graphs.
3. A post-processor ensuring that every graph is a rooted graph where all nodes are reachable from the notional root token.

Our official system placed 6th out of 9 teams with a coarse Enhanced Labeled Attachment Score (ELAS) of 83.57. In a number of unofficial post-evaluation experiments, we make four incremental changes to our pipeline approach:

1. We replace the Stanza pre-processing pipeline with Trankit (Nguyen et al., 2021).

[1] https://universaldependencies.org/u/overview/enhanced-syntax.html

Proceedings of the 17th International Conference on Parsing Technologies (IWPT 2021), pages 204–212
Bangkok, Thailand (online), August 6, 2021.

2. We use XLM-R_{Large} instead of XLM-R_{Base}.

3. We concatenate treebanks from the same language which have more than one training treebank and concatenating English treebanks to the Tamil training data.

4. We introduce a novel multitask model which parses the basic UD tree and enhanced graph in tandem.

All of these additional steps improved our evaluation scores, and for our final system, which incorporates all additional modifications, our evaluation score increases from 83.57 to 88.04. Our code is publicly available.[2]

2 Related Work

In this section, we discuss the relevant literature related to Enhanced Universal Dependencies.

2.1 Enhanced Universal Dependencies

Despite the recent wave of Deep Learning models and accompanying analyses that show that such models learn information about syntax, there is still interest and merit in utilizing hierarchically structured representations such as trees and semantic representations to provide greater supervision about what is taking place in a sentence (Oepen et al., 2019). While dependency trees are often used in downstream applications, their structural restrictions may hinder the representation of content words (Schuster and Manning, 2016). The Enhanced UD representation tries to fill this gap by enabling more expressive graphs in the UD format, which capture phenomena such as added subject relations in control and raising, shared heads and dependents in coordination, the insertion of null nodes for elided predicates, co-reference in relative clause constructions and augmenting modifier relations with prepositional or case-marking information.

Schuster and Manning (2016) build on the Stanford Dependencies (SD) initiative (de Marneffe et al., 2006) and extend certain flavors of the SD dependency graph representations to UD in the form of enhanced UD relations for English. They use a rule-based system that converts basic UD trees to enhanced UD graphs based on dependency structures identified to require enhancement. Nivre et al. (2018) use rule-based and data-driven approaches in a cross-lingual setting for bootstrapping enhanced UD representations in Swedish and Italian and show that both techniques are capable of annotating enhanced dependencies in different languages.

2.2 The IWPT 2020 Shared Task on Parsing Enhanced Universal Dependencies

The first shared task on parsing Enhanced Universal Dependencies (Bouma et al., 2020) brought renewed attention to the problem of predicting enhanced UD graphs. Ten teams submitted to the task. The winning system (Kanerva et al., 2020) utilized the UDify model (Kondratyuk and Straka, 2019), which uses a BERT model (Devlin et al., 2019) as the encoder with multitask classifiers for POS-tagging, morphological prediction and dependency parsing built on top. They developed a system for encoding the enhanced representation into the basic dependencies so it can be predicted in the same way as a basic dependency tree but with enriched dependency types that can then be converted into the enhanced structure. In an unofficial submission shortly after the task deadline, Wang et al. (2020) outperform the winning system using second-order inference methods with Mean-Field Variational Inference.

Most systems used pretrained Transformers to obtain token representations, either by using the Transformer directly (Kanerva et al., 2020; Grünewald and Friedrich, 2020; He and Choi, 2020) or passing the encoded representation to BiLSTM layers where they are combined with other features such as context-free FastText word embeddings (Wang et al., 2020), character features and features obtained from predicted POS tags, morphological features and basic UD trees (Barry et al., 2020), or are used as frozen embeddings (Hershcovich et al., 2020). The only transition-based system among the participating teams (Hershcovich et al., 2020) used a stack-LSTM architecture (Dyer et al., 2015). Ek and Bernardy (2020) and Dehouck et al. (2020) combine basic dependency parsers and a rule-based system to generate EUD graphs from the predicted trees.

3 Official System Overview

This section describes our official system, which is the system we submitted prior to the competition deadline. The architecture of our system is

[2] https://github.com/jbrry/IWPT-2021-shared-task

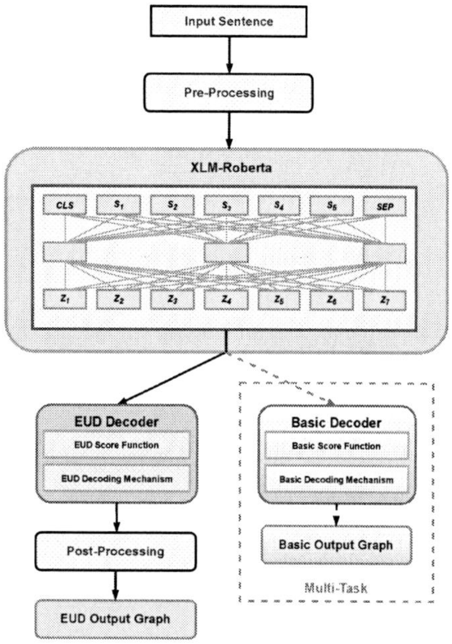

Figure 1: DCU-EPFL Architecture.

shown in Figure 1.[3] The raw text test files for each language contain a mixture of test data covering multiple treebanks, so participants do not know their exact domain. For our official system, we choose the model trained on the treebank with the most amount of training data in terms of sentences for each language to process the test files. This heuristic corresponds to using Czech-PDT for Czech, Dutch-Alpino for Dutch, English-EWT for English, Estonian-EDT for Estonian and Polish-PDB for Polish.

3.1 Pre-processing

For sentence segmentation, tokenization and the prediction of the base UD features (all UD features apart from the enhanced dependency graphs and miscellaneous items in CoNLL-U files), we use the Stanza library (Qi et al., 2020) trained on version 2.7 of the UD treebanks for each treebank released as part of the training data for the shared task.[4] Note that our parser does not pre-suppose any input features other than the input text but we predict the base features using our pre-processing pipeline for completeness and to enable possible additional post-processing which involves altering enhanced dependency labels with lemma information.

3.2 Enhanced UD Parsing

For the enhanced UD parser, we use a Transformer encoder in the form of XLM-R (Conneau et al., 2020) with a first-order arc-factored model which utilizes the edge and label scoring method of (Kiperwasser and Goldberg, 2016). In initial experiments, we found this model to perform better than biaffine attention (Dozat and Manning, 2016) for the task of EUD parsing. This finding was also made by (Lindemann et al., 2019) and (Straka and Straková, 2019) for the task of semantic parsing across numerous Graphbanks (Oepen et al., 2019). Straka and Straková (2019) suggest that biaffine attention may be less suitable for predicting whether an edge exists between any pair of nodes using a predefined threshold and is perhaps more suited for dependency parsing, where words are competing with one another to be classified as the head in a softmax layer. The consistency of these findings across EUD and semantic parsing Graphbanks may provide evidence that enhanced UD is closer to semantic dependency parsing than basic UD parsing.

Parser Implementation Given a sentence x of length n, our model computes vector representations $\mathbf{R} = (\mathbf{r_1}, \mathbf{r_2}, ..., \mathbf{r_n})$ for the predicted tokens $(x_1, x_2, ..., x_n)$. Since the WordPiece tokenization (Wu et al., 2016) of XLM-R differs from the tokenization used in UD, we track the mapping I from XLM-R's k-th sub-word unit of the j-th input token produced by Stanza to the sub-word unit's position $I_{j,k}$ in context of the sentence and we consider the output vector $\mathbf{e}_{\mathbf{I_{j,1}}}$ of the first sub-word unit of each word x_j as its vector representation $(\mathbf{r}_j)$:

$$\begin{aligned}\mathbf{E} &= \mathrm{XLMR}(x_1, x_2, \ldots, x_n)\\ \mathbf{R} &= \mathrm{Filter}(E, \mathbf{I})\end{aligned} \quad (1)$$

where $\mathbf{E} = (\mathbf{e}_1, ..., \mathbf{e}_N)$ are the output vectors of all sub-word units, N being the total number of sub-word units in the sentence, and $\mathrm{Filter}()$ chooses the first embedding for each token. We add a dummy representation of the same dimensionality for the ROOT token to the sequence of vectors $\mathbf{R}$ but mask out predictions from this token. Following Kiperwasser and Goldberg (2016), these representations $\mathbf{R} = (\mathbf{r_1}, \mathbf{r_2}, ..., \mathbf{r_n})$ are then passed to the dependency parsing component, where the feature

[3] For the official system, we did not include the basic dependency parser in a multitask setup.

[4] For Arabic, our Stanza Multi-word Token (MWT) expander predicted MWTs with a span of length 1 for two sentences. In the UD guidelines, MWT span lengths must be larger than one. To pass validation, we trained a UDPipe tokenizer (Straka and Straková, 2017) with Word2Vec embeddings for Arabic instead.

function ϕ is the concatenation of the representations of a potential head word x_h and dependent word x_d, where $\circ$ denotes concatenation:

$$\phi(h, d) = \mathbf{r_h} \circ \mathbf{r_d} \tag{2}$$

Edge Prediction We compute scores for all $n(n-1)$ potential edges (h, d), $h \neq d$, with an MLP:

$$s_{hd}^{(\text{arc})} = MLP^{(\text{arc})}(\phi(h, d)) \tag{3}$$

The edge classifier computes scores for all possible head-dependent pairs, and we compute a sigmoid on the resulting matrix of scores to obtain probabilities. We use an edge prediction threshold of 0.5, i.e. we include all edges with a score above 0.5 in the preliminary EUD graph. This enables words to have multiple heads but it can also lead to words receiving no head, where we manually select the edge that has the highest probability, and to fragmented graphs, see post-processing in Section 3.3.

Label Prediction To label the graph, we then choose a label for each edge using a separate classifier:

$$s_{hd}^{(\text{label})} = MLP^{(\text{label})}(\phi(h, d)) \tag{4}$$

The scores for all possible labels are passed to a softmax layer, which outputs the probability of each label for edge (h, d) and we select the label with the highest probability for each edge.

Loss Function For edge prediction, sigmoid cross-entropy loss is used, and for label prediction, as we want to select the label for each chosen edge, softmax cross-entropy loss is used (Dozat and Manning, 2018). We interpolate between the loss given by the edge classifier and the loss given by the label classifier (Dozat and Manning, 2018; Wang et al., 2020) with a constant λ:

$$\mathcal{L} = \lambda\mathcal{L}^{(label)} + (1 - \lambda)\mathcal{L}^{(edge)} \tag{5}$$

Training details For the empty nodes which are prevalent in enhanced UD graphs, we added them into the graph, and offset the head indices to account for the new token(s) added to the graph. At test time, we did not predict whether an elided token should be added to the graph. Due to time constraints, we trained using the full lexicalized enhanced dependency labels but intend to devise a delexicalization and relexicalization procedure in future work.

Hyperparameter	Size
XLM-R$_{\text{Base}}$ Hidden Size	768
XLM-R$_{\text{Large}}$ Hidden Size	1024
Edge Feedforward	300
Label Feedforward	300
Input Dropout	0.35
Dropout	0.35
Edge Prediction Threshold	0.5
Loss interpolation λ	0.10

Table 1: Hyperparameters of our EUD parsing model.

3.3 Post-processing

In the Enhanced UD guidelines, the predicted structure must be a connected graph where all nodes are reachable from the notional root[5]. After predicting the test files, we use the graph connection tool in (Barry et al., 2020) to make sure that each sentence is a connected graph. Specifically, we repeatedly check for unreachable nodes and the number of unreachable nodes that can be reached from them. We choose the candidate which maximises this number (in the case there are ties, we choose the first node in surface order) and makes it a child of the notional ROOT, i.e. this node becomes an additional root node. System outputs are then validated at level 2 by the UD validator [6] to catch bugs prior to submission.

4 Experiments

In this section, we discuss our official results and then describe post-deadline experiments that improved our submission's score. Model hyperparameters are listed in Table 1. The choice of XLM-R encoder (Base or Large) determines the hyperparameters of the encoder part of our model. In our official submission, we use XLM-R$_{\text{Base}}$. A dropout value of 0.35 is used for the input embeddings as well as for the encoder and MLP networks. A loss interpolation constant λ of 0.1 is used as in (Wang et al., 2020).

4.1 Official Submission

For the official submission, we use the Stanza preprocessing pipeline and our dependency parsing model with XLM-R$_{\text{Base}}$. The results are listed in

[5]In UD, the notional ROOT is the token with ID 0, whereas a root node is any node that has 0 as its head.

[6]`https://github.com/UniversalDependencies/tools/blob/master/validate.py`

Language	[1] Official	[2] [1]+Trankit	[3] [2]+XLM-R$_{Large}$	[4] [3]+Concat	[5] [4]+MTL
Arabic	71.01	78.05(+24.2%)	79.51(+6.6%)	-	81.72(+10.8%)
Bulgarian	92.44	92.47(+0.4%)	93.26(+10.5%)	-	93.59(+4.9%)
Czech	89.93	90.28(+3.5%)	91.06(+8.1%)	91.43(+4.1%)	91.30(-1.5%)
Dutch	81.89	86.51(+25.5%)	87.67(+8.6%)	88.60(+7.5%)	89.51(+7.9%)
English	85.70	85.97(+1.8%)	86.94(+6.9%)	87.46(+3.9%)	87.28(-1.4%)
Estonian	84.35	84.54(+1.2%)	85.92(+8.9%)	86.68(+5.4%)	86.76(+0.6%)
Finnish	89.02	89.34(+2.9%)	90.79(+13.6%)	-	91.16(+4.1%)
French	86.68	86.80(+0.9%)	89.12(+17.6%)	-	90.38(+11.6%)
Italian	92.41	92.44(+0.4%)	93.35(+12.1%)	-	93.47(+1.8%)
Latvian	86.96	86.85(-0.8%)	88.81(+14.9%)	-	89.18(+3.3%)
Lithuanian	78.04	78.44(+1.8%)	82.09(+16.9%)	-	83.47(+7.7%)
Polish	89.17	89.30(+1.2%)	90.20(+8.4%)	91.15(+9.7%)	90.46(-7.8%)
Russian	92.83	93.06(+3.2%)	93.95(+12.8%)	-	94.09(+2.3%)
Slovak	89.59	90.81(+11.7%)	92.33(+16.5%)	-	92.73(+5.2%)
Swedish	85.20	85.98(+5.3%)	88.10(+15.1%)	-	88.64(+4.5%)
Tamil	39.32	40.64(+2.2%)	48.85(+13.8%)	61.14(+24.0%)	62.06(+2.4%)
Ukrainian	86.09	86.30(+1.5%)	89.44(+22.91%)	-	90.91(+13.9%)
Average	83.57	84.58(+6.2%)	86.55(+12.7%)	87.48(+6.9%)	88.04(+4.5%)

Table 2: Evaluation scores on the official test data on the language-specific test files. All runs after **Official** subsume **Trankit** pre-processing and all runs after **Trankit** subsume the **XLM-R$_{Large}$** model. All numbers inside the parentheses are calculated as the relative error reduction of each column and its corresponding previous column.

column [1] of Table 2. Our official submission placed 6th of 9 participants. The overall scores submitted by each team are listed in Table 3. The scores of two teams are close to our overall score: Combo and Unipi placed 4th and 5th with scores of 83.79 and 83.64 compared to our score of 83.57. This grouping is outperformed by the top three submissions TGIF, ShanghaiTech and RobertNLP by a margin from 3.2 ELAS points (RobertNLP vs. Combo) to 5.7 ELAS points (TGIF vs. DCU-EPFL).

4.2 Trankit Pre-processing

In a post-deadline experiment, we replace the Stanza pre-processing pipeline (which uses Word2Vec and FastText embeddings as external input features and a BiLSTM encoder) with Trankit (Nguyen et al., 2021), which uses the Transformer XLM-R as the encoder. The results from adopting Trankit for sentence segmentation and tokenization are listed in column [2] of Table 2. We notice slight improvements for all languages, with notable exceptions being Arabic, Dutch and Slovak, where the better pre-processing accounts for a 24.2%, 25.5% and 11.7% relative error reduction.

4.3 XLM-R$_{Large}$

Our next modification is to leverage the XLM-R$_{Large}$ model. This model has roughly twice as many parameters as the XLM-R$_{Base}$ model used in our official submission. The results for combining Trankit pre-processing and using XML-R$_{Large}$ are listed in column [3] of Table 2. The larger capacity of the model translates to large relative error reductions particularly for Finnish, French, Latvian, Lithuanian, Swedish, Tamil and Ukrainian. Given the improvements seen by adopting both Trankit for pre-processing and the larger XLM-R$_{Large}$ model, we now incorporate these modifications into all further experiments.

4.4 Treebank Concatenation

In our official system, we used just one treebank per language. Our next experiment is to investigate the effect of concatenating all treebanks with enhanced UD annotations for a language. We hypothesize that there could be a positive transfer from learning similar (within-language) treebanks and that it would make our parser more robust to the multiple domains in the test data. This means that for Czech we concatenate the PDT, CAC and FicTree treebanks, for Dutch, Alpino and LassySmall, for English EWT and GUM, and for Estonian EDT

Language	combo	dcu-epfl	fastparse	grew	nuig	robertnlp	shanghaitech	tgif	unipi	off. reference	our best run
Arabic	76.39	71.01	53.74	71.13	0.0	81.58	**82.26**	81.23	77.17	67.35	81.72
Bulgarian	86.67	92.44	78.73	88.83	78.45	93.16	92.52	**93.63**	90.84	85.81	93.59
Czech	89.08	89.93	72.85	87.66	0.0	90.21	91.78	**92.24**	88.73	78.44	91.30
Dutch	87.07	81.89	68.89	84.09	0.0	88.37	88.64	**91.78**	84.14	82.48	89.51
English	84.09	85.70	73.00	85.49	65.40	87.88	87.27	**88.19**	87.11	83.68	87.28
Estonian	84.02	84.35	60.05	78.19	54.03	86.55	86.66	**88.38**	81.27	76.86	86.76
Finnish	87.28	89.02	57.71	85.20	0.0	91.01	90.81	**91.75**	89.62	78.26	91.16
French	87.32	86.68	73.18	83.33	0.0	88.51	88.40	**91.63**	87.43	98.80	90.38
Italian	90.40	92.41	78.32	90.98	0.0	93.28	92.88	93.31	91.81	80.20	**93.47**
Latvian	84.57	86.96	66.43	77.45	56.67	88.82	89.17	**90.23**	83.01	79.32	89.18
Lithuanian	79.75	78.04	48.27	74.62	59.13	80.76	80.87	**86.06**	71.31	75.26	83.47
Polish	87.65	89.17	71.52	78.20	0.0	89.78	90.66	**91.46**	88.31	81.59	90.46
Russian	90.73	92.83	78.56	90.56	66.33	92.64	93.59	94.01	90.90	79.63	**94.09**
Slovak	87.04	89.59	64.28	86.92	67.45	89.66	90.25	**94.96**	86.05	76.42	92.73
Swedish	83.20	85.20	67.26	81.54	63.12	88.03	86.62	**89.90**	84.91	80.98	88.64
Tamil	52.27	39.32	42.53	58.69	0.0	59.33	58.94	**65.58**	51.73	75.44	62.06
Ukrainian	86.92	86.09	63.42	83.90	0.0	88.86	88.94	**92.78**	87.51	77.24	90.91
Average	83.79	83.57	65.81	81.58	30.03	86.97	87.07	**89.24**	83.64	79.87	88.04

Table 3: Evaluation scores on the official test data on the language-specific test files submitted by each team. We also include the official reference system (**off. reference**) which copies the gold tree to the enhanced graph as well as (**our best run**) which is our best post-deadline run, which corresponds to the **+Concat+MTL** run in Table 2. The first and second top scoring models in each language are specified with black and blue color, respectively.

and EWT. For Tamil, we concatenate English EWT and GUM training data to Tamil to address the very poor evaluation score of our official submission, taking inspiration from Wang et al. (2020) who observe substantial positive effects when they add Czech and English data to the Tamil treebank.[7] The results are listed in column [4] of Table 2. Treebank concatenation helps for all languages but most notable is the improvement of over 12 points ELAS or a relative error reduction of 24% for Tamil, the language with the least amount of training data in the task.

4.5 Joint Learning of Basic and Enhanced Dependency Parsing

The official reference system submitted by the shared task organizers which copies the gold trees to the enhanced representation performs very well with 79.87 ELAS (see Table 3). Thus, there is evidence that the basic tree and enhanced graph contain a lot of mutual information. Previous methods which have leveraged the basic representation for producing EUD graphs (see Sec. 2) have focused on using heuristic rules to convert the basic tree to EUD (Schuster and Manning, 2016; Ek and Bernardy, 2020; Dehouck et al., 2020), using the basic tree as input features to the enhanced parsing model (Barry et al., 2020) or converting the enhanced graph to a richer basic representation (Kanerva et al., 2020).

[7]We did not include Czech to reduce training time.

In our final experiment, we try to leverage the information from the basic tree by jointly learning to predict the enhanced graph and the basic tree, testing whether performing basic dependency parsing and EUD parsing in a multitask setup is beneficial for EUD parsing. Given the positive effects seen through concatenation, for those languages where we performed concatenation, we also train multitask models on the concatenated versions of treebanks. We use our EUD parsing model as in Section 3 and integrate with additional basic dependency parsing component (as shown in the right part of Figure 1) which is the biaffine parsing model of Dozat and Manning (2016) and train both parsers jointly. The losses of the two components are combined with equal weight. The results are listed in column [5] of Table 2.

Single Treebanks First, we compare the multitask model to the XLM-R$_{\texttt{Large}}$ run for languages where we did not perform concatenation. Predicting the basic tree and the enhanced graph in a multitask setting yields improvements for all languages, particularly for Arabic, French and Ukrainian.

Multitask Model and Treebank Concatenation When used alongside treebank concatenation, multitask learning can help for Dutch, Estonian and Tamil where it provides additional performance gains. It is interesting to note that concatenation alone is more helpful for Czech and English where we see slight performance drops and multitask learning is not helpful when trained on concatenated Polish treebanks.

The positive contribution of multitask learning for all languages when not performing treebank concatenation, could mean that it would be useful in settings where only one treebank with the enhanced representation is available for a language and the basic tree could be used as auxiliary information to predict the enhanced representation.

Comparison to Official Systems Our best unofficial run `+Concat+MTL` is added to Table 3. Compared to the other official runs, the ELAS scores of this run ranks in second place for 13/17 languages and places first for Italian and Russian.

5 Conclusion

We have described the *DCU-EPFL* submission to the IWPT 2021 Shared Task on Parsing into Enhanced Universal Dependencies. Our approach uses a single multilingual Transformer encoder as well as an enhanced dependency parsing component. Our official system placed 6th out of 9 teams. In post-deadline experiments, we show how our submission can be improved by leveraging better upstream pre-processing, a larger encoder, concatenating treebanks as well as introducing a multitask parser that can parse the basic tree and enhanced graphs jointly.

Acknowledgments

This research is supported by Science Foundation Ireland through the ADAPT Centre for Digital Content Technology, which is funded under the SFI Research Centres Programme (Grant 13/RC/2106) and is co-funded under the European Regional Development Fund. This research is also supported by the Swiss National Science Foundation, grant CRSII5-180320. We would like to thank the shared task organizers as well as the anonymous reviewers for their helpful feedback.

References

James Barry, Joachim Wagner, and Jennifer Foster. 2020. The ADAPT enhanced dependency parser at the IWPT 2020 shared task. In *Proceedings of the 16th International Conference on Parsing Technologies and the IWPT 2020 Shared Task on Parsing into Enhanced Universal Dependencies*, pages 227–235, Online. Association for Computational Linguistics.

Gosse Bouma, Djamé Seddah, and Daniel Zeman. 2020. Overview of the IWPT 2020 shared task on parsing into enhanced Universal Dependencies. In *Proceedings of the 16th International Conference on Parsing Technologies and the IWPT 2020 Shared Task on Parsing into Enhanced Universal Dependencies*, pages 151–161, Online. Association for Computational Linguistics.

Gosse Bouma, Djamé Seddah, and Daniel Zeman. 2021. From raw text to enhanced universal dependencies: The parsing shared task at iwpt 2021. In *Proceedings of the 17th International Conference on Parsing Technologies (IWPT 2021)*, pages 146–157, Bangkok, Thailand (online). Association for Computational Linguistics.

Alexis Conneau, Kartikay Khandelwal, Naman Goyal, Vishrav Chaudhary, Guillaume Wenzek, Francisco Guzmán, Edouard Grave, Myle Ott, Luke Zettlemoyer, and Veselin Stoyanov. 2020. Unsupervised cross-lingual representation learning at scale. In *Proceedings of the 58th Annual Meeting of the Association for Computational Linguistics*, pages 8440–8451, Online. Association for Computational Linguistics.

Mathieu Dehouck, Mark Anderson, and Carlos Gómez-Rodríguez. 2020. Efficient EUD parsing. In *Proceedings of the 16th International Conference on Parsing Technologies and the IWPT 2020 Shared Task on Parsing into Enhanced Universal Dependencies*, pages 192–205, Online. Association for Computational Linguistics.

Jacob Devlin, Ming-Wei Chang, Kenton Lee, and Kristina Toutanova. 2019. BERT: Pre-training of deep bidirectional transformers for language understanding. In *Proceedings of the 2019 Conference of the North American Chapter of the Association for Computational Linguistics: Human Language Technologies, Volume 1 (Long and Short Papers)*, pages 4171–4186, Minneapolis, Minnesota. Association for Computational Linguistics.

Timothy Dozat and Christopher D. Manning. 2016. Deep biaffine attention for neural dependency parsing. *CoRR*, abs/1611.01734.

Timothy Dozat and Christopher D. Manning. 2018. Simpler but more accurate semantic dependency parsing. In *Proceedings of the 56th Annual Meeting of the Association for Computational Linguistics (Volume 2: Short Papers)*, pages 484–490, Melbourne, Australia. Association for Computational Linguistics.

Chris Dyer, Miguel Ballesteros, Wang Ling, Austin Matthews, and Noah A. Smith. 2015. Transition-based dependency parsing with stack long short-term memory. In *Proceedings of the 53rd Annual Meeting of the Association for Computational Linguistics and the 7th International Joint Conference on Natural Language Processing (Volume 1: Long Papers)*, pages 334–343, Beijing, China. Association for Computational Linguistics.

Adam Ek and Jean-Philippe Bernardy. 2020. How much of enhanced UD is contained in UD? In *Proceedings of the 16th International Conference on Parsing Technologies and the IWPT 2020 Shared Task on Parsing into Enhanced Universal Dependencies*, pages 221–226, Online. Association for Computational Linguistics.

Stefan Grünewald and Annemarie Friedrich. 2020. RobertNLP at the IWPT 2020 shared task: Surprisingly simple enhanced UD parsing for English. In *Proceedings of the 16th International Conference on Parsing Technologies and the IWPT 2020 Shared Task on Parsing into Enhanced Universal Dependencies*, pages 245–252, Online. Association for Computational Linguistics.

Han He and Jinho D. Choi. 2020. Adaptation of multilingual transformer encoder for robust enhanced Universal Dependency parsing. In *Proceedings of the 16th International Conference on Parsing Technologies and the IWPT 2020 Shared Task on Parsing into Enhanced Universal Dependencies*, pages 181–191, Online. Association for Computational Linguistics.

Daniel Hershcovich, Miryam de Lhoneux, Artur Kulmizev, Elham Pejhan, and Joakim Nivre. 2020. Køpsala: Transition-based graph parsing via efficient training and effective encoding. In *Proceedings of the 16th International Conference on Parsing Technologies and the IWPT 2020 Shared Task on Parsing into Enhanced Universal Dependencies*, pages 236–244, Online. Association for Computational Linguistics.

Jenna Kanerva, Filip Ginter, and Sampo Pyysalo. 2020. Turku enhanced parser pipeline: From raw text to enhanced graphs in the IWPT 2020 shared task. In *Proceedings of the 16th International Conference on Parsing Technologies and the IWPT 2020 Shared Task on Parsing into Enhanced Universal Dependencies*, pages 162–173, Online. Association for Computational Linguistics.

Eliyahu Kiperwasser and Yoav Goldberg. 2016. Simple and accurate dependency parsing using bidirectional LSTM feature representations. *Transactions of the Association for Computational Linguistics*, 4:313–327.

Dan Kondratyuk and Milan Straka. 2019. 75 languages, 1 model: Parsing Universal Dependencies universally. In *Proceedings of the 2019 Conference on Empirical Methods in Natural Language Processing and the 9th International Joint Conference on Natural Language Processing (EMNLP-IJCNLP)*, pages 2779–2795, Hong Kong, China. Association for Computational Linguistics.

Matthias Lindemann, Jonas Groschwitz, and Alexander Koller. 2019. Compositional semantic parsing across graphbanks. In *Proceedings of the 57th Annual Meeting of the Association for Computational Linguistics*, pages 4576–4585, Florence, Italy. Association for Computational Linguistics.

Yinhan Liu, Myle Ott, Naman Goyal, Jingfei Du, Mandar Joshi, Danqi Chen, Omer Levy, Mike Lewis, Luke Zettlemoyer, and Veselin Stoyanov. 2019. Roberta: A robustly optimized bert pretraining approach.

Marie-Catherine de Marneffe, Bill MacCartney, and Christopher D. Manning. 2006. Generating typed dependency parses from phrase structure trees. In *LREC*.

Minh Van Nguyen, Viet Dac Lai, Amir Pouran Ben Veyseh, and Thien Huu Nguyen. 2021. Trankit: A light-weight transformer-based toolkit for multilingual natural language processing. In *Proceedings of the 16th Conference of the European Chapter of the Association for Computational Linguistics: System Demonstrations*, pages 80–90, Online. Association for Computational Linguistics.

Joakim Nivre, Paola Marongiu, Filip Ginter, Jenna Kanerva, Simonetta Montemagni, Sebastian Schuster, and Maria Simi. 2018. Enhancing Universal Dependency treebanks: A case study. In *Proceedings of the Second Workshop on Universal Dependencies (UDW 2018)*, pages 102–107, Brussels, Belgium. Association for Computational Linguistics.

Stephan Oepen, Omri Abend, Jan Hajic, Daniel Hershcovich, Marco Kuhlmann, Tim O'Gorman, Nianwen Xue, Jayeol Chun, Milan Straka, and Zdenka Uresova. 2019. MRP 2019: Cross-framework meaning representation parsing. In *Proceedings of the Shared Task on Cross-Framework Meaning Representation Parsing at the 2019 Conference on Natural Language Learning*, pages 1–27, Hong Kong. Association for Computational Linguistics.

Peng Qi, Yuhao Zhang, Yuhui Zhang, Jason Bolton, and Christopher D. Manning. 2020. Stanza: A python natural language processing toolkit for many human languages. In *Proceedings of the 58th Annual Meeting of the Association for Computational Linguistics: System Demonstrations*, pages 101–108, Online. Association for Computational Linguistics.

Sebastian Schuster and Christopher D. Manning. 2016. Enhanced English Universal Dependencies: An improved representation for natural language understanding tasks. In *Proceedings of the Tenth International Conference on Language Resources and Evaluation (LREC'16)*, pages 2371–2378, Portorož, Slovenia. European Language Resources Association (ELRA).

Milan Straka and Jana Straková. 2017. Tokenizing, POS tagging, lemmatizing and parsing UD 2.0 with UDPipe. In *Proceedings of the CoNLL 2017 Shared Task: Multilingual Parsing from Raw Text to Universal Dependencies*, pages 88–99, Vancouver, Canada. Association for Computational Linguistics.

Milan Straka and Jana Straková. 2019. ÚFAL MRPipe at MRP 2019: UDPipe goes semantic in the meaning representation parsing shared task. In *Proceedings of the Shared Task on Cross-Framework Meaning Representation Parsing at the 2019 Conference on Natural Language Learning*, pages 127–137, Hong Kong. Association for Computational Linguistics.

Ashish Vaswani, Noam Shazeer, Niki Parmar, Jakob Uszkoreit, Llion Jones, Aidan N Gomez, Ł ukasz Kaiser, and Illia Polosukhin. 2017. Attention is all you need. In *Advances in Neural Information Processing Systems*, volume 30. Curran Associates, Inc.

Xinyu Wang, Yong Jiang, and Kewei Tu. 2020. Enhanced Universal Dependency parsing with second-order inference and mixture of training data. In *Proceedings of the 16th International Conference on Parsing Technologies and the IWPT 2020 Shared Task on Parsing into Enhanced Universal Dependencies*, pages 215–220, Online. Association for Computational Linguistics.

Yonghui Wu, Mike Schuster, Zhifeng Chen, Quoc V. Le, Mohammad Norouzi, Wolfgang Macherey, Maxim Krikun, Yuan Cao, Qin Gao, Klaus Macherey, Jeff Klingner, Apurva Shah, Melvin Johnson, Xiaobing Liu, Łukasz Kaiser, Stephan Gouws, Yoshikiyo Kato, Taku Kudo, Hideto Kazawa, Keith Stevens, George Kurian, Nishant Patil, Wei Wang, Cliff Young, Jason Smith, Jason Riesa, Alex Rudnick, Oriol Vinyals, Greg Corrado, Macduff Hughes, and Jeffrey Dean. 2016. Google's neural machine translation system: Bridging the gap between human and machine translation.

TGIF: Tree-Graph Integrated-Format Parser for Enhanced UD with Two-Stage Generic- to Individual-Language Finetuning

Tianze Shi
Cornell University
tianze@cs.cornell.edu

Lillian Lee
Cornell University
llee@cs.cornell.edu

Abstract

We present our contribution to the IWPT 2021 shared task on parsing into enhanced Universal Dependencies. Our main system component is a hybrid tree-graph parser that integrates (a) predictions of spanning trees for the enhanced graphs with (b) additional graph edges not present in the spanning trees. We also adopt a finetuning strategy where we first train a language-generic parser on the concatenation of data from all available languages, and then, in a second step, finetune on each individual language separately. Additionally, we develop our own complete set of pre-processing modules relevant to the shared task, including tokenization, sentence segmentation, and multiword token expansion, based on pre-trained XLM-R models and our own pre-training of character-level language models. Our submission reaches a macro-average ELAS of 89.24 on the test set. It ranks top among all teams, with a margin of more than 2 absolute ELAS over the next best-performing submission, and best score on 16 out of 17 languages.

1 Introduction

The Universal Dependencies (UD; Nivre et al., 2016, 2020) initiative aims to provide cross-linguistically consistent annotations for dependency-based syntactic analysis, and includes a large collection of treebanks (202 for 114 languages in UD 2.8). Progress on the UD parsing problem has been steady (Zeman et al., 2017, 2018), but existing approaches mostly focus on parsing into *basic* UD trees, where bilexical dependency relations among surface words must form single-rooted trees. While these trees indeed contain rich syntactic information, the adherence to tree representations can be insufficient for certain constructions including coordination, gapping, relative clauses, and argument sharing through control and raising (Schuster and Manning, 2016).

The IWPT 2020 (Bouma et al., 2020) and 2021 (Bouma et al., 2021) shared tasks focus on parsing into *enhanced* UD format, where the representation is connected graphs, rather than rooted trees. The extension from trees to graphs allows direct treatment of a wider range of syntactic phenomena, but it also poses a research challenge: how to design parsers suitable for such enhanced UD graphs.

To address this setting, we propose to use a tree-graph hybrid parser leveraging the following key observation: since an enhanced UD graph must be connected, it must contain a spanning tree as a subgraph. These spanning trees may differ from basic UD trees, but still allow us to use existing techniques developed for dependency parsing, including applying algorithms for finding maximum spanning trees to serve as accurate global decoders. Any additional dependency relations in the enhanced graphs not appearing in the spanning trees are then predicted on a per-edge basis. We find that this tree-graph hybrid approach results in more accurate predictions compared to a dependency graph parser that is combined with postprocessing steps to fix any graph connectivity issues.

Besides the enhanced graphs, the shared task setting poses two additional challenges. Firstly, the evaluation is on 17 languages from 4 language families, and not all the languages have large collections of annotated data: the lowest-resource language, Tamil, contains merely 400 training sentences — more than two magnitudes smaller than what is available for Czech. To facilitate knowledge sharing between high-resource and low-resource languages, we develop a two-stage finetuning strategy: we first train a language-generic model on the concatenation of all available training treebanks from all languages provided by the shared task, and then finetune on each language individually.

Secondly, the shared task demands parsing from raw text. This requires accurate text processing

Proceedings of the 17th International Conference on Parsing Technologies (IWPT 2021), pages 213–224
Bangkok, Thailand (online), August 6, 2021. ©2021 Association for Computational Linguistics

pipelines including modules for tokenization, sentence splitting, and multi-word token expansion, in addition to enhanced UD parsing. We build our own models for all these components; notably, we pre-train character-level masked language models on Wikipedia data, leading to improvements on tokenization, the first component in the text processing pipeline. Our multi-word token expanders combine the strengths of pre-trained learning-based models and rule-based approaches, and achieve robust results, especially on low-resource languages.

Our system submission integrates the aforementioned solutions to the three main challenges given by the shared task, and ranks top among all submissions, with a macro-average EULAS of 90.16 and ELAS of 89.24. Our system gives the best evaluation scores on all languages except for Arabic, and has large margins (more than 5 absolute ELAS) over the second-best systems on Tamil and Lithuanian, which are among languages with the smallest training treebanks.

2 TGIF: Tree-Graph Integrated-Format Parser for Enhanced UD

2.1 Tree and Graph Representations for Enhanced UD

The basic syntactic layer in UD is a single-rooted labeled dependency tree for each sentence, whereas the enhanced UD layer only requires that the set of dependency edges for each sentence form a connected graph. In these connected graphs, each word may have multiple parents, there may be multiple roots for a sentence, and the graphs may contain cycles, but there must exist one path from at least one of the roots to each node.[1]

Accompanying the increase in expressiveness of the enhanced UD representation is the challenge to produce structures that correctly satisfy graph-connectivity constraints during model inference. We summarize the existing solutions proposed for the previous run of the shared task at IWPT 2020 (Bouma et al., 2020) into four main categories:

- *Tree-based*: since the overlap between the enhanced UD graphs and the basic UD trees are typically significant, and any deviations tend to be localized and tied to one of several certain syntactic constructions (e.g, argument sharing in a control structure), one can repurpose tree-based parsers for producing enhanced UD graphs. This category of approaches include packing the additional edges from an enhanced graph into the basic tree (Kanerva et al., 2020) and using either rule-based or learning-based approaches to convert a basic UD tree into an enhanced UD graph (Heinecke, 2020; Dehouck et al., 2020; Attardi et al., 2020; Ek and Bernardy, 2020).[2]
- *Graph-based*: alternatively, one can directly focus on the enhanced UD graph with a semantic dependency graph parser that predicts the existence and label of each candidate dependency edge. But there is generally no guarantee that the set of predicted edges will form a connected graph, so a post-processing step is typically employed to fix any connectivity issues. This category of approaches includes the work of Wang et al. (2020), Barry et al. (2020), and Grünewald and Friedrich (2020).[3]
- *Transition-based*: Hershcovich et al. (2020) adapt a transition-based solution. Their system explicitly handles empty nodes through a specialized transition for inserting them; it relies on additional post-processing to ensure connectivity.
- *Tree-Graph Integrated*: He and Choi (2020) integrate a tree parser and a graph parser,[4] where the tree parser produces the basic UD tree, and the graph parser predicts any additional edges. During inference, all nodes are automatically connected through the tree parser, and the graph parser allows flexibility in producing graph structures.[5]

The tree-based approaches are prone to error propagation, since the predictions of the enhanced layer rely heavily on the accuracy of basic UD tree parsing. The graph-based and transition-based approaches natively produce graph structures, but they require post-processing to ensure connectivity. Our system is a tree-graph integrated-format parser that combines the strengths of the available global inference algorithms for tree parsing and the flexibility of a graph parser, without the need to use post-processing to fix connectivity issues.

[1]Enhanced UD graphs additionally allow insertion of phonologically-empty nodes to recover elided elements in gapping constructions. This is currently beyond the scope our system and we use pre- and post-processing collapsing steps to handle empty nodes (§5).

[2]The same idea has also been applied to the task of conjunction propagation prediction (e.g., Grünewald et al., 2021).

[3]Barry et al.'s (2020) parsers use basic UD trees as features, but the output space is not restricted by the basic trees.

[4]He and Choi (2020) describe their combo as an "ensemble" but we prefer the term "integration" for both their method and ours (which is inspired by theirs), since the two components are not, strictly speaking, targeting same structures.

[5]The main difference from the tree-based approaches is that the search space for additional graph edges is unaffected by the predictions of basic UD trees in an integrated approach.

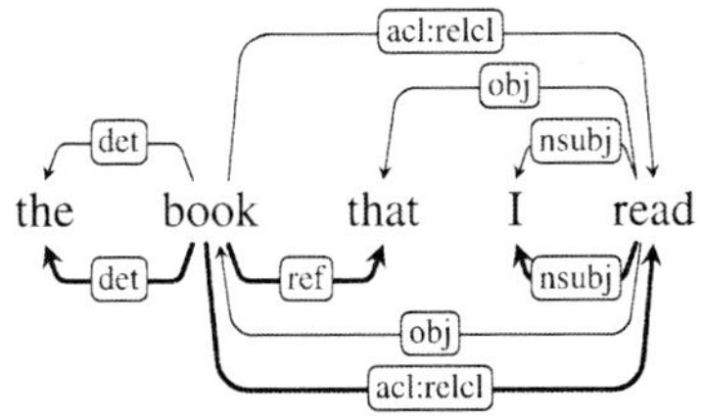

Figure 1: An example with basic UD and enhanced UD annotations above and below the text respectively. The extracted spanning tree (§2.2) is bolded and is different from the basic UD tree.

2.2 Spanning Tree Extraction

A connected graph must contain a spanning tree, and conversely, if we first predict a spanning tree over all nodes, and subsequently add additional edges, then the resulting graph remains connected. Indeed, this property is leveraged in some previously-proposed connectivity post-processing steps (e.g., Wang et al., 2020), but extracting a spanning tree based on scores from graph-prediction models creates a mismatch between training and inference. He and Choi (2020) instead train tree parsers and graph parsers separately and combine their prediction during inference, but their tree parsers are trained on basic UD trees whose edges are not always present in the enhanced UD layer.

Our solution refines He and Choi's (2020) approach: we train tree parsers to predict spanning trees extracted from the enhanced UD graphs, instead of basic UD trees, to minimize train-test mismatch. See Figure 1 for an example. Spanning tree extraction is in essence assignment of unique head nodes to all nodes in a graph, subject to tree constraints. For consistent extraction, we apply the following rules:

- If a node has a unique head in the enhanced graph, there is no ambiguity in head assignment.
- If a basic UD edge is present among the set of incoming edges to a given node, include that basic UD edge in the spanning tree.
- Otherwise, there must be multiple incoming edges, none of which are present in the basic UD tree. We pick the parent node that is the "highest", i.e., the closest to the root node, in the basic tree.

The above head assignment steps do not formally guarantee that the extracted structures will be trees, but empirically, we observe that the extraction results are indeed trees for all training sentences.[6]

2.3 Parameterization

Our parser architecture is adapted from that of Dozat and Manning (2017, 2018), which forms the basis for the prior graph-based approaches in the IWPT 2020 shared task. We predict unlabeled edges and labels separately, and for the unlabeled edges, we use a combination of a tree parser and a graph-edge prediction module.

Representation The first step is to extract contextual representations. For this purpose, we use the pre-trained XLM-R model (Conneau et al., 2020), which is trained on multilingual CommonCrawl data and supports all 17 languages in the shared task. The XLM-R feature extractor is finetuned along with model training. Given a length-n input sentence $x = x_1, \ldots, x_n$ and layer l, we extract

$$[\mathbf{x}_0^l, \mathbf{x}_1^l, \ldots, \mathbf{x}_n^l] = \texttt{XLM-R}^l(\texttt{<s>}, x_1, \ldots, x_n, \texttt{</s>}),$$

where inputs to the XLM-R model are a concatenated sequence of word pieces from each UD word, we denote the layer-l vector corresponding to the last word piece in the word x_i as $\mathbf{x}_i^l$, and the dummy root representations $\mathbf{x}_0$s are taken from the special <s> token at the beginning of the sequence.

Deep Biaffine Function All our parsing components use deep biaffine functions (DBFs), which score the interactions between pairs of words:

$$\begin{aligned}\text{DBF}(i, j) =& \mathbf{v}_i^{\text{head}\top} U \mathbf{v}_j^{\text{mod}} + \mathbf{b}^{\text{head}} \cdot \mathbf{v}_i^{\text{head}} \\ &+ \mathbf{b}^{\text{mod}} \cdot \mathbf{v}_j^{\text{mod}} + b,\end{aligned}$$

where $\mathbf{v}_i^{\text{head}}$ and $\mathbf{v}_j^{\text{mod}}$ are non-linearly transformed vectors from weighted average XLM-R vectors across different layers:

$$\mathbf{v}_i^{\text{head}} = \text{ReLU}\left(W^{\text{head}} \sum_l \frac{e^{\alpha_l^{\text{head}}}}{\sum_{l'} e^{\alpha_{l'}^{\text{head}}}} \mathbf{x}_i^l\right),$$

and $\mathbf{v}_j^{\text{mod}}$ is defined similarly. Each DBF has its own trainable weight matrices U, W^{head}, and W^{mod}, vectors $\mathbf{b}^{\text{head}}$ and $\mathbf{b}^{\text{mod}}$, and scalars b, $\{\alpha_l^{\text{head}}\}$ and $\{\alpha_l^{\text{mod}}\}$.

Tree Parser To estimate the probabilities of head attachment for each token w_j, we define

$$P(\text{head}(w_j) = w_i) = \text{softmax}_i(\text{DBF}^{\text{tree}}(i, j)).$$

The tree parsing models are trained with cross-entropy loss, and we use a non-projective maximum spanning tree algorithm (Chu and Liu, 1965; Edmonds, 1967) for global inference.

[6]Dear Reviewer 1: your question here in the submitted paper caused us to uncover a bug! Fixing it rectified the 4 training sentences that weren't originally getting trees.

Language	Direct Training		Generic	Finetuned
	Graph+Fix	Tree-Graph		
Arabic	80.34	80.30	80.57	**80.63**
Bulgarian	91.81	92.00	91.69	**92.30**
Czech	92.93	**92.98**	92.94	**92.98**
Dutch	92.14	92.13	92.03	**92.21**
English	88.38	88.51	88.44	**88.83**
Estonian	**89.53**	89.42	89.22	89.40
Finnish	91.97	92.10	91.84	**92.48**
French	94.46	94.51	94.26	**95.52**
Italian	93.04	93.24	93.26	**93.41**
Latvian	88.47	88.42	88.38	**89.78**
Lithuanian	90.57	90.63	90.47	**90.85**
Polish	91.28	91.48	91.28	**91.63**
Russian	93.47	**93.50**	93.37	93.47
Slovak	93.70	93.83	94.00	**95.44**
Swedish	90.35	90.48	90.33	**91.57**
Tamil	66.24	66.82	67.35	**68.95**
Ukrainian	92.98	92.94	93.24	**93.89**
Average	89.51	89.61	89.57	**90.20**

Table 1: Dev-set ELAS (%) results, comparing graph parsers with connectivity-fixing postprocessing against tree-graph integrated models (§2) and comparing parsers trained directly on each language, generic-language parsers, and parsers finetuned on individual languages from the generic-language checkpoint (§3).

Graph Parser In addition to the spanning trees, we make independent predictions on the existence of any extra edges in the enhanced UD graphs by

$$P(\exists \text{edge } w_i \to w_j) = \text{sigmoid}(\text{DBF}^{\text{graph}}(i, j)).$$

We train the graph parsing model with a cross entropy objective, and during inference, any edges with probabilities ≥ 0.5 are included in the outputs.

Relation Labeler For each edge in the unlabeled graph, we predict the relation label via

$$P(\text{lbl}(w_i \to w_j) = r) = \text{softmax}_r(\text{DBF}^{\text{rel-}r}(i, j)),$$

where we have as many deep biaffine functions as the number of candidate relation labels in the data. To reduce the large number of potential labels due to lexicalization, the relation labeler operates on a de-lexicalized version of the labels, and then a re-lexicalization step expands the predicted labels into their full forms (§5).

Training The above three components are separately parameterized, and during training, we optimize for the sum of their corresponding cross-entropy loss functions.

2.4 Empirical Comparisons

In Table 1, we compare our tree-graph integrated-format parser with a fully graph-based approach. The graph-based baseline uses the same feature extractor, graph parser, and relation labeler modules, but it omits the tree parser for producing spanning trees, and we apply post-processing steps to ensure connectivity of the output graphs. Our tree-graph integrated-format parser outperforms the graph-based baseline on 12 out of the 17 test languages (binomial test, $p = 0.07$).

3 TGIF: Two-Stage Generic- to Individual-Language Finetuning

In addition to the tree-graph integration approach, our system submission also features a two-stage finetuning strategy. We first train a language-generic model on the concatenation of all available training treebanks in the shared task data regardless of their source languages, and then finetune on each individual language in a second step.

This two-stage finetuning strategy is designed to encourage knowledge sharing across different languages, especially from high-resource languages to lower-resource ones. In our experiment results as reported in Table 1, we find that this strategy is indeed beneficial for the majority of languages, especially those with small training corpora (e.g., 2.13 and 1.01 absolute ELAS improvements on Tamil and French respectively), though this comes at the price of slightly decreased accuracies on high-resource languages (e.g., -0.02 on Estonian and -0.03 on Russian). Additionally, we find that the language-generic model achieves reasonably competitive performance when compared with the set of models directly trained on each individual language. This suggests that practitioners may opt to use a single model for parsing all languages if there is a need to lower disk and memory footprints, without much loss in accuracy.

4 Pre-TGIF: Pre-Training Grants Improvements Full-Stack

Inspired by the recent success of pre-trained language models on a wide range of NLP tasks (Peters et al., 2018; Devlin et al., 2019; Conneau et al., 2020, *inter alia*), we build our own text processing pipeline based on pre-trained language models. Due to limited time and resources, we only focus on components relevant to the shared task, which include tokenization, sentence splitting, and multi-word token (MWT) expansion.

4.1 Tokenizers with Character-Level Masked Language Model Pre-Training

We follow state-of-the-art strategies (Qi et al., 2020; Nguyen et al., 2021) for tokenization and model the task as a tagging problem on sequences of characters. But in contrast to prior methods where tokenization and sentence segmentation are bundled into the same prediction stage, we tackle tokenization in isolation, and for each character, we make a binary prediction as to whether a token ends at the current character position or not.

An innovation in our tokenization is that we fine-tune character-based language models trained on Wikipedia data. In contrast, existing approaches typically use randomly-initialized models (Qi et al., 2020) or use pre-trained models on subword units instead of characters (Nguyen et al., 2021).

We follow Devlin et al. (2019) and pre-train our character-level sequence models using a masked language modeling objective: during training, we randomly replace 15% of the characters with a special mask symbol and the models are trained to predict the identity of those characters in the original texts. Due to computational resource constraints, we adopt a small-sized architecture based on simple recurrent units (Lei et al., 2018).[7] We pre-train our models on Wikipedia data[8] and each model takes roughly 2 days to complete 500k optimization steps on a single GTX 2080Ti GPU.

4.2 Sentence Splitters

We split texts into sentences from sequences of tokens instead of characters (Qi et al., 2020). Our approach resembles that of Nguyen et al. (2021).[9] This allows our models to condense information from a wider range of contexts while still reading the same number of input symbols. The sentence splitters are trained to make binary predictions at each token position on whether a sentence ends there. We adopt the same two-stage finetuning strategy as for our parsing modules based on pre-trained XLM-R feature extractors (§3).

4.3 Multi-Word Token (MWT) Expanders

The UD annotations distinguish between tokens and words. A word corresponds to a consecutive sequence of characters in the surface raw text and may contain one or more syntactically-functioning words. We break down the MWT expansion task into first deciding whether or not to expand a given token and then performing the actual expansion. For the former, we train models to make a binary prediction on each token, and we use pre-trained XLM-R models as our feature extractors.

For the MWT expansion step once the tokens are identified through our classifiers, we use a combination of lexicon- and rule-based approaches. If the token form is seen in the training data, we adopt the most frequently used way to split it into multiple words. Otherwise, we invoke a set of language-specific handwritten rules developed from and tuned on the training data; a typical rule iteratively splits off an identified prefix or suffix from the remainder of the token.

4.4 Lemmatizers

While the shared task requires lemmatized forms for constructing the lexicalized enhanced UD labels, we only need to predict lemmas for a small percentage of words. Empirically, these words tend to be function words and have a unique lemma per word type. Thus, we use a full lexicon-based approach to (incomplete) lemmatization. Whenever a lemma is needed during the label re-lexicalization step, we look the word up in a dictionary extracted from the training data.

4.5 Evaluation

We compare our text-processing pipeline components with two state-of-the-art toolkits, Stanza (Qi et al., 2020) and Trankit (Nguyen et al., 2021) in Table 2. We train our models per-language instead of per-treebank to accommodate the shared task setting, so our models are at a disadvantage when there are multiple training treebanks for a language that have different tokenization/sentence splitting conventions (e.g., English-EWT and English-GUM handle word contractions differently). Despite this, our models are highly competitive in terms of tokenization and MWT expansion, and we achieve significantly better sentence segmentation results across most treebanks. We hypothesize that a sequence-to-sequence MWT expansion approach, similar to the ones underlying Stanza and Trankit,

[7] Simple recurrent units are a fast variant of recurrent neural networks. In our preliminary experiments, they result in lower accuracies than long-short term memory networks (LSTMs), but are 2-5 times faster, depending on sequence lengths.

[8] We extract Wikipedia texts using WikiExtractor (Attardi, 2015) from Wikipedia dumps dated 2021-04-01.

[9] An important difference is that our sentence splitters are aware of token boundaries and the models are restricted from making token-internal sentence splitting decisions.

Treebank	Token			Sentence			Word		
	Stanza	Trankit	Ours	Stanza	Trankit	Ours	Stanza	Trankit	Ours
Arabic-PADT	99.98	99.95	**99.99**	80.43	96.79	**96.87**	97.88	**99.39**	98.70
Bulgarian-BTB	99.93	99.78	**99.95**	97.27	98.79	**99.06**	99.93	99.78	**99.95**
Czech-FicTree	99.97	**99.98**	99.97	98.60	99.50	**99.54**	99.96	**99.98**	99.96
Czech-CAC	**99.99**	**99.99**	**99.99**	**100.00**	**100.00**	**100.00**	99.97	99.98	**99.99**
Dutch-Alpino	**99.96**	99.43	99.86	89.98	90.65	**94.45**	**99.96**	99.43	99.86
Dutch-LassySmall	99.90	99.36	**99.94**	77.95	92.60	**94.23**	99.90	99.36	**99.94**
English-EWT	**99.01**	98.67	98.79	81.13	90.49	**92.70**	**99.01**	98.67	98.79
English-GUM	**99.82**	99.52	98.88	86.35	91.60	**95.11**	**99.82**	99.52	99.18
Estonian-EDT	**99.96**	99.75	99.95	93.32	96.58	**96.60**	**99.96**	99.75	99.95
Estonian-EWT	**99.20**	97.76	98.72	67.14	82.58	**89.37**	**99.20**	97.76	98.72
Finnish-TDT	**99.77**	99.71	99.76	93.05	97.22	**98.26**	**99.73**	99.72	**99.73**
French-Sequoia	**99.90**	99.81	99.88	88.79	94.07	**96.82**	99.58	99.78	**99.84**
Italian-ISDT	**99.91**	99.88	99.90	98.76	**99.07**	**99.07**	99.76	**99.86**	99.83
Latvian-LVTB	**99.82**	99.73	99.80	99.01	98.69	**99.26**	**99.82**	99.73	99.80
Lithuanian-ALKSNIS	99.87	99.84	**99.99**	88.79	95.72	**96.22**	99.87	99.84	**99.99**
Polish-LFG	**99.95**	98.34	99.84	99.83	99.57	**99.88**	**99.95**	98.34	99.89
Polish-PDB	99.87	**99.93**	99.49	98.39	98.71	**99.66**	99.83	**99.92**	99.84
Russian-SynTagRus	99.57	99.71	**99.73**	98.86	99.45	**99.54**	99.57	99.71	**99.73**
Slovak-SNK	**99.97**	99.94	99.95	90.93	**98.49**	96.72	**99.97**	99.94	99.94
Swedish-Talbanken	**99.97**	99.91	**99.97**	98.85	99.26	**99.34**	**99.97**	99.91	**99.97**
Tamil-TTB	99.58	98.33	**99.63**	95.08	**100.00**	**100.00**	91.42	94.44	**95.34**
Ukrainian-IU	99.81	99.77	**99.86**	96.65	97.55	**98.38**	99.79	99.76	**99.84**

Table 2: Test-set F1 scores for tokenization, sentence segmentation, and MWT expansion, comparing Stanza (Qi et al., 2020), Trankit (Nguyen et al., 2021), and our system submission. Our system results are from the shared task official evaluations; Stanza and Trankit results are reported in the Trankit documentation with models trained on UD 2.5. *Caveat*: the results may not be strictly comparable due to treebank version mismatch.

may provide further gains to morphologically-rich languages that cannot be sufficiently modeled via handwritten rules, notably Arabic.

5 Other Technical Notes

Hyperparameters We report our hyperparameters in the Appendix.

Empty nodes Enhanced UD graphs may contain empty nodes in addition to the words in the surface form. Our parser does not support empty nodes, so we follow the official evaluation practice and collapse relation paths with empty nodes into composite relations during training and inference.

Multiple relations In some cases, there can be multiple relations between the same pair of words. We follow Wang et al. (2020) and merge all these relations into a composite label, and re-expand them during inference.

De-lexicalization and re-lexicalization Certain types of relation labels include lexicalized information, resulting in a large relation label set. For example, nmod:in contains a lemma "in" that is taken from the modifier with a case relation. To combat this, we follow Grünewald and Friedrich's (2020) strategy and replace the lemmas[10] with placeholders consisting of their corresponding relation labels. The previous example would result in a delexicalized label of nmod:[case]. During inference, we apply a re-lexicalization step to reconstruct the original full relation labels given our predicted graphs. We discard the lexicalized portions of the relation labels when errors occur either in de-lexicalization (unable to locate the source child labels to match the lemmas) or re-lexicalization (unable to find corresponding placeholder relations).

Sequence length limit Pre-trained language models typically have a limit on their input sequence lengths. The `XLM-R` model has a limit of 512 word pieces. For a small number of sentences longer than that, we discard word-internal word pieces, i.e., keep a prefix and a suffix of word pieces, of the longest words to fit within limit.

Multiple Treebanks Per Language Each language in the shared task can have one or more treebanks for training and/or testing. During evaluation, there is no explicit information regarding the source treebank of the piece of input text. Instead of handpicking a training treebank for each

[10]We find that using lemmas instead of word forms significantly improves coverage of the lexicalized labels.

Language	combo	dcu_epfl	fastparse	grew	nuig	robertnlp	shanghaitech	tgif (Ours)	unipi
Arabic	76.39	71.01	53.74	71.13	–	81.58	**82.26**	81.23	77.13
Bulgarian	86.67	92.44	78.73	88.83	78.45	93.16	92.52	**93.63**	90.84
Czech	89.08	89.93	72.85	87.66	–	90.21	91.78	**92.24**	88.73
Dutch	87.07	81.89	68.89	84.09	–	88.37	88.64	**91.78**	84.14
English	84.09	85.70	73.00	85.49	65.40	87.88	87.27	**88.19**	87.11
Estonian	84.02	84.35	60.05	78.19	54.03	86.55	86.66	**88.38**	81.27
Finnish	87.28	89.02	57.71	85.20	–	91.01	90.81	**91.75**	89.62
French	87.32	86.68	73.18	83.33	–	88.51	88.40	**91.63**	87.43
Italian	90.40	92.41	78.32	90.98	–	93.28	92.88	**93.31**	91.81
Latvian	84.57	86.96	66.43	77.45	56.67	88.82	89.17	**90.23**	83.01
Lithuanian	79.75	78.04	48.27	74.62	59.13	80.76	80.87	**86.06**	71.31
Polish	87.65	89.17	71.52	78.20	–	89.78	90.66	**91.46**	88.31
Russian	90.73	92.83	78.56	90.56	66.33	92.64	93.59	**94.01**	90.90
Slovak	87.04	89.59	64.28	86.92	67.45	89.66	90.25	**94.96**	86.05
Swedish	83.20	85.20	67.26	81.54	63.12	88.03	86.62	**89.90**	84.91
Tamil	52.27	39.32	42.53	58.69	–	59.33	58.94	**65.58**	51.73
Ukrainian	86.92	86.09	63.42	83.90	–	88.86	88.94	**92.78**	87.51
Average	83.79	83.57	65.81	81.58	–	86.97	87.07	**89.24**	83.64
Rank	4	6	8	7	9	3	2	1	5

Table 3: Official ELAS (%) evaluation results. Our submission ranks first on 16 out of the 17 languages.

language, we simple train and validate on the concatenation of all available data for each language.

Training on a single GPU The XLM-R model has large number of parameters, which makes it challenging to finetune on a single GPU. We use a batch size of 1 and accumulate gradients across multiple batches to lower the usage of GPU RAM. When this strategy alone is insufficient, e.g., when training the language-generic model, we additionally freeze the initial embedding layer of the model.

6 Official Evaluation

The shared task performs evaluation on UD treebanks that have enhanced UD annotations across 17 languages: Arabic (Hajič et al., 2009), Bulgarian (Simov et al., 2004), Czech (Hladká et al., 2010; Bejček et al., 2013; Jelínek, 2017), Dutch (van der Beek et al., 2002; Bouma and van Noord, 2017), English (Silveira et al., 2014; Zeldes, 2017), Estonian (Muischnek et al., 2014, 2019), Finnish (Haverinen et al., 2014; Pyysalo et al., 2015), French (Candito et al., 2014; Seddah and Candito, 2016), Italian (Bosco et al., 2013), Latvian (Pretkalniņa et al., 2018), Lithuanian (Bielinskienė et al., 2016), Polish (Patejuk and Przepiórkowski, 2018; Wróblewska, 2018), Russian (Droganova et al., 2018), Slovak (Zeman, 2018), Swedish (Nivre and Megyesi, 2007), Tamil (Ramasamy and Žabokrtský, 2012), Ukrainian (Kotsyba et al., 2016), and multilingual parallel treebanks (Zeman et al., 2017).

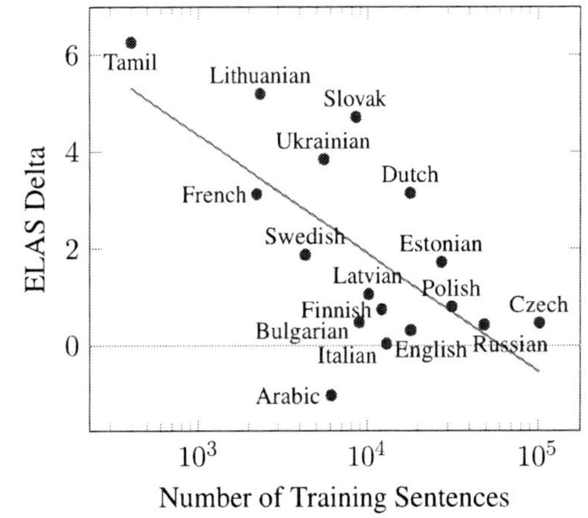

Figure 2: The per-language delta ELAS between our submission and the best performing system other than ours, as a function of (the log of the) number of training sentences. (For Italian, the difference is quite small but still positive.) Our models achieve larger improvements on lower-resource languages.

Table 3 shows the official ELAS evaluation results of all 9 participating systems in the shared task.[11] Our system has the top performance on 16 out of 17 languages, and it is also the best in terms of macro-average across all languages. On average, we outperform the second best system by a margin of more than 2 ELAS points in absolute terms, or more than 15% in relative error reduction.

Figure 2 visualizes the "delta ELAS" between

[11] Reproduced from https://universaldependencies.org/iwpt21/results.html.

our submission and the best result other than ours on a per-language basis, plotted against the training data size for each language. Our system sees larger improvements on lower-resource languages, where we have more than 5-point leads on Tamil and Lithuanian, two languages among those with the smallest number of training sentences.

7 Closing Remarks

Our submission to the IWPT 2021 shared task combines three main techniques: (1) tree-graph integrated-format parsing (graph $\rightarrow$ spanning tree $\rightarrow$ additional edges) (2) two-stage generic-to individual-language finetuning, and (3) pre-processing pipelines powered by language model pre-training. Each of the above contributes to our system performance positively,[12] and by combining all three techniques, our system achieves the best ELAS results on 16 out of 17 languages, as well as top macro-average across all languages, among all system submissions. Additionally, our system shows more relative strengths on lower-resource languages.

Due to time and resource constraints, our system adopts the same set of techniques across all languages and we train a single set of models for our primary submission. We leave it to future work to explore language-specific methods and/or model combination and ensemble techniques to further enhance model accuracies.

Acknowledgements We thank the anonymous reviewers for their constructive and detailed comments, and the task organizers for their flexibility regarding page limits. This work was supported in part by a Bloomberg Data Science Ph.D. Fellowship to Tianze Shi and a gift from Bloomberg to Lillian Lee.

References

Giuseppe Attardi, Daniele Sartiano, and Maria Simi. 2020. Linear neural parsing and hybrid enhancement for enhanced Universal Dependencies. In *Proceedings of the 16th International Conference on Parsing Technologies and the IWPT 2020 Shared Task on Parsing into Enhanced Universal Dependencies*, pages 206–214, Online. Association for Computational Linguistics.

Giusepppe Attardi. 2015. WikiExtractor. `https://github.com/attardi/wikiextractor`.

James Barry, Joachim Wagner, and Jennifer Foster. 2020. The ADAPT enhanced dependency parser at the IWPT 2020 shared task. In *Proceedings of the 16th International Conference on Parsing Technologies and the IWPT 2020 Shared Task on Parsing into Enhanced Universal Dependencies*, pages 227–235, Online. Association for Computational Linguistics.

Eduard Bejček, Eva Hajičová, Jan Hajič, Pavlína Jínová, Václava Kettnerová, Veronika Kolářová, Marie Mikulová, Jiří Mírovský, Anna Nedoluzhko, Jarmila Panevová, Lucie Poláková, Magda Ševčíková, Jan Štěpánek, and Šárka Zikánová. 2013. Prague dependency treebank 3.0.

Agnė Bielinskienė, Loïc Boizou, Jolanta Kovalevskaitė, and Erika Rimkutė. 2016. Lithuanian dependency treebank ALKSNIS. *Human Language Technologies – The Baltic Perspective*, pages 107–114.

Cristina Bosco, Simonetta Montemagni, and Maria Simi. 2013. Converting Italian treebanks: Towards an Italian Stanford dependency treebank. In *Proceedings of the 7th Linguistic Annotation Workshop and Interoperability with Discourse*, pages 61–69, Sofia, Bulgaria. Association for Computational Linguistics.

Gosse Bouma, Djamé Seddah, and Daniel Zeman. 2020. Overview of the IWPT 2020 shared task on parsing into enhanced Universal Dependencies. In *Proceedings of the 16th International Conference on Parsing Technologies and the IWPT 2020 Shared Task on Parsing into Enhanced Universal Dependencies*, pages 151–161, Online. Association for Computational Linguistics.

Gosse Bouma, Djamé Seddah, and Daniel Zeman. 2021. From raw text to enhanced Universal Dependencies: The parsing shared task at IWPT 2021. In *Proceedings of the 17th International Conference on Parsing Technologies (IWPT 2021)*, pages 146–157, Online. Association for Computational Linguistics.

Gosse Bouma and Gertjan van Noord. 2017. Increasing return on annotation investment: The automatic construction of a Universal Dependency treebank for Dutch. In *Proceedings of the NoDaLiDa 2017 Workshop on Universal Dependencies (UDW 2017)*, pages 19–26, Gothenburg, Sweden. Association for Computational Linguistics.

Marie Candito, Guy Perrier, Bruno Guillaume, Corentin Ribeyre, Karën Fort, Djamé Seddah, and Éric de la Clergerie. 2014. Deep Syntax Annotation of the Sequoia French treebank. In *Proceedings of*

[12]Comparing the 3 components: multilingual pre-training has a greater effect than the tree-graph parsing design. Sentence segmentation performance (SSP) doesn't necessarily translate to ELAS, so our SSP's large relative improvement at SS doesn't imply that SS is the biggest contributor to our system.

the Ninth International Conference on Language Resources and Evaluation (LREC-2014), pages 2298–2305, Reykjavik, Iceland. European Languages Resources Association (ELRA).

Yoeng-Jin Chu and Tseng-Hong Liu. 1965. On the shortest arborescence of a directed graph. *Science Sinica*, 14:1396–1400.

Alexis Conneau, Kartikay Khandelwal, Naman Goyal, Vishrav Chaudhary, Guillaume Wenzek, Francisco Guzmán, Edouard Grave, Myle Ott, Luke Zettlemoyer, and Veselin Stoyanov. 2020. Unsupervised cross-lingual representation learning at scale. In *Proceedings of the 58th Annual Meeting of the Association for Computational Linguistics*, pages 8440–8451, Online. Association for Computational Linguistics.

Mathieu Dehouck, Mark Anderson, and Carlos Gómez-Rodríguez. 2020. Efficient EUD parsing. In *Proceedings of the 16th International Conference on Parsing Technologies and the IWPT 2020 Shared Task on Parsing into Enhanced Universal Dependencies*, pages 192–205, Online. Association for Computational Linguistics.

Jacob Devlin, Ming-Wei Chang, Kenton Lee, and Kristina Toutanova. 2019. BERT: Pre-training of deep bidirectional transformers for language understanding. In *Proceedings of the 2019 Conference of the North American Chapter of the Association for Computational Linguistics: Human Language Technologies, Volume 1 (Long and Short Papers)*, pages 4171–4186, Minneapolis, Minnesota. Association for Computational Linguistics.

Timothy Dozat and Christopher D. Manning. 2017. Deep biaffine attention for neural dependency parsing. In *Proceedings of the 5th International Conference on Learning Representations*, Toulon, France. OpenReview.net.

Timothy Dozat and Christopher D. Manning. 2018. Simpler but more accurate semantic dependency parsing. In *Proceedings of the 56th Annual Meeting of the Association for Computational Linguistics (Volume 2: Short Papers)*, pages 484–490, Melbourne, Australia. Association for Computational Linguistics.

Kira Droganova, Olga Lyashevskaya, and Daniel Zeman. 2018. Data conversion and consistency of monolingual corpora: Russian UD treebanks. In *Proceedings of the 17th International Workshop on Treebanks and Linguistic Theories (TLT 2018)*, Oslo, Norway. Linköping University Electronic Press.

Jack Edmonds. 1967. Optimum branchings. *Journal of Research of the National Bureau of Standards*, 71B(4):233–240.

Adam Ek and Jean-Philippe Bernardy. 2020. How much of enhanced UD is contained in UD? In *Proceedings of the 16th International Conference on Parsing Technologies and the IWPT 2020 Shared Task on Parsing into Enhanced Universal Dependencies*, pages 221–226, Online. Association for Computational Linguistics.

Stefan Grünewald and Annemarie Friedrich. 2020. RobertNLP at the IWPT 2020 shared task: Surprisingly simple enhanced UD parsing for English. In *Proceedings of the 16th International Conference on Parsing Technologies and the IWPT 2020 Shared Task on Parsing into Enhanced Universal Dependencies*, pages 245–252, Online. Association for Computational Linguistics.

Stefan Grünewald, Prisca Piccirilli, and Annemarie Friedrich. 2021. Coordinate constructions in English enhanced Universal Dependencies: Analysis and computational modeling. In *Proceedings of the 16th Conference of the European Chapter of the Association for Computational Linguistics: Main Volume*, pages 795–809, Online. Association for Computational Linguistics.

Jan Hajič, Otakar Smrž, Petr Zemánek, Petr Pajas, Jan Šnaidauf, Emanuel Beška, Jakub Kracmar, and Kamila Hassanová. 2009. Prague Arabic dependency treebank 1.0.

Katri Haverinen, Jenna Nyblom, Timo Viljanen, Veronika Laippala, Samuel Kohonen, Anna Missilä, Stina Ojala, Tapio Salakoski, and Filip Ginter. 2014. Building the essential resources for Finnish: The Turku Dependency Treebank. *Language Resources and Evaluation*, 48(3):493–531.

Han He and Jinho D. Choi. 2020. Adaptation of multilingual transformer encoder for robust enhanced universal dependency parsing. In *Proceedings of the 16th International Conference on Parsing Technologies and the IWPT 2020 Shared Task on Parsing into Enhanced Universal Dependencies*, pages 181–191, Online. Association for Computational Linguistics.

Johannes Heinecke. 2020. Hybrid enhanced Universal Dependencies parsing. In *Proceedings of the 16th International Conference on Parsing Technologies and the IWPT 2020 Shared Task on Parsing into Enhanced Universal Dependencies*, pages 174–180, Online. Association for Computational Linguistics.

Daniel Hershcovich, Miryam de Lhoneux, Artur Kulmizev, Elham Pejhan, and Joakim Nivre. 2020. Køpsala: Transition-based graph parsing via efficient training and effective encoding. In *Proceedings of the 16th International Conference on Parsing Technologies and the IWPT 2020 Shared Task on Parsing into Enhanced Universal Dependencies*, pages 236–244, Online. Association for Computational Linguistics.

Barbora Vidová Hladká, Jan Hajič, Jiří Hana, Jaroslava Hlaváčová, Jiří Mírovský, and Jan Raab. 2010. The Czech academic corpus 2.0 guide. *The Prague Bulletin of Mathematical Linguistics*, 89(2008):41–96.

Tomáš Jelínek. 2017. FicTree: A manually annotated treebank of Czech fiction. In *Proceedings of the 17th Conference on Information Technologies - Applications and Theory*, pages 181–185, Martinské Hole, Slovakia.

Jenna Kanerva, Filip Ginter, and Sampo Pyysalo. 2020. Turku enhanced parser pipeline: From raw text to enhanced graphs in the IWPT 2020 shared task. In *Proceedings of the 16th International Conference on Parsing Technologies and the IWPT 2020 Shared Task on Parsing into Enhanced Universal Dependencies*, pages 162–173, Online. Association for Computational Linguistics.

Natalia Kotsyba, Bohdan Moskalevskyi, and Mykhailo Romanenko. 2016. Gold standard Universal Dependencies corpus for Ukrainian. https://github.com/UniversalDependencies/UD_Ukrainian-IU.

Tao Lei, Yu Zhang, Sida I. Wang, Hui Dai, and Yoav Artzi. 2018. Simple recurrent units for highly parallelizable recurrence. In *Proceedings of the 2018 Conference on Empirical Methods in Natural Language Processing*, pages 4470–4481, Brussels, Belgium. Association for Computational Linguistics.

Liyuan Liu, Haoming Jiang, Pengcheng He, Weizhu Chen, Xiaodong Liu, Jianfeng Gao, and Jiawei Han. 2020. On the variance of the adaptive learning rate and beyond. In *Proceedings of the Eighth International Conference on Learning Representations*, Online. OpenReview.net.

Kadri Muischnek, Kaili Müürisep, Tiina Puolakainen, Eleri Aedmaa, Riin Kirt, and Dage Särg. 2014. Estonian dependency treebank and its annotation scheme. In *Proceedings of the 13th Workshop on Treebanks and Linguistic Theories (TLT13)*, pages 285–291, Tübingen, Germany.

Kadri Muischnek, Kaili Müürisep, and Dage Särg. 2019. CG roots of UD treebank of Estonian web language. In *Proceedings of the NoDaLiDa 2019 Workshop on Constraint Grammar-Methods, Tools and Applications*, pages 23–26, Turku, Finland.

Minh Van Nguyen, Viet Dac Lai, Amir Pouran Ben Veyseh, and Thien Huu Nguyen. 2021. Trankit: A light-weight Transformer-based toolkit for multilingual natural language processing. In *Proceedings of the 16th Conference of the European Chapter of the Association for Computational Linguistics: System Demonstrations*, pages 80–90, Online. Association for Computational Linguistics.

Joakim Nivre, Marie-Catherine de Marneffe, Filip Ginter, Yoav Goldberg, Jan Hajič, Christopher D. Manning, Ryan McDonald, Slav Petrov, Sampo Pyysalo, Natalia Silveira, Reut Tsarfaty, and Daniel Zeman. 2016. Universal Dependencies v1: A multilingual treebank collection. In *Proceedings of the Tenth International Conference on Language Resources and Evaluation (LREC'16)*, pages 1659–1666, Portorož, Slovenia. European Language Resources Association.

Joakim Nivre, Marie-Catherine de Marneffe, Filip Ginter, Jan Hajič, Christopher D. Manning, Sampo Pyysalo, Sebastian Schuster, Francis Tyers, and Daniel Zeman. 2020. Universal Dependencies v2: An evergrowing multilingual treebank collection. In *Proceedings of the 12th Language Resources and Evaluation Conference*, pages 4034–4043, Marseille, France. European Language Resources Association.

Joakim Nivre and Beata Megyesi. 2007. Bootstrapping a Swedish treebank using cross-corpus harmonization and annotation projection. In *Proceedings of the 6th International Workshop on Treebanks and Linguistic Theories*, pages 97–102, Bergen, Norway.

Agnieszka Patejuk and Adam Przepiórkowski. 2018. *From Lexical Functional Grammar to Enhanced Universal Dependencies: Linguistically Informed Treebanks of Polish.* Institute of Computer Science, Polish Academy of Sciences, Warsaw.

Matthew Peters, Mark Neumann, Mohit Iyyer, Matt Gardner, Christopher Clark, Kenton Lee, and Luke Zettlemoyer. 2018. Deep contextualized word representations. In *Proceedings of the 2018 Conference of the North American Chapter of the Association for Computational Linguistics: Human Language Technologies, Volume 1 (Long Papers)*, pages 2227–2237, New Orleans, Louisiana. Association for Computational Linguistics.

Lauma Pretkalniņa, Laura Rituma, and Baiba Saulīte. 2018. Deriving enhanced universal dependencies from a hybrid dependency-constituency treebank. In *Proceedings of the 21sh International Conference on Text, Speech, and Dialogue*, pages 95–105, Brno, Czech Republic. Springer.

Sampo Pyysalo, Jenna Kanerva, Anna Missilä, Veronika Laippala, and Filip Ginter. 2015. Universal Dependencies for Finnish. In *Proceedings of the 20th Nordic Conference of Computational Linguistics (NODALIDA 2015)*, pages 163–172, Vilnius, Lithuania. Linköping University Electronic Press, Sweden.

Peng Qi, Yuhao Zhang, Yuhui Zhang, Jason Bolton, and Christopher D. Manning. 2020. Stanza: A Python natural language processing toolkit for many human languages. In *Proceedings of the 58th Annual Meeting of the Association for Computational Linguistics: System Demonstrations*, pages 101–108, Online. Association for Computational Linguistics.

Loganathan Ramasamy and Zdeněk Žabokrtský. 2012. Prague dependency style treebank for Tamil. In *Proceedings of the Eighth International Conference on Language Resources and Evaluation (LREC'12)*, pages 1888–1894, Istanbul, Turkey. European Language Resources Association.

Sebastian Schuster and Christopher D. Manning. 2016. Enhanced English Universal Dependencies: An improved representation for natural language understanding tasks. In *Proceedings of the Tenth International Conference on Language Resources and Evaluation (LREC 2016)*, pages 2371–2378, Portorož, Slovenia. European Language Resources Association.

Djamé Seddah and Marie Candito. 2016. Hard time parsing questions: Building a QuestionBank for French. In *Proceedings of the Tenth International Conference on Language Resources and Evaluation (LREC'16)*, pages 2366–2370, Portorož, Slovenia. European Language Resources Association (ELRA).

Natalia Silveira, Timothy Dozat, Marie-Catherine de Marneffe, Samuel Bowman, Miriam Connor, John Bauer, and Chris Manning. 2014. A gold standard dependency corpus for English. In *Proceedings of the Ninth International Conference on Language Resources and Evaluation (LREC-2014)*, pages 2897–2904, Reykjavik, Iceland. European Languages Resources Association (ELRA).

Kiril Simov, Petya Osenova, Alexander Simov, and Milen Kouylekov. 2004. Design and implementation of the Bulgarian HPSG-based treebank. *Research on Language and Computation*, 2(4):495–522.

Leonoor van der Beek, Gosse Bouma, Rob Malouf, and Gertjan Van Noord. 2002. The Alpino dependency treebank. In *Proceedings of Computational Linguistics in the Netherlands*, Twente, Netherlands.

Xinyu Wang, Yong Jiang, and Kewei Tu. 2020. Enhanced universal dependency parsing with second-order inference and mixture of training data. In *Proceedings of the 16th International Conference on Parsing Technologies and the IWPT 2020 Shared Task on Parsing into Enhanced Universal Dependencies*, pages 215–220, Online. Association for Computational Linguistics.

Alina Wróblewska. 2018. Extended and enhanced Polish dependency bank in Universal Dependencies format. In *Proceedings of the Second Workshop on Universal Dependencies (UDW 2018)*, pages 173–182, Brussels, Belgium. Association for Computational Linguistics.

Amir Zeldes. 2017. The GUM corpus: Creating multilayer resources in the classroom. *Language Resources and Evaluation*, 51(3):581–612.

Daniel Zeman. 2018. Slovak dependency treebank in Universal Dependencies. *Jazykovedný casopis/Journal of Linguistics*, 68(2):385–395.

Daniel Zeman, Jan Hajič, Martin Popel, Martin Potthast, Milan Straka, Filip Ginter, Joakim Nivre, and Slav Petrov. 2018. CoNLL 2018 shared task: Multilingual parsing from raw text to Universal Dependencies. In *Proceedings of the CoNLL 2018 Shared Task: Multilingual Parsing from Raw Text to Universal Dependencies*, pages 1–21, Brussels, Belgium. Association for Computational Linguistics.

Daniel Zeman, Martin Popel, Milan Straka, Jan Hajič, Joakim Nivre, Filip Ginter, Juhani Luotolahti, Sampo Pyysalo, Slav Petrov, Martin Potthast, Francis Tyers, Elena Badmaeva, Memduh Gokirmak, Anna Nedoluzhko, Silvie Cinková, Jan Hajič jr., Jaroslava Hlaváčová, Václava Kettnerová, Zdeňka Urešová, Jenna Kanerva, Stina Ojala, Anna Missilä, Christopher D. Manning, Sebastian Schuster, Siva Reddy, Dima Taji, Nizar Habash, Herman Leung, Marie-Catherine de Marneffe, Manuela Sanguinetti, Maria Simi, Hiroshi Kanayama, Valeria de Paiva, Kira Droganova, Héctor Martínez Alonso, Çağrı Çöltekin, Umut Sulubacak, Hans Uszkoreit, Vivien Macketanz, Aljoscha Burchardt, Kim Harris, Katrin Marheinecke, Georg Rehm, Tolga Kayadelen, Mohammed Attia, Ali Elkahky, Zhuoran Yu, Emily Pitler, Saran Lertpradit, Michael Mandl, Jesse Kirchner, Hector Fernandez Alcalde, Jana Strnadová, Esha Banerjee, Ruli Manurung, Antonio Stella, Atsuko Shimada, Sookyoung Kwak, Gustavo Mendonça, Tatiana Lando, Rattima Nitisaroj, and Josie Li. 2017. CoNLL 2017 shared task: Multilingual parsing from raw text to Universal Dependencies. In *Proceedings of the CoNLL 2017 Shared Task: Multilingual Parsing from Raw Text to Universal Dependencies*, pages 1–19, Vancouver, Canada. Association for Computational Linguistics.

A Hyperparameters

Character-level Language Model Pre-training	
Optimization:	
Optimizer	RAdam (Liu et al., 2020)
Batch size	128
Number of steps	500,000
Initial learning rate	3×10^{-4}
Weight decay	0.1
Gradient clipping	1.0
Simple Recurrent Units:	
Sequence length limit	512
Vocab size	512
Embedding size	256
Hidden size	256
Numer of layers	8
Dropout	0.3
Tokenizer	
Optimization:	
Optimizer	RAdam
Batch size	32
Initial learning rate	5×10^{-5}
Weight decay	0
Gradient clipping	1.0
Multi-layer Perceptrons (MLPs):	
Number of layers	1
Hidden size	500
Dropout	0.5
Sentence Splitter, MWT Expander, and Parser	
Pre-trained model	XLM-R (Large)
Optimization:	
Optimizer	RAdam
Batch size	8
Initial learning rate	1×10^{-5}
Second-stage learning rate	1×10^{-6}
Weight decay	0
Gradient clipping	1.0
Tagger MLPs (Sentence Splitter, MWT Expander):	
Number of layers	1
Hidden size	400
Dropout	0.5
Parser MLPs (Unlabeled Tree and Graph Parsers):	
Number of layers	1
Hidden size	383
Dropout	0.33
Parser MLPs (Relation Labeler):	
Number of layers	1
Hidden size	255
Dropout	0.33

End-to-end mBERT based Seq2seq Enhanced Dependency Parser with Linguistic Typology knowledge

Chinmay Choudhary
National University of Ireland, Galway
c.choudhary1@nuigalway.ie

Colm O'riordan
National University of Ireland, Galway
colm.oriordan@nuigalway.ie

Abstract

We describe the NUIG solution for *IWPT 2021 Shared Task* of Enhanced Dependency (ED) parsing in multiple languages. For this shared task, we propose and evaluate an End-to-end Seq2seq mBERT- based ED parser which predicts the ED-parse tree of a given input sentence as a relative head-position tag-sequence. Our proposed model is a multitasking neural-network which performs five key tasks simultaneously namely *UPOS-tagging*, *UFeat-tagging*, *Lemmatization*, *Dependency-parsing* and *ED-parsing*. Furthermore we utilise the linguistic typology available in the **WALS** database to improve the ability of our proposed end-to-end parser to transfer across languages. Results show that our proposed *Seq2seq ED-parser* performs on par with state-of-the-art *ED-parser* despite having a much simpler design.

1 Introduction

The Enhanced Universal Dependency (EUD) Parsing (Schuster and Manning, 2016; Nivre et al., 2020) framework is an interesting extension of the standard Dependency Parsing framework, which provides additional significant syntactic and semantic knowledge, that is missing in a standard dependency parse-tree. Such additional knowledge can be crucial for numerous downstream NLP tasks.

The *IWPT 2021 Shared Task* (Bouma et al., 2021) requires the participants to perform the enhanced dependency parsing of the given test-sentences, in addition to predicting the sentence-boundaries, token-boundaries, lemmatization, POS-tags, morphological features and the basic dependency relations. The participants are provided with the blind test-corpora in 17 languages, and are expected to perform the enhanced dependency parsing on each sentence within these test corpora and submit the results (in the conllu format).

For this *IWPT 2021 Shared Task* (Bouma et al., 2021) we propose and evaluate the performance an *End-to-end mBERT Based Se2seq ED-Parser* which performs five key tasks namely *UPOS-tagging*, *UFeats-prediction*, *Lemmatization*, *Dependency-parsing* and *Enhanced Dependency-parsing* in multi-tasking settings.

Our proposed model is an extension of the popular UDify model (Kondratyuk and Straka, 2019) which is the state-of-the-art mBERT based multilingual dependency parser, and is inspired by (Li et al., 2018) which is an End-to-end Seq2seq Dependency-Parser. We describe the UDify model in Section 2.

We trained our proposed ED-Parser on a large joint polyglot corpus created by concatenating all the treebanks in the provided training dataset for *IWPT 2021 Shared Task*, and evaluated it on eight of the 17 provided blind test-corpora.

Furthermore, similar to previous approaches (Ammar et al., 2016), we utilized the *Linguistic Typology* knowledge available in **World Atlas of Language System (WALS)** database (Haspelmath, 2009) to improve thc cross-lingual transferring ability of our proposed ED-parser. We fed these typology features together with token-ids into the proposed ED-parser. We describe the architecture of our *End-to-end mBERT Based Se2seq ED-Parser* in detail in Section 3.

2 Background and Related Work

2.1 Seq2seq Dependency Parser

(Li et al., 2018) proposed a Seq2seq architecture to perform the end-to-end dependency parsing. The approach represented the entire dependency parse-tree of a given input-sentence, as a relative head-position tag-seq (of same length as the length of the input sentence). Figure 1 depicts a labelled and an unlabelled parse-tree represented by their re-

Proceedings of the 17th International Conference on Parsing Technologies (IWPT 2021), pages 225–232
Bangkok, Thailand (online), August 6, 2021.

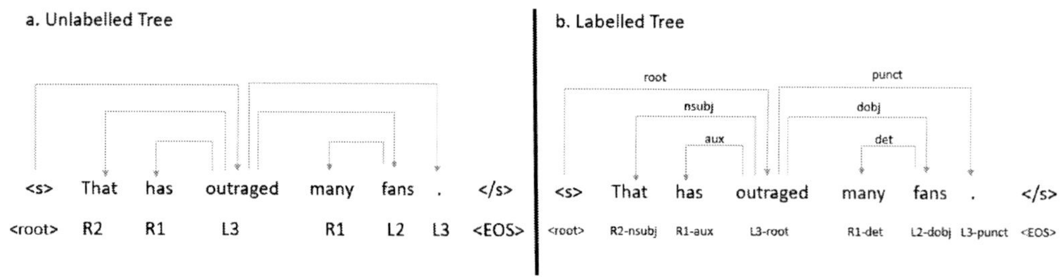

Figure 1: Examples of dependency parse tree being represented as relative head-position tag sequence by (Li et al., 2018)

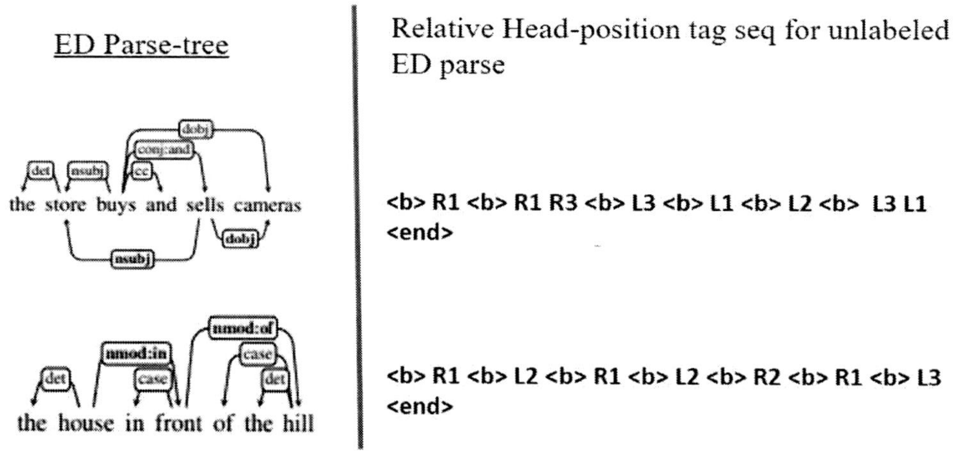

Figure 2: Example Enhanced Dependency Parse trees represented as *Relative Head-position tag-sequences*

spective relative head-position tag-sequences. Subsequently, the approach trains a standard LSTM-based model to predict the relative head-position tag for each token within an input-sentence. Results outlined in the paper show that this end-to-end parser performs as well as the state-of-the-art deep biaffine network (Dozat and Manning, 2016) while being much simpler in design.

2.2 UDify

UDify is an mBERT based multilingual model which simultaneously performs four key language-processing tasks; these tasks are *UPOS-tagging*, *UFeat-tagging*, *Lemmatization* and *Dependency Parsing*, in a multitasking framework. The model utilizes a single shared mBERT based encoder, and four individual task-specific decoders, for each of the four tasks respectively.

The *mBERT Encoder* takes in the entire sentence as input, tokenizes it using pre-trained the Word-Piece Tokenizer (Wu et al., 2016) and subsequently outputs mBERT (Wu and Dredze, 2019) based contextualized-embeddings for each word within the input-sentence. We refer to original UDify (Kondratyuk and Straka, 2019) paper for a detailed description of the mechanism of computing/fine-tuning such contextualized embeddings.

The decoders for both the *UPOS-tagging* and *UFeat-tagging* tasks adopt a standard sequence-tagging architecture with a softmax layer on the top. These decoders accept the contextual embeddings generated from the mBERT Encoder for each word in the input sentence, and predicts its UPOS/Ufeats tag.

For the *Lemmatization* task as well, the model uses a standard sequence-tagger which predicts a class-tag representing a unique edit script, for each word. An edit-script is simply the sequence of character operations to transform a word form to its lemma-form.

For dependency-parsing, the model adopts the popular deep biaffine architecture (Dozat and Manning, 2016) for graph-based parsing, with LSTM-encoder been replaced by the shared *mBERT En-*

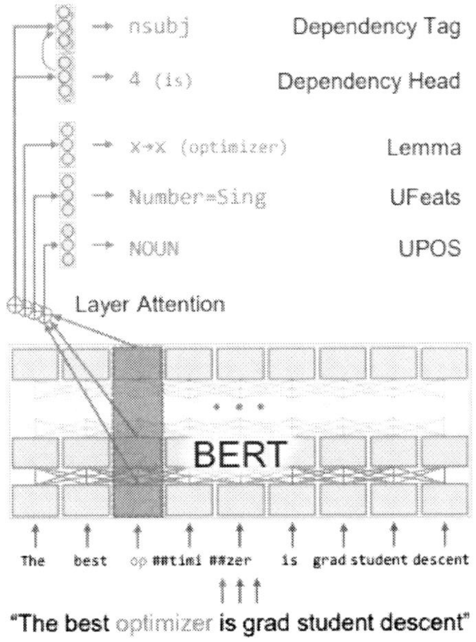

Figure 3: UDify model architecture. Figure from (Kondratyuk and Straka, 2019).

coder.

Hyper-parameter	Value
Dropout prob.	0.01
Bach-size	32
Number of steps per epoch	Size of training corpus / 32
Epochs	150
BERT Model	bert_multi_cased_L-12_H-768_A-12

Table 1: Hyper-parameters

3 mBERT based Seq2seq ED Parser

Figure 2b depicts the architecture of the proposed ED parser. Our proposed *End-to-end ED Parser* is an extension of the UDify (Kondratyuk and Straka, 2019) model described in section 2.2, with one additional component namely the *Relative Head Sequence predictor* which predicts the relative head-position of the tag-sequence representing the unlabelled enhanced-dependency parse-tree of the input sentence (as the fifth auxiliary task in the multitasking UDify model).

3.1 ED parse-tree as relative head-position tag sequence

Given a sentence of length T, its unlabelled ED parse-tree can be represented by a relative-head tag-seq of length $\hat{T}$ such that $\hat{T} \geq 2T + 1$. Figure 2 depicts the representations of sample unlabelled enhanced-dependency parse-trees as their relative sequences of relative head-position tags. Here, the tag $< b >$ represents the next-token whose heads are pointed by the subsequently predicted relative-head position tags (until the next $< b >$ tag is predicted).

3.2 Relative Head Sequence predictor

As evident in Figure 2b, our *Relative Head Sequence predictor* is a standard LSTM based Seq2seq neural-network (Sutskever et al., 2014) which takes in the entire input-sentence encoding vector as input, and sequentially predicts the relative head-position tag-sequence, one tag at a time.

3.2.1 Input sentence-encoding

The sentence-encoding $e^X \in R^d$ of any input sentence $X = x_1, x_2, ...x_T$ is computed by applying equation 1.

$$e^X = W * [BERT(X); TY_l] + b \qquad (1)$$

Here $BERT(X)$ is the output embedding-vector from the UDify's shared mBERT encoder for the end-of-sentence token $< /s >$ of input-sentence and TY_l is a *Linguistic-typology* vector of language l being parsed. Each value within TY_l represents a single typology-feature from *WALS* (Haspelmath, 2009) database having a specific integer value. Equation 1 involves the concatenation of the *BERT-output* and the *Typology* vectors, followed by dimension reduction through a feed-forward network. Feeding typology features together with the input sentence could improve the cross-lingual transferring ability of the multilingual model, as shown by (Ammar et al., 2016).

For the proposed model, we use all the word-order and constituency features in WALS (Haspelmath, 2009) database excluding trivially redundant features as excluded by (Takamura et al., 2016).

3.2.2 Training

We trained our *mBERT based Seq2seq ED Parser* on a single large joint-polyglot corpus, created by concatenating all the treebanks available in the training dataset provided for the *IWPT 2021 Shared task*.

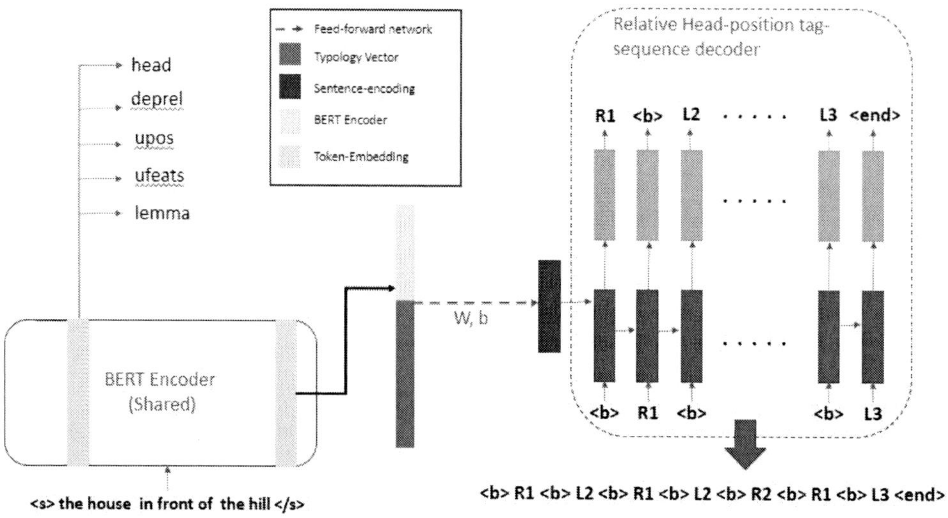

Figure 4: Architecture of the *Relative Head-position Sequence predictor*

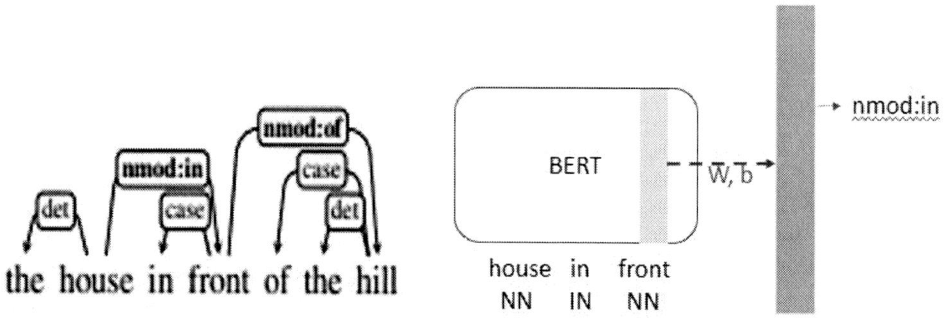

Figure 5: Architecture of the *Label predictor*

Before each training epoch, we randomly shuffle all sentences in our polyglot training corpus, and subsequently feed mixed batches of sentences from this shuffled corpus into the model being trained, where each batch may contain sentences from any language or treebank (as done by authors of UDify (Kondratyuk and Straka, 2019)).

We optimized the weights of our multitasking model by minimizing the total loss as the sum of sparse cross-entropy losses for all five tasks namely *UPOS-tagging*, *UFeat-tagging*, *Lemmatization*, *Dependency Parsing* and *Relative Head-position Sequence prediction*.

3.2.3 Predicting

The ED parsing of any unknown input-sentence $X = x_1, x_2, ...x_T$ can be performed by extracting the most probable correct relative head-position tag-sequence. The correct relative head-position tag-sequence would satisfy following constraints.

1. Sequence should start with $< b >$ and end with $< end >$.

2. For each word in $x_i \in X$, the relative head-position tag assigned to it should be within the range of the sentence. For example, within the sentence **"the house in front of the hill"**, the word '*the*' can not have tags L_2, L_3, L_4, L_5, L_6 and the word '*hill*' can not have any right tags, as these are outside the range of the sentence.

3. The label sequence should not generate any cycles within the dependency tree.

4. One of the words should have the head at $< root >$ token.

Language	**UPOS**	**UFeats**	**Lemmas**	**UAS**	**LAS**	**ELAS**
Bulgarian	98.81	35.97	97.40	93.37	90.03	78.45
English	95.17	32.77	95.76	87.07	84.46	65.40
Estonian	96.49	35.04	95.55	85.41	82.46	54.03
Latvian	96.12	35.61	95.45	88.51	85.19	56.67
Lithuanian	93.40	30.09	92.66	78.25	73.52	59.13
Russian	98.25	36.32	97.49	92.67	91.01	66.33
Slovak	96.62	22.68	94.61	90.09	87.49	67.45
Swedish	96.05	33.56	92.46	85.64	82.18	63.12

Table 2: Results achieved by our proposed End-to-end ED-parser

Model	**UPOS**	**UFeats**	**Lemmas**	**UAS**	**LAS**	**EULAS**	**ELAS**
combo	97.62	94.95	94.39	91.55	89.14	86.41	85.01
dcu-epfl	96.32	91.81	95.15	87.44	84.3	87.67	86.89
fastparse	97.24	93.0	95.84	78.23	72.44	69.42	67.07
grew	97.24	93.0	95.84	89.6	87.03	85.18	82.95
robertnlp	97.89	94.06	0.01	93.15	90.4	89.25	88.44
shanghaitech	0.46	32.78	0.01	4.18	1.27	89.76	88.37
tgif	0.46	32.81	0.01	10.93	0.94	91.45	90.67
unipi	96.37	91.75	95.17	90.55	87.98	85.96	84.42
nuig	**96.36**	**32.75**	**95.17**	**87.63**	**84.54**	**67.21**	**63.82**

Table 3: Average results achieved by all ED parsers

5. The sequence should contain the number of $< b >$ tags equal to number of tokens in the input sentence X.

We used dynamic programming with beam-search to efficiently extract the most probable relative head-position tag-sequence which satisfies the above listed relative head-position tag-sequence, out of all possible sequences.

3.3 Label Predictor

Figure 2c depicts the architecture of our *Label predictor* model. It is an mBERT based multi-class classifier with a softmax layer on top. The model takes as input the token-seq segment from the input sentence ranging from head to tail, as well as its corresponding predicted POS-tag sequence. The model outputs the probabilities of all possible ED dependency labels to be assigned to the given relation.

The *Label-predictor* is trained on all ED relationships available in training dataset for *IWPT 2021 Shared task*. The parameters of the mBERT encoder of our *Label predictor* are initialized with the parameters of the fine-tuned mBERT encoder of our *Relative Head-position tag-sequences*.

4 Experiments

As already explained, our proposed *End-to-end Seq2seq ED-parser* is trained on a large joint polyglot corpus created by concatenating all the treebanks in the provided training dataset for *IWPT 2021 Shared Task*. We evaluated our parser on test corpora provided for the *IWPT 2021 Shared Task* in eight distinct languages namely *Bulgarian, Estonian, English, Latvian, Lithuanian, Russian, Slovak* and *Swedish*. We outline the results achieved by our proposed model in detail in Section 5. Table 1 outlines hyper-parameters used in the experiments. These values are obtained by minimizing the training loss for *English-EWT Corpus* provided in the *dev* dataset provided for *IWPT 2021 Shared Task*.

5 Results and Conclusion

Table 2 outlines results achieved by our proposed *End-to-end BERT Based Se2seq ED-Parser* on all eight blind test-corpora on which the model is evaluated, as calculated by the evaluation script for the shared task.

Appendix A compares the results achieved by our *ED-parser* with the results achieved by the other participants of *IWPT 2021 Shared tasks*. Table 3 outlines the average results achieved by all the models proposed in *IWPT 2021 Shared task* for all eight test-languages. It is evident that our models performs on par with other state-of-the-art ED-parsers despite the fact that its much simpler in design as it is an end-to-end design, and thus is much easier to train and implement.

References

Waleed Ammar, George Mulcaire, Miguel Ballesteros, Chris Dyer, and Noah A Smith. 2016. Many languages, one parser. *Transactions of the Association for Computational Linguistics*, 4:431–444.

Gosse Bouma, Djamé Seddah, and Daniel Zeman. 2021. From raw text to enhanced universal dependencies: The parsing shared task at iwpt 2021. In *Proceedings of the 17th International Conference on Parsing Technologies (IWPT 2021)*, pages 146–157, Bangkok, Thailand (online). Association for Computational Linguistics.

Timothy Dozat and Christopher D Manning. 2016. Deep biaffine attention for neural dependency parsing. *arXiv preprint arXiv:1611.01734*.

Martin Haspelmath. 2009. *The typological database of the World Atlas of Language Structures*. Berlin: Walter de Gruyter.

Dan Kondratyuk and Milan Straka. 2019. 75 languages, 1 model: Parsing universal dependencies universally. *arXiv preprint arXiv:1904.02099*.

Zuchao Li, Jiaxun Cai, Shexia He, and Hai Zhao. 2018. Seq2seq dependency parsing. In *Proceedings of the 27th International Conference on Computational Linguistics*, pages 3203–3214.

Joakim Nivre, Marie-Catherine de Marneffe, Filip Ginter, Jan Hajič, Christopher D. Manning, Sampo Pyysalo, Sebastian Schuster, Francis Tyers, and Daniel Zeman. 2020. Universal Dependencies v2: An evergrowing multilingual treebank collection. In *Proceedings of the Twelfth International Conference on Language Resources and Evaluation (LREC 2020)*, pages 4027–4036, Paris, France. European Language Resources Association.

Sebastian Schuster and Christopher D Manning. 2016. Enhanced english universal dependencies: An improved representation for natural language understanding tasks. In *Proceedings of the Tenth International Conference on Language Resources and Evaluation (LREC'16)*, pages 2371–2378.

Ilya Sutskever, Oriol Vinyals, and Quoc V Le. 2014. Sequence to sequence learning with neural networks. In *Advances in neural information processing systems*, pages 3104–3112.

Hiroya Takamura, Ryo Nagata, and Yoshifumi Kawasaki. 2016. Discriminative analysis of linguistic features for typological study. In *Proceedings of the Tenth International Conference on Language Resources and Evaluation (LREC'16)*, pages 69–76.

Shijie Wu and Mark Dredze. 2019. Beto, bentz, becas: The surprising cross-lingual effectiveness of bert. *arXiv preprint arXiv:1904.09077*.

Yonghui Wu, Mike Schuster, Zhifeng Chen, Quoc V Le, Mohammad Norouzi, Wolfgang Macherey, Maxim Krikun, Yuan Cao, Qin Gao, Klaus Macherey, et al. 2016. Google's neural machine translation system: Bridging the gap between human and machine translation. *arXiv preprint arXiv:1609.08144*.

A Results

This section compares the results achieved by our *ED-parser* with the results achieved by the other participants of *IWPT 2021 Shared tasks.*

Table 4: Results of all participants of *IWPT 2021 Shared Task*

Begin of Table							
Language	**Models**	**UPOS**	**UFeats**	**Lemma**	**UAS**	**LAS**	**ELAS**
Bulgarian	combo	98.72	97.23	97.25	92.98	89.52	86.67
	dcu-epfl	98.89	97.57	97.30	93.25	90.19	92.44
	fastparse	99.15	97.95	97.97	87.85	83.39	78.73
	grew	99.15	97.95	97.97	94.36	91.62	88.83
	robertnlp	99.13	98.31	0.01	96.30	94.15	93.16
	shanghaitech	0.00	35.92	0.01	5.80	1.54	92.52
	tgif	0.00	35.98	0.01	10.58	1.13	93.63
	unipi	98.81	97.57	97.40	95.29	92.71	90.84
	nuig	**98.81**	**35.97**	**97.40**	**93.37**	**90.03**	**78.45**
English	combo	95.74	93.54	95.26	89.61	87.22	84.09
	dcu-epfl	94.96	93.53	95.66	86.45	83.64	85.70
	fastparse	95.85	94.16	96.04	82.36	77.99	73.00
	grew	95.85	94.16	96.04	89.22	86.83	85.49
	robertnlp	96.24	94.44	0.00	90.79	88.48	87.88
	shanghaitech	0.28	32.80	0.00	3.71	1.24	87.27
	tgif	0.28	32.76	0.00	7.86	1.08	88.19
	unipi	95.17	93.70	95.76	90.64	88.47	87.11
	nuig	**95.17**	**32.77**	**95.76**	**87.07**	**84.46**	**65.40**
Estonian	combo	97.42	96.57	86.09	90.00	87.53	84.02
	dcu-epfl	96.46	95.30	95.58	85.31	82.35	84.35
	fastparse	96.89	95.78	94.90	71.70	64.50	60.05
	grew	96.89	95.78	94.90	86.62	83.85	78.19
	robertnlp	97.09	96.46	0.00	90.02	87.59	86.55
	shanghaitech	0.12	34.99	0.00	3.67	1.16	86.66
	tgif	0.12	35.08	0.01	11.86	0.82	88.38
	unipi	96.49	95.33	95.55	87.11	84.14	81.27
	nuig	**96.49**	**35.04**	**95.55**	**85.41**	**82.46**	**54.03**
Latvian	combo	97.35	94.97	96.53	92.91	90.25	84.57
	dcu-epfl	95.95	93.59	95.34	88.47	85.10	86.96
	fastparse	96.28	93.79	95.81	78.37	72.03	66.43
	grew	96.28	93.79	95.81	88.32	85.27	77.45
	robertnlp	97.61	95.18	0.03	93.62	91.25	88.82
	shanghaitech	0.58	35.57	0.03	4.22	1.42	89.17
	tgif	0.56	35.62	0.03	10.37	0.97	90.23
	unipi	96.12	93.45	95.45	89.90	86.63	83.01
	nuig	**96.12**	**35.61**	**95.45**	**88.51**	**85.19**	**56.67**
Lithuanian	combo	97.26	95.05	93.76	88.03	84.75	79.75
	dcu-epfl	93.47	87.74	92.71	78.36	73.25	78.04
	fastparse	95.97	91.07	93.61	61.39	53.55	48.27
	grew	95.97	91.07	93.61	82.54	78.65	74.62
	robertnlp	97.42	93.20	0.00	90.49	83.27	80.76

	shanghaitech	1.51	30.12	0.00	5.12	1.77	80.87
	tgif	1.51	30.20	0.00	10.89	1.24	86.06
	unipi	93.40	87.14	92.66	82.75	78.31	71.31
	nuig	**93.40**	**30.09**	**92.66**	**78.25**	**73.52**	**59.13**
Russian	combo	98.94	98.04	98.16	95.37	94.29	90.73
	dcu-epfl	98.19	87.67	97.39	92.61	90.97	92.83
	fastparse	98.86	88.97	98.33	87.09	83.23	78.56
	grew	98.86	88.97	98.33	94.22	92.97	90.56
	robertnlp	99.06	89.51	0.00	95.65	94.64	92.64
	shanghaitech	0.02	36.35	0.00	3.35	0.73	93.59
	tgif	0.02	36.37	0.00	13.81	0.51	94.01
	unipi	98.25	87.52	97.49	94.51	93.32	90.90
	nuig	**98.25**	**36.32**	**97.49**	**92.67**	**91.01**	**66.33**
Slovak	combo	97.88	95.03	95.61	93.19	91.72	87.04
	dcu-epfl	96.55	91.15	94.72	89.27	86.60	89.59
	fastparse	97.67	93.42	96.47	78.23	71.71	64.28
	grew	97.67	93.42	96.47	92.27	90.45	86.92
	robertnlp	98.28	95.54	0.00	96.16	93.88	89.66
	shanghaitech	1.19	22.69	0.00	6.06	1.96	90.25
	tgif	1.17	22.69	0.00	13.67	1.60	94.96
	unipi	96.62	91.44	94.61	93.32	91.75	86.05
	nuig	**96.62**	**22.68**	**94.61**	**90.09**	**87.49**	**67.45**
Swedish	combo	97.67	89.19	92.45	90.31	87.82	83.20
	dcu-epfl	96.12	87.92	92.47	85.83	82.30	85.20
	fastparse	97.25	88.82	93.60	78.88	73.11	67.26
	grew	97.25	88.82	93.60	89.26	86.59	81.54
	robertnlp	98.30	89.87	0.00	92.15	89.92	88.03
	shanghaitech	0.00	33.79	0.00	1.55	0.34	86.62
	tgif	0.00	33.79	0.00	8.42	0.20	89.90
	unipi	96.07	87.83	92.47	90.86	88.53	84.91
	nuig	**96.05**	**33.56**	**92.46**	**85.64**	**82.18**	**63.12**
Language	**Models**	**UPOS**	**UFeats**	**Lemmas**	**UAS**	**LAS**	**ELAS**

Author Index

Association for Computational Linguistics
209 N. Eighth Street
Stroudsburg, Pennsylvania 18360

ISBN 978-1-7138-3377-2

9 781713 833772

CURRAN ASSOCIATES INC.
proceedings.com